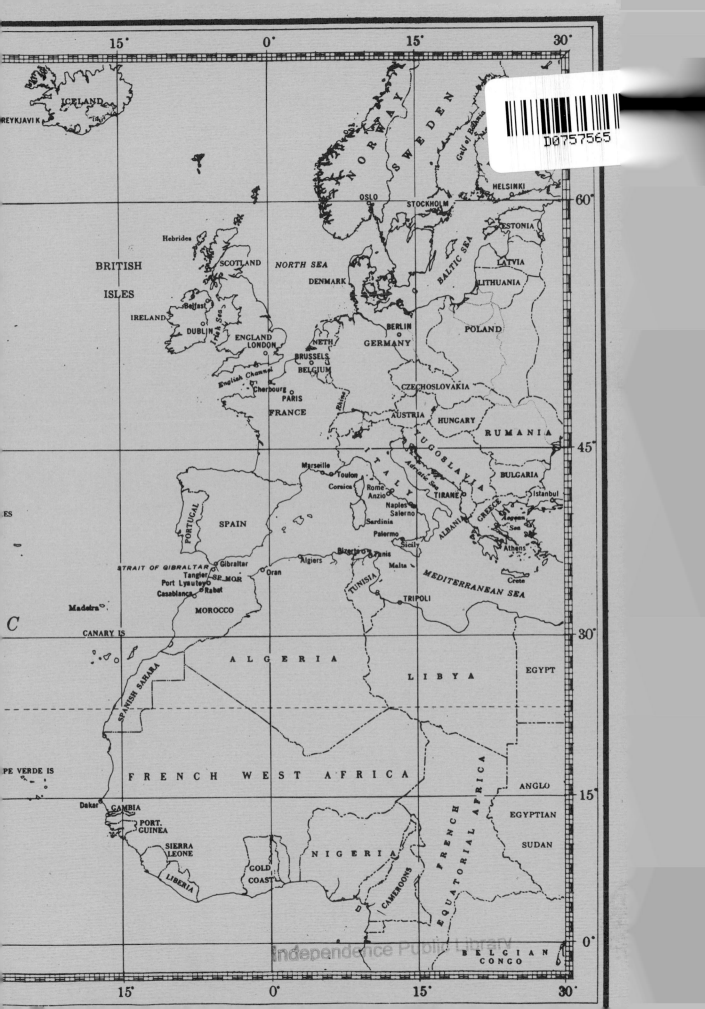

*The U.S. Coast Guard in World War II*

IN MEMORY OF THE MEN AND WOMEN
OF THE UNITED STATES COAST GUARD
WHO SERVED THEIR COUNTRY
IN WORLD WAR II A.D. 1941-1945

# The U.S. COAST GUARD in WORLD WAR II

## Malcolm F. Willoughby

LIEUTENANT, UNITED STATES COAST GUARD RESERVE (TEMPORARY)

NAVAL INSTITUTE PRESS—ANNAPOLIS, MARYLAND

To all members of
The United States Coast Guard
Regular, Reserve, and Temporary Reserve
who served their Country during World War II
this book is respectfully dedicated

Revised printing, 1989

Library of Congress Catalogue No. 57-9314
ISBN 0-87021-774-7

PRINTED IN THE UNITED STATES OF AMERICA

# FOREWORD TO THE REPRINTED EDITION

WORLD WAR II was the test of fire that forged the modern Coast Guard. From the very beginning, Coast Guardsmen participated in almost every phase of the maritime war. The cutter *Northland* made the first naval capture in September 1941 when it intercepted a group of German radio operators off Greenland. The service's first combat death occurred on board the transport *Leonard Wood* when the ship was attacked by Japanese planes at Singapore the day after the bombing of Pearl Harbor.

Coast Guardsmen were in every major amphibious assault of the war. At the Normandy invasion Coast Guardsmen not only landed thousands of men on the beach, they rescued 1,500 who were stranded in the surf. In the Pacific, First Class Signalman Douglas Munro posthumously won a Congressional Medal of Honor at Guadalcanal when he helped rescue three companies of Marines who were trapped on the beach.

At sea, Coast Guard manned vessels and aircraft sank eleven U-boats during the Battle of the North Atlantic. Most of these victories came early in the war when the campaign against the wolf packs was still in doubt.

On shore, Coast Guard men and women performed numerous less publicized but no less vital tasks. Thousands of merchant ships that had been hurriedly built for the war effort needed inspection. Merchant mariners needed training and certification. Our coasts needed to be patrolled. In fact, a Coast Guard petty officer intercepted an enemy sabotage team on Long Island during June 1942. Ten thousand women volunteered for service, thus freeing men for combat duty.

I would need hundreds of pages just to begin to tell the Coast Guard's story during World War II. Fortunately for the service, Malcolm Willoughby has done just that. The book was originally published in 1957. Although it has long been out of print, the demand for this work earns it the right to be called a classic. I thank the Naval Institute Press for helping us to launch our bicentennial celebration by once again making this fine book available to the American public.

ADMIRAL PAUL A. YOST
*Commandant, U. S. Coast Guard*

4 August, 1989

v

# FOREWORD TO THE FIRST EDITION

It was probably given to few men to be able to visualize on November 1st, 1941 what lay ahead for the Coast Guard when President Roosevelt signed the Executive Order placing the Coast Guard under the jurisdiction of the Navy for the duration of the emergency. The far-seeing probably recognized that this, for us, was the beginning of World War II; that even these foresaw the growth and ever-changing scope of the Coast Guard in the following years implies an omniscience beyond the reach of ordinary man. We should remember that these were still the days when "measures short of war" still conditioned our thinking.

The next month hardly offered a period of preparation and integration but December 7th, 1941 found the Coast Guard, if not ready, at least willing and able. Mushrooming growth, multiplicity of assignments, demands on personnel and equipment presented problems of overwhelming magnitude, but problems that were met in stride and brought to solution. The resolution of these problems led to a brilliant record of accomplishment that now finds its way into national and Coast Guard history.

That much of this record was made possible by the distinguished leadership of the Commandant of the Coast Guard, Admiral Russell R. Waesche, needs little amplification here. If difficult times bring forth great men, we need go no farther for an example to prove our point. The foresight, the courage and the resilience of Admiral Waesche beggars the imagination. The thousands of us who knew him or served under him owe a debt of gratitude we can never hope to repay.

It was Admiral Waesche who foresaw that these were to be the great times and that such times needed to be chronicled for all time. For that burden he ordered the establishment of the Historical Section of the Coast Guard charged with the duty of preparing and preserving the records of the events that were to follow. From this section, under the able guidance of F. R. Eldridge and his associates, came the basic material out of which grew this volume.

Times and circumstance brought forth the author of this history of the Coast Guard in World War II. Mr. Willoughby was a Coast Guard officer in the Temporary Reserve. Like the thousands of other "Temporaries" he found time and energy, beyond his normal pursuits, to devote hours, days and weeks to service to the Coast Guard. His interest in this history stems from the work he did in preparation of some of the Monographs of the Historical Section. That this busy man has undertaken this task almost as a "labor of love" is a credit to him and benefit to all of us. All Coast Guardsmen, past and present, extend to him our everlasting thanks and a hearty "Well Done."

Vice Admiral Alfred C. Richmond
*Commandant, U. S. Coast Guard*

10 May, 1956

# INTRODUCTION

ADAPTABILITY is a characteristic of the American fighting man that has enabled this country's Armed Forces to emerge triumphant in every major war we have fought. Adaptability is synonymous with the operations of the United States Coast Guard.

In peace, this Service is dedicated to enforcement of our commercial laws, and the insurance of safety of life at sea. In war, the Coast Guard team continues its peacetime mission, but in addition, "joins the Navy" as an integral part of the maritime force of this nation.

I am highly pleased that this history of the Coast Guard in World War II has been prepared for general distribution to the American people. It is the story of a valiant Service, which, in the usual reporting of the maritime aspects of the War, sometimes lost its identity because it was grouped with the "Navy". This volume tells the story of the Coast Guard in World War II, showing its metamorphosis from its peacetime missions to its wartime missions.

The Coast Guard is an old Service, and one rightfully proud of its record. Its prewar nucleus of officers and men performed a gigantic task in administering and building the wartime efficiency of this fighting Service. In wartime operations Coast Guardsmen performed individual acts of heroism as valorous as those of any other of the Armed Services. The selfless devotion to duty of the Coast Guard rescue teams, which on innumerable occasions risked their lives in saving those of others, as well as the performance of their duties as part of the Navy's fighting force, deserves the Nation's hearty "Well Done!"

But beyond this, recognition of the thousands upon thousands of Coast Guardsmen, including the Temporary Reserves and other primarily volunteer personnel, is long overdue. Routine work, seldom involving dramatic incidents, often goes unrecognized. This work, however, acting as a deterrent to sabotage, espionage, and subversive activities of every nature, contributed immeasurably to our wartime successes. We can only speculate on the incidents which might have occurred had these loyal American citizens not patrolled the beaches and supervised the handling of ships at the docks of our country during the War. We can chronicle the incidents in which they reacted to emergencies; we can only speculate as to the innumerable emergencies that they prevented.

Admiral Russell R. Waesche, the wartime Commandant of the United States Coast Guard, was a man I held in the highest esteem. It was my privilege to have many of his combatant units under my command during the War. Their dependability made them an important part of our team. I know of no instance wherein they did not acquit themselves in the highest traditions of their Service, or prove themselves worthy of their Service motto, *Semper Paratus*—"Always Ready".

C. W. NIMITZ
*Fleet Admiral, USN*

# PREFACE

This is a history of the United States Coast Guard's participation in World War II, but not a history of the war itself. Although the Coast Guard was, and is, the smallest of the armed forces of the United States, its contribution to the ultimate victory was important. The influence of this Service was felt strongly at home, in the Atlantic and Pacific oceans, and in all foreign areas where the Navy, of which it was an integral part, landed troops.

The story of the Coast Guard at war is replete with incidents which, in combat or otherwise, demonstrated consummate skill, great devotion to duty, and heroism worthy of special mention in any wartime history of the Service. Coast Guardsmen who received awards are listed in Appendix A. Many who played parts in outstanding exploits are mentioned in the text. Yet, because of space limitations it has been impossible to include them all.

For similar reasons, many Coast Guard vessels and Navy and Army ships which the Coast Guard manned are not specifically named. Many plodded faithfully through their assigned duties, contributing to successful effort without becoming involved in significant happenings. In general, however, vessels concerned with the more important events are specified, and, when the name of the commanding officer at the time is clearly ascertainable, it is also recorded. But in far too many instances available sources do not reveal who was commanding at the time of the incident, and for the sake of accuracy it has been necessary to omit his name. To each who should have been mentioned the author offers his apologies. Ranks and ratings changed over the war period. Throughout these pages, the rank or rating held at the time mentioned is uniformly given regardless of further attainments. Photographs are all official Coast Guard photographs unless otherwise stated. Maps and art work are by Mr. W. M. Shannon.

The World War II historical undertaking of the Coast Guard had its inception in a directive of 9 March, 1945, by Captain Ellis Reed-Hill, USCG, then Chief, Public Relations Division, calling for appointment of a District Coast Guard Historical Officer in each Naval District and outlining the work to be accomplished. Each Historical Officer was to write or supervise the writing of a "first narrative" from official records on each subdivision of Coast Guard activity in his District. In addition, ship histories were to be prepared. Invasion records and narratives were to be assembled at Headquarters. Historical Officers were appointed and the work was well underway when Captain Reed-Hill was succeeded as Chief, Public Information Division, by Captain Samuel F. Gray, USCG.

As a subdivision under Public Relations (later Public Information) a Historical Section was set up at Headquarters under Lieutenant Commander Frank R. Eldridge, USCGR(T), who was appointed Chief, Historical Section. The Historical Officers in each District were directly responsible to him. The excellent work of these officers who collected and submitted the basic material is acknowledged.

The "narratives," ship histories, and combat data were the basis for Monographs at a national level covering each subdivision of Coast Guard wartime activity. These were eventually written by, or under the direction of, Lieutenant Commander Eldridge. The authors of the Monographs are:

CAPT E. M. Kent, USCG
    Naval Engineering
CAPT R. R. Tinkham, USCG
    Civil Engineering
LCDR F. R. Arzt, USCG
    Legal
LCDR Malcolm Stuart Boylan, USCGR (T)
    Auxiliary
LCDR Frank R. Eldridge, USCGR(T)
    Aids to Navigation
    Assistance II
    Lost Cutters
    Pacific Landings
    Personnel
    Public Relations
    Transports and Escorts
    Weather Patrol
LCDR T. J. LeBlanc, USCG
    Medical
LCDR Clyde T. Solt, USCG(Ret)
    Communications
LT V. E. Howard, USCGR
    Intelligence
LT F. C. Riley, USCG
    Personnel

LT Malcolm F. Willoughby, USCGR(T)
    Finance
    Port Security
    Temporary Reserve
LT Dorothea Wyatt,* USCGR(W)
    Women's Reserve
LTJG Elaine Morrell, USCGR(W)
    Assistance I
Slc Dr. Walter C. Richardson,† USCGI.
    Alaska
    Aviation; Beach Patrol
S2c Edna R. Parrott, USCGR(W)
    Loran I
Mr. Joseph E. Coker
    Communications Engineering
Miss Pauline DeBrodes‡
    Greenland Patrol
    Landings in France
    Marine Inspection
    North African Landings
    Sicily-Italy Landings
Mr. Ralph C. Smith‡
    Loran II

These Monographs have been the chief source of information in preparing this history. However, it has been necessary to study other sources for background and other information. The exceptionally fine *History of United States Naval Operations in World War II*, volumes I to IX, by Rear Admiral Samuel Eliot Morison, USNR, was particularly valuable and interesting. *Battle Report*, volumes II, IV and V, by Captain Walter Karig, USNR, provided much helpful information. General Eisenhower's Official Report on European Operations also furnished valuable and useful material. Acknowledgment with thanks is given to *Harper's Magazine*, Little Brown and Company, and General Robert L. Eichelberger, USA, for permission to use quotations from works by Nicholas Monsarrat, Admiral Morison and General Eichelberger, respectively.

Throughout this historical endeavor, the author has had the benefit of helpful cooperation from Captain L. H. Morine, USCG, and Captain O. A. Peterson, USCG, who respectively succeeded Captain Gray as Chief, Public Information Division, and from Commander A. E. Carlson, USCG, Assistant Chief of that Division. To all of these officers, the author gives his sincere and profound thanks.

MALCOLM F. WILLOUGHBY

Boston, Massachusetts

* Professor of History, Goucher College.   † Professor of History, Louisiana State University.
‡ Historical Section, Headquarters.

# TABLE OF CONTENTS

# LIST OF ILLUSTRATIONS

# MAPS AND DIAGRAMS

*The U.S. Coast Guard in World War II*

# PROLOGUE

In presenting the history of the United States Coast Guard in World War II, it is fitting and desirable to outline very briefly the establishment and growth of the Service which became known as the Coast Guard in 1915. How this branch of our armed forces fitted into the pattern of our great war effort and how it contributed to final victory will become clear. The story of the Coast Guard through its earlier years is full of salty interest, the details of which must be omitted in a work of this sort due to space limitations and adherence to the subject at hand. The reader who wishes to enjoy those details is referred to an excellent work, *The United States Coast Guard, 1790-1915*, by Captain Stephen H. Evans, USCG, published by the United States Naval Institute.

What is now the United States Coast Guard had its beginning in 1789 when Congress passed the first Tariff Act. This law was to be enforced by Alexander Hamilton, first Secretary of the Treasury. One of the most painless methods of furnishing badly needed money to the new Treasury was by indirect taxation through an import tariff and tonnage dues on shipping entering our ports. Merchants soon complained that goods, evidently of European origin, were appearing on the market at such low prices it was obvious that the import duty on them had not been paid. Unless smuggling were checked, one of these sources of revenue would dry up.

Hamilton needed boats to stop smugglers from unloading their goods before the arrival of their vessels in port and the clandestine transferring of such goods by small vessels to land. Supported by information from the collectors, Hamilton, on 22 April 1790, asked Congress to authorize construction of "ten boats" to enforce the law. He estimated that savings in revenues would much more than compensate for the expense of the vessels. He wrote: "The utility of an establishment of this nature must depend on the exertion, vigilance and fidelity of those to whom the charge of the boats shall be confided. . . . To procure such . . . it will, in the opinion of the Secretary, be advisable that

they be commissioned as officers of the Navy. This will not only induce fit men, the more readily to engage, but will attach them to their duty by a nicer sense of honor." Hamilton referred to the various State Navies or to a revival of the Continental Navy (dissolved in 1785), and not to the U. S. Navy which was not created until 1798.

On 4 August 1790, Congress authorized construction of the ten boats, and specified in some detail that they were for use in waters extending from New England to Georgia. Thus, the United States Revenue Marine was born. The original cutters, ranging in keel length from 36 to 40 feet and armed with swivel guns, were *Massachusetts, Scammel, Argus, Vigilant, General Greene, Active, Virginia, Diligence, South Carolina,* and *Pickering.* They proved too small, however, for the duties assigned them, and within a decade other vessels of greater size were provided.

The Act of 2 March 1798 provided that the cutters "shall, whenever the President shall so direct, cooperate with the Navy of the U. S." When the quasi-war with France began that year, 20 vessels of the newly formed Navy were sent to prey on French commerce and destroy that nation's privateers. Upon decision to extend operations against France to waters of the West Indies, the President placed eight cutters of the Revenue Marine under orders of the Secretary of the Navy to augment four Navy fleets. These cutters patrolled from Nantucket to Cape Henry, and later escorted vessels and attacked French privateers in the vicinity of the West Indies. Twenty vessels were made prizes by these augmented fleets. Vessels of the Revenue Marine, unaided, captured 16 of these 20.

The Act of 25 February 1799, authorized the President to place in the Naval Establishment and to employ accordingly, any and all vessels which, as revenue cutters, had been increased in force and employed in defense of the coast. Under this law, the Coast Guard has fought side by side with the Navy in every one of the nation's wars at sea.

Peace with the French in 1801 found the

Revenue Marine with 17 vessels, many experienced officers, well-trained crews, and an enviable record in peace and war.

In 1807 a law was enacted forbidding the entry of slaves into the United States. The Revenue Marine—and later the Navy—took an active part in enforcing this law. The efforts to suppress the slave trade did not cease until the Civil War.

A brief period of retrenchment after the quasi-war with France was found to be false economy. Ten new revenue cutters were built and manned, and after helping enforce newly imposed embargoes, these cutters helped carry the naval burden in the War of 1812.

The Revenue Marine in 1812 consisted of 16 vessels. These operated with numerous small gunboats escorting convoys, attacking or warding off attacks of privateers, and engaging armed flotillas sent out by British squadrons. Nine cutters, averaging 125 tons, with crews of 15 to 30, and armed with 6 to 10 light guns, took 14 prizes. There were many exciting engagements between the revenue cutters and the British, in some of which the former came off second best, but the entire record was creditable and in keeping with the high standards of the Service.

Shortly after the end of these hostilities, two new cutters, *Alabama* and *Louisiana,* were built on Baltimore clipper lines, with high sterns and low bows. In August 1819, while "protecting the merchant vessels of the United States and their crews from piratical aggressions and depredations," they fought the Mexican privateer *Bravo* in the Gulf of Mexico and took her after a brief engagement. Later, they destroyed Patterson's town on Breton Island, a notorious pirates' den, thus practically putting an end to organized piracy on the Gulf Coast, though unorganized depredations continued sporadically. In 1822 *Alabama* took three slavers, and *Louisiana* joined an American and a British naval vessel in capturing five pirate vessels.

The Revenue Marine was also concerned with duties other than enforcing revenue laws. In 1799 it was instructed to see that state quarantine statutes were strictly observed; in 1818 it began enforcement of the neutrality laws which prohibited certain foreign ships remaining in United States waters. During the attempt to nullify the Tariff Act by the State of South Carolina in 1832, five cutters were ordered to Charleston Harbor "to

take possession of any vessel arriving from a foreign port, and defend her against any attempt to dispossess the Customs Officers of her custody until all the requirements of the law have been complied with." The silent influence exerted by the presence of these cutters was a strong factor in the solution of the problems which menaced peace.

On 16 December 1831, before the Charleston incident, Secretary of the Treasury John McLane had designated seven cutters to render assistance to vessels in distress and to save life and property at sea by patrolling areas near their stations during winter. In 1837, the Congress authorized employment of public vessels to cruise the coast in severe weather and afford aid to distressed navigators. Six years later, cutter personnel were instructed to assist in the preservation of property found on board wrecked vessels and to rescue cargoes for the benefit of their owners. Thus, the primary function of law enforcement was supplemented by an equally important one, that of providing maritime safety. These, together with maintenance of military readiness, constitute the three principal roles of the Service today.

Meanwhile, in 1836, the Seminole War had broken out. Eight cutters cooperated with the Army and Navy in blockading rivers, carrying dispatches, transporting troops and ammunition, and providing landing parties for the defense of settlements menaced by the Indians. "Their prompt and helpful cooperation with the Army," wrote an officer under whom they operated, "has called forth the highest commendations from commanding generals, who take occasion to eulogize the service rendered by the cutters."

In the 1840's, the Revenue Marine suffered again from "economies", but this was followed very soon by construction of new cutters. There was also experimentation with iron vessels and side-wheelers which, at the time, met with little success.

Eleven cutters, consisting of six schooners and five steamers, took active part in the Mexican War of 1846-1848, cooperating chiefly with armies under Generals Taylor and Scott. For the first time in war, several cutters operated as a unit under command of Revenue Marine officers. Others operated as part of a naval fleet. The cutter *Forward,* serving with the Navy, played a brilliant part. On 13 October 1846 she and *McLane* participated in the amphibious operations at the mouth of the Alvarado River. Commodore Connor was moved to say in his official report: "I am gratified to bear witness to the valuable services of the Revenue Schooner *Forward,* commanded by Captain H. B. Nones, and to the skill and gallantry of her officers and men." As a result of the Mexican War, we took over California. The discovery of gold in the next year, and the subsequent inrush of the '49ers, made the extension of revenue cutter service to the West Coast of paramount significance. The brig-rigged cutter *Lawrence* (Captain Alex V. Fraser), journeyed around the Horn to San Francisco, taking about a year for the trip.

From the end of the Mexican War until the Navy's Paraguayan Expedition in 1858, the cutters were busy hunting slavers as well as attending to their other duties. The iron side-wheel cutter *Harriet Lane* joined 14 naval vessels in this expedition. The purpose of this fleet was to impress Latin-Americans and pave the way for a treaty of "amity and commerce" and granting of free trading rights to United States merchant vessels.

*Harriet Lane* fired the first shot in the Civil War. The steamer *Nashville,* lying off Charleston Bar waiting to run in just before the bombardment of Fort Sumter in April 1861, refused to show her colors. A shot across *Nashville's* bows had the desired effect. The cutter later took part in the expedition to relieve Fort Sumter, and participated in the attack on Forts Clark and Hatteras, which were Confederate blockade-running bases on Hatteras Inlet. Capture of these forts provided the first Union victory of the Civil War.

The Revenue Marine expanded in the Civil War through the purchase of a number of tugs, small craft, yachts, and seagoing steamers. Six new screw steamers were built, each bearing six guns. In all, the Revenue Marine had 25 vessels by November 1864. The cutter *Miami* was President Lincoln's personal transport and saw action at Willoughby Point. Other vessels rendered valuable service in the James River, Chesapeake Bay, and waters of North Carolina, and cooperated with the Army and Navy on the South Atlantic coast. During all this time the cutters were also busily engaged in safeguarding the collection of badly needed revenues.

In 1867, Alaska was purchased from Russia. The revenue cutter *Lincoln* was the first American vessel to arrive there. In all but one subsequent year, one or more cutters were assigned to the Alaska patrol. They rendered aid to shipping, cared for the shipwrecked, and assisted destitute stranded natives to return to their homes when driven ashore. Public Health surgeons detailed to cutters prescribed for and aided the sick, treating thousands of cases annually.

The next 30 years saw the Revenue Cutter Service, as it came to be called, engaged in its peacetime duties related to law enforcement, Bering Sea patrol, safety at sea, and similar activities. It suffered at times from economy measures, but the net result was moderate expansion, better vessels, and better-trained personnel.

When the Spanish-American War broke out in 1898 the cutter *McCulloch* was bound for San Francisco from the East Coast of the United States, via Europe and the Suez Canal. She made a quick run to Hong Kong after overhaul at Singapore, and followed directions to join Commodore Dewey; she accompanied him on his operations against Manila. It was *McCulloch* that carried the first news of the victory at Manila Bay to Hong Kong.

Cooperating with the Navy during this war were 13 revenue cutters carrying 61 guns, and manned by 98 officers and 562 enlisted men. Eight of these cutters were in Sampson's fleet on the Havana blockade, one (*McCulloch*) was in Dewey's fleet, and four cooperated with the Navy on the Pacific coast. Three others, with 25 officers and 210 men, had been ordered to operate with the Navy, but the war ended before they could be equipped and sent to combat areas.

At the Battle of Cardenas on 11 May 1898, cutter *Hudson* sustained the fight against the enemy gunboats and shore batteries side by side with the Navy torpedo boat *Winslow.* With *Winslow* badly damaged and helpless, *Hudson* courageously stood by her in the center of the hottest fire of the action, made fast a line, and towed *Winslow* out of gun range. Each of *Hudson's* officers received a gold or silver medal of honor, and each crew member a bronze medal. These were the only gold and silver medals bestowed by Congress for services during the Spanish-American War.

The Revenue Cutter Service continued its peacetime functions in the years following the Spanish-

American War. In 1912, following the sinking of the steamship *Titanic* by collision with an iceberg, an ice patrol in the North Atlantic was instituted. In 1914, a formal convention at London prescribed permanent and systematic patrol. This agreement was signed by the principal maritime powers. The object of this patrol was to locate icebergs and field ice nearest to the transatlantic shipping lanes, and to send out frequent messages giving vessels information regarding ice menaces to navigation. This patrol was the responsibility of the Revenue Cutter Service, soon to become part of the Coast Guard. This patrol has been altered or discontinued during subsequent periods of war.

The Revenue Cutter Service continued as an entity until 1915, when it was combined with the Lifesaving Service, which had also been operated under the Treasury Department. The combined organization received a new name—"United States Coast Guard".

The establishment of the Lifesaving Service may be said to have been in 1785, the date of the founding of the Massachusetts Humane Society. This society built small houses of refuge along the coast, but lifeboats were not connected with them until 1807. It was still another 40 years before the United States Government showed an interest in this type of service.

In 1848 Congress appropriated $10,000 for eight small boathouses to be placed along the New Jersey shore line. These were the first lifesaving stations in America under government operation. In short order these stations proved their value in rescue operations, and in 1849 other stations were established on Long Island. Gradually, such stations became generally installed along our shores.

The story of the Lifesaving Service is one of daring and skill. Men of this service learned early that "Regulations say you have to go out, *but they don't say you have to come back.*" Statistics show that through the combined efforts of this Service and the Revenue Cutter Service, 203,609 lives had been saved in the 70 years from 1871 to 1941. Property valued at $1,784,738,124 also was saved from "Davy Jones' Locker." In addition, succor was afforded to 48,023 persons. The annual averages for these 70 years was 2,868 lives saved; $25,137,157 worth of property saved; and 676 persons afforded succor. Men of the Coast Guard

and predecessor Services were, and still are, unsurpassed anywhere in the handling of small boats.

When a state of war with Germany was declared on 6 April 1917, the Coast Guard immediately went into action with the Navy. It augmented the Navy by 15 cruising cutters, over 200 commissioned officers, and almost 5,000 warrant officers and enlisted men. Coast Guard vessels hunted submarines and raiders, and guarded troop transports, our most precious cargo. Of 138 commissioned line officers, 24 commanded combatant naval vessels in the European war zone, five commanded combatant ships attached to the American Patrol Detachment in the Caribbean, and 23 commanded combatant ships attached to naval districts. Five officers were in charge of large training camps and six were in aviation, two of the latter commanding air stations.

One squadron of six cutters was based at Gibraltar, performing escort duty between there and the British Isles as well as in the Mediterranean. Other cutters operated in the vicinity of the Azores, off Nova Scotia, in the Caribbean, and in United States coastal waters. There were many deeds of daring and heroism. Noteworthy was the case of the cutter *Seneca*, escorting a convoy to be met by the British naval sloop *Cowslip*, out of Gibraltar on 28 April 1918. The latter was torpedoed, and despite a warning to stay away because of the presence of submarines, *Seneca* risked her own safety, and following the laws and traditions of her Service succeeded in sending off small boats and rescuing two officers and 79 enlisted men.

On another occasion, the British collier *Wellington*, in a convoy escorted by *Seneca*, was torpedoed and had her forefoot blown away. The victims abandoned ship, but *Wellington* did not sink. Men from *Seneca* boarded her together with a few of her own crew. They got up steam and headed for Brest at eight knots. However, a gale caused trouble and she finally sank. Men from the U. S. destroyer *Warrington*, which was standing by, picked up 15 men, of whom eight were Coast Guardsmen. Eleven of *Seneca*'s crew were lost. Of this exploit the British Admiralty said: "Seldom in the annals of the sea, has there been exhibited such self-abnegation, such cool courage and such unfailing diligence in the face of almost unsurmountable difficulties. America is to be congratulated."

On the stormy night of 26 September 1918, cutter *Tampa*, bound for Milford Haven, having escorted a convoy to Gibraltar, disappeared with a loud explosion, leaving no trace other than some floating wreckage. It is believed that she was torpedoed by a German submarine. Two bodies, clad in naval uniforms, were found, but these were never identified. One hundred and fifteen men died that night—111 Coast Guardsmen and four Navy sailors. During World War I, Coast Guardsmen suffered the greatest loss in proportion to numerical strength of any of the Armed Services.

Following World War I, the experiment of prohibition added many problems to the work of the Coast Guard. While enforcement of the laws against smuggling alcoholic beverages was Coast Guard duty, and its connection with the unpopular law was unpleasant and often dangerous, funds were allotted for expansion with a generosity never before equaled. The Service was greatly augmented and improved, especially in the fields of communications and intelligence.

In 1939, the Coast Guard took over additional duties—maintenance and operation of aids to navigation. Originally, lighthouses were built and supported locally, but promptly upon the organization of the Federal Government provisions were made for lighthouse maintenance. An act was passed at the first session of Congress and approved 7 August 1789, which provided that the maintenance of aids to navigation generally "shall be defrayed out of the Treasury of the United States." Cession of the lighthouses to the Federal Government took place between 1789 and 1795, and thus the Lighthouse Service was established.

Alexander Hamilton directed the details at the outset. In 1820, supervision was turned over to the Fifth Auditor of the Treasury. The organization of the Lighthouse Board occurred in 1852. This Board remained under the Treasury Department until 1 July 1903 when, with other activities relating to navigation, it was transferred to the Department of Commerce and Labor. Later, when this department was partitioned into the Department of Commerce and the Department of Labor, the Lighthouse Board was placed under the Department of Commerce.

The Lighthouse Board was terminated in 1910, and a simple bureau form of organization was substituted. The Bureau of Lighthouses continued, greatly increasing the efficiency of the navigational aids system, until 1 July 1939, when the entire Lighthouse Service was merged with the Coast Guard. This vastly increased the scope of that branch of the Government Service. The merger was most logical, for certainly the function of the Lighthouse Service is, and always has been, to contribute to the safety of life and property at sea.

The Coast Guard is thus a merger of three important Government services, all concerned with the safety of those who go down to the sea in ships, and the ships themselves. The new Coast Guard organization, including the Lighthouse Service, continued its peacetime duties on an augmented scale under the Treasury Department.

The separate field organization of the former lifesaving activities was, at the same time, integrated with other functions of the Coast Guard. The grouping of shore stations, including lifeboat (lifesaving) stations and light stations and certain bases, which was put into effect at this time, proved of practical value shortly afterward when the Coast Guard was given the task of organizing the Beach Patrol in 1942. This integrated system of shore establishments then became the key of our entire coastal defense system.

The Coast Guard's function of maritime safety had scarcely been augmented by the additional responsibilities of the maintenance and operation of aids to navigation when the tocsins of war were sounded in Europe with the invasion of Poland by Germany on 1 September 1939. During the next two years, in keeping with the maintenance of military readiness, the scope of Coast Guard responsibility increased in detail after detail. New duties included the patrol of anchorages to enforce anchorage rules, and the supervision of the loading of explosives, gasoline and fuel (dangerous cargoes).

A National Emergency was proclaimed by President Roosevelt on 8 September 1939. On 27 June 1940, the President called for additional measures within the limits of peacetime authorizations. Eleven months later, on 27 May 1941, an Unlimited National Emergency was proclaimed. Because of the situation in the Pacific, Coast Guard operations at Hawaii were transferred by Executive Order on 16 August 1941, to the service and jurisdiction of the Secretary of the Navy, and thereafter Coast Guard units in Hawaii operated as part of the Navy. Events of 1941 pointed unmistakably toward war.

During these two years of emergency, the Battle of the Atlantic developed; the Neutrality Patrol was organized and made effective; convoys traversed the North Atlantic; German submarines became a fearful menace; and shipping was sunk in increasing numbers. Demands upon the Coast Guard expanded rapidly, requiring an expansion of the Coast Guard itself which, in September 1939, consisted of 17,022 persons (11,384 military and 5,638 civilian); 332 vessels; 50 aircraft; 818 field units; and Headquarters at Washington, D.C. Paralleling the great expansion of Coast Guard functions, the Service had increased from these 1939 figures to 29,978 persons (25,002 military and 4,976 civilian) by December 1941.

During this period, the Coast Guard actively participated in operations in the Atlantic, primarily on the Greenland Patrol and in escort-of-convoy duties. The Navy was in need of more vessels than it had available, and the large Coast Guard cutters were admirably qualified for this type of duty. Many were assigned to cooperate with the Navy, under Navy orders, and performed valuable service. In 1940, the Coast Guard, cooperating with the Weather Observation Service, used its newly modernized cutters to establish an Atlantic Weather Observation Service. Cutters took turns patrolling certain weather stations between Bermuda and the Azores, usually for 30-day periods, and their daily reports were designed primarily for the protection of the rapidly increasing transatlantic air commerce.

Control of dangerous cargoes inaugurated in 1939 came none too soon. In the calendar year 1940, our total exports of ammunition and explosives reached $56,449,969; by April of 1941 they had reached $31,262,827 for a third of that year. Between 1 January 1940 and 30 June 1946, some 15,500,000 tons of explosives and ammunition were handled under Coast Guard supervision without a major casualty or loss of life. The navigable waterfront real property of the United States which these regulations were designed to protect was valued in 1942 at $3,777,263,184, with an additional $895,486,576 of personal property in waterfront warehouses.

This immediate prewar era saw groundwork laid for the great expansion in personnel which a war would require. The Coast Guard Reserve and Auxiliary Act was passed 23 June 1939. It provided for an organization of civilian yacht and motorboat owners for the advancement of safety on navigable waters and an increase in efficiency in operating such vessels. By an Act of 19 February 1941 (revised March, 1941) this organization became the Coast Guard Auxiliary. A Coast Guard Reserve modeled after the Naval Reserve, but with both regular and "temporary" members, was authorized by the same Act. By December 1941, the Auxiliary had 5,205 members, 4,524 boats, and 216 flotillas. The regular Reserve had a nucleus of 245 officers and about 1,366 enlisted men, upon which was built the tremendous wartime expansion of personnel serving "for the duration", with pay.

By 1 November 1941, the war situation had become critical. It seemed only a matter of time before the United States would become involved in hostilities. On that day, Executive Order 8929 transferred the entire Coast Guard to the Navy, and directed it to operate as part of the Navy. It did so until 1 January 1946.

The attack by Japanese air forces on Pearl Harbor on the morning of 7 December 1941, was followed on 8 December by joint resolutions passed by the Congress and approved by the President, that a state of war existed with Japan. On 11 December similar resolutions were passed and approved declaring that a state of war existed with Germany and Italy.

It was inevitable that the Coast Guard should undergo a great and rapid expansion in personnel, vessels, bases, housing facilities, and equipment. Basically, all this rested upon personnel. On 7 December 1941, Coast Guard personnel, military and civilian, totaled about 29,000. The peak was reached about 30 June 1944, with 175,000 regulars and regular reservists. Throughout the entire war period there was constant and urgent demand for Coast Guardsmen at sea. This grew as the war tempo increased right up to final victory. Simultaneously, there was great need for them on shore in connection with tremendously important port security duties. The Auxiliary and Reserve Act, as amended in June 1942, paved the way for a satisfactory solution to this problem. It provided for two broad classifications of reservists—regular and temporary—with the temporary members at full or part time with or without pay. The great majority of these temporary reservists were volunteers who served part time (minimum 12 hours a week) without pay. In June 1944, temporary reserve personnel reached 51,173 actively enrolled, of which 44,307 were serving part time without pay. It is estimated that this number released 8,250 full time Coast Guardsmen for other duty.

Another group of reservists also effectively released men for combat duty. Public Law 773, signed by the President on 23 November 1942, amended the Auxiliary and Reserve Act and authorized replacement of officers and men for duty at sea by women in the shore establishment of the Coast Guard. The Women's Reserve was thus established as a branch of the Coast Guard Reserve, and members became known as SPARS. Starting from nothing, the Women's Reserve on 3 June 1944, numbered 8,371, of whom 771 were officers and 7,600 were enlisted personnel. By the close of 1944, over 11,000 women had signed enlistment contracts, though many had been rejected.

The primary purpose underlying the entire temporary reserve activity was the release of regulars and regular reservists for duty at sea and in combat areas. Yet, this demand could not be met at the expense of the security of our ports, through which vast amounts of war materials, equipment, munitions, and men were pouring to the battle areas. There could be no stoppage through fire, sabotage, or neglect along our waterfronts. Therefore, the port security program was immensely important, and it became one of the Coast Guard's major wartime efforts. It related not only to shore patrol and harbor patrol protection for the waterfront facilities so vital to shipments overseas, but to every phase of the safety of vessels in port. For proper prosecution, it initially required large regular and regular reserve personnel. Gradually this work was taken over by the great majority of the 50,000 temporary reservists. Throughout the war there were no waterfront conflagrations or great disasters of any kind in port areas under Coast Guard responsibility. This is proof of the effectiveness of the program and the devotion to duty of those who accepted the task of keeping our ports safe.

The successful prosecution of the war would have been jeopardized without adequate protection for American ships and the men in them. One central agency experienced in the consideration and development of safety standards at sea was needed.

The President, by Executive Order on 1 March 1942, placed the authority and responsibility for the protection of American merchant ships and seamen directly upon the Commandant of the Coast Guard. To assist in carrying out this responsibility, this order transferred from the Secretary of Commerce to the Commandant, certain safety-at-sea functions of the former Bureau of Marine Inspection and Navigation. Thus, another agency related to safety of lives and property at sea logically became part of the Coast Guard.

The mounting war effort required rapid and vast expansion in floating equipment. When we entered the war the Coast Guard had 168 vessels which bore names and were 100 feet or over in length. Included in this group were seven 327-footers, four 240-footers, twenty-two 165-footers, and thirty-three vessels 125 feet in length. There were also 39 lightships. During the war the Coast Guard acquired 156 more vessels of the name class, and 339 of the numbered class. Thus, the total Coast Guard fleet comprised 802 vessels of 65 feet or over, plus a large number of smaller craft—7,960 at the peak on 1 January 1943. In addition both the Army and Navy needed Coast Guard personnel to man many of their vessels. In all, 351 Navy vessels and 288 Army craft were so manned, and it is therefore evident that Coast Guardsmen fully manned 1,441 vessels longer than 65 feet during the war.

It is estimated that at the close of 1943, some 406 Coast Guard and Coast Guard-manned vessels were actively engaged in antisubmarine or escort duty, and that 42,698 out of a total of 171,493 regulars and regular reservists were serving afloat. By 30 June 1945, Coast Guard personnel at sea numbered 80,476 out of 171,168; 49,283 of them were in 288 Navy vessels, 6,851 in 262 Army ships, and 24,342 in 802 Coast Guard vessels. Navy craft manned by Coast Guardsmen included 22 transports, 9 auxiliary transports, 15 cargo ships, 5 auxiliary cargo attack ships, 18 gasoline tankers, 28 landing craft (infantry), 76 landing ships (tank), 30 destroyer escorts, 75 patrol frigates, and 33 miscellaneous smaller craft. The wartime total was 351. These figures afford some conception of the great wartime increase in personnel and vessel activity, as well as the breadth of operations at sea. It is noteworthy that the Coast Guard participated in every amphibious operation by United

States military forces during World War II.

During the early stages of the war the major effort of the Coast Guard at sea was in the Atlantic. Beginning with the assignment of large cutters to Navy Task Forces operating the "Neutrality Patrol" in the " 'twixt wind and water" days from 1939 through 1941, this effort steadily mounted until it was climaxed by intensive escort-of-convoy duty and the Normandy Invasion. It included antisubmarine combat in the Atlantic and the landings in North Africa, Sicily, Italy, and France, with the Coast Guard lending invaluable service to the Army and Navy by cooperating effectively in all of these invasions. Throughout the period, attention to the duty of assistance and rescue was never relaxed.

While these Atlantic and Mediterranean operations were being carried on, the effort in the Pacific was increasing in tempo and scope, and the Coast Guard was called upon to cooperate with the Army and Navy in those campaigns. As Coast Guardsmen are experts in small craft handling, there were, in addition to the manning program already mentioned, constant demands for them to operate landing craft of all descriptions. As successes in the Atlantic area and in Europe made it possible to shift emphasis, this was done, and the Coast Guard gradually moved its chief combat effort to the Pacific.

The Battle of the Atlantic was chiefly a contest between German submarines and Allied air and surface craft. It was in that theatre of war that most submarine sinkings took place. However, many were sunk in other areas. During the entire war, in all theatres, the Allied surface ships and aircraft sank a combined total of 996 enemy submarines. These comprised 781 German, 130 Japanese, and 85 Italian undersea craft. By far the largest numbers were accounted for by British and European Allied surface vessels, which sent 323 Axis submarines to the bottom. Aircraft of the British Empire and its European Allies took a toll of 233 enemy underwater attackers. The United States Navy sank 130 with its surface vessels and 96 with its airplanes. United States Army aircraft disposed of 63. The Coast Guard was responsible for 12 submarines which never rose again, 11 being sunk by cutters or Coast Guard-manned Navy vessels, and the other by one of its planes. The Coast Guard also assisted in several other sinkings.

Fifty-nine enemy submarines were victims of collisions or some other type of marine disaster; 33 struck mines; and 47 disappeared without any definite proof of the cause. By years, enemy submarine sinkings were:

| 1939 | 1940 | 1941 | 1942 | 1943 | 1944 |
|------|------|------|------|------|------|
| 9 | 42 | 56 | 126 | 285 | 296 |

In the 7½ months of 1945 until V-J Day, 182 enemy submarines were sunk. These sinkings were all confirmed by enemy records uncovered after the war.

The Coast Guard suffered its casualties. In all, it lost 11 of its own name vessels of 65 feet or more in length; 5 numbered vessels 65 to 100 feet long; and 12 Navy vessels which were wholly manned by the Coast Guard at the time. Most of the 572 Coast Guardsmen listed as killed in action were crew members of these 28 vessels. Some other Navy vessels which were sunk had some Coast Guardsmen in their crews. Total personnel losses from all operations were 72 officers and 966 enlisted men.

In this great combat effort, it was essential that shipping in our ports be efficiently and expeditiously handled to avoid harmful delays and congestion of any sort. It was the Coast Guard's responsibility, through its clearance and anchorage activities, to make sure that shipping flowed in and out of our ports smoothly, efficiently, and confidentially. Control of shipping movements, in cooperation with the Naval Port Directors, was an important contribution of the Coast Guard toward successful prosecution of the war.

Behind all of these operations were the necessary logistics which, because of the great expansion of the Service, presented numerous major problems for which the Coast Guard had no precedents. Solutions were often by trial and error, but almost always were ultimately satisfactory. These problems concerned recruiting, training, transportation, finance, supply, commissary, bases, and housing. Much legal work was involved. The health and welfare of Coast Guardsmen were essential to efficiency and morale. The Public Health Service provided doctors who served well and faithfully, and the Navy furnished chaplains for larger shore establishments.

In summary, the accomplishments of the Coast Guard in World War II contributed importantly to final victory. The Coast Guard was returned to the Treasury Department on 1 January 1946, pursuant to Executive Order 9666, dated 28 December 1945. Upon this occasion, the Secretary of the Navy paid tribute to the distinguished war record of the Coast Guard in the following words:

> During the arduous war years, the Coast Guard has earned the highest respect and deepest appreciation of the Navy and Marine Corps. Its performance of duty has been without exception in keeping with the highest traditions of the naval service.

In the pages which follow, these wartime activities of the Coast Guard are taken up separately and presented as a brief history of what this Service accomplished. Because operations were so numerous and took place in such widely diversified areas under very different circumstances, a chronological presentation is impracticable. Therefore, the reader should keep in mind the many activities engaged in simultaneously with the particular subject with which he is at any moment concerned.

Part I

Development of the Wartime
Organization of the Coast Guard

# Chapter I

# THE MEN BEHIND THE GUNS

THE ENTIRE wartime effort of the Coast Guard depended primarily upon the men and women who joined this Service to do their bit toward defeating the enemies of the United States and protecting their country. Although operating as part of the Navy throughout the war, the Coast Guard never lost its identity. Coast Guardsmen were always identified from Navy personnel by the shield on the sleeve of the uniform.

In many respects the Coast Guard and the Naval Services were similar, but the smaller Service manned and operated no submarines and few combat vessels larger than frigates and 327-foot cutters other than some attack transports, cargo ships, and tankers. On the other hand the Coast Guard was entirely responsible for the security of our ports and the vessels and facilities within them; enforced navigation and maritime safety laws; and was responsible for aids to navigation and maritime safety at sea.

As shown in the Prologue, the wartime duties of the Coast Guard underwent tremendous expansion to meet the demands upon this Service. It was necessary to augment personnel commensurately with the increase in scope of activity. This expansion had to be accompanied by intensive and widespread training programs, and by a great increase in housing facilities, and stations of various types. In the earlier days, especially, personnel growth exceeded that of training and housing, creating rather serious problems, but demands were soon met by the Finance, Civil Engineering, and Legal Divisions.

Enlisted personnel formed the great bulk of Coast Guardsmen, of course. The regulars, through voluntary enlistment, had increased from about 17,000 to nearly 30,000 by the time of Pearl Harbor. Enlistment of regulars was suspended between 1 February 1942 and 7 August 1945, when only reservists were accepted. This was necessary because a regular "hitch" generally was for three years, and the Coast Guard did not wish to find itself with thousands of excess officers and enlisted men and women whose contracts had not expired when the war ended. As regular and reserve enlistments had about the same requirements, we shall be concerned only with the latter during the war period.

Naturally, the highest type of recruit was desired, and a high school education was generally standard. However, to get sufficient enlistments it was necessary from time to time, to accept those who had only grammar school education, and to waive some minor physical defects that would not interfere with proper performance of duty. No person who had a police record was enlisted, though misdemeanors such as traffic violations were disregarded.

Enlisted personnel were recruited from all over the country and from practically every conceivable civilian occupation. Most had no prior military training, and little or no knowledge of nautical matters. Procurement was carried out through recruiting stations located throughout the country. These were manned by a commissioned, warrant, or chief petty officer, and several enlisted men, depending upon the quotas assigned to the particular station. Mobile recruiting units reached into the more remote localities and added greatly to the effectiveness of the recruiting program.

In addition to enlisting applicants at their stations, the men and women assigned to these recruiting stations went out to contact prospects, and engaged in intensive publicity drives. No opportunity to publicize the Coast Guard was overlooked in this effort to interest men and women in enlisting. Radio, newspapers, magazines, and other publicity media were used. Various organizations were visited to obtain the support of the leaders in making known to their members the advantages of joining the Coast Guard. Many advertising campaigns were undertaken and numerous speeches delivered, always with a view of obtaining recruits in quality as well as quantity. The Public Relations Office of each Coast Guard district cooperated in all of these programs. The custom of having pictures of recruits printed in their hometown papers was particularly successful.

Recruiting continued throughout the war, with changing conditions altering the program from time to time. At first, when a great need for enlisted men existed, there were no restrictions on the number to be recruited. Later, quotas for each district were specified. The induction program under the Selective Service System extended from 1 February to 1 December 1943, during which period recruitment was only for men under 18 or over 38 years of age. Coast Guard representatives were assigned to induction stations to process Coast Guard inductees. Between December 1943 and March 1944 no male enlistments were accepted. However, SPAR recruiting, which began 1 July 1943, continued until 13 August 1945, when all reserve enlisting activities terminated.

After physical examination and other details were satisfactorily accomplished, the enlistees were sworn in and transferred to a training or receiving station. At times, recruiting was achieved so rapidly that enlistees were placed immediately on inactive duty until such time as the training stations could receive them.

Basic training of enlisted men before the war had been conducted at Port Townsend, Washington; New Orleans, Louisiana; and at the Coast Guard Yard at Curtis Bay, Maryland. These training stations were augmented in the first six months of the war by the addition of recruit training stations at Alameda, California; and Manhattan Beach, New York. The period of basic training was reduced to about one month in order to handle the greatly increased numbers of recruits. However, the urgency for men was so great at that time that many newly enlisted personnel were assigned directly to units without prior training.

As more and more men were brought into the Service, the existing recruit training stations were augmented by many district training stations. These were operated during periods of peak recruitment,

and were decommissioned when the need had passed. They all had the same objective—to prepare recruits for duty by instructing them in Coast Guard customs and traditions; by teaching them discipline through intensive military drills and other means; by showing them how to wear and care for their uniforms; by preparing the men physically through medical examinations and physical training; and by teaching them seamanship, military courtesy, and the use of firearms.

Advanced training for enlisted personnel consisted of programs of study for advancement or change in rate. This was provided by the Coast Guard Institute at Groton, Connecticut, and at training stations as well as at specialty schools. Manning stations also conducted training to qualify personnel in ratings held by them, but in which they were not proficient. Various correspondence courses were provided for men interested in self-improvement. Another important method of training for advancement was to send men to various training stations and private schools throughout the country for special instruction to qualify them for ratings such as radarman, soundman, ship's cook, radioman, and electrician's mate.

Training was a continually changing process because of the changing conditions of the war. For example, after the invasion scare in the early part of the war, the need for beach patrol stations greatly decreased, and at the same time Coast Guardsmen were badly needed for manning ships. Many a boatswain's mate on beach patrol had never been in a ship. When needed, he was assigned to a manning unit and trained for eventual transfer afloat. Manning units also trained personnel in new ratings after need for their old ratings had passed.

Visual aids training through use of motion pictures, slides, charts, and mock-ups, begun early in 1943, was particularly successful. Subject coverage was wide. Films on a great variety of subjects were available in all districts. This type of training, in which the Coast Guard was assisted by the Navy, was uniform and well conceived.

Every officer and enlisted man in the Coast Guard was subjected to some form of basic, advanced, or refresher course training at one time or another. The program was administered very successfully, though many difficult problems required solution.

ALEXANDER HAMILTON . . . . first Secretary of the Treasury, and founder of the
Revenue Marine, later the Coast Guard.

ADMIRAL RUSSELL R. WAESCHE, USCG . . . . Commandant of the Coast Guard throughout World War II.

CUTTER *MASSACHUSETTS* . . . . built in 1791 at Newburyport, Massachusetts, was the first of a long line of distinguished cutters.—*Painting by Hunter Wood*

*HUDSON* RESCUING DISABLED *WINSLOW* . . . . from under the Batteries at Cardenas, Cuba.—*Painting by Muller*

A WOUNDED TANKER SUCCUMBS . . . . a common sight at sea in the early days of the Battle of the Atlantic.

*NORTHWIND* . . . . on Bering Sea Expedition in 1953.

The advent of war did not change the type of officer needed for the regular career service. Nationwide publicity programs were undertaken to acquaint qualified young men with the opportunities and advantages of a career as an officer. Throughout the period of hostilities, the Coast Guard continued training cadets at the Coast Guard Academy for regular commissions, because officers who were to spend their lives in the Service required much more technical knowledge and military training than did reserve officers. Consequently, the only change in the regular officer procurement program was a reduction of the period of cadet training from four to three years, which increased the number of yearly graduates. These cadets were awarded a bachelor of science degree and an ensign's commission in the regular service.

Most officers appointed during the war were given reserve commissions or warrant appointments. The types of occupations they had had in civilian life varied almost as much as the number of officers themselves. The Coast Guard needed officers with special training as well as those with a nautical background. With early expansion, an immediate need arose for officers for special and general duty. Consequently, appointments were made from among qualified applicants, regardless of age, who had college degrees and considerable experience in such fields as yachting, law, and engineering. Announcements concerning the availability of reserve officer appointments were made locally to the press, over the radio, and through other media. Upon receipt of applications, district officer procurement boards examined the applicants by written and oral tests, and sent recommendations on those best fitted to Headquarters at Washington, D.C., where the final selections were made. The ranks to which they were appointed depended chiefly upon their qualifications and ages, and ranged between warrant officer and captain. As soon as possible, it was arranged for officer candidates to have training before appointment. Between February 1942, and September 1945, the vast majority of men selected for appointment were first sent to the Coast Guard Academy for a four-month Reserve Training Course. As the officer procurement program really got under way, the reservists were generally college graduates not over 30 years old. As the war progressed, however, there were fewer and fewer men available with

college educations. Toward the end of the war, outstanding enlisted men who had even less than high school educations were accepted by the Coast Guard for appointments.

In general, the Coast Guard provided basic, refresher, and advanced training for its regular and reserve officers, as well as for its enlisted personnel.

Basic training of officers was conducted at the Coast Guard Academy at New London, and at the Training Station, St. Augustine, Florida. The Academy courses were primarily designed to train men and women in the basic requirements of service life, and some of the duties they would be immediately called upon to perform. Courses were given in such important fields as navigation, gunnery, seamanship, and communications. To supplement classroom instruction, short cruises were provided in small vessels for practical instruction.

The Coast Guard Training Station, St. Augustine, Florida, provided an indoctrination course for commissioned officers without previous training. It became increasingly apparent that the earlier officers who had been assigned directly to duty needed some form of indoctrination. Thus, beginning in September 1942, instruction was given them in such fundamentals as customs and traditions of the Service, military drill, use of firearms, and military courtesy. When the program ended in April 1944, some 1,078 officers had completed the courses.

Beginning in 1943 and ending February 1944, about 300 enlisted men were given the opportunity to go to college in the Navy V-12 program to finish their education, and then receive Coast Guard commissions. In September 1943, an Academy Preparatory School was established at the Training Station in Groton, Connecticut, for qualified enlisted men, and later for civilians as well. This course, which prepared men for competitive examination for a regular cadet appointment, was completed by 373 men before its discontinuance in May 1946.

When the manning program got under way about July 1943—to man destroyer escorts, transports, cargo vessels, tankers, landing craft, and frigates—units were established at Norfolk, Miami, Camp Bradford, and Alameda. Many officers without previous sea experience were assigned to these units, and it was necessary to indoctrinate and train them in their respective billets.

Advanced training was given officers available for special assignments at both Service and private schools. Resident courses of up to three years duration in colleges and universities were taken by officers who were outstanding in special subjects. The prewar post-graduate training program, designed to provide officers with highly technical training in engineering, business administration, law, etc., continued throughout the war. Special advanced courses in gunnery, damage control, fire-fighting, navigation, loran, radar, engineering, and aviation, running from a few days to several months, were also provided at Navy and Coast Guard facilities. The Coast Guard Institute and the United States Armed Forces Institute provided correspondence courses covering a large number of professional and academic subjects. In 1944 special courses were provided at the Coast Guard Academy to give officers the opportunity to brush up on many professional subjects.

With this great influx of men from all walks of life into the Service, and the consequent rapid readjustment required of them, certain morale problems were inescapable. It was absolutely essential that a serious effort be made to raise the level of morale in many quarters. Wartime conditions created much discontent, and this had to be overcome by the establishment of a Military Morale Division. This resulted in such developments as Coast Guard Welfare; the appointment of military morale officers at Headquarters and in district offices; appropriation of morale funds by Congress; and authorization of ships service stores with the use of their profits for recreation and entertainment. This all added up to an extremely valuable contribution to the success of wartime personnel administration, for those in the Service realized that the Coast Guard was doing everything feasible to ease personal hardships. A rotation policy proved of great assistance to morale. It became the policy of the Coast Guard to rotate to shore establishments all personnel with over 18 months of sea duty or assignments overseas if they so desired. Otherwise, many men would have served overseas throughout the entire war while others never would have left shore establishments.

In the early days of the war, Navy chaplains assigned to Navy units, were requested from time to time to lend their services to the Coast Guard. As the war progressed, districts found it necessary to request the assignment of Navy chaplains on a full time basis, and the Navy granted this request. Their services were of great benefit to the personnel, not only for their needed religious services and spiritual advice, but also for the help they gave to the distressed and troubled.

In the summer and fall of 1942, there came to the women of America an opportunity to participate directly in the war effort as members of the Armed Services. With the authorization of women's reserves for the Army, Navy, Marine Corps, and Coast Guard, women answered the call to volunteer. On 23 November 1942, the President signed Public Law 773, which amended the Coast Guard Auxiliary and Reserve Act of 1941, and established the Women's Reserve as a branch of the Coast Guard Reserve, with authority to enlist and appoint women to serve during the war and for six months thereafter. Members were to be trained and qualified for duty in the continental shore establishments to release male personnel for sea duty.

The Coast Guard selected Dorothy C. Stratton, Dean of Women on leave from Purdue University and a lieutenant in the Women's Naval Reserve, to head its Women's Reserve. It was she who suggested that members be known as SPARS; the term was derived from the Coast Guard motto "Semper Paratus", and its translation, Always Ready. She anticipated that SPARS would be particularly useful as yeomen, storekeepers, receptionists, messengers, mail clerks, telephone and teletype operators, radio operators and technicians, drivers of light motor vehicles, pharmacists mates, cooks, and stewards.

The establishment of the machinery to recruit women immediately followed. Many preliminary decisions had already been made. The Navy, Marine Corps, and Coast Guard agreed to recruit and train the members of their Women's Reserves together. In the early months, existing facilities in the Office of Naval Officer Procurement were used for recruiting the women, and they were trained in the Naval Training Schools established for the WAVES. The original SPAR complement, to be attained by April 1944, was set at 8,000 enlisted women and 400 officers.

Recruiting began in December 1942. As agreed by the Navy and Coast Guard, the Women's Reserve received its first 15 officers and 153 enlisted personnel by transfer from the Navy. During the first half of 1943, some SPAR officers were assigned to many Naval Officer Procurement offices where interviewing aid was required. The needs of the Coast Guard were made known by the Recruiting and Public Relations Divisions through publicity programs. Educational requirements for both officer and enlisted personnel were about the same as those for men.

Two months after the authorization of the SPARS, 531 women had enlisted, and 121 had become officers. Recruiters did well; by May 1943, SPARS numbered 333 officers and 2,838 enlisted personnel. It was found that many women whose brothers, sweethearts, or husbands were in the service decided that civilian life and work were not enough, and they turned to enlistment as a way of working more closely in spirit with their men. However, recruiting of women was not always easy, and it ran into many obstacles such as:

(1) High wages paid by war industries.
(2) Recruiting agreement with the War Manpower Commission and Office of War Information not to seek or enlist women in certain kinds of work without clearance.
(3) Objections of parents and men friends.
(4) Fear of regimentation and having social activities curtailed.
(5) Reluctance to accept idea of "being sent anywhere."
(6) Lethargic attitude of many women concerning their part in the war effort.

These objections were countered as far as possible. When the Coast Guard Training Station for enlisted SPARS was opened at a Palm Beach hotel, recruiting officers were able to offer the prospect of boot training "under glorious Florida skies." This met with some success.

On 1 July 1943, the Coast Guard withdrew from the joint recruiting agreement, and thereafter women applicants were interviewed and enlisted at Coast Guard recruiting stations. Medical facilities and officers of the Public Health Service were available for examination of the applicants. Recruiting went forward with renewed enthusiasm.

During the 12 months, from 1 July 1943 to 1 July 1944, some 11,558 qualified women made application to join the SPARS. Of these, 62 percent were accepted, and three-fourths of these, or about 5,020, actually enlisted. Early in this period,

a request was made of District Coast Guard Officers to indicate what additional SPAR personnel were needed and desired, and the replies indicated an increase of 81 percent. This shows with what genuine success the Women's Reserve was accomplishing its function. In December 1943, an increased SPAR complement was announced—1,200 officers and 12,000 enlisted women, as against 489 and 6,103, respectively, then existing. The SPARS were proving their worth, and more were wanted. By 3 June 1944, the Women's Reserve had 771 officers and 7,600 enlisted personnel.

It was requisite, of course, that virtually all of the SPARS undergo training and indoctrination. Initially, the use of Navy WAVE schools for SPAR training was extremely helpful, for Coast Guard training stations were just being established and expanded. First recruit indoctrination training began on 17 February 1943 at the Naval Training Station, The Bronx, New York (Hunter College). On completion of this 5-week training period the SPARS were sent to active duty. New drafts followed at 2-week intervals. Some SPARS, selected for special training, were sent to WAVE yeoman schools at Cedar Falls, Iowa; or Stillwater, Oklahoma; to storekeeper schools at Bloomington, Indiana; Boston, Massachusetts; or Milledgeville, Georgia; and to radio schools at Madison, Wisconsin; or Oxford, Ohio.

The Coast Guard established its own training schools for SPARS in mid-1943. The principal indoctrination courses were given at the Palm Beach Biltmore Hotel in Florida, which had been leased by the Coast Guard for the purpose. By the time this station was established approximately 20 percent of Women's Reserve members had received indoctrination in Navy schools and half of this number had had advanced training in Navy schools for specialty ratings. Indoctrination courses for both recruit and officer candidates included lessons in military etiquette and customs, insignia, naval history, ships and aircraft, naval organization and Navy Regulations. In these 5-week courses, pace was rapid, the regimentation great, and the amount of individualism practically *nil*. Specialty training for those with necessary aptitudes followed, with courses running from 4 to 12 weeks.

In the first four months of the SPAR program many officer candidates were commissioned directly from civilian life. Beginning in March 1943, candidates attended the Naval Reserve Midshipmen's School (Women's Reserve) at Northampton, Massachusetts, for initial indoctrination, and then went to the Coast Guard Academy at New London for final indoctrination. Some, however, were chosen for eight weeks of communications training at Northampton before attending the Academy. Throughout the Officer Procurement program for SPARS, preference was given candidates with college training. Those with knowledge of personnel, finance, and communications were particularly desired. By mid-1943, all women officer candidates except those taking communications courses at Northampton were being trained at the Coast Guard Academy. It is interesting to note that, by the time SPAR officer training terminated in November 1944, about 21 percent of all SPAR general duty officers had come from the enlisted ranks.

As it became evident that SPAR officers would be valuable in Pay and Supply, a class in that type of training was established at Palm Beach in October 1943. Candidates were selected from qualified enlisted SPARS. Subjects of instruction included pay, disbursing (including travel), allotment accounting, commuted ration mess, general mess, clothing, and procurement (including transportation and stores).

On 27 September 1944, an amendment to the basic Reserve Act removed some restrictions on locations where SPARS could serve. Thereafter, they could be assigned upon their request to duty in Hawaii and Alaska and to the American Area. A gratifying number requested and were assigned to such duty.

The members of the Women's Reserve, officers and enlisted personnel, gave highly satisfactory service from the inception of the program to the end of the war and for several months thereafter. They fully lived up to expectations, and were invaluable to the war effort. They carried a heavy load in the work of the shore establishment, releasing men for sea duty who otherwise would have been anchored to desks. They gained the full respect of their shipmates in the Coast Guard, and the country can be proud of their efficient and patriotic service.

Another group which started in a small way and later contributed greatly to the war effort comprised members of the Coast Guard Auxiliary, established in 1939. This was a volunteer non-military organization of yacht and motorboat owners. It grew slowly until Pearl Harbor, which brought about increased Auxiliary activity. The Seattle flotillas began to patrol that very night, and many patrols were soon established elsewhere, the Auxiliarists putting in many hours a week patrolling in their own vessels. By June 1942, there were approximately 11,500 members enrolled in the Auxiliary, and 9,500 boats were organized into about 44 flotillas. As the war tempo increased and port security responsibilities grew, it became evident that the civilian status of the Auxiliary would prevent the most effective wartime use of its personnel. Not only did the Auxiliarist lack military authority, but going out on antisubmarine patrol as civilians subjected them, if captured, to being executed as spies. Besides, in some flotillas the yachting spirit still predominated. The need for militarization was very apparent, and accordingly the majority of Auxiliarists were later enrolled in the Coast Guard Temporary Reserve.

The Temporary Reserve, established by the Auxiliary and Reserve Act of 19 February 1941, as amended in June 1942, was unique in the annals of United States military service. There were eventually about 50,000 members aside from "Coast Guard Police", most of whom served on a voluntary, part-time basis, without pay. With reference to this component of the Reserve, Admiral Waesche, wartime Commandant of the Coast Guard, wrote:

All the wars in which America has been concerned have produced bodies of civilian volunteers whose careers are interwoven with the particular contests which engendered them. The Minute Men of 1775 were citizen soldiers; so were the Texas Rurales who fought the Mexicans along the Rio Grande long before war was officially declared. In this category may be placed a major part of the Rough Riders who fought at San Juan Hill in 1898. Even in the First World War the utilization of part-time citizen levies was under consideration when the conflict abruptly terminated.

Now, in the present struggle, by far the greatest which our country has been fated to endure, we hail the advent of a group of devoted citizenry not dissimilar to those just mentioned and certainly yielding nothing to their predecessors in zeal and thoroughness. The men and women of the Volunteer Port Security Force in the U. S. Coast

Guard have proved themselves worthy successors to the bodies of patriotic volunteers who rendered similar service in all previous crises of our national history.

Although Admiral Waesche referred specifically to the Volunteer Port Security Force, his remarks applied equally to all volunteer temporary members of the Coast Guard Reserve. These volunteers set up a wholly new, practical application of patriotism.

At first any Auxiliary member could volunteer the services of his boat, himself, and his crew (if any) for temporary service in the Temporary Reserve. Thus, the Coast Guard was able to draw on trained Auxiliarists for the performance of regular Coast Guard duties afloat on a military basis, and the Auxiliary became chiefly a source of personnel supply.

The program for Temporary Reservists on full-time duty with pay was originally established to facilitate the acquisition of badly needed reserve boats and men from the Auxiliary, because the need for small patrol craft in the early days was extremely urgent. Men were enrolled for "temporary duty" for specific periods such as three or five months, and usually were assigned to their own vessels. They were not transferred from their particular boat, or out of the district. Their duty was chiefly with the Coastal Picket Fleet (mentioned presently) between June and November 1942. This type of duty for Temporary Reservists was then discontinued.

The final set-up for the Temporary Reserve was established 29 October 1942, when these six categories were designated:

(1) From the Auxiliary: in a part-time voluntary capacity and in a no-pay status. (Usually units afloat.)

(2) Volunteer Port Security Force: in a part-time voluntary capacity and in a no-pay status. (Usually guard details on piers, wharves, and other harbor facilities.)

(3) From Pilot Associations: on a non-military pay basis, but receiving usual pay from the Association by whom they were employed.

(4) Civil Service Employes: on a full-time basis without military pay, but with pay from Coast Guard Civil Service appropriations.

(5) Merchant Marine Inspectors: on a full-time basis without military pay, but with pay from Coast Guard Civil Service appropriations.

(6) Coast Guard Police: on a full-time basis without military pay, but receiving regular pay from the shipyard or war plant by which they were employed.

Enrollments in category (1) began in June 1942, progressed slowly, and were chiefly for duty in Coast Guard Reserve craft patrolling harbor, river, and inlet waters along the Atlantic Coast. These cooperated in the earlier days with the Auxiliary, which was carrying out similar patrols. However, Temporary Reservists began to fill the crews, and except in two districts, Auxiliary patrols ceased after 1 January, 1943.

While the need for Temporary Reservists on water patrols was acute, demand for patrol of waterfront facilities on the landside was urgent. This was first recognized at Philadelphia and steps were taken as early as May 1942, for the creation of a "Volunteer Port Security Force" there. The plan was to establish a full-time regiment of part-time volunteers to guard vessels, wharves, piers, and other waterfront facilities as a precaution against sabotage, fire, unauthorized persons, and anything else which might endanger waterfront properties and personnel. This force of men, inducted into the Temporary Reserve under category (2) apart from the Auxiliary, became effective in December 1942. The plan was so successful that similar forces varying little in organization were established in 22 United States ports.

While engaged on active duty a temporary member of the Reserve had the same power, authority, rights, and privileges as members of the regular Coast Guard of similar rank, grade, or rating, in the execution of assigned duty. He was entitled to the same military courtesy and privileges, and was governed by the same military procedures and practices as regular personnel, and to the same extent.

Recruiting of Temporary Reservists (generally called TRs) was not easy, and aggressiveness was needed in most areas. The Auxiliary provided a nucleus of men well qualified in small-boat handling. But demands became greater and greater as pressure grew for sending regulars to sea. Especially when Volunteer Port Security (VPSF) units became a necessity, concerted drives for recruits had to be instituted. A "good press" was very beneficial in this effort. Local merchants in many areas donated their advertising space for recruiting purposes. Regular recruiting offices were set up, and mobile units assisted greatly in outlying areas.

The bulk of the volunteer, unpaid Temporary Reservists were men who, for some reason, could not enter full-time service in the Armed Forces but who, nevertheless, because of their patriotism, abilities, and desire to do their bit, were willing to guarantee at least 12 hours of duty each week. Many gave considerably more time, often as much as 40 or 50 hours a week over an extended period. Ages ran from 17 to over 70. Enrollment did not change draft status; while in some sections men subject to draft were denied enrollment, they were accepted in others. All were subject to physical examination, but waivers were quite liberal. Many who, because of minor disabilities, would have been excluded from the regular Service were thus able to serve their country. There was a vital job to be done, and the volunteers selected themselves to do it. The great majority served well, for which their only recompense was a calm conscience and the comradeship of men pulling together with common purpose.

These men assumed their duties with the understanding that there would be no pay or other benefits. They came from all walks of life. A typical boat crew might include a business executive, an automobile mechanic, a school teacher, a salesman, and a printer. Clergymen gave valuable time. Bank presidents stood watches on coal docks with their office boys. A former Governor of Maine, and Arthur Fiedler, famous conductor of the Boston Pops Orchestra, were seamen on the Boston Harbor Patrol; a seaman on guard duty at Portland, Maine, became Governor of that State while on active duty. This was typical of all districts. Veterans of World War I were prominent in the rosters; most were too old to serve in the regular Armed Forces, and found the Temporary Reserve a practical outlet for their patriotism.

Virtually all of the 50,000 TRs who served had to be trained before they could become effective and trusted with their assignments, for it was essential that they be efficient even from their first watch or patrol. Training became one of the broadest and most important activities in this branch of the Coast Guard. Upon it depended to a large extent the efficiency of the entire personnel. Boatmen received training in all phases of small-boat handling and in first aid, military courtesy, motor mechanics, and fire prevention and protection. Men in guard details (VPSF) and a large number of boatmen were instructed in the use and care of small arms, in port security, fire-fighting, unarmed combat, chemical warfare, and infantry drill. The diligence of the instructors and the conscientiousness of the "students" were largely responsible for the efficiency of the units which contributed so much to the excellent port security record of the Coast Guard throughout the war.

As these men became trained and ready for duty, they were assigned to patrol boats and guard units. By the end of 1942, boats in many areas were manned entirely by Temporary Reservists on a 24-hour basis, and the number of boats and areas covered increased steadily until late 1943, when maximum coverage was attained. By early 1944, most waterfront areas in our principal harbors were effectively covered by VPSF or similar units. Temporary Reservists, for the most part, took over the duties of guarding the ports. Thus, they were an integral part of the entire port security activity, which is more generally treated in later chapters.

We have endeavored to outline briefly the personnel problems and their solutions in building up the Coast Guard on an effective wartime scale, and to give an indication of the breadth of Coast Guard contribution to the effort of the Armed Services. The total military strength at the peak, including the Auxiliary, was 239,422. The regulars, the regular reservists, the SPARS, and the Temporary Reservists comprised the active personnel. Once on duty, their functions were all part of the business of winning the war and, at the same time, as far as possible, carrying on the peacetime functions of the Coast Guard.

An efficient administrative system welded together this personnel and its far-flung and varied activities. Under the President, as Commander-in-Chief, came the Secretary of the Navy, to whom the Chief of Naval Operations was responsible. Next in the chain of command for the Coast Guard was the Commandant, Admiral Russell R. Waesche, who served with high efficiency in that capacity throughout the war. Directly under him were the Assistant Commandant and the District Coast Guard Commanders who were known through most of the war as District Coast Guard Officers. The Coast Guard Districts were made coextensive with, and became part of, their respective Naval Districts. Close liasion between the District Coast Guard Officers (DCGO) and the Navy Commandants of the naval districts was always requisite. The second in command of each district was the Assistant District Coast Guard Officer, under whom most members of the DCGO Staff served; these latter headed one or more of the various activities in the district, such as Port Security, Aids to Navigation, Vessel Operations, or Finance. Large Coast Guard vessels operating at sea always came under the operating command of the Navy commander of the Task Units or Task Forces to which they were attached; but the District Coast Guard Officers remained responsible for every phase of their logistical support.

At the Coast Guard Headquarters in Washington, D.C., there was also a carefully set up organization responsible for the over-all administration of the Coast Guard. Under the Commandant was the Assistant Commandant, to whom practically all administrative officers for each broad activity were responsible. These officers oversaw all district activities in their particular fields, and had their own administrative staffs at Headquarters. Liaison between and coordination of these various subdivisions were, of course, highly important, and were aggressively pursued.

This organization grew from its relatively small size before the war to its ultimate, by various stages in which trial and error played a considerable part. The Coast Guard had no precedent for much of this organization. Certain set-ups for various functions were established and, after a while, shortcomings would become evident, calling for further change and experiment. The great expansion during this process complicated the problem and often drew organization changes along with it. However, by late 1943 the approximate peak of expansion had been reached, much experimentation had been completed, and, in the meantime, administrative and operational functions had been quite well executed. Administratively, the Coast Guard reached maturity, and on 1 January 1944, an *Organization Manual* was published and distributed setting forth in detail the chain of command and duties of all Headquarters and district administrative officers. Duties will be mentioned as

necessary in the chapters which follow, but the administrative organization relating to chain of command is set forth below; there was little change of any importance from this date onward.

COAST GUARD HEADQUARTERS ORGANIZATION

The Commandant
    Advisory Board
    Merchant Marine Council
    Administrative Management Division
    Public Relations Division
    Special Assistants
Assistant Commandant
    Office Services Division
Statistical Division
Chief Personnel Officer
   Assistant Chief Personnel Officer
    Auxiliary Division
    Civilian Personnel Division
    Enlisted Assignment Division
    Medical Division
    Military Morale Division
    Officer Assignment Division
    Personnel Procurement Division
    Temporary Reserve Division
    Training Division
    Women's Reserve Division
Inspector in Chief (Inspection Division)
Chief Intelligence Officer (Intelligence Division)
Chief Counsel (Legal Division)
Chief Operations Officer
    Operations Planning Officer
    Aids to Navigation Division
    Allowance Division
    Aviation Division
    Beach Patrol Division
    Communications Division
    Merchant Marine Inspection Division
    Merchant Marine Personnel Division
    Ordnance and Gunnery Division
    Port Security Division
Chief Finance and Supply Officer
   Assistant Chief Finance and Supply Officer
    Administrative Assistant
    Planning and Procedures Officer
    Accounting Division
    Budget and Reports Division
    Supply Division
Engineer in Chief
   Assistant Engineer in Chief
    Aeronautical Engineering Division
    Communications Engineering Division
    Civil Engineering Division
    Naval Engineering Division
    Contract Services Division
    Materiel Reports Division

COAST GUARD DISTRICT ORGANIZATION

The Commandant
Assistant Commandant

District Coast Guard Officer
  Public Relations Officer
  Assistant District Coast Guard Officer
    Office Services Supervisor
    Personnel Officer
      Military Morale Officer
      Personnel Procurement Officer
      Records and Assignments Officer
      Temporary Reserve Personnel Officer
      Training Officer
      Civilian Personnel Officer
      District Director of the Auxiliary
    Medical Officer
    Engineer Officer
      Civil Engineer Officer
      Communications Engineer Officer
      Marine Engineer Officer
    Operations Officer (ADCGO)
      Aids to Navigation Officer
      Beach Patrol Officer
      Communications Officer
      Marine Inspection Officer
      Ordnance and Gunnery Officer
      Port Security Officer
      Vessel Operations Officer
    Intelligence Officer
    Law Officer
    Finance and Supply Officer
      Budget and Accounting Officer
      Clothing Officer
      Commissary Officer
      Pay and Disbursing Officer
      Supply Officer
      Transportation Officer

With the transfer of the Coast Guard to the Navy, and realignment of the districts, use of the term "Coast Guard Districts" ceased, and the term "Naval Districts" became standard. Reference will be made to Naval Districts especially in Parts II and III, and the following summary of districts and their headquarters ports will be helpful.

| Naval District | Headquarters |
|---|---|
| First | Boston, Massachusetts |
| Third | New York, New York |
| Fourth | Philadelphia, Pennsylvania |
| Fifth | Norfolk, Virginia |
| Sixth | Charleston, South Carolina |
| Seventh | Miami, Florida |
| Eighth | New Orleans, Louisiana |
| Ninth | (Great Lakes, Illinois) |
| St. Louis* | St. Louis, Missouri |
| Chicago* | Chicago, Illinois |
| Cleveland* | Cleveland, Ohio |
| Tenth | San Juan, Puerto Rico |
| Eleventh | San Diego, California |
| Twelfth | San Francisco, California |
| Thirteenth | Seattle, Washington |
| Fourteenth | Honolulu, Hawaii, T.H. |
| Seventeenth | Ketchikan, Alaska |

Note: There were no Second, Fifteenth, or Sixteenth Districts.
* For Coast Guard purposes, the Ninth Naval District was further subdivided. Each subdivision had its own DCGO. On 31 December 1943, the Chicago and Cleveland subdivisions were merged.

This outline of personnel and organization shows in a general way how the problem was met to carry out efficiently the four broadly classified functions of military readiness, assistance, marine safety, and law enforcement. As stated earlier by 30 June 1945, some 80,476 regular and reserve Coast Guardsmen were serving afloat out of a total of some 171,168. Thus, it took 1.13 regular and regular reserve men ashore to support each man at sea. The shore establishment had SPARS and Temporary Reservists in the approximate ratio of 0.3 to one man afloat. The work of the shore establishment was vital, not only in providing logistical support to the men at sea, but also in carrying out training and in successfully performing the important functions of all phases of port security and merchant marine and maritime safety in all its many aspects.

These were the men behind the guns, and the men and women behind the men behind the guns, all performing vital service, with their work coordinated through a carefully conceived administrative and operational organization. Also behind the men at sea, and those affording security at home, were logistical activities which assumed substantial proportions, such as medical, law, public information, finance, and engineering, and which deserve much more than passing mention.

Chapter 2

# LOGISTICS AND OTHER
# VITAL SERVICES

W EBSTER defines *logistics* as "that branch of military art which embraces all details of moving or supplying armies." The term applies to naval forces ashore and afloat. Without this support, military forces would be impotent. Other non-operational but important services, not strictly within that definition, also are of utmost consequence to the proper maintenance and servicing of military forces.

The primary function of much of the Coast Guard shore establishment was to provide all necessary logistical support to the men and ships at sea, and to operational shore units such as lighthouses, beach patrol stations, lifeboat stations, bases, training stations, and port security forces. Vital to all operations were the health and welfare of personnel at sea and ashore. Procurement, conversion, construction, and maintenance of Coast Guard vessels, bases, offices, and buildings was a herculean task of supreme importance. Legal matters relating especially to real estate required efficient handling, as well as all phases of pay, disbursing, clothing, commissary, and supply. Constructive information for the public regarding the Coast Guard and its personnel was needed to promote recruiting and good public relations. These vital services required a large number of well trained officers and enlisted personnel. Many were later transferred to sea, and others, through the rotation process, left sea and combat duty to fill the vacancies.

We shall not dwell at length on details of these activities, though many chapters could be devoted to them. A broad perspective on the Coast Guard's wartime history, however, requires some comprehension of those fields of endeavor.

First, let us consider medical aspects. Before the war, the Coast Guard had no organized medical activities within the districts proper. At the Coast Guard Academy infirmary there were three medical officers and one dental officer; at the Fort Trumbull Training Station, New London, there were one medical and one dental officer; and at the Curtis Bay Depot, there was one dental officer. Medical officers were also assigned to sea duty in cutters basing at Honolulu, T.H.; Cordova and Juneau, Alaska; and San Juan, Puerto Rico. In addition, a medical and a dental officer were assigned to the Coast Guard dispensary, Unalaska, Alaska, to care for personnel of the Bering Sea Patrol Force. Early in 1941 medical officers were assigned to sea duty in cutters on Neutrality Patrol and Weather Patrol in the Atlantic; cadet practice cruise vessels; and in one cutter then basing on Lisbon, Portugal. There were over 200 local physicians with appointments as Acting Assistant Surgeons in the Public Health Service who rendered medical relief to Coast Guard personnel in isolated communities.

In August 1941, Coast Guard Headquarters completed arrangements with the Public Health Service for the assignment of eight full-time reserve medical officers to eight district offices. They performed physical examinations for new Reserve personnel, and worked for months without suitable quarters or adequate equipment.

Following Pearl Harbor, recruiting stations were opened throughout the country, placing a greater load on medical officers and Marine Hospitals. To relieve this pressure, the Public Health Service appointed over 300 local, independent physicians who performed physical examinations on a fee basis for reserve enlistees. Additional medical and dental officers for recruit examination were assigned by Headquarters to district offices.

All this greatly increased administrative work,

and by September 1942, a District Medical Officer was assigned to each district. He was primarily charged and occupied with planning and providing effective medical service for the greatly expanded district activities. Still more medical and dental personnel were needed to meet requirements; the complement of pharmacist's mates was woefully inadequate and remained so until well into 1944.

This tabulation, showing the strength of professional Public Health Service personnel with the Coast Guard clearly illustrates the rapid expansion:

| Year | Medical Officers | Dental Officers | Nurse Officers |
|------|------------------|-----------------|----------------|
| 1940 | 19  | 6   | 0  |
| 1941 | 30  | 16  | 0  |
| 1942 | 85  | 47  | 0  |
| 1943 | 286 | 132 | 0  |
| 1944 | 384 | 170 | 33 |
| 1945 | 409 | 190 | 37 |
| 1946 | 132 | 69  | 12 |
| 1947 | 28  | 29  | 8  |

The organization of the Beach Patrol and the Temporary Reserve in 1942 brought into sharp focus the lack of medical and dental personnel. The number of physical examinations per district in the first three months of 1942 averaged almost 50 per month. Thereafter, this figure jumped tenfold. The Public Health Service responded gratifyingly for additional professional personnel, and Coast Guard infirmaries began to operate throughout the United States, Alaska, Hawaii, and Puerto Rico.

To relieve the shortage of pharmacist's mates, arrangements were made with Columbia University School of Pharmacy in New York City to provide basic training for that rating. This was an adjunct to the regularly established Hospital Corps Training School at Groton, Connecticut. Six classes of 200 male students were graduated at Columbia between 15 April 1942 and January 1944, and two classes of 100 SPARS each were graduated in 1944.

Although adequate medical and dental personnel were a long time coming, and procurement of proper equipment was painfully slow, the needs of the Coast Guard were ultimately met. During this period of expansion, every effort was made to provide adequate facilities at sea, and hospitalization cases were, for the most part, taken care of in Marine Hospitals.

Close liaison was requisite between the District

Medical Officers and their respective Marine Hospitals, as well as the Medical Departments of the Army and Navy. Medical treatment of Coast Guard personnel in Army and Navy facilities was generally interchangeable as conditions required. As an example, these figures for one typical 1945 week in the First Naval District indicate distribution of hospitalized Coast Guard personnel over the various facilities:

| | |
|---|---:|
| U. S. Marine Hospital, Brighton (Boston), Massachusetts | 186 |
| U. S. Marine Hospital, Portland, Maine | 28 |
| U. S. Marine Hospital, Vineyard Haven, Massachusetts | 3 |
| U. S. Naval Hospital, Chelsea, Massachusetts | 54 |
| U. S. Naval Hospital, Newport, Rhode Island | 22 |
| U. S. Naval Hospital, Portsmouth, New Hampshire | 4 |
| U. S. Naval Hospital, Springfield, Massachusetts | 20 |
| Infirmaries of DCGO, First Naval District | 18 |
| | 335 |
| Total Personnel Attached to the District | 7,316 |

To decrease the high cost of hospitalization, sick bays were established at units of sufficient size. Where large groups of Coast Guard personnel were assembled, special dispensaries and infirmaries were set up, with medical, dental, and nursing staffs being supplied by the Public Health Service.

In all, 663 Public Health officers were assigned to the Coast Guard from 7 December 1941 to 2 September 1945, comprising 413 medical, 195 dental, 6 engineer, and 49 nurse officers. During that period practically all of the medical officers and 77 dental officers were assigned on one or more occasions to duty afloat.

Several special studies were undertaken by the Coast Guard medical organization. One was a study of war fatigue among officers and enlisted personnel of seagoing units. This was made through personal visits on board vessels and through questionnaires. As a result of the findings, the Board made specific recommendations relating to time limitations for various types of sea duty, and these recommendations had much to do with establishing the personnel rotation program.

Soon after Pearl Harbor, a Tuberculosis Control Program was inaugurated with Dr. Herman E. Hilleboe of the Public Health Service in charge. Inability to obtain adequate equipment retarded development of the program, but units were finally established at several training stations, and a mobile unit assisted greatly in reaching smaller and inaccessible units. The program was efficiently executed and proved highly valuable. Between July 1942 and January 1946, 156,727 chest x-ray examinations were made. Of 141,523 actual readings, some 140,506 were essentially negative, 431 showed some form of tubercular condition, 156 showed suspected tubercular condition, and 1,264 conditions other than tubercular were revealed.

The actual range of medical activity was very broad. The Coast Guard picked up many survivors from torpedoed vessels and wrecked planes, provided first aid treatment, and rushed them to hospitals. Availability of ambulances was important. Medical and dental attention was given dependents of Coast Guardsmen whenever facilities were available. Prevention of disease by immunizations, vaccinations, and inoculations was important, as well as timely medical, surgical, and dental treatment resulting in absence of epidemics and an extremely low morbidity and mortality rate. Routine sanitary inspections were made of barracks, galleys, and mess halls. Safe water supply, fumigation, proper handling and preparation of food, sewerage disposal, insect control, and refrigeration were problems of the Medical Division. It was imperative that small floating units be provided with adequate first aid kits and facilities. There was much correspondence relative to Veterans Administration and Red Cross inquiries, medical histories, and claims.

Mention of a few experiences of medical officers will show their devotion to duty and efficient conduct of assignments. Some incidents referred to will receive more detailed mention in later chapters. On 29 January 1942, the cutter *Alexander Hamilton*, in heavy seas, had just released a tow to a Navy tug near Iceland where submarines were known to be operating. A mine field was close by. Suddenly the cutter was jarred by an explosion. The medical officer, Dr. James A. Finger, was in his stateroom. At the sick bay he found there was some crowding because of the large number of casualties, the small space, and absence of electric power. He and the pharmacist's mates administered morphine, and applied temporary bandages and splints to the injured. The order to abandon ship was then received. Injured men were placed in all available lifeboats, with a pharmacist's mate

in each boat. The men were picked up and reached shore; the injured were taken to local residences, then removed by ambulances to the U. S. Army Base Hospital. The cutter which had been taken under tow capsized and sank some hours later.

Cutter *Muskeget*, on weather station in early September 1942, disappeared without a trace. All hands, including Dr. Haskell D. Rosenblum, were lost.

When the transport *Dorchester* was torpedoed and sunk off Greenland on 3 February 1943, cutters *Escanaba* and *Comanche* saved 225 men. Utter disregard of self in devotion to duty, plus resourcefulness and coolness under fire are seen in the medical report of Dr. L. Ray Howard, medical officer on board *Comanche*. Within an improvised hospital ward in a tossing ship pursued by submarines, the men, oblivious of their own safety, worked swiftly and efficiently in darkness, to save human life. After the first hour the doctor and chief pharmacist's mate found it impossible to carry out promptly the various treatments required for each patient, because of the large number of survivors being brought on board who needed attention. Crew members were hastily trained to help in teams of three or four, with satisfactory results.

On the morning of 17 April 1943, cutter *Spencer*, escorting a North Atlantic convoy, followed a submarine sound ·contact and eventually discovered *U-175*, apparently damaged by her depth charges, breaking surface off her port bow. *Spencer*, assisted by cutter *Duane*, opened fired on the submarine, which was in a sinking condition. Survivors abandoned ship and were rescued by the cutters. One man remained on board, however, and shelled *Spencer*, resulting in 27 casualties, including one death. The medical officer, Dr. John J. Davies, received a shrapnel wound in the right forearm, but during the next 72 hours, despite his wound, he gave medical care to the 26 surviving casualties and to two wounded prisoners from the submarine.

Cutter *Escanaba* blew up and sank within three minutes in the North Atlantic on 13 June 1943. All but two of the entire crew of 103 were lost, including Dr. Ralph R. Nix.

The *USS Serpens*, a Coast Guard-manned ammunition ship of 14,250 tons, exploded while loading depth charges off Lunga Beach, Guadalcanal, on 29 January 1945. Medical officer Dr. Harry

M. Levin, 7 other officers, 188 crewmen, and 57 Army personnel lost their lives. Only two officers and eight men survived.

Coast Guard-manned transports participated in European, African, and Pacific invasions and amphibious operations, each with its medical officer and staff. These went ashore with the invasion forces to care for wounded men on the beach, and tended many hundreds of wounded when they were brought on board their own vessels. Many vessels suffered casualties to their own men when under fire. For instance the *USS Callaway*, a Coast Guard-manned transport, was struck in Lingayen Gulf by a kamikaze on 9 January 1945, killing 29 men and wounding about 25. Dr. Benjamin H. Wolfman was the medical officer at the time. This vessel later took over 300 casualties from the beach at Iwo Jima.

Dr. Vernon G. Guenther and one other medical officer were assigned to a group of LSTs which took part in the invasion of Iwo Jima. These vessels remained anchored close off the island so that the amphibious truck drivers could return to the ships for ammunition as necessary. A number of wounded taken on board Dr. Guenther's LST during the invasion were given emergency care pending further transfer. This unit later participated at Okinawa where it was attacked several times by Japanese planes.

Doctors Leon Holloman and Romeo J. Gentile were medical officers of a flotilla of 24 LCIs which crossed the Atlantic to North Africa in 1943. Illness in any vessel necessitated transferring a doctor to another vessel while under way.

This flotilla took part later in the landings at Sicily. The LCIs proceeded to the beach under heavy fire from shore and air. A bomb ripped off the stern anchor cable of the vessel to which Dr. Holloman was attached, and destroyed the foward part of the ship including the surgical unit. When the ship was abandoned the entire complement went ashore as United States warships pounded the enemy and finally silenced their batteries. Dr. Holloman joined a Naval Beach Party surgical unit and worked all D-Day aiding the wounded. Next day he and several pharmacist's mates went from one ship to another, administering first aid to his flotilla and to casualties from the beach. A few weeks later, there was repeat performance in the Salerno landings.

These are but a few incidents out of hundreds involving the Coast Guard's Medical Division which are worthy of historical record.

The breadth and rapid expansion of Coast Guard activity have been outlined so it is not difficult to comprehend the importance and scope of the Finance and Supply Division. Throughout the war, transfers of officers and enlisted personnel from the shore establishments to sea and vice versa meant a certain, and often troublesome, rotation in this field. Every floating unit and every unit on shore was the concern of the Finance and Supply Officers. In most cases, these units were too small to justify a Finance Officer of their own. Yet each unit, large or small, was directly or indirectly affected by budgeting and accounting, pay and disbursing, clothing, supply, commissary, transportation, and war bonds—the subdivisions of Finance and Supply. Possibly few persons in this Division were heroes in that work, but they certainly were unsung.

Heading this Division at Headquarters was the Chief Finance and Supply Officer, responsible to the Assistant Commandant; under him were staff officers such as Chief of the Accounting Division, Chief of the Supply Division, and Chief of Budget and Reports Division. Cooperating directly with them in each district was a District Finance and Supply Officer, under whom were the officers heading up the various subdivisions. All men of the Coast Guard had to be paid, clothed, fed, and transported, and this was the responsibility of these officers. All units had to be supplied with necessary equipment, but this had first to be procured in a highly competitive market where the Navy and Army enjoyed top priorities. With these officers also rested procurement of space for offices, barracks, training stations, bases, and such at a rate required by rapid growth. Budget Officers had to anticipate further expansion and demands for funds incidental thereto, and to exercise control over spending.

Before the war this activity was the work of a relatively small group, because the Coast Guard was small. As war threatened and developed, pay clerks and chief pay clerks were trained to take over additional duties of greater scope. Many enlisted storekeepers who were thoroughly grounded in their respective duties were commissioned for finance and supply duty. Reserve officers, commissioned from civilian status, were indoctrinated in pay and supply procedures in a school at the Coast Guard Yard, Curtis Bay, Maryland.

SPARS were given indoctrination and training at the Palm Beach Pay and Supply School. Upon graduation, they were commissioned as ensigns and assigned to shore establishments throughout the United States, and later in Alaska and Hawaii. They served as commissary, clothing, assistant disbursing, war bond, and ship's store officers, and in many other capacities, rendering excellent service throughout their tour of duty. Thus, many male pay and supply officers were made available for important assignments with the combat forces. Many enlisted SPARS trained for yeoman and storekeeper ratings in Finance, and proved efficient and valuable.

At the peak of Coast Guard expansion there were 827 officers specializing in Finance and Supply—regular, reserve, and SPAR officers numbering 401, 292, and 134 respectively. The total number of personnel in this activity reached almost 9,000.

The Budget Estimate of each district required the anticipation of the needs of the various departments of the district, and the funds needed were specified. These estimates were the basis of that part of the budget which Headquarters prepared and presented in turn to the proper Congressional Committees, so that funds might be appropriated and later allotted to the district concerned. The matter was complicated because the establishment and operation of a shore or floating unit during the expansion period created expenditures which could not be anticipated, and for which funds had to be appropriated, obligations incurred, and payments recorded. Allotments covered pay, and a long list of general expenditures such as repairs to vessels, fuel and water, rebuilding and repairing stations, aids to navigation, recruiting, etc. A systematic control of expenditures was maintained and allotments could not be exceeded.

The Pay Accounts Section maintained and prepared the pay accounts for all military personnel. The Disbursing Section audited all public vouchers; reconciled Treasury statements; prepared and issued checks for all military and civilian payrolls; and maintained accounts and prepared returns. SPARS were particularly useful in Pay

and Disbursing, and by the end of the war they largely "manned" these offices. For instance, the Fourth District in December 1942, had 23 males and no SPARS in this Section. In June 1945, there were 9 males and 23 SPARS.

An outstanding incident relating to Pay and Disbursing occurred in the Third Naval District, when the forward part of a Coast Guard-manned destroyer escort was towed in from the Atlantic. What remained of the vessel after the stern had been blown off and sunk by a German torpedo, arrived in New York on a Sunday morning, with surviving personnel. The men were in urgent need of funds and clothing; they had not been paid for a long time, and many of their belongings and their pay records had been lost. The District Duty Officer telephoned the Disbursing Officer who, with a couple of storekeepers, went to the wreck, reconstructed the pay accounts, and paid the men that same Sunday afternoon.

Before the war, clothing for enlisted personnel, except chief petty officers, was requisitioned from the Navy. With the declaration of a National Emergency in September 1939, district clothing lockers were established to provide a readily accessible local supply of uniforms and small stores. They did their own accounting and reporting. Later, however, loss of great quantities of Navy clothing at Pearl Harbor and other factors caused a serious shortage. New recruits came in faster than they could be clothed. It was not until late in 1942 that this condition was relieved, nor was it corrected until well into 1943. One factor which assisted materially, was the establishment of a Coast Guard Clothing Depot at New York in mid-1942. The officer in charge negotiated Coast Guard contracts for the manufacture of cloth and the production of uniforms and accessories.

A shortage of officers' (and chief petty officers') uniforms also developed in commercial establishments due to the increased demand and scarcity of materials. The Clothing Depot successfully alleviated this shortage through contracts. With the advent of the Temporary Reservists and the SPARS, the clothing problem intensified; these 60,000-odd personnel had to be properly and promptly uniformed. SPAR uniforms were originally procured from the Navy, but by mid-1943 they were handled by the Coast Guard. After October 1943, the Navy again furnished Coast Guard personnel with clothing and small stores, except special items. SPARS were employed in most clothing offices, but men were always retained for lifting and other heavy work.

All of the supply officers had their hands full. They were responsible for procurement of virtually all supplies and equipment needed in their districts. They had to locate sources of supply; prepare and negotiate contracts; and prepare requisitions, purchase orders, and vouchers to liquidate procurement obligations. They acted as property officers and provided for the delivery, distribution, and inspection of all purchases other than foodstuffs. They were greatly concerned with priorities for critical materials for which competition was murderous. Late in the war and afterwards, supply officers were responsible for storing, reporting, and disposal of surplus property. Close liaison with other district officers was requisite.

Almost always there were special circumstances surrounding supply relationships with large cutters. Most of these vessels operating in the North Atlantic were attached to the First Naval District for logistics purposes, and their outfitting, supplies, and equipment were the responsibility of the District Supply Section. Early in the war, bases were established in Greenland and Newfoundland, and the task of completely outfitting these also fell upon this Section. Personnel of these bases and vessels had to be provided with special winter clothing.

Procurement, a most important supply function, covered a wide range, and included supplies, equipment, vessels, office space, real estate, telephone, and other services, and virtually everything else except clothing and commissary items. An example of the frustrating pressure for procurement put upon supply officers at times came to light in a report from the First Naval District written in September 1942, which is quoted verbatim:

We received from the Commander, Greenland Patrol, a list of items on 23 September, 1942, to be purchased by the District Coast Guard Officer and put on board ship bound for Greenland on 1 October. That is a little more than a week away. These items constitute material for construction and equipment of a radio station and a 50-man barracks, as far as we can make out. Considering the state of the procurement market these days, this is a most flattering tribute to the reputation of our procurement office. But before we start assembling this material, we must find out who is

going to pay for it. Admiral Smith's request received 23 September for a complete radio station and barracks was approved by Headquarters on 26 September, and it appears that we will make shipment of the complete outfit in less than a week. This is snappy work on the part of Headquarters, New York Store, and District Supply Officer.

The acquisition of real estate through construction or lease was a major task for the Supply Section. Space was urgently needed for offices, barracks, bases, training stations, coastal lookouts, recreation halls, repair shops, garages, warehouses, and many other shore units. The Law Officer was always consulted regarding leases, and the legality of the papers was passed upon by him. An indication of the rather hectic days of establishing beach patrols is the following excerpt from a Thirteenth District report of 27 March 1943:

Improvements have been completed or are nearing completion in a number of beach patrol stations. These include a new type of water supply at Ozette Beach; new barracks and dog houses at Lapush; a new laundry and barracks building at Kalaloch; a new forge shed, 60 dog kennels, a work house, sentry box and a new hot water heating plant at Ocean Park; repairs to galley and cabins at Rockaway; remodeling of bath houses and completion of two shelter houses at Taft; barracks and plumbing, new mess hall and galley, and a reservoir at Heceta Head; a bath room at Coos Bay; barracks at Coquille River; new barracks, water system, generator refrigeration, and remodeling of present buildings at Pistol River; repairs and refrigeration for a restaurant leased at Brookings; and permanent shelters at Florence.

Feeding the Coast Guard during the war, keeping commissary supplies adequate, records and finances straight, and the men satisfied, was little less than a herculean job in itself. The food situation with the commuted ration messes in isolated communities, dependent upon local merchants for their supplies, became increasingly desperate due to rationing and shortages. Army and Navy marketing centers became available in June 1943, for the procurement and distribution of commissary supplies and provisions, but deliveries were restricted to units of 2,000 or more men. Few Coast Guard units were of sufficient size to benefit, for the nature of Coast Guard activity required a large number of small units. The problem was solved by the establishment of Coast Guard Commissary Warehouses, strategically located to serve the greatest possible number of activities with a minimum of transportation. These warehouses proved capable of supplying provisions for all Coast Guard general and commuted ration messes in the continental United States.

Prior to the establishment of separate sections, transportation relating to equipment and supplies generally came under the direction of the Supply Officer. If related to personnel or dependents, it came under the Personnel Officer. One of the first "Transportation Officers" was assigned by Headquarters in August 1942, to the First Naval District. He was responsible to the Supply Officer. In most districts, Transportation Offices were set up early in 1943, and were separated from Supply, but remained under the jurisdiction of the District Finance and Supply Officer.

The duties of this Section were chiefly to arrange transportation of personnel and dependents; to issue Regular and Temporary Reserve meal tickets; and to make reservations through all means of travel within the United States. Also included was the moving of the household effects of eligible personnel, picking up, packing, crating, and shipping these effects, and unpacking and uncrating at the destination. The Section was responsible for obtaining and purchasing all motor vehicle parts for all units in the district, keeping motor vehicle records, correspondence relating to vehicles, and assignment of vehicles. It arranged for the transportation of all materials and supplies and, in the First District, the area of responsibility included Greenland, Newfoundland, Iceland, and Bermuda, as well as within the district itself.

The tremendous volume of work done by Transportation Sections is evident from these First Naval District figures covering the two-year period from September 1943 to September 1945.

| | |
|---|---:|
| Requests for transportation of personnel | 68,454 |
| Requests for transportation, materials and supplies | 36,395 |
| Men flown North | 1,455 |
| Material and supply shipments sent North | 714 |
| Transportation requests issued | 5,614 |
| Meal tickets issued | 4,069 |
| Groups of 15 or more men transported (11,690 men) | 347 |
| Pullman reservations | 8,480 |
| Hotel reservations | 244 |
| Authorizations for moving dependents | 819 |
| Authorizations for movement of household effects | 669 |

Coast Guard motor transport on shore came under this Section. Expansion of the Coast Guard, with the attendant establishment of new units in isolated localities, required transportation of personnel in increasing numbers. The maintenance of security patrols along the coasts necessitated the procurement of many types of vehicles not previously employed by the Coast Guard. Some vehicles, such as jeeps, command cars, and other types, which were developed for the Army, were procured in great numbers and used extensively. There were midget scout cars, panel trucks, troop transport trucks, marsh buggies, trailers of various types, and fire pump trailers. Central garages were established in advantageous locations in each district for the maintenance and repair of motor vehicles, and motor pools were set up with tight control over movements and assignments. Later, a preventive maintenance program was instituted to extend the longevity of motorized equipment through regular periodic inspections and the immediate correction of minor defects.

These vehicles were assigned to beach patrols and lifeboat stations for hauling equipment. They were used to assist the Post Office Department, transport personnel, household effects, materials, supplies, and commissary stores, and served countless other purposes. Ambulances were also under the control of the Transportation Officer.

One very serious problem was solved by the Transportation Unit of the Third Naval District. The Supply Depot in New York had a requisition for a large amount of radar equipment for installation in several combat ships being constructed on the West Coast. Delivery could have been made in time under normal procedures, but the construction of the vessels had been accelerated under orders of the Bureau of Ships, and they were completed far ahead of schedule, in order to participate in a large amphibious operation. Railroads could not possibly meet the deadline requirements. The Transportation Officer, Third Naval District, obtained permission from Headquarters to transport the equipment by truck. Transportation of this fragile radar equipment required the greatest care. With fourteen vehicles, operated by experienced men, the convoy led by the Transportation Officer himself, proceeded for San Francisco, and arrived in time to beat the deadline set by the Navy Department. A return load was secured from the Army-Navy Consolidated Freight Depot in San Francisco.

It was natural that the sale of War Bonds came within the jurisdiction of the Finance Officer. Until late in 1943 purchase was generally left to the service man's initiative, but in cooperation with the Treasury Department a bond allotment program for Coast Guardsmen was then organized. A War Bond Officer was appointed in each district, and the commanding officer of each unit was usually made responsible for the success of his own particular program. Most units were visited by the War Bond Officer. Total figures for the Coast Guard are unavailable, but First Naval District experience can be cited as an example of the effort's success. At the inception of the program, less than 12 percent of the personnel attached to the District had made Savings Bond allotments. By V-J Day, the percentage had risen to 82.3 percent.

The transfer of the Coast Guard to the Navy created some legal problems, and activity of the Law Officers increased greatly. Most of the attorneys in the Legal Division were transferred to the Coast Guard Reserve. Many officer candidates with backgrounds in law were given commissions. In 1942, District Law Officers were appointed, and ultimately there were about 80 lawyer officers in the district offices. There were many legal problems arising from the military and civil law enforcement activities, the port security program, the merchant seaman training program, and the integration of the former Bureau of Marine Inspection and Navigation. These became responsibilities of the Legal Divisions. The Law Officer served as the general advisor of the District Coast Guard Officer on legal matters, and was a member of his staff. He had cognizance of contracts, real estate, courts and boards, law enforcement and review, marine casualty investigation and review, tort claims of and against the Government, and fines, penalties, and forfeitures.

On 15 March 1946, the Public Information Division at Headquarters (Public Relations Division before June 1945) prepared a report on its work during 1945. This report, with 19 exhibits and 17 representative photographs, was entered in the national competition held by the American Public Relations Association, and was selected as "representing one of the most meritorious public relations performances in 1945." The Public In-

formation Division, headed during the war by Captain Ellis Reed-Hill, was awarded a Silver Anvil (anvil of public opinion) mounted on a walnut pedestal. The report listed eight "Public Information Objectives":

(1) To acquaint the public with the work of the Coast Guard, the part it has played in the war and the peacetime duties it performs for the Treasury.

(2) To build up morale among men of the Coast Guard, especially those overseas, by giving them due public recognition for services rendered. To publicize medal winners, to build morale of families back home.

(3) To cooperate with other publicity officials in supplying radio talent, musicians, men for incentive speeches, bond rallies, etc.

(4) To keep material for historical purposes —written by combat correspondents and pictures by combat photographers.

(5) To review all material for censorship clearance and national security.

(6) To show benefits of the service and to urge young men and women to join the Coast Guard in the service of their country.

(7) To correct misimpressions of the service by reporting faithfully.

(8) To stress accuracy and quality of work, and to conform to American traditions which are generally accepted among Public Relations men.

The public relations work of the Coast Guard started from scratch and grew with the Service during the war until it had reached a scope and excellence that warranted the highest national recognition among public relations men.

The effective use of recognized media in reaching the public is the primary function of the public relations man. These include newspapers, magazines, pamphlets, and books, the radio, the motion picture, the public forum, and meetings of civic bodies. The printed word and the appeal to the eye through photographs, drawings, paintings, and graphic art are extensively used.

Emphasis on hometown media and publication of stories and photographs of local Coast Guardsmen gave Coast Guard publicity unique appeal. This activity reached a peak in 1945, when the Coast Guard processed an average of 330 Coast Guardsmen's photographs daily and mailed a daily average of 3.13 prints to each of some 332 newspapers.

Most public relations work "in the field" came within three classifications—correspondent, photographic, and graphic art. The Correspondent Section gathered and distributed information about the Coast Guard's role in the war in the form of news stories, feature articles, and magazine pieces. Correspondents were mostly enlisted men with newspaper or writing backgrounds, who sent stories and articles to Headquarters for processing and distribution to a wide variety of printed media. They were assigned to various cutters, and to many Coast Guard-manned Navy craft.

The Photographic Section was highly developed. Wherever there was action, men of this unit were on the job, turning out first rate pictures which were consistently shown on front pages with the first battle dispatches. While much photographic developing was done in the field, most of the processing was done in the laboratory at Headquarters. This laboratory operated 24 hours a day, with a daily average of about 2,500 prints. On 16 January 1945, the Coast Guard had 101 cameramen afloat and 84 ashore. By the end of the war, over 80,000 negatives of historical and technical value were in the film library at Headquarters. Motion pictures also proved effective, and many combat pictures were produced. A full length musical feature film, "Tars and Spars" (Columbia Pictures), was shown throughout the United States.

H. F. Cattel of the New York *Mirror* wrote on 29 September 1945: "I want to take the opportunity to say that the Coast Guard press and foto coverage was the best of all services. . . . It certainly merits the highest praise."

The Coast Guard maintained a Graphic Unit at White Plains, N.Y., where posters and exhibit material were prepared. Several Coast Guard artists, including Ken Riley, Hunter Wood, and Anton Otto Fischer, produced outstanding work, much of it on the spot in actual combat.

Emphasis on participation of the individual Coast Guardsman in battle proved a good antidote for the widespread mistaken notion that the Coast Guard stayed close to home, and had little to do with the fighting.

The Civil Engineering Division had a real job on its hands, particularly in the days of great expansion. This Division, organized during the period of limited national emergency with civilian personnel previously engaged chiefly in civil engineering for the former Lighthouse Service, carried out all the engineering projects for the Coast Guard shore establishments.

The Civil Engineering Division, headed by the Chief of Civil Engineering at Headquarters, initiated and executed all engineering requirements of whatever type, pertaining to shore establishments, including fixed structures on submarine sites. This work included investigations and surveys preliminary to acquisition of property, and the design, construction, installation, and maintenance of structures, appurtenances, utilities, and equipment essential to operation of shore facilities. It involved roads, reservoirs, wharves, water supply, sewage disposal, power and heating plants, compressors, marine railways, and apparatus for all types of aids to navigation.

The first major undertaking was the provision of shore facilities for receiving and training recruits for both the Coast Guard and merchant marine. Next came housing for SPARS, buildings at the Academy, bases and moorings for Captains of the Port and coastal picket patrols, and for fireboat stations. As the war progressed, regional supply depots and clothing lockers were established; garages for motor pools were provided; as well as telephone section stations, weather reporting stations, and rifle ranges. Concurrently, many lookout stations and towers were constructed to supplement the coastal network of lighthouses and lifeboat stations. On the organizing of the Beach Patrol, it was necessary to provide housing and living facilities for the men, kennels for their dogs, and barns of their horses, over the entire periphery of the continental coastline. Of great importance were the organization and the outstanding performance of Construction Detachments operating outside the continental United States. In practically all districts separate field parties and construction units were set up from which details were dispatched. Loran and radio stations, both major projects, will be covered in some detail in a later chapter.

The volume of work done is indicated in figures for the fiscal year 1944. There were 7,839 projects completed at a total cost of $6,360,130, not including work at the Coast Guard Academy, and Coast Guard Yard at Curtis Bay. In all, during the war, the Civil Engineering Division planned and carried out a wide variety of projects, covering all shores and waterways of the continental United States, and extending to advance bases in the North Atlantic, the Caribbean Sea, and to all of the combat areas of the Pacific. One measure of the extent of these projects was their cost; close to $75 million, to which was added projects planned and executed for the Navy and War Shipping Administration amounting to approximately $21 million. However, the diversity and multiplicity of projects were more significant than the cost.

The Coast Guard Naval Engineering Division saw that the Coast Guard had the ships it needed, insofar as was humanly and financially possible. Before the war the Division of Marine Engineering had been responsible for all propulsion machinery and related items; the Division of Construction and Repair had cognizance of hull and all related items outside of machinery space. These two were combined into Naval Engineering. On the invasion of the Low Countries by Germany in 1940, Congress appropriated funds to fully outfit the Coast Guard fleet in accordance with Navy war plans. These plans called for the conversion of 33 cutters, 50 coastal patrol boats, 65 local patrol boats, and 61 tenders for war purposes. In May 1941, the United States assumed the defense of Greenland. A year later, designs were laid down for four of the Wind Class icebreakers—the heaviest yet to be constructed. Many additional vessels were procured and converted to war use. Construction began on 39 new *Cactus*-class buoy tenders, and these required eventual conversion.

Shortly after the declaration of war, a vast program was undertaken to augment the Coast Guard fleet. A total of 495 vessels were purchased and 2,834 vessels were enrolled in the Reserve. Plans were drawn up for conversion of the larger craft, and for the armament of smaller vessels, and the bulk of the equipment was procured. Local field units undertook completion of assigned projects.

The Naval Engineering Division initiated plans during the war for the construction of 89 new Coast Guard vessels ranging from 73-foot river tenders to the 290-foot icebreaker *Mackinaw*, and including icebreakers, tenders, cruising cutters,

tugs, river craft, and lightships. It was also responsible for the planning and construction of 230 83-foot cutters; 15 64-foot cutters; 64 50-foot cutters; 478 38-foot picket boats; and 171 fire barges and fireboats of varying sizes. For the most part, regular naval architects and regular shipbuilders were employed, under the supervision of the Naval Engineering Division. In addition, 83 vessels acquired by loan, charter, or purchase, were converted. These included trawlers, ferryboats, yachts, Government vessels, passenger ships, tugs, freighters, subchasers, whalers, lake freighters, fishing boats and schooners.

The activities of the Buoy Section increased tremendously to meet Navy demands and, at the same time, carry on normal buoy construction and the upkeep work of the Aids to Navigation Division. Inasmuch as the Coast Guard maintained established standards for buoys and related equipment, the Navy procured great quantities of buoyage to mark restricted areas, ranges, and offshore and advanced bases. These numbered 5,500 for the Pacific, 200 for the Caribbean, and 1,100 for the Atlantic. About a dozen private concerns produced buoys under contract.

The Naval Engineering Division purchased and distributed special equipment in mass quantities for fireboats, such as pumps, monitors, valves, hose, fire-fighting tools, and clothing, and made great strides in perfecting old fire-fighting apparatus and developing new devices and procedures. It conducted joint studies concerning research, development, and design of air-sea rescue craft and equipment. Particular attention was paid to damage control in Coast Guard cutters. In designing new vessels great care was taken to make them as resistant as possible to damage and casualties without requiring the particular attention of crew members. The improvement and design of abandonship equipment was important in order to reduce the large loss of life due to torpedoing of warships and merchant vessels.

The work carried on by the various divisions mentioned in this chapter was obviously vital to the successful prosecution of the war, and a knowledge of it is helpful in gaining a true comprehension of the wartime work of the Coast Guard. Let us now devote our attention to the various operational phases, examining first how the Coast Guard promoted security at home.

Part II

Security at Home

# Chapter 3

# COAST GUARD AVIATION

COAST GUARD AVIATION in World War II was chiefly concerned with patrol and rescue. These two functions were almost inseparable, for whichever purpose a mission served, the other was almost sure to be involved, directly or indirectly. Patrols were, in the final analysis, to protect our shores and coastwise shipping, but no opportunity to save life or property at sea was ever overlooked, and many opportunities arose. Several rescues incidental to patrol will be mentioned in this chapter; other cases of assistance by air will receive comment under other appropriate subjects.

As early as 1915, three imaginative Coast Guard officers at Hampton Roads, Virginia, conceived a plan for an air patrol to search for disabled vessels along the Atlantic seaboard which were in need of assistance. Captain B. M. Chiswell, then in command of cutter *Onondaga*, and two of his junior officers, Lieutenants Norman B. Hall and Elmer F. Stone, presented the plan to the officer in charge of Curtis Field. As a result, a plane was secured on loan. The experiment was so successful that it received official blessing, and thus Coast Guard aviation was born. Stone became a pilot with the *USS Huntington*, and later, in 1919, was a co-pilot in the Navy's NC-4 which made the first transatlantic crossing by air.

The Navy Deficiency Act of 29 August 1916, authorized the establishment of 10 Coast Guard Air Stations, but no funds were appropriated for them until 1924, when, in conjunction with the effort to stop rum running, the project received an appropriation of $13,000,000. In the meantime, aviation had occupied the attention of many Coast Guard officers, and some spasmodic flying had been done with borrowed planes. In 1921, the Commandant, then Rear Admiral W. E. Reynolds, set forth the particular functions of the aviation program, and seven distinct duties were enumerated:

(1) Experimental flights for locating schools of fish.
(2) Reconnaissance of land and water areas in surveying, mapping, or determining routes for lines of communications.
(3) Assistance in flood control and relief work for the Western River region.
(4) Emergency transportation services for government officials to remote or inaccessible locations.
(5) Enforcement of Federal maritime laws.
(6) Patrol duty. (Location of illicit stills in the swamp areas of the South became important, especially in the Prohibition Era.)
(7) General humanitarian work along the coasts.

During the period of "spasmodic flying", there were many cases of assistance rendered, which proved beyond doubt the value of aviation in the Coast Guard's normal peacetime work. The first formal Coast Guard aviation unit was established at Gloucester, Massachusetts, in 1925. The services of the Gloucester seaplane in checking rum running were indispensable. Experimental radio equipment was installed, and this greatly increased effectiveness. In 1926, the Coast Guard procured five planes of its own. After this, the aviation branch grew steadily and rapidly. By 1933, the Service had 13 planes and 14 aviators; three years later there were 45 planes and 27 aviators on active assignment. In the period between 1927 and 1934, the number of flights for all Coast Guard Air Stations combined increased from 258 to 1,200. Miles cruised in 1927 were 28,325; in 1934 they totaled 219,572. Cases of assistance rendered went from 12 to 44, and hours flown increased from 366 to 2,752. Nine Coast Guard Air Stations were finally established:

| Air Station | Commissioned |
|---|---|
| St. Petersburg, Florida | August, 1934 |
| Biloxi, Mississippi | December, 1934 |
| Salem, Massachusetts* | February, 1935 |
| Port Angeles, Washington | August, 1935 |
| San Diego, California | April, 1937 |
| Brooklyn, New York | April, 1938 |
| Elizabeth City, North Carolina | August, 1940 |
| San Francisco, California | November, 1940 |
| Miami, Florida | June, 1942 |

* Superseding Gloucester

The aviation branch became an integral part of the national organization. It was primarily designed to carry on the traditional and time-honored duty of the Service, that of the protection and saving of life and property. Stations were strategically located to enable the greatest rescue service. The operational areas of the stations approximated an average of 500 miles of seacoast and its navigable waters and adjacent territory. Adequate protection of airborne traffic was thus guaranteed. When an accident occurred, the nearest Coast Guard Air Station was ready with immediate assistance. The important wartime role of the aviation branch in national defense was really incidental to this original objective.

With the outbreak of European hostilities in 1939, the United States organized the Coast Neutrality Patrol, for which Coast Guard aviation was largely responsible, and regular Coast Guard air patrols were organized in 1940. Upon our declaration of war on 8 December 1941, the activities of all coastal air stations, both Navy and Coast Guard, were greatly increased. Demands upon the normal peacetime patrols were rapidly increased. Coast Guard planes were soon actively engaged in antisubmarine patrol and convoy or convoy escort duties, in addition to their regular rescue operations. The latter increased in scope commensurately with the wartime hazards at sea.

Before Pearl Harbor, three major types of planes were used, the twin-engine amphibian; the Hall flying boat (PH-2); and the single engine observation scout plane, designated SOC-4. These had speeds of 150, 160, and 195 miles an hour, and cruising ranges of about 700, 2,070, and 1,000 miles respectively. Although particularly adapted for use on cutters, the SOC-4 was convertible to land operations. With the advent of war, many new types of planes were perfected. Grumman amphibians (J4F and JRF), observation scouts

(SOC-4), and Navy VOS type gradually supplanted the older models in the Coast Guard.

In September 1944, fewer than 70 planes were owned by the Coast Guard, but at the end of that year Coast Guard personnel were operating 151 planes, including some assigned by the Navy. Of these, the JRF, PBM, and PBY (patrol bomber types) were the most adaptable to Coast Guard use. One of the most popular rescue planes was the stripped down *Catalina* (PBY5A) which was equipped with droppable life rafts, "Gibson Girl" transmitters, shipwreck kits, markers, smoke and light buoys, as well as other emergency equipment. Blimps and helicopters completed the normal standard aircraft complement. Helicopters were particularly helpful in certain types of rescue operations. Equipped eventually with rescue hoists and special pickup harness, the helicopters were able to pick up, from the air, stretcher cases from vessels on which there was no room for landing. The hoists permitted rescue from land or sea in about one-tenth the time theretofore required.

From the beginning of hostilities in 1941 to June 1943, Coast Guard aircraft delivered 61 bombing attacks on enemy submarines, located over 1,000 survivors, and actually rescued 95 persons without assistance. During fiscal year 1943, over 11,000 flights were made, including administrative, test, training, assistance, ambulance, law enforcement, and patrol flights. These involved sorties against enemy submarines, aerial coverage of merchant and naval vessels, and numerous reconnaissance patrols over the offshore waters of the continental United States, Greenland, Labrador, Alaska, Canada, Mexico, the West Indies, and Cuba.

From the Spring of 1942 until the threat of enemy raids along the coast diminished, the air stations were primarily engaged in antisubmarine patrols and auxiliary missions. In general, the duty consisted of patrol and scouting activity off the principal ports and coastal waters, and from 100 to 200 miles at sea. The port approaches were especially important. Convoy escort duty was performed to the extent that cruising radius of the planes permitted. Uppermost in the purpose of these patrols (and also those from Naval Air Stations) was protection of shipping from hostile submarines. Special scouting was done in connection with the arrival and departure of United States and allied naval and merchant vessels. Suspicious craft were investigated in an effort to discover ships refueling enemy submarines, especially in waters off the First Naval District where numerous fishermen worked far offshore.

The actual operation of Coast Guard aviation came under the direction of the Navy Area Commanders who, in turn, operated under the Commander of the respective Sea Frontiers. The Coast Guard, therefore, had no operational control, and its function was logistical—providing personnel, planes, and small stores for the air stations, and maintaining the buildings and plants.

On 5 October 1943, Patrol Bomber Squadron Six, the only naval squadron manned entirely by Coast Guard personnel, and an important and colorful unit, was commissioned for active antisubmarine patrol and convoy coverage in southwest Greenland, with detachments operating in the Canadian Arctic, Iceland, and Newfoundland. It was really a part of the Greenland Patrol. Since its activity was more closely related to that Patrol than to operations concerning safety at home, the story of that Squadron is related in Chapter 7. Patrols made in northeast Greenland were for ice observation, evidence of enemy landing, and weather station operation.

Most air patrol work was hard, routinized, and without special excitement. Regular harbor, inshore, and offshore patrols, often as far as 500 or 600 miles out at sea, were not very spectacular; much of the pleasure of flying was lost in the constant vigil which was required. Pilots were continually on the lookout for obstructions, derelicts, or surface craft that had to be identified. Nevertheless, every pilot had his thrilling moments. At any time a routine patrol might be interrupted by a radio message sending the plane out on an emergency mission; a ship might be lost, a boat wrecked, or a vessel sinking and its crew in dire need of assistance. "Mercy flights" gained an enviable reputation.

The early war days were neither easy nor satisfying for Coast Guard aviation. For example, the first station order received by the Air Station at Elizabeth City, North Carolina, from the Navy after the declaration of war was for an air patrol of "steamer lanes and offshore approaches to Chesapeake Capes; on alert for enemy submarines." This patrol, extending 50 miles to sea

and south to Cape Lookout, was maintained every day that weather conditions permitted. Thirteen pilots and ten planes were available for antisubmarine patrols, but positive achievements in repelling enemy operations off the coast were largely negated because the planes were unarmed. Merchant vessels were being sunk daily, while pilots stood by helplessly, unable to do more than turn in an outraged report. Despite requests for modern planes, adequately armed for combatting submarines, it was not until 22 January 1942, that armed planes were assigned to the Station. Two, equipped with machine guns and bomb racks, were then received, but they were poorly adapted for submarine warfare. It was December 1943, before adequate fighting planes were procured. By then, the submarine danger was largely past.

Primarily, the efforts of the Coast Guard Air Stations were directed to antisubmarine patrols during 1942, 1943, and the early part of 1944. Daily inshore patrols protected the important harbors and the approaches to the sea. Offshore patrols covered other sections of the coasts. Many enemy submarines were contacted. Several were attacked and damaged or disabled. Action reports record numerous attacks which drove submarines from the coastal areas.

Actually, however, most aviation units performed a greater service in rescuing or aiding survivors as a by-product of antisubmarine patrols, than in scaring off submarines. The patrols were, for the most part, little less than harassing agents. Day after day, pilots gave what assistance they could to the victims of torpedoed vessels. Seaplanes could land in the water and pick up survivors, but the others could only pause in their patrol to stand by until other rescue craft came. Many rescues not covered in this chapter are detailed in Chapter 8.

A noteworthy service developed by Coast Guard aviation, especially in the lower Atlantic Coast and Gulf areas, was a hurricane warning system used to warn small craft. When hurricanes threatened, Coast Guard planes dropped warning blocks to offshore vessels not equipped with radio. These were particularly valuable to local fishermen, yacht owners, and vessels engaged in the sponge fishing industry. Many vessels reached shelter which might otherwise have been caught in dangerous storms.

By October 1944, the submarine menace along the Atlantic Sea Frontier had largely disappeared, though occasional sinkings continued. Coast Guard aviation had generally ceased antisubmarine patrols at that time, and the organization underwent transition to an integral part of the newly organized Air-Sea Rescue Forces. As naval, air force, and merchant marine operations daily increased, the number of planes and vessels requiring assistance grew constantly. It was to facilitate saving the lives of countless aviators and seamen that Air-Sea Rescue was born. Thereafter, wartime air activity was almost entirely confined to rescue operations, the normal peacetime function of this branch of the Service.

The first Air-Sea Rescue unit was established at San Diego, California, in December 1943. The regular National Air-Sea Rescue Agency was established at Washington on 22 February 1944, and its administration was placed under the Coast Guard. Maximum coordination of all rescue efforts of the Army, Navy, and Coast Guard was the major responsibility of each regional Air-Sea Rescue Task Unit, headed by the commanding officer of the Coast Guard Air Station. Except as this Agency was concerned with rescues before the end of the war, it was primarily a postwar organization. Upon receipt of information from any source that an accident had occurred, the sector headquarters sent out an appropriate search from the nearest task unit or, if the situation warranted, indicated a general "alert" for the entire section area. Thus, all services, operating under a unified command, coordinated their activities in a general search.

The outstanding work of Coast Guard aviation remained little known to the general public during the war. Only when some dramatic incident was publicized was it given any general acclaim. Yet, operations reached large proportions during the war years. While statistics are incomplete, several interesting and informative figures taken from Aircraft Operations Reports can be cited to show the scope of operations by the nine Coast Guard Air Stations. In the fiscal years 1943 and 1944, Coast Guard planes spent a total of 131,277 hours in flight. There were 42,282 training, test, patrol, and administrative flights, and 1,295 assistance flights. A total of 12,365,072 miles was cruised, and an area of 85,957,671 square miles was searched. In all, 207,522 vessels and planes were identified; 194 vessels and planes assisted; 207 disabled or overdue planes and vessels were assisted; 659 persons received assistance; and 175 medical cases were transported. Other persons transported totaled 4,422, and cases of assistance to other government departments numbered 305.

In January 1942, a Coast Guard plane from the Salem Air Station was ordered up when the Navy Information Center requested information about the sinking of an unidentified tanker. The plane sighted the partly sunk vessel in a vertical position, with its bow extending about 20 feet above the water. The area was searched for survivors and enemy craft. A life raft and lifeboats with survivors were located within five miles of the derelict. The plane informed five nearby commercial fishing vessels of the situation, and they picked up the survivors.

From time to time pilots would chance the dangers of crashing and effect successful landings in order to give succor to the dying or helpless. The first such landing by an Elizabeth City plane was made by an unarmed PH-No. 183 on 1 May 1942, when 13 survivors were saved after drifting at sea for six days. Two men, one seriously injured, were flown to Norfolk, while the remaining 11 were picked up by a Coast Guard cutter. The next day, another offshore landing saved the lives of two men adrift on a raft. Perhaps the most spectacular rescue from Elizabeth City was made in July 1942, when Lieutenant Richard L. Burke and his co-pilot Lieutenant R. W. Blouin picked up seven German survivors from the submarine *Dergin*, which had been sunk by an Army plane. Burke was awarded his second Distinguished Flying Cross for this exploit.

On 3 April 1943, Lieutenant J. N. Schrader, while patrolling out of the Miami Air Station in an OS2U3, received a radio message to search for survivors of the torpedoed tanker *Gulfstate*. Upon sighting the remains of the wreck, he was able to spot three groups of survivors. Dropping his depth charges, he came down in the water and picked up the three men in the first group. He taxied to the second group, gave them a rubber raft for support, and went on to the assistance of the third group, one of whom was badly burned. Taking this man on board his already overloaded plane, Schrader stood by to protect the drifting survivors from sharks until other planes arrived.

Long before Pearl Harbor, Coast Guard aviators operated in Greenland from cutter-based planes. Without *Northland's* plane, the South Greenland Survey Expedition could not satisfactorily have made its survey. After war was declared, Coast Guard planes, flying from cutters, maintained antisubmarine patrols over wide areas of the ocean. In their flights on coastal patrol and over convoy lanes, the Greenland airmen's toughest battles were against the elements—gales, icy rains, heavy fogs, and unexpected storms. Coming down on the Ice Cap presented new dangers in the form of treacherous crevasses and the sudden popping open of ice which had appeared solid enough for a landing.

Lieutenant John A. Pritchard, Jr., a Coast Guard aviator, operating from his mother ship, *Northland,* successfully flew the hazardous air lanes of the North Atlantic for nine months in his amphibian. In November 1942, three Canadian airmen came down on the Greenland Ice Cap, not far inland from the coast. The Coast Guard was assigned to rescue them, and Lieutenant Pritchard led a rescue party ashore to hunt in the icy wasteland. *Northland*, anchored in a fjord at the edge of the Ice Cap, fired flares and star shells and broadcast a Morse code message: "Move back from the edge of the glacier and bear south to meet landing party." The Canadians went wild with joy. It was their 14th day of torture and suspense, and they had almost given up hope.

Using skis and snowshoes, the Coast Guard shore party, after many hardships in sub-zero weather, finally found the Canadians and carried them to the cutter. The stranded men were on the verge of collapse and almost frozen. They had made a bonfire of their parkas in a desperate attempt to attract attention. Taken on board *Northland*, they were rushed to the sick bay and treated for shock and exposure. The Canadian Government presented a plaque to the Coast Guard to commemorate the rescue.

Five days later, *Northland* received word that the crew of a Flying Fortress, lost two weeks previously on the Ice Cap, had contacted U. S. Army planes. These flyers were about 40 miles from Comanche Bay. The Coast Guard was asked to attempt rescue. *Northland* ploughed her way through the ice as far as possible toward the scene of the disaster. Lieutenant Pritchard asked permission to fly to the rescue, proposing to land his J2F on the snow and ice with pontoons, which would work like runners. His plane soon roared out of the fog and climbed 2,000 feet to the Ice Cap, as Radioman Benjamin A. Bottoms sent a message to the grounded plane that they were landing. The stranded Army flyers signaled that it was dangerous, but Pritchard ignored their warning and landed safely. He then set out on foot to pick up the survivors four miles away.

He found the men, who were almost starved and half frozen, but they received him with joyous shouts. One man had a broken arm and two others were also suffering from injuries, but they were walking casualties. These received first attention. Assisted by the sturdiest, Pritchard led the three back to his plane, but could fly with only two. The third man, Corporal L. A. Hayworth, waited for a return trip the next day. The plane reached *Northland* after dark, but Pritchard landed successfully with the aid of the cutter's searchlight.

Next morning Pritchard and Bottoms took off in a blinding snowstorm for the third man on the Ice Cap. Despite warnings from *Northland* just before landing that bad weather was setting in, and despite orders to go back, Pritchard repeated his splendid performance of the day before, and took the remaining airman on his plane. Bottoms sent a message to the cutter that they had the passenger and were in the air again. On board the cutter, anxious men awaited the hum of the returning plane. Messages from the plane suddenly stopped. The storm had grown worse, and somewhere on the return flight the pilot had lost his way. Searching parties were driven back by the howling gale.

On 4 December 1942, five volunteers from *Northland* went ashore under the leadership of Ensign Richard L. Fuller, USCG, to locate Pritchard's plane. These men waged a stirring fight for several days on snowshoes. On the night of the second day they and *Northland* saw a light northeast of Atterbury Dome, on the Ice Cap, and two days later were able to investigate. An assumed position of the plane had been given them, but a careful, heroic search of several days failed to locate it. The party broke camp on 11 December, and after a long, tortuous journey, they returned to the beach and *Northland*. Since the cutter had no plane, ultimate rescue of the rest of the Flying Fortress men was accomplished by a Navy and an Army plane under Lieutenant Bernard Dunlop,

USNR, and Colonel Bernt Balchen, U. S. Army, respectively.

Four months later, Colonel Balchen flew over Pritchard's lost plane and reported it 6 to 8 miles from its originally reported position. Lieutenant Pritchard and Radioman Bottoms were listed as missing in action, and in 1943 each received a post-humous award of the Distinguished Flying Cross.

On 28 November 1943, an AT-7 plane was reported lost, and several planes based at Narsarssuak (Patrol Bomber Squadron Six) conducted a search over a wide area. Lieutenant A. W. Weuker finally located the wrecked plane on the edge of the Sukkertoppen Ice Cap on 1 December 1943. On the second flight six days later, Weuker marked the spot with flag stakes; on 21 December photographs were finally taken successfully to guide a rescue party. A Coast Guard PBY-5A directed the actual rescue party on 5 January 1944 over the last 10 miles to the wreckage, dropped provisions to the rescuers, and two days later contacted the rescue group on the return trek and again dropped provisions.

Coast Guard planes and surface craft often co-operated in rescues as well as in attacks. Two officers and 20 enlisted men on board the 110-foot British trawler *HMS Strathella,* disabled in a heavy storm, faced death after being adrift in the North Atlantic for over a month. They were dramatically rescued on 13 February 1944 by the combined efforts of a Coast Guard PBY-5A plane and the cutter *Modoc.* Lieutenant Commander John J. McCubbin, USCG, was on a routine air patrol to check ice conditions and deliver mail, when he sighted a red flare in position 60° 03′ N, 45° 24′ W, west of Cape Farewell. He requested the ship's identity by blinker, received her name in like manner, and was told of these victims being adrift for five weeks. Food was very low, all the drinking water gone, and it was impossible for them to send radio messages. McCubbin radioed to shore and within an hour *Modoc* was speeding to the rescue. The latter towed *Strathella* 100 miles safely to the Greenland base.

A case of cooperation in attack was that of Coast Guard plane No. 00796 from Elizabeth City Air Station. This plane was escorting the U. S. tanker *William A. Rockefeller,* 14,054 tons, at 1217 on 28 June 1942. It was on the port beam of the tanker, in position 35° 07′ N, 75° 07′ W, about 40 miles off Cape Hatteras, when the pilot saw a tremendous explosion and the tanker burst into flames. At the same moment a submerged submarine running at about 30 feet was sighted 3,000 yards on the tanker's port beam. The plane, which was 1,200 feet above the burning ship, made a full throttle dive on the sub, but by the time it had arrived at the bomb release point, the submarine had disappeared. The plane dropped two depth charges at one second intervals, set for 50-foot depth, in the best ascertainable position, with no visible results. The pilot then dived to *CGC-470,* which was distant about five miles. This vessel turned toward the scene and the pilot dropped two smoke lights on the spot where the depth charges had detonated. *CGC-470* then laid seven depth charges around the smoke lights with no visible results, after which she began picking up survivors from the lifeboat. The plane directed her to one man on top of an overturned lifeboat and another clinging to a piece of wreckage. There were no casualties, and the entire crew of 50 was saved.

A short time later, on 1 August 1942, a Coast Guard Utility Amphibian J4F (Aircraft V-212), piloted by Chief Aviation Pilot Henry Clark White, bombed a German submarine in the Gulf of Mexico about 100 miles south of Houma, Louisiana. Chief White, with Radioman First Class George Henderson Boggs, Jr., as his only crew-man, was patrolling an assigned area near a buoy marking a sunken United Fruit ship. At 1337, White sighted on his starboard bow a surfaced and stopped submarine. Boggs sent an SSS message, indicating position.

Chief White thought that circling and making the attack from the stern would be most effective; but while he was circling the submarine began to submerge. Therefore, he started his attack im-mediately from abeam at an altitude of 1,500 feet and one-half mile distant. As the submarine was going under fast, White went into a 50° dive and released his bomb from an altitude of 250 feet. The submarine had been visible during the entire approach, and though under when the bomb was released, it was clearly seen.

Boggs, with his head out the window, saw the bomb strike the water and explode in what appeared to be a direct hit. White pulled out of the dive and came around to observe results; no debris was seen, but various patches of oil coming to the surface bore witness to heavy damage, at least.

After the attack, two Army observation planes came on the scene, and White's relief arrived. White remained in the vicinity for about an hour and then departed. It later developed that he had made a direct hit, and the submarine *U-166* had been completely destroyed. It was the only submarine sunk by a Coast Guard plane during the war. For his exploit, White, then a Lieutenant, was awarded the Distinguished Flying Cross, and Boggs received the Air Medal for his participation in the sinking.

The age of the helicopter for Coast Guard rescue work was only beginning in these war years. It was determined that the helicopter, while suitable for certain types of operations, had decided limitations. It was best adaptable to law enforcement work, observational patrols, transportation of personnel and supplies between ship and shore, and general distress and rescue duties. It merely supplemented other air operations. The spotlight of public interest in helicopters for the Coast Guard was first turned on when the Air Station at Brooklyn, New York, was designated as a helicopter training base 19 November 1943.

Several spectacular rescues were made by helicopter. In a trainer from Floyd Bennett Field, Lieutenant (jg) W. C. Bolton, USCG, rescued a boy from a sand bar off Jamaica Bay, New York. The official service debut of this type of aircraft, however, came on 3 January 1944. Commander F. A. Erickson, USCG, commanding officer of Floyd Bennett Field, made an emergency flight to take two cases of blood plasma from The Battery to a hospital at Sandy Hook, New Jersey, where survivors from the explosion of destroyer *USS Turner*, off New York Harbor, had been taken. The limited space for landing at the hospital required the services of a helicopter, and this flight was instrumental in saving several lives of naval personnel.

Eventually a helicopter was assigned to each Coast Guard Air Station and its services were valuable. For instance, the record shows that at the Brooklyn Air Station, in the first quarter of 1945, there were 147 assistance flights by helicop-

ter in which a total of 1,123 miles were cruised.

In May 1943, a Salem plane on patrol intercepted a message regarding a plane down at sea north of Peaked Hill Bar at the tip of Cape Cod. Proceeding to the scene, the pilot located an overturned lifeboat and a man on a life raft nearby. Three planes were circling overhead. The only vessel in sight was a disabled trawler, from which two dories were rowing toward the life raft. The Coast Guard plane dropped its depth charges clear of the scene, and landed on the water a mile off the beach. It taxied to the dory, which had picked up the survivor of the plane crash who was suffering from head injuries and exposure. He was taken on board the Salem plane and flown to the Naval Air Station, at Squantum.

After the hurricane of 14 September 1944, an amphibian from Salem was the first plane under Commander Northern Air Patrol to go out. A photographic survey was made of the damage along the coast, and an unsuccessful search was conducted for the Vineyard Sound Lightship which was later discovered to have foundered at her mooring.

In September 1943, Ensign W. M. Braswell, flying from the Miami Air Station, and still in a weakened condition from recent hospitalization, landed near a Pan American plane that had crashed in Biscayne Bay. Risking his own life, he swam to the submerged plane, unstrapped the pilot, and, with the aid of his radioman, rescued the pilot and two other survivors. Artificial respiration brought all three unconscious men to life before they were turned over to the Coast Guard crash boat for medical treatment. Rescues of this character indicated more than a mere strict responsibility to duty.

One rescue during patrol by a plane from the St. Petersburg Station is another example of how patrol and rescue duties were combined. In December 1944, Ensign F. T. Merritt accomplished a dramatic rescue of a Navy pilot who apparently had collided with a tow plane during a practice gunnery exercise and had been forced to bail out. Returning from a routine administrative flight to Cuba, Merritt and his crew were instructed to search for survivors of an Army Liberator. While thus engaged they spotted and investigated an SOS dye marker about 20 miles off Daytona Beach. An injured fighter pilot was discovered on a life raft. Merritt effected a safe landing, picked up the injured pilot and delivered him safely to the hospital at his Daytona base.

Sometimes Coast Guard planes had work well inland from the coast. Typical of the harmonious coordination of all types of Air-Sea Rescue units was the rescue of six members of the crew of a Navy patrol plane which crashed in the fog about 130 miles northeast of Seattle. The rescue necessitated a 6-day search from 14 to 20 January 1945, over the rugged Cascade Mountains under the most trying weather conditions. Amid snow and rain, without shelter or rest, Army, Navy, Coast Guard, and Forest Service crews searched. By the 17th, four men had been found. The Army and Navy secured search operations after that, but the Coast Guard and Forest Service continued the at-tempt until the other two members were rescued. The lives of five of the six men were saved.

As an example of Air-Sea Rescue experience in the later days of the war after most antisubmarine patrols had been secured, the records of the Northern California sector of the Western Sea Frontier may be mentioned. Of the total of 38 crashes, involving 37 planes and 98 persons, from March 1944 to January 1945, 42 persons were saved, 51 were beyond help, and only five were lost who might have been saved.

Coast Guard aviation proved itself time and again during these crucial war years. While air patrols were largely preventive and few tangible results can be cited, the number of lives and the value of property saved were, in the aggregate, highly impressive. The airmen, in their devotion to duty and in their efficient execution of assignments, fully lived up to the fine traditions of the Service.

# Chapter 4

# THE BEACH POUNDERS

Among the many activities of the Coast Guard in World War II was the operation of a security force for the protection of our coasts and inland waterways. A Beach Patrol organization was established soon after the outbreak of hostilities as a supplement to Port Security. Originally, this came under the jurisdiction of the Captains of the Port. During the critical years 1942 and 1943, when our shores were constantly subject to acts of sabotage and enemy attack, the Beach Patrol was one of the most important phases of national defense.

Many Beach Patrol responsibilities were "regular business" for the Coast Guard. For years it had maintained patrols on certain vital sections of the coast, as well as manned a large number of lookout posts. The original Life Saving Service had always patrolled the beaches in the regular line of duty. Hundreds of Coast Guardsmen were long accustomed to the tireless vigilance of lookout, harbor, and revenue patrols. It was logical that the new organization should be built upon the foundation already established by this Service.

Although somewhat comparable to the earlier lifesaving beach patrols of peacetime, the new system was fundamentally different both in origin and operational functions. Primarily a security force, it was designed, in its broader aspects, to protect American shores against sabotage, enemy submarines, enemy landings, and "fifth column" activities along the coast. Actually, it had three basic functions: (a) to detect and observe enemy vessels operating in coastal waters and to transmit information thus obtained to the appropriate Navy and Army commands as a basis for naval action against the enemy; (b) to report attempts of landing by the enemy and to assist in preventing such activity; and (c) to prevent communication between persons on shore and the enemy at sea.

Subsidiary objectives were numerous. Two were of fundamental importance. The Beach Patrol served as a most useful agency in rescuing survivors of our own and friendly vessels sunk by the enemy; it also acted as a unified guard force in policing the prohibited or restricted areas of the coast. The former work was of incalculable service. In the innumerable rescues of ships' crews and grounded aviators alone, the Beach Patrol more than justified its operation.

In the initial months of the war, patrols were conducted about as in peacetime, but they were placed under the responsibility of the local Captain of the Port, and were augmented to some extent. The Beach Patrol fitted into the early basic pattern of defense organization. By General Orders of 3 February 1941, all coast areas had been organized into defense divisions known as "Naval Coastal Frontiers". On 6 February 1942, these became "Sea Frontiers", with Defense Commands of Army and Navy troops established in each area generally, to guard the coast and prevent enemy invasion of our shores. The Army defended the land areas while the Navy was responsible for maintaining inshore and offshore patrols. As an integral part of the United States Navy, the Coast Guard took its logical place in this scheme of things.

Right from the outset of the war, the German submarine menace became increasingly alarming. Japanese undersea craft also were a very potent threat. Submarine activity along the Atlantic seaboard was painfully evident. The situation at sea became acute, even before Naval and Coast Guard offshore patrols were prepared to cope with it. The entire coast was, in effect, open to possible raids by the new, all-powerful, far-ranging submarines of the enemy. The need for more highly organized security was urgent. Unless adequate defense precautions were taken, saboteur landings could become common. In those days, actual invasion of our shores was not beyond the realm of possibility.

Numerous instances of industrial sabotage did more than reports of investigating committees possibly could, to convince America of the growing gravity of conditions. In the words of J. Edgar Hoover, head of the Federal Bureau of Investigation, Americanism was on trial: "The spy, the saboteur, the subverter must be met and conquered". It was generally felt that, as U-boat depredations grew steadily worse, there would at least be isolated attempts to test our defenses. Intelligence reports indicated comprehensive German plans for landing agents on our coasts. Still, it took a few graphic incidents to initiate full action.

The first incident of successful saboteur landing came on 13 June 1942. Shortly before midnight, a German submarine surfaced about 500 yards off the beach at Amagansett, Long Island. The weather was thick and the visibility poor. Under cover of fog, a rubber boat was launched from the sub and four men with four large boxes landed silently on the sandy shore.

John C. Cullen, seaman second class, of the Amagansett Coast Guard Station which maintained a regular patrol, was on his nightly 6-mile easterly trek. Surprising the group on the beach, Cullen stopped and questioned the leader. Two other men in the background, speaking in German, at once aroused his suspicions, but being alone, he could do little more than cleverly lead the spokesman into self-incriminating statements. Alarmed, the German at first threatened, then attempted to bribe Cullen, who feigned a friendly acceptance of $260. Having made up his mind, Cullen started away. As soon as he was enveloped in fog he raced to his station to report the incident. When an armed group of Coast Guardsmen reached the spot they found no trace of the men, but next morning they found the four cases buried on the beach. It developed that these men had ample funds of American currency, as well as high explosives, detonators, timing devices, and such, designed at the special school of sabotage near Berlin, where they had been trained. The FBI took up the case and later succeeded in apprehending all four German saboteurs.

Four days later, on 17 June 1942, four more German agents were put ashore from a U-boat on Ponte Vedra Beach, on the coast 15 miles southeast of Jacksonville, Florida. These men were reported by local fishermen, who found hidden boxes that contained their incriminating paraphernalia—small boxes of bombs and incendiary devices. These saboteurs, too, were later seized by FBI officials. Of the eight, six were executed, one was given life imprisonment, the other thirty years.

Nor was this all. Much later, near Machias on the coast of Maine, two men were landed from a German submarine, and might have been unnoticed had it not been for an alert boy. These, also, were arrested later.

The first two landings justified immediate action. The importance of the beach patrol was no longer questioned, and within a month the new Coast Guard organization was under way, as recommended by the FBI.

At about this time, and before the new organization was an actuality, it became known that the Germans had acquired property at Martha's Vineyard, Massachusetts, and that German submarines had been observed hovering in the vicinity. Grave concern was expressed as to the adequacy of the existing patrols, and their extension was requested.

After preliminary Army-Navy-Coast Guard conferences, comprehensive surveys were made of strategic sections of the coast. District Coast Guard Officers cooperated by submitting complete analyses of existing defense arrangements in their respective regions. It was agreed that an extended chain of coastal patrols and lookouts would be required to fully protect the coastline against the landing of foreign agents by surface craft.

By directive of 25 July 1942, Coast Guard Headquarters authorized all Naval Districts adjacent to the coast to institute an organized beach patrol system. They were directed to maintain well equipped beach forces in all areas where terrain would permit. Patrolmen were to be properly armed and fully instructed in the execution of their duties. Provision was made for the establishment of an efficient system of communications to enable each patrol promptly to relay its reports or signals to the proper Coast Guard authorities.

On 30 July 1942, the Vice Chief of Naval Operations informed commanders of the Sea Frontiers that the beaches and inlets of the Atlantic, Gulf, and Pacific Coast would be patrolled by the Coast Guard whenever and wherever possible. Plans and organization progressed. All patrol activities were integrated with the work of the FBI, the Army, and various local services such as state and local police. Coordination for complete coastal defense was the keystone of the organization. The ultimate success of the Beach Patrol was due as much to the sustained cooperation of the several agencies involved as it was to the constant vigilance of the individual patrols.

The Army, Navy, and FBI all had tangible interests in coastal defense. The Army was basically charged with responsibility for the defense of the beaches and for the conduct of any military operations involved in repelling enemy invasion. This included Army reconnaissance and patrol activity. The Navy was responsible for the protection of coastwise merchant shipping against submarine attack, for the rescue of merchant seamen, and for protection of the various sea lanes vital to the defenses of the United States. The Navy was to support the Army as necessary in repelling any attacks upon coastal objectives, and to operate an intelligence division within the elements of sea defense. The FBI was primarily concerned with the detection of evidence of either subversive activity along the coast or attempted landings of enemy agents. Its success in the apprehension of spies and saboteurs was predicated, in part, upon the receipt of information gained by both Army and Navy Intelligence.

Because of these interwoven responsibilities, the Beach Patrol and Coastal Lookout Organization was closely integrated with the military coast defenses and the anti-aircraft warning system. The specific function of the Coast Guard on beach patrol was to guard the coast, not to repel military invasion. A Headquarters directive clarified this: "These beach patrols are not intended as a military protection of our coastline, as this is the function of the Army. The beach patrols are more in the nature of outposts to report activities along the coastline and are not to repel hostile armed units. The function of the Army in this connection is not to guard against surreptitious acts, but rather to furnish the armed forces required to resist any attempt by armed enemy forces or parties to penetrate the coastline by force."

The "Coastal Information System" which was built around the Beach Patrol was one of the most important contributions of this activity toward security of our coast areas. The extensive chain of Coast Guard lifeboat stations, lighthouses, and lookouts provided the basis for intercommunication all along the coast. These were later improved through the addition of some new stations and many lookout towers.

The regular stations had established telephone communication, but in most districts these were inadequate to meet the increased wartime demands. Means had to be provided for almost instant contact between patrolmen on the beach and their local patrol stations for the immediate reporting of incidents. It was also imperative that those stations communicate with other stations, section offices, district headquarters, and other appropriate military centers, including Naval Intelligence.

In general, the beach patrol communications system included a plowed-in special beach wire, metallic telephone, and common battery circuit. Commando jack boxes were distributed along the beaches at 1,200 or 1,500 foot intervals, and, finally, patrolmen were equipped with portable hand-set telephones which could be conveniently plugged into any commando jack box to establish immediate communication with their stations.

Problems in setting up the necessary equipment were legion. Suffice it to say that thousands of miles of land lines and hundreds of miles of submarine cable were efficiently laid, and a great amount of equipment installed, to enable this system to function smoothly. These were, of course, tied in with the regular Bell system. Command lines were also installed as needed. Thus, the Beach Patrol functioned as an official organ to act as the eyes and ears of the Army and Navy in the capacity of a reporting agency. It was essential to both activities.

As normal procedure, information reported by lookouts or patrols was speedily dispatched through intermediate channels to the headquarters of the Naval District, the Sea Frontier, and the Defense Command. In each echelon of command, adjacent Army and Navy units were notified and the nearest representative of the FBI contacted. Information immediately reported included: vessels in distress, aircraft crashes, landings, flashing lights, flares, fires, naval vessels, unidentified aircraft or ships, gunfire, explosions, bombings, splashes, hostile or suspicious vehicles or individuals, submarine mines, land mines, demolitions, obstacles, chemicals, sabotage, flotsam, wreckage, and unusual objects.

Organization under the new system required an independent, national Beach Patrol Division at Headquarters. This was set up under the capable direction of Captain Raymond J. Mauerman, who was later succeeded by Captain A. M. Martinson, Captain G. W. Bloom, and Lieutenant Commander C. G. Gardner. Conforming to Headquarters' specifications, each district set up its beach patrol organization as it desired. Administrative divisions were established under direction of a special Beach Patrol Officer who was responsible for seeing that all units and local stations properly carried out their specific functions. To assure complete unity of operations, the Beach Patrol was separated administratively from the other activities of the districts.

A great many new Coast Guard stations were opened during the autumn of 1942, often with temporary quarters hurriedly erected to provide necessary accommodations until permanent constructions were completed. In the First Naval District alone, 57 coastal lookout towers and outposts were built by the Civil Engineering Division. Estimates based on a unit cost of $835 per man called for an appropriation of $720,000 for the first 192 stations established. An additional $12,525,000 was needed in September for the completion of the program.

The establishment of an effective coverage of several thousand miles of beach under conditions which sometimes seemed almost insurmountable, was by no means a simple task. The undertaking involved not only the relatively easy patrolling of long stretches of open, sandy beach but also the guarding of unusual coastal terrain: sand dunes, inlets, rivers and rocky cliffs; the rugged and heavily forested areas of the Pacific Northwest; the treacherous shore of New England, with its wild, indented coasts of Maine; the isolated Keys of Florida, and the swampy mosquito-infested regions of the Gulf. Along many sections of the coast, mounted patrols, or even foot patrols, were virtually impossible, as in the remote and unpopulated barrier islands of the Charleston (Sixth) District or in the swampy, isolated jungles of

southern Louisiana. In fact, no attempt was made to establish complete coverage of the more inaccessible regions. Boat patrols supplemented beach patrols in many areas which could not be covered by the latter. Where foot patrols or mounted patrols were impracticable, or where coastal conditions permitted, motorized patrols were organized. This was particularly true in Maine, Washington, and Florida.

Altogether, ten districts maintained a Beach Patrol organization which, at its peak, employed approximately 24,000 officers and men. Extended beach patrol coverage totaled about 3,700 miles, exclusive of areas covered by strategically located lookout towers.

By boat, jeep, truck, on foot, and on horseback, Coast Guardsmen tirelessly patrolled the Atlantic, Gulf, and Pacific Coasts. Most areas were under constant surveillance by the close of 1943. Night patrols operated from a continuous chain of stations extending from Maine to Florida, from Key West to Corpus Christi, and from Southern California to Puget Sound. Concentrated coverage was given the more vulnerable coastal sections. In many regions, where danger of invasion or sabotage activity was greatest, a full 24-hour beach coverage was undertaken. Elsewhere, patrols were maintained only during darkness, or in daylight hours of low visibility. Continuous lookout watches, however, were maintained both day and night.

Usually, patrolmen traveled in pairs, covering two miles or less, and were armed with rifles or sidearms and equipped with flashlights and Very pistols. Mounted patrolmen usually carried portable radio receiver-transmitter sets, a compass, a whistle, and often, both pistol and rifle. Periodic reporting by telephone every quarter of a mile assured the necessary vigilance. Patrols were generally required to cover distances between their report posts within an allotted time; failure to make a report brought immediate investigation to that point.

The very nature of the Beach Patrol required careful selection of personnel. The work was hard and exacting, with little reward, save personal satisfaction in a job well done. Despite the many difficulties encountered and overcome, morale was universally high. Adequate facilities were sometimes lacking, but the spirit of cooperation was widespread. Neither material equipment nor com-

TRAINEES LINE UP FOR INSPECTION . . . . this, they learned, was only the beginning.

LIFEBOAT HANDLING . . . . an all-important part of training. Seamen learn all about
raising and lowering a lifeboat from an old hand.

SPAR CADETS GO TO SEA . . . . a welcome break in routine of classroom lectures.

CAPTAIN DOROTHY C. STRATTON, USCGR(W) . . . . who headed the Women's Reserve.

SPARS ON PARADE PASS WASHINGTON MONUMENT.

AERIAL BOMBS FOR HITLER'S HORDES . . . . a Temporary Reserve unit in Boston became expert in supervising the loading of explosives.

COAST GUARD TEMPORARY RESERVES . . . . attending an indoctrination lecture.

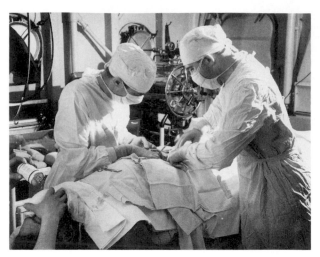

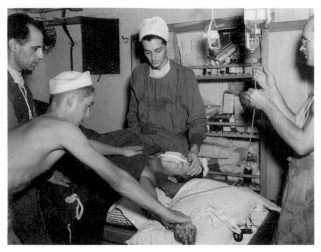

AN APPENDECTOMY AT SEA . . . . Dr. John J. Davies, USPHS and Chief Pharmacist's Mate Leo Legault perform emergency operation.

WOUNDED MARINE RECEIVES BLOOD PLASMA . . . . on board a Coast Guard-manned transport in Southern Pacific theatre.

MID-OCEAN TRANSFER FROM SHIP TO SHIP . . . . an injured merchant seaman is hauled to a Coast Guard ship for medical treatment.

SHIP'S DOCTOR ON MERCY MISSION . . . . takes a ride in boatswain's chair to treat injured seaman in merchantman.

COAST GUARD CUTTER *INGHAM* . . . . on convoy duty in the North Atlantic.

ARTIST'S CONCEPTION OF *SPENCER* FIGHTING A U-BOAT . . . . Hunter Wood, Coast Guard artist of the
Public Relations Division, depicted a mid-Atlantic attack in this watercolor.

A FAMOUS ON-THE-SCENE PICTURE . . . . a Coast Guardsman makes the supreme sacrifice at his battle station.

RELEASING MEN FOR SEA DUTY . . . . SPARS served as "ship's cooks" in many shore establishments.

SPARS MADE EXCELLENT RADIO OPERATORS . . . . they helped to relieve the persistent shortage of radiomen.

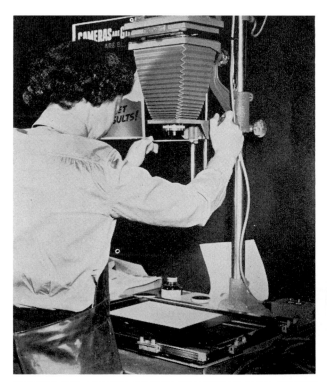

PUBLIC RELATIONS PHOTOGRAPHIC LABORATORY . . . . a SPAR makes prints for home town paper distribution.

SPAR LABORATORY TECHNICIAN . . . . many SPARS continued their civilian professions in the Medical Division.

fort were fundamentally prerequisites for efficiency. Rather, it was the prevailing attitude of the officers and men that made for the success of the Beach Patrol. Since the personnel were well chosen, the feeling of obligation to duty was strong. From the very beginning, men were impressed with the seriousness of the work. Districts frequently selected the patrol units from among members of the native neighborhood—men familiar with the local geography of the coast. Thus, many guarded their own communities.

The work was routinized and seldom spectacular. The methodical tramp, tramp of weary feet plodding their beats back and forth, in fair weather and foul, stood as a constant reminder that the military duties on the home front were often as essential to victory as the more exciting activities of the far-flung battle line. Often the routine was most rigorous. Some posts were completely isolated from civilization. Without thought of leave or liberty, these men worked seven days a week, often 10 to 14 hours a day. In the thickly wooded sections of Washington and Oregon they did their own cooking and managed the general upkeep of their stations. Jungles were penetrated; new trails were blazed through the forests. Not infrequently the beach lay 200 or 300 feet below the upland. Steep ascents were difficult; open, rocky beaches left the men exposed to blinding snow and rain in winter or to the blistering heat of summer.

In describing his patrol area, one patrolman working at Duxbury, Massachusetts, near Plymouth, said: "The beach itself is annoying rather than dangerous. During most of the year it is covered with round, slippery rocks concealed by slimy kelp; it is strewn with lobster-pots, barrels, ships' fenders, water-logged mattresses, flotsam, jetsam, and just plain skudge."

Procedures in repelling landings by the enemy were specific and standardized. Capture of the offenders was vital. This would prevent fulfillment of their mission and enable authorities to obtain the maximum of desired information. Preservation of all evidence of possible sabotage was requisite. A landing party was to be challenged once or twice before threat was indicated. If the challenge went unheeded, a shot was fired overhead or into the ground. Only when the party attempted to run or escape was the guard to shoot to kill. The intent was to stop the party, not to create casualties. But if the challenge went unheeded and hostile intent was apparent, patrols were directed to open direct fire. The second patrolman was available to turn in an alarm when the culprit was under control.

Very pistols and flash reports were used in critical cases. Beach Patrol "Red Flash" reports cleared all telephone lines for important calls, and obtained immediate attention. The reporter then gave the code name of the beach, the number of his jack box, the source of information, nature of the incident, its location, and urgency. Full written reports always followed these emergency calls or signals.

The value of trained dogs in assisting the beach patrols and in sensing and controlling unauthorized persons was recognized. Soon after Pearl Harbor, the institution of Dogs for Defense, Incorporated, was founded. It eventually became the official procurement agency for all dogs employed by the armed forces. In mid-1942, the Coast Guard instituted its dog program, and Dogs for Defense provided in all about 2,000 dogs for Beach Patrol during its operation.

Dogs were given intensive training at the Elkins Park Training Station in Pennsylvania, on the 300-acre estate of P. A. B. Widener, and at Hilton Head, South Carolina, where horses were also trained. A few of the districts maintained kennels for special training of dogs. It also became necessary to recruit men specially qualified for dog handling. Later, other men were selected from existing complements to be trained as dog specialists. Special training schools for dog handlers were opened at Elkins Park and Hilton Head.

About the last of August 1942, dog patrols were begun in the Fourth Naval District, at Brigantine, New Jersey, with 30 dogs trained at Elkins Park. They were immediately successful. Within a year over 1,800 dogs were on active duty in the various districts.

Altogether the Coast Guard used 18 breeds of dogs. Because of their greater size, strength, adaptability, and general intelligence, the German Shepherds, Doberman Pinschers, and Airdales were favored by all branches of the military, but the German Shepherd proved most adaptable to beach patrol duties.

Dog patrols were maintained only at night.

Usually, one patrolman and his dog worked together as a team, the dog always under leash. These normally covered about one mile of beach, and replaced earlier two-man patrols, thus reducing personnel requirements. Dogs showed unusual alertness and they easily sensed the presence of strangers. They were also formidable adversaries. A fifty to seventy-five pound dog, attacking with teeth bared, was often a more dangerous adversary than a man with a gun.

In the early days of dog patrol, some of the dogs were not well-trained, but made very good pets and so were handled and spoiled. Later, more experienced and better trained dogs became available, men were trained in handling them, and these dogs proved more valuable. One man on patrol near Plymouth, Massachusetts, was prevented from walking off a cliff on a black night by the refusal of his dog to advance further. At times, the dogs were less helpful, especially on three occasions in the same area when they picked up skunk trails and brought the men so close that the latter were "skunked" in the ensuing combat.

After about a year of successful operation, Headquarters directed gradual curtailment of dog patrols. In the autumn of 1943, the dog schools were closed and the patrols were reduced almost 75 percent. However, this did not anticipate immediate discontinuance of the dog program. Many dogs were retained on special guard duty or assigned to necessary, limited patrols. Surplus animals were released to the Army or Navy. The dog patrols had been most important, efficient, and popular.

During September 1942, the use of horses for Beach Patrol was authorized. By 30 June 1943, about 2,990 horses were on active duty, virtually all of them furnished by the Army, without expense to the Coast Guard except for maintenance. At the peak, in September 1943, the number of horses in Coast Guard service reached 3,222. The Army Remount Service provided all riding gear but the Coast Guard had to equip its riders. It was necessary to enlist horse-personnel, and this progressed rapidly in 1943. Stabling arrangements were made for quartering horses in suitable localities, and Army Remount Officers, acting in an advisory capacity, were assigned to each of the eight Districts in which horses were used. The horses were trained at Elkins Park and Hilton Head, as were most of the dogs.

Horse patrols got under way in November 1942 on the East and Gulf Coasts. Headquarters approved the use of horses as practicable in lieu of foot patrols along shores where the terrain was suitable. The types of patrol naturally varied, however, with the local conditions of the different districts. For example, in the Sixth District mounted patrols were used almost exclusively. None were used in the First and Third Districts. It was estimated that a mounted Coast Guardsman could patrol twice the distance covered by a footman without impairing the effectiveness of the patrol. Two mounted patrolmen, traveling about 100 feet apart, normally covered a two-mile front.

To augment these patrols, special appeals were made for horsemen to join the Temporary Reserve on a voluntary, unpaid basis. They were asked to provide their own mounts, as well as the feed, stabling, and veterinary facilities necessary for the maintenance of the horses. However, few were willing to contribute all this, plus their own services, without charge, and on 18 September 1942, this program was canceled. Nevertheless, some such patrols had been established, and since they functioned successfully, they were continued. An efficient mounted unit of 96 men and 60 privately owned mounts at Grand Cheniere in the New Orleans (Eighth) District proved the plan sound.

In many isolated coastal sections, mounted horsemen were much more practical than any other type of patrol. They could traverse difficult ground more rapidly than either footmen or motor vehicles, run down suspects more easily, and carry reports with greater speed to remote points where ordinary communications were unavailable. Furthermore, horses were more alert than men to unusual circumstances, and could detect the presence of strangers long before the rider was aware of them. In congested areas such as the popular New Jersey beaches, horsemen proved useful in controlling crowds and in maintaining a sharp lookout over heavily trafficked junctions.

When Beach Patrol was curtailed in 1944, surplus mounts were disposed of at public auction through the services of the Procurement Division of the Treasury.

As in other activities, the Beach Patrol Organization was constantly under pressure for the release of men for combat duty at sea. Here, the Temporary Reserve was found extremely useful in filling in for the men so transferred. The Temporary Reserve was expanded to relieve such situations, and in some areas these volunteers went into the beach stations and coastal lookouts and carried on these functions after many of the regular and regular Reserve personnel had been transferred to sea.

In most areas, the use of these volunteers was impracticable in actually patrolling the beaches because, being employed in civilian occupations and devoting 12 hours a week to the Coast Guard, they could not work far from their homes. Rugged, isolated Oregon coast areas, the isolated beaches of South Carolina, the Florida keys, and the bayous of the Gulf coast could not be reached by these men for intermittent, temporary duty. However, where Beach Patrol was conducted in reasonable proximity to centers of population, Temporary Reservists were used to excellent advantage. In the First Naval District about 1,500 of these volunteers were engaged in patrolling the beaches, often with dogs; manning coastal lookout towers; maintaining sentry watches or telephone watches at beach stations; and performing station base duties. In the Third District, fewer were used, chiefly in the lookouts of the north Jersey shore. The Fourth District employed a great many in coastal lookouts, especially along the south Jersey coast and at Capes May and Henlopen. About 15 percent of the Temporary Reserves in the Lake Michigan area served in lifeboat stations, many on lookout duty. Some were used on beach patrols in other districts.

Although prevention of enemy landings was an important mission, beach patrols were more than preventive. Positive results were contributed to the safety and general welfare of the community in every area where they operated. Part of the assignment was guarding prohibited or restricted beach zones. Thousands of suspects were challenged and forced to justify their presence on the coast. Many others were apprehended for further investigation by intelligence authorities or the FBI. Countless incidents of a suspicious or questionable nature were reported. True, many were "false alarms", but a great number were of inestimable value to intelligence units throughout the country whose duty it was to evaluate this body of information. The slightest matter of significant importance was faithfully reported.

Patrolmen and patrol boats recovered flotsam and jetsam, discovered booby traps, mines, bombs, and other dangerous contrivances of the enemy, and turned over to proper authorities valuable articles or bits of wreckage which were found along the beaches. Coast Guardsmen were constantly available for all kinds of assistance to local agencies. They aided in blackout and defense exercises, helped supervise air raid drills, and actively cooperated with the Army, Navy, Marine, and civil authorities in ordinary law enforcement. Among the many public services rendered was that of fire control. Beach fires were prevalent in various coastal regions. The most common sabotage device encountered, and chiefly on the Pacific Coast, was the lighted cigarette with attached matches, which was employed in innumerable cases to start beach or forest fires. Patrols were often able to spot fires in time to prevent their spreading into dangerous proportions. Organized assistance in fighting fire, or relief work in flooded regions, and during storms or hurricanes were frequently the most exciting work of the patrolman.

The most outstanding work of the Beach Patrol was in its traditional role of life saving. Foot or boat patrols were in a position to sight vessels in distress or to spot planes as they were forced into crash landings. In fact, if not in form, patrols became an important rescue agency. On many remote beachheads or on isolated islands, Coast Guard patrolmen and lookout watchmen were the only people present for this kind of work. The mounted service proved especially valuable because on several occasions horsemen were able to locate bodies that were missed by the foot patrolman. Furthermore, the efficient beach communications system enabled alarms to be turned in quickly enough to bring almost immediate assistance. Official reports are filled with instances of outstanding service rendered by patrolmen in saving the lives of shipwrecked sailors or airplane crews that had been forced down or had crashed.

Since all movement was watched and reported, planes were seldom unseen along the coast in clear weather. There were numerous times when beach patrolmen directly or indirectly saved persons from drowning. They were responsible for sending assistance to small craft in distress in the areas under their jurisdiction. In innumerable instances, patrolmen off the beach manned surfboats which put out to rescue survivors of wrecked or grounded vessels, often "through surf and storm and howling gale." They discovered persons in the water, and, applying artificial respiration, brought them back to life.

One example will illustrate the high degree of efficiency attained by patrols. In April 1943, a small Navy boat with 10 or 12 armed personnel tried to make an unidentified landing on the eastern side of the Cape Cod Canal. The beach patrol intervened and successfully prevented the landing. The incident doubtless came as a surprise to both parties, but it was conclusive proof that the Coast Guard was on the alert.

The Beach Patrols, both mounted and foot, materially strengthened the rescue work of the Coast Guard. One of the outstanding achievements in the Fifth District was the reporting of the disaster of the Greek steamer *Louise*, which broke up just offshore near the Little Kinakeet Coast Guard Station. The mounted patrol discovered the first of the 11 bodies washed ashore. This report made it possible for two lives to be saved.

At various times Army aviators were rescued from the Grand Cheniere swamps, in Louisiana near the Texas line. Coast Guardsman Joseph Klein, seaman first class, was awarded the Navy and Marine Corps Medal for heroism in one such rescue. Probably the toughest job accomplished by the Grand Cheniere unit was the rescue of survivors of a B-26 bomber which crashed just off the coast. The crew wandered into the swamps in search of assistance and became hopelessly lost. The entire ridge was methodically searched by Coast Guardsmen before all the men were found. During this unit's short period of existence, its men saved more than 35 lives.

Many lookout tower and station watches were dull and uneventful, of course, as were most Beach Patrols. An "alert" was always welcome, and routine was occasionally broken by incidents serious, humorous, or just annoying. An example of welcome relief is an "alert" at Brace's Cove, Gloucester, on the ocean side of Eastern Point. The telephone rang in the lookout shack and the officer at Popple's Point barracks said: "Three men on a raft in your area. Find out about them." The men were instantly alerted and excitement ran high. Were they saboteurs, survivors of a torpedoing, or adventurers in trouble? Each man did his best to be the first to discover the raft, and a wide area was searched to no avail. On return to the lookout shack it was discovered to have been a false alarm. But the monotony of the watch had been broken.

On 11 June 1942, four lifeboats were sighted containing survivors of the torpedoed tanker *F. W. Abrams* by the Beach Patrol of the Ocracoke, North Carolina, Lifeboat Station. The patrolmen signaled them the best place to land on the beach. All 36 survivors were carried by motor truck to the Ocracoke Station where they were afforded succor. Incidents of this sort were common that year.

An outstanding instance of rescue by a Beach Patrol was that of the Russian steamship *Lamut,* on 2 April 1943. The vessel had gone aground at 2300 the previous night. This proved a very busy day for the Coast Guard along the Washington (State) shore, where rain, wind, and waves combined to harry the traveler by sea and sky. On the morning of that day, Coast Guardsmen from the Lapush Beach Patrol Station, about 35 miles south of Cape Flattery, were carrying out their usual duties along the rugged coast line. At 0730 patrolmen found wreckage on the beach. As they walked southward they sighted part of the mast and the top of a ship's funnel lying behind the rocks just offshore from Teahwhit Head, and at 0750 they discovered the body of a woman that had washed ashore. One of the patrolmen left to report the wreck to the Lapush Station which relayed the message by telephone to the Quillayute River Lifeboat Station to the northward.

The latter unit dispatched a motor lifeboat which arrived at 0900 off the shore where the wrecked vessel lay. Because of heavy seas and the rocks surrounding *Lamut*, the lifeboat could not approach closer than 125 yards, so she returned to the station, where personnel then decided to attempt a rescue by land. Meanwhile, in addition to the regular beach patrolmen, special details had been sent out from the Lapush Station to search for survivors and casualties along the shore from Cape Johnson to Taylor's Point. The wrecked ship was reached by this party at 1125, and the vessel was found to be lodged between a small island of rock and a high cliff jutting out from the mainland. The best available rescue point was on top of a precipitous cliff about 50 feet above a small cove where most of the survivors were, having reached the cove by means of a line from ship to shore. The other survivors were still on board.

The rescue party had no way of reaching the Russian crew except by using a light makeshift line weighted with a rock. The survivors tied a heavier line to it and one line succeeded another until one strong enough to support a person was stretched up to the cliff top. One by one, the women first, the survivors were ferried across the rocks to an undercut ledge about halfway up the face of the cliff, and from there they were taken to the top, then lowered down the other side of the precipice. One of the women survivors, injured on board ship, was taken up in a basket stretcher. The first victim was brought to the top at 1215. An hour later men from the Quillayute Station arrived to assist. A bos'n's chair and lines were used and the last of the survivors were brought in safely at 1720. In all, 47 officers and men and seven women were assisted.

Throughout these operations, Coast Guard planes circled in search of other possible victims. *Lamut's* survivors were taken to the two Coast Guard stations, arriving at about 1920, where they were bathed, fed, given dry clothing, and furnished with temporary sleeping quarters. This one incident justified the full two years of hard, routinized activity at the stations concerned.

On 27 October 1943, when beach patrolmen reported that a large freighter was going aground at Belmar, New Jersey, a crew from the Shark River Lifeboat Station was dispatched with beach apparatus, and practically met the ship as she struck! On arrival at the scene the crew set up a breeches buoy and transferred six men ashore. They then stood by and maintained patrols and watches pending culmination of a severe northeast storm.

The danger of enemy landings declined during the summer of 1943. It was felt that full beach coverage was no longer necessary. As the submarine menace diminished in the Gulf of Mexico, changes were made along that Coast. Many stations were eliminated, and some were consolidated with the coastal lookout system. Men released from beach patrol were eagerly taken up for combat duty at sea. At the turn of the year, some curtailment was made in the northeastern Atlantic and Pacific Coast areas. Many foot patrols and the less necessary boat patrols were the first to go. Mounted and dog units were relaxed very little at this time, however, because they provided maximum beach coverage with a minimum of manpower. Considerable reduction in patrols everywhere was effected beginning in April 1944. But to leave uninhabited sections entirely unguarded would merely have been inviting trouble. Important patrols continued, and a screen of observation posts or lookout stations along the seaboard was retained. Finally, the Coast Guard patrol force reverted to its former peacetime status.

The sum total of Beach Patrol contributions to the important achievements of the Coast Guard at war was by no means insignificant. It is impossible to estimate what would have been the ultimate results had our coasts remained unguarded. That the Beach Patrol was effective is proved by comprehension of the efficiency of the coastal information system for which it was primarily responsible, of its rescue operations, and of possible dire contingencies which never arose. No major saboteur landings occurred. The military did not have to oppose the enemy on home shores.

Obviously, there is no way of knowing how many spies, despite all possible precautions, eluded the patrols by slipping into the country via the route of the eight apprehended saboteurs of 1942. Let the positive achievements of the security program and the fact that our shores were well guarded be remembered in any evaluation of the Beach Patrol.

# Chapter 5

# THE SECURITY OF OUR PORTS

ONE OF THE MOST important activities of the Coast Guard during World War II was Port Security. This was built around the already established "Captain of the Port" organization which grew in scope to an almost undreamed of extent.

Brief mention of the beginning and early growth of this organization is appropriate.

In time of war the Coast Guard, though part of the Navy, maintains its identity. In World War I it continued to *enforce* the rules and regulations governing the anchorage and movement of vessels in various harbors. Due to the great increase in shipping at New York and the consequent expansion of anchorage activity and shipment of explosives, the operational officer in charge there was termed the "Captain of the Port."

In 1918, jurisdiction over the anchorage and movement of vessels in certain harbors passed from the War Department to the Treasury Department. The Secretary of the Treasury designated Coast Guard officers as Captains of the Ports of New York, Philadelphia, Norfolk, and Sault Ste. Marie, and additional appointments followed at six other ports. After the war, officers in charge of Coast Guard port activities at the principal harbors continued to be known as Captains of the Port. They continued law enforcement, supervision of explosives loading, and anchorage duties in waters under their jurisdictions.

The scope of operations gradually broadened. For instance, in the fiscal year ended 30 June 1935, Coast Guardsmen under Captain of the Port of New York inspected 9,219 vessels at anchorages; warned 327 vessels for violations; supervised the transfer of 16,460,000 pounds of explosives; transported 2,261 aliens; furnished daily transportation to Customs Inspectors, Public Health officers, and other officials to Quarantine; patrolled three regattas and one launching; and engaged in extensive icebreaking operations.

Thus, when World War II began in September 1939, the Captain of the Port organization had already expanded considerably. Yet, duties remained largely within the two classifications: (a) enforcement of anchorage regulations and control of the movement of vessels; and (b) supervision of the loading and unloading of explosives in specified areas.

On 8 September 1939, President Roosevelt proclaimed a National Emergency. This required proper observance, safeguarding and enforcement of United States neutrality, and the strengthening of our national defense within the limits of peacetime authorizations. The war in Europe tremendously increased the responsibilities of the Captains of the Port, both as to scope of duties and workload.

Captain of the Port duties expanded almost immediately. Pursuant to the Neutrality Act, the Coast Guard was directed to furnish the White House, and the State, Treasury, and Navy Departments, as well as other interested agencies, a daily report of the movement of all foreign merchant vessels, public vessels, and aircraft within United State ports. A few days later domestic vessels with domestic cargo, passenger vessels in coastwise and foreign trade, tugs, barges, and bay, sound, or river vessels were also included. Late in 1939 the responsibility for sealing radios and checking armaments of belligerent vessels arriving in port was added to these duties. COTP (Captain of the Port) personnel boarded such vessels and gained much valuable information. Masters of those ships were given a form letter of instructions relating to the radio, repairs, alterations, installations of armaments, gun emplacements, degaussing, ammunition, and explosives.

President Roosevelt issued a proclamation on 27 June 1940, calling for additional measures within the limits of peacetime authorization provided by the so-called Espionage Act of 1917. Pursuant to this, the Secretary of the Treasury immediately issued *Anchorage Regulations* which reaffirmed all existing rules and regulations, and stated that they would be enforced by the Captain of the Port, or his equivalent. They also provided that movements of vessels between points within a port, and the movement, loading, or discharging of explosives or other dangerous cargo, should be under the supervision and control of the Captain of the Port, or his equivalent. That officer was authorized to inspect and search any vessel, or person, or package therein; to place guards in vessels and remove unauthorized persons therefrom; to take full possession or control of any vessel for the collector of customs when necessary to secure safety against damage or injury; and to prevent damage or injury to any harbor or waters of the United States. The regulations stated further that all lighters, barges, ferries, tugs, motor boats, sail boats, and similar craft might be required to have special licenses, and that these licenses might be revoked for infractions of the regulations or any act inimical to the interests of the United States; they stipulated that no vessel should depart from any United States port on a voyage requiring clearance by the Customs Officer unless authorized by the latter at the port of departure.

Because the Treasury Department would necessarily assume some functions previously vested in other agencies, the Commandant of the Coast Guard called a conference. Represented were Departments of the Treasury, War, Navy, and Commerce, the Interstate Commerce Commission, the Association of American Railways, the Bureau of Explosives, the American Association of Port Authorities, the New York City Fire Department, the American Petroleum Institute, and the Standard Oil Company of New York. Need was stressed for uniformity in Federal regulations in major ports and for the elimination of existing varying rules. There was, however, a desire to adhere as closely as possible to procedures normally followed by the various regulatory agencies, and to receive advice and assistance from the latter in adopting new or amending old regulations. There was much to be done in smoothing out the rules for handling explosives and dangerous materials, and in determining jurisdiction of agencies involved.

The functioning of the Coast Guard as "Federal Police" for law enforcement in United States harbor waters would continue. Close cooperation with the local police on shore was requisite. With the waterfront as the Coast Guard's bailiwick, and with most of the power plants, even in interior cities such as Pittsburgh and Cincinnati, located on the waterfront for easier access to coal and oil barges, the borderline between police and Coast Guard authority had to be worked out. At that time, policing of piers could not be undertaken by the Coast Guard for lack of sufficient personnel.

The first step in identification of longshoremen came at New York in mid-1940. A system was inaugurated for ascertaining the nationality, and obtaining fingerprints, of longshoremen and granting them permits. This system was later extended to other ports.

On 20 September 1940, it was arranged with the State Department that licensed exporters of explosives be required to report to Coast Guard Headquarters all shipments for export, including all pertinent details. Authorities concerned were then properly notified.

The "Dangerous Cargo Act" followed on 9 October 1940, making the provisions of the International Convention for Safety at Sea relating to the carriage of explosives and dangerous goods more effective. Every vessel in United States waters, except public vessels and tankers, was thus brought under supervision, and regulations became very strict.

On 29 October 1940, the Secretary of the Treasury issued "Anchorage Grounds for Certain Ports of the United States and Rules and Regulations Relating Thereto." These expanded and refined previous regulations, and the resulting enforcement and supervision duties increased the responsibilities of the Captains of the Port.

On 5 November 1940, Captains of the Port were designated at the following 29 key ports. At each port the primary duties at the time were enforcement of all regulations, and supervision of explosives. The key ports were as follows:

| | |
|---|---|
| Portland, Maine | Miami, Florida |
| Boston, Massachusetts | Key West, Florida |
| New York, New York | Mobile, Alabama |
| Philadelphia, Pennsylvania | Gulfport, Mississippi |
| Baltimore, Maryland | New Orleans, Louisiana |
| Norfolk, Virginia | Galveston, Texas |
| Charleston, South Carolina | San Juan, Puerto Rico |
| Port Everglades, Florida | Sault Ste. Marie, Michigan |

Detroit, Michigan
Cleveland, Ohio
Chicago, Illinois
Duluth, Minnesota
San Diego, California

San Pedro, California
San Francisco, California
Seattle, Washington
Astoria, Oregon
Ketchikan, Alaska

Honolulu, Hawaii

This system set up effective law enforcement machinery on a fairly uniform basis, subject only to variations due to local conditions.

On 25 March 1941, a further step was taken, designating as "Headquarters Ports" those listed above, except Port Everglades, Gulfport, San Diego, and San Pedro, and in addition included 11 other ports:

Rockland, Maine
Portsmouth, New Hampshire
New London, Connecticut
Atlantic City, New Jersey
Tampa, Florida

Los Angeles, California
Buffalo, New York
Marquette, Michigan
Oswego, New York
St. Louis, Missouri

Port Arthur, Texas

Sub-ports under the Headquarters Ports were also designated, and most of these were later assigned Assistant Captains of the Port (ACOTPs). Thus, the entire seacoast, Great Lakes shores, and navigable mid-Western rivers, as well as the waters of Alaska, Hawaii, Puerto Rico, and the Virgin Islands, became the responsibility of these officers.

Another development affecting Port Security was the United States Coast Guard Auxiliary and Reserve Act of 19 February 1941 (later amended in June 1942) which repealed the Coast Guard Reserve Act of 1939 and established the Coast Guard Reserve as a military component. The former non-militarized civilian reserve became the Auxiliary. Under this Act, the regular Reservists later constituted that part of the Coast Guard personnel who served "for the duration" full time, with pay. The "Temporary Reservists", created by this Act but not activated until after June 1942, were principally part time unpaid volunteers who were chiefly and importantly connected with the Port Security effort as outlined in the next chapter.

It will be remembered that upon the declaration of *World War I*, United States Customs officers took possession of German ships in United States ports, and that widespread destruction of ships and machinery, and other acts of sabotage had been perpetrated. With this in mind, and through a desire to keep fully informed, Captains of the Port kept a close check on movements of Italian and German vessels within their jurisdictions.

In March 1941, the COTP, Norfolk, Virginia, received information of evidence of sabotage being committed in Italian vessels at Wilmington, North Carolina, and at Baltimore. An inspection of three Italian vessels at Hampton Roads showed that much damage had been done to their machinery by the Italian crews. COTP inspections of Italian ships followed at various American ports, and the first really warlike episodes involving the COTPs resulted. On 30 March 1941, Italian and German vessels were taken into protective custody in United States ports. Country-wide seizure was made at piers or anchorages, using Coast Guard vessels and Captain of the Port details. The seizures were so timed and executed, and the dispersion of the boarding and steaming crews was so complete, that no resistance or violence was possible. Later, seizure extended to vessels of some other nations. From 29 March to 5 April 1941, 27 Italian vessels with 850 officers and crew were seized and 35 Danish vessels with 470 officers and crew were taken into protective custody. Later still, 15 French vessels were taken. They were reconditioned for Maritime Commission service.

By May 1941, heavy shipments of lend-lease goods were going overseas, and an alarming proportion failed to reach their destinations due to war at sea. The Axis nations were having increasing successes on the fields of battle. The invasion of Britain was expected. Involvement of the United States became more probable. On 27 May 1941, the President proclaimed an Unlimited National Emergency, and with this came greatly increased demands for the security of our ports. The Neutrality Patrol became a full scale operation. Small patrol vessels and personnel to man them were needed with increasing urgency, many to augment fleets for patrol duty under Captains of the Port. The Coast Guard began to take over boats from members of the Auxiliary.

Particular attention was paid to the safety of waterfront oil properties, and 1941 was a year for many consultations with civilian safety agencies and for the formulation of rules and regulations for the safety of such properties. Out of these surveys, particularly those at Los Angeles, grew a manual or set of standards, approved by the Navy and Coast Guard, and adopted by the oil terminal operators, for the conduct of their plants during the emergency.

The shipment of explosives increased greatly in many ports. This brought about surveys to discover better and safer locations for loading points. Regulations for the movement and inspection of neutral and belligerent ships became tighter. Regulations enforced by the boarding officers for purely defensively armed vessels included securing of guns, stowing of ammunition, and sealing of the radio. Carriers of belligerent nations taking on explosives found COTP personnel on the docks and in the holds enforcing safety measures and blocking possible sabotage.

The attack on Pearl Harbor on the morning of 7 December 1941, was followed by the declaration of war on Japan, and a state of war with Germany and Italy. The Coast Guard was prepared to undertake the security measures which were bound to expand tremendously under actual war conditions. The President, by Executive Order, empowered the Coast Guard to place guards upon waterfront installations whenever necessary to protect national defense premises, materials, and utilities. This was the forerunner of later directives which gave the Coast Guard prime responsibility for waterfront security.

At first, because of insufficient Coast Guard personnel, the primary burden of guarding facilities was placed upon their owners and operators to install guards and anything else necessary for proper protection. However, supervision was furnished by COTP. Adequate attainment of necessary expansion took 15 months, and the needs of the Port Security program during that period naturally grew faster than the Coast Guard's ability to fully meet them. Through the ports and harbors of the United States and its possessions, were to flow almost undreamed-of numbers of men, and quantities of materials and supplies to the fighting fronts overseas.

The keynote of Axis success in Norway and elsewhere had been a specialized army smuggled into the country before the actual invasion. This army, once inside, would attack and disrupt lines of supply and communications by sabotage on unguarded installations and facilities, thus so weakening the aggressed country that it was comparatively helpless. If acts of sabotage in the United States were to be committed, they would most certainly be directed at the waterfronts and installations where vitally needed supplies were stored awaiting shipment to beleaguered countries. Therefore, protection of harbors and facilities to prevent acts of sabotage and carelessness of individuals was vital. As Port Security was a relatively new task of great magnitude, it could not emerge as an organization overnight, but was the product of trial and error, experimentation, careful thought, and clever utilization of tools and organizations already in existence.

With both landside and waterside responsibility, the Captains of the Port insured that no suspicious boats were lurking in the vicinity of shipping and waterfront property. Through the establishment of boat patrols they attempted to detect and prevent any surreptitious landing of persons from boats, and took other measures to safeguard property against sabotage or other dangers.

To attain the objective of the Port Security program, the Captains of the Port eventually built an organization with the following broad scope of responsibilities which thereafter remained virtually unchanged:

(1) Control of the anchorage and movement of all vessels in port.
(2) Issuance of Coast Guard identification cards, and supervision of ingress and egress to vessels and waterfront facilities.
(3) Fire prevention measures, including inspections, recommendations, and enforcement.
(4) Fire-fighting activities, including use of fireboats, trailer pumps, and other extinguishing agents.
(5) Supervision of the loading and stowage of explosives and military ammunition.
(6) Boarding and examination of vessels in port.
(7) Sealing of vessels' radios.
(8) Licensing of vessels for movement in local waters and for departure therefrom.
(9) Guarding of important facilities.
(10) Enforcement of all regulations governing vessels and waterfront security.
(11) Maintenance of water patrols.
(12) General enforcement of Federal laws on navigable waters, and other miscellaneous duties.

The period from mid-1942 to mid-1943 was that of greatest expansion in the Port Security forces. Eventually, Port Security absorbed about 22 percent of the total Coast Guard manpower, even aside from the Temporary Reservists. The peak in personnel, equipment, and training was reached about March 1943. The number of commissioned officers in Port Security and enlisted personnel *on shore* on 20 August 1942 numbered 13,429. It had increased to 28,482 by 7 July 1943. Enlisted personnel attached to Port Security Floating Units on 15 December 1942 was 9,232, and this figure remained fairly static. These numbers later declined, but the deficiency was made up by Temporary Reservists.

As the war tempo increased and traffic in the many ports changed, Captain of the Port units were added at some places and discontinued at others. There was nothing static about this organization. By the beginning of 1943 there were 75 Captains of the Port and about 90 Assistant Captains of the Port. At the end of that fiscal year there were 99 and 146 respectively. On 25 February 1944, the numbers had declined to 75 and 91, respectively.

There was substantial success in integrating this far-flung Port Security organization into a coordinated and relatively uniform system. Considering the wide variety of duties, and the varying problems and local conditions at the different ports, a remarkable degree of uniformity was achieved. The Captains of the Port were carefully instructed as to Headquarters policies. To further coordinate activities, a District Port Security Officer was appointed for each district. Every effort was made to publicize regulations. They were printed and distributed to ships' officers, operators, and other interested parties. Posters were placed upon waterfront structures and vessels in large numbers.

Throughout virtually the entire war period, the Coast Guard was short of personnel. Active recruiting brought in many tens of thousands, but these had to be trained before they were of value. Though Port Security, greatly expanding, needed more and more men, so did the fleets at sea, the invasion forces, and other units operating far from continental United States. The demand for men at sea was so great that it was continuously necessary to draw from men trained in and engaged in Port Security. COTPs trained men and placed them on duty as soon as they were of value, only to have them transferred and replaced by others

needing training. It was a continuing problem, and a serious one. As has been stated, the situation was partly relieved by the use of Temporary Reservists. It was also alleviated to a considerable degree by the advent of the Women's Reserve, and the use of SPARS at shore installations. These relieved to a great extent the shortage of office personnel, released a great many men for sea duty, and did their work efficiently and satisfactorily.

The foregoing account of the growth of the Captain of the Port organization and the Port Security program indicates the magnitude and importance of this branch of Coast Guard activity. It will now be interesting to examine more carefully some of the activities which were integral parts of the Port Security effort.

With the coming of war, fire prevention and fire protection problems multiplied many times, and were particularly acute in our port cities because of the vulnerability of waterfront installations and shipping to fires, from acts of sabotage, incendiary bombings, and acts of carelessness. The lifeblood of the fighting forces was the ever-increasing flow of men, ammunition, and supplies. The port facilities from which these moved were very vital links between the home front and the fighting front. Destruction by fire or sabotage would not only have eliminated greatly needed supplies but would have seriously delayed the transfer of supplies from the transportation systems on land to the supply line of ships, to say nothing of the loss of vital storage and handling facilities. One of the greatest problems in Port Security was that of safeguarding our extensive waterfront facilities in important coastal and interior port cities against destruction by fire or other causes. Success of this effort required cooperation with military, naval, and Department of Justice intelligence organizations, as well as with state and municipal public safety agencies, and underwriters' associations.

Normally, the fire protection of ports is a municipal function. In time of war, the whole picture changes with the huge increase in shipping. The municipality usually has neither the men nor the money to care adequately for the intensified situation. Thus, augmentation of fire-fighting equipment and men by the Coast Guard was requisite for port safety.

In early 1942, the 83,000-ton French luxury

liner *Normandie* was at New York undergoing conversion into a transport. On 9 February, fire broke out and spread rapidly through the vessel. After several hours of fire-fighting the flames were extinguished, but so many tons of water had been poured into her that she capsized at her pier. This disaster, mentioned later in greater detail, was a major factor in bringing about the Coast Guard's great fire prevention effort, as well as Executive Order No. 9074 of 25 February 1942, placing the responsibility for the security of our ports.

The fire-fighting program was one of the first to receive attention. An intensive fireboat program was inaugurated. At the beginning, municipal fire departments throughout the United States had in service only 44 fireboats in 20 major cities. The need for additional fireboats was great, and the time short. Conversion of existing vessels into fireboats was undertaken, and 103 small Hanley boats were built on order. By 25 February 1944, the Coast Guard had built or converted 253 fireboats and placed them in service in 132 ports. It was the largest fleet of its kind in the world. The fireboats were well-equipped, and some were fitted with radio.

Great care was taken in locating the fireboat stations strategically. At extremely hazardous locations where explosives or dangerous cargoes were being handled, a fireboat constantly remained at the scene. It was vital that Coast Guard fireboats cooperate fully with the municipal departments, for they *supplemented* the city apparatus. In many ports, the city fire alarm system was tied in with Captain of the Port headquarters. A large number of small fire pumps were placed in picket and patrol boats operating within harbors, to permit extinguishment of small fires which might be discovered during patrols. Fireboat pumps were used to good advantage in pumping out craft in a sinking condition and keeping them afloat until they were placed on marine railways or otherwise secured.

A considerable amount of land fire-fighting equipment was also acquired and assigned to Captains of the Port. These consisted of 500-gallon-per-minute trailer pumps and motorized vehicles for towing them. On 1 July 1943, there were 260 units of this type located strategically in waterfront areas. The Coast Guard also rendered valuable assistance to municipal departments at serious fires

located outside the jurisdiction of the Coast Guard.

Much emphasis was placed on fire prevention work. In each Captain of the Port organization, men trained in this type of work made periodic inspections of all waterfront facilities under Coast Guard responsibility, searching for fire hazards, checking the condition of fire-fighting appliances and alarm devices, and enforcing rules of good practice in handling and storing cargo. Reinspections were numerous.

Though the Coast Guard had many men with years of fire-fighting experience, instruction was necessary in the newer and broader aspects of Port Security work. A training station for this purpose was established at Fort McHenry, Baltimore, Maryland. The full 6-week course included fire-fighting, fire prevention, anti-sabotage work, legal aspects of Port Security, vessel security, guarding, handling of explosives and hazardous cargo, ship construction, seamanship, close-order drill, and physical training. Actual fires were built on shore and on board a special ship, and extinguished during the course of training. Many trainees went back to their units to become instructors.

The record in the one-year period between 1 October 1942 to 30 September 1943, is representative. The Coast Guard responded to 91.65 percent of waterfront alarms in all districts combined; discovered 25.46 percent; and extinguished or assisted others to extinguish 41.21 percent. (Workmen at the scene extinguished many incipient fires though alarms might have been sounded.) The greatest known causes of waterfront and ship fires were welding and cutting. These started 15.78 percent of the fires. Next in line were heating appliances such as ovens, dryers, etc., which caused 13.06 percent. Smoking and careless use of matches as a cause of fire were surprisingly a poor third, at 10.84 percent. Enforcement of non-smoking regulations obviously was instrumental in this low ratio. As a tribute to the efficiency of the explosives program, detonation of explosives caused but .04 percent of all fires. Vessel fires constituted nearly one-third of the total.

Action involving fire details was varied, as mention of a few will show. Loss of $100,000 resulted in September 1943, from one welding fire at the Western Pipe and Steel Company in the Los Angeles Harbor area. The *CG-30080-F* (fireboat) and trailer unit #3 were dispatched to the fire in hull 139 (*USS Bangust*). It was centered in the completely equipped radar and intercommunication control room. Heat from bulkhead welding had caused the plastic instrument board to ignite. The room was locked and gas masks had to be used because of the dense, acrid smoke.

At Portland, Oregon, the Russian steamer *Djurma* had been inspected prior to welding operations in April 1943. The contractor disregarded a Coast Guard warning that welding could not be performed in certain places on board until these were cleared of highly combustible cargo. After the inspecting force had departed, however, welding started in those places. Sparks from the welding torch penetrated a steel bulkhead, and ignited paper used for lining. The resulting blaze occurred amid clouds of highly explosive floor dust raised in the process of loading.

In October 1943, two oil barges collided near New Orleans, and an empty one came to rest partly on top of the other which was full. Because of the possibility of explosion, a Coast Guard fireboat was dispatched to the scene before separating them. She pumped 70 tons of water into one section of the empty barge, thus reducing the weight on the full barge, and when the vessels were finally parted, sprayed the contact points to avoid sparking.

A dangerous explosion and fire occurred at 0100 at an oil refinery at Beaumont, Texas, endangering the entire, extensive tank area. A Captain of the Port fire detail responded with equipment. All but one of the oil line breaks feeding the fire were shut off by company employees. The other break which was feeding an enormous quantity of fuel to the fire had not been reached due to the intense heat. Coast Guardsmen, assisted by refinery workers, put four 2½-inch hose lines into service. Within five minutes the area was cooled sufficiently to allow the Port Security Officer, COTP, Port Arthur, equipped with an asbestos suit and protected by a water shield, to cut off the valve at the base of the butane-pentane tank, and the flames immediately abated.

On 28 February 1945, a fire occurred in the tug *W. W. Werner* while moored alongside barges at the Standard Oil Company docks at Baton Rouge.

The *CG-36028-F*, stationed at this facility, made fast to the burning tug which had been abandoned by its crew, cast off the mooring lines, and towed her across the Mississippi River fighting the fire en route. The fire was brought under control in 45 minutes.

Incipient fires which started after work had ceased for the night were not easy to discover. In some West Coast ports, especially during hot, dry weather, fire danger on piers increased. It became the custom in some Twelfth and Thirteenth District ports to wash down the piers after dry, hot days, partly to extinguish any smouldering cigarette butts and lessen the fire hazard. There were virtually no night fires after this practice was adopted.

The growth of responsibility and activity in Captain of the Port supervision of the loading of explosives and handling of dangerous cargoes has been outlined. Early jurisdictional uncertainties in responsibility between the Interstate Commerce Commission, local fire departments, and the Coast Guard were satisfactorily settled, and regulations became complete, specific, and tough.

The Army, Navy, and other agencies concerned, continually sought the advice and counsel of the Coast Guard relative to safe practices in the transportation, loading and stowage of explosives and dangerous cargoes. The value of supervision was proven on many occasions. The Coast Guard constantly checked and improved the procedures and supervision rendered by its field forces in the various ports where such loading was carried on.

In the earlier days there was much to be done in educating the Army, Navy, steamship operators, and operators of privately owned facilities who often were ignorant of regulations regarding this activity. After long experience, explosives loading became an old story to handlers, and familiarity seemed to breed contempt among the longshoremen. The Coast Guard had to be especially alert to insure continued gentle and careful handling.

The Coast Guard conducted classes in handling, stowage, and transportation of explosives and other dangerous articles to further efficiency in this field, and supervision details were thoroughly trained. In virtually every important United States port the Captains of the Port surveyed piers and evaluated locations to determine the best and safest facilities for explosives loading. Terminals were usually chosen or constructed in isolated localities. Explosives-laden vessels were not permitted to remain in port any longer than necessary, and were escorted to sea.

Even before the outbreak of hostilities, the desirability of identifying persons frequenting our waterfronts was recognized. Fear of sabotage and subversive acts was strong. The first identification card in the New York area was issued 23 October 1940. By the latter part of 1941 identification cards were being issued in quantity. After Pearl Harbor, issuance became a very important activity for the Captains of the Port. Wartime regulations required that each individual have a card as a prerequisite to his admission to the waterfront. These identification cards were just that—they were not "passes." Captains of the Port set up offices to perform most of the identification work, with the larger offices handling around 200 applicants a day. In some places, mobile identification units went directly to plants or shipyards and, sometimes to large buildings adjacent to the waterfront, and processed the applicants. The *screening* of applicants came under Coast Guard Intelligence, and most information resulting in exclusion came from that source.

Four types of cards were used. Most were white cards, issued to United States citizens and citizens of friendly nations whose presence on waterfronts or vessels was required in connection with their livelihoods. Buff cards went to those having only occasional business on board vessels and facilities. Green cards, for temporary use and having expiration dates, went to persons needing identification for a single visit or trip or for the duration of a particular job. If issued to an enemy alien, they were stamped "Enemy Alien." Pink cards were issued to enemy aliens and so stamped, to seamen of foreign vessels, as well as to citizens of countries hostile to the United States or associated with or dominated by hostile countries such as France or Finland. In the case of persons denied access, notice of such exclusion was sent to all districts to forestall issuance elsewhere of cards to those persons.

Identification of all persons having legitimate business on waterfronts of the entire United States was a huge job. Time was required for processing and screening. The total number of cards issued

in the United States is not available, but some idea of the magnitude of the task may be had from the fact that files at Boston contained applications and personal records of about 150,000 persons to whom cards had been issued, including 10,000 who received permits for handling explosives. At New York, the Identification Detail fingerprinted and issued credentials to more than 2,500,000 persons.

Where congestion of anchorages was likely, the Captain of the Port made regular inspections and required any movements he deemed necessary. He was also responsible for the departure and movement of practically all non-public vessels. The Anchorage Regulations authorized inspection and search of any vessels or persons therein and the removal of any person not specifically authorized to go or to remain on board. Every person on board any vessel within territorial waters had to carry satisfactory identification.

The Captain of the Port Anchorage and Ship Movement Activity was very important, especially at New York where about 60 percent of the country's wartime waterborne traffic was handled. At the peak, as many as 195 ships were recorded as passing in and out of this harbor daily. This work at New York and elsewhere included anchorage patrols which enforced rules and regulations, provided information, assisted in emergencies, and watched closely for anything not "right" at the various anchorage areas. COTP offices at principal ports maintained a chart room in which were shown the locations of ships in the port, shifts of positions, and movements into and out of the port. The type, kind of load, and classification of every vessel were recorded. Another section issued flag hoists to coastwise shipping, small boats, and fishing craft. In major ports, this office also facilitated planning with the Navy Port Director for control of inbound and outbound convoy movements; on problems concerning anchorages for large Naval units; and for clearing anchorage areas to expedite the sailing of troop transports, carriers, and other craft.

By the Spring of 1942, the situation in the Atlantic and along our Atlantic Coast, and later the Gulf Coast, became extremely critical. As evidence of the closeness of the war to our shores, survivors by the thousands were being brought to

East Coast ports. Large quantities of urgently needed oil, materials and munitions were failing to reach their destinations. This made it vital that nothing should occur in our ports to hinder the flow of supplies overseas.

Defense of shipping against submarines offshore called for coastal picket vessels. This initiated the effort to procure small craft, and this was prosecuted with vigor. At first most of the vessels procured went on offshore duty. Later as numerous additional vessels were obtained, the Captains of the Port took them over for systematic harbor patrol, since security of harbor waters required this. These boats were, for the most part, taken into the Coast Guard Reserve and became "CGR" boats.

For the greatest effectiveness, offshore and harbor patrol craft cooperated with the beach patrols where possible. All three patrols concentrated on the safety of coastal waters, shores, and ports, and there was a close tie in their operations. Each activity supplemented the others. Originally, Beach Patrol was part of the Port Security organization, but it was soon set up separately.

In the waters under their jurisdiction Captains of the Port set up boat patrol areas with specific limits, and assigned vessels to cover those areas, with particular emphasis on patrol of vital portions. These areas generally included all piers of importance, navy yards, war industries on the waterfront, power plants on tidewater, coal and lumber yards, bridge areas, anchorages both regular and for explosives, and important channels. It was also necessary to protect and watch inlets and rivers, and even the smaller harbors along the coasts where fishermen were active, and places where landings could be made by subversive agents. Later, the piers, wharves, and other landside facilities were patrolled and guarded by men on shore in addition to the waterside patrols.

Thus, harbor waters were well covered as long as necessary. The earliest patrols were carried on by such men as the Coast Guard had available, but they were few, and Auxiliarists augmented the patrols in their own craft. The increasing war tempo brought about greater need for military patrols, more efficiently executed and with wider coverage. In the latter part of 1942, Temporary Reservists began taking over these patrols, and by early 1943, patrols were handled by these men in most ports. It developed chiefly into a Temporary Reserve

activity, and remained so as long as patrols were needed. This will be covered in some detail in the next chapter.

Good cooperation between the Captains of the Port and Navy and Coast Guard Intelligence was essential. Before full development of Coast Guard Intelligence, some Captains of the Port temporarily established their own intelligence divisions.

The chief function of Intelligence was to receive promptly from every possible source all information concerning activities in or near coastal areas; to evaluate it in the light of existing military conditions; and to disseminate information to all appropriate action agencies. The COTP organization was an action agency when actual or threatened incidents involved the security of the port. Intelligence operated as a clearing house and repository for information. It maintained liaison with the Office of Naval Intelligence and other Governmental agencies; it planned and conducted investigations of Coast Guard personnel (except Coast Guard Police); and maintained fingerprint identification and other intelligence records. It furnished, through appropriate channels, information in response to requests by District Officers and Captains of the Port regarding individuals and organizations. Many intelligence investigations were made as a result of information gathered and passed along by COTP personnel and details.

Excellent cooperation with the various military and civilian agencies was achieved in most ports. Probably the most highly organized coordination was at New York. The Office of Coordinator of the Port of New York was established early in 1942. This office cleared a considerable volume of telephone and written communications with a minimum of red tape and with almost complete elimination of "through channels" technique. All marine fire-fighting facilities there were coordinated. This involved understanding between the Coast Guard, the waterfront municipalities in New Jersey, towboat operators, and the New York Fire Department. A particularly close relationship existed with the fire departments, and some officers and men worked with the New York firemen to gain working knowledge of operational methods. In a spirit of friendly give and take, the Coordinator held regularly scheduled meetings with representatives of the following:

U. S. Coast Guard
U. S. Army
U. S. Navy
U. S. Customs
War Shipping Administration
New York City Dept. of Marine and Aviation

New York City Police Department
New York City Fire Department
Fire Underwriters' Association
Other municipal and private groups

Occasional meetings were also held with Civilian Defense authorities and many other interested agencies. These meetings led to elimination or avoidance of unrelated action, cross purposes, and confusion between the several organizations.

The Coordinator's force inspected all piers, wharves, and other waterfront facilities in the district under Coast Guard jurisdiction for security and fire protection. It was the Coordinator's duty to cooperate and correct unsatisfactory conditions if possible. If action were needed, the COTP, in whom compulsion was vested, wrote the responsible party requesting correction of the defects.

A summary of the work of the Coordinator's Office for one month gives an idea of its activity. During December 1943, two investigators of his office inspected 169 vessels on which some 959 welding machines were in operation, and 926 welders, 197 burners, and 1,125 fire watchers were working. The investigators discovered and corrected on the spot 21 minor violations, and investigated one complaint. Twelve new welding concerns were contacted, Coast Guard Regulations discussed, and a copy of the Regulations left with each concern.

Regulations for the security of vessels in port were approved by the President on 31 December 1942, and signed by the Coast Guard Commandant 1 January 1943. These regulations provided for the necessary security, promoted cooperation between groups responsible for vessel security, and insured the basis for uniform administration. They stated: "In time of war, merchant vessels become vital auxiliaries to the armed forces. The safety of a merchant vessel in port in wartime depends on the effort and the cooperation of those groups responsible for safety, and they are: the officers and crew; guards; the terminal organization; those handling cargo; the terminal owners; the local municipal authorities; and the Coast Guard."

The purpose of the regulations was to insure the safety of all vessels in port while anchored, or while moored to docks, piers, wharves, or other waterfront facilities. Nothing in the rules relieved masters, owners, or operators and agents of ships from their primary responsibility for the security of their vessels. Any evidence of sabotage or subversive activity involving any vessel or facility was to be reported immediately to the FBI and the Captain of the Port, or to their respective representatives.

Vessels were required to have ship guards, cargo guards, and fire guards, in addition to the crew requirements for manning. It was provided that cargo guards should be maintained continuously in each cargo space when working explosives or other dangerous articles, except inflammable or combustible liquid cargo in bulk. A fire guard was required whenever welding, cutting, or riveting was in progress. Provisions were made for gangway guards and roving guards. Duties were specific. Guards were to be provided by the master, owner, operator, or agent, except where guards were provided by military authority, and could be required for any vessel in the discretion of the Captain of the Port. As soon as the personnel situation allowed, the Coast Guard furnished most of these guards.

Fire guards kept fire extinguishers as well as hoses with running water handy at all welding or cutting operations, and inspected the surrounding areas to be sure of no threat from combustible materials. They were thoroughly familiar with the location of fire alarm boxes and telephones, and with the procedure for sending in alarms of fire.

Persons boarding vessels were required to have acceptable means of identification (preferably a Coast Guard Identification Card), an acceptable pass, and a legitimate reason for boarding. Except where safety or necessary repairs required otherwise, vessels at anchor or moored to facilities were required to have steam pressure in at least one main boiler sufficient to operate the engines and essential auxiliaries and to allow movement.

The regulations specified a wide variety of precautionary measures which had to be meticulously observed by vessels in port. Because of the importance of petroleum and its products to the war effort, special notes were included covering care of hose and terminal loading and discharge procedures. Pollutions frequently occurred at oil docks and terminals where vessels were moored taking on or discharging oil. It was especially necessary to be vigilant at such locations, not only for the protection of the vessels, but also of the shore facilities themselves. Thorough inspections were required before and after loading of all cargo.

Probably there were no two divisions of the Coast Guard whose functions and problems so closely paralleled each other in many respects as did the Port Security and Marine Inspection activities. Both were interested in the security of the ship. The Port Security Division was interested from the standpoint of security from external influences; the Marine Inspection Division from the standpoint of technical considerations within the vessel itself. There was close correlation between the two, especially in the matter of tankers.

The principal medium of the Captains of the Port for the checking of factors relating to the security of vessels in port was the inspection program, and that for the enforcement of the regulations was the guard detail. These guards at first were regular Coast Guardsmen, but as Temporary Reservists became an effective factor, they took over the major portion of guard work in most of the ports.

Pilot operations were an integral part of Port Security. At the end of 1942, virtually all port pilots were enrolled in the Temporary Reserve and continued in their pilot capacity until the latter part of 1945, operating under their respective Captains of the Port. Their record was one of outstanding success, and is commented upon in the following chapter.

Inbound vessels other than those of the Navy entering our major ports were identified, boarded, and examined by Coast Guard boarding officers operating from Examination Vessels or by boarding parties to verify their innocent character. These boarding officers were alert for any and all violations. Boarding was done chiefly from picket boats maintained at the boarding stations. In high winds and choppy seas, with pitching, rolling, spray, and often on icy decks, boarding required good seamanship, agile men, and great care, for most boarding was done while vessels were under way.

Boarding of vessels for the enforcement of the

Navigation, Steamboat Inspection, and Motorboat Laws, and the enforcement of Customs Laws is a regular peacetime function of the Coast Guard. In wartime, additional duties concerned the security of the port and the vessels therein, and the necessity of close examination of ships, cargo, crew, and equipment.

Boarding officers called the master's attention to violations and reported serious violations and cases of non-compliance. They checked everything of a suspicious nature; recorded various data regarding the vessel; checked the ship's documents; and informed the master of traffic regulations, gate signals, and other special orders. Usually, a detail for radio sealing and armament inspection accompanied these officers. Excepted from regular inspection were incoming vessels of a coastwise nature on a regular coastwise run.

Fishing vessels habitually using a port were boarded inside the harbor by a detail which inspected cargo, fuel, and crew, and attended to radio sealing. Food and fuel were checked to prevent or detect transfer of such items to enemy ships. In outlying harbors and small ports, this checking was done by patrol craft if no regular boarding officer was maintained.

The nature of the work of the Captains of the Port required prompt and efficient communication with every unit under their jurisdiction in the event of emergency. In the principal ports, these officers established their own communications systems. Emergencies involving the fire division, patrol boats, pier guards, explosives details, and others might occur at any time, and required prompt action. Many scout and patrol cars and jeeps were radio-equipped. Patrol and pilot boats, as well as most fireboats, were generally equipped with five- or ten-watt transmitter-receivers. At larger ports, it was necessary for the COTP to communicate by radiotelephone or landline with the Examination Vessel.

To facilitate communication between the Captain of the Port, units ashore and afloat, and also between shore units and merchant or other vessels, some signal stations were established. At Boston a signal station at the Coast Guard Base was wholly operated by Temporary Reservists throughout its two-year existence. Several lookout stations were set up in New York Harbor. Equipped with telautograph, visual signaling, telephones, and field glasses, the men kept constant vigil over the principal Upper Bay anchorages; informed the COTP chart room of arrivals, departures, and movements of vessels within the anchorages; and communicated with the vessels in emergencies. They recorded and reported all information of value.

Operations in Port Security have been summarized. For the most part, they were conducted efficiently and with only the normal operational problems to be expected when many new fields are entered without a great fund of experience, and where developments depend on trial and error.

Port Security generally gave the impression of walking docks during dull watches, patrolling waters day and night where nothing happened, and inspection after inspection, without real opportunities for action or heroism. While that was usually true, and many men in this duty never encountered excitement involving danger, there were plenty of exceptions. When things happened, the Port Security men, be they regulars, regular Reservists or Temporary Reservists, met their emergencies and dangers involving personal risk with efficiency and courage.

Richard L. Cariens, Motor Machinist's Mate First Class, received an award for heroism in connection with an explosion which occurred on Army Boat *234* on 21 September 1943 at Charleston, South Carolina. After the explosion, the *CG-30041-F* (fireboat) went into immediate action. A civilian who had been blown into the water was rescued by a Coast Guardsman. The fire was still burning but under control when Cariens went below to repair a damaged gas line through which gasoline was running into the engineroom and bilges. Overcome by gasoline fumes on the first attempt, he went below a second time with a gas mask and stopped the flow in two breaks. Coast Guard details removed explosives from the deck and secured the codes and confidential papers. For his heroism, Cariens received the Navy and Marine Corps Medal.

Charles D. Rogers, Specialist First Class, was the outstanding COTP New York Port Security hero. At 0215 on 21 September 1945 he was on roving patrol checking the security of piers and other vital spots. He discovered flames licking their way from beneath one of several tank cars on a siding of the Central Railroad of New Jersey. He turned in alarms and then checked the contents of the cars. He discovered that the dripping tank car was filled with an acid used as a basis for high explosives and was likely to blow up at any moment; one of the next two cars contained high test gasoline, and the other liquid chlorine. Regardless of this, he procured a shovel and began fighting the fire.

The ground area surrounding the cars was aflame, and the exposed gas mixture gave off noxious, suffocating, and irritating vapors. Rogers' citation, awarding him the Navy and Marine Corps Medal, said: "Rogers, with this knowledge, shoveling sand and dirt on the fire, worked his way beneath the tank car, without gas mask, in an attempt to shut off the flow. The soles of his shoes were badly burned as a result of those efforts. Rogers persuaded the brakeman and the locomotive engineer, against their fear of explosion, to uncouple and detach the flaming and leaking tank car from the tank cars of chlorine and gasoline and move them away from the fire. The hazard of explosion was thus lessened." Port Security men and the municipal fire department then joined the fight. More than 50 men had to have their burned-off shoes replaced. The acid gave off a deadly gas. Had it gotten out of control and had the wind been just so, a large part of the nearby population would have been wiped out. An explosion from such ingredients, compounded by acid and gas, would have caused a major catastrophe.

The first security watches on board a British vessel at Boston occurred on 14 August 1942. The British transport *Aquitania* was undergoing repairs and alterations. The Commandant of the First Naval District requested that the Captain of the Port assume responsibilty for the security of this vessel. During the 24 days this vessel was in port, the COTP established a fire detail which extinguished 36 different fires on board this ship. Similar requests were made at various times for 11 other vessels owned or operated by the British. The men on the majority of these watches were Temporary Reservists who volunteered to perform this task in addition to other regular weekly duties. This expedient proved highly effective in fire prevention.

The great Halifax explosion of World War I was not forgotten in World War II. It was a potent influence in the extreme caution with which explosives vessels were loaded and moved in all United States ports. The Coast Guard Munitions Detail at New York was thoroughly trained, and at the peak of activity, it included 44 commissioned Munitions Supervisors and 450 enlisted men. Escorts were provided for all explosives movements within the harbor.

Despite all precautions, two incidents in the New York area could have had serious consequences. While a stevedore was loading aircraft bomb fuzes from the tray to a stowage magazine, one of the fuzes detonated in his arms. There was much excitement. A pile of dunnage caught fire. The lives of everyone for miles around were seriously endangered. Although struck in the groin by flying fragments, a Coast Guard seaman, Sandow Holdman, quickly extinguished the blaze with a fire extinguisher and a ship's hose.

The second incident, which involved the near collision of a blazing tanker with ammunition-laden vessels, occurred in January 1945. At 0045, a burning tanker was sighted about one mile off the pier where it had been anchored the previous night because of dense fog. The vessel seemed to be headed directly for the pier. Crews of the vessels berthed at the pier were alerted. Coast Guard munitions men stood by with fire axes ready to cut the mooring lines should that become necessary. The tanker continued its apparent "sail into oblivion" straight as an arrow towards the munitions pier. Then, seemingly out of nowhere, a gallant, rugged Navy tug appeared. It rammed against the fiercely blazing tanker just in time to prevent its smashing into the pier. Blazing benzol immediately encompassed the pier pilings and two vessels at the outer berths. The tanker soon grounded. Quick, expert, and heroic action by Coast Guardsmen and Navy men extinguished the surface fire and pier piling blaze in short order, and another catastrophe had been averted!

Earlier in this chapter the *Normandie* incident was mentioned. It had a profound influence upon all fire prevention and fire-fighting measures which the Coast Guard later put into effect in the Port Security effort. The 83,000-ton French luxury liner *Normandie* had remained in an idle status at Pier 88, North River, New York, from August

1939 until this incident in February, 1942. Since May 1941, a Coast Guard detail of 150 men had stood watches on board her to insure her safety and to learn the details of her operation. The Chief of Naval Operations had ordered the French crew removed in December 1941. Thereafter, the Coast Guardsmen, besides standing security guard, performed all tasks relating to maintenance of the ship in idle status. Jurisdiction then changed rapidly. The Maritime Commission took possession on 16 December 1941, with the Coast Guard detail remaining on duty. The Navy took over possession on 24 December 1941, and reconversion into a troop ship began. Two weeks later the Army took title, and on 27 January 1942, the Navy took over again.

Conversion was rushed, and on the day of the fire, 2,500 civilians were engaged in the work. The contract called for the highest degree of care to protect the vessel from fire.

On 8 February, the day before the fire, the prospective Navy commander ordered, among other things, removal of four large metal stanchions in the salon which held light fixtures. Two were removed without incident. Piled around the other two were highly inflammable kapok life preservers. These were moved so that the men could walk around the stanchions. There were no fire watchers when the last two stanchions were cut. When the last was practically down, the foreman turned his back and walked away. This last burning was done without a shield and without observation by the foreman.

A small flame was observed darting upward from the bales of life preservers near the base of the stanchion. The frantic cry of "Fire!" echoed throughout the salon where 21 persons were assembled. Men vainly attempted to put out the fire with their hands. In the space of minutes the blaze was beyond control and the dense smoke made it necessary to abandon the salon. There were no extinguishers nearby, and lack of water made hoses inoperative.

After a delay due to inoperation of the ship's fire alarm system, a policeman on the pier was requested to sound an alarm, which he did, at 1449. The Coast Guard fire brigade arrived on the scene, and observed the fire spreading rapidly. Two minutes after the alarm, New York City fire apparatus arrived. Due to smoke in the boiler room, it was necessary to secure the Scotch boilers. Soon after 1500, all light and power in the ship failed, putting everything below decks in darkness. City firemen were unfamiliar with the maze of passageways. Darkness and smoke hindered their efforts. By 1615 there were 36 pieces of city apparatus at the fire, including three fireboats. Private tugs also fought the fire. In four hours of firefighting operations, over 839,000 gallons of water had been poured into *Normandie*. The huge vessel gradually listed. The fire, which had never penetrated to the lower decks, was under control and largely out at 1800, though small fires still burned for two more hours. When the fire was out, 255 persons, including enlisted personnel of the Coast Guard and Navy, workers in the ship, and city firemen, had received medical treatment for burns, smoke inhalation, exposure, and other ills.

By 2100 the list had increased to 20 degrees, and by 2300 to 40 degrees. Orders were given to abandon ship at midnight, and at 0245 on 10 February 1942, the great vessel capsized and came to rest on her port side at an angle of 80 degrees.

This incident brought about investigations by the House and Senate Naval Affairs Committees. From these investigations came constructive suggestions and regulations. Many specific recommendations were made which underlay rules and regulations for Port Security later adopted and almost uniformly enforced by the Coast Guard.

After months of tedious effort and huge expense, American skill and ingenuity floated *Normandie*. A Coast Guard security detail was maintained on the vessel after she was raised and while en route to Bayonne, New Jersey. This detail remained for three rat-ridden years at Gowanus Bay until 20 October 1945, when the detail was secured prior to cutting the vessel to pieces.

One aftermath of this catastrophe was the almost immediate organization of a nationwide fire prevention and fire-fighting program; the establishment of fire schools; intensive training of men for the fire-fighting forces; enlistment of firemen; and inauguration of the fireboat program which finally resulted in the Coast Guard operating 253 vessels of that type.

Three major fire incidents involving fireboats are worthy of mention. In the New York area one of the most spectacular involved the Panamanian steamship *El Estero*. She had completed loading about 1,500 tons of high explosives and was about to sail. The amount of explosives on board was about equal to that which wrecked Halifax in World War I. At 1720 on 24 April 1943, a fire started in her boiler room and bilges when an oil feed pipe was punctured. Because of inaccessibility the fire was exceedingly difficult to attack. It spread rapidly. An alarm was sounded and the Coast Guard Munitions Supervisor on board immediately assumed command. He directed his men in a valiant attempt to extinguish the blaze. Flames leaped to the superstructure. To stay below for any time would have been suicide. Coast Guard, Jersey City, and New York firemen worked courageously, but the danger of explosion and attending disaster was great, and the Captain of the Port ordered the ship scuttled. However, because of the fire, the sea cocks were inaccessible.

*El Estero* was then cut adrift and towed by Coast Guard, city, and private tugs into the bay while fireboats alongside stuck to the job of flooding her. The Coast Guard gave telephone alarms throughout the Metropolitan area advising precautions taken under a "Yellow" air raid alarm, and commercial radios broadcast the warning of possible explosion. Regular air raid mobilization was effected. Meanwhile, *El Estero* was being flooded and towed to a spacious area where damage would be less if she "blew". With the fireboats and other Coast Guardsmen at the scene, it was "Praise the Lord and Sink the Ammunition!" A half mile northwest of Robbins Reef Lighthouse, all hands were ordered off the burning vessel, the decks of which were then awash. At 2100, after some minor explosions, the vessel foundered in 35 feet of water, and the fire was quickly extinguished.

Lieutenant Commander John T. Stanley, USCG, on board *El Estero*, was on his first day of duty as Munitions Officer. For his heroic part he was later awarded the Legion of Merit. The citation read, in part: "For exceptionally meritorious conduct during fire fighting operations aboard a merchant vessel loaded with explosives. . . . Realizing the ever present danger of an explosion, Lt. Comdr. Stanley boarded the burning vessel and for three hours directed a large detail of men engaged in controlling and extinguishing the fire; by his calm and courageous leadership he inspired the personnel under his command and skillfully coordinated their activities, thereby preventing an explosion which might have done incalculable damage to other vessels and vital installations in the harbor."

A serious waterfront fire occurred on 11 August 1944, at Pier 4, Hoboken. Cargo on this large, modern pier included drums of Kolloxiline (inflammable, and explosive if overheated) awaiting loading on SS *Nathaniel Alexander*, berthed alongside. Large cases containing automobile parts were being loaded at the time. One was towed along the concrete floor past the drums by a chisel truck. The driver saw a tongue of flame at his side and, deserting his truck, ran away in time to avoid a moderate explosion of one drum, followed by more as other drums became involved. Fire-fighting by longshoremen was insufficient, and three alarms were sounded. Coast Guard lookout towers reported the fire and explosions. In five minutes the entire sea end of the pier was in flames. Meanwhile, Hoboken and New York City firemen and large Coast Guard details went into action. Coast Guard fireboats and tugs were rescuing men in the water. *Nathaniel Alexander* caught fire eight minutes after the alarm, was towed to safety within ten minutes, and the fire on board her was extinguished.

Commercial tugs and Coast Guard fireboats pumped water on the blazing pier structure. Several men were injured, and two stevedores and a watchman lost their lives. The fire was under control in five hours, but burned well into the next day. Port Security assistance, a major element in subduing the disastrous $1,500,000 fire, involved 22 officers, 785 enlisted men, 32 patrol boats, 9 fireboats, 3 large tugs, 6 trailer pumps, 19 units of breathing apparatus, and a large variety of other small equipment.

At 0857 on 5 February 1945, the Port of New York suffered one of the worst wartime tragedies in its history, when two ships collided off Stapleton, Staten Island; one burst into a raging inferno. At about 0855 the Panamanian freighter *Clio* was outbound with a cargo of water ballast. To maneuver between a U. S. Navy vessel, *KA-75* and U. S. tanker *Spring Hill*, both anchored, *Clio* swung to port toward the main ship channel. Suddenly her master saw the opening blocked by several invasion barges being brought alongside *KA-75*. The master frantically endeavored to swing his vessel hard to starboard, but momentum, combined with a strong ebb current, carried him toward the port side of *Spring Hill*.

Collision was imminent. Port and starboard anchors were immediately dropped and the engines reversed, but the bow of *Clio* rammed the port side of *Spring Hill* forward of the bridge, leaving a large gaping hole in number three port wing tank. Laden with a cargo of high octane gasoline, *Spring Hill* was immediately enveloped in flames. *Clio* backed away. Flaming gasoline from the ruptured tank covered the surface of the water, spreading rapidly downstream with the current and enveloping the Norwegian tanker *Vivi*, loaded with diesel oil which, fortunately, did not burn. Many of *Spring Hill's* crew were trapped below decks; others, as well as the Naval Armed Guard, jumped overboard with life jackets into the icy waters. Attempts to release lifeboats were futile. Crew members of *Vivi* did likewise, though a small detail remained. With steam already up, *Vivi* proceeded through the blazing water, dragging both anchors.

Coast Guardsmen at the Pier 18 Signal Tower promptly reported the incident, and all available cutters, fireboats, and small craft were dispatched to render assistance. Working with high efficiency, Coast Guard fireboats, New York City fireboats and commercial tugs extinguished the blaze in two hours.

There were several well-executed rescues. A CGR vessel was nearby when the fire started. John Zeigler, Chief Boatswain's Mate, with his two men directed his craft toward the stricken *Spring Hill*, and rescued 35 survivors from the flaming but icy water. At one time, a line fouled the Coast Guard vessel's propeller, causing a helpless drift toward the flames. It was freed in the nick of time. Lt. W. A. George in *CG-64309*, going out to patrol, saved about 23 seamen from certain death by expert seamanship and utter disregard of hazards. This fire caused the death of more than 15 seamen, and in all about 85 survivors were brought in to Pier 18, given first aid, and taken to the hospital. Three died soon after arrival at the pier.

Two attempts at sabotage at New York are of interest. In fighting this threat, nothing could be taken for granted. Shortly after our entrance into the war, the commanding officer of the Munitions Detail was inspecting two ships which were loading ammunition at Gravesend Bay. They had wooden sheathing between the skin and the holds. He noticed that some knots in the boards had been dislodged, and had his men rip down some boards. They found cotton on the ship's skin, and light Manila rope strands combed down to bare fibre lying around. A check on the ship's history revealed that it had never carried cotton. And a check on the cotton disclosed a certain chemical treatment making it self-igniting in high temperatures.

On another ship this same officer found a shackle pin on the head block of a boom that had been unscrewed to the last thread. The lanyard keeping it in place had been cut almost through during the night. A sling of explosives might have been dropped as a result, with disastrous effect.

During the war, over 100,000,000 tons of shipping was handled at Philadelphia, one of the world's largest fresh water ports. Yet, despite all the heavy wartime pressures, the accident rate was reduced, no incidents of sabotage occurred, and few waterfront fires raged out of control. A job for the fireboats occurred early in the morning of 29 August 1942. The wooden steamship *John Cadwalader* caught fire and, unaccountably, the blaze spread with amazing speed to all parts of the ship, which was soon a raging inferno. Coast Guard fireboats arrived immediately and Coast Guardsmen policed the area. Ammunition on board exploded with the heat of the flames. After seven hours of continuous battle, the fire was extinguished. Though the vessel was almost a complete loss, the pier and pier cargo were undamaged. One crew member from Liverpool was detained for further action, as his behavior indicated that he had had a very important part in causing the fire.

The Delaware River Patrol of the Philadelphia COTP had a diversion in June 1942. The *SS Empire Woodcock* had a fire in a hold from spontaneous combustion in cotton bales wetted during a shower while loading. Men of this patrol with $CO_2$ equipment departed their base on board a cutter and contacted the vessel at Marcus Hook. Steam was forced into the hold, and then firemen entered the hold and extinguished the flames. Coast Guard personnel attending this fire received commendation from the British Consul.

There was an unusual emergency in the evening of 6 September 1943, which involved the Coast Guard. The Pennsylvania Railroad's "Congres-sional Limited" was wrecked in North Philadelphia. The Captain of the Port immediately dispatched 120 men, some of whom were the first military group to reach the scene. They went to work immediately under the direction of the Philadelphia Police, releasing many trapped passengers, removing bodies, carrying injured persons to waiting ambulances, guarding and gathering personal property of passengers, and preventing looting. The men threw a cordon around two wrecked cars, patrolled the wreckage, installed lighting equipment, and assisted firemen in handling hose lines. Morphine syrettes, blankets, and other medical supplies were donated. The Coast Guard also furnished housing for some of the injured. The detail remained on duty until 0030 on 7 September, when nothing further remained to be done.

On an earlier occasion, there had been a wreck of three trains on the Baltimore and Ohio Railroad near Dickerson, Maryland. Lieutenant Commander Harold D. Rice of the Temporary Reserve received commendation from the Secretary of the Navy with the right to wear the Navy Commendation Medal. His citation read in part: "Unhesitatingly going to the aid of several passengers imprisoned beneath the wreckage and in imminent danger of burning to death, Lieutenant Commander Rice risked his life by repeatedly crawling beneath a mass of heavy pipes and assisting in bringing out the wounded. Lieutenant Commander Rice's courageous initiative and utter disregard for his own personal safety undoubtedly saved the lives of many who otherwise might have perished. His gallant conduct was in keeping with the highest traditions of the United States Naval Service."

The duties of the Examination Vessel (Lightship #105) at the Virginia Capes were chiefly identifying and boarding incoming and outgoing merchant craft. Most examination vessels did rigorous duty but were spared the difficulties of collision. Not so at the Virginia Capes. She was struck several times while on station, sometimes with considerable damage. On 20 July 1944 at 2120, she was accidentally rammed and sunk by two barges under tow. All hands abandoned ship in boats and were picked up by nearby naval craft. Fortunately, none of the men were injured, but all personal gear was lost.

Fires on the Norfolk waterfront were 85 percent

under those of prewar days, but there were some troublesome cases. At 0430 on 30 January 1944, there was a serious fire, and seven municipal engines and two truck companies responded. However, the blaze could be fought effectively only from the waterside. The Coast Guard sent five fireboats and five picket boats with pumps, and the blaze was finally extinguished. The fireboats alone pumped water for 34 hours. The officer-in-charge of the fireboat unit received commendation from the Commandant and from the District Coast Guard Officer.

One evening in June 1942, the American tanker *Robert C. Tuttle*, loaded with fortified fuel oil and in a damaged and leaking condition due to collision, was brought into lower Chesapeake Bay. Fire broke out near the pump room, and this was followed by explosions. All piping and valves were smashed, and she was very nearly broken in two. Water and foam were used without avail in an effort to quench the flames. About midnight, two tons of dry ice in blocks about 12 inches cubed, were dropped into the hold. The fire then diminished in that tank. The use of dry ice was a successful experiment, and the fire was extinguished in less than two hours after the first application. In all, about five tons were used. The vessel carried nearly 100,000 barrels of very dangerous crude oil, all of which was removed, though every bit of machinery was out of order.

On 1 June 1943, the American freighter *John Morgan*, loaded with explosives, and Navy tanker *Montana* collided in convoy off the Virginia Capes. Fire resulted in both ships, and *Morgan* blew up and sank almost immediately. The Coast Guard tug *Acushnet* was dispatched and fought the fire in the tanker. She was joined by naval craft. This fire burned two days, but *Montana* was finally towed to Lynnhaven anchorage.

There were two disastrous fires at Charleston, South Carolina, which taxed the seven fireboats and the shore units there. On 6 October 1944, the Southern Railway Pier #2, used by the United Fruit Company, was almost destroyed by fire. The pier could not be saved, and all efforts were concentrated on preventing spread of the fire. The Chief of the Fire Department credited the Coast Guard with saving the adjoining facilities. Another fire at a warehouse caused $500,000 loss.

A noteworthy case of rescue involved Captain of the Port personnel on 15 March 1942. An oil tanker was torpedoed off Southport, North Carolina, and immediately burst into flames. Several boats from the Captain of the Port, Wilmington, North Carolina, including boats of the Auxiliary, worked for hours rescuing severely burned and wounded men from the sinking tanker.

At a fire in Jacksonville, Florida, on 12 February 1943, 50 men responded with two fireboats and other equipment. Due to wind and the inflammable contents, three Atlantic Coast Line warehouses were destroyed with loss of $100,000. A Coast Guard seaman suffered fractures of both legs as well as multiple bruises and contusions. The city fireboat was trapped in the fire area, but the Coast Guard towed her away and sprayed water over her during the process.

Another serious episode occurred at Jacksonville on 6 October 1943. An empty steel oil barge previously used for transporting gasoline, was moored at a dock and under repair. A violent explosion during welding operations caused fire in the barge. Twelve shipyard workers were killed and a score injured. Four Coast Guard fireboats, 6 patrol boats, and 60 Coast Guardsmen assisted in combatting this fire and in rescue operations.

Many Greek sponge fishermen, including numerous aliens, operated on the west coast of Florida. Several fishing vessels, supposedly Cuban, were boarded close to the coast, but there were no fish on board and all hands were loafing. It was possible that they were endeavoring to land aliens, for the nature of the coast invited it. The best that could be done in this type of case was a careful check, for not enough men were available to give the coast complete coverage.

The Aransas Pass, Texas, Captain of the Port detail was notified by the Harbor Entrance Control Post at 0200 one night that *YP-159* was in a sinking condition three miles off the entrance to Aransas Pass Inlet. *CG-38365* was dispatched and assisted the vessel to Port Aransas. The vessel had lost her shaft and wheel and was taking in considerable water. Here was a case where a fireboat saved a vessel with her pumps. *CG-50084-F* lay alongside, pumped *YP-159* dry, and continued the operation until emergency repairs had been made.

A Navy LST was proceeding downstream near New Orleans on 20 October 1944. The tug *Alexander MacKensie*, with nine oil barges, was headed upstream. They collided, and the LST and two of the barges caught fire. The damaged barges spilled about 100,000 gallons of crude oil into the river, and this became ignited. Two Coast Guard fireboats, a picket boat, and a cutter were dispatched from New Orleans. On their arrival at the scene, the fire in the LST had been extinguished, but the other fires were extinguished by Coast Guard details. The cutter secured the barges torn adrift by the collision. The oil, which constituted a serious fire hazard, was broken up and passed through the port. Two fireboats were assigned to the intake of the water purification plant, and for 36 hours they washed the oil away from the intake, preventing its entry into the city water supply.

The Captain of the Port at Galveston was notified in April 1944, that several boats had capsized near a causeway, and many persons had drowned, in a very sudden and fierce squall. All available boats were dispatched from the Galveston Lifeboat Station. During the day's operations 37 persons were rescued from peril and four skiffs and one motor launch were recovered. The search for bodies of the eight missing persons continued for six days until all were accounted for. The Coast Guard recovered four.

The Great Lakes area also had its few cases of possible sabotage. Late in July 1942, a bridge tender on a highway bridge at Toledo, Ohio, came across a package of material evidence of the operation of Nazi agents in Toledo. This was turned over to Coast Guard District headquarters by the Assistant Port Security Officer, and in turn to the FBI.

On the night of 22 August 1944, the Captain of the Port at Sturgeon Bay, Wisconsin, was informed by the mayor that every fire hydrant near the shipyards was opened and the caps of the hydrants damaged so that no appreciable water pressure could have been delivered in case of a fire.

There were many steel mills, oil tanks and refineries, and railroad properties, but few piers on the Chicago waterfront. The area included many war plants and about 20 shipyards. The Captain of the Port's principal duty here was to provide adequate boat patrols to assure the security of these areas, and to maintain efficient fire prevention and fire-fighting programs. Furnishing guards on Lake

vessels was important in the earlier days. Also, two guards were placed in each Navy vessel for the trip from shipyard to tidewater.

On 26 July 1943, at Indiana Harbor, the Canadian tanker *Bruce Hudson* with steam up ready for departure, caught fire after she was fully loaded with high test gasoline. The fire was probably caused by fumes which had not been properly dispensed. It was extinguished by Coast Guardsmen after a one-and-a-half-hour battle. Four of the vessel's crew, including the master, were killed.

The Ninth (St. Louis) District was one of navigable rivers. A great volume of traffic essential to the war effort transited the Mississippi River and its major tributaries. Much of this consisted of newly built, medium-sized naval vessels on their way to tidewater.

The larger cities and the nearly 6,500 miles of navigable waterways required security. Fireboat protection was particularly necessary at important points. Of major concern was the security of bridges. The sabotage of any bridge would have immeasurably delayed the transit of craft to tidewater. Later, an important Coast Guard duty was the furnishing of pilots to craft transiting the river. In some areas jeep patrols went along and stopped bridge traffic while vessels passed under, to prevent anything being dropped from the bridges.

Flood relief by the Coast Guard in the Mississippi Valley reached large proportions on several occasions during the war. These activities involved loading sandbags for levees, repairing levees, evacuating people and livestock, saving stored crops, and other incidental duty. In May 1943, floods drove 155,000 persons from their homes, along the major rivers of the Ninth (St. Louis) District and crop loss was about $5,000,000. All available personnel and equipment in the District turned to flood relief work. Surf boats and communications trucks were sent from the Cleveland and Chicago Districts to augment equipment on the scene.

In April of 1944, disastrous floods along the Mississippi, Missouri, and Illinois Rivers again heavily taxed the facilities of the Coast Guard. Over 1,500,000 acres were flooded, thousands of families made homeless, and thousands of buildings damaged or destroyed. In the Ohio and Mississippi Valley floods of 1945, the Coast Guard rescued over 10,000 people and saved thousands of head of cattle. The Coast Guard transported food, medical supplies, mail, household effects, and such throughout the area. When residents of a Louisville suburban community lost their fight to keep flood waters behind a dike hurriedly built of sandbags, Coast Guardsmen were standing by to evacuate 35 families as water rose 12 feet in a few hours.

Port Security activity at Puerto Rico centralized at San Juan, where there were 14 piers. Duty consisted chiefly of pier guard, fire prevention, and fire-fighting. There were no outstanding episodes. The section had its share of small fires, and a few large ones. However, an unusual accident occurred at Guayanilla, on the south coast, in November 1942, when a pipe line of the West India Oil Company broke, flooding a section of the Playa with 16,000 gallons of gasoline. The Coast Guard established patrols, preventing fire until the local fire department washed the area.

The destruction by fire of the Hammond Lumber Company pier was the most serious event at Los Angeles Harbor affecting the security of the port. Several Navy personnel lost their lives and about 26 were injured. Three LSTs were considerably damaged. Captain of the Port forces responded with fireboats and trailer pumps. In 15 hours the fire was brought under control. The origin of the fire was undetermined, but carelessness at lumber yards, especially in the early days, was notorious.

The *Manuel Espinosa* incident at San Francisco in April 1943, involved interesting activity for the Coast Guard. The vessel was an old 135-foot one-masted lumber "schooner" with motor, and it was under Panamanian registry. She had been loaded with 350 tons of dangerous cargo for Central and South American ports. The Coast Guard Explosives Detail had supervised the loading of 9,420 cases of fuzes aboard her. *Manuel Espinosa* sailed on 4 April. Fifty or sixty miles out, encountering heavy weather, she began to leak, and headed back to port for repairs. She was forced to stay outside until morning due to fog. The rough water was too much, and she started to sink. The crew were promptly saved by Coast Guard motor lifeboats and picket boats. Currents tossed the vessel about on the bottom and she broke open, disgorging most of her cargo of dynamite. The cased explosives popped up to the surface and were carried into San Francisco by the incoming tide. Shipping was stopped, and all COTP and lifeboat station craft, together with some Navy patrol boats, went to work gathering up the floating cases of dynamite. Then the tide changed, carrying the explosives out to sea again. On the next incoming tide cases were strewn along the beach south of San Francisco, and were picked up from the shore. This went on for several days, but for many months an occasional floating case would be found. Floating low in the water, they were not easily observed. All those recovered were turned over to the Commanding Officer of Fort Baker.

A great munitions center in the Twelfth District was that at Port Chicago in Suisun Bay, near Vallejo, about 30 miles from San Francisco. Coast Guard explosives loading details had been assigned there, but were withdrawn on 1 November 1943, at the request of the Navy Inspector of Ordnance in Charge, Naval Ammunition Depot at Mare Island. On 17 July 1944, the steamships *Quinalt Victory* and *E. A. Bryan* were loading ammunition at Port Chicago. The Coast Guard's only responsibility at the port was to furnish a standby fireboat and a patrol boat. Suddenly, at 2219, the *E. A. Bryan's* cargo of about 5,000 tons of ammunition exploded. This terrific explosion destroyed both vessels and was felt for 200 miles. Damage extended for 10 miles and there were isolated cases of broken windows 50 miles away. The pier and buildings of Port Chicago were extensively damaged, and all aids to navigation in the vicinity were ruined. Coast Guard fireboat *CG-60014-F* was destroyed and its crew of five killed. The patrol boat was damaged and its crew of four injured. Thousands of persons, mostly naval personnel, were injured, and about 325 lives were lost.

The Coast Guard immediately established patrols in the area which were maintained for several days. Traffic was temporarily stopped. The patrols searched for bodies, eventually recovering 67, and removed a tremendous amount of debris from the water. When the channel was opened, Coast Guard boats escorted vessels through the affected area.

At Seattle cooperation between the Coast Guard fire-fighting units and the undermanned local fire department was outstanding. Local fire chiefs assisted in Coast Guard training. The Coast Guard manned a regular city fire truck as well as the city-owned fireboat *Duwamish*. The crew were quartered in the new city fire station and were subsisted by the city department. Pharmacist's mates attended all major fires to administer first aid.

There was a large fire on 30 May 1943, involving and largely destroying four Seattle waterfront manufacturing facilities. Starting from a watchman's wood stove, the fire spread rapidly. The Municipal Fire Department and the Coast Guard surrounded the burning structure and prevented further spreading. COTP units, which pumped 2½ million gallons of water into the fire from the bay, probably prevented a conflagration.

Another serious fire occurred on the Seattle waterfront, just below the District Coast Guard Office, on 26 April 1944. The facility was a large, unsprinklered warehouse on a pier, and contained essential war commodities. The fire was first spotted by an officer in the Captain of the Port Office. The Duty Officer promptly dispatched three 50-foot fire barges and the fireboat *Duwamish* to the scene. In addition, 25 men, a troop transport, and a pumping unit were sent from the Base, as well as 75 men from the COTP. These were en route before any alarm was received on the ticker by the Seattle Fire Department. Discernible, of course, from the District Coast Guard Office, the fire was seen to rise from the interior of the superstructure, and within six or seven minutes traveled the entire length of the 525-foot roof top. The fireboats, barges, and personnel during this time were seen converging on the fire. It was fought and extinguished chiefly from the waterside. As the fire was under control 25 minutes after discovery, it was an excellent example of response and action.

Honolulu became of major importance as a stopping point for the tremendously expanded transpacific aviation operations. Enormous tonnages of explosives and dangerous cargoes went into the Hawaiian Islands, and a vigilant harbor patrol was required at Honolulu because of the restricted, and crowded wooden piers. Fire prevention was of great importance, and several boats were converted into fire boats. Various coastal lookouts in the Islands were manned under direction of the Captains of the Port. Though partially relieved by SPARS in January 1945, COTP personnel shortage in Hawaii was acute throughout the war.

At Honolulu several ship fires were detected and extinguished before serious damage resulted.

On one occasion, in May 1944, Captain of the Port personnel distinguished themselves in helping to put out fires in a nest of Navy LSTs at Pearl Harbor. Fire started from an explosion in one LST, and was fought with four fireboats and two picket boats for 24 hours. Four men were seriously burned, and 27 men in the fire-fighting detail were cited by the Commandant for displaying "courage and outstanding devotion to duty."

The navigable waters in Alaska are very extensive, and there was much wartime traffic to be controlled and protected. Small ports are scattered along the coast principally between Kodiak and Ketchikan. At 14 of them there were COTPs or ACOTPs. Distances, however, were considerable, transportation poor, and facilities inadequate. Port Security developed slowly. Though most waterfront properties were fire hazards, fire-fighting equipment was far from sufficient. Drunken natives added to the chance of fire due to carelessness. Usual Port Security measures were taken on a relatively small scale, and there were no outstanding occurrences.

There was gradual curtailment of activity throughout the country as the war progressed and the enemy became less effective. By the end of 1944, Captain of the Port units remained at only about 35 major ports, where wartime traffic was mostly still on the increase. The remaining units made no curtailment in their wide variety of activities except identification. Most of these units carried right on until after V-E Day. V-J Day brought about a virtual end to Port Security except for supervision of explosives loading and unloading, minimum fire protection measures, and the ordinary peacetime activities usually connected with the Captain of the Port.

While operations against an acknowledged enemy may be evaluated in terms of actual tangible accomplishments, Port Security, on the other hand, was *PREVENTIVE* from every standpoint, and the success of the entire undertaking must be expressed in terms of *what did not happen.* During the Port Security program, no injury or damage of *great* importance occurred to any facility or vessel for which the Coast Guard was responsible. Undoubtedly other things definitely would have happened except for the vigilance of the Coast Guard; the training given its men; its equipment; the long, tedious water and pier patrols; the care in loading explosives; the control of vessel movements; and all the other positive activities of this branch of the armed forces. There were many dangers from within, chiefly from sabotage or the threat of sabotage, carelessness, and negligence. The Coast Guard and the Federal Bureau of Investigation were effective bulwarks against these. As for sabotage accomplished, the United States was exceedingly fortunate.

In conclusion, it may be said that the entire Coast Guard Port Security program was well organized and well executed, despite what, at times, seemed insurmountable obstacles. In the whole effort, mistakes were fewer than might logically have been expected, and the full effectiveness of the entire program is evident when the war record of our ports and the shipping which they handled are carefully weighed and evaluated in terms of *what did not happen.*

Chapter 6

# THE TEMPORARY RESERVE
# IN PORT SECURITY

In the preceding pages some reference has been made to the Temporary Reserve. This component of the Coast Guard became extremely important in the whole Port Security program—so important, in fact, that without it Port Security and the manning program at sea would have suffered measurably. How this part of the Coast Guard Reserve came into being and the personnel who comprised it were described earlier. In the pages immediately preceding we have reviewed the Port Security program. It is now appropriate to consider how the Temporary Reservists (TRs) fitted into this important activity.

With shifts in offensive operations overseas, the Coast Guard, as coordinator of port activities, had to be ready well in advance to provide the means of expediting an accelerated movement of men and war materials through the Nation's major war ports. The size of the Port Security job is indicated by the fact that within the continental United States alone there were more than 21,000 miles of port waterfront, about 8,000 waterfront facilities, and millions of square feet of docks, piers, and other storage and loading spaces. *One-fifth* of the entire Coast Guard personnel was required to safeguard these littoral establishments. These heavy responsibilities required more men than the Coast Guard was able to muster from its regular ranks, and yet, those whom it did have were urgently needed in combat areas and at sea. It was into this picture that the growing numbers of volunteer, unpaid Temporary Reservists began to fit so well. Eventually totaling about 50,000, they released men for duty elsewhere, and gradually took over the various Port Security responsibilities without the slightest loss of efficiency.

While their principal duty was boat patrol and guard work on waterfront facilities, Temporary Reservists also engaged in other phases of Port Security. The various subdivisions of activity for which the Port Security officers were normally responsible may be summarized as follows:

| | |
|---|---|
| Clearance and Anchorage | Harbor Patrol |
| Explosives Loading | Plant Guards (Under Navy) |
| Fire Division | Guard Detail |
| Identification | Pilots |
| Communications | Beach Patrol |
| Boarding | Miscellaneous |

Although not all of these Port Security activities were necessarily covered by Temporary Reservists in each district, there was no phase in which they did not function in one district or another. Probably the broadest coverage was in the First Naval District wherein the approximately 10,000 TRs contributed service to every Port Security activity.

Demands in some districts resulted in their taking over duties not generally performed in others. For instance, more than 1,000 were engaged in Beach Patrol in New England. They stood regular watches in lifeboat stations, patrolled beaches, and manned coastal lookout towers. In many districts they stood coastal lookout watches. At Charleston, South Carolina, a group of Temporary Reserve officers became the official Boarding Officers. The First Naval District was the only one in the United States where TRs were used in the supervision of explosives loading. Specially trained, they comprised 40 percent of all explosives loading details at the Boston Port of Embarkation for a period of 22 months. There was similar activity for a short while at Davisville, Rhode Island.

Boston also had the only Radio Sealing Unit manned wholly by these volunteers. For two years, 26 men did all radio sealing in Boston Harbor, boarding ships at their docks or anchorages under all conditions of weather. One flotilla at Boston consisted of men with special skills ranging from plumbing to diving. A corps of pharmacist's mates at Seattle, Washington, did valuable sick bay work there. Weather Bureau men enrolled as TR Chief Aerographers Mates (Civil Service pay) were assigned to Weather Patrol in the North Atlantic. They operated out of Boston and were the only Temporary Reservists so utilized.

The only signal station in the United States wholly manned by Temporary Reservists was maintained by them at the Coast Guard Base, Boston, from 6 July 1943 to 15 June 1945. This unit, consisting of 72 men, mostly rated signalmen, stood 12-hour watches of four to five men. They also maintained a tower watch over upper Boston Harbor where shipping and piers were most congested. They handled about 7,000 visual messages, discovered certainly six and probably eight fires, corrected by blinker or reported about 500 hoist and nameboard violations, and observed and sent help to about 20 small craft in trouble.

One of the earliest vital requirements was for men and craft to perform patrol for rescue work, and to track submarines and reduce their effectiveness against our coastal merchant shipping. The first Temporary Reservists, enrolled for a specific period of months on full time with pay, were employed almost wholly in the Coastal Pickets on offshore patrol. While there was some Coastal Picket activity on the Pacific coast, most activity was off the Atlantic shores. The Navy, short of small craft, called upon the Coast Guard to procure urgently needed motor and sailing yachts and other vessels suitable for offshore duty.

The vessels were procured chiefly from Auxiliary members. They became "Coast Guard Reserve" boats and were largely manned by these early TRs. By 22 December 1942, the Coast Guard had acquired and placed in operation some 2,093 of these boats, many of them in use as Coastal Pickets. Actual operation of the Coastal Picket Force rested with the Navy under the Commanders of the several Sea Frontiers. Vessels assigned to this duty were attached to conveniently located bases. Before Temporary Reservists ceased participation in this activity, about 5,000 had served.

In order to be most effective in offshore areas, the Coastal Picket fleet, mostly sailing yachts with a scattering of motor cruisers, cooperated closely with naval vessels and airplanes, particularly in rescue work. Planes finding survivors usually endeavored to locate surface craft in the vicinity, be they fishermen, naval vessels, Coast Guard patrol boats, or merchant ships, and indicate to them the location of survivors. Rescues were then made by the surface craft, which, without the planes, probably would not have sighted the victims.

An example of such cooperation may be mentioned. In mid-1942, a Coast Guard plane from Elizabeth City, North Carolina, was scouting offshore near Diamond Shoal. At about 0940 the plane's radioman intercepted a message from another Coast Guard plane that survivors in a lifeboat had been spotted about 30 miles due east of Oregon Inlet. A Coastal Picket vessel was sighted on the horizon and the plane proceeded to its location, informing it of the situation by Aldis lamp. A message block was dropped on the patrol boat with all available information regarding the lifeboat. While the plane remained on position, the picket proceeded to the location of the boat, picking up survivors at 1415.

This offshore duty was probably the most rugged and punishing of all engaged in by Temporary Reservists except weather patrol in the North Atlantic. Patrols were often dull and monotonous, and many times craft would return to their bases without having seen or heard a sign of the enemy or any survivors. Yet, they had to be out there in large numbers to remain "on top" of enemy submarines and keep them down. The larger sailing vessels without auxiliary motors, known as the "Corsair Fleet," worked far offshore. Because they moved noiselessly through the water, they were better than motor vessels for listening, had greater cruising radius, and could stand heavy weather better. Time and again when storms approached, the motor craft were ordered in, but not so the sailing vessels!

Coastal Pickets were really an extension of the Coastal Information System which was built around the Beach Patrol organization. Investigation was important, and they kept authorities advised of every activity heard or observed. The pickets made scores of contacts by sound device and tracked them down as long as contact could be maintained. Oil slicks were discovered and checked. Gunfire was heard and investigated. Convoys were notified of the presence of a submarine, thus allowing changes of course to avoid danger. Some submarines were located and properly depth-charged. Disabled vessels were towed in, ill persons taken ashore, and plane crash victims removed from the water.

The Atlantic, especially off New England and New York, became very boisterous as the winter of 1942-43 approached. Continuous gales piled up mountainous, unrelenting seas, and the cold became intense. The weather notwithstanding, the "Corsair Fleet" held to offshore positions. It seemed as if these vessels were continuously on their beams-end, making living conditions almost intolerable. At this time, and shortly before Temporary Reservists were relieved of Coastal Picket duty, an epic experience involved the 100 percent TR-manned 58-foot yawl *CGR-3070* and her nine-man crew.

It was the last day of a tough week-old patrol. Under storm sails, this vessel was tossed in seas which had been making up for two days. Water boiled across her decks. Her bow was momentarily buried under green water, but with reassuring buoyancy she shook it off and slowly started to climb the face of the next onrushing roller. Hours passed thus, and the wind stepped up to a full gale. Suddenly, with a terrific impact, *CGR-3070* was heeled over on her side by a giant comber and a sudden burst of wind. She attempted valiantly to right herself, but another mighty sea struck too soon and knocked her down. Seas filled her mizzen sail and snapped the mast. She was at the mercy of the storm as solid green water pounded her from stem to stern. Water cascaded into the living quarters and the engineroom. The crew cut away the broken rigging, torn canvas, and splintered mizzen mast that were holding her down. The vessel regained an even keel, and the first battle with the elements had been won!

The boat above and below decks was a shambles. The skipper, Chief Boatswain's Mate Curtis Arnall, estimated his position as near Nantucket Shoals. Upon learning that the main engine and generator were out of commission due to submersion in salt water, he used the radiotelephone to report the condition of his vessel, request a fix on his position, and ask for a tow to facilitate rapid transfer and hospitalization for one of his crew

who had suffered broken ribs and another with a badly battered head.

Coast Guard radiomen all along the Atlantic coast picked up the message. The operator at the Greenport Base of *CGR-3070* tried unsuccessfully to reach the yawl. Two motor lifeboats attempting to battle the storm were driven back. Other units were contacted, and a widespread search was instituted involving a large cutter and two planes. A Coast Guard PBY flying boat sighted the stricken craft, and the cutter was given her position.

On board the Coastal Picket, salt water had ruined much of the food, water became dangerously low, and a rationing program was put into effect. The hull was still sound and buoyant. Water was pumped from the cabin, emergency repairs were made, and a jury sail was rigged.

A Navy PBY spotted the vessel and contacted surface craft, but the latter could not find *CGR-3070* in the dark of night. Additional Army and Navy planes were sent in search. Another cutter started out from Boston. Finally a British destroyer came upon *CGR-3070* about 200 miles east of the position where she had been sighted the night before. Though seas were running high, a towline was made secure, and towing toward Halifax began. The jubilance of the Coast Guardsmen, however, was shortlived. The towline parted, and the yawl was again lost in the darkness. *CGR-3070* continued to wallow in the gale-whipped seas for several days without special occurrence. Then a naval ship of a convoy escort force sighted her heading straight for the deep-laden tankers and freighters. Recognition signals by means of blinker were exchanged and the yawl, running before the gale and partly out of control, miraculously blundered her way through the convoy. That was all!

For the next seven days the gale continued. The Naval authorities feared the little ship had foundered. Yet, something urged continuation of the search which now involved 14 Canadian planes and 11 U. S. Army planes. At dusk on the tenth day after the mishap, a U. S. naval vessel contacted the yawl by blinker, but the weather would not permit close approach. Although the ship broadcast the yawl's position contact had been lost by morning. *CGR-3070* was in poor condition. The men were hungry and nearly exhausted and two were injured, but they kept grimly on. Fortunately, the high winds moderated somewhat, and naval planes from Bermuda joined the hunt.

Fourteen days after the mishap, an Army B-17 located the vessel heading due west 350 miles east of Nag's Head, North Carolina, apparently under control, making slow progress under jib-sail only. The plane dropped supplies by parachute 150 feet ahead of her. In attempting to haul the package on board the lines parted and the boxed food sank. Contact was lost again, and the men aboard the yawl resumed their long vigil.

On the twentieth day a vessel was sighted from *CGR-3070*. There was verbal contact with the ship, which turned out to be a Coast Guard cutter. Fog thickened, a heavy rain squall struck, and the yawl disappeared again. But the cutter notified Operations ashore, and planes and blimps were pressed into action. Final discovery of *CGR-3070* was by blimp about 15 miles east of Ocracoke Inlet. Contact was maintained, a cutter took the yawl in tow and landed the bearded crew at the Ocracoke Section Base. The men walked off the vessel despite their weakened condition, and all were home for Christmas.

This saga of the seas embraced air-sea rescue facilities from Boston, Massachusetts, to Charleston, South Carolina, and eastward to Bermuda. Aircraft of the U. S. Army and Navy and of the Canadian Air Force, and surface craft of the Coast Guard, U. S. Navy, and the British Navy were involved. Undoubtedly, the search for *CGR-3070* was the biggest manhunt and attempted rescue on the Atlantic during World War II. The little Coastal Picket covered about 3,100 miles, and was at sea for 27 days, 20 of them under the most trying conditions. Yet, she almost certainly would have entered Ocracoke Inlet under her own jury rig had she not been picked up in the last 15 miles by the blimp and cutter.

While most Coastal Pickets did not run into such difficulties, the Temporary Reservists on board them endured rugged service, and were definitely instrumental in reducing destruction by submarines. Temporary Reservists officially ceased Coastal Picket work 15 December 1942, and regulars or regular Reservists took over. The activity was discontinued eleven months later.

Another special class of Temporary Reservists consisted of the "Coast Guard Police." The Navy recognized a special need for military control of plant guards employed at shipyards and other facilities having Navy and Coast Guard contracts. There was great danger from sabotage and activity of subversive agents in virtually every shipyard or other facility devoted to such work. Thus, the Navy utilized the Auxiliary and Reserve Act as amended in June 1942 permitting temporary enrollment in the Reserve on a full or part-time basis without military pay. Plant guards were enrolled by the Coast Guard, trained by the Navy (except in the Thirteenth District), operated under the Navy, and continued to be paid by the companies employing them. Except for the military basis of operations, military law and discipline, they continued guarding the plants about the same as before. Plant guards reached their peak in June 1943, with 80 commissioned officers, 842 Chief Warrant and Warrant officers, and 23,941 enlisted men.

As plants completed their contracts the Coast Guard Police there were disenrolled. The number of plants completing contracts accelerated rapidly early in 1944. By mid-year, the Police had been reduced to 2,736, and all were disenrolled by August. These men, as a whole, served admirably, and functioned as intended.

The most important activity of the volunteer, unpaid Temporary Reservists, who formed the bulk of the TRs, was divided into two types; (a) waterside patrol and (b) landside patrol of piers and other waterfront facilities. Both were an integral part of the Port Security program, and often were correlated. The primary purpose of each was the same—to protect waterfront facilities against injury from sabotage, subversive actions, and negligence, and through safety in the ports, to expedite the passage of troops and war materiel to the fighting fronts.

The civilian Auxiliary was establishing harbor patrols by small craft in harbors, rivers, and inlets in 1942, but after June of that year enrollments in the Temporary Reserve began and harbor patrols in Coast Guard Reserve boats were gradually taken over by members of that Reserve. As this activity grew, attention was also directed to the establishment of Temporary Reserve units for landside patrol of docks, piers, and other waterfront installations.

This activity had its beginning at Philadelphia, with the organization of the Volunteer Port Security Force (VPSF). After much preliminary work which involved many talks at Washington, approval was given to a plan developed by Donald F. Jenks and Dimitri F. White of Philadelphia. Despite many official qualms, enrollment of volunteers was authorized. A commanding officer was selected on 29 July 1942, followed by selection of staff members. Money was raised to finance the project, and on 19 September 1942, there was a mass induction of the first enrollees.

As thorough indoctrination was required before duty could be performed, the Training Officer had a real job on his hands. School facilities were obtained and classes began. By 6 November 1942, 700 were engaged in, or had completed, training, and the first actual duty was performed on 23 December 1942. Enrollments and training continued virtually throughout the war period. The experiment at Philadelphia proved so successful after a fair trial, that the value of similar units at other ports became obvious. This required organization and centralized authority, and a Volunteer Port Security Division was set up at Coast Guard Headquarters in Washington, D.C. This was followed by an energetic expansion of the Volunteer Port Security Forces. Eventually, such forces, with combined enrollments of over 20,000, were set up in these 22 major ports of the United States:

| | |
|---|---|
| Philadelphia, Pa. | Galveston, Texas |
| Baltimore, Md. | Houston, Texas |
| Washington, D.C. | Corpus Christi, Texas |
| Charleston, S.C. | Duluth, Minn. |
| Savannah, Ga. | San Juan, Puerto Rico |
| Jacksonville, Fla. | Los Angeles, Calif. |
| Miami, Fla. | San Diego, Calif. |
| Tampa, Fla. | San Francisco, Calif. |
| Port Everglades, Fla. | Oakland, Calif. |
| Mobile, Ala. | Seattle, Wash. |
| New Orleans, La. | Portland, Ore. |

In the First and Third Naval Districts (Boston, New York, etc.), Guard Details, with exactly the same duty as Volunteer Port Security Forces, were organized from the Auxiliary and operated as details rather than as separate regimental organizations.

The Philadelphia Regiment was the first and largest VPSF, and since the others with only slight variations due to local conditions, were patterned after it, its structure is presented as an example.

The original plan called for six hours of service once a week. This was later changed to six hours each six days in order to provide rotation. At the outset there were 152 officers and 1,000 men. The latter group was later increased. Each platoon had an ensign, two boatswains, four chief boatswain's mates, four boatswain's mates first class, and sixteen seamen. They were divided into two watches of two squads of six men each, with a boatswain for each watch. Thirty-six platoons were built up and ultimately the size of the platoons was increased. Squads were augmented to 10 men. This method avoided the placing of completely inexperienced squads on duty and the officer proportion was properly reduced.

The waterfront was divided into six areas. Platoons were assigned in cycles and rotated until the men were familiar with all; thereupon assignments became permanent. The units were then placed under Area command, comparable to a battalion organization. Eventually, the Regiment was organized into 24 companies, providing more effective control. Additional coverage was gained, first by increasing the length of each watch to eight hours, and then by accelerating rotation to one watch in five days.

In all these organizations, a staff of able and intelligent men and women was behind the men performing the Port Security duties. They worked hard, and often rendered extraordinary service. Women Temporary Reservists were extremely useful. Officers headed up these various departments:

| | |
|---|---|
| Personnel | Transportation |
| Operations | Security |
| Regimental | Military Training |
|   Training and | Finance |
|   Military | Enrollment |
|   Inspection | Supply |
| Fire Drill | Recruiting |
| Public Relations | Women's Transportation |
| Legal | Women's Office Detail |

Much of the duty ashore involved the control of entrances to piers. All persons were required to present proper identification and to show they had legitimate business there. This was especially important where persons wished to visit ships. Guards roved the piers at regular intervals. They had to know everything about the pier, its cargo, equipment, and hazards, as well as the location of all emergency apparatus such as fire extinguishers, hoses, telephones, and alarm boxes. They were required to know, in case of fire, exactly what to do in the promptest manner—sound the alarm, direct apparatus, remove obstacles, and lend assistance in extinguishing the blaze. The security of vessels in port required trained Ship, Gangway, Roving, Cargo, and Fire Guards. All VPSF men observed, and corrected if possible, any violations on their premises.

One of the most important duties was to guard against fire. The Coast Guard furnished fire watchers, whose duty it was to attend all jobs where welding or cutting were being done on board ship, and to have extinguishers and hoses with running water always handy. In many ports, such "hot work" was forbidden unless attended by a Coast Guard fire watcher.

Because of the urgency of nation-wide fire prevention and control, classes for the study of this were established at the Coast Guard Fire School adjacent to Fort McHenry, near Baltimore. It was a school of experimentation and scientific fire-fighting. Subjects were fire knowledge, fire-fighting and prevention, Port Security problems, morale, discipline, and Coast Guard legislation. Over 400 officers and men of the VPSF units and Temporary Reserve units afloat completed these courses. Most returned to their units to train other men, and branch schools were established in various districts.

With this as a background, it will be interesting to review some of the experiences of various Volunteer Port Security Forces.

After the establishment of these units, real progress was quickly made, and landside guard duty was gradually taken over effectively by these unpaid volunteers. By October 1944, Temporary Reservists were manning all posts on piers along the Boston waterfront without the assistance of any regulars. Complete coverage was also attained at Portland and Providence. In 1944, the Boston volunteers furnished 147,470 watch standers representing about 1,180,000 hours of duty. In the entire District, 305,809 watches were stood for a total of 3,113,100 hours of duty, including boat patrol. Only 6.4 percent of this time was spent for administrative work.

British transports were often at Boston for repair and overhaul. There was special need for watches in these vessels to prevent, detect, or control fire, to stand fire watches when welding or cutting was being done, and generally to look after the security of the vessel so that there might be no "*Normandie* incident" at Boston. These watches were undertaken by Temporary Reservists as *extra* duty. In one typical 10-day emergency in the fall of 1943, TRs furnished 2,795 men, of whom 1,600 were guard detail men and the rest boatmen. Many fires were discovered in these vessels, but none reached more than very minor proportions.

At 0341 on 16 January 1945, there was a serious fire on board a Norwegian steamship at a pier in upper Boston Harbor. Ensign (T) George H. Falvey arrived at the scene seven minutes after the alarm was given and took charge of operations. In removing ammunition from the burning vessel, he was assisted by seven other Temporary Reservists who had been sleeping at the Base awaiting their regular watch. The District Coast Guard Officer wrote: "Ensign Falvey demonstrated excellent judgment and ability in handling the situation, and to the Temporary Reservists assisting him, I give thanks for the extra measure of service put forth by them to prevent what otherwise might have been a catastrophe."

The Girard Point area, Philadelphia, was rather typical of guard areas. This was located on the bank of the Schuylkill River near its confluence with the Delaware River. The Point is served by the Pennsylvania Railroad which has a large freight yard nearby. There are three piers and a large grain elevator. The piers were not covered, and were exposed to the weather. The VPSF men at their own expense constructed a barracks which proved a morale booster. By the Fall of 1944, the average number of ships there had increased from two or three to six or seven. Fire watch at the grain elevator was vital.

The monotony of watches was broken now and then. One time a wild bull got loose, but available records do not indicate what, if any, constructive steps were taken by the VPSF men on duty. Discovery of a time bomb failed to scare the TRs, but caused plenty of concern to the experts who were called in. A gangway guard on board a Liberty ship was attacked by a drunken and abusive messboy who wielded a large butcher knife. The Coast Guardsman drew his gun and, assisted by the ship's officers, subdued the boy.

One TR in another area, intervening at the request of the crew, stopped a vicious fight between

THE END OF THE PATROL . . . . five beach pounders
head toward their base and chow.

MAN AND DOG ON LONELY VIGIL . . . . dogs proved
loyal, keen, and trustworthy assistants.

HORSE PATROL ALONG AN ISOLATED BEACH . . . . constantly alert for attempted landings,
unauthorized persons, or signs of distress.

READY TO TAKE OFF ON PATROL

SUSPICIOUS **OBJECT SIGHTED**

SHIP UNDER COAST GUARD'S WATCHFUL EYE . . . . vessel is framed between pontoon and depth bomb.

LIEUTENANT JOHN A. PRITCHARD JR. (*Left*)

CHECKING SIGHTS OF A MACHINE GUN

MOUNTED TEMPORARY RESERVISTS OF THE BEACH PATROL . . . . awaiting
inspection at a southern patrol base.

RUSSIAN STEAMER *LAMUT* POUNDS TO PIECES . . . . Coast Guardsmen work on nearby rocks to
perform a thrilling and challenging rescue.

*EL ESTERO* RESTS HARMLESSLY NEAR ROBBINS REEF . . . . sinking of this burning vessel which was loaded with explosives prevented possible disaster to the New York metropolitan area. Her *Baker* flag still flies.

*NORMANDIE* AT THE HEIGHT OF THE FIRE . . . . the Coast Guard, Navy, City Fire Department and workers fought this disastrous fire, pouring thousands of tons of water into the ship which finally capsized her.

FIRE RAGES IN *SPRING HILL* AT NEW YORK . . . . a fireboat attacks the inferno with spray and foam.

COAST GUARDSMEN FIGHT WATERFRONT FIRE AT CHARLESTON . . . . Temporary Reservists and regulars fought fires together as a single team. A high pressure stream from jeep-drawn pumper proves effective in this blaze.

BARGE OFFICE CHART ROOM . . . . where an accurate check of ships' movements in New York harbor was maintained.

FIREBOAT STANDS BY AS AERIAL BOMBS ARE LOADED . . . . every precaution was taken in loading explosives.

DOCK PATROL FOILED SABOTEURS, DISCOURAGED NEGLIGENCE . . . . four Coast Guardsmen keep pier and ship under guard.

COAST GUARD PILOT CLIMBS ON BOARD A MERCHANT VESSEL . . . . he will take the ship through the channel to its anchorage in New York harbor.

ETERNAL VIGILANCE ON THE WATERFRONT
. . . . safety of piers in port was a heavy responsibility.

"IDENTIFICATION, PLEASE" . . . . gangway guard requires identification before permitting stranger to board ship.

ENTRANCE GUARD AT PORT OF EMBARKATION PIER . . . . ready to check credentials of all who enter.

DAY'S END, AFTER STOWING AMMUNITION . . . . watchful Coast Guardsman checks workmen.

A COASTAL PICKET ON ANTI-SUBMARINE PATROL
. . . . many patriotic yachtsmen provided vessels which were
used to detect presence of submarines.

ALERT WATCH ON BOARD A COASTAL PICKET
. . . . the "Corsair Fleet" maintained constant lookout for
enemy attempts to molest Allied shipping.

COAST GUARD WINGS HOVER OVER CONVOY . . . . homeward bound vessels are seen safely to port.

two crew members of *Manuel Calvo* without resorting to the use of weapons or threats. A TR Chief Boatswain's Mate, noting that a carpenter working in the hold of a ship was pinned under a crate with one leg almost severed, immediately descended to the scene. Disregarding his own personal risk from overhanging cargo, he applied a tourniquet. His poise and presence of mind were especially commended. Another received a Commanding Officer's commendation for discovering an Army land mine in the hold of a Liberty ship, and for prompt and efficient action in clearing and protecting the scene until Army Intelligence took over.

A boatswain's mate acted promptly and resourcefully when, at the risk of life or limb, he leaped into icy water from Pier 82 to save the life of a seaman who had fallen overboard from an allied vessel. In another incident, through an explosion in her tanks, the *John Carver* was seriously damaged and sank at her berth. The conduct of the Coast Guardsmen on duty was commended. The presence of mind of the Coxswain, Allen S. Cuthbert, the action taken by him, and his refusal to abandon his post on board the ship won citations from the Regimental Commanding Officer and the Commandant of the Coast Guard.

From a pier where valuable cargo was being loaded, a boatswain saw a blazing drum floating with the tide toward the wooden piling substructure of the pier. His prompt action prevented possible destruction of millions of dollars worth of war materials. In another incident on a cold, rainy night, a group of longshoremen made themselves a tent shelter of packing cases and paper, ran a "mule" into it, and kept the engine on for warmth. The inflammable structure caught fire. But for prompt action by the volunteer Coast Guard sentries, pier, ships, and cargo might have been destroyed.

An interesting incident occurred at Philadelphia on 11 November 1944. Charles M. Merbitz, Boatswain's Mate First Class, was making his rounds in *Castillo Ampudia*. On going forward he found a deckload of bales of cork. Working back, he approached a ladder and noticed something in a dunnage barrel beneath it. He requested a nearby crew member to remove a piece of canvas, and discovered a man there. Drawing his gun, he noticed a second man under a bale of cork. He blew his whistle for

help, and the two men, both Germans, were taken without trouble. They were well-supplied with food. Proper authorities including the Area Commander were notified.

The Area Commander immediately boarded the vessel, arriving at the same time as a detail of regular Coast Guardsmen and five FBI men. The two prisoners were put in separate cabins and interrogated. Guards were posted. The older of the two Germans talked freely while the younger refused to talk. After the FBI gave up, the Area Commander stayed in the cabin with the younger man under guard for several hours, talking chiefly with the guards about what the United States thought of Germany. The prisoner finally broke down and talked freely in perfect English. The FBI then came in and talked with him, and the two men were taken away in their custody.

These men had escaped from a western prisoner-of-war camp, and had worked their way through Canada to New York and Philadelphia. Apparently in communication with the underground in this country, they were liberally supplied with money and food. *Castillo Bellver*, due to sail the very morning the Germans had arrived, had been moved to another berth and the incoming *Castillo Ampudia* had taken her place. Since the ship had appeared fully loaded, the fugitives had made a natural mistake.

Prevention, discovery, and control of waterfront fires was a highly important Port Security function. Instances of alertness and proper action by Temporary Reservists were numerous in virtually all ports. Space permits mention of only a few typical examples. One was when a VPSF member discovered a fire one afternoon at New Orleans. Seeing flames issuing from the crew's quarters of a derrick barge at a wharf, he quickly extinguished them himself before they caused more than negligible damage. Fire broke out in a warehouse near the same waterfront early one evening, and was discovered by workmen. A general alarm was sounded, and 30 members of the VPSF were mobilized. They had all roadways and hydrants cleared when the city fire engines arrived; some manned a hose to guard against fires set by sparks and embers; and all were praised by police and firemen.

Men on duty at Pier 48 in Philadelphia on 1 July 1944, heard an explosion at 0215 across

Delaware Avenue, in another warehouse. The watch notified the Fire Department and the Duty Officer, and requested additional men from the latter. The Fire Department was promptly at the scene, and extra VPSF men arrived. Several explosions occurred as the fire increased in intensity, and falling sparks endangered the piers. Fire pumpers were made ready and stood by. Since sparks and embers were flying, men with water hoses were dispatched to the roofs of Piers 53 and 55. All fire equipment was poised for use, and three fireboats stood by. Water was played on portions of the roof of Pier 53. The steamer *Castillo Bellver,* lying at a pier, was moved from danger. The effectiveness of the VPSF effort prevented spread of the flames and untold damage to valuable facilities.

In the Great Lakes area, Temporary Reservists were involved in various ways in Port Security. For varying periods they performed general guard duty and sentry duty, and for a time served as guards on board Great Lakes vessels. They had their share of fire experiences. A notable case came in December 1943, at Erie, Pennsylvania, where a very serious fire completely destroyed the Baker Building. Several city firemen were killed when the north wall fell. Temporary Reservists helped materially in removing debris to get at the bodies of the firemen, and helped to recover mail in the flooded basement of the neighboring Post Office Building.

The breadth of Temporary Reserve participation in Port Security is evidenced by a unique VPSF regiment at San Juan, Puerto Rico. It was one of the finest of the 22 VPSF units. In this community of 200,000, there were relatively few with the necessary education and bi-lingual ability, and men for day duty were scarce. Nevertheless, final enrollment reached about 455. By early 1944, the VPSF had taken over about 50 percent of all Coast Guard waterfront posts, and by the year-end, all posts were covered. Probably in no other place where TRs operated was there such an interesting miscellaneous mixture of ship stevedoring and terminal personnel of various nationalities and languages.

The scope of accomplishment there is summarized:

(1) Fires discovered, extinguished, or fought (alone or in conjunction with other military or civilian services) .............................27

(2) Lives saved or first aid given in cases that might have cost a life (including stopping knife-fights and other fights) .........................45

(3) Thefts prevented or successfully investigated (omitting cases of petty thievery) ............22

(4) Persons caught photographing waterfront or engaged in suspicious activities ..................6

All but two of the fires were discovered and controlled in their incipient stages; but for quick discovery and action a number could have had serious consequences.

Fires sometimes have peculiar origins. One man patrolling a pier at San Juan saw smoke rising from a pile of thousands of bags of spoiled potatoes, on the apron of the pier. He summoned help, and upon removal of the top bags, the heat was so intense that the hand could not be held near. The Base sent a fireboat and a VPSF detail. Hose lines were connected and the detail cooled the bags until stevedores could spread them over the apron.

The most serious San Juan fire during VPSF operation occurred in July 1944. At 0200, a police officer notified a VPSF guard at Pier 3 Gate of smoke issuing from Tony & Al's Grill across the street. After investigation, the Insular Fire Department and Coast Guard were immediately notified, and the door broken down. The smoke inside was dense, and flames were coming through the east wall. It was a critical area, with a warehouse next door storing tar paper and paints, and with cafes and night clubs nearby. Insular fire engines arrived and laid hose, but there was no water in the hydrants. The pumpers went to the piers, but it took some time to pump the sea water. Flames spread throughout the building. The VPSF arranged for and provided a water screen between the burning areas and the piers, and at no time were the latter menaced. Coast Guard, Navy, and Army pumpers and fireboats arrived and finally smothered the flames which had burned out half a block. Without this military assistance, damage would have been far greater. The Captain of the Port, San Juan, commended the TRs.

Pacific Coast units were organized in the principal ports, and their experiences were similar to those mentioned. The Seattle VPSF finally engaged in 24 different types of duty, and unusual activities included drivers, messengers, masters-at-arms, radio dispatchers, communications, radio maintenance and repair, pharmacist's mates, traffic control, junior officers of the deck, and service in fire barges. In April 1945, about 1,000 Seattle VPSF members were thrown into a waterfront search for Joe Bill, a 32-year-old fugitive Alaskan Eskimo, who was sought on a first degree murder warrant charging him with the brutal sex-slaying of a five-year-old girl. Despite great vigilance, he was not apprehended by the Regiment.

Most duty was monotonous and unspectacular, but the absence of serious occurrences, disasters, and conflagrations in the waterfront areas bore mute testimony to the efficiency with which the men performed their duties. When emergencies did arise, the men handled the situations well.

The Women Temporary Reservists, known as "TR SPARS", were also of great assistance. The Act approved 23 November 1942, amending the Coast Guard Auxiliary and Reserve Act of 1941, authorized a Women's Reserve as a branch of the Coast Guard Reserve. Just as the existing Act authorized the use of men as temporary members of the Reserve, so was the use of women authorized on the same basis. The units afloat and ashore grew, and the burden of "paper work" and transportation increased commensurately. Men, who could well be used in patrol boats, on guard duty, and in administrative activities, found themselves spending their duty hours at typewriters, working on records, and doing all the office detail. TR SPARS moved in and released them. Eventually, there were over 2,000 women TRs.

These women performed a wide range of duties. First and foremost was typing and clerical work at VPSF, flotilla, and district headquarters, including correspondence, unit and training records, service records, watch schedules, log copying, mimeographing, and working on publications. Next came provision of transportation for men going to or returning from duty where regular means were lacking. Some TR SPARS provided chow for men on waterfront duty, using mobile units. Others were messengers, automobile mechanics, and quartermasters. When the Temporary Reservists went on unassigned status, the women did the necessary clerical work in winding up the affairs of regiments and flotillas. They deserved and received the fullest appreciation from the men with whom they served. The women successfully carried a heavy load and, through release of men for more arduous duties, contributed as much toward the war effort as the men they released. Their work was truly invaluable.

In many coastal areas, Temporary Reservists were used in manning coastal lookouts. This type of duty was monotonous, unexciting, and was not conducive to outstanding incidents. The efficacy of so using TRs is summed up in comment by the District Coast Guard Officer of the Fourth Naval District, who said: "It has been reliably reported by the commanding officers of the key stations that the Temporary Reservists performing this tower watch duty have more than demonstrated their competence and reliability. These men show far keener interest in the assignment than the regular personnel who are inclined to treat the duty as an onerous task. . . ." Throughout their period of beach duty they spotted surface and air craft in trouble and sent aid, and in some cases provided men for surfboats engaged in rescue activity. They submitted much valuable information to Captains of the Port.

We have outlined Port Security activities of the Temporary Reservists ashore. About equally important was the waterside patrol carried on by the floating units. If proper security were to be achieved, the harbor waters, where shipping was active, and where ships of all kinds were being built for the "bridge of ships" and for the coming naval offensives, had to be equally well guarded and watched. This applied also to the harbor entrances, inlets, and rivers where all water traffic had to be carefully checked and identified. No person or vessel without proper identification or legitimate business should roam these important waters. This security work could be done only by floating units. The first active duty by volunteer Temporary Reservists enrolled from the Auxiliary was harbor patrol. As the tempo of the war increased, aggressive recruiting of Temporary Reservists was undertaken to handle the patrols on a 24-hour basis.

While harbor patrol duties differed slightly depending upon local circumstances, basically the purposes were the same everywhere. It was the duty of the men in patrol craft to watch constantly for fire; for unauthorized persons and pleasure craft with improper papers or none at all; to check or report unidentified vessels; to remove menaces to navigation; to watch for accidents and render assistance to persons or craft in difficulty; to assist at plane crashes; to recover bodies and wreckage; and to observe and report anything which did not appear "right." Duties also included policing and clearing channels for the movement of troopships; patrolling ammunition ships; keeping vessels away from the location of diving operations; preventing craft from entering restricted areas; and performing various special assignments such as transporting customs officers, Coast Guard pilots, load line inspectors, and Boarding Officers.

The first harbor patrol was done by the Auxiliary, a group of yachtsmen using their own vessels and carrying a regular Coast Guard petty officer for authority. These patrols worked well in the early days of the emergency, but were inadequate under the stress of wartime demands. The Coast Guard needed complete jurisidiction over a vast number of small craft, and every effort was made to have Auxiliary owners transfer their boats to the Coast Guard Reserve for full time service through sale, charter, or gift. About 1,000 boats, mostly from the 9,500 available Auxiliary craft, were taken into the Coast Guard Reserve for harbor patrol, and were designated "CGR" boats. Temporary Reservists enrolled from the Auxiliary, chiefly for floating units, finally numbered about 30,000, and formed the largest group of TRs.

The fiscal year ending 30 June 1942, had witnessed complete transition of the Coast Guard from its peacetime role as the nation's maritime police under the Treasury Department to its traditional wartime role as a service operating as part of the Navy. The second half of 1942 saw the transition of most active Auxiliarists to the militarized Temporary Reserve. Virtually all early duty by TRs was confined to operation of patrol craft.

Training boatmen was as important as training the VPSF. It was far more intricate, covered a wider field, and took considerably more time. Practically all trainees were required to attend classes before assuming responsibilities, but training usually had to continue "on the job."

CGR boats were used well into 1944, when a return to the owners began. The CGR boats were replaced where practicable and necessary with regular 38-foot picket boats. The CGR boats were mostly converted pleasure craft given a coat of grey paint, with large white letters and numbers

on bows and stern, and equipped with coal stoves for heating purposes, and with radiotelephones, small arms, and sometimes fire pumps. Sizes of the boats ranged from 26 to 60 feet, and designs were numerous. In most areas crews were provided on a 24-hour basis, 7 days a week, the men usually doing 12 hours of duty at a stretch. Boats on a full time basis operated an average of 21 hours a day, cruising at around 4 knots. Thus, each traveled about 80 miles a day, or about 25,000 miles a year allowing for normal layup due to repairs. This is about as much use as a summertime yachtsman would give his boat in 12 to 15 years! It is not surprising that these boats took plenty of punishment.

Boarding was an important function for Boston Temporary Reservists. All boarding of fishermen and larger vessels at Boston was done either from the Outer Examination Vessel (regulars) well outside the harbor, or from the floating Boston Lifeboat Station moored inside Deer Island. Personnel of the latter station boarded outgoing vessels as directed by the Captain of the Port and the Harbor Entrance Control Post, and also boarded such incoming vessels as had not been boarded from the Outer Vessel.

The Boston Lifeboat Station was continuously manned by about 10 regulars and 30 Temporary Reservists. A patrol boat, a picket boat, and a gig, chiefly manned by TRs, were attached here for transportation and boarding purposes. The Boarding Officers were regulars, but were accompanied and transported by TRs who made out armament reports, and checked crew lists, sealed radios, and checked ships' papers, fuel, cargo, food, and ID cards. Boarding merchant vessels while proceeding at 5 to 10 knots, in all weathers over a two-year period, and handling their boats without accident, was outstandingly good seamanship. Between 1 January 1943 and 31 March 1945, Boarding Officers were put on board some 5,000 vessels, and TRs boarded a total of 21,526 vessels, which included freighters, tankers, colliers, and a very large number of fishing vessels.

A primary peacetime duty of the Coast Guard is assistance and salvage. While in wartime the chief responsibility of patrol craft lay in all phases of protection to shipping and port facilities, the saving of life and property still remained very important. Cases of assistance and salvage became almost routine. TRs in virtually every port participated in the rescue of persons from precarious situations, and in the recovery of property. Victims of plane crashes were assisted, and small craft grounded, waterlogged, overturned, or broken away from moorings were saved. Seaworthy craft and Navy planes on the water in dangerous situations were assisted. Patrol boats with fire pumps gave valuable assistance at waterfront fires. Each case required alertness, attention to duty, good seamanship, and keen intuition as to the right things to do in emergency, and many required an exact administration of first aid. "Routine" cases worthy of mention are too numerous to permit coverage in this work, though some involving unusual circumstances, individual heroism, or particular success against odds are recounted.

There were very few collisions involving patrol craft. One at Boston was notable. Early one morning, while *CG-45001* was on patrol off famed T Wharf, she and a pilot boat collided. The bowsprit of the latter swept the whole wheelhouse off the patrol boat, and it was placed not so gently on the after cabin deck. Everything in the wheelhouse was wrecked. The Coast Guard decided to have the damage repaired; an estimate from a local boatyard was $1,800 and the time required, three months. Not pleased with this prospect, permission was requested by the flotilla operating the boat—and granted—for the unit to undertake its own repair work. The craft was back on patrol in two weeks at a cost to the Coast Guard of about $6. This work was done entirely by the men of the flotilla on their own time.

First Naval District boat patrol experience probably was not very different from that of other districts, except possibly in scope. A summary of outstanding accomplishments of boat patrol in this District is interesting. It indicates the types of incidents having direct bearing on the relationship of boat patrol to the security of harbor waters. These outstanding accomplishments included:

(1) An estimated 1,500 obstructions to navigation removed or disposed of

(2) An estimated 45 waterfront fires discovered, controlled, reported, or fought

(3) An estimated 12 cases of burning material prevented from floating under piers, including a lighted float blowing under a pier piled with ammunition

(4) An estimated 300 cases of assistance rendered to small craft in distress, most involving towing

(5) Numerous cases of rescue of people from water, mostly from overturned pleasure craft or unseaworthy craft

(6) An estimated 12 cases of assistance rendered to planes forced to land in the water

(7) An estimated 10 persons apprehended while taking photographs

(8) An estimated 20 cases of assistance rendered to larger craft

(9) Three cases of deserters from merchant vessels apprehended in or on the water

(10) Many cases of investigation with intent to rescue persons, recover property

(11) An uncounted number of pleasure craft checked for permits and ID cards

(12) Uncounted cases or reports of aids to navigation extinguished, out of position, or otherwise needing attention

(13) An estimated 12 cases of dragging for bodies or lost property

(14) An uncounted number of boardings of fishing vessels at smaller ports.

The carrying out of assignments in the normal course of patrol, already summarized, were in addition to the foregoing. The presence of boats on patrol doubtless prevented many incidents which, fortunately, never happened.

In March, 1944, a bus carrying 18 war workers skidded off the Market Street Bridge and into the Passaic River at Passaic, New Jersey, carrying all to their deaths in 18 feet of water. A Temporary Reserve-manned patrol boat was dispatched to the scene from the Port Newark Base, and despite blinding snow, sleet and rain, negotiated the several miles of Passaic River channels in fast time. The Commanding Officer of the Base arrived quickly by automobile and took charge of salvage operations. Several unsuccessful efforts without divers were made to raise the bus; the chains and cables broke under the weight of the vehicle. Four divers arrived and worked from a float alongside the patrol boat until well into the night. Cables were rigged between the bus and the wrecking crane which had come by barge, and the wreckage raised sufficiently to permit removal of the bodies.

On the morning of 3 January 1944, U. S.

destroyer *Turner* was at anchor 3 miles north of Ambrose Lightship. At about 0620 a terrific explosion in the vessel shook the whole area. The initial explosion was followed by several more. Immediately, six boats manned partly by Temporary Reservists at the Rockaway Lifeboat Station, and six others at the Sandy Hook Lifeboat Station were dispatched to the scene. Two 83-footers which were near at the time of the explosion returned to Sandy Hook with survivors at 0740. *CG-83343* went in with 45. Thirty-nine were picked up by pilot boat *CGR-1904* and taken to the Base at Stapleton, Staten Island. Other Coast Guard vessels recovered several more survivors and much debris. The Sandy Hook Station took care of immediate first aid and hospitalization, assisted later by 11 Navy nurses and six enlisted Navy men. Of the 160 survivors, 156 were rescued by the Coast Guard in accord with the traditions of the Service.

An unusual flotilla, that at Thunderbolt, Georgia, was composed entirely of fishermen and shrimpers, who served more than 30,000 man-hours each month. Their boats carried ship-to-shore radio, and they kept in constant touch with the Navy, informing it of any suspicious objects or occurrences observed while carrying on their livelihood. These men operated their own vessels at no expense to the Coast Guard, and performed their fair share of rescues.

A shortage of Coast Guard Boarding Officers at Charleston, South Carolina, was relieved by the Temporary Reserve. Several officers from the units afloat and the VPSF formed a group which took over entirely the duty of boarding merchant ships entering Charleston Harbor. It was the only port in the United States where volunteers assumed the duties of Boarding Officers. Seven covered the assignment on a 24-hour basis, and conducted boarding by picket boat at any hour and in all kinds of weather. They deserve much credit for a difficult and confining duty satisfactorily performed.

Temporary Reservists were active in the Great Lakes and mid-West river areas, where traffic was of great importance to the war effort. Its huge movements of grain, iron ore, coal, petroleum products and general freight were essential to the prosecution of the war. Shipbuilding attained large proportions. It was essential that the great steel centers be fed every bit of ore which could be transported, and it was necessary that the lake and river waterways be kept open and safe. The Coast Guard's 24 hours a day vigil in all sections was of vital necessity. Traffic stoppage could have had a serious effect upon the speedy conduct of hostilities. Temporary Reservists, relieving hundreds of regulars for sea duty, stepped in to guard the shore line, docks, vessels, and bridges, and to patrol the harbors and man the lookouts.

During a heavy gale on 12 December 1943, three fishermen were reported adrift on an ice floe in Big Bay DeNoc, Lake Michigan. With the valuable assistance of four Temporary Reservists who cooperated in the rescue, Coast Guardsmen of the St. Joseph Lifeboat Station successfully launched a boat under the most trying conditions. Ensign (T) Walter Hornstein received commendation from the District Coast Guard Officer, and Chief Machinist's Mate (T) Marvin A. Merrill and Chief Machinist's Mate (T) George S. Campbell received citations for "services to the Coast Guard in assisting in the launching of the St. Joseph Coast Guard Station lifeboat during a 44-mile an hour gale and . . . devotion to duty during the succeeding 11 hours on 12 December 1943, while aboard said lifeboat."

On another occasion, a pipe line on the dock of the Standard Oil Company at Cleveland broke and gasoline drained into the Cuyahoga River. While this facility was the responsibility of the Army, the Coast Guard was vitally interested because of the hazardous exposure to other waterfront facilities. A Coast Guard fireboat was dispatched to the scene and stood by. Temporary Reservists were strategically stationed at key points along the dock and the Jefferson Street Bridge. All traffic passing over the bridge was stopped and warned against smoking. Standby and patrol continued throughout the night, until the hazardous condition had passed.

Another outstanding episode at Cleveland involved Temporary Reservists. On the afternoon of 20 October 1944, there was an explosion of liquid gas stored in tanks of the East Ohio Gas Company, followed by fire and numerous smaller explosions. There ensued one of the greatest holocausts in Cleveland's history. Hundreds of homes were completely destroyed by the explosion; over 150 persons lost their lives; and property damage was $5,000,000 to $7,000,000. While the facility was not under Coast Guard cognizance, the fire was of such proportions as to endanger the entire waterfront. All available Coast Guard personnel and equipment responded to an urgent call. By radio, telephone, and word of mouth, all available Temporary Reservists were ordered to report to the Captain of the Port. Cleveland, Lorain, and Fairport units promptly furnished 453, who assisted Navy and other personnel in preventing spread of fire, policed the area, protected merchant shops from looting, and uncovered several bodies. Coast Guard efforts also prevented the explosion of five tanks of highly noxious and explosive material stored in an adjoining plant. In three days all danger had passed and Coast Guard activity there was secured.

The Ninth (St. Louis) District included the great mid-West area of navigable rivers extending from Pittsburgh to Minneapolis and south to Memphis. A great volume of river traffic essential to the war transited the Mississippi River and the major tributaries. The larger cities and the 5,000 miles of shore on these rivers required security. About 2,500 Temporary Reservists enrolled from the Auxiliary handled the job, operating under 20 Captains of the Port. Duties generally were boat patrol of rivers at strategic localities, boat maintenance, fireboat operation, jeep patrols, guard and sentry duties, boarding and inspection details, telephone watches, identification cards, and special pilot assignments.

One duty related to rescue and salvage was peculiar to this District. The Mississippi River and its major tributaries have the disastrous habit of overflowing their banks and inundating vast areas of rich farmlands, cities, and towns. Floods occur in some sections almost every year, but the war years seemed to have more than their share. Rescue of persons and protection of property under flood conditions was a Coast Guard function, and Temporary Reservists assisted very materially, though their service was necessarily confined to their immediate vicinities. They aided the regular Coast Guardsmen in all flood relief activities such as loading sandbags and repair to levees, evacuating people and livestock, and saving stored crops.

At widely scattered ports, TRs were used in fireboats to augment the regular crews, and at some places, notably in the Seattle area, fireboats or fire barges were entirely manned by the volunteers.

Thirteenth Naval District Auxiliarists and Temporary Reservists cooperated in rescue and salvage operations in the sinking of the ferry *May* on the night of 10 February 1943. The sinking resulted in the loss of nine lives. The vessel was operating between Russel Moorage and the Vancouver shipyards, carrying 16 passengers and 3 crew. Inclement weather, heavy wind, and rain, as well as a generally unstable condition of the vessel, coupled with a crowding of passengers to the lee side for shelter, caused the vessel to capsize and sink. Five passengers in the wheelhouse above the main deckhouse contributed to a topheavy condition. *CG-Phantom*, fireboat *CG-55010-F*, and *CGR-1317* were dispatched at 2356 on first word of the disaster. Meanwhile, *CGA-7701* with two Auxiliarists had proceeded to the sunken vessel and had begun dragging operations. Three bodies were recovered. Nine of the ten survivors were rescued in a small rowboat by an employee of the Russel Towboat and Moorage Company.

Many Temporary Reservists suffered minor injuries while on duty, or while going to or from duty. Chief Boatswain's Mate (T) H. Louis Tupper, seriously injured in an explosion on board *CGR-06462* at Cager's Inlet in August 1943, used crutches for six months. Many TRs were victims of automobile accidents between home and place of duty. An approximately complete record of those who died during their term of active duty, whether or not directly or indirectly as a result of duty, and of those injured during period of duty, shows the following numbers:

| | Died | Injured |
|---|---|---|
| First District | 20 | 14 |
| Third District | 18 | 4 |
| Fourth District | 6 | 0 |
| Fifth District | 7 | 4 |
| Sixth District | 1 | 1 |
| Seventh District | 6 | 0 |
| Eighth District | 9 | 0 |
| Ninth District | 33 | 0 |
| Tenth District | 3 | 1 |
| Eleventh District | 9 | 1 |
| Twelfth District | 13 | 6 |
| Thirteenth District | 12 | 10 |
| Total | 137 | 41 |

The Temporary Reservists afloat contributed immensely to the security of our ports. Their presence doubtless discouraged many acts of sabotage and other subversive acts. When emergencies did arise, the patrol boats were there to cope with them, and their crews usually distinguished themselves.

When hurricanes threatened or struck, the TRs pitched in as one integrated unit, regardless of their regular type of duty. During the war period, there were four hurricanes in which Auxiliarists or TRs played some part. In southern areas, hurricane possibilities were foreseen, and advance mobilization plans were made. Even in New York, where hurricanes seldom occur, instructions were issued. These proved their value. The intensity of all hurricanes was great in the areas affected, but by far the most extensive was the Hatteras to New England hurricane. A brief account of this blow will show how the Temporary Reservists functioned in these emergencies.

This destructive tropical hurricane roared northward over the Atlantic Ocean on 14 September 1944. Moving with great fury from near Cape Hatteras to the Virginia Capes, it resulted in the sinking of U. S. destroyer *Warrington,* and the capsizing and sinking of two 125-foot Coast Guard vessels, *Jackson* and *Bedloe,* with heavy loss of life. Leaving in its wake flooded coastal sections, disrupted communications systems and power lines, damaged roofs, fallen trees, and general destruction, the storm swept up the Atlantic coast over New Jersey and New York, and on to New England. The Weather Bureau gave ample warning of its approach.

Army, Navy, Coast Guard, and some local civilian organizations made ready. Householders were warned, and thousands were evacuated from low-lying coastal areas. Small craft were checked, and sheltered if possible. Vessel crews were aided in handling extra lines at wharves. From treacherous Cape Hatteras to Portland, Maine, the Coast Guard called out about 7,000 Temporary Reservists for any hurricane duty that might become necessary. Many Reservists were immediately posted at critical points. In the First Naval District alone, between 1,500 and 2,000 reported.

Experience at one Coast Guard station is enlightening. At Lewes, Cape Henlopen, the tide began to break over the bulkhead in front of the main Coast Guard Lifeboat Station building at 1645. At 1700 an attempt was made to launch the pulling surfboat as a precautionary measure for saving the lives of personnel, but due to the huge

waves breaking against them the doors could not be opened. When sea water rose to two feet on the first floor, all hands were ordered to the second floor. At 1730 the water tank, detached boathouse, garages, and all smaller buildings were carried away completely. At 1740 the main building was moved 20 feet from its foundation. The water outside was too deep to attempt reaching safety at Brigantine City. At 2030 the water began to subside.

Along the beaches to the northeast, where beach cottages were tumbled about at all angles, a tremendous amount of work was done. TRs recovered several bodies. During the height of the storm, the men were continually exposed to the danger of sweeping tide water, high winds, and flying debris. They evacuated stranded residents flooded out of their homes; aided in disconnecting broken gas and water mains; and guarded downed power lines. First aid was rendered as needed.

Damage in New England alone reached $100,000,000, and over 30 lives were lost. In southern New England, many small craft were blown ashore and destroyed, but TRs did excellent work not only in saving and securing many boats, but in saving lives and property generally. The Reservists in various areas along these shores assisted in clearing roads of fallen trees, branches, wires, and debris; aided persons in stalled motor cars; shut off escaping gas in damaged houses; and helped people to shelter.

The full fury of the storm was felt at Martha's Vineyard, where the Vineyard Sound district was especially hard hit. Torrential rains accompanied the high winds, and a roaring surf with 20-foot breakers smashed at the entire New England coast line. Vineyard Lightship, clinging tenaciously to her moorings off Cuttyhunk, was torn by these tremendous seas, the entire superstructure was ripped clean from her deck, and she foundered with the loss of all hands.

Woods Hole, Massachusetts, was in the center of a hard hit area. Before the storm struck, TRs were posted over an extensive territory and roving patrols were established. The local Flotilla Commander and an assistant toured the area and at the first and second stations found all men on duty. At Woods Hole Drawbridge, the rain, wind, and rising tide had become so terrific that identification of the men was prevented. It was impossible for a man to stand without support. At a nearby dock, all TRs were assisting three fishermen to make secure.

As the Flotilla Commander proceeded in the pitch darkness over the highway bordering the Sound, he encountered falling tree limbs and wires. The sea was breaking over the road, demolishing the bath houses. Good-sized stones were flying through the surf. The man on duty was instructed to allow no more cars through.

The next point of check was at some boat sheds. The six men there were being blown around, but were trying to bolster the doors which were beginning to give way under the pressure of the wind. The tide had risen to dock level. The Commander telephoned the Base, but due to the noise of the wind he could not be heard. On returning to the boat sheds, he found them collapsing. Wreckage, including portions of boats, buildings, branches, and various unidentified objects, was being washed up the main street from the Sound. Still the tide rose.

At Falmouth, trees were falling and wires, torn down by the trees, were shorting and shooting sparks. A telephone pole was burning despite the drenching, driving downpour. At a railroad crossing, the Commander and his assistant found the crossing signals shorted, with lights on and bells ringing, holding up cars on each side. Having determined that no train was approaching, they cleared the traffic.

The noise of the hurricane made the night hideous. The wind reached its peak with gusts of over 100 miles. The Commander, upon trying to cross a railroad bridge, was picked up by the wind, carried back and deposited on a lawn.

Finally, the wind gradually dropped and the worst was over. The Flotilla Commander, relieved, started home and crossed a bridge bare seconds before it went out in a surge of angry water.

Temporary Reservists in the entire affected area acquitted themselves in an outstanding manner, again demonstrating their versatility and devotion to duty.

In 1939, weather reporting and observation were undertaken by the Coast Guard and in February 1941, five cutters were serving as Weather Patrol vessels. This immensely valuable activity continued during the war, and was of great benefit to surface craft and transatlantic planes. The cutters operated out of Boston, and their wartime operational tasks were assigned by the Navy; however, the Coast Guard continued to be responsible for all logistics.

Weather ships, almost "sitting ducks" while on patrol, were open to attack by enemy submarines or surface vessels, and there were many encounters. One cutter, *Muskeget*, was lost without a trace in September 1942. The weather ships kept at sea in all kinds of weather to cruise in a small radius in complete isolation for a month at a time—dodging submarines and battling storms—to send their reports to Base stations from six to eight times daily.

Every effort was made to improve the results of these patrols. In February 1944, it was agreed that weather observing personnel would consist of four men in each vessel out of a group of 30 Weather Bureau men and six Aerographer's Mates who were former Weather Bureau men. Encouragement was offered Weather Bureau personnel to enroll in the Temporary Reserve for part time duty on Civil Service pay, as Chief Aerographer's Mates; active duty to be for the duration of each patrol. Enrollments were effective 15 April 1944, and about 125 men enrolled. Many had done similar work in the cutters as civilians.

The principal duty of the weather men was the preparation and release of balloons with instruments and radio devices for registering and transmitting information on temperature, humidity, and barometric pressures, recording the readings, and submitting reports on their observations.

The successful use of Weather Bureau men as Temporary Reservists was matched on a far larger scale by the pilots. In World War II, the mechanics of war became increasingly technical. Practically all lines of action, and particularly piloting, had to adhere more strictly to military procedures. As an aid to well-organized operation, pilots of a given port in the normal course of events, belong to a single Pilot Association, through which their operations are handled and controlled. The pilots have the responsibility for safe navigation of vessels requiring pilotage from the time of leaving the open waters off a port until returning to those waters. Most associations own one or more pilot boats which lie off the entrance, sometimes for a week at a time, with pilots available for those who may need them.

A chain of events in the early days of the war emphasized the necessity for gearing pilotage to the machinery of war. The Coast Guard was authorized to assume complete military control of the State pilots, and this was accepted by all State pilot associations. On 4 December 1942, a directive authorized the enrollment of pilots in the Temporary Reserve. The "senior pilot", or head of each association, became Senior Coast Guard Officer attached, and was directly responsible to the District Coast Guard Officer, cooperating with the Captain of the Port. Enrollment of pilots was accomplished in December 1942, and virtually all were commissioned. Pilot boats became "CGR" vessels. There were no radical changes in pilotage procedures. The pilots served without military pay, but received remuneration exactly as before in the matter of pilotage fees. This whole change was vital in the interest of Port Security; the safeguarding of important war information; and the coordination of the existing State pilot system in accordance with wartime requirements.

Most piloting in our wartime shipping ports was "run-of-the-mill" business for these officers, and there were very few special incidents in which they were involved. The story of the pilots in one port might be that of all, except that local conditions and problems altered details.

The duties of the pilots at Portland, Maine, were, for the most part, similar to those in other ports of comparable size, and are summarized:

(1) General pilot service for vessels entering and leaving port.

(2) Free pilot service to public vessels of certain classifications.

(3) Transportation of: (a) personnel between examination vessels, (b) coastwise pilots from anchorages to dock, (c) coastwise pilots from ships eastward bound or westward bound, between outer waters and port, and (d) compass adjusters.

(4) Handling of vessels for compass adjusters in inner harbor, and for degaussing range test runs of each new merchant ship built at South Portland.

(5) Pilotage for ships seeking Portland for shelter on Navy or Coast Guard orders due to enemy action or other causes off-shore (half-rate).

(6) Informing of pleasure craft and fishing vessels of rules, regulations, and procedures on leaving or entering Portland Harbor.

(7) Keeping informed of Army and Navy underwater installations, and protecting them by keeping to the swept channel.

(8) Carrying convoy instructions from Port Director's office to designated ships due to sail, or in transit off the coast. Carrying degaussing sheets for testing degaussing systems of each vessel entering or leaving port, and delivering sheets each day to degaussing range. Picking up crew lists for COTP when vessels sailed unexpectedly, as well as papers relating to changes of crew.

During operation by the Coast Guard, Boston pilots completed an estimated 15,000 piloting assignments, representing about 231,000,000 tons of shipping and involving about 7,000 convoy vessels. Despite special hazards of a narrow channel, tricky currents, a single gate, and temperamental winds, they succeeded in carrying out their assignments without accident, which is a tribute to their skill and dependability.

One of the outstanding achievements of these Boston pilots was their efficient handling of convoys leaving the harbor. The 24 pilots were at times faced with the necessity of piloting as many as 40 vessels making up a convoy. This is how the problem was solved. Twenty-four vessels moving first each had a pilot. When the first vessel had been taken to a point where a pilot was no longer necessary, a Coast Guard picket boat removed him, picked up the second and third pilots, and took them back to the 25th, 26th, and 27th ships which had not, at that time, been called upon to move. This process was followed until all vessels had been provided with pilots.

New York, the leading wartime shipping port, provided great activity for the Coast Guard pilots. There were two pilot groups at New York. One numbering 108 consisted of the "New York Pilots", and the other, totaling 14 (later 20) were the "Hell Gate Pilots". Work of the latter was highly specialized.

The Pilot Command Office compiled and forwarded information on ship movements to other military agencies; handled convoys and independent ships; and handled matters pertaining to vessel identification. The Office was informed of expected convoy arrivals and departures, so that the required pilots would be at the pilot station in plenty of season. The New York pilot station was in exposed water, and boarding and removal of pilots was often accomplished under the most adverse conditions of weather and sea.

After the Pilot Command received the necessary convoy information on arrivals, pilots were notified, given the needed data, and transported to the pilot station to await their charges. Armed with all the required information, the pilots were taken by launch to their vessels, which they boarded and directed up the channel to quarantine and eventually to berth or anchorage.

The time schedule on departures informed the pilots in advance where each ship was located, its time to get under way, and the time for passing through the gate and various points in the channel. Two hours before sailing time, the pilot arrived, checked identification signals, and saw that all was in readiness.

On 15 December 1942, the Hell Gate Pilots (originally established in 1757) began to function under the Coast Guard, but remained an entity because of their highly specialized work. The 16-mile East River between Long Island Sound and New York Harbor, is really a tidal channel. This treacherous passage, and particularly Hell Gate which is its most dangerous part, has long been recognized as the biggest water traffic problem in New York waters. Aside from narrow, confined channels, tricky currents, and mid-stream rocky areas, there are 22 changes of course in the 16-mile run! The series of abrupt turns added together result in some of the worst tidal currents navigators and pilots have to face anywhere. The current in the narrow West Passage of Welfare Island attains a mill-race velocity of 4.6 to 5.2 knots. Above Welfare Island, the river makes two turns of about 90° each in less than a mile. This is Hell Gate, notorious for its narrow width, treacherous currents, boilers, and limited visibility. At ebb tide there are whirlpools and suction points that can spin a good-sized vessel out of control and carry her onto jagged rocks that abound in the vicinity. Yet, to save ships and lives, the East River had to be used. Maneuvering a heavy ship there demanded exacting skill and steel-steady nerves. To these Hell Gate Pilots, this greatest undertaking in their history was all in their day's work, but the tremendous volume of waterborne traffic to come was to tax their abilities to the utmost.

To facilitate safe pilotage, a traffic warning system was established. The principal components were a lookout on Triborough Bridge, and a light control tower on Hell Gate Bridge, with flashing warning lights visible from the east and west approaches to Hell Gate. Boats of the Harbor Patrol Fleet were radio-equipped for communication with the control tower. A loud speaker system enabled the pilots to know the exact type, speed, and position of unseen approaching vessels, and thus formulate and execute a course change without endangering their ships. In case of an accident or a traffic tie-up, patrol boats warned approaching craft and interested harbor authorities.

In addition to controlling his ship as it proceeded, the pilot continuously had to anticipate his moves and those of others a mile in advance. Vessels were often entirely unfamiliar, and pilots had no knowledge of how they "handled." At one time, during a peak of traffic, 37 ships passed through Hell Gate in 30 minutes. With slack water lasting four to eight minutes, the first ship through experienced a head tide while the last ship had a fair tide! Between 1 January 1942 and 31 May 1945, the Hell Gate Pilots took 14,539 vessels through without the loss of a ship, and with only a few minor, and no serious, accidents. The successful accomplishment of the wartime assignments of these temporary members of the Coast Guard Reserve is a highlight in Coast Guard wartime annals.

While pilot activity in most other Naval Districts varied little, the Ninth (St. Louis) District experience was somewhat different. There, the most important duty was the safe and expeditious delivery of 2,388 Navy and Army vessels from their builders' yards on the rivers and Great Lakes to salt water. Some traveled 2,600 miles. Forty-nine licensed river pilots were commissioned and 43 assistants were enlisted in the Temporary Reserve.

With military victory in Europe on 8 May 1945, came immediate cessation of many TR activities. Port Security measures were eased and most VPSF units either had been, or were then, placed in an unassigned status. By mid-June all harbor patrols had been secured, and virtually all TRs went unassigned, with disenrollment following in September 1945.

In evaluating the contribution by the Temporary Reservists toward the war effort it must be recognized that their use was primarily to release regulars and regular Reservists for duty at sea, on foreign stations, and in the invasion forces. About one full-time man was released for every six TRs. This means that the approximately 50,000 volunteers made available about 8,250 regulars or regular Reservists for sea duty, or about 20 percent of those Coast Guardsmen so engaged. In terms of vessels, one could say that 8 transports, 22 destroyer escorts and patrol frigates, 24 landing craft of all types, and 10 miscellaneous craft were "manned" by those released by TR activity. Thus, these Temporary Reservists made a definite contribution toward the effectiveness of the United States Coast Guard in its seagoing operations against the enemy.

Part III

Safety at Sea

# Chapter 7

# THE GREENLAND PATROL

FURTHERANCE of safety at sea is prominent among Coast Guard duties in peace and war. This takes many forms. It includes aids to navigation both visual and audible; communications; assistance; marine inspection; weather patrol; and the alleviation of dangers from the elements as well as from the enemy, wherever possible. Thus far, we have discussed Coast Guard activities chiefly related to security at home; now we shall turn farther afield and consider wartime safety at sea. The Greenland Patrol, carried out by the Coast Guard, concerned safety at sea in many of its phases, including the prevention of hostile action against vessels and seamen of the United States and friendly nations.

This Patrol was very broad in its operations—so broad that the story of the activity necessarily includes episodes and experiences that logically could be included in the story of Coast Guard Aviation, such as that of Lieutenant Pritchard; in assistance such as the case of *USS Cherokee*; and in the Battle of the Atlantic, involving the loss of cutter *Escanaba*. Where is the historian to draw the line? For the "Greenland Patrol", while essentially *just that*, combined these and many other things.

The Greenland Patrol was formally established on 1 June 1941, a year and three-quarters after war had started in Europe, and six months before Pearl Harbor. Let us review briefly the conditions and events which brought about its establishment, and which determined its purposes.

Early in the war the Nazis knew the importance of Greenland as a weather forecasting base for Europe. They patrolled its coasts with weather planes from which they sent advance information to their submarines, surface vessels, and air forces. The trapped German battleships *Scharnhorst* and *Gneisenau* were able to slip out of harbor under the cover of a heavy fog and maneuver their way unmolested within 15 miles of Britain's Dover coast because of such advance information. The Nazis had been suspiciously accurate in their weather forecasts that controlled their bombings of Britain. German radio stations in Greenland were sending information to Berlin several times a day, and informing their submarines in Greenland waters of weather conditions, as well as Allied ship movements in lanes close to Cape Farewell, the southern tip of Greenland.

After the German invasion of Denmark on 9 April 1940, the United States became seriously concerned about its defenses against attack in the North Atlantic. Greenland, a Danish island, presented a double threat. Hitler might get control of it, establish weather stations, air and other military bases, and strike Allied ships on the northern route. He might use defenseless Greenland as a springboard to attack the Western Hemisphere. Canada, like the United States, had no North Atlantic outposts. It was not until the 50 "obsolete" destroyers (World War I four-pipers) were traded that we acquired a base on Newfoundland at Argentia; this eventually became one of the strategic centers of the war.

Many Coast Guard ships were adapted for operations in ice. Numerous Coast Guard officers were experts in Arctic navigation through long association with the International Ice Patrol in the North Atlantic, and the Bering Sea Patrol in Alaska. In May 1940 cutter *Comanche*, which had made numerous ice observation patrols, was detailed to transport Mr. James K. Penfield, the first American Consul to Ivigtut, Greenland. As a result of negotiations with the Danish Minister to Washington the consulate had just been opened at Godthaab.

The cryolite mine at Ivigtut was an important concern of our Consul. Cryolite is an essential mineral in the production of aluminum, which was urgently needed in our aircraft building program.

The mine, less than a mile from the sea, was vulnerable to attack. We could take no chances with that mine! The United States agreed not only to sell armaments to Greenland in 1940, but ex-Coast Guard personnel, trained in the use of firearms, were sent to guard the cryolite mine. Cutters patrolled the west and east coast, and in August 1940, *Duane* carried a party to make an air survey of Greenland's west coast. *Northland* (Commander Edward H. "Iceberg" Smith), cruised the east coast looking for European military occupation or activity; explored the many fjords; and organized the data into charts for a "Greenland Pilot."

Greenland had significance as a possible air base, and preliminary conversations with this in mind were begun in the Fall of 1940. On 17 March 1941 as soon as ice conditions permitted, the South Greenland Survey Expedition, composed of representatives of the State, Treasury, Navy, and War Departments, sailed from Boston for Greenland in the cutter *Cayuga*. The mission was to locate and recommend sites for airfields, seaplane bases, radio stations, meteorological stations, and aids to navigation, and to furnish hydrographic information. Arriving at Godthaab on 31 March 1941, the party left 7 April in *Cayuga* to visit points on the west coast.

Throughout the Expedition's cruise of about two months, the Coast Guard made every effort to assist. On 17 May, *Northland* relieved *Cayuga*. Commander Smith, in the former, reported that the cruise further confirmed his contention that Coast Guard cutters were the best adaptable naval ships for the Greenland sector, and that all such ships should be equipped with a plane. The ship-based plane proved of great service to the work of the Expedition. The plane reported ice conditions, and, among other things, the airmen made photographs of various tentative building sites.

Acceptable Greenland charts were not available. The Coast Guard made new charts, and uncharted areas were surveyed and recorded. Locations were verified or corrected; cutters ran up one side of the many fjords and down the other, making soundings. There were no effective aids to navigation. Mapping and charting of certain important areas, including approaches to proposed airfields was also accomplished.

As a result of this Expedition, it was decided to construct landing fields at Narsarssuak at the head of the Julianehaab Fjord, and at Kipisako, near Ivigtut, with seaplane bases at other locations. A central radio and aerological station was planned for Akia Island, near Kipisako, with a secondary observing station elsewhere. These stations proved invaluable to Allied forces. The meteorological information, on the basis of which General Eisenhower set D-Day for the Normandy invasion, came largely from Greenland.

At this juncture it should be mentioned that Commander Smith, as a lieutenant commander, had studied abroad and in this country under outstanding scholars, and is said to have passed the Harvard examinations for a Ph.D. in oceanography with extremely high marks. Because of his great knowledge of Arcticphenomena, especially ice and icebergs, he became fondly referred to as "Iceberg" Smith. He gained renown as one of the world's foremost scientists.

On 9 April 1941, by agreement with the Danish Minister, the United States undertook the defense of Greenland under the Act of Havana of 30 July 1940. This authorized the United States to accept responsibility for Western Hemisphere defense. It gave us the right to locate and construct air fields for the defense of Greenland and the American continent as long as the emergency lasted. Denmark still retained its sovereignty over the "defense areas." The United States respected all of Greenland's laws, regulations, and customs, and safeguarded the welfare of its inhabitants. A similar agreement was made with Iceland a few months later.

Meanwhile, American neutrality in the European war was coming to a practical end. President Roosevelt had announced that the defense of Great Britain was vital to the defense of the United States. On 11 March 1941, the Lend-Lease Act had become law. Food was urgently needed by the British people, whom Hitler was trying to starve into surrender by his submarine warfare. The first Lend-Lease food transfer had been authorized 16 April 1941. In the succeeding eight months a million tons of American food was sent across the ocean, effectively tiding Great Britain over her most serious food crisis.

Enraged at our success, Hitler sent the giant battleship *Bismarck*, accompanied by the cruiser *Prinz Eugen,* to raid the Allied food convoys and to destroy the United Nations' supply lines. The speed and power of *Bismarck* made her a deadly menace; not only was she the most powerful ship afloat, and so honeycombed with water-tight compartments as to be almost "unsinkable", but she was far larger than the 35,000 tons which official German sources gave as her displacement. No sooner had these German warships left Norway on this mission, than 46 Allied warships took up the chase. There followed one of the most spectacular sea battles of the war.

On 21 May 1941, seventeen Allied food ships returning to Europe were reported attacked and some torpedoed, 150 miles southeast of Cape Farewell, Greenland. *Northland* had rendezvoused with cutter *Modoc* at sea and was on her way to Boston, when both vessels were ordered to search for survivors of these attacks. *Modoc* learned from a tanker in a passing convoy that she had intercepted weak signals from the boats of *Marconi* which had been sunk the previous day 100 miles south of the main convoy. *Northland* proceeded to the scene of the main sinkings with full lights and colors displayed, broadcasting her position and purpose each hour. Throughout the period of search, visibility in mist, fog, and rain seldom exceeded two miles.

At noon on the 22nd, she reached the reported position 57° 41′ N, 41° 21′ W. Shortly afterward, Commander Smith in *Northland* sighted several bodies in life jackets, along with oil on the surface, wreckage, and debris. Two empty lifeboats and an empty life raft were found; a second raft was discerned, burnt and charred. At 1900 three vessels of the convoy were sighted, and it was learned that they had taken 53 survivors from these boats and rafts. A few miles to the southeast, the cutter found an abandoned tanker, *British Security*, completely burned and wallowing in the swell with decks awash—a gaping hole just forward of her bridge. Altogether, 120 persons were rescued by the convoy vessels.

*Modoc*, unsuccessful in locating *Marconi's* boats, joined *Northland*, and the two cutters searched the area. A British trawler had informed them earlier that eight ships had been torpedoed by 12 U-boats, and that 140 men were still unaccounted for. In the meantime, cutter *General Greene*, Chief Boatswain C. L. Jordan, on an oceanographic survey off Newfoundland, having intercepted a message from Headquarters, decided to join the search for *Marconi* survivors. Meanwhile *Bismarck* was reported to be only 100 miles to the eastward.

The search continued, but by the 24th, *Modoc* and *General Greene* had worked into the vicinity of an air attack incidental to the *Bismarck* battle, in which eight planes and three naval vessels were involved. The cutters, under jurisdiction of the Treasury, were unmolested for they were a familiar sight in these regions. Nevertheless, anti-aircraft missiles from *Bismarck* narrowly missed *Modoc's* bow. British planes were inflicting damage on the German warship, reducing her speed until British battleships could come up. *Modoc* narrowly escaped attack during the evening by HMS *Prince of Wales*, which, fortunately, identified the cutter in time.

During an interlude, *General Greene* worked an area which had not then been searched by British vessels. On the 26th she picked up a *Marconi* lifeboat containing a chief petty officer and 19 men, who had been buffeted about by strong winds, snow, and rough seas for six days. In the afternoon they found another lifeboat with 19 survivors, who told a story of acute suffering and of having one of their number die in agony after drinking sea water.

On the same day, *General Greene's* officers saw four large battleships speeding northward; they heard heavy gunfire and observed thick smoke. The British ships had caught up with *Bismarck*. Hit many times and barely holding her own, the latter had received the following message from Berlin: "All our thoughts are with our victorious comrades. Hitler." From *Bismarck* went the reply: "Ship unmaneuverable; we shall fight to the last shell. Lutjens." It was at this time that the British battleship *Hood* blew up with all hands as a result of a salvo from the invisible *Bismarck* which touched off her magazines. On the 27th, *Bismarck* was southwest of Ireland attempting desperately to make a French port. Her guns were silenced, her mast blown away, and smoke and flames poured skyward. She finally turned over and sank with only 110 survivors out of a crew of 2,400.

The search for the unaccounted-for *Marconi* survivors was continued by *Northland* until the 31st, when further search was abandoned. In reporting the activity during the eleven days of search, Commander Smith wrote: "It is fortunate that there were no accidents and mistaken identities when all parties concerned were more or less on a hair trigger. It is equally certain, however, that both the British and German ships knew of our presence through our lights and regular radio broadcasts, and if any casualty had resulted it could fairly have been termed as plainly an overt act."

The Battle of the Atlantic was moving toward a climax, and the Royal Navy was trying to guard the already huge volume of North Atlantic shipping by itself. Against this background of great violence, the South Greenland Patrol, with cutters *Modoc, Comanche,* and *Raritan,* and the ex-Coast and Geodetic Survey ship *Bowdoin,* was established 1 June 1941, under the command of Commander Harold G. Belford. One month later, the Northeast Greenland Patrol with cutter *Northland,* the ex-Interior Department vessel *North Star,* and *USS Bear,* was organized under Commander Edward H. Smith, with Commander Carl Christian von Paulsen as second in command. Both patrols, consolidated in October of that year, became the Greenland Patrol, Task Force 24.8, under Commander Smith, operating under Commander-in-Chief, U. S. Atlantic Fleet.

Admiral Samuel Eliot Morison, USNR, in his excellent History of Naval Operations in World War II, writes that Smith "received orders from the Chief of Naval Operations, to do a little of everything—the Coast Guard is used to that." This "everything" meant keeping the convoy routes open for surface vessels, and the air routes for planes; breaking ice; finding leads in the ice for the Greenland convoys of merchant ships and transports; escorting such ships; rescuing survivors of submarine attacks; constructing and maintaining aids to navigation; reporting weather and ice conditions; and maintaining air and surface patrols. In addition, Commander Smith was to discover and destroy enemy weather and radio stations in Greenland; continue the hydrographic survey; maintain communications among the several United States and Greenland government posts; bring supplies to the Eskimos and the small Danish settlements; escort cryolite ships; and perform rescue missions for vessels in distress and crashed planes. Really, quite an assignment! "These duties", writes Morison, "the Coast Guard performed with exemplary fortitude and faithfulness throughout the war."

It took some time to organize regular patrols, and the first weeks of official patrol were relatively uneventful. However, on 4 September 1941, the destroyer *USS Greer* was sunk by a German submarine while carrying mail to Iceland. On 12 September, the day following the President's warning to the Axis nations to stay out of American waters or take the consequences, Commander Smith noticed an apparently innocent fishing vessel. He recalled having been informed by some members of a Sledge Patrol of faithful Danes and Eskimos, that they had seen a party landing in a lonely fjord. Commander Smith stopped the fishing vessel and sent out a boarding party, who took her into a small body of water called McKenzie Bay, halfway up the east Greenland coast, to look her over.

At first the 27 persons on board, most of them Danish hunters and Norwegian trappers, claimed to be a fishing and hunting party. The leader of the expedition was a scientist. The one woman on board said she was a nurse. "Have you dropped off any men?" a Coast Guard officer asked. "No," answered everybody. After more questioning, however, these adventurers realized they were up against men who could not be bluffed. One of the crew said that two sets of "hunters" had been dropped off, one with radio equipment near the entrance of Franz Joseph Fjord, about 500 miles north of McKenzie Bay. The fishing vessel was identified as the Norwegian trawler *Buskoe,* controlled by German interests and servicing a radio station in Greenland.

Commander Smith immediately placed a prize crew on board the Norwegian. Examination revealed that the vessel was equipped with a main transmitter and a portable transmitter, a main receiver and a portable receiver, a portable engine-generator, and a control panel. The vessel was believed to be engaged in sending weather reports and information on Allied shipping to German U-boats and Axis-controlled territory.

Leaving *Buskoe* with the prize crew, *Northland,* now under command of Commander C. C. von Paulsen, set out to find the suspected radio station on the east coast of Greenland. The following night, the cutter anchored in a fjord about five miles from the place. Twelve men, led by Lieutenant Leroy McCluskey, were assigned to attack and capture the radio station. About midnight the landing party proceeded in a small boat to within

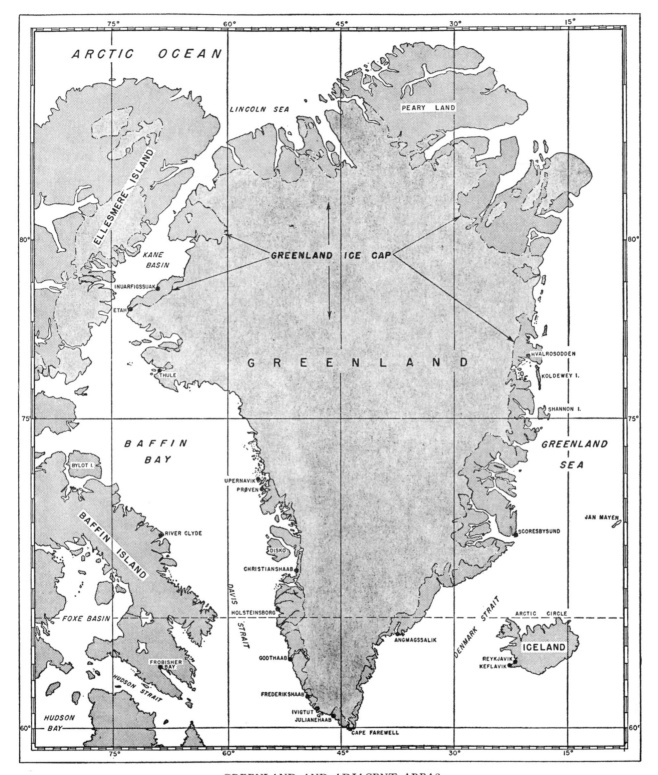

GREENLAND AND ADJACENT AREAS

a mile of the station. Making their way through pitch darkness and over icy ground, they at last found the so-called hunters' shack which had been described to them as the site of the radio station. Lieutenant McCluskey surrounded the shack with his commandos and, gun in hand, kicked in the door of the building and rushed in upon three men who were resting in their bunks. The German radiomen quickly surrendered and told all they knew. Their radio equipment and code were also taken. Under pretense of building a fire to make coffee for the Americans, the radiomen tried to burn some papers, but the Coast Guard party was too quick for the Nazis and the papers were seized. They turned out to be confidential instructions—Hitler's plans for radio stations in the far north—and of considerable value to the Coast Guard.

Discovery of the trawler and the radio station had been most timely, for their weather reports were just being made ready for transmission to Olso, Norway. The captured vessel, with her crew and passengers, was taken to Boston for internment. Coast Guard seizure of *Buskoe* was the first naval capture by the United States during the period of emergency; we were not officially at war at the time.

When we entered the war on 8 December 1941, the Greenland bases were already in operation, but more small ships with a long cruising radius were needed. Commander Smith found them along the fishing docks in Boston. They were taken over by the Coast Guard, camouflaged blue and white, and given Eskimo names for animals—*Aivik, Aklak, Alatok, Amarok, Arluk, Atak, Arvek, Nanok, Natsek,* and *Nogak.* They were commanded by young officers, three of the regular Coast Guard and seven of the Reserve.

One of many results of Commander Smith's trip in 1941 was the establishment of a dog-team patrol whose duty it was to observe and report any person who was not an authorized resident of northeast Greenland. This "Sledge Patrol", organized late in 1941, was made up of faithful Danes and Eskimos whose knowledge of the terrain and its inhabitants was unsurpassed. In that great expanse of snow and ice, where it is difficult to recognize people at even a short distance, only natives covering the territory on sleds, and well acquainted with the regular inhabitants were likely to detect a stranger. The Danes were, for the most part, hunters who lived in wooden shacks situated at varying intervals, sometimes a hundred miles apart. For their fresh food they depended chiefly on what they caught.

The Sledge Patrol worked in close cooperation with the Coast Guard, the U. S. Army, and the Greenland Administration which was wholly isolated from the government in Denmark. Sledge Patrol members were eventually accorded military status, working as a unit of the U. S. Army.

The Coast Guard learned that almost every other shack was at that time a weather station sending information by radio to Denmark. The first thing we did after the Danish invasion was to dismantle these stations to cut off weather and other information from the Germans.

It might be pointed out at this juncture that for nearly two years afterwards there were suspicions that enemy radio shacks still existed in Greenland. While all shacks and strangers, especially those in northeast Greenland, were systematically inspected and checked by the Sledge Patrol, it was suspected that Nazis were still operating weather stations when some Army fliers, asking for weather information in secret code, were answered *in secret code* and ran into a heavy storm which caused them to crash. These were the same fliers for whom Lieutenant Pritchard gave his life in his attempt to rescue them. The false information apparently was sent from a German submarine or radio station on the Greenland east coast.

While the Coast Guard was concerned with discovering and destroying German weather radio stations, it also set up some establishments for the United States. Aids to navigation in Greenland were few and far between. Working parties under Coast Guard officers constructed much needed aids. The first, under Lieutenant (jg) Carl W. Rom built Gamatron Radiobeacon Station during the winter of 1941-42. A second party under Lieutenant Joseph W. Havlicek established Simiutak Light Station, Karjartalik Light and Radiobeacon Station, and Cruncher Island Light and Radiobeacon Station, from April to December 1942. A third party, headed by Lieutenant Frank P. Ishmeal, USCGR, installed the rest of the Greenland aids, completed various repair projects, and designed the Army-Navy Administration Building at Narsarssuak, about 50 miles up Skov Fjord. Many cutters took turns serving as workships for these jobs and in transporting men and their supplies.

Convoy traffic increased greatly after the United States officially entered the war. Long range German planes patrolled the east coast of Greenland and thus air attack in the area was a threat through 1942. The number of Coast Guard vessels on Greenland Patrol also grew, as did the number assigned to weather patrol in the North Atlantic. These two activities were closely related and often blended together.

Greenland Patrol cutters made many thrilling rescues. One came on 15 June 1942. *Escanaba*, bound from Cape Cod to Halifax, while hurrying to rejoin her convoy after attacking a submarine, saw flares and rockets indicating a submarine attack on the convoy. Firing star shells, the cutter came to the position where *USS Cherokee* (fleet tug) had gone down and survivors were milling around in the freezing water. Rescue operations started immediately in pitch darkness with a volunteer crew in a monomoy surfboat. Twenty survivors were taken from the water and brought on board. Several other vessels present unfortunately showed lights during this operation. This brought rescue work to a halt to avoid submarine attack.

With the great increase in convoys, and in the war tempo at sea, came many contacts with the enemy, and Coast Guard vessels made every effort to run the enemy down. While *Northland* was patrolling a circular area with a 60-mile radius in Davis Strait on 18 June 1942, she made an underwater contact and leapt to the attack. The contact was on a bearing 265 degress at a range of 2,300 yards. A minute later a firmer contact at 1,900 yards was made. The cutter headed straight for the submarine and dropped five 300-pound depth charges. Turbulent water, oil and air bubbles appeared close to the first charge and there was an oil slick 100 yards in diameter. After the second and third charges, reverberatory noises were heard and felt, and oil bubbles continued to rise in profusion. The cutter continued the search for 14 hours before leaving for emergency repairs at Iceland. Although German records discovered after the war gave no report of a submarine lost in this position, perhaps this sub was one of those whose fate the Nazis classified as "unknown."

There were numerous attacks on convoys, of course. Only a few can be chosen for special comment; many worthy of mention must be omitted because of space limitations. One attack occurred on 25 August 1942. Cutter *Mojave* was escorting the U. S. Army transport *Chatham* from Sydney, Nova Scotia, to Greenland in one group of convoy S-G6, while cutters *Mohawk* and *Algonquin* were escorting steamships *Laramie*, *Biscaya*, *Arlyn*, *Alcoa Guard*, and *USS Harjurand* in another group. At 0900, when near the north end of Belle Isle Strait, *Chatham* was torpedoed.

Twelve hours later, at about 2100, when off Chateau Bay, an alarm was sounded in *Mohawk* and all hands took their battle stations. Personnel in the CPO quarters and in the fireroom heard a hissing or whining sound pass under the ship, undoubtedly the sound of a torpedo. This was neither reported to the bridge nor picked up by the QC (underwater sound) operator. Thirty-five minutes after the first alarm, an explosion was heard. A faint white glow was seen on *Laramie's* bow. A second explosion rent the air about five seconds later followed by another white glow near *Laramie* or *Arlyn*. *Mohawk* rushed to her station on the convoy's left flank. A minute later a third explosion thundered off the cutter's port bow.

*Laramie*, a Navy tanker, sent up two white rockets. *Mohawk*, speeding to her assistance, and finding her down by the head and listing to port, proceeded down the moon in search of the submarine; she hunted unsuccessfully until 2300. Meanwhile, *Laramie* and *Algonquin* were firing projectiles and star shells.

The situation had become confused. *Algonquin* escorting two ships, was heading southeast, but *Mohawk* did not follow. The submarine which had sunk *Chatham* had remained in the vicinity, giving rise to the belief that if injured *Laramie* were left unattended, the sub might finish her off. *Arlyn* had been sunk, but no word of this had been received until 2259. *Mohawk* sighted red flares; if these were from lifeboats, it was assumed they could be only 5 miles from shore and assistance, therefore, was not needed. *Mohawk* followed an oil slick and finally caught up with *Laramie* shortly before midnight. The cutter, being told of an underwater echo 2,000 yards distant, ran down the bearing but established no contact. She dropped four depth charges as an embarrassing attack. At 0100 *Mohawk* asked a naval patrol plane to look for possible survivors of *Arlyn*, five miles southeast of Chateau Bay. She continued escorting

*Laramie* until relieved by *USS Bristol. Laramie* and other remaining vessels of the convoy were then safely escorted to port in Greenland.

Many such experiences were had by Coast Guard-manned convoy escorts. A Greenland Patrol billet was certainly no sinecure; it was "guarding the coast" with a vengeance.

The appearance of oil on the surface of the water following the explosion of a depth charge did not necessarily mean the U-boat had been destroyed. The explosion might have merely ruptured the portion of the outer hull where the fuel oil was stored, and so produced an oil slick. Sometimes submarine crews themselves released oil to simulate destruction when they felt the explosions too near them. The subs were tough; there were cases where depth charges tore away conning towers with men clinging to them, and yet the subs subsequently limped back to port! Whales and icebergs, contacted on the underwater sound apparatus or radar, were often mistaken for submarines. Many depth charge attacks, however, served to keep the subs down and were at least protective.

In November 1942, *Northland* (Captain Charles W. Thomas) arrived at the Norwegian island of Jan Mayen, well north of Iceland, to establish a high frequency direction finder station (HF/DF). *Northland* landed 41 officers and men with 30 tons of stores and equipment under extremely difficult conditions, both geographic and weatherwise. The Norwegians on the island called the U. S. radio station there "New Chicago" because it was protected from aerial attack by machine guns!

To appreciate duty in Greenland waters, some mention of ice conditions will be helpful. During certain seasons the southeast coast of Greenland is surrounded by a belt of "storis" 20 to 30 miles wide; this is loose pack ice of small icebergs or growlers, sprinkled with a few larger icebergs. Small bergs are about the size of a Greyhound bus, while large ones could cover several city blocks. Even the sturdiest vessels, especially built for icebreaking, were constantly damaged by this heavy Arctic ice. Bent propeller blades caused the vessel to vibrate, and operations would have to be suspended during repairs. Many cutters made temporary repairs themselves and continued on their missions. The Coast Guard's Greenland Patrol served logistically all the Army, Navy,

and Coast Guard bases in Greenland. Food and clothing for the men had to be brought in, whether or not the fjords were frozen. In some places fjords froze to a thickness of six to eight feet. The cutters found leads through this ice or broke it, so supply ships could get through.

A ship in a clear course of water one minute might find its way blocked the next, so swiftly did the ice situation change at times, especially with high winds and swift currents. Surrounded by ice, the cutter would have to send out or call for a plane to survey the area for miles around, looking for leads through which open water could be reached. Without such information from a plane, a cutter might follow one of several leads only to be again surrounded by ice. Smoke flares were first used in July 1943 by PBYs to show the position of leads. Where planes were not available, vessels sometimes were obliged to spend weeks in the ice, always in danger of being crushed.

The escort vessels experienced great difficulty in keeping track of their convoy ships when fog combined with ice to cause more trouble. Bringing stragglers lost in the fog back into line was, therefore, an important part of routine escort duty.

The trawlers taken over by the Coast Guard for work around Greenland and in the North Atlantic were thoroughly uncomfortable, cramped, and wet; but they were generally good sea boats and they performed their duties well. Few ran into serious situations, but *Natsek* was lost on 17 December 1942, without a trace.

A group of three vessels was to proceed from Narsarssuak, Greenland, to Boston. This group comprised *USS Bluebird* (256 gross-ton-minesweeper) commanded by Lieutenant Commander James F. Baldwin, USNR, who was senior officer; converted trawler *Natsek* (Lieutenant (jg) Thomas S. LaFarge, Jr., USCGR); and converted trawler *Nanok* (Lieutenant Magnus G. Magnusson).

In conference on 13 December, it was decided that *Bluebird* would lead, and the three would proceed in column. *Bluebird* and *Natsek* got under way about 0800; *Nanok* was delayed half an hour to receive mail and passengers. *Bluebird*, while proceeding down Skov Fjord, closed cutter *North Star* which was proceeding up the Fjord, to receive mail, and then closed a trawler to receive a passenger. During this time, *Nanok* joined *Natsek* and, receiving no signal from *Bluebird*, the two proceeded to sea. When *Bluebird* was ready to proceed, the other two were three or four miles ahead, and an attempt by her to communicate with the trawlers by blinker failed. *Natsek* and *Nanok* with speed exceeding that of *Bluebird*, soon parted company with the latter. The trawlers kept together, and on 17 December, at about 0100, they sighted Belle Isle Strait.

About 0215 snow began to fall and Belle Isle Light became obscured. The commanding officers of the two trawlers conferred by hailing back and forth, and decided to proceed during darkness through the Strait as long as their positions were known. *Natsek* was to lead and keep *Nanok* informed of water depth, since the latter's fathometer was inoperative. The weather thickened, and in heavy snow the two vessels soon lost visual contact with each other.

About 0245 *Nanok* stopped and lay to for about four hours; then, determining her position, she proceeded. When Point Amour Light was abeam the weather cleared; the wind hauled to the west and within an hour reached gale force. Spray, whipped up by the high wind, froze and formed ice on the ship. By nightfall of that day (still the 17th), *Nanok* was west of Rich Point with heavy ice conditions prevailing. For three days *Nanok's* crew worked long hours to break ice from the ship's structure to prevent dangerous accumulation. On the 22nd she passed south of Cape Sable, the southwestern tip of Nova Scotia, and continued toward Boston. *Bluebird* followed *Nanok* in, arriving at Boston on 26 December.

Nothing more was ever heard of *Natsek*. She was seaworthy, only a year old, 116 feet long and of 225 gross tons. Search by air and surface failed to discover trace of her. The most probable cause of foundering was structural damage which might have destroyed watertight integrity, or loss of stability from ice accumulation. Possibly the work of freeing the ship from ice was not started in time or pursued with enough vigor. We shall never know.

*Natsek's* commanding officer, Thomas S. La-Farge, Jr., USCGR, was a grandson of John LaFarge, the noted painter. He was himself an artist and had joined the Coast Guard Reserve to paint while performing his regular duties. With his experience as a yachtsman, he had accepted one of these tough commands. Even during his one year of Greenland duty, he had turned in many fine paintings for Coast Guard Public Relations exhibits.

In Chapter 3, the story of Lieutenant Pritchard's thrilling attempt to rescue the crew of an Army Flying Fortress from the Ice Cap was told, and how this brave officer lost his life in the attempt. It will be recalled that Ensign Richard L. Fuller led an expedition to find Pritchard's plane. An aftermath of all this came on 14 January 1943, when Ensign Fuller, with a civilian dog driver, Mr. Johan Johansen, again set out for the Ice Cap Station near Comanche Bay, this time in an attempt to rescue the ditched Army plane. Running by compass, they reached the Ice Cap Station that evening.

They found Sergeants Joe Liston and Arthur Hall there in a station unfit for human habitation. Buried under five feet of snow, the roof was dripping like a shower; the water on the deck was two inches deep, there were no sanitary facilities. The only light was one gasoline lantern. A blizzard began. Fuller and Johansen returned to the Beach Head Station, but the Army men remained in the wretched hovel until 25 January. Then they were able to make the Beach Head Station on skis dropped by a plane.

Six days later, Fuller and Johansen again set out for the reported position of the missing PN-9E. They reached the Ice Cap Station, but the first three days of February were unfit for travel. They set out on 4 February in a stiff northerly wind, with good visibility and the temperature 12° below zero. At midday a B-17 from Ikateq dropped supplies and equipment, all of which were cached, except trail flags and a "walkie-talkie." The next day they continued on toward the reported position of the downed plane, aided by a B-17 which gave directions as it flew over, accompanied by two PBYs. The Army planes then flew to where all but three of the survivors were camped, six miles from their plane; Colonel Bernt Balchen, U. S. Army, landed a PBY and evacuated them.

When about 12 miles from the wrecked plane, Fuller was informed by the B-17, which dropped a tent and some clothing, that there had been no signs of life for several days from the three survivors remaining with the downed PN-9E. That night, wind made it difficult to pitch the tent; in the process Ensign Fuller froze his right foot. Next morning he decided to turn back because of this, as well as poor visibility and a shortage of dog food. For two days he and Johansen ran on compass from flag to flag back to the Ice Cap Station. There, a 3-day hurricane with extreme cold caused the death of several dogs. Gales and snowstorms bogged the men down for the rest of February. Dog food and heating fuel became scarce and on the night of 2 March, with the situation becoming desperate, they reached the Beach Head Station with only three dogs pulling. Eight of the original 15 dogs had perished, and four were crippled. They remained at Beach Head Station until May, digging for fuel and food in the caches, and keeping the tunnels in the living quarters clear.

Pharmacist Hearn amputated two of Fuller's frozen toes and extracted the offending teeth of two men who had developed severe toothaches. On 8 May 1943, all Coast Guard personnel were removed from Comanche Bay. All members of the trail party were commended by their superior officers for their attempts to rescue the Army fliers from the Ice Cap. Ensign Fuller received the Navy and Marine Corps Medal, and the other members were recommended for official commendation. This expedition had to be evaluated more in terms of heroism than accomplishment.

While this effort was in progress, several other events took place. In a remarkable rescue at sea on 3 February 1943, *Escanaba* (Lieutenant Commander Carl U. Peterson) and *Comanche* (Lieutenant Commander R. R. Curry) saved a total of 225 men out of 299 who were rescued from the transport *Dorchester*, which had been attacked by a submarine about 150 miles south of Cape Farewell. *Dorchester*, with 904 men on board, was one of three vessels which these cutters were escorting from St. Johns, Newfoundland, to Greenland. She was torpedoed shortly after midnight and sank soon afterwards. The cutters worked in absolute darkness for more than eight hours, rescuing men in the water as submarines hovered nearby. Many men died of shock in the freezing water. Cutters *Duane* and *Tampa* tried to locate and attack the submarines and also searched for survivors.

It was here that the retriever method of rescue was first used. The majority of men in the water at this latitude were absolutely helpless and unable to climb up sea ladders or cargo nets slung over the side. It was futile to throw them lines. Instead, Coast Guardsmen were lowered over the side in rubber suits. They acted as retrievers, helping the men into boats or onto rafts by securing bowlines under their arms so that they could be pulled up over the side. These retrievers were in and out of the water for hours. Some swam long distances to save men who otherwise would have been lost. The work had to be done fast because of the freezing water and the presence of enemy submarines.

Individual heroism in this operation was commonplace, and resulted in many decorations. It was in *Dorchester* that three chaplains gained immortality by giving up their life jackets to others and going down with the ship. Of the 133 survivors picked up by *Escanaba*, one died soon after being taken on board. Twelve bodies were also recovered. *Comanche* rescued 93 men. A few months later, on 13 June 1943, *Escanaba* herself was destroyed, as is explained in Chapter 14.

Soon after the *Dorchester* incident, while escorting a convoy on 20 March 1943, cutter *Modoc* received a report from cutter *Algonquin* that the British vessel *Svend Foyne*, in convoy, had collided with an iceberg at 0450 the previous day about 100 miles south of Cape Farewell. The cutters immediately began search in the indicated area. Shortly after midnight on the 21st, they contacted cutter *Aivik* and verified the stricken vessel's position; they learned that passengers and crew had abandoned ship and were drifting in lifeboats and rafts. *HMS Hastings*, contacted by the cutters, also joined the search.

*Svend Foyne* was finally sighted in a group of two large and several small icebergs. Nearby were several lifeboats and cutter *Frederick Lee*. At 0133, *Modoc* maneuvered alongside one lifeboat and took on board 25 survivors—a difficult operation due to the deep roll of the vessel and the helplessness of the victims. At 0143 another lifeboat was located, and in 15 minutes, 16 more survivors had been rescued under similar difficulties. The other vessels also picked up survivors. *Modoc* found a raft 40 minutes later with men so weak they could not make lines fast; two or three fell into the freezing water and were drowned. Only two could be saved by *Modoc*. *Aivik* finally went alongside the raft and took off the rest. Three of *Modoc's* crew, Leonard W. Campbell, Chief Boatswain's Mate, John T. Hendrix, Chief Electrician's Mate, and William F. Coultas, Seaman First Class, particularly, distinguished themselves in these rescues by voluntarily going down the nets and attempting to secure lines about those struggling in the water. They were later awarded the Navy and Marine Corps Medal.

The rescue vessels took turns searching for other survivors and screening the other ships from possible submarine attack. At 0920, *Modoc* discontinued the search and *Hastings*, with 16 survivors, departed for Iceland. The other vessels transferred their survivors to *Modoc* for transportation to St. Johns. There were 22 from *Algonquin*, 42 from *Aivik*, and 20 from *Frederick Lee;* with those in *Modoc* and *Hastings*, the total rescued was 144.

One small group, known as the Canadian Arctic Task Unit, had as its mission the assistance and support of the U. S. Army in its area, through exercising Naval control over, and safeguarding, merchant vessels there. Coast Guard station vessels of this group were *Aklak* at Chimo and *Arluk* at Frobisher. The mission included arranging shipping schedules, routing, and providing escort, air coverage, and antisubmarine air sweeps if needed. The open period was short, July to October. The station ships, with *USS Bear*, which had no definite station in 1943, met Sydney-Greenland convoys and escorted vessels bound for the Canadian Arctic to a safe and sheltered position, usually in lower Frobisher Bay. There destinations were checked, mail was distributed, and the group was split under local escort as required.

Planes patrolled at every opportunity along the entrance to Hudson Strait and Frobisher Bay. They made the first ice survey on 30 May 1943, and these surveys continued as long as planes were available. Vessels were assisted through and around ice fields, leads were pointed out, and general limits of the ice fields to be encountered were indicated. Ice surveys of important portions of Labrador and Baffin Land as well as various hydrographic surveys were accomplished during the summer of 1943.

In the Spring of 1943, a German weather and radio station was finally uncovered on the east coast of Greenland. Three members of the Sledge Patrol, noticing two tiny black spots moving along the ridge of a mountain in the coastal region,

searched an empty cabin nearby. Sleeping bags, German uniforms, weapons, and food convinced them it was being used by the enemy. An alarm was sent out. A few nights later the Nazis appeared at another Sledge Patrol station. Challenged by a guard, they opened fire with automatic rifles and machine guns. The Danes, outnumbered, fled. One Dane was killed later when he returned unwittingly to this captured station; with his ears covered by a parka, he failed to hear the Nazi command to halt. The next day, another Sledge Patrol member walked into a Nazi trap. Directed to guide the Germans to a nearby Sledge Patrol station, the Dane cunningly persuaded the Nazis to divide into two parties and sent one on a long roundabout route to the station. Then he overpowered and took prisoner the one remaining Nazi left to guard him. The Dane delivered him safely into U. S. custody after a fabulous 40-day, 300-mile journey over the ice.

A task force of Coast Guard bombers, together with cutters *North Star* and *Northland*, sailed from Narsarssuak on 1 July 1943 to search out the enemy base from which the Nazis had come. Three Danes with 40 dogs completed this expedition, which arrived at Angmagssalik on 10 July. *North Star* became trapped and damaged in the ice there and had to proceed with *Northland* to Reykjavik, Iceland, for repairs. Undamaged *Northland* remained at Reykjavik but 14 hours and again headed for East Greenland to search for an enemy supply ship believed still afloat in Hansa Bay. En route, she fired on a German Junkers bomber without result.

Arriving at Shannon Island on 21 July, *Northland* sent up her plane for air reconnaissance. It was found that the Danish Sledge Patrol station, 30 miles to the south at Hansa Bay on Sabine Island, had been completely destroyed by fire. A landing force investigated and found indications of intended permanent Nazi occupation, but no actual occupation. All main buildings were burned; there was evidence everywhere of a bitter fight and subsequent hurried evacuation, evidently by air. It developed that Colonel Bernt Balchen, USA, had attacked the site by air on 25 May, apparently with complete success.

Only one German officer was eventually found; he identified himself as Dr. Rudolph Sennse, "assistant surgeon" and physician of the Nazi expedition. He had lost his dogs and sledge in an ice crevasse while scouting, and on return to camp had found the Americans there. He had been the Gestapo man of the Germans' Sabine Island garrison, and he was to take back information about the land and its people. Dr. Sennse had been ranging over northeast Greenland, as far south as Scorseby Sound, when Colonel Balchen bombed the Sabine Island installation. With his comrades gone, the station destroyed, and *Northland* present, he decided to give himself up rather than face starvation. Captain Charles W. Thomas of *Northland* had Sennse placed under guard and quartered him in the sick bay. This incident set off an intensified search for other Nazis and their installations.

On 23 July 1943, *North Star,* proceeding from Iceland to northeast Greenland, encountered a German reconnaissance plane north of Jan Mayen Island. This plane engaged in a machine gun duel with the cutter's gunners, was hit, and disappeared over the horizon, trailing heavy black smoke.

In Chapter 3, Coast Guard Patrol Bombing Squadron Six was mentioned. This special squadron, assigned to the Greenland Patrol, was probably the most colorful of all the Coast Guard aviation units. It was commissioned on 5 October 1943 at Argentia, Newfoundland, and sent to Narsarssuak, Greenland, to relieve Bombing Squadron 126. Its first commanding officer was Commander D. B. McDiarmid, USCG. The position of this unit was singular, its organization distinctive, its work colorful and dramatic. Personnel were entirely Coast Guard, but Navy planes were used.

The functions of Bombing Squadron Six were fivefold: air coverage for convoys, antisubmarine patrol, mail delivery, rescue duties, and observational surveys of ice conditions. Administrative control was vested in the Commander, Fleet Air Wing Nine, with the exception of personnel matters, which were under the immediate direction of Coast Guard Headquarters. The main base was at Narsarssuak, but detachments operated from Argentia and Reykjavik, and in the Canadian Arctic. After six months of operation (April 1944) the Squadron had 12 operational PBY-5A type Catalina planes based at Narsarssuak, and 5 officers, 24 aviators, 4 aviation pilots, and 152 enlisted men, including the pilots.

It was common for planes to fly under the most

trying weather conditions over several thousands of square miles of Greenland ice caps in a single rescue search. On routine patrols the bombers not infrequently sighted stranded vessels, or crews which had sometimes been adrift for weeks in the stormy northern seas. Radioed messages would send Coast Guard cutters speeding to the rescue.

There were operational difficulties, of course. Greenland weather and terrain limited aviation activities. The island has a mountain range of some 15,000 feet elevation extending around the entire coast, with fjords and harbors closed during the winter months by pack ice. About 85 percent of the interior is covered by a great ice cap of almost unbelievable thickness. The main squadron base had a single concrete runway down a sheltered fjord, and seven Quonset huts housed all activities including maintenance shops and barracks. Personnel were rotated frequently because of the rigorous duty. Two planes, assigned to the Canadian Arctic during summer and autumn, operated chiefly over Labrador, Cumberland Island, and Baffin Land, and were engaged primarily in rescue, reconnaissance, and coverage missions. Patrol and observation flights carried these planes as far north as the Ugaba, Frobisher, and Hudson Bays.

The duties of Bombing Squadron Six required mostly high altitude flying; the extensive ice caps made landing on about 90 percent of the island impractical, if not impossible. Flying at high danger point, with wind velocities sometimes as great as 120 to 185 miles an hour, far from landing bases, required high courage and expert skill; well trained pilots and crews were necessary. The men selected for this duty contributed more glory and renown to Coast Guard aviation.

This Squadron flew 6,235 hours between August 1943, and the end of November 1944; this represented 638,998 miles cruised, an area of 3,213,605 square miles searched, and many assistance flights and memorable rescues. Assistance rendered to grounded crews or pilots usually consisted of spotting survivors, dropping emergency kits and supplies, and marking the spot for later rescue. Most flights, however, were routine convoy coverages and ice patrols. For a period of three months in 1944 Lieutenant C. H. Allen maintained an average of more than 100 hours a month in the air over difficult Arctic terrain. The two Iceland planes under Lieutenant Commander G. R.

Evans, flew 410 hours during 60 flights in about the same period. Some 20 percent of this was night flying and about 15 percent was instrument flying under the most trying conditions of snow, ice, sleet, and rain. Several 300 to 400-mile reconnaissance flights were made in extremely low temperatures with unheated planes. During fiscal year 1944, the Squadron aided 43 planes and vessels, and rescued or assisted 47 persons. One medical case and 87 other persons were transported. Of the other 1,153 flights, 71 were for assistance, 346 for antisubmarine patrol and convoy coverage, and 736 were routine missions.

Vessels on Greenland Patrol in October 1943, when activity was close to its peak, were the original cutters *Northland, North Star, Modoc, Comanche, Raritan;* USS *Bear,* and the Coast and Geodetic ship *Bowdoin;* and converted trawlers *Aivik, Aklak, Alatok, Amarok, Arluk, Arvek, Atak, Nanok,* and *Nogak.* In addition were cutters *Active, Algonquin, Arundel, Faunce, Frederick Lee, Laurel, Manitou, Mohawk, Mojave, Storis, Tahoma, Tampa,* and *Travis.* There were the Coast Guard-manned naval vessels *Albatross, Bluebird,* and SCs *527, 528, 688, 689, 704,* and *705.*

On 21 November 1943, the Greenland Patrol was placed under command of Commodore Earl G. Rose, USCG.

Just one week later, an AT-7 plane was reported lost. Commander McDiarmid (Commanding Patrol Bombing Squadron Six) began a search two days later, covering an area of 6,000 square miles for two days. Lieutenant (jg) B. B. Dameron, Lieutenant D. M. Morrell, Lieutenant A. W. Weuker, R. E. Asterberg, C.A.P., Lieutenant A. F. Perkins, and Lieutenant Commander R. R. Johnson all joined the search. It was Weuker who finally located the wrecked plane on the edge of the Sukkertoppen Ice Cap at 65° 52′ N, 50° 22′ W, on 1 December. Black debris was seen scattered with a smudge on the snow north of it. On a second flight, on the 7th, Weuker was able to mark the spot with flag stakes. Final verification did not come until the 21st when photographs were successfully taken to guide the actual rescue party. A Coast Guard PBY-5A directed this party on 5 January 1944 over the last 10 miles to the wreckage; dropped provisions; and otherwise assisted.

Heroism and tragedy marked the rescue by *Comanche* (Lieutenant Langford Anderson) on 15-16 December 1943, of 29 men and a dog from the 1685-ton Army freighter *Nevada.* The stricken vessel had been abandoned about 1300 on the 15th when her forepeak and No. 1 hold became flooded and pumps could not keep up with the inflow of water. She finally went down in a raging gale about 200 miles southwest of Cape Farewell, Greenland. Detached at 1352 on the 15th from escorting a Newfoundland-to-Greenland convoy, *Comanche* set out to aid the foundering ship in bad weather which turned into a furious storm as early darkness fell.

The wind reached 60 miles an hour, whipping up huge seas. Heavy snow squalls cut visibility to zero. *Comanche* reached *Nevada* after seven hours, to find the wallowing freighter down by the bow with a 30° list. Receiving no answer to the usual challenge, Lieutenant Anderson illuminated the vessel with his searchlight and identified it. The boat falls were empty and the ship appeared to have been abandoned. Two red flares downwind signified the location of the lifeboats, and the cutter proceeded in their direction. At 2231, with the storm at the height of its fury, the cutter sighted a lifeboat containing about 30 men who had been fighting the raging seas for nine hours. They were praying and singing, with shouts of "Thank God!" rising above the howl of the gale. All hands in *Comanche* were ordered to rescue stations, and volunteers in rubber suits stood by to dive overboard.

The chances of bringing the lifeboat alongside in those heavy seas were slight. One minute it lay in the trough far below the cutter's rail, and the next it would be lifted high above her deck on the crest of a comber. After many attempts, a sea painter was passed by heaving line, making it possible to bring the boat along the starboard side. Three men were hauled on board. Then the sea pitched the lifeboat under *Comanche's* No. 1 lifeboat which was rigged out. Three other survivors leaped on their boat's gunwale, preparing to jump to the cutter on the next upsurge, despite orders from *Comanche* to remain seated. Falling into the sea, one sank immediately and the other two drifted away. The lifeboat was cut loose while *Comanche* headed for the men in the water.

As the drowning men were held in the searchlight, four volunteers in rubber suits, with bowlines under their arms, were lowered over the side one by one. William G. Mitchell, Storekeeper First Class, was the first to dive into the heavy seas in an effort to rescue the two men struggling in the water. He was smashed unconscious against the side of the cutter and hauled back. Arthur Nickerson, Carpenter's Mate First Class, dived next. He nearly succeeded, but after getting his legs around the survivor and being hauled to the ship's side, he too was battered into unconsciousness, and hauled on board. The survivor had slipped from his grasp. Robert C. Vile, Fireman First Class, was third. After reaching his man and towing him to the cutter's side Vile, in turn, was battered and beaten by the sea into a state of helplessness; his man slipped away, and when last seen, was apparently dead, floating face down supported by a life preserver. Vile was pulled to safety with difficulty.

The second survivor was still alive, so *Comanche* headed for him. Philip Feldman, Fireman First Class, volunteered to go over the side. Poised on the rail in a rubber suit, Feldman was about to dive. In the darkness a sudden snow squall hid the man from view, and at the same moment the cutter's searchlight burned out. By the time the squall had passed and new carbons were placed in the searchlight, the man in the water could not be found.

Meanwhile the lifeboat with 26 men had been temporarily lost, but was soon located. Two unsuccessful attempts were made to pass a line by a shoulder line-throwing gun. At last a heaving line was thrown into the lifeboat and a sea painter made fast to a thwart. The surging sea pulled the thwart loose but not until several survivors had been hauled to the cutter on the ends of long bowlines passed over their heads and under their arms. Despite four interruptions when thwarts were pulled out, the remaining men were pulled one by one to safety. The last man placed his line around "Grondal", the mascot dog of *Nevada*, and consented to be saved only after the dog had been rescued.

Later, on the 17th and 18th, *Storis*, *Modoc*, and *Tampa* joined in the search for additional survivors, but abandoned it on the 19th. It was learned that Captain George P. Turiga, with 31 of his crew, had been in a second lifeboat which had capsized on leaving the ship. Two rafts on the *Nevada* had also been cut loose, and some men were seen to scramble on board them, but there was no chance for men to live on rafts in that storm. Boarding and salvage work was impossible in the heavy seas and towing the steamer could not be undertaken. On 18 December 1943, *Nevada* sank in position 55° 27′ N, 47° 13′ W. Later, Mitchell, Nickerson, and Vile received the Navy and Marine Corps Medal, while Feldman's action was recorded under "Meritorious Conduct" in his service record. All were highly commended by Lieutenant Anderson.

Weather patrol might be considered a subsidiary activity of the Greenland Patrol. This was carried out in the North Atlantic by various Coast Guard vessels. Weather observations proved so valuable that in the Spring of 1944 the number of stations was increased from two to six. On patrol 24 hours a day, these vessels, besides sending in weather reports six or eight times daily, were on the lookout for enemy aircraft, surface ships or submarines, sudden storms, and ditched planes. They acted as plane guards serving a growing number of American and British transatlantic flights. It was estimated that, during 1944, there was a daily average of 54 flights across the North Atlantic or in the Greenland area, exclusive of 50 Naval Air Transport flights a month between Newfoundland, the Azores, and Europe, and about 100 flights a month by chartered commercial planes. Stations in the Greenland area during 1943 were in Davis Strait, Denmark Strait, and south of Cape Farewell. All stations kept in touch with every plane in the area by radio. This activity is treated separately in Chapter 9.

The battle with the German weather and shipping observation expeditions to Greenland came to its climax between July and October of 1944. Four cutters finally smashed through ice packs a few hundred miles south of the North Pole, to break up a determined Nazi effort to establish fortified bases on the northeast coast of Greenland. Concerned were *Northland* and *Storis*, and the newly commissioned icebreakers *Southwind* and *Eastwind*. Together, they captured 60 Germans, routed three German trawlers, and destroyed two enemy weather and radio stations.

The Sledge Patrol had reported a Nazi weather and radio station in the neighborhood of Shannon

Island. The Sledge Patrol officer had been surprised by a Nazi officer while observing the station and had shot the German in a gun duel.

In July, *Northland* and *Storis* were sent to the area to furnish supplies for the Sledge Patrol and to destroy the reported station.

The cutters carried some Army personnel for a joint Army-Coast Guard landing force. A platoon of 24 men under Lieutenant Philip S. Pepe and Ensign Benjamin D. Fleet from *Northland* joined a *Storis* landing party of 15 under command of Lieutenant (jg) LeWayne N. Felts for the attack. The 25 Army men were commanded by Captain Bruce M. Minnick and Second Lieutenant Robert C. Nelson. It was planned for the party to land on the island and attempt to go overland from the south to the Nazi installation which was known to be fortified with machine guns, rifles, and grenades.

As the ice pack had moved into the bay in front of Cape Sussi, the location of the enemy base, the landing force hoped to surprise the Nazis. Unfortunately, bad weather bringing heavy snow, sleet and mushed-out trails, made it impossible to penetrate inland more than six miles. A stronger force was put ashore three days later. Part of this group was to make a base camp on the way to Cape Sussi from which the attacking Americans could operate, but weather spoiled these plans, too. Eventually, the landing force, worn and weatherbeaten, arrived at Cape Sussi. Meanwhile, a shift of the wind had opened leads through the ice pack in the bay, so *Northland* moved around the island and sent another landing party ashore.

The Americans found a deserted Nazi building, so well camouflaged that it could be seen only from a certain angle. Smashed instruments indicated a hasty flight. Search disclosed that ice caves nearby contained a large stock of gasoline, food and ammunition. Parts of a radio capable of direct communication with Germany were discovered. The Americans fired the base, and returned to their ship.

As the cutters were leaving, *Northland's* lookout reported a vessel caught in the ice about four miles away. Heavy pack ice prevented close approach, but from the air the vessel appeared to have been abandoned. An investigation party of 16 men under Lieutenant F. H. Harmon went over the ice to the vessel and reported back that she was a 155-foot armed Nazi trawler, beset and crushed by the ice. She was gutted by fire, and an explosion had holed her badly. It was evident that the German crew and other expeditionary passengers had moved all food, ammunition, and supplies to the ice and to the building where they had lived for some time. Two anti-aircraft guns had been removed from the ship and set up nearby on the ice. Parachute cylinders indicated that the men had been supplied by air. This vessel was believed to be *Coberg*, carrying one of the apparently three separate German expeditions to northeast Greenland.

A second Nazi vessel was disposed of 1 September by *Northland*, after a 70-mile race through twisting paths between ice floes off Great Koldewey Island. For seven hours, the cutter chased this Nazi trawler toward the southernmost tip of Great Koldewey, where the German became blocked by a long finger of ice. Spotted 7½ miles away by a *Northland* lookout in the early Arctic dawn, the Nazi was challenged, but instead of answering she altered her course and attempted to dodge into the ice pack. *Northland* immediately gave chase, and although the enemy ship was faster, managed to keep within about 10,000 yards. Whenever the trawler, appearing intermittently between ice and floes, came within range, *Northland* fired. As the range closed rapidly, the cutter began continuous fire with her forward gun. Unreadable signals from the trawler were observed at 1001, and again at 1014 when the Nazi was told to stop. However, the enemy kept her speed, and the shelling continued. No hits were observed. Finally, the cutter gained valuable yardage and her shells began dropping uncomfortably close to the fleeing craft.

Lieutenant Commander R. W. Butcher, commanding *Northland*, feared the trawler might round the tip of Great Koldewey and enter clear water where her superior speed would enable her to escape. As the enemy reached the turning point she suddenly stopped, enabling *Northland* to come rapidly within effective gun range. Shells splashed up the wake of the trawler. Two explosions at 1042, one forward and one aft, suddenly ripped the enemy craft. The Nazis had scuttled their ship rather than have her fall into American hands. She sank in three minutes in 23 fathoms of water. As three lifeboats pulled swiftly toward the beach,

*Northland's* 20-mms were manned to stop any overland escape. The cutter anchored 500 yards from the tip of the island. The lifeboats came alongside with eight officers and 20 enlisted men. These Germans surrendered and were taken on board *Northland*. A Nazi commander dramatically handed over his sword to Lieutenant Commander Butcher, who later had it framed and hung in *Northland's* wardroom.

About four months after her commissioning, the new icebreaker *Eastwind* was engaged on Greenland Patrol, and accounted for the third German trawler. *Eastwind* was flagship of the Task Unit carrying out the operation against the weather and radio stations of the Nazis. Both were under command of Captain Charles W. Thomas, who had formerly commanded *Northland*. On 2 October 1944, while off Shannon Island 600 miles north of Iceland, Captain Thomas sent his plane northward on reconnaissance. It returned with word of a "big ship" about 100 miles away. The commanding officer knew it was an enemy ship, and that he must destroy or capture her.

*Eastwind* immediately started northward to make contact. Estimating the enemy's probable course, the icebreaker was headed to intercept. She ran all night, meeting new ice which became harder and thicker. At daybreak a solid, heavy wall of the main polar pack stretched across the horizon. The plane was sent again on reconnaissance and, on return, the observer reported what appeared to be building materials on North Little Koldewey Island.

Captain Thomas pushed through 12 miles of pack ice under cover of darkness to make a night landing and surprise the enemy's rear. Ice was broken so the boats could get to shore, and at 0400 the landing party, under command of Lieutenant (jg) Alden Lewis hit the beach. Taken by surprise and outnumbered, the entire force of 12 Germans surrendered. They were placed on board *Eastwind*, together with virtually all the equipment, including well-built housing, valuable radio and meteorological equipment, tons of food and munitions, and countless miscellaneous items. Important top-secret documents, which the Nazi commander unsuccessfully attempted to destroy, were also taken.

These documents revealed that the German naval transport *Externsteine* had landed these men, and it was doubtless that ship which the plane had spotted. Several unsuccessful reconnaissance flights were followed by one on 14 October which located the ship frozen solid in a consolidated field of polar ice about 10 miles off Shannon Island. *Southwind*, which had joined the Task Unit, and *Eastwind* started to close in. The latter was able to follow leads to within seven miles of the objective. Picking up the target by radar, she crushed her way laboriously through the ice for five miles. Three salvos were then fired, taking care to hit around the ship but not the ship itself. A blinker message from the enemy read: "We give up."

The icebreaker progressed to within 200 yards of *Externsteine*, and a landing force crossed the intervening ice to receive the vessel's surrender. All the prisoners, except for the captain and chief engineer, were taken on board. A prize crew of 32 men from *Eastwind* boarded the captured vessel. The icebreaker broke *Externsteine* free, and the two proceeded to Hochstetter Bay to rendezvous with *Southwind* which had been ordered there because of a damaged propeller.

The captured vessel was unofficially renamed *Eastbreeze* by the 32 men who became a permanent crew, with Lieutenant Curtis Howard in command. New equipment was installed. She was readied for patrol work, but this lasted only a few days. She was then sent to Reykjavik, Iceland, where she arrived on 30 October, and reached Boston on 14 December. Taken over by the Navy, she became *USS Callo*.

After the *Externsteine* incident, there was little of a combat nature to occupy the Greenland Patrol. Thereafter, operations were largely security patrol and rescue activity.

As a result of the Greenland Patrol with surface ships and planes, the enemy was prevented from attempting an invasion of the Western Hemisphere on the scale of the invasion of Norway, and those enemy expeditions that did arrive in Greenland were thoroughly routed. Without these bases in Greenland, German U-boat attacks, especially on the northern convoy routes, were greatly restricted. In short, the men who kept Greenland free, not only protected America from invasion, but denied the enemy vital weather and shipping information. The Greenland Patrol was a positive factor in winning the Atlantic Battle.

# Chapter 8

# RESCUES AT SEA

A BRIEF OUTLINE of how saving life and property at sea developed as a duty of the old Revenue Marine was given in the Prologue to this history. This has been a major responsibility of the Coast Guard and its predecessor organizations almost since the first. In the preceding pages, it has been made clear how the saving of life and property was interwoven with all the other duties which devolved upon the Coast Guard. This was a corollary duty in virtually every activity, whether it be Greenland Patrol, convoy escort, weather patrol, air reconnaissance, aids to navigation, port security in its various phases, small boat patrol, beach patrol, or direct combat. This traditional role of the Coast Guard was always present.

There were infrequent times when, cruel as it may seem, importance of some work at hand subordinated this function. For instance, sinking a submarine to prevent a future loss of ships and lives sometimes appeared more vital than saving a half dozen lives at some particular moment.

Throughout the war, it was virtually impossible to separate saving of life and property from the other activities. This is evident from accounts already given. Yet, even though such episodes were often incidental to other operations, daring, selfless devotion to duty, superb seamanship, and downright heroism were so frequent and so outstanding as to merit special mention. Even so, space limitations require omission of many cases which

deserve lasting tribute in any wartime history of the Coast Guard.

What was the scope of these rescue operations? Some idea may be gained from an examination of the record of soldiers and seamen saved during the European phase of World War II. In all, 4,243 military personnel and merchant seamen were saved by the Coast Guard. These included 1,658 survivors of enemy torpedoings along the Atlantic Coast, in the Gulf of Mexico, and in the Caribbean Sea, who were brought in by Coast Guard vessels and planes. In addition Coast Guard cutters saved 810 in the North Atlantic, and 115 in the Mediterranean. Furthermore, 1,660 were hauled to safety by invasion rescue cutters of the Coast Guard in the English Channel during the assault on Normandy. Hundreds of others were rescued by Coast Guard-manned Navy vessels, and through joint action by the Coast Guard and other services.

Of the 4,453,061 United States soldiers embarked by ship to fight the Axis in Europe and Africa, only 3,594 were lost at sea—a truly amazing record. This record was better than the record in World War I, despite the greater deadliness of U-boats, bombing planes, and mines in the later war.

Here is a list of the more important sinkings of vessels bearing Army troops, with the date and location of sinking, as well as the number of lives lost in each.

| Name of Vessel | Date | Location | Lives Lost |
|---|---|---|---|
| Rohna | 26 November 1943 | Off Djidjelli, Algeria | 1,015 |
| Leopoldville | 24 December 1944 | Off Cherbourg, France | 764 |
| Paul Hamilton | 20 April 1944 | Off Algiers | 504 |
| Dorchester | 3 February 1943 | Off Greenland | 404 |
| Henry R. Mallory | 7 February 1943 | Off Greenland | 86 |
| H. G. Blaisdel | 29 June 1944 | English Channel | 76 |
| J. W. McAndrews | 13 March 1945 | Off Azores | 68 |
| William B. Woods | 9 March 1944 | North of Palermo, Sicily | 51 |
| Cherokee | 15 June 1942 | East of Boston | 20 |

| | | | | |
|---|---|---|---|---|
| *LST 313* | 10 July | 1943 | Mediterranean | 20 |
| *Sicilien* | 7 June | 1942 | South of Haiti | **19** |
| *Coamo* | * December | 1942 | Atlantic Ocean | **16** |
| *Daniel C. French* | 3 March | 1944 | Off Bizerte, Tunisia | **14** |
| *Samuel J. Tilden* | 2 December | 1943 | Bari, Italy | 14 |
| *Empire Javelin* | 28 December | 1944 | Off Cherbourg, France | 14 |
| *Uruguay* | 12 February | 1943 | Northeast of Bermuda | 13 |
| *Louise Lykes* | 11 January | 1943 | Atlantic Ocean | 10 |
| | | | 23 other vessels | 486 |
| | | | | |
| | | | **Total** | 3,594 |

* Date uncertain

The Coast Guard's most intense lifesaving activity was in the dark days of early 1942, when Nazi submarines were running rampant along the Atlantic and Gulf Coasts, picking off freighters and tankers even within sight of land. Offshore patrol cutters and craft from lifeboat stations rescued survivors from ships of all leading maritime nations. During the period of the war, 674 United States merchant ships (total gross tonnage 4,156,849) were lost on all oceans. Of this total tonnage only one-fourth, or 1,081,417, were being escorted or in convoy when sunk.

The following accounts of certain rescues form some of the most thrilling pages in the history of the Coast Guard.

Six months before the United States entered the war, cutter *Duane,* while on weather observation patrol in the North Atlantic, picked up an SOS radio call from the British steamship *Tresillian.* This vessel was being shelled by a German submarine. Reaching the reported position by daylight of 14 June 1941, the cutter began searching for survivors, working to eastward. Three U. S. Navy flying boats soon signaled that assistance was needed, and the cutter proceeded 20 miles farther eastward, as indicated by the planes. There, two drifting lifeboats filled with survivors were sighted, and the victims were taken on board. These proved to be *Tresillian's* entire crew. Had it not been for the cooperation of the Navy planes, however, *Duane* might never have found the lifeboats, as they had drifted 20 miles from the scene of the sinking.

On 7 December 1941, the day of Pearl Harbor, the 6,256-ton American freighter *Mauna Ala* was ordered back to port after having started for Australia. She was groping her way along our darkened Pacific Coast during a blackout test on 10 December 1941, unaware that all lighted aids to navigation had been blacked out. Mistaking her position, she ran aground on Clatsop Beach, Oregon, and lay in moderately heavy ground swells. Cutter *Onondaga,* patrolling north of Columbia River Lightship, was directed to the scene by radio direction finder bearings, and by a searchlight at Fort Stevens. At *Onondaga's* request, *Mauna Ala's* navigational lights were relighted and the cutter closed in. Repeated efforts by *Onondaga* and other craft to float the vessel failed. The stranded ship began to take water and break up. Thirty-six persons on board were removed, and the million dollar vessel, with its $100,000 cargo, became another victim of the sea.

An early indication of enemy barbarism with no concern for human life was recognized on 14 January 1942. An enemy submarine torpedoed the Panamanian tanker *Norness* which was carrying fuel oil from New York to Halifax. Cutter *Argo,* then at Newport, Rhode Island, was ordered to the scene, about 150 miles distant. After several hours at full speed she reached the unfortunate tanker, a grim sight with stern submerged and bow still projecting 40 feet above water. *Argo* sighted a capsized motor launch, and three rafts, on one of which (under the hovering Navy Blimp K6) were huddled 6 frightened survivors, their drawn faces reflecting the ordeal through which they had passed. These 6, who were rescued, were all that remained of a crew of 40.

Four days later, an enemy submarine torpedoed and then shelled an American tanker, but failed to sink her. The tanker eventually escaped. After what appeared to be a lethal torpedoing off the North Carolina coast on 19 January 1942, three crew members of the tanker *Malay* left the vessel in a lifeboat. No others abandoned ship. When

FLYING OVER TREACHEROUS TERRAIN . . . . a Coast Guard plane searches the rugged Greenland coast.

CUTTER *NORTH STAR* HEADS FOR GREENLAND WATERS . . . . a worthy veteran of Arctic and Antarctic ice.

ICING WAS A SERIOUS PROBLEM . . . . it could cause loss of stability and make vital equipment useless until freed.

CONVERTED TRAWLER *NATSEK* . . . . lost without a trace, possibly a victim of ice.

CUTTER *NORTHLAND* ON GREENLAND PATROL . . . . plane on after deck made many valuable reconnaissance flights.

ARMED GERMAN TRAWLER *EXTERNSTEINE* IN THE ICE . . . . *Eastwind* broke her free and placed a prize crew on board.

ICEBREAKER *EASTWIND* IN HER ELEMENT . . . . ice was no barrier between her and the Nazis.

BAFFIN BAY FJORD FROM THE AIR . . . . flying over
such territory was dangerous business.

COAST GUARD VESSELS IN THE FAR NORTH . . . .
a cutter and a seagoing tug in a Greenland fjord.

COAST GUARD PLANE PATROLS GREENLAND COAST . . . . this photograph was taken by
Lieutenant Thomas S. La Farge, skipper of ill-fated *Natsek*.

ABANDONED NAZI TRAWLER BELIEVED TO BE
*COBERG* . . . . landing party from *Northland*, in background, inspects icebound, crushed, and gutted vessel.

GERMAN RADIO SHACK ON SHANNON ISLAND,
GREENLAND . . . . Coast Guardsmen from cutter surround
the recently abandoned installation before destroying it.

END OF A NAZI RADIO-WEATHER STATION . . . . a file of bewildered Germans
surrenders to a Coast Guard landing force.

SURVIVORS OF TORPEDOED VESSEL ARE DRAWN ALONGSIDE . . . . half-frozen and fighting to keep their grip on a tossing life raft.

MID-ATLANTIC SWIMMER IS RESCUED . . . . Earl N. Phillips fell from his ship in westbound convoy and was picked **up by** Coast Guard-manned destroyer escort.

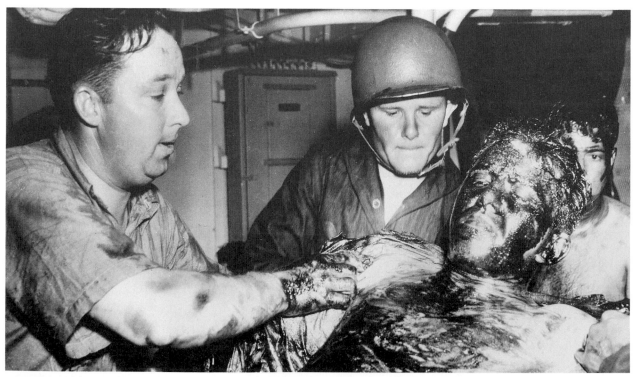

AN OIL-COVERED *LANSDALE* SAILOR IS RESCUED . . . . Coast Guard-manned DEs *Menges* and *Newell* rescued 230 men from ill-fated destroyer *Lansdale* off the coast of North Africa.

TO THE RESCUE, FRIEND OR FOE . . . . German sailors from sunken submarine just before being taken on board Coast Guard cutter.

TIME-HONORED BREECHES BUOY SAVES STRANDED CREW . . . . men of the Virginia Beach Lifeboat Station save thirteen crew members from grounded vessel.

*HENRY R. MALLORY* SURVIVOR REACHES SAFETY . . . . *Bibb* saved 202 lives after U-Boat
sent *Mallory* to the bottom of the Atlantic.

DAMAGED DESTROYER ESCORT *MENGES* IS TOWED TO PORT . . . . shortly after the *Lansdale* rescue *Menges* herself suffered a Nazi torpedo hit which carried away a third of her hull. Later, she and bowless *Holder* were joined to produce
a single DE—named *Menges.*

boats from the Oregon Inlet and other Coast Guard stations arrived, the master, who had remained on board with 34 crew members, reported that his vessel had been unmercifully shelled subsequent to the torpedoing.

*Malay* then got under way and headed for port. Later, the enemy again appeared and began a further bombardment of the already badly crippled vessel. *Malay* was struck amidships, leaving a gaping hole and flooding No. 7 tank. She remained afloat, however. Eluding the enemy, she raced with all the speed she could make, and limped into Norfolk under her own power. One crew member was killed during the shelling; three were seriously injured. The injured were taken on board a motor lifeboat from the Oregon Inlet Lifeboat Station.

On 23 January 1942, when 12 miles south of Hatteras, the British tanker *Empire Gem* was torpedoed and burst into flames. Motor Lifeboat No. *4464* of the Hatteras Inlet Lifeboat Station was sent to the scene, and after arrival, maneuvered around the burning tanker and stood by as close as possible until midnight. As there were no signs of life, she left to search for lifeboats which might have been launched. As if the danger of drowning was not enough when a ship was sinking, an added hazard was often thrown in for good measure, and both fire and water raced to claim lives. Motor Lifeboat No. *5426* from the Ocracoke Lifeboat Station was proceeding to the assistance of steamship *Venore* at 2030 that same night when she received orders to change her course and proceed to *Empire Gem*. She arrived at the scene at 0300 the next morning. The crew sighted three men on the tanker's bow, away from the fire which extended from amidships to the stern.

Finding it impossible, in the heavy seas, to get near enough to take the men off, this lifeboat stood by to await dawn. At 0700 the lifeboat got close to the tanker, and the three imperiled men jumped overboard. The lifeboat crew picked up two of them, and barely missed the third man who was swept into the burning oil and sank.

After a fruitless search, the Hatteras boat returned to the burning tanker and contacted the Ocracoke lifeboat. The two survivors, who were *Empire Gem's* master and radioman, were transferred from the Ocracoke boat to that from Hatteras and departed for Hatteras Inlet. The

Ocracoke lifeboat remained to search for life rafts which might have put out from the ship. A third motor lifeboat was ordered out from Oregon Inlet Lifeboat Station, 75 miles away, but arrived too late to assist effectively.

Three days later, on 27 January 1942, a dual role of bombing the enemy from the air and bringing aid to survivors was played by Coast Guard airplane V-175, piloted by Lieutenant Commander R. L. Burke from the Elizabeth City (N.C.) Air Station. The plane received a distress call from the 7,096-ton American tanker *Frances E. Powell* that she was being overhauled by a submarine, eight miles off Currituck Light, south of Virginia Beach. The tanker was sunk soon afterward. A Coast Guard-piloted J2F-5 plane first sighted the submarine and dropped two depth charges within 100 feet of the submerged marauder. Then Commander Burke in the V-175 dropped a grapnel with 100 feet of line and two life jackets to buoy the spot so that destroyers could later depth charge the area. It seemed likely that the enemy had been damaged because Burke later saw and photographed what appeared to be a distress buoy from a submarine. All but four of the tanker's crew of 32 were eventually saved by surface craft brought to the scene by the two planes.

The Coast Guard performed another rescue on 3 February 1942, this time off Lewes, Delaware. The sinking Panamanian (United Fruit) freighter *San Gil*, from Santa Marta, Colombia to Philadelphia with bananas, sent an SOS which was intercepted by cutter *Nike* at 2400. *Nike* immediately proceeded to the scene and took on board the 39 crew members and one passenger. A surfboat from the Ocean City (N.J.) Lifeboat Station also arrived and towed *San Gil's* two empty lifeboats to that station.

The American tanker *China Arrow* (8,403 tons), was torpedoed on 5 February 1942 just southeast of Ocean City, Maryland. She was en route to New York from Beaumont, Texas. Her crew of 37 escaped unscathed in their three lifeboats, but were adrift two days before being picked up by *Nike* with the assistance of Coast Guard aircraft. The cutter took them to Lewes, Delaware; they were unaffected, except by exposure.

The 5,000-ton Brazilian steamship *Buarque*, carrying a general cargo, 11 passengers, and a crew of 74, fell victim to an enemy submarine 10 days later. En route from Rio de Janeiro to New York, 34 crew members and 8 passengers lost their lives. Cutter *Calypso*, with a Coast Guard plane as spotter, located two of her lifeboats carrying 42 survivors, and took them on board. Insufficiently clad, the victims were suffering severely from exposure and cold.

On the following day, 16 February 1942, Coast Guardsmen on board cutter *Woodbury*, patrolling off the Chesapeake Bay entrance, heard a deafening explosion and immediately proceeded to the locality. They found a lifeboat with 11 survivors, and after further search, three more lifeboats containing the rest of the crew of 40 of the United States tanker *E. H. Blum*. The latter had been traveling in ballast from Philadelphia to Port Arthur, Texas, when she was either torpedoed or struck a mine. The survivors were taken to the Navy Section Base, Little Creek, Virginia, and two injured men were hospitalized at Norfolk. Eventually, *Blum* was salvaged; her two halves, which remained afloat, were towed to Philadelphia and rejoined, and the ship later returned into service.

From Cape Canaveral, the Florida eastern shore forms one side of the Florida Straits which stretch about 40 miles east to the Bahama Banks. Here deep water flows close to the Florida coast. Thousands of ships annually travel the Gulf Stream, funneling through the Straits, and wartime traffic became heavy. These narrow waters were a natural "happy hunting ground" for enemy submarines. Before sufficient naval strength became available to ward off undersea attacks, 24 ships had been sunk there. From these ships, 504 men were saved. Coast Guard lifeboat stations and their crews were often the sole hope of submarine victims. They proved themselves worthy, time and again.

On the night of 19 February 1942, the American tanker *Pan Massachusetts* was torpedoed by a submarine in a storm-swept sea at the north end of the Florida Straits. "Flames sighted 20 miles, 142 degrees from Cape Canaveral," a calm voice reported from the lighthouse at that Cape. Cutter *Forward*, sent to investigate, found that the process of abandoning ship on board the burning tanker had been complicated by the swiftly spreading blaze. The flaming lifeboats were useless. The 38 crewmen had leaped overboard into a sea of fire. A British passenger vessel, *Elizabeth Massey*,

only a short distance away when the torpedo struck, had put over a lifeboat.

*Forward* took the lifeboat in tow and moved slowly through the wreckage. As a survivor was spotted, the British seamen in the lifeboat cast loose from the cutter, picked their way to the struggling victim—usually thickly caked with oil —and took him on board. Then, avoiding the flaming oil, they would maneuver back to the cutter. All bodies recovered were placed on board *Forward*, and all 18 survivors on board *Elizabeth Massey*, which then proceeded to Jacksonville.

Three more ships went down two nights later, two off Jupiter Inlet, and one southeast of Cape Canaveral. The first was the 5,287-ton American tanker *Republic*, which was hit late on the night of 21 February. Twenty-two of her crew made shore in a lifeboat just south of Jupiter Inlet. Seven others were picked up by a passing steamer and taken to Port Everglades, where they were turned over to the Coast Guard.

During efforts to save *Republic*, a second tanker, *Cities Service Empire* (8,103 tons) was torpedoed farther off shore early in the morning of the 22nd. Cutter *Vigilant* was the first vessel to reach her, arriving at 0800. Passing 36 survivors, who had taken to life rafts and could be attended to later, Lieutenant L. R. Daniels, Commanding Officer of *Vigilant*, nosed his ship up to the blazing *Empire's* bow where he had seen three men fouled in the lifeboat falls. Crawling on board the lifeboat, Coast Guardsmen battled flames as they labored to work the victims free. Two were brought on board, but as rescue crews started back for the third, the tanker exploded and sank, spraying *Vigilant* from stem to stern with unignited oil. Lifeboats from Fort Pierce Lifeboat Station assisted in the search for bodies; seven were recovered, including that of the man Lieutenant Daniels and his crew had almost saved. Meanwhile, the U. S. Navy destroyer *Biddle* had taken the 36 crew members from their life rafts about a mile away.

Finally, while details from the Palm Beach Auxiliary and the Lake Worth Lifeboat Station were taking soundings at the scene of the *Republic* disaster, tanker *W. D. Anderson*, 10,227 tons, was attacked nearby. It took the Auxiliary less than 40 minutes to organize a search of the area. Only one crewman escaped from this sinking. The search was finally abandoned after rescuing the lone survivor, who had seen the torpedo track and leaped to safety before the explosion.

A six weeks lull ensued along the east coast of Florida due partly to measures taken by a handful of ships and 18 Coast Guard planes. Nine planes from the Air Station at St. Petersburg and nine from that at Miami were divided into three squadrons. Based at Banana River, they patrolled day and night in conjunction with the Navy.

Meanwhile, elsewhere along the Atlantic coast, enemy submarines were raising havoc with our shipping, much of which was still unescorted in convoy. The American freighter *Marore*, 8,215 tons, with a cargo of precious iron ore, had set out from Chile and, eluding the enemy, had reached a position off Big Kinnakeet (N.C.) Lifeboat Station on 26 February 1942, when a torpedo blasted her and sent her to the bottom. Shortly afterward, the lifeboat station lookout saw a small boat rigged with a sail endeavoring to make shore. A motor surfboat from the station went to meet it, and, finding on board the master and 13 crew members of *Marore*, helped them to land in safety. Three or four of the crew were lost.

The lookout of the Shark River Lifeboat Station on the New Jersey coast, while scanning the ocean from his lookout tower on 28 February 1942, sighted what appeared to be a ship afire. A picket boat and motor lifeboat from Shark River and Manasquan were immediately sent out at top speed toward the burning vessel. On arrival at 0200, the picket boat found the Standard Oil Company tanker *R. P. Resor*, 7,451 tons, afire from bow to stern. Apparently the ship had been hit above the waterline with one or more shells which exploded, setting the oil on fire. Oil seemed to be pouring from the ship faster than the fire could burn it. Blazing oil had spread from the bow toward the south for a distance of 500 feet.

The Coast Guard boat cruised as closely as possible to the burning vessel, when voices were heard crying for help. The smoke that arose was, at times, blinding; and the heat was so intense that the Coast Guardsmen were almost overcome. Nevertheless, they brought their boat close to the inferno in an effort to reach the victims, who were threatened with envelopment by the flames. Suddenly there bobbed up before the Coast Guard boat a man so thickly covered with oil as to be almost unrecognizable as a human being. He must have been three times his normal weight, making it difficult to gain a firm hold on his slippery, oil soaked clothing. The crew were unable to pull him on board.

The heat was growing more intense with the passing seconds and the strength of the life savers was taxed to the limit. After much effort, the men succeeded in tying a line under the armpits of the helpless victim and towed him from the white-hot sides of the burning vessel. Paint on the side of the Coast Guard boat had begun to blister. The man, with his extra weight, towed under; the boat was stopped, and the four Coast Guardsmen finally pulled him on board. The lifeboat headed again toward the burning tanker to rescue additional victims. Another oil soaked man was found, and clinging desperately to a life raft. Two crew members went over the side into the sea of oil to rescue this man, who was too exhausted to get on board without help. Both survivors were stripped of their oil soaked clothing, wrapped in blankets, given coffee, and otherwise made comfortable in the cabin. Although the station boat searched the rest of the night, no other members of the 49-man tanker crew were found.

The sinkings continued. At least 30 vessels, aggregating 166,578 tons of American merchant shipping, were lost in February of 1942, compared with 23 vessels of 127,642 tons sunk in January. March 1942 came in like a lion in the battle against subs. During the month 30 more American merchant vessels totaling 193,987 tons were sunk, of which only two (11,533 tons) were in convoy.

The Coast Guard cutter *Calypso* performed a splendid piece of rescue work when she rushed to the aid of the 7,000-ton Brazilian freighter *Arabutan*, torpedoed without warning well off the Virginia Capes on 7 March 1942, while bound from Norfolk to Trinidad with coal and coke. The freighter sank in 20 minutes. The 54 crew members, drifting in their lifeboats, were constantly endangered by continued enemy fire. When *Calypso* arrived shortly after midnight, she began searching for survivors in total darkness and a heavy wind. The crew of the cutter, in great danger from enemy torpedoes, scanned the heavy seas all night in their determination to find survivors. Next day an assisting Coast Guard plane, V-183, sighted them and directed the cutter to the spot about two hours distant. Within 15 minutes of her arrival, *Calypso* had taken on board all 54 survivors from four lifeboats, and was on her way out of the danger zone and headed for Norfolk. One man of the freighter's crew had been killed in the torpedoing.

Three more sinkings followed off the Atlantic coast within the next five days. The 6,676-ton American tanker *Gulftrade,* from Port Arthur, Texas to Philadelphia with oil, was broken in two by an enemy torpedo on 9 March 1942, a half mile off Barnegat Light. While cutter *Antietam* was picking up the 16 survivors from the crew of 34, the submarine fired a torpedo at the cutter, which passed within 20 feet of her bow. Two days later, the Norwegian steamship *Hvosleff* was torpedoed off Fenwick Island Light Station near Cape Henlopen. The survivors, in a lifeboat, landed on the beach nearby. Coast Guardsmen assisted and transported them to the Lewes Lifeboat Station.

The next day, the American tanker *John D. Gill,* 11,641 tons, was torpedoed while bound from Philadelphia to Texas with a cargo of gasoline and oil. She was found early in the morning by a Coast Guard motor lifeboat from Oak Island (S.C.) Lifeboat Station. The tanker was afire and sinking, about 25 miles east of Cape Fear. Any survivors had apparently already taken to lifeboats and rafts. The motor lifeboat, the *CG-186,* and cutter *Agassiz,* began their search. Through fire, smoke, and oil, the Coast Guardsmen combed the area in every direction and were rewarded at daybreak by sighting a red flare. Upon investigation it was found to have come from a life raft with 11 survivors. The exhausted men, clinging to the raft, were taken on board and rushed to Southport, South Carolina, by *CG-186;* the motor lifeboat and the cutter continued the search for many hours. *Agassiz* found 14 bodies and took them to Southport. Later it was learned that 15 more survivors had been picked up by a passing tanker and taken to Charleston, South Carolina. Altogether, 26 of the tanker's 49-man crew were saved.

Two other March sinkings were noteworthy. On the night of 16 March the 7,118-ton tanker *Olean* was torpedoed 15 miles south of Cape Lookout, North Carolina, while en route from Norfolk to Houston. A motor lifeboat from the Cape Lookout Lifeboat Station arrived at the scene about 0330, and later, one arrived from Fort Macon Lifeboat Station. After a careful search,

the Coast Guardsmen saw a dim light flicker for only two or three seconds, but that was enough. In a few moments, 20 survivors were found in a lifeboat. Ten of the most seriously injured were placed in the Fort Macon boat together with five from another life raft, and these proceeded to Beaufort, North Carolina, the nearest point where medical aid was available. Later, three more survivors and one body were located by a plane. In all, six persons lost their lives and 36 were saved.

The tug *Menomenee* and three barges were attacked simultaneously and shelled by an enemy submarine off Metomkin Inlet Lifeboat Station, 50 miles north of Cape Charles, Virginia, on 31 March 1942. A lookout there reported a small boat drifting two miles offshore that night, and two motor lifeboats rushed to the scene. They found one of the barges belching smoke and fire, with shells from the submarine still bursting about her. The tug, and the barges *Allegheny* and *Barnegat* sank soon after the attack, and only the barge *Ontario* remained afloat. The crew of the tug had been picked up by *Northern Sun,* a passing tanker. The crew of *Ontario,* those seen by the lookout, were found and saved. Then a motor lifeboat set out at top speed to search for the survivors of the two sunken barges. The intrepid Coast Guardsmen went into the thick of the enemy shelling attack on the now waterlogged *Ontario.* Here they found the crews of the other barges and took them on board. Thus, all nine in the three barge crews were saved by the Coast Guardsmen while one barge was still under attack.

In April, American merchant ship losses reached 38 ships totalling 203,303 tons. None of those sunk was in convoy. There simply were not enough escort vessels at that time to handle all coastal shipping. On 11 April 1942, the thirteenth day after the 8,272-ton motorship *City of New York* had been torpedoed off North Carolina, a lifeboat with 11 of her survivors came within sight of *CG-455.* Cold, hunger, thirst, and mental torture had racked these unfortunate victims as they had drifted hopelessly day after day. But, contrary to their superstitions, rescue came on the thirteenth day. One saved was Miriam Etter, aged three, whose mother had died in the boat; a sailor had also succumbed to the harrowing experience. Another boat load of survivors from the same vessel reached Norfolk after a similar ordeal during which the wife of a Yugoslav consular official had given birth to a child in the open lifeboat.

Events following the torpedoing and sinking of the Panamanian freighter *Chenango* on 20 April, 55 miles southeast of Oregon Inlet, North Carolina, brought home the horrors of submarine warfare. There were only two survivors. *Chenango* sank in two minutes, so quickly that no boats could be launched. After shelling the stricken vessel, the submarine deliberately cruised through the 15 or 20 survivors struggling in the water, drowning many and leaving all but two to the sharks. The two managed to reach an improvised life raft, but there were no oars and the raft drifted away from the other victims.

Twelve days later, on 2 May 1942, these two starving, blistering, sunburned, semi-conscious, and emaciated men were sighted by an Army bomber. The Coast Guard's Elizabeth City Air Station was notified and Lieutenant Commander R. L. Burke then flew from that station and searched the reported location off shore. He finally sighted the raft and made a successful sea landing. Incipient thunderstorms were evident, and there were confused cross seas with waves four to six feet high.

Burke taxied the plane up the wind beyond the bouncing, heaving raft and cut both engines, then drifted downwind close to the raft. Burke had to start his engines to get the plane close enough to the raft to heave a line to it. One man was delirious and thought the plane was starting up to take off and was going to leave him behind. He screamed and jumped overboard into the shark-infested waters, but was recovered. A line was tossed to the raft which acted as a sea drogue for the drifting plane, and Burke was able to pull the two close and get them on board. A pharmacist's mate on the plane dressed their wounds and administered sedatives while the plane flew to the Naval Air Station, Norfolk, Virginia, turning the survivors over to Navy doctors and intelligence officers there.

Such cases of drifting for days and weeks brought inconceivable hardship on the hapless victims, and their rescues were true acts of mercy. Cooperation between Coast Guard and Navy units, both air and surface, led to saving 13 men who had been adrift in the Atlantic for 17 days. Their ship, *Pipestone County*, from Trinidad to Boston, had been torpedoed without warning far to the east of the Virginia Capes on 21 April 1942. She sank in 20 minutes. A Coast Guard plane from Elizabeth City was scouting far offshore on 7 May. The radioman intercepted a message saying survivors in a lifeboat had been spotted from another Coast Guard plane 30 miles east of Oregon Inlet. The first plane, sighting cutter *Calypso* on the horizon, flew over her and at 1010 reported the situation by message block dropped on board.

Fifteen minutes later *Calypso* picked up a message from the plane pilot stating that he was circling over the lifeboat and giving its exact position. The cutter changed course and steered for the plane; she was further directed by a Navy blimp which had taken station over the lifeboat. Meanwhile, the 13 men received their first fresh provisions in 17 days from another Elizabeth City plane.

Three hours after receiving the first message, and 33 miles from her original position, *Calypso* reached the lifeboat and picked up the boatload of *Pipestone County* survivors. These said that the rest of the crew had put off in three other lifeboats which had become separated the first day. The cutter sank the lifeboat by gunfire and took the survivors to the Naval Operating Base, Norfolk. Passing craft farther at sea had rescued some of the others and taken them to Boston. The vessel's master, who was in the latter group, reported that 46 men had been on board; most were saved. One of the four lifeboats was never found.

On 26 April 1942, Andrew J. Cupples, AAM 1c, attached to the St. Petersburg Coast Guard Air Station, was returning from patrol in his plane to Key West. He sighted an oil slick nine miles from Marquesas Key, which proved to be U. S. destroyer *Sturtevant* sinking stern first with only a bit of her bow still above water. One lifeboat was afloat picking up survivors. The vessel was inside a recently laid mine-field. No ships were in the vicinity and Cupples, without a radioman, proceeded 20 miles to Key West and made his report. Refueling, and taking on a radioman, he took off again and sighted a rescue boat five or six miles from the scene. He directed it to the lifeboat and rafts containing survivors, and radioed for a second boat, when the first proved inadequate to carry all the survivors. Small craft took 137 survivors to Key West. Three were dead and 12 missing in this mishap. Cupples was recommended for commendation by his commanding officer.

At about this time, German submarine commanders again centered their attention on Cape Canaveral, Florida. Fifty miles from the nearest lifeboat station at Ponce de Leon Inlet, and well isolated from any village or town, Canaveral was truly the wolf-pack's heaven. Lying offshore, U-boats picked up silhouettes of ships in the flashing light from Cape Canaveral Lighthouse, and sent torpedoes crashing into them. Within a two-week period, 151 survivors from torpedoed vessels received first aid, medical assistance, food, and clothing at that lighthouse, which had become a veritable house of refuge. To reduce the silhouettes, Cape Canaveral Light was dimmed; shortly afterwards, on 9 May 1942, the power of all lights along the coast was reduced.

Lieutenant Commander W. B. Scheibel departed Elizabeth City on 1 May in a Coast Guard plane to search for a lifeboat containing starving survivors of an unknown torpedoed vessel. A heavy smoke pall from swamp fires, carried seaward by a moderate westerly wind, cut visibility to three or four miles. A grid search was begun, and at 1332 a lifeboat from the British *Empire Drum* with 13 survivors was sighted. The exhausted men had been adrift for a week. The plane notified its station and dropped emergency rations, medical supplies, and blankets. One injured delirious man was on board. The plane landed and took him and one other survivor to Norfolk. Surface vessels rescued the others.

Two cargo vessels and a tanker were torpedoed on the 4th and 5th of May, this time off the southern Florida coast. First was the steamship *Eclipse*, off Boynton Inlet. She was loaded with essential war supplies worth millions of dollars. Her master had become suspicious and had deliberately run her aground in an attempt to dodge what he thought was a submarine. He was right. However, the Nazi did not fire his torpedo until *Eclipse* had pulled herself off and was again gaining headway. Just after the torpedo struck her side, the vessel went aground again, still off Boynton Inlet and in full view of spectators on shore. Coast Guard Auxiliary members were alerted and reached the scene within a few minutes.

The commercial tug *Ontario* was in the vicinity with a tow. The Commanding Officer of Base Six at Fort Lauderdale, on orders from his District Coast Guard Officer, went on board this tug while still at sea with her tow. Because of the grounded vessel's cargo, it was essential that *Eclipse* be pulled from the shoal; those supplies were needed by the fighting men on the other side of the world. The Coast Guardsman explained the situation to the tug's captain and asked that *Ontario* release her tow and hurry to the aid of *Eclipse*. Under strong persuasion coupled with a threat to commandeer the tug, *Ontario* secured her tow, put about, and steamed for Boynton Inlet. *Eclipse* was finally pulled off the bar. *Ontario* and another tug, *Bafshe*, took her to Port Everglades.

While the tugs and escorts were en route, the 8,327-ton American *Java Arrow*, a straggler behind its convoy all the way from New York, was torpedoed off Bethel Shoals, presumably by the same raider that had blasted *Eclipse*. Also, word was received of the torpedoed steamship *Delisle* (3,478 tons), aground off Jupiter Inlet Light. The tugs and their escorts were ordered to proceed to *Java Arrow*, since she was in greater danger than *Delisle*. Auxiliary men came back from *Java Arrow*, which was also loaded with war supplies, with the report that she could be salvaged. The master and her crew had been removed. Lieutenant Maurice G. Field went on board from Fort Pierce Lifeboat Station, and directed the initial preparations for salvaging, while awaiting the arrival of the two tugs. The crew were returned to the ship.

Field's plan was to cut the anchor chain at a 6-fathom shackle, linking the shackle to a towline. A Fort Pierce acetylene torch operator was routed out of bed at midnight, rushed to the scene, and cut the chain. The eerie light of the blue flamed acetylene torch, with no other illumination except flashlights, was too much for the *Java Arrow* crew, most of them veterans of one or more torpedoings. They demanded to be returned to the beach. Lieutenant Field went ashore, where, from West Palm Beach, he directed *Java Arrow*, her tow, and escort, during the 4-day trip to Port Everglades. Two other vessels were sunk in that vicinity while *Java Arrow* was making port.

Still another tanker, *Lubra Foil*, was hit on its way into Port Everglades *in full view* of the salvage fleet. One of *Java Arrow's* escorts together with Auxiliary and Coast Guard vessels from Lake Worth Inlet Lifeboat Station, managed to pull 31 survivors from flaming wreckage in a debris-littered sea, leaving the blazing *Lubra Foil* to drift northward for two days before she sank. The escort then returned to *Java Arrow*, and the salvage party proceeded to Port Everglades. Other sinkings kept things lively.

Lifeboat stations and District Headquarters during this time worked around the clock. Officers and men barely had time to eat; sleep was out of the question. One assignment had scarcely been completed before another took its place. Late in May, two Mexican tankers were attacked, one off Miami and the other off the Florida Keys; three Coast Guard Auxiliary flotillas brought in 22 survivors out of *Portero del Llano's* crew of 35, and seven days later cutter *Nemesis* brought in 28 survivors from the other, *Faja de Oro*. A few days after this, Mexico formally declared war on the Axis.

The United States tanker *David McKelvey*, 6,821 tons, was torpedoed and sunk off the Mississippi River Delta on 14 May 1942. A Coast Guard plane from Biloxi Air Station proceeded to its reported position, located an oil slick 15 miles to the eastward, and discovered the tanker afloat but on fire. Tanker *Norsol* was approaching, and was told that some of the crew were still on the burning vessel. Twenty-five of the 42 crew members were saved. Two days later the same plane proceeded to almost the same position where the American tanker *William C. McTarnahan*, 7,305 tons, had been struck by two torpedoes. Two lifeboats and four rafts with 28 persons on board were three miles away. The plane flew five miles to inform some fishing boats which then effected the rescue. This tanker stayed afloat, was salvaged, and reconditioned.

There was another similar rescue five days later. Another plane from Biloxi Air Station proceeded to the position of the sunken American freighter *Heredia*, 4,732 tons. Her masts showed above water, well south of Atchafalaya Bay, Louisiana. About a mile to the west eight men and a small boy were on a raft made from a hatch cover; four more men were a half mile to the eastward; still more men as well as a small girl were near the mast; and five were clinging to bits of wreckage. There was also one body supported by a life preserver. The pilot requested his station to send aid, and dropped message blocks to the survivors telling them aid was coming. He then proceeded to six

fishing boats, five miles northwestward, which went to the scene and took all survivors on board.

The British steamship *Peisander* was torpedoed on 17 May 1942, about 300 miles off Bermuda. All 61 members of the crew got away in three lifeboats. Two of these boats, with 43 survivors, were found and towed in by *CGR-37* and a motor lifeboat of the Maddaket (Nantucket) Lifeboat Station, but the third boat, with 18 survivors, was still missing. This was sighted by a Navy plane and word was relayed through Boston to cutter *General Greene*. The latter was ordered, on 24 May, to search for this boat. Fog hampered this operation, but at 0945 on the 25th the cutter found the third lifeboat near Nantucket Shoals. At the same moment, the lookout sighted a submarine which was crash diving across the cutter's bow. *General Greene* tried to ram, but the sub was too deep; she then closed in on a sound contact and dropped three depth charges. An oil slick 400 feet in diameter appeared. Unable to pick up the sound again during the next 25 minutes, the cutter broke off the attack and took on board the 18 occupants of the lifeboat.

These survivors explained that the submarine had been tagging the lifeboat, and had sent two torpedoes into the American freighter *Plow City*, 3,282 tons, when that vessel had attempted a rescue on 21 May. One crew member had been killed. The other 30 crewmen were picked up five days later by *USS Sapphire*, a converted yacht.

*General Greene* took the 18 survivors and their lifeboat to Nantucket Harbor. Here she collected the other 43 survivors of *Peisander* and carried them all to Newport, Rhode Island.

The Panamanian tanker *Persephone*, traveling in convoy from the Dutch West Indies to New York, was torpedoed in daylight on 25 May 1942, 2½ miles from Barnegat, New Jersey. First on the spot was patrol boat *CG-159*, an escort. Those on board *CG-159* had seen the tanker hit when about four miles from Barnegat Lightship Gas Buoy. This Coast Guard boat proceeded at full speed toward the stricken vessel and, arriving within 10 minutes, immediately began circling, looking for survivors.

Meanwhile, four picket boats were ordered out from Barnegat Lifeboat Station, and arrived at the scene about 20 minutes after *CG-159*. The first took on board 14 crew members from a life raft; the second rescued a man in the water; the third picked up 12 men from a partly submerged life raft. These two vessels returned promptly to Barnegat Lifeboat Station with their 26 men while the other boats stayed for further search. The master of *Persephone* was taken off soon afterward by *CG-159* which then searched two hours for the submarine. Meanwhile, two boats had returned to search for the nine missing men, but without success. Following this, *CG-159* sent men on board the damaged tanker to salvage the ship's papers and mail, 23 bags of which were turned over to the Barnegat Station. On shore, all survivors were cleaned of oil, fed, and given medical attention; six were hospitalized.

Although the peak of United States merchant vessel sinkings was reached in June 1942, the number of vessels sunk off our coasts declined in that month. Of the 44 United States (233,416 tons) vessels sunk in all areas in May 1942, 20 had gone down off our coasts. Only 10 percent of all were under escort. During June of that year, when 51 United States merchant vessels totaling 289,790 tons were sunk (18 percent in convoy) only 13 of the sinkings were off our shores. The submarine was gradually being driven from our coasts by the increased use of convoys as escorts became available, and especially by better protection from the air.

The enemy was also active on the West Coast. On the afternoon of 7 June 1942, the United States steamship *Coast Trader,* 3,286 tons, was torpedoed well off the entrance of the Strait of Juan de Fuca and Cape Flattery, Washington. A Coast Guard plane from the Port Angeles (Washington) Coast Guard Air Station proceeded to search for survivors. A Canadian plane had sighted rafts about 0530 on the morning of 9 June, and dropped a flare. At 0552 the Coast Guard plane sighted one empty raft and two others carrying together some 20 persons, and dropped a float. The Canadian corvette *Edmundston* picked up the survivors.

While on weather patrol off the Grand Banks on 16 June 1942, *USS Sea Cloud,* Coast Guard-manned, picked up eight survivors of the Portuguese fishing schooner *Maria de Gloria.* The latter had been sunk without warning on 6 June, and the survivors had been adrift in their small boat for 10 days. One other survivor had died of wounds

and another, becoming crazed, had jumped overboard. When the fishing vessel sank, 44 men had taken to lifeboats. The remaining 34 were never heard from, and doubtless perished from hunger, thirst, and exhaustion after drifting about with ever-diminishing hope of rescue.

Thirty-three persons lost their lives, and 14 were rescued when the British tanker *Empire Mica* was torpedoed in the Gulf of Mexico, 40 miles off Apalachicola, Florida, on 29 June 1942. Most of the crew were trapped below decks by scattered debris and impassable flames. A half crazed seaman jumped overboard but managed to swim ahead of the advancing flames and was subsequently picked up by a lifeboat in which 13 other men had managed to escape. The rest of the crew either perished on board, or in the flaming oil that surrounded the doomed tanker. The drifting lifeboat was located by the Coast Guard Auxiliary vessels *Countess* and *Sea Dream,* which took the survivors to Apalachicola.

The downtrend in the sinkings of American merchant craft had now definitely set in. Only 41 United States merchant vessels (245,762 tons) were sunk in July 1942, and only five of these were off the Atlantic or Gulf Coasts. The submarine war had moved far afield, and the sinkings were mostly from submarines or bombings of vessels on their way to Murmansk; in the Barents or Kara Seas; off Iceland or Australia; or in the North Atlantic, or North Pacific. The Coast Guard figured in some, but by no means all, of the rescue activities.

After one of the most dramatic rescues of a tanker's crew off the Florida Keys, the tanker itself was finally salvaged. On 8 July 1942, Dr. E. E. Kitchens and Mr. E. R. Smith, both of the Miami Coast Guard Auxiliary, were in their yachts at Craig, in the lower Florida Keys. They interrupted their leisure to rescue survivors from the American tanker *James A. Moffett, Jr.,* which had been torpedoed and set afire off Tennessee Reef Light. They took on full crews of regular Coast Guardsmen from the local station and struck out in heavy seas for *Moffett,* eight miles off shore. Kitchens, starting back with 14 survivors from the burning tanker, found 16 more. All were brought to safety. Smith, with 12 survivors, stayed behind to investigate. He found the skipper, the only casualty, with his body caught in the lifeboat falls.

Kitchens was commended by the Commandant.

*R. M. Parker, Jr.,* a 6,779-ton tanker, was the only American vessel sunk in United States waters during August. She went down in the Gulf of Mexico, and all 44 crewmen were saved. Altogether, 18 United States merchant vessels, totaling 116,552 tons, were sunk in August.

Two foreign ships, *Manzanillo* and *Santiago de Cuba* traveling in convoy from Key West on 12 August 1942, were the last submarine victims in Florida waters for nearly a year. *Manzanillo* was carrying Coast Guard personnel and special equipment to an advance Coast Guard base in Cuba. Two Coast Guard radiomen and all *Manzanillo's* officers were lost. The rest of the 16 men killed in the attack were in *Santiago de Cuba.* Survivors were picked up by other vessels in the convoy, while a Coast Guard picket boat recovered all bodies.

When the British steamship *Arletta* was torpedoed a few days earlier, on 5 August, while en route from Scotland to Halifax, 36 crewmen met death. A Coast Guard amphibious patrol plane located the five survivors and led *Menemsha,* Coast Guard weather patrol vessel, to the drifting life rafts, one of which carried four survivors. All were suffering from exposure and hunger after being adrift 15 days. They were taken to Marine Hospital, Boston (Brighton), Massachusetts.

Only a 1,281-ton barge, *Druid,* was sunk in United States coastal waters during September 1942. This sinking occurred off the coast of Virginia, on the 21st. All the rest of the September sinkings were in distant areas. In October, only two ships were sunk in coastal waters. One, the United States tanker *Larry Doheny,* was torpedoed off California and 38 out of 44 on board were saved. A second, United States tanker *Camden,* was torpedoed 10 October off Oregon, and 47 of the 48 on board were rescued. Thereafter, merchant vessel sinkings were less frequent and, for the most part, in distant waters. Only 12 out of 174 United States vessels sunk throughout the world during 1943 went down in United States coastal areas.

Early in January 1943, Coast Guard headquarters at Ketchikan, Alaska, received word that a Lockheed plane owned by Gillam Airlines, Inc., was missing on a flight from Seattle. A search was organized, but no definite word was had until 3 February when patrol boat *CGR-232* found two

survivors on the shores of Boca de Quadia. These two men believed they could lead a rescue party back to the others. They said the Lockheed had crashed on a mountain 5 January, and that snow had hidden it from searching planes. A rescue group was organized to base in cutter *McLane.* A plane pilot located the camp on 4 February and dropped food and blankets. Then a shore party started out from Smeaton Bay. Meanwhile, the body of Harold Gillam, pilot of the wrecked plane, was found. He had apparently started out to find help and had died of exposure. The two remaining survivors and the body of a girl were reached on 5 February. The survivors were taken by toboggan and sled to *McLane* at Badger Bay. The girl's body was recovered later.

Sinkings in American coastal waters may have declined greatly, but convoys in the North Atlantic still had their troubles, especially in the first half of 1943. On 7 February 1943, the cutter *Bibb* rescued 202 survivors from the sunken freighter *Henry R. Mallory,* and later took on board 33 victims from the torpedoed Greek ship *Kalliopi.* Both vessels were attacked in convoy SC-118 which *Bibb* was escorting off Iceland. On the same day cutter *Ingham,* also an escort of this convoy, picked up 33 survivors from three merchant vessels of the convoy, *Henry R. Mallory,* tanker *Robert E. Hopkins,* and freighter *West Portal,* and some from freighter *Jeremiah Van Rennselar,* torpedoed in another convoy on the 2nd.

Regardless of war, the traditional role of lifesaving engaged Coast Guardsmen whenever the occasion demanded. Rough seas and high winds slowed rescue operations on 5 March 1943, when the American freighter *Hartwelson,* 3,078 tons, ran aground on Bantam Rock off the Maine coast. Damariscove Island Lifeboat Station, 1½ miles to the northeast, sent a lifeboat which arrived at the scene at 0800. Sea conditions and shallow water around the freighter, however, made it impossible to get alongside until the sea became calmer. The steamer reported by blinker that those on board were all right. A second lifeboat from Kennebec River Lifeboat Station arrived at 1000; later another from Burnt Island Station and a naval vessel joined them.

Heavy seas caused *Hartwelson* to begin breaking up, and prevented getting a line on board. But her crew, on instructions, drifted a line secured to a ring preserver to leeward, which was picked up by the naval vessel. During this operation a line fouled the propeller of the Kennebec boat. This lifeboat, without propulsion, was damaged when hurled helplessly against the naval vessel by the waves. Cutter *Ilex* arrived after dark, at 1835. By then the freighter had broken in two and the after section had sunk. At 1922 the cutter started pumping oil overboard to windward of *Hartwelson.* Ten minutes later a small boat left the cutter for the wreck. From a position 35 yards from the wreck, a line was shot to the ship and a two-inch line was hauled in. The stranded men were secured to this line, lowered over the side, and pulled into the lifeboat. This boat and the Damariscove lifeboat transferred the entire crew of 35 to *Ilex,* and thus safety.

Two tankers, running blacked out, collided off Lake Worth Inlet, Florida, on 2 October 1943. The explosion and fire which followed cost 33 lives. Observers on shore thought a huge transport or freighter had been torpedoed. All anti-submarine vessels in the vicinity were ordered to the scene. Only the northbound *Gulfland,* 5,277 tons, was carrying cargo. However, blazing aviation gasoline from her was sprayed over the southbound *Gulf Belle.* The heat was so intense that only a few men, who were on deck and were hurled into the ocean by the impact, were saved.

As Coast Guard Auxiliary vessels from West Palm Beach neared the scene, they were met by a wall of flame. Despite this barrier to effective rescue, the Coast Guard saved 29, and the Navy, 54 crew members. The only living thing found on board either wreck some days later was a dog which became the mascot of the Port Everglades Coast Guard fireboat. *Gulfland* drifted aground in Hobe Sound and burned for 52 days and nights. *Gulf Belle,* the blaze partially under control, was towed to the sea buoy off Port Everglades where, due to ammunition stored on board, she threatened to blow up at any minute. Under these hazardous conditions Lieutenant (jg) Sidney Carter won the Navy and Marine Corps Medal for directing the fire fighting operations which finally saved her.

By no means were all rescues at sea an aftermath of enemy action. Convoy NK-588, consisting of the merchant vessel *Tydol Gas* and three escorts, *USS St. Augustine* (PG-54) and cutters *Thetis* and *Argo,* the latter commanded by Lieutenant (jg) Eliot Winslow, USCGR, left New York on the morning of 6 January 1944. They were to rendezvous with additional merchant vessels off Norfolk the next day. That night, all ships were running darkened; the moon was nearly full and visibility was good. At about 2200 *St. Augustine* established radar contact on a vessel in a sector which was normally *Argo's,* and proceeded to investigate. At 6,000 yards she challenged by blinker and later by flashing her running lights but received no answer. She turned sharply to port and increased speed to full ahead, getting into a dangerous position in relation to the other vessel, *Camas Meadows.* Those in *Argo* watched them approach each other; the silhouettes never separated in the moonlight. The vessels collided, the bow of *Camas Meadows* striking *St. Augustine* about midships on the starboard side, penetrating her hull 10 to 15 feet and rupturing the boiler or steam lines, allowing live steam to escape.

*Camas Meadows'* radio operator did not wait for his captain to OK a message, but radioed that the ship had been torpedoed. At once, *Argo* started searching; the search took her three miles away before another message canceling the first stated the vessels had, instead, collided and that *St. Augustine* was sunk! The error lost valuable rescue time, and cost many lives. *St. Augustine* sank in five minutes at about 2330.

By then, *Camas Meadows* was running with all lights; *Argo,* approaching, signaled her by blinker and was told that survivors were to the left of *Argo.* At 2350 the cutter saw the first survivors waving a red light. From midnight to 0200 *Argo* picked up survivors, with rough water hindering operations. Some of her men jumped overside into a life raft to put lines around men too weak to lift themselves up. In all *Argo* saved 23 men.

Meanwhile, *Tydol Gas* was ordered to heave to. *Thetis* was busy, too, with her rescues. Her searchlights picked up a crowded raft, so she abandoned her attempt to recover a body she had sighted, and managed to bring the raft along her port side. Lines were passed, but the men on the raft could not hold them, nor could *Thetis's* crew grab the survivors because oil made the men heavy and slippery. Two of *Thetis's* crew dropped into the raft to pass lines around the men. Of the 13 taken on board, one responded to artificial respiration and joined six others who lived; the other six died.

Several other vessels also assisted; *USS Allegheny* found 20 bodies, *USS SC-1321* recovered 17 bodies, *USS SC-1354* took in 17 bodies, and *CG-83314* recovered seven. *St. Augustine's* sailing list showed 145 persons, of whom only 30 survived. In recognition of their parts in the rescue, two officers and two men of *Thetis* and two officers of *Argo* received letters of commendation. Navy and Marine Corps medals were awarded to four men in *Argo*.

There were rescues far afield under stress of intensive combat. Many are mentioned in other chapters. For example, *USS Menges* (DE-320) and *USS Newell* (DE-322), both Coast Guard-manned, between them rescued 230 Navy personnel out of 277 on board the U. S. destroyer *Lansdale* (Lieutenant Commander D. M. Swift, USN). This rescue occurred on 20 April 1944, while the men-of-war were escorting a Bizerte-bound convoy in the Mediterranean. To begin the incident the ammunition freighter *Paul Hamilton,* was struck by aerial torpedoes and exploded with a tremendous flash of light which lasted about six seconds. About 504 men were killed, including 498 who were part of a specially trained demolition squad that was en route to the Anzio beachhead. Later, several enemy planes flew in over *Lansdale*. While the latter was firing on the first Nazi plane, a second spotted the destroyer and sank her. No flame or fire accompanied *Lansdale's* sinking.

*Menges* shot down one Nazi plane and rescued its pilot and radio operator. They were on a life raft with a light blinking, which they failed to extinguish when ordered to do so. After the enemy planes had departed, *Menges* and *Newell* launched lifeboats to search for survivors, and these ships accounted for many of the rescues. Meanwhile, survivors able to swim the short distance to the two DEs, were rescued by lines or life jackets thrown them. Most had on inflated life belts. Some

Coast Guardsmen went over the side on nets and pulled survivors on board. *Menges* succeeded in rescuing 119 men, while *Newell* saved 111. Most were uninjured, though many were suffering from shock. Among those rescued was Lieutenant Robert M. Morgenthau, USNR, Executive Officer of *Lansdale* and son of the Secretary of the Treasury.

As the war progressed and the Allied nations gained the upper hand, opportunities for rescue at sea became less frequent. During the 7½ months of the war in 1945, only 30 United States merchant vessels (233,981 tons) were sunk. But three were within Coast Guard operation areas. The American tanker *Atlantic States* was torpedoed (later salvaged) off Massachusetts on 5 April. All 57 crew members were saved. The 8,300-ton steamer *Swift-scout* was sunk off Virginia on 18 April, and of the 47 on board, 46 were saved. Finally, on 5 May 1945, only three days before V-E Day, the 5,353-ton collier *Black Point* was torpedoed four miles southeast of Point Judith, Rhode Island, and sank in 20 minutes. Several 83-footers, cutters *Hornbeam* and *Hibiscus,* and lifeboats and motorboats from all nearby stations were dispatched to the area. Twelve lives were lost on the collier. The rest of the crew were taken to Point Judith and Watch Hill. A thorough search of the area, continued by the Navy, resulted in the sinking of an enemy subarine within a few hours of the incident.

We have seen that rescues were an important part of Coast Guard operations in all areas and under all conditions. They were pursued with persistence, courage, and heroism. Rescues were always performed *after* the unfortunate event. But it was also a function of the Coast Guard to *prevent*, as far as was humanly possible, the incidents which brought about the *need* for rescue. In the next chapter we shall consider some of the various preventive functions which were carried out by the Coast Guard.

# Chapter 9

# NEW RESPONSIBILITIES
# FOR SAFETY AT SEA

SINCE SAFETY at sea has always been of major concern to the Coast Guard, it seemed most logical to transfer to that Service certain activities from other agencies also related to that field of endeavor. Thus, efforts along that line were consolidated in the one Service. It was pointed out in the Prologue that, in July 1939, the Lighthouse Service was transferred to the Coast Guard. Its primary mission was to contribute to the safety of navigation for all vessels through a system of aids to navigation. These included lighthouses, lightships, fog signals (audible, radio, etc.), radiobeacons, unattended lights, buoys, daymarks, and so forth, to assist vessels in determining their positions, avoiding dangers, and identifying locations along the coasts in all weathers. Under the Coast Guard, this activity became the Aids to Navigation Division.

War in Europe began shortly after the Coast Guard took over the responsibility for the maintenance of some 29,606 aids to navigation. Subsequently, Coast Guard operations were naturally forced primarily into other channels. As the war progressed, the Neutrality Patrol and expanding Port Security received top priority. Aids to Navigation was the one branch of Coast Guard work which, from an operational standpoint, suffered materially as a result of the war, since the Navy command effort was not directed toward development of this aspect of the Service. As a result there was little opportunity to effect a proper wartime coordination between the activities formerly performed by the Lighthouse Service and the normal operations of the Coast Guard.

Another responsibility concerning safety at sea not only for surface ships, but for transatlantic planes as well, devolved upon the Coast Guard.

On 25 January 1940, in cooperation with the United States Weather Bureau, an Ocean Weather Service was established primarily for the safety of transatlantic traffic. This activity developed throughout the war and became a very efficient and vital service. It has already received some mention.

Finally, by Executive Order 9083 of 28 February 1942, certain safety-at-sea functions of the former Bureau of Marine Inspection and Navigation came temporarily under the Coast Guard. These were chiefly the inspection and certification of construction of merchant vessels, and the licensing and certification of merchant marine officers, pilots, and seamen. These became permanent duties of the Coast Guard on 16 July 1946.

Taking these three basic functions together, the role of the Coast Guard in promoting safety at sea increased greatly.

First to be taken over, as we have seen, was Aids to Navigation, adding 5,000 personnel to the Coast Guard. For the most part, Lighthouse Depots became Coast Guard bases where Aids to Navigation work continued as before, but some of these facilities were also useful to the Coast Guard in connection with other regular functions. The Lighthouse Service was a *major* activity. The 29,606 aids to navigation which were transferred to the jurisdiction of the Coast Guard included 9,862 lighted aids, comprising 1,801 lights of 200 candlepower or more, 6,180 lights of less candlepower, 30 lightships, and 1,881 lighted buoys of all kinds. There were 1,764 fog signals, consisting of 141 radiobeacons, 570 sound fog signals (in air) and 9 submarine fog signals, and 676 lighted and 368 unlighted buoys with whistles, bells, gongs, or trumpets. There were 13,468 silent and unlighted buoys, and 5,188 daymarks. These aids were serviced by a large number of tenders.

This responsibility was undertaken as of 1 July 1939, just two months before World War II started in Europe. While the transfer was made as smoothly as possible in a merger of this magnitude, there were countless administrative, operational, personnel, supply, and financial problems which required prompt attention and solution without interference with other Coast Guard functions.

The greatest immediate problem concerned personnel. Most lighthouse keepers were "career men" in their field. Keeping lighthouses was often work handed down from generation to generation by simple, honest, dependable civilians who lived somewhat isolated lives, took pride in their responsibilities, and loved that kind of life. Not only the keepers, but others connected with the depots, tenders, and the general establishment, had a natural reluctance to change from one long-established Service to another. Personnel could choose between induction into the Coast Guard's military grades and ratings, with appropriate promotion and pay increase, or retention of their civil service status; many preferred the latter and retained that status for many years.

But personnel were more and more militarized, acquired regular Coast Guard ratings, and lost their identity with the Lighthouse Service as such. Militarized personnel were subject to transfer from one Coast Guard activity to another, and a morale problem was created when men, who loved lighthouse work, found themselves transferred to beach patrol, port security, or combat assignments, and when boatswain's mates who wanted to be at sea, or fighting the enemy far afield, were transferred to lighthouses on quiet shores.

Lighthouse Districts were combined with the Coast Guard Districts to facilitate administration and operation. The Lighthouse Division had its Chief and his Staff at Headquarters in Washington. Superintendents of former Lighthouse Districts became assistants to the District Commanders for the administration of lighthouse functions, and were called District Aids to Navigation Officers. Whenever possible, they moved their offices to Coast Guard District headquarters. Consolidation increased efficiency through the coordinated use of personnel, vessels, boats, and supplies.

Physical assimilation by the Coast Guard of aids to navigation came when war developments in Europe and the North Atlantic made it clear that the United States was heading toward involvement. During the two and one-half years from initial consolidation until Pearl Harbor, new installations of aids to navigation were made and antisubmarine nets were installed at many naval bases in the continental United States. An extensive aids to navigation system was installed at Midway.

Early participation in helping to equip naval defense establishments was the Service's first contact with many far-flung areas outside our borders. This was an introduction to the work of tender-class cutters in the Pacific as we later advanced, taking island after island from the Japanese, from Guadalcanal to Tokyo. Marking and lighting channels in the newly acquired Pacific bases was essential. In areas such as Greenland, which were virtually unmarked, charting, and the establishment of new aids were requisite.

Installations were also made at San Juan and Vieques Sound, Puerto Rico, and at newly acquired bases (leased from Great Britain) at Newfoundland, Bermuda, Antigua, St. Lucia, Trinidad and Jamaica; also at Kodiak, Alaska, Kanoehoe Bay, Hawaii, and at Wake, Palmyra, Johnston, Guam, and Samoa Islands in the Pacific. During the fiscal year 1940, some 1,581 new aids were established, and 767 old aids were discontinued. The new establishments needed all types of navigational aids from daymarks to lights, and these had to be maintained and serviced.

Under the Coast Guard, lighthouse tenders became known as buoy tenders. They relieved buoys annually, replaced and recharged batteries, installed acetylene accumulators, established new aids, and supplied lighthouses. The routine was never monotonous. Work was often done in treacherous waters, near dangerous shoals, in fog, and in storms. The nature of the equipment made the task of the buoy men hazardous as well as highly specialized. Winter activities in northern latitudes were especially gruelling, as sharp winds blew icy water on the men as they worked, and the rolling ship with its slippery deck made each movement one of danger.

During the transition period, as the threat of our involvement in the war grew, plans were made for Alaskan defense. In 1941 it was decided to develop and protect the Inside Passage of Southeastern Alaska—the main artery of communication with the United States. This called for measures to deny this waterway to the enemy in event of war, through location of minefields or by the employment of surface craft at strategic points, while at the same time making it available to our own and friendly nations. Plans were developed for the suppression of coastal aids when they were not required for our own uses.

This, in general, was the aids to navigation situation facing the Coast Guard as we entered the conflict. War urgency and Navy policy dictated that, as the war progressed, the even tenor of the ways of lighthouses, buoys, and tenders be broken; that other activities receive priority; and that except for the most urgent items of maintenance, work be largely confined to changes made necessary by the exigencies of war. Tenders, normally engaged continuously for attending aids, had to be extensively used in transporting materials and personnel for defense works, salvage operations, and icebreaking, as well as marking new wrecks, adjusting aids to mark special areas, and maintaining harbor protection such as submarine nets. This, in itself, led to the neglect of usual servicing.

The advent of war on 7 December 1941 brought about the extinguishment or reduction in power of lights and lighted buoys, removal of some buoys, and other alterations in many areas. Some lights, fog signals, and radiobeacons in Alaska, for example, were discontinued. Aids were extinguished around Kodiak, Sitka, and Dutch Harbor. But by 30 December 1941, aids in the Inside Passage had to be relighted as the waters were extremely dangerous and aids were needed for safe operation of our own vessels. The same was true in many other areas. Soon, further reductions became unnecessary because of careful measures taken in each district to accomplish prompt blackout in case of emergency.

There was an obvious need for extensive military operations in widely scattered parts of the world, some of which had never been adequately marked with aids to navigation or well charted. This presented another immediate problem.

The grouping of shore stations, including lifeboat stations, light stations, and certain other bases became, as we have seen, the key to our entire coastal defense system during World War II. The need for patrolling a large part of our continental coastline to guard against subversive landings was soon emphasized by the saboteur landings at Amagansett and Ponte Vedra Beaches, and later at Machias, already mentioned in Chapter 4. Lighthouses and Aids to Navigation personnel were fully utilized in this work.

Discoveries and inventions in the field of television and other electronic devices were quickly directed toward immediate military problems. The result was the development of several systems of electronic signals applicable to air and sea navigation and to the detection of approaching aircraft and ships before they became visible. As the practicality of these devices was demonstrated it became, to a large extent, the duty of the Coast Guard to install and maintain such equipment at fixed points throughout the North Atlantic and the Northern and Western Pacific. The number of radiobeacons increased from 141 in 1939 to 197 in 1948, and to these were added radar beacons, loran, and other electronic devices.

Accomplishments of the Aids to Navigation Division during the war can be very briefly summarized. In the fiscal year ending 30 June 1942, war operations made necessary the withdrawal of certain lightships from their stations and their employment in other fields. Immediately after the war started, dimout and blackout of aids (including radiobeacons) were initiated in cooperation with the Army and Navy. Many aids—especially buoys for new harbor channels, minefields, defense and restricted areas, swept channels, and convoy routes—were provided and placed in connection with offshore Naval bases and other military operations. The western end of the Intracoastal Waterway from Matagorda Bay to Aransas Bay, Texas, was completed and well marked with aids.

During the next twelve-month period, the number of aids to navigation increased by 1,120 to a total of 33,557. These met the wartime needs of shipping in the Intracoastal Waterway along the Atlantic and Gulf coasts, and in marking approaches to military establishments, swept channels, and other critical areas. The buoyage system of the Mississippi River and its tributaries was expanded to assure safe and expeditious movement of military craft to tidewater from builders' yards on the Great Lakes and the rivers.

The fiscal year preceding 30 June 1944 found aids to navigation installed at outlying Greenland bases and in diverse combat areas. Loran (*LOng-RAnge Navigation*) stations were established on our coasts and in other Atlantic and Pacific areas. These enabled navigators of air and surface craft to fix their positions under all weather conditions.

As a result of wartime discoveries in electronics, three important new types of aids were developed. Loran, a pulse system of electronic signals furnishing reliable longitude and latitude positions over greater areas than those covered by radio systems, eventually was operated from 49 stations in 11 chains, from Greenland to Tokyo. (Loran is the subject of Chapter 11.) Radar beacons were fixed frequency transponders which provided coded response to radar interrogation on the proper frequency; this gave a navigational fix by means of simultaneous display of both range and bearing information. Forty-five radar beacons were operated during the war. Finally, Anrac was a remote control radio system transmitting specially coded ultra-high frequency signals to special receivers mounted on buoys or other aids, which started or stopped the operation of lights and fog signals.

In order to meet increased shipping needs, the marking of channels in the Mississippi River Basin and on the Intracoastal Waterways continued. As the war situation along our coasts improved, relaxation of the dimout and blackout of aids to navigation, with a return to practically normal operation was permitted.

During the fiscal year 1945 there was a net increase of 2,286 aids, and the total reached 36,540. Cessation of hostilities in the Atlantic following V-E Day resulted in the removal of aids used primarily for war purposes, but the increased demand throughout the Pacific more than offset this temporarily. Lightships which had been removed during the war were returned to their former stations on the Atlantic Coast, and all lighted aids were returned to fully lighted status as quickly as practicable.

The Fourteenth (Honolulu) Naval District, as such, concerned itself chiefly with Hawaiian waters, and had relatively little to do with aids to navigation in Pacific invasion areas. These were furnished by direct issue from Coast Guard Headquarters. Technical assistance from the Coast Guard was requested by the Commander, Service Forces, Pacific (COMSERVPAC), on several oc-

casions, and finally Commander C. N. Daniel, USCG, was assigned to the Navy as Coast Guard Liaison Officer for aids to navigation for all Pacific and invasion bases. As the United States forces pushed on toward Japan from late 1942 until final victory, aids to navigation of various types and functions were established in the advancing forward areas.

The second new responsibility for safety at sea which the Coast Guard assumed was Weather Patrol. Weather reporting by vessels had been established as a distinct project back in 1906, when the masters of about 50 vessels agreed to take daily observations at a fixed hour when in prescribed ocean locations, and to forward the results by "wireless" to the Weather Bureau in Washington.

The development of radio equipment for vessels had brought about a considerable improvement in charting storms at sea. The Coast Guard had always cooperated with the Weather Bureau in this. It was not until the 1935 hurricane season, however, that a well organized network of stations was set up by the Coast Guard in cooperation with the Weather Bureau, to take observations of weather and sea conditions during the hurricane season. Selected stations were equipped to send reports. The Coast Guard was originally drawn into collaboration with the Weather Bureau when it took over the operation and maintenance of coastal landlines including those formerly operated by the Weather Bureau, and lines of the storm warning service operated by the Army Signal Corps. It was, therefore, necessary for the Coast Guard to render certain service to the Weather Bureau. This had been done for about three decades in a most harmonious manner on the part of the two Services. During World War II, the Coast Guard provided extensive supplementary weather reporting service.

However, until 1939 weather reporting was handled, for the most part, by the Weather Bureau. This reporting was done by civilian personnel, and, except for the cooperation mentioned, the activity was independent of the Coast Guard. But in 1939 weather reporting and observation was also undertaken by the Coast Guard. On 25 January 1940, the Coast Guard, cooperating with the Weather Observation Service, was authorized to use its newly modernized cutters to establish (at the request of the Weather Bureau) an Atlantic Weather

Observation Service. Cutters *Bibb* and *Duane* were the first on station. Their daily weather reports were designed primarily to protect the rapidly increasing transatlantic air commerce.

During 1940 when Great Britain was suffering great ship losses, and the transportation by sea of planes became critical, risks were boldly taken to fly American bombers directly from Newfoundland to England. A third ocean weather station, about 500 miles northeast of Newfoundland thus became necessary.

By February 1941, five Coast Guard cutters were serving as Weather Patrol vessels, taking turns patrolling two weather stations about 10 miles square between Bermuda and the Azores, usually for 21-day periods. Due to war conditions in the Atlantic, these cutters operating out of Boston, were relieved of their usual patrol and cruising duties, and Weather Patrol became a full-time assignment. In November 1941, when the Coast Guard was transferred to the Navy, the schedules of the Weather Patrol ships *Hamilton, Mojave, Spencer, Bibb,* and *Duane* were not affected. These ships continued to operate for a while under the jurisdiction of the Commandant of the Coast Guard. In January 1942, all Weather Patrol vessels became the responsibility of the District Coast Guard Officer, First Naval District, so far as personnel, upkeep, internal control, and other logistics were concerned, but the vessels themselves continued to operate under the Commandant. In the Fall of 1942, operations were finally shifted to the command of CTF-24, U. S. Navy, though logistics responsibility remained unchanged throughout the war.

The original vessels on Weather Patrol were 327-foot cutters, but war developments increased demand for these vessels elsewhere, and they were finally replaced by other craft taken over by the Coast Guard. In August 1942, the duty was being performed by cargo type vessels *Manasquan, Manhasset, Menemsha, Monomoy,* and *Muskeget,* and by *Sea Cloud,* the former yacht of Ambassador Joseph E. Davies. While on patrol they were open to attack by enemy submarines or surface craft. If so attacked, they were instructed to depend upon vessels of the North Atlantic Fleet for assistance and support. They were, in fact, almost "sitting ducks." *Muskeget* with 121 on board was lost without a trace 9 September 1942. Her

loss testifies to the ruggedness of this duty and the heroism of the men who kept at sea in all kinds of weather, to cruise about in a small radius in complete isolation for a month at a time, dodging submarines and battling storms, winter and summer, to send in the required reports.

The strategic importance of meteorological observations from station vessels in the Atlantic was emphasized in 1943 by the Chief of the Weather Bureau in Washington, who said:

"The necessity for maintaining meteorological station vessels in the Atlantic was reviewed by the joint Meteorological Committee under the Joint United States Chiefs of Staff, Washington. It was the unanimous opinion of Army and Navy representatives that the weather reports from these vessels were among the most vital meteorological information for war operations of the United Nations. The reports were considered indispensable not only for certain plans and operations of the armed forces, but also for the British military activities. The need of more than two station ships in the Atlantic had been repeatedly stressed by British and American transport interests. Upon these two station vessels, depended in large measure, the analysis of weather conditions over the vast expanse of the Atlantic. There were no alternative stations from which to obtain synoptic reports as was the case over most continental regions. The difficulty and hardships of service on these station vessels was fully recognized but the value of their reports more than compensated for those difficulties, and the men so serving were performing duties of high priority in the war effort."

Fighter planes were being flown across the Atlantic by way of United States Army airdromes, bridging the ocean from Labrador to Greenland to Iceland. This required more Coast Guard-manned plane guard and weather stations—one midway between Labrador and Greenland in Davis Strait, and the other in Denmark Strait, between southern Greenland and Iceland. Just before invasion of Normandy in June 1944, three additional stations, requested by the Army, were located far out in mid-Atlantic. The British Navy also established a one ship weather station about 50 miles west of the British Isles. In the air raids over Europe, the Normandy invasion, and other Allied operations, the weather data provided by these vessels was utilized. Weather reports were forwarded by radio to base stations from six to eight times daily. These reports were assembled and analyzed by various weather establishments, principally by the Army Air Force. Ships and planes also sent warnings of head winds, storms, icing conditions, and such. Many of the weather observation cutters encountered submarines close to their stations.

To minimize the time needed for travel from station to base, the ships used advanced naval bases for a while, particularly Argentia, Newfoundland.

By May 1945, 16 stations had been established north of 15° N latitude to give adequate weather observation and air-sea rescue facilities. Six more were between the equator and 15° N in the Atlantic. Eleven of the stations were operated by a task force of 26 frigates based at Argentia, Newfoundland, rotating on a schedule which permitted their visiting Bermuda, Greenland, Iceland, and Boston.

Weather information was so vital that every effort was made to improve the results of the patrols. Some of the converted steamers, slow and sluggish, were replaced by buoy tenders such as *Conifer, Evergreen,* and *Sorrel.* These were better sea boats. Finally, almost any available vessel of adequate size was used, and the ships ranged from buoy tenders to the 425-foot, 10,000-ton oiler *Big Horn.* As frigates became available, there was a shift to that type of vessel.

The weather ships usually stayed at sea for 21 days, and then were in port about 10 days for supplies, repairs, and rest. There was a feeling that reports and observations could be improved upon. To promote smoother functioning, plans were made with the Weather Bureau in February 1944, for better administration and greater accuracy in reports. Accordingly, arrangements were made for the assignment of aerographer's mates to the local Weather Bureau office during in-port periods for the purpose of checking reports made during the patrol just completed.

Also in February 1944, a conference was held at Boston on board the weather ship *Asterion,* between representatives of the Coast Guard and the Weather Bureau, to determine the manner of selection of weather observing personnel for the North Atlantic Weather Patrol. The Commanding Officer of *Asterion* had recommended that these men be militarized to still further their efficiency,

and then integrated with the officers and men with whom they were to serve. It was agreed that the weather units of specified vessels would consist of a group of 30 Weather Bureau men and 6 aerographer's mates, who were former Weather Bureau men. Four would be assigned to each vessel. Encouragement was offered personnel of the Weather Bureau to enroll in the Coast Guard Temporary Reserve for part time service as Chief Aerographer's Mates, to be on active duty for the duration of each patrol. About 125 men enrolled on this basis, and thus the Temporary Reserve became actively involved in this important duty. Enrollments were effective 15 April 1944.

The Weather Bureau did not force any man to accept duty on "ocean weather." Asked if they would be willing to accept the assignment, and knowing the need, most accepted. These men had been doing essential work as weather men before entering the Temporary Reserve. Many had gone out in weather ships as civilians during a period of almost a year before enrollment. Because of experience and professional ability, all were enrolled as chiefs except a few who were commissioned.

Although numerous chief aerographer's mates stayed with one vessel for many months, most were "one trippers", making one cruise in one vessel, and being reassigned for the next patrol.

The principal duty of the weather men was the preparation and release of balloons with instruments and radio devices for registering and transmitting information. RADIOSONDES measured upper air temperature, pressure and humidity at various computed altitudes. This information was obtained by sending a midget radio transmitter aloft on a small free balloon. The transmitter sent data to the surface observer automatically. PIBALS measured the direction and intensity of winds aloft by tracking the movement of a small free balloon having an assumed ascentional rate. Tracking was done visually with a special type of instrument known as a theodolite. This was also done by RAWINS, whereby a small balloon carrying a radar reflector was tracked by a standard radar on board ships. These observations were transmitted by each weather vessel to Radio Washington on regular schedules, and then forwarded to the Weather Bureau, for national and international distribution.

The release of balloons sounds simple to the uninitiated; it was anything but that. The weather specialists were highly conscientious in their duty, and observations were missed only when high winds made it impossible to release the balloons. Many releases were made at sea which would have seemed impossible on land. Ingenuity was responsible for much of this success. Occasionally, an observation would be missed when the weather was so bad that the ship could not be headed into the wind to attempt the radiosonde release. However, one aerographer's mate stated that in his 26 months of service, only two observations were missed in vessels in which he sailed. In both cases, waves were breaking over the boat deck, and the commanding officer felt that the risk to his men was not worth the observation.

While most patrols lasted 21 days, after which Boston or another port was made for about a week, some vessels were away for months at a stretch. Many times, these vessels were out of sight of land for a month or more, and life became very monotonous. One outstanding instance was a vessel which left Boston on 22 December. She stopped at Argentia one day for fuel; proceeded toward station; stopped to escort a leaking vessel back to Argentia; proceeded again toward station; sprang a leak herself, and returned to Argentia for repairs. She proceeded to station one week later, where she spent 22 days; went to Iceland for fuel; staying a week, and back on station another 21 days. From there she returned to Argentia for 10 days, spent more time on station, and then went to Boston. She had been at sea for 70 out of 90 days.

For six full months there was only one liberty period for *Big Horn,* and that was at Argentia.

While on station the weather ships were ideally situated to undertake rescue work when things went wrong in their general areas. There were many, many cases of rescue, not only while on station, but while en route to and from stations and bases. Some instances are mentioned in other chapters.

The weather program which was started as a war measure had proved so valuable that it was continued in operation. In September 1946, the interested North Atlantic nations agreed at London that a minimum of 13 ocean weather stations, maintained by the Coast Guard, were required.

Five others were to be operated by the British and two by Brazil.

In the Pacific, ocean weather stations were manned by Navy vessels of various types until the frigates, manned by the Coast Guard, began to operate in the Pacific area about June 1944. Some of these frigates took up ocean weather duty. At the peak of activity there were 20 Pacific Ocean weather stations, mostly maintained by Navy manned vessels.

The third new responsibility looking to safety at sea that was undertaken by the Coast Guard was Marine Inspection. The Bureau of Marine Inspection and Navigation really had its inception in 1824, when Congress directed the Secretary of the Treasury to investigate steamboat disasters, particularly boiler explosions in Mississippi River steamboats, which were causing the loss of an increasing number of lives. No legislation resulted at that time because it was felt that it would do mischief rather than prevent disasters. There was little progress in that direction until 1838 when, by Act of Congress, owners and masters of steam vessels were required to employ skilled engineers, as well as provide lifeboats, fire pumps, hose, signal lights, and other safety equipment, and to have hulls inspected annually and boilers semiannually.

The "Steamboat Act" of 30 August 1852 provided for nine supervising inspectors who were to be experts in the construction and operation of commercial craft. Each had his own territory. Local inspectors, acting under the supervising inspectors, issued licenses to the engineers and pilots of passenger vessels.

In 1871, Congress established the Office of Supervisory Inspector General, under the Treasury Department; officers and crews of cargo vessels were then afforded the same protection given previously to passenger ships. Pilot rules were also authorized and formulated. By 1881 all privately-owned foreign steam vessels carrying passengers for hire from our ports were subject to the steamboat laws.

From time to time, the scope of inspectors' duties was extended. In 1903 the Steamboat Inspection Service was transferred along with the Lighthouse Service from the Treasury Department to the Department of Commerce and Labor. There followed a special session of supervising inspectors to modernize operations in keeping with developments in marine transportation. Later, additional responsibilities including measures for the prevention and extinguishment of fire, the prescribing of lifesaving equipment, and the licensing of operators of certain vessels of up to 15 gross tons propelled by gas, gasoline, petroleum, or electricity were added. On 9 June 1910, the Motor Boat Act was approved.

The Steamboat Inspection Service stayed with the Department of Commerce when Commerce and Labor separated in 1913. On 30 June 1932, the Steamboat Inspection Service and the Bureau of Navigation of the Department of Commerce (which enforced the laws relating to hiring, discharge, and conduct of American seamen), were consolidated into the Bureau of Navigation and Marine Inspection. After the *Morro Castle* was destroyed by fire off Asbury Park, New Jersey, in 1934, the organization was set up under revised regulations. A technical staff was created in 1936 to pass on plans and specifications for passenger vessels and the name was changed to Bureau of Marine Inspection and Navigation.

Enemy attacks on American seamen and ships just prior to and after our entry into the war indicated the urgent need for immediate measures to provide more effective safety precautions in order to meet the conditions of modern warfare. A central agency experienced in the consideration and development of safety standards at sea, was found desirable. This was the reason behind Executive Order 9083 of 28 February 1942, which placed the authority and responsibility for the protection of American merchant ships and seamen directly upon the Commandant of the Coast Guard. The Bureau of Marine Inspection and Navigation was thus transferred to the Coast Guard.

The duties of Merchant Marine Inspection, now assumed by the Coast Guard, included:

(1) Approving plans for merchant ships and their equipment;

(2) Inspection of vessels to check on stability, fire control or fireproofing, lifesaving and fire-fighting equipment and other details;

(3) The administration of the load line;

(4) The administration and enforcement of laws pertaining to the numbering, equipment, and operation of motorboats;

(5) Enforcement of manning requirements;

(6) Issuance of certificates of inspection;

(7) Examination, licensing and certification of Merchant Marine personnel including masters, pilots, engineers, staff officers, and seamen;

(8) Signing on, discharge, and supervising the living conditions of merchant seamen;

(9) Investigation of marine casualties;

(10) Preparation and publication of rules and regulations to provide protection to passengers, officers and crews of American ships;

(11) Merchant Marine Council activities.

This, it will be readily admitted, added greatly and importantly to the duties of the Coast Guard.

Blueprints of plans for new vessels dealing with hull structure, main power plant, auxiliaries, piping systems, electrical equipment, and installation were submitted to highly trained naval architects and engineers of the Coast Guard, who checked to make sure that they conformed with all requirements. Full compliance with rules and regulations for the class of vessel and service intended was mandatory. Contracts and plans which were reviewed at Coast Guard Headquarters involved construction, alteration, and repair of merchant vessels, and, in most cases, vessels for the War Department and other agencies of the Government. Headquarters also reviewed the basic safety characteristics, as well as all details of the adequacy and arrangement of the vessel and its equipment.

From the moment the keel of a new ship was laid until the vessel retired from active duty, the Coast Guard watched over that vessel's career—testing, inspecting, examining, safeguarding. Each vessel was inspected at various stages of building, and lifesaving and fire-fighting devices were tested. Because of the huge acceleration and expansion in the construction of ships in 1942, there was a tremendous increase in the activity of the inspector. Gross tonnage of merchant vessels of 1,000 tons or more increased from 6,720,042 on 15 December 1941 to 26,146,500 on 20 August 1945. If, to this, were added the 4,156,849 gross tons lost during the war, the total tonnage *increase* was 23,583,307. Every ton of this shipping had to be inspected by the Coast Guard.

The Coast Guard was the technical advisor to the U. S. Army on merchant marine matters. Additional armament on an Army transport affected her stability, and ballast had to be provided to offset it, so Army transports were inspected and inclined to test their stability. All United States and foreign troopships carrying U. S. troops were Coast Guard inspected.

Boiler plates were inspected and tested at the mills, and completed boilers were inspected at the place of manufacture. Lifeboats, rafts, ring buoys, and other items of safety equipment were inspected at the factories.

All United States merchant vessels were inspected annually. In 1943, inspections were completed on 6,883 vessels, including transports. To facilitate operations of vessels in war areas, inspectors were assigned to duty at foreign war zone ports. Stationary installations, such as boilers and unfired pressure vessels and other appurtenances at veterans' hospitals, Government penitentiaries, forts, Army cantonments, Federal buildings, and such were inspected and tested each year by Coast Guard Marine inspectors.

Load line certificates were issued to American ships by the American Bureau of Shipping. The load line is a 9-inch line on the side of a ship which indicates the maximum draft to which she can be loaded. If the ship is overloaded, this load line is submerged and the ship is legally unseaworthy. The Coast Guard was required to check the load line of all United States and foreign ships using American ports, to see that no vessel was overloaded. If it were, the Coast Guard prevented the ship sailing.

A Board of Investigation was convened by the Secretary of the Navy in 1943 to inquire into the design and methods of construction of welded steel merchant vessels. Several such vessels had broken in half at sea. A specific case was the Standard Oil tanker *Esso Manhattan* which, on 29 March 1943, broke in two. The vessel jack-knifed and the bow dug under an oncoming wave. The crew abandoned ship, and lifeboats were picked up by cutter *Kimball*. The vessel floated in two parts, and was towed to port, the sections rewelded, and the vessel returned to service. The interim report of the Board on 3 June 1944 stated that the speed and volume required of the shipbuilding program could not have been achieved without an early and general adoption of welded construction of merchant ships. Imperfect welding underlay most of these mishaps. Contrary to popular impression, hull fractures were not confined to Liberty ships.

Abandoning ship correctly took practice. Quick thinking and fast action often meant the difference between life and death. Lifeboat training programs drilled men in handling lifeboats and equipment so that they would know exactly what to do if their ship were torpedoed.

To insure safe operation, an adequate crew both as to number and qualifications was required; no vessel was supposed to put to sea unless manned as required by the inspection certificate. Waivers were, however, issued in emergencies, and, as the war progressed, full crews became the exception rather than the rule. The Coast Guard's choice was between getting materials where they were needed to win the war, and risking some element of danger through undermanning. With the return of peace, waivers became the exception.

Ships were reboarded from time to time to check on their continued seaworthiness and the efficiency of their crews. As a result of these inspections, examinations, instructions, and drills, crews acquired a thorough familiarity with their duties and with the use of emergency equipment —this latter being especially important as many new devices were being constantly added for increased safety.

Coast Guard inspectors visited transports leaving United States ports with American troops to explain and demonstrate emergency equipment, conduct fire and boat drills, and see that all devices were in good condition and ready for immediate use. Wartime safety requirements controlled the safe loading, stowing, and inspection of cargo to insure against shifting and loss at sea, and to prevent sagging and hogging stresses which might capsize or break the vessel in heavy weather.

A Merchant Marine Council was created on 1 June 1942 to study and make recommendations for the efficiency and welfare of merchant seamen, and the improvement in efficiency of safety equipment on board merchant vessels. A panel of experts was chosen from the country's outstanding leaders in every phase of maritime activity. This Council constituted a forum where various elements of the industry could express opinions on proposals and actions of the Coast Guard affecting their interests.

During World War II the Coast Guard maintained the individual files of about 500,000 merchant seamen. Each file contained a complete history of the seamen's employment on board U. S. merchant vessels, and a record of all documents issued to him by the shipping commissioners and Merchant Marine inspectors at the various ports where he had shipped. Also collected and maintained were records of all cases arising from alleged misconduct, incompetency, or negligence, of Merchant Marine personnel, looking toward revocation or suspension of licenses or certificates. Coast Guard officers concerned, were informed about when and where the accused seaman would next arrive in the United States, and the action to be taken.

The sad duty of notifying the next of kin of all Merchant Marine personnel reported dead or missing also fell upon the Coast Guard. The latter also furnished such information to the Red Cross, War Shipping Administration, Office of the Provost Marshal, and operators of the vessels concerned.

Written examinations meeting uniform standards were prescribed and offered to Merchant Marine officer candidates throughout the country. Special examinations were developed and distributed periodically for prospective licensed officers in Maritime Service Training Stations. Officers of the Merchant Marine were awarded licenses, and seamen were given certificates of service, after successfully passing tests given by the Coast Guard.

Hearing Units were created to investigate marine casualties including collisions, groundings, strandings, heavy weather damage, and war casualties. Many lessons were learned from the careful study and analysis of casualties. These units also investigated cases involving misconduct, negligence, inattention to duty, and various other faults on the part of the Merchant Marine personnel. Wartime conditions brought about a great increase in crew trouble and marine casualties, and segregation of this activity into a special unit was constructive from all angles. This investigating, which had been formerly done by the Office of Marine Inspection, was placed under the jurisdiction of the Hearing Unit for more efficient and expeditious handling, and to allow the Marine Inspection office to devote its efforts exclusively to marine inspection work.

Few experienced men were available for this activity and training courses had to be instituted. Young officers were often utilized in this work.

Throughout the activity, there was the problem of young ensigns with only four or five weeks of training, sitting in judgment on masters and other experienced seafarers who had spent their lives at sea and in command of ships, and who with some reason heartily resented this situation. Yet there seemed to be no alternative.

There were Hearing Units in all major United States ports and in the several foreign war areas. The foreign Units, in addition, made decisions regarding temporary repairs to damaged merchant vessels, so that the ships could be made seaworthy until they could reach a place where regular repair work was done. By the end of 1944, foreign hearing units were operating in about 30 foreign locations, including the Southwest Pacific.

In June 1944, General Dwight D. Eisenhower asked for a high ranking officer who was thoroughly familiar with merchant marine problems to become a member of his Staff. This was when the invasion of Europe was giving rise to many problems involving thousands of merchant ships and seamen. Captain Halert C. Shepheard, USCG, Chief of the Merchant Marine Inspection Division of the Coast Guard, was recommended and appointed. He promptly departed for England.

Interviews with survivors of torpedoed merchant vessels often brought excellent suggestions for the improvement of lifesaving equipment. A crew member did not mind the precaution of having the frequent drills once he had experienced a torpedoing. Drinking water and protective clothing were two items frequently emphasized by survivors. As a result, all lifeboats were equipped with 10 quarts of drinking water. Many deaths from exposure in frigid waters gave rise to the use of rubber immersion suits for those compelled to abandon ship at sea. These contained all the desirable features of the old exposure suits and, in addition, kept the wearer upright, with his head and shoulders well above the water. Safer electric lights, replacing the calcium water lights which could ignite a sea of oil, enabled the wearer to be easily spotted and rescued at night. After one survivor told of signaling a passing ship by tearing off the lid of a tin can and catching the reflection of the sun on its surface, the inspectors added mirrors to lifeboat equipment. Parachute flares and other safety devices were also added.

Thus, many new safety measures were based squarely upon the experience and needs of survivors.

Difficulty in launching lifeboats, especially on loaded tankers which immediately gushed burning oil all around the vessel when torpedoed raised many problems. Getting a lifeboat into the sea from the sloping deck of a burning or sinking ship with a decided list, was exceedingly difficult. Davits were continually improved, and it eventually became possible to launch lifeboats despite the vessel's list. Under new safety rules American ships carried their lifeboats in the outward position so that they could be lowered more quickly. Enough lifeboats to take care of the entire crew were carried on each side of a cargo ship so that either set would be sufficient in case of a heavy list. "Skates" were provided to help a lifeboat slide over projections when a vessel listed. All lifeboats carried at least one mast and a set of sails so that, with a good wind, a boat could sail 2,000 miles if necessary, and reach port.

There were many other improvements. Red or chrome-colored lifeboat sails made spotting from the surface or air much easier. Yellow dyes spread on the water could be easily seen from the air; these saved Eddie Rickenbacker in November 1942, when he was forced down at sea on a transpacific flight. Better lifeboats had grab rails, skates, and skids, while some had motor propulsion. Life rafts of sufficient capacity to accommodate all persons on board became required equipment. Provision of food in lifeboats received much study, resulting in tremendous improvement. Embarkation ladders and lifesaving nets were required over the ship's side for easy boarding of lifeboats and rafts, and also for rescuing survivors from the sea.

The Coast Guard issued many publications and manuals during the war. These were generally distributed among merchant officers and seamen, and gave the best advice obtainable on what to do in emergency. Undoubtedly, these saved many lives.

These new responsibilities for adding to safety at sea greatly increased the influence of the Coast Guard, and fitted logically with its other duties.

# Chapter 10

# COAST GUARD COMMUNICATIONS

THE COAST GUARD COMMUNICATIONS SYSTEM satisfactorily met peak requirements in World War II. It consisted of an integrated network extending along the coasts of the continental United States and throughout the North Atlantic, Gulf of Mexico, Caribbean Sea, and Alaska, and the middle and northeast sectors of the North Pacific. In general, it consisted of land based and lightship radio facilities; 17 communications centers; over 60 direction finder stations; 49 Loran stations; 98 post offices ashore and 196 afloat; landline service of over 1,700 miles of leased telegraph circuits; 1,968 miles of owned circuits (serving 4,807 stations); 1,849 units (excluding Headquarters); and radio facilities in its vessels, aircraft, and mobile units. The system was so interwoven that the many Coast Guard functions were smoothly and flexibly coordinated, facilitating any required action, whether for purposes of combat; a vessel or aircraft in distress; rescue of survivors; relief in floods, hurricanes, or other disasters; or other emergency.

Wartime Coast Guard communications, however, were chiefly an expansion of the prewar communications system, to which were added many adaptations of new types of equipment to keep pace with progress in the field and to meet the increasing and finer demands occasioned by the war. To comprehend the problems, limitations, and achievements, it is desirable to present to the reader a little background history relating to the various subdivisions of the communications activity. Technical details, of interest to the student of this highly technical subject, are generally omitted as this review is not intended to present a treatise on the subject.

The Coast Guard's various communications activities since the establishment of its landline services in 1878, and the use of radio afloat since 1903, proved of inestimable value in the performance of its peacetime functions. The Service had kept abreast of developments and improvements, while consistently maintaining high operational standards, under the competent guidance of such outstanding pioneers and leaders in the field of communications as Walton, Waesche, and Webster. The degree of readiness for wartime activation which Coast Guard Communications was thereby able to maintain, was ultimately reflected in the creditable manner in which the numerous additional wartime duties were assumed.

Its many years of experience in the field of emergency communications was recognized by the Secretary of the Navy when, under authority of Executive Order, he issued his directive of 6 June 1942, charging the Coast Guard with the task of providing adequate military and safety distress communications for the Merchant Marine. The peacetime training of Coast Guard personnel in Navy communications procedures and techniques greatly facilitated the assumption of wartime duties when the Coast Guard operated under the Navy.

Some idea of the breadth of Coast Guard participation in World War II has been given, as well as the degree to which war had become mechanized. Far-flung operations, 100-ship convoys, great fleet actions, large-scale amphibious operations, and other activities were extremely complicated in comparison with the war experience of former years. The importance of communications within these forces, and with other units, as well as between the forces and their bases cannot be overestimated. A breakdown of communications might well mean a breakdown of an entire operation. Accuracy and promptness were essentials, and the responsibilities of Communications Officers were heavy.

To appreciate Coast Guard Communications in World War II, it will be helpful to review briefly the developments in the prewar period.

While the Lifesaving Service had actively used coastal landlines since 1878, and the Revenue Cutter Service had used "wireless telegraphy" in its vessels since 1903, the various phases of these two methods of communication were first coordinated and operationally organized under the Coast Guard by the 1927 *Communications Instructions*. These charged the Coast Guard with the construction, operation, maintenance, and supply of all Coast Guard communications facilities, and the instruction and training of the necessary personnel. The Coast Guard Communications Service was designated as having cognizance of Coast Guard communications by telegraph, telephone, cable, radio-telegraph, radiocompass, visual and underwater signals, sound telegraph, as well as registered and secret publications, codes and ciphers. Detailed instructions were given on organization, operation, and administration.

The *mission* of the Coast Guard Communications Service, as established in the 1927 instructions, was:

(1) To receive information relative to distress direct from its source;

(2) To provide for receipt of distress information expeditiously by all means of and from all sources available;

(3) To provide for the dissemination of distress information to all possible sources of aid with the utmost speed and accuracy;

(4) To handle orders and information accurately, rapidly, and secretly when necessary to, from, and between our units afloat, in the air, and on shore;

(5) To develop, procure, install, maintain, and operate all apparatus necessary to the efficient handling of communications.

Communications Officers were specified as commissioned or chief warrant officers (chief radio electricians) and designated to assist division and force commanders in communications. Communications centers were established at Headquarters and under each division commander. Each division center was operated under the direction of the communications officer, whose duties included transmission of messages, their routing, coding, decoding, placing them in proper form, fixing priority of dispatches, filing, recording, and effecting delivery. They also maintained records of telephone, telegraph, and mail addresses of all Coast Guard vessels, stations, offices, personnel on special assignments, ship-owners and agents, and central law enforcement agencies in their divisions. At first, these centers were required to guard the distress frequency, but later this was taken over by other units not subject to troublesome local electrical interference.

*Communications Instructions*, as they stood on 15 December 1930, further defined the organization, mission, and policies of the Coast Guard communications system. With some alterations, these were patterned as closely as possible after the *Navy Communications Instructions* in order to provide for operation as part of the Navy, whenever required, and to facilitate communications between the two Services at all times.

The Secretaries of the Navy and Treasury on 30 September 1936, fully realizing the necessity for full cooperation in communications between the Navy and the Coast Guard, signed a declaration of policy which was to prove highly effective in developing the Coast Guard communications system along lines which further facilitated smooth and efficient integration as part of the Navy organization in time of war. When World War II began, the transition to wartime operation under the Navy was effected quickly and with practically no confusion.

The wartime communications organization operated under the Chief, Communications Division, whose office was at Headquarters in Washington, D.C. His office was divided into various subsections and units which were concerned with the several phases of communications work. These, for the most part, had their counterparts in the district organizations, and are briefly outlined.

The Operations Section had three subsections: (a) Shore Stations and Ships, (b) Statistical, Analysis, and Accounting, and (c) Aeronautics. These functioned virtually as one in developing and administering communications operating plans. They instructed field personnel on operating plans and procedures, prepared communications publications and maintained records of all shore unit activities, made recommendations for any changes in shore units and facilities, and advised on equipment and personnel. They also kept informed of field operations; handled the program for safety and distress communications; developed, improved, and administered the direction finder networks program, the direction finder calibrating transmitters, and visual communications; and monitored radio stations and radiobeacons.

The Special Projects and Plans Unit handled special assignments and studied special problems. It collected historical data on Coast Guard communications, and performed assignments relating to interdepartmental committees.

The Electronic Equipment Subsection saw that all units afloat and ashore had the necessary radio and other electronic equipment needed for efficient operation. It assigned radio and underwater sound and Loran shipborne receivers to floating and shore units as needed. This Subsection also maintained records of all stocks of electronic equipment installed in Coast Guard units; considered improvements in communications equipment; and kept abreast of scientific developments.

The Radio Frequencies Subsection, through appropriate applications and protests to the Interdepartment Radio Advisory Committee, obtained and protected frequencies needed by the Coast Guard. It made general frequency studies, and advised the Chief Communications Officer on effective use of Coast Guard frequencies.

The Landlines and Cables Subsection prepared Headquarters programs on the development and operation of the landlines system; prepared letters and instructions on landline and cable operating policy; determined operational needs for commercial services; and actively administered the "long lines" program. It also reviewed contracts and controlled suballotment funds; estimated budgets for commercial service; and maintained records of landlines and cable facilities at Coast Guard units.

The more important duties of the Postal Affairs Subsection included the establishment and administration of Coast Guard units of the Navy postal service; bonding of its mails clerks; maintenance of records; and handling of claims and complaints based on the mishandling of mail by Coast Guard personnel.

The Weather Reporting Subsection arranged and established weather reporting facilities at shore units at the request of the Weather Bureau or Navy Department; maintained necessary records; and cooperated with the Weather Bureau and other agencies interested in weather. It kept informed regarding the Weather Patrol and procedures of communications with Radio Washington. It handled instructions about the display of storm signals; collaborated on problems in instruction relating to weather broadcasts and transmission of weather data to air stations; made recommendations on the procurement of equipment, facilities, and aerological personnel; as well as provided local aerological services at air stations.

The Administrative Subsection concerned itself with personnel complements at communications units, and with personnel records, training, and promotion of communications specialists.

The Office Services Subsection maintained the Division files, provided messenger, duplicating, and drafting services, and obtained office equipment and supplies for Division use.

The Registered Publications Unit was established at Headquarters late in 1924, when the Coast Guard was undergoing expansion because of its law enforcement duties. To provide the necessary wartime security, certain documents, especially cryptographic publications and devices, were assigned secret or confidential classifications. Continuous accountability was required.

The Communications Security Subsection prepared allowance lists and arranged for the distribution of registered publications and non-registered classified publications to Coast Guard units. It considered cases of compromise of classified matter by personnel, and advised the Navy on code publications applicable to the Coast Guard.

The Communication Center transmitted and received messages in connection with Headquarters activities. Virtually all of the operations were conducted on teletype linked with Navy Radio Washington, Coast Guard Radio Washington, as well as with the commercial teletype (TWX) and Western Union. In meeting peak wartime requirements the Center was operated continuously. It prepared stencils and distributed all general messages to the "Standard Distribution List," and to a mailing list of some 85 units. It kept files and records; delivered unclassified dispatches; checked Headquarters teletype bills; and reviewed field reports of traffic involving tolls. A Coding Board encoded and decoded all classified dispatches sent and received by Headquarters. The Headquarters

Communication Center handled up to 24,000 messages in one month. During 1944 and 1945 it handled this amazingly similar traffic:

|  | 1944 | 1945 |
|---|---|---|
| Total number of messages | 245,689 | 248,403 |
| Total number of words | 8,650,946 | 8,465,538 |
| Average number of messages per month | 20,474 | 20,700 |
| Average number of words per month | 720,912 | 705,461 |
| Average number of messages per day | 682.5 | 690.0 |
| Average number of words per day | 24,034 | 23,515 |

The requirements and responsibilities of the Communications Division grew with the years, particularly during the war. Among the duties of the District Communications Officers set forth in the 1 January 1944 *Organization Manual* were the direction of the operation of the Communication Center; Coding Board; the central switchboard service in the District Office, and the primary radio station of the district. They were to generally administer other communications facilities, including radio direction finder stations, mobile communications units, and the operations of the weather reporting facilities in the district. It was their responsibility to keep completely informed of all district communications activities through field visits, inspections, and reports, and also of any changes relating to communications. These officers were to administer the naval postal facilities handling Coast Guard mail; to maintain liaison with other communications agencies; and to provide for the security, safekeeping, and distribution of registered publications in the District. They reviewed or initiated requests for personnel, equipment, supplies, and facilities.

Radiomen require extensive specialized training, and this became a major concern to Communications. The commissioning of 25 destroyers in 1924-1926 for the suppression of rum-running had given the Coast Guard its first experience in handling the communications of a large force. With the resulting great increase in personnel, it was necessary to obtain operators as quickly as possible. This meant enlisting men who had seen only Navy, Army, or commercial service. The result was a non-uniform group, with widely varying conceptions of procedure. The experience gained at this time probably did more than anything else to emphasize the necessity for careful and thorough training of radio operators in Navy pro-

cedure. A program of intensive training was established and never relinquished. From a humble beginning at the State Pier and at Fort Trumbull, New London, Connecticut, the radio school grew, and was eventually moved to Atlantic City on 29 June 1942. Training of Coast Guard radiomen reached its peak in the truly magnificent accomplishments of this Atlantic City Training Station Radio School during World War II. At the end of the fiscal year 1939, the Coast Guard had an authorized radioman complement of 938 and an "on board" count of 596. By August 1945, the authorized complement for enlisted communications personnel was well over 16,000. During the war, the school graduated 5,510 male radiomen and 386 SPAR radiomen; and 101 male officers and 510 male enlisted men were trained in high frequency direction finding. In addition 145 male and 60 SPAR officers were graduated in general communications training.

Throughout the war there was a critical shortage of radiomen. Vessels had to be manned, and the drain on radiomen was especially acute in early 1943. The situation was somewhat relieved by SPAR radiomen, the first of whom became available after training at the University of Wisconsin. These SPARS were usually made supervisors as soon as others followed. In a few months the SPARS had relieved many men, and eventually most of the men on shore assignments were so relieved. SPAR officers were placed in charge of many activities, particularly in district offices. It is believed that the First Naval District was the first to have an all-SPAR Communications Center. Many SPARS became as adaptable to radio communications as men, but they excelled rather generally as teletype operators.

Of the total enlisted male and SPAR personnel in Coast Guard communications during the war, 78.7 percent were Reserves. This percentage does not include Temporary Reservists who served full or part time in radio sealing; nor does it include the many hundreds who performed allied communications duties such as telephone switchboard operators, mail clerks (other than Specialists (M)), messengers, and such.

A very important part of Coast Guard work has been *landline* communications. Earlier in this history we have commented upon the "coastal information system"—really an outgrowth of this. It will be interesting to trace briefly the establishment and development of this phase of communications, for the landlines proved a vital link in our coastal chain of defense and rescue efforts.

Under the Act of 3 March 1873, a storm signal service was established at several lifesaving stations on the Atlantic coast. This was operated for the benefit of seamen by the Army Signal Corps. The Corps constructed telegraph lines for communication between these stations to facilitate the coordination of lifesaving activities in event of marine disaster. In 1878 telephones were placed on the telegraph lines. It is believed that the Life Saving Service (now the Coast Guard) was thus the first such institution in the world to introduce the telephone as a lifesaving medium. The effectiveness of this innovation was immediately and completely demonstrated. In the next 10 years a large number of stations were connected into the system.

On its establishment in 1890 the Weather Bureau took over the weather and storm warning work, together with the telegraph lines, while the Life Saving Service absorbed the telephone lines. During the following 25 years the telephone system was greatly expanded.

In 1916, when rumbles of war in Europe were becoming louder in the United States, it was recommended that, for the purpose of saving life and property at sea, and for national defense and for administration in time of war, the various means of communication along our coasts under the several executive departments be coordinated, and that the Coast Guard bring the then existing telephone system of coastal communications to a high state of efficiency. This would include all Coast Guard stations and important lighthouses. This program was completed late in 1918, with the assistance of the American Telephone and Telegraph Company and associated systems. There were difficulties; most of the work was done during wartime with attendant scarcities of materials and personnel, often in out-of-the-way places, sparsely settled localities, marshes, sand dunes, and across stretches of water. Several radio-compass stations were established on shore by the Navy, and landline communication to many of these stations was furnished over Coast Guard facilities.

A few landlines, retained by the Weather Bureau, were finally transferred to the Coast Guard in 1929, together with some of the Weather Bureau personnel who had maintained these lines. By 1933 the Coast Guard owned and operated a coastal communications system consisting of telephone and telegraph lines totaling about 1,493 miles of pole line, 2,512 miles of open wire aerial circuits, 31 miles of aerial and underground cables, and 585 miles of submarine cable.

In improving this communications system, it was necessary to lay submarine cables in certain localities. In World War I, the Coast Guard had no cable ship. What little cable laying was done in that period was accomplished by the Western Union cable ship *Robert Clowrie* and a converted menhaden trawler *John A. Palmer, Jr.,* operated by the Navy. In October 1919, the latter was turned over to the Coast Guard and renamed *Pequot.* She laid cables along the Atlantic Coast for over two years. In April 1922, the minelayer *General Samuel M. Mills* was acquired and renamed *Pequot,* and the old vessel of that name was decommissioned. The second *Pequot* engaged in extensive cable laying operations for the Coast Guard until placed out of commission in 1946.

This whole system was efficiently maintained, and wires and cables renewed and replaced as needed. The developing emergency of 1939 found the system generally in good condition; scarcely any cables were over 10 years old. The lines, combined with a modern inside plant, adequately met normal requirements of the Service. By the time of Pearl Harbor these facilities connected lighthouses and lifeboat stations to commercial telephone facilities.

With the advent of war, the institution of beach patrol, and the rapid expansion of military activity, immediate additions to the regular Coast Guard coastal landline system became mandatory. Over 1,500 miles of additional telephone circuits were buried along the outer beaches, with reporting stations at quarter-mile intervals. On many beaches, "commando jacks" were installed where patrolmen could plug in hand sets which they carried as part of their equipment. Isolated sections, not served by commercial systems, required lines, and new coastal Army and Navy units needed telephone and teletype facilities. The prewar circuit of the Coast Guard system of some 4,400 miles, was expanded to about 12,000 miles.

This required immediate installation of hundreds of miles of pole lines, wire and cable, and demanded the eventual enlistment and training of over 500 additional linemen, cable splicers, and other installation and maintenance personnel.

While this expanded system thoroughly covered many sections of our coasts, there were still many areas lacking these facilities. This necessitated providing new landline radio communications along many miles of coast line.

Wire installations along many beaches were accomplished with the use of special plows, tractors, splicing equipment, and other supplies. About 4,000 miles of wire were laid in this manner. Installations were usually made parallel to, and close to, the beaches along routes traveled by the patrolmen. There were many difficulties. Obstructions under the surface made it impossible to bury cable in some localities. Sometimes storms cut away the beaches and washed out or broke the cables. In moving the line back from such areas, heavy beach grass, underbrush, and heavy timber often caused complications. Tough beach grass occasionally penetrated the rubber jacket of the cable and grounded out the circuits. Special equipment was often required to clear out many areas for the standard cable laying plows. In the West, gophers liked the soft plowed earth and burrowed there, gnawing cables if they interfered with their burrowing, thus disrupting service. Much cable, therefore, frequently had to be renewed. In some areas where cables could not be laid, patrolmen were equipped with "walkie-talkies" or similar two-way voice communication radio sets, and their stations were equipped with the necessary apparatus. Even radio equipped motor vehicles were available if needed.

In the Pacific Northwest, with vast areas densely wooded with immense heavy timber, and no commercial facilities within many miles, it was sometimes necessary to cut right-of-way through dense spruce and hemlock for long distances. Such clearing was a major logging operation requiring the enlistment in the Coast Guard of trained lumbermen.

In meeting the requirements of port security in thickly populated and congested harbor sectors, special telephone circuits were extended to thousands of posts located among warehouses, docks, and other facilities. These were constantly ready to flash word in the event that sabotage activities were detected, fires discovered, or other emergencies observed.

The Coast Guard, of course, operated the regular coastal radio stations for communicating with its own cutters, motorboats, and motor vehicles. The motorboats operating on harbor patrol and along inaccessible shore lines were radio equipped, thereby completing a far reaching system that, in its entirety, thoroughly covered our coast line.

During 1945 marked changes were made in the landlines system. Abolishment or curtailment of the beach patrol in many areas meant elimination of several thousand miles of temporary beach patrol circuits.

In assuming responsibility for a coastal network of radio direction finder stations, the Coast Guard put into operation about 7,500 miles of teletypewriter circuits to interconnect these stations. Voice command circuits were also needed for radio direction finder services and the rapidly developing air-sea rescue operations. A further increase in circuits was brought about after 1 July 1945 through the establishment of permanent network service in place of that previously provided by Navy leased temporary wartime circuits.

Of equal importance to Coast Guard communications was shipborne radio. A brief outline of its development will add to the interest of the wartime experience. In March 1899, Marconi succeeded in transmitting messages by "wireless" across the English Channel. On 12 December 1901, he transmitted signals across the North Atlantic. In the following years the United States Army, Navy, Weather Bureau, and Revenue Cutter Service (forerunner of the Coast Guard) actively experimented and progressed with "wireless" as a regular means of communication on land and at sea. An installation in cutter *Grant* in 1903 succeeded in ship-shore communication.

Gradually, additional installations were made in other vessels and the transmission of messages became more successful. In 1904-1905 shore wireless stations were being established. General installations were recommended in 1904 for the larger revenue cutters. In 1907, $30,000 was approved for installing radio (as it became known in 1906) apparatus in up to 12 revenue cutters. *Algonquin* was the first to be so equipped, and by 1909, installations had been made in most of the large cutters.

Until 1912, there was no general concerted idea

regarding frequencies and wave lengths. Finally, the 600 meters (500 k.c.) wave length was established for general calling and distress. For several years, "wireless" operators of the Revenue Cutter Service were landline telegraphers, hired for the purpose, who used the American Morse Code. In Europe, another code—the International (Continental) Code—was employed, and for some years both codes were used by American coastal radio stations and by United States vessels.

It is believed that the first distress call by an American vessel was sent on 10 December 1905, by Relief Lightship #58 at the Nantucket Shoals Station. This consisted of the word "H-E-L-P", followed in both codes by a request for aid. The lightship had developed a leak in the fireroom and because her pumps were insufficient to keep ahead of the water, her fires were drowned out. The tender *Azalea*, in a heavy gale, reached the lightship and towed her toward New Bedford, but the stricken craft foundered 18 miles from her station.

In 1908, when the "White Squadron" of the United States Navy went around the world, there were 97 radio stations on the United States coasts, of which 40 were operated by the Navy, 16 by the Army, and the rest privately. Sixty-four Navy vessels and 62 private United States vessels were radio-equipped, as were most transatlantic passenger liners.

By Act of Congress of 4 May 1910, every passenger ship and any other ship carrying 50 persons or more, leaving any port of the United States, was required to be equipped with radio. This resulted chiefly from experience in the collision of the liner *Republic* with the steamer *Florida* off Nantucket in January 1909. *Republic's* radio operator, Jack Binns, who summoned help, was among the last of the 761 survivors to be removed; he was taken on board a boat from cutter *Gresham*. This was an early episode in a long series of rescues where Coast Guard communications played an ever-increasingly important part.

Necessity for further improvement in apparatus and methods was emphasized when over 1,500 lives were lost in the *Titanic* disaster of April 1912. That vessel, on her maiden voyage, sank after striking an iceberg. This disaster led to the organization of the International Ice Patrol, conducted by the Coast Guard from 1913 until World War II.

In 1923, when the Coast Guard became active

in combatting the smuggling of liquor into the United States, some 250 small patrol vessels were radio-equipped. For the smaller boats, special equipment had to be developed and produced. This program cost about $2,000,000.

Transmitters and receivers developed in 1938 for use at lifeboat stations and in motor lifeboats marked a great improvement in this type of equipment by providing a complete two-way system for operation between the stations and boats, utilizing radiophone or C.W. telegraphy. With the developing world crisis in 1939, which accounted for close coordination with the Navy in communication matters, it became evident that shipborne equipment of the Coast Guard should be of Navy type to facilitate replacement and interchange of parts. Later, Radar, Loran, and Sonar equipment was installed in practically every Coast Guard vessel of size.

With the increase in use of small craft in the early days of the war, it became necessary by 1942 to obtain additional, low power two-way voice communication equipment. Cutters generally were furnished new standard radio-telephone transmitter-receiver sets during 1941-1943. For equipping survival lifeboats, the Coast Guard obtained special transmitters which would automatically send "SOS" or submarine warning "SSS" messages; these could also be keyed manually. A wide variety of other transmitting and receiving sets for special uses were acquired, furnished, and installed.

When the need for Amphibious Task Group flagships arose during 1944 and 1945, the Navy converted the six 327-foot cutters *Bibb, Campbell, Duane, Ingham, Spencer,* and *Taney.* The mission of these vessels was to serve as headquarters ships and, therefore, as communication control ships in amphibious operations. Every electronic device known to be of value in the performance of such duty was provided. Installations were made on a grand scale, and these ships were virtually floating radio stations. They represented the ultimate in shipborne electronic equipment operated by the Coast Guard during the war. These cutters performed the tasks of flagships for landing operations from landing craft, for a large combined force of minesweepers, minelayers, and net layers, and for a Transport Area screening group or groups during landing operations.

Radio stations on shore were vital in the proper

performance of Coast Guard communications. However, before the smuggling suppression operations of 1924, there was no need of Coast Guard-operated shore stations as existing facilities were adequate. With the great expansion of 1924 incident to the suppression of smuggling, and the large increase in the number of Coast Guard small craft, there was need for a more far-reaching radio communication service than Navy or commercial facilities provided. To meet this requirement a shore radio station was established at Rockaway Point Coast Guard Station, New York. This was so successful that soon afterward additional units were established at Nahant, Massachusetts; New London, Connecticut; Cape May, New Jersey; Cape Henry, Virginia; Fernandina and Fort Lauderdale, Florida; Mobile, Alabama; San Francisco and San Pedro, California; and Port Angeles and Anacortes, Washington. These continued to function in the prewar period.

Radio Washington was established late in 1933 at Fort Hunt, Virginia, as a radio monitoring station. During World War II, Radio Washington performed many important services. Among these was the handling of the constant flow of traffic to and from the Commander, North Atlantic Patrol. It maintained constant communication with Coast Guard vessels of the Atlantic Weather Observation Service. The scheduled collection and transmission of data by up to 13 weather patrol ships in the Atlantic from the equator to Greenland kept its three circuits fully loaded.

The force of Coast Guard cutters and other vessels which were organized into the Greenland Patrol in 1942 was augmented by the Operating Base Radio Station at Narsarssuak, Greenland, which was the nerve center of the network of the other bases and activities in Greenland. The operation of this station posed one of the most perplexing communications problems experienced during the war. With this station situated in a spot surrounded by lofty mountains, communications on high frequencies were erratic and highly uncertain; total "blackouts" were frequent.

Satisfactory results were obtained only upon the installation of low frequency equipment, whereupon Argentia and the various Greenland units were worked with practically no interruption, and service for the Coast Guard Air Patrol Squadron of PBY-5-A8s was successfully accomplished on different frequencies. Through this station, the Commander, Greenland Patrol, was able to keep in touch with men and ships in the vast stretches of Arctic ice and snow where no other means of communication were available. Because of this communications network, the Danish patrolman who stumbled across a Nazi weather station was able to announce his discovery to American authorities who took appropriate action in driving the enemy out of Greenland. This network also made possible the coordination of HF/DF (high frequency direction finding) and Loran operations in the area, and the consolidation of weather reports from outlying stations by the central base.

Radio communications were vitally important in weather reporting by the Coast Guard's weather ships. Weather information did much to eliminate accidents and disasters, and to minimize the seriousness of their consequences. The development of shipborne radio equipment made it possible to obtain weather information over the vast ocean areas. This was used to good advantage by the Coast Guard in its far flung theatres of operations, such as the North Atlantic Ice Patrol before war conditions required its discontinuance, and in its Alaskan operations.

As war approached and developed, the weather activities of the Coast Guard increased greatly and were divided into two main categories: (a) special reporting from both land stations and ships at sea, similar to that done before the war, and (b) regularly scheduled reporting from selected shore stations and from certain Coast Guard vessels patrolling defined areas. It is evident that good communications were vital to this activity.

Increased aircraft patrol along the coasts made an increase in the number of coastal weather reporting stations necessary. Nine were established on the East Coast and nine on the West Coast. The Coast Guard furnished the personnel; the Weather Bureau trained them; the Bureau or the Navy provided the meteorological equipment; and the Civil Aeronautics Administration installed the teletype facilities. All coastal weather reporting stations made hourly reports to the Weather Bureau over the national teletype circuit.

The fixed shore stations sometimes required supplementary communications in certain areas. The Coast Guard, in 1933, recognized the need for, and value of, mobile radio stations capable of communicating over comparatively long distances in relief operations during floods and other emergencies. A fleet of communications trucks was obtained and completely equipped as emergency radio stations. Eighteen were eventually placed in service, and distributed throughout the various districts, ready for emergency use. Their crews consisted of four to six men. Equipment varied with the years and was kept up to date, but basically consisted of a main transmitter and associated receivers, as well as secondary equipment, field land telephone sets which could be connected into Coast Guard or commercial circuits, and high intensity searchlights. These trucks were supplemented by auxiliary trucks for "leg work", and by light field trucks equipped for monitoring and direction finding.

While communications trucks were developed chiefly for use in coordinating the operations of units engaged in flood relief in the Ohio and Mississippi River areas, they proved adaptable for many uses in the wartime operation of the Coast Guard's communications system. They were especially useful in searching inland for crashed planes. For instance, on 25 May 1944, the communications truck of the Thirteenth District played a leading role in search operations which resulted in finding one survivor and the removal of several bodies from a TBF-1 plane which had crashed in the thickly wooded, steep, and rugged terrain near Port Angeles, Washington.

The same truck later participated in extensive operations for many days after a Navy Ventura medium bomber crashed in the Mount Baker National Forest on 14 January 1945. This truck, which was necessarily stationed in a virtual bowl, the sides of which were lofty and densely wooded mountains, handled a large amount of Army, Navy and Coast Guard radio traffic, through Navy and Coast Guard stations, and between the truck and searching planes. The five occupants of the plane had parachuted to the ground, and all were found, four of them still alive. This truck also provided power for electric equipment and lights installed at the temporary operating base camp. It was agreed that, of all units in the search, the truck proved the most valuable.

World War II shore operations required the equipping of a vast number of motor vehicles and other units, as well as Captain of the Port offices with radio equipment for voice transmission. Frequency modulated equipment came into rather general use for this purpose, proving especially satisfactory in connection with Captain of the Port, Harbor Patrol, and Beach Patrol activities.

Coast Guard aviation, as we have seen, played a most valuable role during the years of war. Here, efficient communications were of paramount importance. The development of radio in Coast Guard planes can be covered briefly.

The first radio equipment used by the Coast Guard in aircraft was installed in a biplane type seaplane borrowed from the Navy and operated from Ten Pound Island, Gloucester, Massachusetts in 1925. Experimentation with this equipment resulted in important recommendations by Lieutenant Commander E. F. Stone, USCG, looking toward the development of radio in Coast Guard aviation.

Experimentation and refinement of equipment continued from this beginning. On 13 June 1929, the plane *Yellow Bird* took off from Old Orchard Beach, Maine on an attempted transatlantic flight. A Coast Guard plane flying over the scene broadcast the event by voice radio. These transmissions were received by commercial ground equipment and carried over a national radio hookup. Reception was of such (then) good quality that every word was picked up, relayed over the broadcasting network, and received clearly by many thousands of listeners. It is believed that this was the first successful broadcast of this nature.

In 1931 three Douglas amphibians, and in 1932 five flying boats, were acquired by the Coast Guard for offshore patrol and rescue work. Since no radio suitable for these planes existed, the right kind of apparatus had to be developed. Experimentation and trial resulted in two-way radiotelegraph and radiotelephone capable of communication over distances up to hundreds of miles under the frequently adverse conditions encountered in over-ocean flying. Direction finding equipment for navigational, homing, and guiding purposes was also needed. The radio communication and radio direction finding equipment developed by the Coast Guard in meeting the requirements of these aircraft was probably the most complete, and by far the most versatile, airborne equipment in use during the period 1931-1935.

Acquisition in 1935 of 15 JF-2 Grumman amphibians, which were smaller than the patrol planes previously equipped, required radio apparatus incorporating features theretofore unknown to aircraft communications. It was necessary to develop equipment weighing not over 138 pounds which would do everything required of the 300-pound equipment then in use. With good cooperation from manufacturers' engineers, the problem was satisfactorily solved.

Radio direction finders comprised part of the standard radio equipment of all Coast Guard planes after 1931. Thus, in poor visibility, the planes could instruct vessels in distress, or ships with injured persons, to transmit radio signals at frequent intervals to guide the plane directly to the objective, even if the position given by the vessel were inaccurate, as often proved to be the case. The direction finders also enabled aviators to take bearings on fixed radio stations in checking their own positions.

In 1937 and 1938, the Coast Guard had some success in obtaining bearings from two commercial airplanes which were flying from Bermuda to New York. While not sufficiently accurate for navigational purposes, they assisted greatly in determining the general position of the planes— vitally important in case of emergency. The cutter *General Greene* succeeded in complete monitoring reception of transmission by two other commercial planes during transatlantic survey flights. In January 1939, after loss of the Imperial Airways plane *Cavalier* on the New York-Bermuda run, the Coast Guard instructed its New York air station to maintain continuous radio guard of Bermuda flights.

In January 1940, the Civil Aeronautics Administration assumed the responsibility for handling communications through their new station WSY in the New York area. The Coast Guard assumed responsibility for coordinating activities of all agencies, Government or otherwise, that would be involved in safety operations relating to airlines, shipping companies, communications companies, and the Maritime Exchange. Thus, organized safety measures for transatlantic flights took a substantial step forward. In connection with this, Coast Guard Headquarters transmitted, via Radio Washington, distress messages to Coast Guard vessels on special duty such as ice patrol, weather

service, or other missions, which might be in a position to assist the aircraft in distress. In May 1942, these operations had to cease due to war conditions, but many features of the plan were incorporated in the postwar air-sea rescue organization, in which communications play an extremely important part.

Planning for what became air-sea rescue, and later search and rescue, actually began at a Washington conference in June 1943. Out of this came a Liaison Committee of Emergency Rescue Equipment of the Office of Research and Development, Navy Department, and a Communications Coordinating Committee with three members representing the Coast Guard, the Army Air Force, and the Air Transport Command. Prompted by reports of the continued loss of life among trained airplane crews at sea—apparently caused by lack of a coordinated air-sea rescue organization and by inadequate communications facilities and equipment—the Communications Coordinating Committee began study in July 1943, with a view toward proposing recommendations for saving lives and at the same time improving the morale of crews operating planes over the ocean.

The resulting recommendations provided a sound foundation for a system to enhance safety of life at sea, not only for military and non-military aircraft, but for surface craft as well. Plans called for the improvement of radio transmitters to increase communication range. Many tests of radio and direction finding equipment were conducted under direction of this Committee, some with cooperation from the Federal Communications Commission. Special consideration was given the matter of further developing direction finder equipment to assist in locating distressed personnel and rescuing them within a matter of hours instead of days, or even weeks. The Committee made specific recommendations pertinent to the necessary communications facilities for an air-sea rescue organization. Most of these were incorporated in the joint communications plan ultimately adopted in Joint Army and Navy Plan 107.

The original Air-Sea Rescue (Search and Rescue) organization was established in the Coast Guard by the Secretary of the Navy in accordance with a Joint Chiefs of Staff request of 15 February 1944. Actual functioning began slowly. *The Air-Sea Rescue Manual* which included doctrine which had then been developed on search and

DRY TORTUGAS LIGHTHOUSE, FLORIDA . . . . wartime demands were not allowed to affect efficiency in maintenance and operation of primary lighthouses.

CAPE HENRY LIGHTHOUSE . . . . which guards the entrance to Hampton Roads and Chesapeake Bay. In the right background is the old abandoned lighthouse.

TILLAMOOK ROCK LIGHT STATION, OREGON . . . . servicing of such seaswept stations, difficult under ordinary circumstances, was a challenge with the wartime shortage of tenders.

BUOY TENDER APPROACHES BUOY FOR INSPECTION . . . . thousands of buoys were serviced
annually by the tenders' all-weather crews.

LIGHT BUOY IS HOISTED TO DECK OF TENDER
. . . . all aids to navigation were kept in top condition to
guide ships carrying men and materiel to fighting fronts.

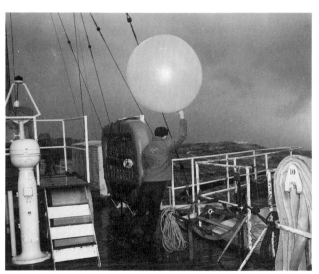

OCEAN WEATHER OBSERVATIONS FROM CUTTER
*DUANE* . . . . about to release 100 gram balloon to which
copper wire is attached for tracking by ship's radar.

*BIG HORN* OF THE OCEAN WEATHER FLEET . . . . only one liberty in six months for the crew of this busy vessel.

NO DETAILS OVERLOOKED BY THE MARINE IN-
SPECTORS . . . . safety at sea depended on inspection and
correction of faulty boilers, equipment and machinery.

BOAT DRILL ON BOARD TANKER *THOMAS F. CUN-
NINGHAM* . . . . all hands must understand **and take part**
in this vital duty. Taken at Colombo, Ceylon.

HEARING UNIT IN SESSION . . . . these units investigated marine casualties, reached just findings,
and gathered highly valuable information.

THE OLD AND THE NEW . . . . (*Left*) first Coast Guard shore radio station, 1924.
(*Right*) Coast Guard Administration and Radio Laboratory today.

REVENUE CUTTER *GRANT*, RADIO PIONEER . . . .
first U. S. vessel to make practical use of "wireless telegraphy."

TWENTY-FOUR YEARS OF CABLE LAYING . . . .
cable ship *Pequot*, a former Army mine planter.

A CORNER IN "RADIO WASHINGTON," ALEXANDRIA, VIRGINIA . . . . Coast Guard radio stations
were well equipped to handle the heavy traffic required of them.

INTERIOR OF A COAST GUARD COMMUNICATIONS
TRUCK . . . . a radioman takes a routine field strength
measurement.

KEEPING CONTACT WITH SHIPS IN HIS CONVOY
. . . . communication by voice radio between ships was often
essential to well-ordered team work.

RADIO-EQUIPPED PLANES FACILITATED MANY RESCUES . . . . numerous survivors owed their lives to radio by
which planes directed surface craft to their rafts and boats.

OPERATORS AT LORAN STATION ON TIME EQUIP-
MENT . . . . specially trained men were moved in as soon
as a station became operative.

NAVIGATOR OBTAINS DATA FROM LORAN RE-
CEIVER INDICATOR . . . . on board ship positional data
are noted. Loran chart and tables lie handy on the work shelf.

LORAN STATION ON A SMALL PACIFIC ATOLL . . . . almost complete isolation at such a
station was a great mental challenge to those who manned it.

AT ADAK, ALASKA . . . . Loran station under construction.

THE LORAN STATION AT ATTU . . . . service at the single master station at the western extremity of the Aleutians was rugged duty.

COAST GUARD-MANNED *USS MENKAR* . . . . she carried construction material, equipment and personnel for the Loran stations in the southwest Pacific.

AERIAL VIEW OF LORAN STATION AT SAIPAN . . . . a peaceful scene on an island where some of the most vicious Pacific fighting occurred.

rescue, detailed instructions on communications procedures for aircraft safety and related subjects, and rescue techniques and procedures, was issued on 20 June 1945. Full activity was largely a post-war development.

A study of over 60 flight reports, many of which dealt with enemy action, reveals various stories of communications illustrating the importance of efficient radio and visual contact. Some typical instances are reviewed.

Lieutenant Commander William B. Scheibel was piloting a plane from Elizabeth City Air Station on 7 May 1942. While scouting offshore from Corolla Light to Diamond Shoal at about 0940, his radioman, Brocklehurst, intercepted a message from another Coast Guard plane that survivors, in a lifeboat, had been identified by Ensign Perry, piloting another plane, about 30 miles due east of Oregon Inlet. Lieutenant Commander Scheibel sighted a Coast Guard patrol boat on the horizon, and proceeded over it; by Aldis lamp he advised it of the situation. A message block with all available information about the lifeboat was dropped on the patrol boat. The patrol boat then proceeded to the spot, picked up the survivors, and reported the situation by radio.

Ten days later another plane piloted by Lieutenant (jg) E. B. Ing, transmitted messages for destroyer *Ellis* and cutter *Dione* to home on the position of a sunken submarine about 50 miles off Elizabeth City. Contact was successfully made. The plane stood by while *Ellis* dropped a pattern of seven depth charges, bringing increased oil to the surface. The plane guided *Ellis* to the proper spot in which to attack by means of float lights. Good results were reported.

On the same day, another Coast Guard plane, piloted by Lieutenant Commander R. L. Burke, proceeded to contact *Ellis* and *Dione* to further develop a damaged U-boat contact made by Ensign Perry. The plane dropped a float light to mark the position where oil bubbles were observed moving slowly out to sea. Another float light was dropped on the new position. The plane used blinker to request *Ellis* to steer a course down the oil slick, and indicated it would zoom the exact place where bubbles were coming up. At twilight the underwater flash of an explosion was seen about 200 yards from the last depth charged position and a large agitated mass of air bubbles rose

to the surface. *Ellis* was asked by blinker to buoy the last spot, since it was believed the U-boat had been finished off; the plane would return early next morning. At the time it was thought that the U-boat had committed hari-kari and destroyed itself.

Two days later, a plane piloted by Lieutenant (jg) J. D. Hudgens on regular patrol out of the Biloxi Air Station, proceeded to a point near Ship Shoal Buoy where Hudgens located a number of survivors from a ship sunk by a submarine. Message blocks were dropped to the survivors informing them of impending assistance. Proceeding to the vicinity of a group of six fishing vessels operating five miles to the northeastward of the survivors, the plane dropped message blocks informing the fishermen of the survivors and requesting them to follow the plane to the scene, where it would indicate the location by diving. The fishermen immediately complied. All survivors were picked up, 11 of them by *J. Edward Treakle*, 10 by *Shearwater*, 2 by *Pam Car*. One dead man was recovered by *Conquest*. The antiquated but reliable method of using message blocks probably saved 23 lives.

Communications were not always satisfactory. On 15 July 1942, Lieutenant Commander R. R. Johnson was piloting a plane from Brooklyn Air Station, searching for a lifeboat with survivors which had been sighted previously by an Army plane. At 1315 Johnson located the lifeboat with six men on board, under way on a westerly course with a small sail set. After dropping a shipwreck kit to the lifeboat, the plane informed the Naval Air Station at New York of the circumstances, and was told that a surface unit was en route. The plane continued to circle the lifeboat and at 1545 a Navy blimp was sighted; at 1605 when about six miles west of the plane, the blimp changed course and proceeded to the position of the lifeboat.

The pilot reported to the Naval Air Station that all attempts to communicate with the blimp by radio or flashing light were unsuccessful. Then at 1635 Johnson sighted a surface craft about 18 miles westward on a northeasterly course and, after several attempts to raise the vessel on 3,000 kc., the plane proceeded on an intercept course leaving the blimp to mark the location of the lifeboat. The plane returned to the lifeboat and informed the survivors that surface craft would arrive shortly. *PC 495* took the survivors on board at 1910. Obviously, a general air-sea rescue communications plan was urgent, and such a plan was, of course, placed in effect later on.

Direction finding has been mentioned. This important branch of communications deserves more than passing comment. The first Coast Guard use of a shipborne radio direction finder (then called radiocompass) came in 1919 during the International Ice Patrol. Electrician (first class) J. A. McCarron on board cutter *Androscoggin,* improvised a loop antenna which he held in position by hand, and through the directional properties of this loop, used in conjunction with the radio receiver, determined the direction from which the signals from the relieving cutter *Tallapoosa* were coming, thus effecting quick contact during poor visibility. In 1921, cutter *Tampa* was equipped with a Navy type direction finder, and other installations followed.

During 1925-1927, eleven 100-foot patrol boats and thirty-two 125-footers were acquired; direction finders of a special type were needed for the smaller craft. These were developed and the first installation was made in *McLane.* Similar equipment was soon installed in the others. As usual with new devices, experimentation resulted in great improvements, and in 1928-1929, better equipment was generally placed in Coast Guard vessels. An extensive radio direction finder installation and modernization program, completed in 1934, included over 125 vessels of all types ranging from 100-foot patrol boats to destroyers.

The 1929 liquor smuggler had at his command, on both ship and shore, the newly developed and very efficient high frequency radio communication —over great distances with very low power— equipment which could be operated with a fair degree of secrecy. The use of this equipment became so general that the Coast Guard was forced to develop the means of locating such stations in its anti-smuggling operations. Little was known about direction finding on other than low frequencies, and the Coast Guard had to develop its own equipment. Much credit for this new and highly specialized development is due Lieutenant Frank M. Meals who was in charge of the field activities of the Coast Guard's Radio Intelligence at the time.

For detecting clandestine radio communications, the Coast Guard developed in 1930 a small portable direction finder which could be used in public without revealing its nature. The equipment was concealed in a conventional leather suitcase, and the signal, when received at right angles to the sides of the suitcase, was emitted by a small concealed loud speaker unit.

On 1 July 1941, certain medium frequency radio direction finder stations were turned over to the Coast Guard by the Navy, and these were then manned by the Coast Guard. Operational control reverted to the Navy on 1 November 1941, since the Coast Guard was then operating as part of the Navy. These stations were located at:

| | |
|---|---|
| Cape Elizabeth, Maine | Point Fermin, California |
| North Truro, Massachusetts | Point Hueneme, California |
| Fire Island, New York | Point Montara, California |
| Cape May, New Jersey | Empire, Oregon |
| Bethany Beach, Delaware | Klipsan Beach, Washington |
| Virginia Beach, Virginia | Tatoosh, Washington |
| Cape Lookout, North Carolina | |

However, on 1 August 1944, the Navy specifically transferred to the Coast Guard the operational control of the Coast Guard-manned stations listed above, plus those at:

| | |
|---|---|
| Surfside, Massachusetts | Point Reyes, California |
| Cape Hatteras, North Carolina | St. George, California |
| Point Arguello, California | Fort Stevens, Oregon |
| Farallon Islands, California | |

The following stations were added later bringing the total to 25:

Winter Harbor, Maine
Amagansett, New York
Poyners Hill, North Carolina
DuPont, South Carolina
Imperial Beach, California

The direction finder networks consisted of these stations and sub-net control and net control stations operated under direction of the Commandant. The respective District Coast Guard Officers were responsible for operations and for logistic and administrative control. The prescribed mission of the nets was to: (a) detect and obtain bearings on enemy transmissions; (b) obtain bearings on vessels and aircraft in distress and on emergency portable transmitting equipment; and (c) to furnish navigational assistance to ships and aircraft. The system comprised five networks: (1) West Coast of the United States; (2) Alaska-Aleutian Area;

(3) Atlantic Coast of the United States; (4) Hawaiian Area; and (5) other Pacific Island areas as necessary. These and the radio station networks were tied together by teletype or radio circuits into an efficient system which could immediately be alerted in case a vessel or aircraft might become imperiled. Later, the medium frequency service was wholly discontinued and the entire service was provided by high frequency equipment, familiarly known as HF/DF, or "Huff Duff."

With the installation of Navy Type DAQ high frequency radio direction finding equipment in Coast Guard vessels for use in tracking German submarines, it became necessary to train personnel for operating the equipment. The Coast Guard had no facilities of its own for such training, and the first men to be so trained in this new technique were a group of 14 rated radiomen who graduated from the Navy School at Cheltingham, Maryland, in January 1943. One additional class followed, and in May 1943, the school was moved to Casco Bay, Maine. Training was started there in June and continued for two years. During this interval about 300 Coast Guardsmen were graduated.

During the period March to August 1945, inclusive, radio direction finder stations took many bearings in connection with actual or potential distress cases. Omitting the Hawaiian network, these stations took bearings on a total of 328 actual and 203 potential distress cases involving vessels. They also took 398 bearings in actual and 2,820 in potential distress cases involving aircraft. From bearings taken, Evaluation Centers were able to provide 613 fixes.

The ending of hostilities; the use of Loran as a navigational aid; and an acute shortage of personnel following demobilization, brought about operational reduction. Thereafter the system was concerned only with obtaining bearings on distressed vessels or aircraft in connection with the newly established Search and Rescue activity.

As a result of its many years of experience in the field of distress communications, the Coast Guard was naturally designated by the Navy during the war as the agency charged with the responsibility for providing adequate merchant marine safety and distress communications when coastal commercial communication facilities were closed down for security reasons.

A lesson in the conduct of distress communications has come from every major distress case at sea in the twentieth century. This was particularly true in the *Republic-Florida* collision of 1909, already mentioned, and in the *Vestris* disaster on 12 November 1928. The latter case marked the inauguration in the Coast Guard of the collection and compilation of facts relating to such communications. In 1929 a series of distress communications studies was begun, and between then and 1939 a total of 35 cases were studied. Particular attention was paid to collecting statistics during 1932-1934. Special emphasis was placed upon the value of the lessons learned in each case and how these lessons might apply to future problems.

This work was suspended in 1939, but in July 1944, submission of reports by the District Coast Guard Offices was resumed. By the end of that year, 50 cases had been reported, 45 of these from the Third (New York) District. Some reports were made in 1945, but late that year all districts were required to submit regular reports of complete distress communications data for use in studies of all major cases—those involving loss of life, ships, or planes—and other cases in the district commanders' discretion. Thus, the Coast Guard actively pursued a policy of making each experience in distress communications a contribution toward more effective attainments in the future.

When war started in Europe on 3 September 1939, the Secretary of the Treasury charged the Coast Guard with enforcement of neutrality in radio communications by belligerent countries. The Proclamation of Neutrality dated 5 September 1939, prohibited general use of radio and signal apparatus by belligerent vessels while in waters subject to jurisdiction of the United States. The only such communications permitted were calls regarding distress, safe navigation, arrival, and departure.

When, under Presidential Proclamation of 27 June 1940, certain portions of the Espionage Act of 1917 became effective, radio sealing activities were extended to include vessels of both foreign and domestic registry, and enforcement with the cooperation of the Customs Service became the Coast Guard's responsibility. This responsibility and these duties continued throughout the war, and ceased on 17 September 1945.

The work of the radio sealing units was about evenly divided between boarding ships at dock, and ships at anchorage. Jeeps and picket boats, respectively, were used for transportation. The work was carried on at all ports of consequence. It was done in all kinds of weather, with the worst conditions prevailing in winter with heavy winds, and in northern latitudes, below-zero temperatures, making boarding from picket boats particularly difficult. In Boston this work was done by the Temporary Reserve.

The principal duty was boarding cargo vessels of various nationalities, as well as fishing craft. Under orders from the Captain of the Port, the boarders made sure that all transmitting apparatus on board was closed up and sealed with wire and a lead USCG seal, so that it would not be used at unauthorized times. Such apparatus included main, emergency, and lifeboat transmitters, and even in some cases, radiating receivers which could be trailed by submarine radio direction finders. Apparatus was inspected and sealed in vessels entering port. Similar action was taken in vessels where service work had been done on radio equipment under Coast Guard authority to break the seal for repairs. This work came thick and fast when convoys were making up and operators wished to assure themselves of the efficiency of their equipment. Often, ships were under way before the sealers could leave.

Marine radiobeacons are special radio transmitters installed at lighthouses, in lightships, and at other strategic points for automatically sending out symmetrically radiated signals on which a navigator takes bearings with his shipboard direction finder. Intersection of cross bearings provides a "fix." The first radiobeacons were established by the Lighthouse Service in 1921. Radiobeacons are currently operated on the 15 even frequencies within the 285-315 kc. band, thus providing a separation of two kilocycles. This close separation permits operation by geographically adjacent beacons only through the use of interlocking time schedules and frequency stability. Proper operation of these beacons requires careful monitoring.

A radio monitoring station was established in 1933 at Fort Hunt, Virginia, and moved to Fairfax County, Virginia, in 1941. Its purpose was to monitor frequencies with specially prepared equipment. It was instrumental in keeping all Coast Guard transmitters on assigned frequencies through regular and random checking. It measured frequencies of the transmitters of other Services which often got off their assigned frequencies and drifted onto those of the Coast Guard, and it sometimes also determined the frequencies of clandestine and enemy stations.

On 2 October 1944, Headquarters published the first "approved list" of radiobeacon monitoring stations, giving the location of each and what radiobeacons were to be monitored by each. By May 1946 there were 30 monitoring stations checking on 190 radiobeacons in the United States, Puerto Rico, Alaska and Hawaii.

Of the multitude of electronic devices which were developed during the war, those of the pulse operated types designated as "Radar" and "Loran" were probably the most valuable insofar as Coast Guard operations were concerned. In the development, establishment, and operation of these and other electronic aids, the Coast Guard had definite responsibilities in which it was directly and vitally concerned.

Before the Spring of 1944, the Coast Guard had made no practical application of shore based radar. At that time, a prominent manufacturer, with permission from the Coast Guard, set up experimental equipment at Straitsmouth Lifeboat Station, Rockport, Massachusetts, and at Highland Lifeboat Station at North Truro, Massachusetts and, with the Army's permission, on Army property at Deer Island, Boston Harbor. These formed a 40-mile triangle covering the approaches and entrance to Boston Harbor. Installations were completed in December 1944, and offered to the Coast Guard for its use in conducting tests to determine the capabilities and limitations of the equipment then in use, and to develop possible uses by the Coast Guard such as in plotting air and surface traffic entering or leaving a particular area, or as an aid in lookout activity. This development, however, was too late to have important wartime significance.

Some Ice Patrol experimentation with radar as a means of detecting the presence of icebergs took place late in the war. Results were unsatisfactory, but further research was recommended.

One more phase of the communications activity, rather remotely related to the rest, was that of postal affairs. During World War II the handling of mail for personnel ashore and afloat was a major problem, both within the United States and at foreign stations. By mid-1942 the Coast Guard had established Navy post offices at two shore units and on board four vessels. Coast Guard personnel performing postal duties were nominated and bonded through the Navy, as Navy mail clerks and assistant mail clerks. In September 1942, a General Agreement was made between the Post Office and Navy Departments concerning Navy, Marine Corps, and Coast Guard postal services, and in November of that year the Navy Postal Service was transferred to the cognizance of the Director, Naval Communications.

At that time the rapidly expanding world-wide postal requirements made the need of a mail section at Headquarters obvious. A Postal Affairs Subsection was established there under the Chief, Communications Division. Lieutenant Commander J. A. McCullough, a postal inspector in civilian life, headed the section and supervised, along lines of the Navy Postal Service, the entire Coast Guard postal program during the war.

In all, 98 post offices were established on shore, with the peak in 1943 and 1944, and 196 post offices were set up afloat, with the peak in 1944 and 1945. Many mail specialists were recruited from postal employees. In meeting wartime requirements, the Coast Guard had about 860 bonded mail clerks, of whom 348 were Specialists (M) including 35 SPARS. In some Districts, the volume of mail handled reached 15,000 to 20,000 pieces a day for extended periods. Money orders were handled, and, in general, these post offices provided full postal service. Night service was maintained at major ports to enable prompt delivery of mail to incoming Coast Guard vessels regardless of the hour of arrival. SPARS were used at many shore offices to handle the large volume of insufficiently or inaccurately addressed mail, and the mail of transferred personnel. In May 1944, the Mail Sections were transferred from Communications to Office Services, but functioned as formerly.

Loran was one of the most revolutionary of long range navigational aids since the invention of the magnetic compass. An electronic device, it was strictly an aid to navigation and is worthy of chapter treatment.

# Chapter 11

# THE STORY OF LORAN

LORAN, a name derived from *LOng RAnge Navigation*, is a system whereby a vessel or plane with special charts, and with suitable equipment comparatively simple to operate, may determine its position in all weathers even at a great distance from shore.

This new electronics development is a method of navigation having a long effective range. It is reliable up to 800 miles from the transmitting station in daytime and 1,400 miles at night. Loran uses a wave length similar to that used at night for long-range radio communications. Its waves are reflected from the ionosphere and follow the earth's surface as do the familiar radio broadcasting waves. The speed and time of travel of these radio waves are very reliable and stable. The basic characteristic of the Loran system is that it utilizes pulse transmission, which permits measurement of the time of travel of the signals.

In this new system, demonstrated to be practical beyond doubt, an infinite number of lines of position are laced over the earth's surface by radio. To provide the necessary signals, ground stations are appropriately located to cover the area to be served. Two shore stations, a "master" and a "slave", operating as a Loran "pair", lay down a set of these lines of position over a portion of the earth.

Reduced to simple terms, a pulse is sent out by the master station. This is received by the slave station and by the vessel or plane seeking to establish its position. After a brief interval following receipt of the pulse by the slave, the slave sends out its pulse, which is also received by the vessel or plane. This cycle is repeated continuously. The navigator selects a pair of signals. By means of a Loran receiver-indicator on board the ship or plane, connected to an ordinary antenna, he measures electronically the difference in time of travel of the radio waves from the two ground stations. With the use of Loran charts for the areas served by these stations, a line of position is deduced from this time difference. A second line of position is similarly determined using another "pair" of stations. The intersection of these two lines provides a "fix".

The *time difference*, which determines *distance*, but not the direction of the waves, is the factor that provides the line of position. Since the speed of travel of radio waves is much more stable and reliable than any other radio wave propagation characteristic, this accounts in part for the high order of accuracy of the Loran system. The average operator requires about two minutes to obtain the readings which provide a line of position.

Let us go back to the beginning of this highly important discovery. As the war in Europe swung into full stride, the development of what was first known as the "radio obstacle detector" occurred in 1940. Under the coined name "Radar", it became an important defense against the blitz in England; the RAF rose and rose again, forewarned in time by precision radio detection that the enemy was coming over.

Very early in 1941, the English were known to have a pulse transmitting type of navigational aid which operated on a very high frequency with a range believed to exceed radar's 50 to 100 miles. Radiation Laboratory and Bell Telephone Laboratory scientists visited England and gathered privately a few salient facts, but the British Government was not, at that time of great national peril, disclosing any military secrets to a neutral. These scientists returned and began development of a high frequency, short wave system. They were not at all sure what they were attempting to

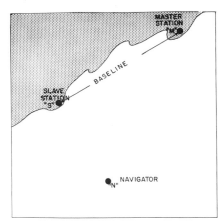

STEP I

NAVIGATOR ABOARD SHIP AT "N" IS WITHIN RANGE OF
STATIONS "M" AND "S" AND IS ABOUT TO RECEIVE LORAN
SIGNALS.

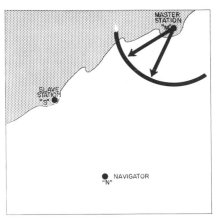

STEP II

LORAN TRANSMISSION CYCLE IS BEGUN BY "MASTER"
STATION. PULSE IS RADIATED IN ALL DIRECTIONS AND
TRAVELS TOWARD BOTH "SLAVE" STATION AND NAVIGATOR.

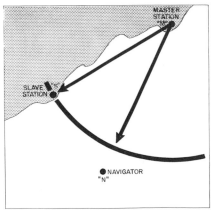

STEP III

PULSE TRANSMITTED BY "MASTER" STATION ARRIVES AT
"SLAVE" BUT HAS NOT YET REACHED THE NAVIGATOR.

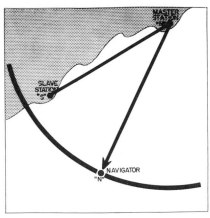

STEP IV

PULSE FROM "MASTER" STATION ARRIVES AT POSITION OF
NAVIGATOR. "SLAVE" STATION HAS ALREADY RECEIVED
"MASTER" PULSE AND IS WAITING FOR PROPER AMOUNT OF
TIME TO ELAPSE BEFORE TRANSMITTING TO ASSURE CORRECT
SYNCHRONIZATION WITH "MASTER".

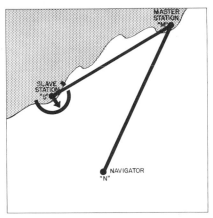

STEP V

AFTER WAITING FOR THE PROPER AMOUNT OF TIME TO
ASSURE CORRECT SYNCHRONIZATION, THE "SLAVE" TRANS-
MITS ITS PULSE. THE NAVIGATOR HAS ALREADY RECEIVED
THE PULSE FROM THE "MASTER" STATION.

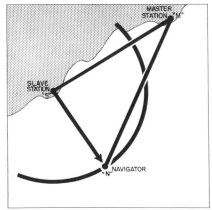

STEP VI

"SLAVE" PULSE ARRIVES AT NAVIGATORS POSITION. SINCE
NAVIGATOR HAS ALREADY RECEIVED THE SIGNAL FROM THE
"MASTER" STATION, LORAN READING IS TAKEN BY
MEASURING THE TIME ELAPSED BETWEEN THE ARRIVAL OF
THE MASTER AND SLAVE PULSES. AFTER BOTH SIGNALS
HAVE TRAVELLED THROUGHOUT THEIR EFFECTIVE RANGE,
THE CYCLE IS REPEATED.

## SEQUENCE OF OPERATION OF LORAN TRANSMITTING STATIONS

do; they might develop an improved radar, or a harbor entrance locator for convoys, or almost anything. They were simply searching for something that might serve the nation in the event war actually came to the United States.

To implement their experimentation, the scientists requested use of two inactive Coast Guard lifeboat stations. As a result, on 24 March 1941, the Treasury Department granted a permit to the National Defense Research Committee (NDRC) of the Council of National Defense to use one at Montauk, Long Island, New York, and one at Fenwick Island, Delaware. This was the Coast Guard's first contact with what was to become Loran—a revolutionary aid to navigation.

The scientists of the NDRC drew plans for a new type of transmitter and a receiver based on the principles of television, using the cathode ray tube to display the pulses generated by the transmitters. These transmitters were constructed and installed at the Montauk and Fenwick stations. The receivers were set up at the Bell Telephone Laboratory's Transoceanic Monitor Station at Manahawkin, New Jersey. Testing was begun to determine the range of the pulsed waves when bounced off the lower E-layer of the heaviside layer below the ionosphere, the region above the earth's surface in which ionization takes place. At first, no attempt was made to achieve synchronization between the two transmitting units. A monitor-observer at Manahawkin reported the quality of the pulses on the air to the two transmitting units. As late as November 1941, only occasional synchronization was being achieved, and it was difficult to keep the transmitters on the air with any regularity or to obtain maximum reception of pulses from Montauk at any time.

Then came Pearl Harbor. Soon afterward, Rear Admiral Julius A. Furer, USN, Coordinator of Research and Development for the Secretary of the Navy, felt that there was a definite possibility that a long range navigational aid might be developed as a result of the tests. At a meeting of the Joint Chiefs of Staff late in March 1942, the scant results of medium frequency, long range tests were presented. A plan was made for a chain of stations to be constructed, installed, and operated by NDRC, the results to be submitted to whomever was most interested. It was decided that some of the test units should be constructed along the

United States and Canadian Atlantic coast. This required the cooperation of the Canadians which was forthcoming in early May 1942.

Beginning in that month, Coast Guard personnel participated actively in the development of Loran. When the Vice Chief of Naval Operations requested the services of a ranking Coast Guard officer possessing radio and electronics experience, neither Captain Lawrence M. Harding, USCG, who was assigned, nor his immediate superiors had any idea what his assignment involved. The utmost secrecy was maintained not only at this time, but through most of the war. Captain Harding was ordered to temporary duty in Cambridge, Massachusetts.

May 1942 was probably the turning point in the development of Loran. The Radiation Laboratory, Cambridge, Massachusetts, was beginning to arrive at tentative technical means for evolving a long range navigational aid, and Admiral Furer was alert to the naval possibilities of such a device. However, he recognized that in order to apply the technical developments of the Radiation Laboratory effectively to the needs of the Navy, it would be essential for the Navy to actively guide and assist in the work.

The far-seeing and practical naval viewpoints of Admiral Furer, Captain Furth, and Captain Harding, and the cooperative personal efforts of Mr. Melville Eastham, Dr. Alfred Loomis, and others, eventually made possible the development and application to the war effort, of a practical system of long range navigation. It was accomplished in an amazingly short time. The active and aggressive sponsorship of the project by the Navy, and the cooperative response of the leaders of the NDRC to Navy guidance, made Loran effective for general use over a very considerable period of the war. There were many difficulties and rough spots, but on the whole, amazingly rapid application followed from the foresight of these leaders.

Upon reporting to the Chief of Naval Operations, Captain Harding was given orders of great latitude. He was to be the naval representative to the Radiation Laboratory itself, and to undertake any necessary field activities. He was to determine by any suitable means, whether the transmission of long range pulse waves could be developed into anything of immediate value to a nation whose merchant shipping was being sent to the bottom at an alarming rate, and whose Navy, after Pearl Harbor, was totally inadequate to cope with the demands of convoy coverage. Captain Harding took up his temporary duty at the Radiation Laboratory on 3 June 1942.

About 15 May 1942, Mr. Don Fink, of the Radiation Laboratory, had returned from Canada with the assurance of cooperation from the Royal Canadian Navy. Early in June, at a consultation between representatives of the Radiation Laboratory, Captain Harding, and Commander Worth, RCNR, in Cambridge, it was planned that the two already partially established experimental stations at Fenwick and Montauk would be Units #1 and #2 respectively, and that Units #3 and #4 would be located along the coast of Nova Scotia. Sites were to be tentatively selected and agreed upon between Captain Harding representing the Navy, Commander Worth, representing the Royal Canadian Navy, and Mr. Eastham, representing the Radiation Laboratory. The Royal Canadian Navy appointed Lieutenant Commander Argyle, RCN, as Canadian Liaison Officer for the project.

To obtain concrete data on the behavior of the pulse transmissions, Mr. Jack Pierce desired to observe them from some mobile test unit. Captain Harding was also extremely anxious to ascertain for the Navy, as soon as possible, whether the whole project had practical, immediate value in the war effort. The Navy could well use a precision aid to navigation extending beyond the radiobeacon's 200 mile radius, if it could be applied with sufficient speed to the actual wartime problems of navigators.

Captain Harding, therefore, arranged for observations and tests to be made from a Navy blimp during June, and, more important, he arranged to have receiving equipment installed in a Coast Guard weather ship, *USS Manasquan*, so that an adequate navigational test might be made. The test, which lasted one month, was conducted by Messrs. Davidson and Duvall. At about this time, Captain Harding coined the word "Loran" as a convenient designator for the project. This was accepted by both the Navy and the Radiation Laboratory.

If the experiments in *Manasquan* proved that a practically correct line of position could be obtained from the pulse transmissions of one pair of stations at times when celestial navigation was impossible, it would be reasonable to assume that navigational fixes could be achieved when within range of two pairs of transmitting units, and *in all kinds of weather*.

In June, Lieutenant Commander Argyle and Mr. Waldschmitt selected the site for Unit #3 at Baccaro, Nova Scotia, and for #4 near Deming, Nova Scotia. Since the Radiation Laboratory was handling all construction costs for the two stations, contracts had been quickly let to local contractors, and no time was lost in beginning the work. The sites were swiftly cleared for construction. Supplies, expedited by United States Navy sponsorship, arrived in the middle of June; ground was broken at Baccaro on 19 June and at Deming eight days later.

While the work on the Nova Scotia stations proceeded and field tests were being arranged, further thought was given to installations to serve additional important sectors of the North Atlantic. Conferences between the Radiation Laboratory and Captain Harding resulted in proposals by the latter that instead of a continuous chain of stations as the Radiation Laboratory suggested, certain key sectors be served by groups of stations, partly to conserve time. Careful studies made by Captain Harding, the Radiation Laboratory, and the famous explorer Commander Donald B. MacMillan, USNR, furnished invaluable assistance in spanning the difficult gaps from Nova Scotia eastward toward Europe. By the end of June, the areas had been tentatively determined.

It was at this point that the Radiation Laboratory realized it lacked the trained personnel to man the stations if tests proved the value of Loran. The Laboratory requested that Captain Harding obtain personnel from the Navy or Coast Guard to man a proposed Greenland station, and also the units at Fenwick and Montauk. These men as well as some Canadians were, according to plan, to be trained at the Laboratory and at the two stations in operation.

A survey party to determine sites for two more stations, #5 and #6, consisted of Commander MacMillan, Captain Harding, and Mr. Don Fink of the Laboratory. This party departed Quonset, Rhode Island, by seaplane on 15 July 1942, and picked up Waldschmitt and Argyle at Shediac, New Brunswick, en route to Newfoundland. Captain Harding conceived the idea of a preliminary survey of the coastline by plane, supplemented by trips by small boat and afoot. This proved to be very efficient.

The party examined a site for station #5 near Bona Vista, Newfoundland, on a point jutting out to sea; it approved the location, and made arrangements for cooperation from a local contractor. Two days later, the party proceeded to Battle Harbor, Labrador, where they were ferried ashore in a small boat by the local tycoon, a friend of Commander MacMillan named Stanley Brazil, who put the party up at his house. The next day, they surveyed the shoreline in Brazil's launch, *Lily*. A site for station #6 was chosen after a thorough survey ashore, and the location was christened Loran Point. Brazil became the local representative of the Laboratory to receive consignments.

The men were stormbound for two days before flying to Goose Bay, Labrador, to arrange for the Canadian McNamarra Construction Company to act as general representatives and contractors. The party then returned by way of Shediac to Quonset Point.

Results of the tests made in *Manasquan*, completed 17 July, awaited Captain Harding on his return to Cambridge. They were most satisfactory. Ground waves were efficient up to 680 miles in the daytime when the reflecting heaviside layer was affected by the sun, and up to 1,300 miles at night when that layer was reflecting the sky waves to earth. The 1950 kilocycle frequency was found suitable. The results were considered adequate preliminary proof that Loran was practical.

A Navy directive for the project resulted, calling for a complete trial system of the units at Fenwick and Montauk, Bona Vista and Battle Harbor, and one later at Greenland. These, with the Royal Canadian Navy units at Baccaro and Deming, would give complete skeleton coverage of the Northwest Atlantic area. Construction of the units was pursued with vigor.

The next project was the Greenland Station, #7 in the seven-unit Northwest Atlantic chain. This involved many problems, frustrations, and hardships. Captain Harding conducted airborne and surface craft surveys along the southwest coast of Greenland, and selected the best compromise site near a primitive collection of Eskimo igloos called Frederiksdal on the Danish charts.

This was the only satisfactory technical possibility between Cape Farewell and Cape Desolation. Despite problems of strong winds, field ice, and Greenland government objections to naval establishments near Eskimo settlements, the Eskimos, who respected Commander MacMillan, gave friendly cooperation, and the project was completed.

The Greenland unit was the first erected entirely by the Armed Services. However, Mr. Whipple and Mr. Waldschmitt gave technical advice on the installation of the transmitting and receiving equipment, which was furnished by the Radiation Laboratory. Originally, the Army Engineers agreed to construct the buildings. However, early in October, the Army announced that the site was unsatisfactory and that it would not afford the support the Navy had expected. The Vice Chief of Naval Operations called a hurried meeting attended by Captain von Paulsen, USCG, (Captain Harding was in the Pacific), Commander MacMillan, USNR, Lieutenant D. G. Cowie, and Messrs. Waldschmitt, Tierny, and Fink of the Laboratory. On 13 October this meeting decided that the Navy would undertake construction.

The freighter *Norlaga* was chartered to carry equipment, materials, and supplies, and scheduled to sail at midnight on 15 October. In the short interval, the Coast Guard and Navy got a construction crew together and on board the freighter. At the Quonset Point Supply Depot Mr. Tierny and Mr. Waldschmitt obtained replacements, spares, and special pieces of equipment far exceeding what was then thought necessary, but their foresight later paid big dividends. Navy trucks, commandeered for the purpose, moved supplies and materials to the ship in a steady stream for two days. The Navy did an excellent job of packing and shipping. *Norlaga* sailed on schedule!

The Coast Guard installation and operation crew, under Lieutenant Clark and Chief Radioman Samuel Michaels, accompanied by Mr. Waldschmitt, sailed for Greenland in the ill-fated *Dorchester*, and arrived near Frederiksdal on 11 November 1942.

The party was amazed to find that the Army Engineers considered the site ideal, and that construction supplies had already been dispatched to the site! They were ready to proceed with the work, and after the misunderstanding was resolved, construction became something of a joint Army-Navy proposition.

*Norlaga*, cutter *Raritan* and *USS Bluebird* with 12 Army construction crewmen and Mr. Waldschmitt arrived at the Frederiksdal site on 7 December. With no suitable dock, a barge was towed to the anchored *Norlaga*. Supplies were loaded on the barge which was then towed to the shore, beached, unloaded, and kedged off at high tide. Work was delayed by a heavy gale. Since darkness is almost constant at that time of year, electric outdoor floodlights were set up to assist operations. The native Eskimo villagers were fascinated, and dropped everything to watch. All material had to be hauled two miles overland from the beach to the site. This work was completed by the 11th, and all was ready, with tents up, when *Bluebird* and *Raritan* brought construction materials on 13 December.

The next week, the second of the terrific gales which constantly plagued the Greenland party blew away the tents. Supplies were blown all about the site. On 20 December, at the tail of the gale, cutter *Aklak* arrived escorting *Tintagel*, a sorry old wreck of a freighter which was carrying additional supplies. Due to the gale and the freighter's uncomfortable position far up a fjord, it was necessary to unload quickly and get her out. All hands, regardless of rating or assignment, turned to unloading, and worked without rest until Christmas night, when the job was completed. Meanwhile, a second set of tents had blown away.

By the last day of the year, the Army construction crew and Coast Guardsmen had erected specified Armour type of structures, and all hands moved gratefully into the wooden buildings. But this luxury lasted less than 24 hours! On the night of 1 January and the next morning, a furious 162-mile wind carried away many supplies and completely demolished the wooden buildings, literally blowing them off Greenland! In Lieutenant Clark's formal report, he wrote: "When last seen, buildings were headed in the general direction of Boston, Massachusetts." All hands took refuge in the church at Frederiksdal, making their way there by clinging to a steel cable towed by tractor.

A Coast Guard crew rebuilt the unit under direction of Mr. Waldschmitt and Lieutenant Clark. Captain Harding, with great foresight, had included five Quonset huts in the material originally sent to Frederiksdal. Because of the Army Engineers' readiness to undertake construction of wooden buildings, there had been efforts to sidetrack the huts, but Clark and Waldschmitt had resisted them. The huts were now salvaged from the debris. Nearby frozen sand was dynamited, and under great difficulties a 6-foot deep trench was dug in order to install the huts securely. By 12 January, four huts had been set up and partly buried in the sand. Since storms had blown away all the original covering of sheet metal, tarpaper and wooden strips were used. These eventually proved more weatherproof than the metal. The sides of the huts were then covered with sand and turf, and wood and plyboard were put across the tops. Antenna masts were erected with nine guy wires to a pole, and a Beverage antenna installed. The system proved satisfactory.

On 23 January 1943, *Raritan* and the barge arrived to pick up the construction crew and their equipment, and *Nogak* arrived with Michaels and Coast Guard radiomen. These vessels removed all but the station crew and seven Coast Guard construction men on the 26th. As each piece of technical equipment was installed it was put into operation, and the station was on the air for the first time on 11 March. First satisfactory synchronization was achieved on 30 May. The station was officially turned over to Lieutenant Clark and his Coast Guard crew about 6 July.

Our development of Loran did not escape the British. Early in 1943 the British Admiralty began to take an active interest in its North Atlantic performance. With more and larger convoys transiting the North Atlantic and making the fearful Murmansk run when the Battle of the Atlantic was at its peak, it was evident to the Admiralty that an extension of the Loran system across the Atlantic was most desirable.

At a meeting of the Combined Chiefs of Staff in Washington, D.C., a three-unit chain for the Northeast Atlantic was pronounced necessary and agreed upon, with close cooperation to exist between the United States and Royal Navies. The Admiralty agreed to construct, maintain, supply, and operate the three units; the United States Navy agreed to furnish technical Loran equipment; and the British would lean heavily upon the United States for technical advice and training of personnel.

Captain Harding was, at the time, on temporary duty on General Eisenhower's staff in North Africa. The Admiralty requested his services. He reported there for temporary duty, and, with the assistance of Lieutenant (jg) Jack D. Roberts, USNR, he conducted surveys in Iceland, the Faeroe Islands, and the Hebrides—remote, inaccessible and exposed areas, most of them under regular air surveillance and frequent attack by enemy air forces—and selected three sites. Actual work was begun promptly by the Royal Navy, and Captain Harding and Lieutenant Roberts returned to the United States.

The United States Navy purchased the required technical equipment from the Radiation Laboratory and saw to its delivery. This was the Laboratory's only official connection with the project. Training of personnel for the Admiralty was accomplished at the Loran School (Navy) at the Massachusetts Institute of Technology, Cambridge, Massachusetts. As requested by the Royal Navy, Coast Guard technical personnel were assigned to assist in setting up the stations and getting them on the air. The first of these, Radio Electrician Everett B. Kopp, USCG, and Chief Radio Technician Theodore C. LeBaron, USCGR, were sent to Vik, Iceland, in October 1943. In two months they had installed, adjusted, tested, and turned over to the Royal Navy the operation of the first of these "U-K" units.

At about the same time, a second station at Skuvanes Head in the Faeroes went on the air, but synchronization was not achieved for some time. The Admiralty appealed for technical advice, and Lieutenant (jg) T. D. Winters, USCGR, was ordered to London as technical adviser. It was also requested that Kopp and LeBaron be retained, and they were sent to Skuvanes Head to solve the synchronization difficulty.

On 11 February 1944, Chief Radioman A. Yasinsac, USCG, arrived at Mangersta in the Hebrides to assist with that station. Kopp and LeBaron were already there and had completed most of the work. Yasinsac remained until good, solid signals were observed 24 hours a day. Initial operation of these "U-K" stations was complicated by difficulty in obtaining qualified British personnel. The whole project, however, was an example of harmonious cooperation under great pressure. All Coast Guardsmen who had been loaned to the British were back in the United States and on other

duty by the end of May 1944, and the Atlantic chain was an accomplished fact.

In summary, the Atlantic Loran stations were:

| Location | Operated by |
| --- | --- |
| Fenwick Island, Delaware | U. S. Coast Guard |
| Montauk Point, Long Island, New York | U. S. Coast Guard |
| Baccaro, Nova Scotia | Royal Canadian Navy |
| Deming, Nova Scotia | Royal Canadian Navy |
| Bona Vista, Newfoundland | U. S. Coast Guard |
| Battle Harbor, Labrador | U. S. Coast Guard |
| Frederiksdal, Greenland | U. S. Coast Guard |
| Vik, Iceland | Royal Navy |
| Skuvanes Head, Faeroe Islands | Royal Navy |
| Mangersta, Hebrides | Royal Navy |

—— and ——

| | |
| --- | --- |
| Sankaty Head, Nantucket, Mass. (Monitor) | U. S. Coast Guard |

The Radiation Laboratory continued with transmission range extension experiments to improve daytime performance. A large number of cutters and ships of the United States Atlantic Fleet were being equipped with Loran receiving sets. Ships at sea reported good, useable sky-waves at 2,000 to 3,000 miles from the baselines of the various pairs of stations in operation. Training of Loran operating personnel became stabilized. The school was transferred from the jurisdiction of the National Defense Research Committee to the Senior Naval Officer at Massachusetts Institute of Technology, and the name was changed to Naval Training School (Navigation), with quarters at 19 Deerfield Street, Boston. Expansion of requirements caused further transfer in March 1944, to Groton, Connecticut. Eventually, these trainees voyaged east and west to the farthermost reaches of American and British Naval control.

Creation of the Atlantic chain, including the period of initial experimentation, took from March 1941 until May 1944. We have seen that Loran tests indicated the system was practical as early as July 1942, and have followed the development of the Atlantic stations. The establishment of some Loran chains in Pacific areas took place concurrently with developments in the Atlantic.

The first of these projects was a chain for the Bering Sea, in western Alaska. It was the first full-scale program for Loran stations in which the Coast Guard undertook both construction and operation. Normally, this area had prolonged periods of bad weather which hampered navigation. The Army and Navy were operating there, confronted with the problem of dislodging the Japanese in

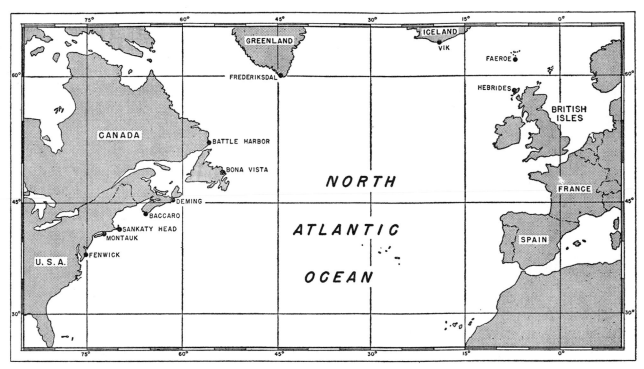

NORTH ATLANTIC LORAN CHAINS

the westernmost island of the Aleutians, and of making full use of the Alaskan area for military activities directed toward the western Pacific.

In September 1942, two months after the *Manasquan* tests, a survey party comprised of representatives of the Army Air Force, the Coast Guard, and the Radiation Laboratory went into the Bering Sea and selected Loran sites on St. Matthew, St. Paul, and Umnak Islands. On 28 January 1943, the Coast Guard was directed to establish stations at these sites. Headquarters organized a special Construction Detachment A (Unit 26) to construct and man the stations. The permanent manning crews were to be used also as the construction force, and each slave station was to have one officer and 18 men.

Lieutenant Commander John F. Martin, USCGR, was designated as commanding officer and sent to MIT for a course in Loran work. An order of 19 February 1943, called for the simultaneous construction of four stations. The project required the procurement of substantial amounts of construction equipment, tools, supplies, and technical apparatus, as well as special foods and clothing for life on the northern islands. All were finally assembled at Seattle. Forty-six men with construction experience and two civil engineering

officers, Ensigns David R. Permar and John J. O'Meara, were assigned to this project. Trained technicians and operators were drawn from the Loran school.

Most of the materials, equipment, and crew departed Seattle for Dutch Harbor, Alaska, in *USS Henry Failing* and *Jonathan Harrington* on 12 April 1943. Unloading began on arrival 25 April, and a detachment headquarters was set up. Cutter (buoy tender) *Clover* stood by to transport personnel and material to the various sites.

*Clover* departed Dutch Harbor for Umnak Island on 12 May, towing a landing barge. Just outside Dutch Harbor, however, the barge capsized because of the "excessive" speed of 10 knots, and it was returned to the harbor for reconditioning. Since that would delay operations, plans were changed and *Clover* left on 21 May for St. Paul Island, 250 miles distant, where unloading would be done by barges belonging to the Army garrison there.

Two trips to St. Paul Island were required to transport the 450 tons of materiel—trucks, cranes, bulldozers, concrete mixers, Quonset huts, lumber, cement, pipe, and other items, as well as electronic equipment such as antennae, transmitters, timers, switchboards, generators, and other things needed to make a completely self-sustaining station. The shoreline of the island consisted of rocky cliffs and ledges rising to a height of about 45 feet. The site was on a promontory with the sea on its west and south sides. Unloading was done by barge, and the materials were hauled by truck from the dock to the end of the existing road. The remainder of the haul was over rocky terrain, and transportation was furnished by two Army tractors with trailers, and by sledges built by the crew. Heavy snow covered the entire island; when it melted, conditions were deplorable.

When the technical equipment was unpacked, it was discovered that the Loran timers and transmitters were in poor condition. Defective parts and poor connections caused trouble, and a shortage of spare parts and test equipment caused difficulty in getting the station on the air. On 31 May 1943, Coast Guard plane PBY-189, under command of Lieutenant Commander Richard Baxter, with Ensign Harold Bennett as co-pilot, reported for duty to transport the commanding officer of the Loran Construction Detachment, as well as mail, personnel, supplies, and materials to the various sites.

Conditions at St. Matthew Island were observed from this plane. St. Matthew was the northernmost site, 200 miles north of St. Paul Island, and over 400 miles north of Dutch Harbor. At the proper time, *Clover* loaded materials and the construction crew and, with the landing barge, sailed for St. Matthew on 17 June. Here, since snow and ice covered the site, and the tundra, which was 18 inches to eight feet thick, was unstable when not frozen, it was necessary to prepare unusually elaborate foundations for the structures. Technical equipment was in a condition similar to that at St. Paul, and several trips for spare parts were required before the station began testing on 11 September. While tests were being conducted, five enlisted men set out on an errand from St. Matthew Island in a small surfboat for a 9-mile journey along the shore to an Army weather station. Despite a calm sea, the men, boat, and equipment disappeared without a trace. Only a 5-gallon oil can known to have been in the boat was ever found—mute testimony to tragedy.

On 5 June, *Clover* set out from Dutch Harbor with equipment, materials, and a construction crew for Umnak Island. A landing was made there, and

supplies were transported ashore by barge, and a temporary camp was established in the village of Nikolski. The site at Cape Starr was five miles away. There was no road over the rugged terrain and all hauling had to be done when the ground was dry or frozen. The Army had an air station at the island, and vessels arrived at least once a month throughout the year. From this station, a squadron of fighter planes in 1942 had knocked down several Jap planes which had attacked Dutch Harbor. Ten-hour transmissions from this chain began on 18 October, and by July 1944, transmissions were on a 24-hour basis.

During the first winter, difficulties were caused chiefly by weather. Snow was heavy and continuous; drifts varied from 3 to 25 feet in depth. Several blizzards lasted 10 days, and men lost their bearings even when traveling only 50 feet from hut to hut. Guide ropes rectified this difficulty. Men were rotated after a year of service.

There was a light station at Cape Sarichef, on Umnak Island, 80 miles northeast of Dutch Harbor. A monitor station was established here toward the end of 1943. Personnel were housed at the light station. However, because electronic results were poor, the monitor was decommissioned in December 1944, and its duties were taken over by a temporary monitor station which had been established in July of that year at St. George Island, one of the Pribilof group.

The crew of plane PBY-189 played an important part in building the Alaskan Loran chain. It made 96 flights, and of 354 hours of flying, mostly under adverse weather conditions, 200 flying hours required instrument flying. As there were no handling facilities at the three destinations, it was necessary to anchor the plane in the open sea. During this period, the plane rescued four injured men from an Army plane wrecked in the Bering Sea.

On completion, the Alaska chain comprised:

| | | |
|---|---|---|
| St. Matthew Island | Unit #5 | Single Slave |
| St. Paul Island | Unit #60 | Double Master |
| Umnak Island | Unit #40 | Single Slave |
| Cape Sarichef* | Unit #25 | Monitor |
| St. George Island | Unit #95 | Monitor |

* Replaced by St. George Island Station

The Japanese had occupied two of the Aleutian Islands—Attu and Kiska. The United States Navy and Army had driven the Japs off Attu, the westernmost of the islands in a hard-fought battle of two weeks duration ending in success on 29 May 1943. Kiska was evacuated by the Japs on 28-29 July of that year. All of the Aleutian Islands were then in American hands.

On 18 July, the first United States air attack on Paramushiro occurred when six planes took off from Attu and completed the 2,000-mile round trip. A second raid was made on 11 August. On 15 August, American and Canadian troops had landed on Kiska Island and found the enemy had deserted it. The weather was so uncertain, however, both over the Aleutians from which the bombers had to fly, and over the Kuriles which were fogbound most of the year, that bombing was hazardous and uncertain. Loran was a means of reducing the hazards of navigation. The Bering Sea stations were still under construction but nearing completion when, in the late summer of 1943, it was decided to expand Loran coverage in Alaska through a second chain in the Western Aleutians.

Site surveys were made by Coast Guard plane late in August, and sites were chosen at Adak Island, roughly 400 miles west of Dutch Harbor; at Amchitka Island, 180 miles west of Adak; and at Attu, 250 miles west of Amchitka.

Because the work would be carried on in the winter and temporary construction personnel had proved only moderately satisfactory, Construction Detachment A (Unit 26) was assigned to this work. It consisted of eight officers and 130 men, and these were subdivided into four detachments. Personnel of each subdivision included a construction officer, carpenter's mates, motor machinist's mates, cook, pharmacist's mate, electrician's mates, and seamen, making each unit self-sufficient. A headquarters unit consisted of 4 officers and 10 enlisted men including yeomen, storekeepers, and general duty men. The entire detachment was under command of Lieutenant Commander J. F. Martin.

Supplies, personnel, and equipment were assembled at Seattle. Advance arrangements were made at the three locations for the housing and messing of personnel and for storing gear. With preliminary arrangements completed, *SS George Flavel* left Seattle about 1 November for Adak and Attu by way of Ketchikan and Dutch Harbor, with personnel and supplies. Cargo movements between Dutch Harbor and the Loran sites were handled by buoy tender *Cedar*.

On 15 November 1943, Lieutenant Commander Martin was relieved by Lieutenant (jg) Garrett Horder, and assigned to survey work for southwest Pacific stations. He returned to Dutch Harbor in a JRF airplane assigned to Loran work in Alaska and the Aleutians, transferring to another plane for Kodiak. The short-range JRF had just been pronounced inadequate for work in the bad weather there, and had been ordered to Port Angeles, Washington. The JRF left Dutch Harbor, also for Kodiak, 20 minutes before Martin's plane. After leaving Port Heiden it was never heard from again.

The Adak station (monitor) was built at the top of a steep 634-foot hill, 340 feet above the nearest road. The chief problem encountered was getting the cargo up the hill; gear was hauled over the ground on Athey wagons—a slow process. The buildings were erected on spaces dug out of the hillside, and were well banked with soil to reduce surface exposed to the very high prevailing winds. When the station was turned over to the regular manning personnel, supplies were obtained from the Naval Operating Base being developed on the island.

Material for the master station at Attu was unloaded from *George Flavel* at Massacre Bay on 7 December 1943. Attu is about 40 miles long east to west, and 20 miles wide. The site was midway on the south side, at Theodore Point. Materials and equipment were moved 11 miles by barge from Massacre Bay to a rocky beach near the site. Transportation to the site required the conquering of steep grades, with the last mile over an abrupt 1,600-foot hill. There were 7 to 10 feet of snow on the ground.

Cutter *Citrus*, which relieved *Clover*, arrived with the construction crew consisting of Chief Boatswain's Mate William Goodwin and 80 men, and commanded by Lieutenant Thomas Kiely. Cargo was taken ashore by ship's boats, LCMs, and pontoon barges. Four barges were lost in the process due to difficult landing conditions and the suddenness of storms. Chief Goodwin designed, and the men built, a bobsled capable of carrying 20 tons, which almost made the difference between success and failure in transportation of materials and equipment. A bulldozer was rigged as a caterpillar, to pull the bobsled. Even this rig could not get over the steepest part of the route until a road with two switchbacks had been built. While working on this road, a bulldozer operator, William A. Baughman, seaman first class, was killed when the vehicle rolled down the side of the hill.

Work at the site began 11 January 1944. Despite extremely cold weather, blizzards, and deeply frozen ground, the station was on the air and testing 11 February, with a complement of about 23 men. Navy ships supplied this station after it was placed in operation, sending supplies ashore by dory. The supplies were hauled up a 230-foot hill, with steep incline, on a cart pulled by cable and winch. Station personnel spent much of their time handling such deliveries.

While the Attu station was being built, construction of a slave station began at Amchitka Island, under the direction of Ensign O'Meara. Eleven months earlier, the Army had landed there and begun construction of what became a major base. A fighter strip had been completed on 16 February, from which planes soon began bombing Kiska. The cargo for the Loran station was landed on 10 December 1943. Building proceeded normally. The site on St. Makarius Point was far removed from the Army installation in order to avoid interference from other radio stations.

The Aleutian chain was on the air by mid-February 1944, and all were operating on a 24-hour basis by early June. To summarize, it consisted of:

| Attu | Unit #62 | Single Master |
| Amchitka | Unit #63 | Single Slave |
| Adak | Unit #64 | Monitor |

The western Aleutian Loran units were highly important and useful. Many officers including those attached to the Fleet Task Force, which made frequent raids on the Kurile Islands, stretching northward from the main Japanese islands, held Loran in high esteem as an all-weather aid to navigation. For example, a vessel performing guard ship duty was able to keep her station through two weeks of adverse weather, using daytime sky waves. Navigators on patrol missions made by Navy Catalinas used Loran extensively. It gave drift data free from the inaccuracies of drift sights taken on the ocean's surface. A Ventura bomber, while on a mission over the Kuriles, was hit by a burst of antiaircraft fire which threw the plane over on its back and destroyed its radar, compass, and other instruments. The Loran gear was still operative, however, and by homing on a line of position from

rate 0, the plane reached its home base. The value of Loran was recognized by the Commanding General of the Army Air Forces in their attacks on the Kuriles, when he forbade his bombers to take off on missions to the westward unless their Loran sets had been checked and found working properly.

The invasions of Tarawa, Makin, and Abemama in the Gilbert Islands took place in November 1943, just as construction of the Aleutian stations was getting under way. Other operations between Hawaii and Australia were in progress. Guns were blazing in the Gilberts when, on 12 November, it was decided by the Joint Loran Planning Committee of the Joint Chiefs of Staff that Loran coverage should be provided in the area southwest of the Hawaiian Islands. Through these waters passed the all important supply route from Hawaii to Australia.

Sites chosen were on Kauai for a monitor station, and on the islands of Hawaii and French Frigate Shoals for single slave stations. The island of Niihau was chosen for a double master station. These were along a 600-mile line through the entire Hawaiian group.

Newly created Construction Detachment C (Unit 80) was assigned to the project, first under Lieutenant Commander Frank L. Busse and then under Lieutenant Commander Merton W. Stoffle. Work began late in March 1944. Problems there differed from those in Alaska. The terrain was different, the climate was tropical, and buildings and other features needed to be altered to provide reasonable comforts. Here, also, there was a possibility of attack by sea or air. This meant some dispersion, concealment, and camouflage of buildings.

French Frigate Shoals are 400 miles west-northwest of Kauai and Niihau. The Loran site was on Government owned East Island, a sandy expanse over coral reef rising but 10 feet above sea level. The island was uninhabited except by gooney birds. Approaches had to be buoyed, and bad weather delayed progress in landing cargo.

The station at Niihau was the first to be started. The others were simultaneously built soon afterward with no major difficulties. The chain as a whole was completed and tests begun on 22 July 1944. It went on the air 23 July; system accuracy tests were completed 4 November; and the District Coast Guard Officer, 14th Naval

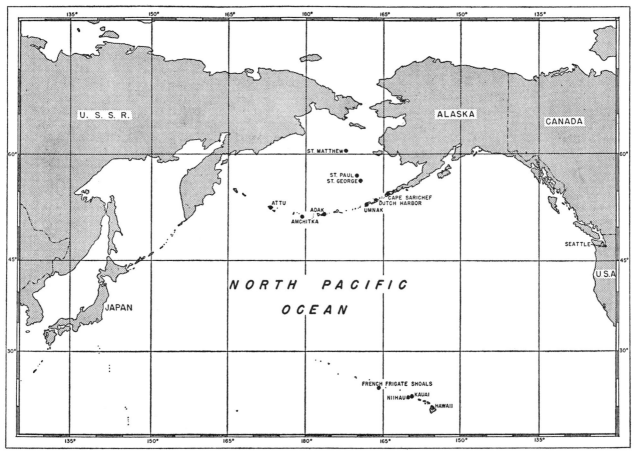

LOCATIONS OF FIRST PACIFIC LORAN STATIONS

District (Honolulu) took it over on 8 November. The Hawaiian chain was made up of:

| | | |
|---|---|---|
| French Frigate Shoals | Unit #204 | Single Slave |
| Niihau | Unit #205 | Double Master |
| Hawaii | Unit #206 | Single Slave |
| Kauai | Unit #207 | Monitor |

The many new Loran stations required increasing numbers of trained men. By July 1944, the Loran School at Groton, Connecticut, was turning out 20 rated "radiomen Loran" every 5 weeks in its 10-week course, to man the four new stations being built every 10 weeks. Loran was growing up.

Headquarters recognized the need for the supervision of construction work from a point much closer to activities than Washington, D.C. As a consequence Command Unit # 203, headed by Lieutenant Commander John F. Martin, was established in April 1944, to take charge of all Loran construction in the Pacific. A fixed base was required for administrative work, as a receiving and shipping point for construction personnel and ma-

terials, and for storage of materials and equipment. Accordingly, a base was established at Sand Island, in Honolulu Harbor, adjacent to the Coast Guard aids to navigation depot. The base was designed to house 350 men, and to store materials for three Loran chains. After finishing the Hawaiian stations, Construction Detachment C (Unit 80) built the Loran portion of the base before going to the Marianas. The Sand Island Base became the depot from which all construction materials were procured.

Working in conjunction with this base were the Advanced Base Section of Coast Guard Headquarters Civil Engineering Division; the construction detachment supply officers at the Coast Guard Supply Depot, Alameda, California; and the District Supply personnel at Seattle. Coast Guard planes were assigned to this unit for survey, transportation, and signal check purposes. A Liberty-type cargo vessel was acquired by the Coast Guard to handle material and equipment for Loran work.

This vessel, *USS Menkar* (AK-123), 445 feet long, was transferred from the Navy to the Coast Guard in October, 1944, and placed in command of Lieutenant Commander Niels P. Thomsen, USCG, with a full Coast Guard crew. Three days after its first arrival at Sand Island, *Menkar* was headed for the Marianas with Loran materials.

Later on, progress in the Pacific was such that in January 1945, a similar advanced base was established at Guam, near the scene of later Loran construction, and Command Unit #203 departed for that base.

The Armed Forces of the United States were gradually pushing their way through the South Pacific and securing first one and then another of the several large island groups. Loran had proven so valuable that it became an established policy to go into these areas with Loran chains at the earliest possible moment. The new aid to navigation would be vitally important in the ensuing operations nearer the Philippines and Japan. United States planes had bombed Wake Island and the Japanese mandated Marshall Islands, and the Army and Marine forces had landed at Roi and Kwajalein. A chain in the Phoenix Islands, midway between Hawaii and Australia, would serve naval and air operations over a wide and important area in which the Army Air Transport Command was operating planes.

This chain was authorized on 5 February 1944. Construction Detachment D (Unit 211) consisting of 8 officers and 130 men was formally commissioned on 7 April 1944, to build the chain. Lieutenant George L. Kelly became the commanding officer. The project called for a master station at Gardner Island, a monitor at Canton Island, and slave stations at Baker and Atafu Islands. Canton Island was chosen as the base of operations, and units arrived there in May.

The Baker Island slave station was the first to be built. Buoy tender *Balsam* carried all materials and supplies for this installation in one load except for technical equipment, and reached Baker on 6 June, towing an LCM. On that day a message that 12 aviators from a crashed PBM plane were down off Howland Island, 31 miles to the north was received. *Balsam* arrived with her tow at the scene, and the LCM, manned by men of the construction detachment under Lieutenant (jg) Bobby D. Pomeroy, rescued the aviators

under difficult circumstances. The survivors were later transferred to a Navy submarine chaser from Canton Island, and *Balsam* returned to Baker Island. Landing materials at Baker took two weeks, and was complicated by high winds, torrential rains, and treacherous surf.

Baker Island was ready for testing on 20 August. On 19 September the remaining construction men were ready to leave. Net tender *Spicewood* arrived to remove the men and construction equipment. When the barge was loaded with about 30 tons of gear and ready to shove off, it broached to, but a tractor operator, thinking quickly, pushed the stern outward. En route to *Spicewood*, one motor in the barge failed, then the rudder gears gave way. The barge was maneuvered alongside the tender. Soon, mooring bits gave way, then the ramp cable parted and the ramp fell down. In attempting to raise the ramp, James O. McKeehan, boatswain's mate second class, was lost in the sea. Two shipmates, Kenneth E. Foreman, boatswain's mate first class and Joseph Letko, motor machinist's mate second class, dived into the shark infested water to save him, but no trace of him was ever found. The barge, having become useless and taking water rapidly, was finally sunk by gunfire.

The Baker Island station began operations on 28 September.

At this time, the position of Loran stations was accurately determined in advance of actual construction, in order to enable the Hydrographic Office to proceed with the preparation of special Loran charts, each of which had to go through the press several times because of the many colors required. Thus, exactness in setting up the transmitters was essential. The Hydrographic Office survey ship *Sumner* was in the Pacific surveying prospective Loran sites and establishing the exact latitude and longitude of the points where antennae were to be erected. The Loran charts were then begun; the stations themselves being constructed later.

In establishing the Phoenix chain, the Coast Guard was faced for the first time with the possibility that the Japanese might attempt a commando or similar attack upon an isolated station in order to gain possession of equipment. Despite the secret nature of the basic principles of Loran, the Japs were probably aware of the existence of the system and would be anxious to obtain details.

As it was not expected that station crews could offer sustained resistance to a large landing force, demolition procedure was prescribed. Other security measures made use of sentries, dogs, machine guns, grenades, and other light weapons.

A landing party arrived in *Balsam* at Gardner Island on 24 July 1944, to begin work at the site of the master station. Materials and equipment arrived about 1 September. Actual operation began in December. The Atafu slave station was in the process of building from May until December. Cargo for this station was loaded at Canton Island in a Navy net tender and a large steel barge which the tender towed. The trip covered 360 miles. When they were nearing Atafu, a tropical squall struck. The LCMs, which were being carried, broke loose. The net tender, being unable to pick them up in the heavy seas, put crews on board, and the LCMs finished the last 40 miles under their own power.

When the construction crew reached shore, the Polynesian village elders insisted upon vacating and making available to them the eight native houses until a camp could be set up at the site. Their hospitality was gratefully accepted for the four days spent in unloading, during which time the natives' amazement at the mobile equipment and other gear was almost unbelievable.

Stations of the Phoenix chain went on the air on 29 September 1944. System accuracy tests were completed on 15 November; and the District Coast Guard Officer, 14th Naval District, took over the chain on 16 December. Completion of the chain provided Loran coverage for practically all of the Pacific war front as it then existed, and over all important targets. By this time, shipboard and airborne Loran receivers were installed in over 1,000 surface vessels and 7,000 aircraft, with production and installation picking up rapidly. More than 50,000 receivers were then in production.

The Phoenix chain stations were:

| Baker Island | Unit #91 | Single Slave |
| Gardner Island | Unit #92 | Double Master |
| Atafu | Unit #93 | Single Slave |
| Canton Island | Unit #94 | Monitor |

All Japanese had been driven from the Gilbert and Marshall Islands, northwest of the Phoenix group, soon after construction had been begun on the Hawaiian and Phoenix Island stations. It was, therefore, possible to undertake the Marshall-Gilbert Loran chain. The campaign in those islands was part of the general military plan for a further advance toward the Philippines. Our forces had established bases and airfields in the Marshalls, Admiralties, and in north central New Guinea. These threatened enemy bases in the Carolines, in the eastern Netherland East Indies, and southern Philippines. Japanese air strength in the Carolines was deteriorating, and because of this the Japs were strengthening their positions in the Marianas. Allied military preparations urgently required good Loran coverage from stations in the Marshalls. Thus, Loran followed the trend of Pacific warfare, which was moving from the Hawaii-Australia alignment to one extending from Hawaii toward the Philippines.

The Marshall-Gilbert chain extended from the Makin Atoll through the Majuro Atoll to the Kwajalein Atoll, a distance of 450 miles in a southeast-northwest direction. It consisted of a single slave at Kwajalein and at Bikati (Varsity) Island of the Makin Atoll, a double master station at Rogeron (Loraine) Island of the Majuro Atoll, and a monitor at Enigu (Marilyn) Island of the Majuro Atoll. These stations were built by Construction Detachment A (Unit 26), which had built the two Alaska chains. Surveys were made in November 1943, and the bulk of the personnel arrived at Majuro on 28 June 1944.

Delays plagued the construction force. Cargo intended for the two Majuro stations, which had been shipped in *Rutland Victory*, was delayed two months or more, due to the rerouting of the vessel by the Commander, Forward Area, for operational reasons. This cargo was reloaded in other ships as many as five times before finally arriving at the site! In the course of all this handling, many pieces of cargo were lost. The cargo intended for Makin was similarly delayed some six weeks.

A vessel with Loran equipment reached Eniwetok Atoll, where United States forces had landed after the capture of Kwajalein. Preparations for the Saipan invasion were in full swing there, and the ammunition which formed an important part of the vessels' cargo was vitally needed. Consequently, the Navy unloaded the Loran equipment and supplies onto lighters, barges, and LCTs. All the cement, lumber, commissary supplies, and a good portion of the tools disappeared. A considerable period of time elapsed before transportation was available for the rest of the materials destined for the use of this detachment. The construction force at Kwajalein, while awaiting arrival of their material were, however, able to do a great deal of preliminary work.

The greatest difficulty in construction of the Marshall-Gilbert stations was brought about through the many missing items lost in the frequent handlings. Despite the troubles, this chain went on the air on 29 September, tests began by 15 October, and on 16 December all were operative and placed in commission under the District Coast Guard Officer, 14th Naval District, together with those of the Phoenix chain.

The chain comprised:

| | | | |
|---|---|---|---|
| Kwajalein | (Kwadack) | Unit #82 | Single Slave |
| Majuro | (Rogeron) | Unit #83 | Double Master |
| Makin | (Bikati) | Unit #84 | Single Slave |
| Majuro | (Enigu) | Unit #85 | Monitor |

The Pacific military campaign progressed relentlessly. After the Marshalls and Gilberts had been secured, the Navy, with Army and Marine units, pushed into the Marianas. The campaign was viciously prosecuted and viciously resisted. The power of the naval assault was tremendous. Only after the most intensive fighting did Saipan, Guam, and Tinian fall to American arms. Saipan, a mountainous island with an extinct volcano 1,554 feet high, had a prewar population of 19,000, of which 16,000 were Japanese. It was completely in possession of American forces by 9 July 1944. Guam was secured in mid-August.

Loran stations in these islands were urgently needed to cover the approaches to the Philippines and Japan. Pursuing the established policy, the Coast Guard moved in soon after occupation, and surveyed for Loran sites in September and October. Sites were chosen for a single master station on Saipan Island; a single master station on Potangeras Island in the Ulithi Islands; a double slave station on Cocos Island (Guam); and a monitor station at Ritidian Point, Guam. These islands were approximately 1,200 miles east of the Philippines, and extended in a northeast-southwest line about 500 miles long.

Preparation of airfields was begun immediately after occupation, and American planes were soon ready for a long range bombing offensive. In bombing Japan, it was necessary to route the flights far to the west of those islands, because of the presence of Japanese forces in the islands between the Marianas and Japan. This meant 1,500 miles of open water flight with no radio or radar check points until within 100 miles of Japan. Accurate navigation was essential, and Loran signals offered the solution for such air operations. Loran became the navigational aid upon which the navigators leaned most heavily.

Construction of the chain was assigned to Construction Detachment C (Unit 80), commanded by Lieutenant Commander Merton W. Stoffle, which had built the Hawaiian chain. *Menkar*, with construction material, reached Saipan on 31 October 1944. Work was begun on 5 November. Army Ground Forces realized the urgency of establishing Loran service, and promptly cooperated. The station was ready to go on the air 16 November, but there were as yet no other stations with which it could operate.

The urgent need for Loran stations was soon demonstrated. On 25 November one hundred and eleven B-29s bombed Tokyo; it was the first bombing attack on that city since the Doolittle raid in 1942, and the first of many raids which were literally to obliterate every target in Japan worth bombing. As this station was close to the Marianas airfield which was used by the B-29s, enemy air raids were frequent and there was considerable danger from falling shrapnel due to American anti-aircraft firing.

At Cocos, a small island two miles off the town of Merizo on the south end of Guam, a double slave station was begun on 11 November under direction of Lieutenant (jg) Marshall T. Munz. Cocos Island was 700 feet long, 500 feet wide, low, sandy, and densely covered with tropical growth. A channel that would accommodate LCMs and LCVPs had to be blasted through the reefs on the south shore, to allow gear to be landed without danger of wetting. The station paired with Saipan and went on the air 27 November.

The Ulithi station was not operative for another month. While it was not customary to operate only two stations of a chain without the third station, the Guam-Saipan stations during this interval provided Loran rate which gave planes and vessels the benefit of a single line of position which could be combined with dead reckoning, and which proved extremely useful.

On 11 November, *Menkar* arrived at Apra

Harbor with materials for the monitor station. These were put ashore with some difficulty through the terrific wreckage still remaining from the naval and air bombardment. The cargo was hauled by trucks and other vehicles for 30 miles along the shore road and then inland through the heavily wooded country to the Loran site on Ritidian Point at the northern end of Guam. Lieutenant Ralph L. Bernard and his crew did an excellent job, and this station was operating on 4 December.

The Ulithi Atoll was about 380 miles southwest of Guam. It was surveyed with the cooperation of Commodore Oliver O. Kessing, USN, Island Commander of the Atoll. The most desirable islands of the group were very crowded. Potangeras seemed the most likely island, but additional time would be required in clearing the ground. This objection was removed when Commodore Kessing offered to have the ground cleared by the 88th Navy Construction Battalion. *Menkar* picked up the necessary equipment and the detachment which had built the Saipan station, reached Ulithi on 13 December. This single master station was on the air on 26 December, pairing with the Cocos station. The Ulithi unit was put into operation in less time than any other station in the Pacific.

This chain was completed in February 1945, and commissioned on 1 March. The signals were used immediately by the 21st Bomber Command.

Heavy bombers attacked Tokyo and other Japanese industrial cities from the United States bases at Saipan, Tinian, and Guam. The B-29s could make the flight to Tokyo and return, but about halfway from Guam to Tokyo was Iwo Jima, held by the Japanese. As its three airfields would serve far better if in American hands, Iwo Jima became the next American military objective. Plans for this new amphibious assault, along with bombing attacks on the Japanese mainland, made the Marianas Loran stations extremely important. These were:

| | | |
|---|---|---|
| Guam (Cocos) | Unit #336 | Double Slave |
| Saipan | Unit #337 | Single Master |
| Ulithi (Potangeras I.) | Unit #338 | Single Master |
| Ritidian Point (Guam) | Unit #339 | Monitor |

With a change of headquarters of Commander-in-Chief, Pacific (CincPac) and Commander-in-Chief Pacific Ocean Area (CincPoa) from Pearl Harbor to Guam at the beginning of 1945, the Coast Guard moved its Command Unit #203 to Guam. It will be recalled that this unit was responsible for Loran construction. This unit, then commanded by Lieutenant Commander K. W. Donnell, was made operationally responsible to Commander in Chief, Pacific Ocean Area, and Commander in Chief, Southwest Pacific Area, and was itself responsible for the movement and operation of the three construction detachments, the plane, *Menkar,* the Advance Base Staging Detachment, and the Charting Element (which issued temporary Loran charts in advance of stations becoming operative). All matters of design, siting, and supervision of construction, and the testing of stations in the Pacific were also the responsibility of this unit.

With the further progress of United States forces which were now carrying the campaign to the Philippines, it was desirable to provide closer Loran coverage for the Mindanao area. The importance of stations in this area was so great in the planning of military operations, that the Navy's Seventh Amphibious Force made landings to secure territory for that sole purpose. Mobile Loran units went on the air on 1 December 1944 at Pulo Anna, Palau, and Morotai to provide service pending the establishment of permanent stations. In January, steps were taken to erect and maintain three fixed stations at these places to replace the mobile units.

Accordingly, a double master station was set up at Pulo Anna Island; a single slave station on Ngesebus (Peleliu) Island; a single slave at Pangeo (Morotai); and a monitor station on the former Japanese island of Angaur. This chain followed the northerly swing of military operations. The work was assigned to Construction Detachment D (Unit 211), Lieutenant Gary S. Morgan, which had built the Phoenix chain. Construction began on 5 March when *Menkar* arrived at Angaur at the southerly extremity of the Palau Islands. The station relieved the mobile unit on 2 April.

All cargo had reached the Ngesebus site by 14 March, and work began immediately. Only 14 days later, the station was ready to go on the air. So close was this station to the scene of fighting that during the invasion of the Jap-held island to the north, men in the elevated tower could see the

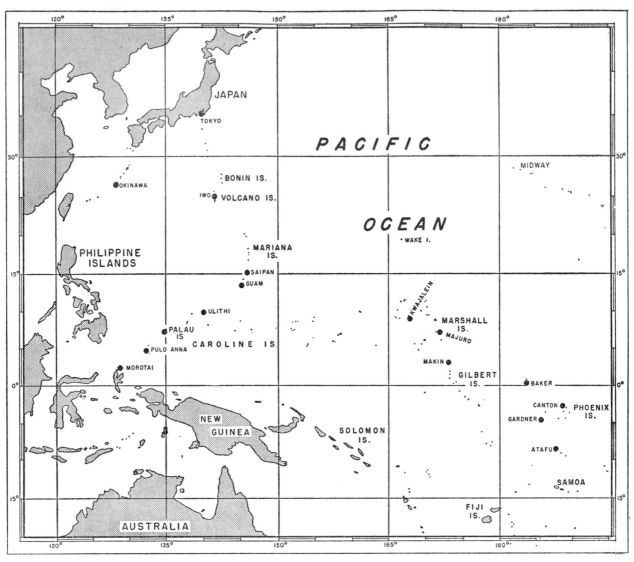

LORAN SITES IN APPROACHES TO JAPAN

men going ashore, the bombers blasting the targets, and fighters strafing installations. When these
nearby islands were in Allied hands, the Loran
personnel felt more secure in their isolated position. The mobile stations were picked up by
*Menkar* and taken to sites in the west Philippines.

*Menkar* reached Pulo Anna on 9 March and
landed construction equipment and personnel for
the double master station. Pulo Anna was a palm-
studded island 200 miles southwest of Angaur
and Peleliu, roughly half a mile long and a
quarter mile wide. On 16 March, *Menkar* arrived
at the naval base at the south end of the island of
Morotai with material for the single slave station
there. Japanese forces, which were in a bad way,

were still in the interior of this mountainous,
jungle-covered, 50 mile long island. A small
United States Army force close by the Loran site
and station, maintained a perimeter against them.

Landing conditions at Pangeo Beach on Morotai
were poor, but unloading was attempted. Shallow
water and high breaking surf made operations
hazardous, and on striking the beach both barges
broached. Thereafter, *Menkar* returned to anchorage, and in relatively calm water unloaded cargo
into LCTs. Even so, when *Menkar's* LCMs went
alongside for hoisting, nothing could eliminate the
rolling and pitching of the ship. While hoisting,
George Ybarra, Seaman Second Class, of *Menkar*,
was crushed to death between the ship and an

LCM. *Menkar* returned to Pangeo Beach with her LCMs and the LCTs. The former were successfully unloaded. After many unsuccessful attempts, one LCT finally landed and was unloaded. Heavy seas prevented the other from doing so, and she transferred her cargo to LCMs which finally got the remaining cargo ashore in somewhat moderated weather. Manning personnel arrived on 7 April, and the station went on the air on 28 April. The mobile unit was discontinued. All units in the chain were operative by May and commissioned 22 June 1945.

The stations of the Palau-Morotai chain were:

| Angaur | Unit #346 | Monitor |
| Pulo Anna | Unit #344 | Double Master |
| Ngesebus (Peleliu) | Unit #343 | Single Slave |
| Morotai (Pangeo) | Unit #345 | Single Slave |

With the assaults upon Iwo Jima and Okinawa well under way, the time was approaching when the network of Loran stations could be expanded even farther toward Japan. New stations of the Japan Loran chain would provide navigational aid for the bombers which were concentrating on the main islands of the Japanese Empire, and for the amphibious units in their projected assault upon Japan.

Iwo Jima, 700 miles south of Tokyo, and Okinawa, about the same distance southwest of that city, were satisfactory locations for Loran stations. A third station to complete the chain would be erected at some point in the general vicinity of Tokyo when this became possible.

Siting surveys of Iwo Jima and Okinawa were made long before the islands were fully secured, and the Coast Guard parties carrying out this work were under fire on several occasions. On completion, this chain consisted of a double master station at Iwo Jima; a single slave at Okinawa; and later, a single slave on O Shima, an island in the entrance to Tokyo Bay.

A very small, rocky island known as Kangoku Iwa, one and a quarter miles northwest of Iwo Jima, was chosen as one site. It consisted wholly of rocks ranging in size from six feet in diameter down to the size of a man's fist. There was no sand. *Menkar* reached the island on 20 April 1945, just two months after the Marines had first landed, and by 23 April, all supplies, materials, and the construction detail were ashore. Construction started the next day. This double master station

was ready to go on the air on 5 May, but it could not be put into operation until its paired station at Okinawa was completed.

The Tenth Army and the Amphibious Marines had invaded Okinawa on 1 April. A siting party visited Okinawa and completed its work by 3 May. The site chosen was Ike Shima, an island about one mile square, five miles off the east coast of Okinawa, and 325 miles south of the Japanese mainland. There was an ideal, well protected, sandy landing beach.

*Menkar*, which arrived at Ike Shima on 10 May, received a noisy welcome. Enemy aircraft were reported over the area five times during the night, and each time all hands were called to battle stations. The following day was quiet, and discharging operations were conducted in fair weather and a favorable sea. Work was discontinued one hour before sunset to prepare for anti-aircraft defense. There were three air raids in the area that night. On 12 May work was again commenced at sunrise. General quarters sounded at 1912 as the ship was warned of approaching enemy aircraft. Anti-aircraft fire was observed in the vicinity but no aircraft were visible.

On the third day unloading proceeded, but general quarters was called at 1915. Shortly afterward, there was heavy anti-aircraft fire to the northeast, the direction from which the attack was approaching. The group of attacking planes split up and the two sections attacked from the north and east. *Menkar's* immediate concern was the attack coming from the east, as she was anchored east of Okinawa. Only seconds later, there was the sound of aircraft approaching from that direction. Enemy planes were over Ichi Banare Island and coming in over the forward part of *Menkar*. As anti-aircraft batteries on shore opened fire, the attacking plane dropped a stick of four bombs which straddled the ship. The plane veered sharply to the south. The heavy anti-aircraft fire broke up the attack, and the planes did not return. There was no serious damage to the ship. One member of the crew, F. E. Koeber, Boatswain's Mate First Class, was injured when a bomb fragment entered his left hand.

The discharge of cargo was accelerated on 14 May so that *Menkar* might get away from the anchorage in the afternoon. On 16 May while she was anchored in Katchin Wan Harbor, Okinawa, there were three alerts. Two days later, while the ship was still anchored there, a report of "enemy air attack imminent" brought the crew to battle stations. A plane was reported by the after gun watch. All guns which could bear started tracking. When the plane reached 160° relative, it was identified as an "Oscar" by the recognition team.

When the plane reached 100° relative, at a range of 800 yards, it banked to the left and dived directly towards *Menkar*. The order to open fire was given, and all the starboard batteries, including the forward and after 40 mms, opened fire. In 30 seconds *Menkar* expended 441 rounds of 20 mm., and 155 rounds of 40 mm. ammunition. Many bursts were seen to explode on the plane. The plane disintegrated and struck the water alongside the merchant ship *Uriah Rose*, 300 yards distant.

The gear for the Okinawa station which *Menkar* had landed was transported to the north end of the island over a very narrow road. Work started on the station on 15 May, under direction of Lieutenant (jg) Wilson Mulheim. This slave station was on the air by 27 May, pairing with Iwo Jima, 730 miles away. A system check began on 5 June and continued through 12 June. This was 25 days before organized Japanese resistance on the island ceased.

Construction of the third station of the Japan chain at O Shima had to wait until appropriate territory was captured. On 14 August 1945, the Japanese offered to surrender. American planes flew the Japanese delegation from Ike Shima to Manila to hear General MacArthur's terms. Two hundred C-54s flew the initial occupying force into Tokyo. On 2 September 1945, orders were issued

to proceed with the construction of a slave station at O Shima, 60 miles south of Tokyo, to pair with the Iwo Jima station. O Shima went on the air on 1 December 1945. The Japan chain finally consisted of:

| Iwo Jima | (Kangoku Iwa) | Unit #348 | Double Master |
|----------|---------------|-----------|---------------|
| Tokyo | (O Shima) | Unit #349 | Single Slave |
| Okinawa | (Ike Shima) | Unit #350 | Single Slave |

Soon after cessation of hostilities, it was planned to establish a China Sea Loran chain. Various difficulties were encountered, however, and since the war was over, the project was abandoned.

When the construction detachments headed eastward, with their destination the Pacific coast ports of the United States, they left behind them an achievement of which all might be proud. Taking an electronic system of position finding which had been developed under the pressure of war necessity, and the intricate parts of which were manufactured in all haste, this group of civil engineers had gone to far-off islands, the remoteness of which could hardly be exceeded. They had landed on open beaches; had established camps; assembled transmitting equipment; installed power plants; and placed in operation all the living and other facilities which would make it possible for the permanent crews to provide continuous Loran service. The magnitude of the problem overcome in the establishment of the individual stations was exceeded only by the magnitude of the task in general, for the stations which these crews erected provided Loran service for practically the entire Pacific area in which combat operations were performed. It was a job "well done."

# Chapter 12

# COAST GUARD MEN AND NAVY SHIPS

Partially as a result of the disastrous attack on the naval vessels at Pearl Harbor, the U. S. Navy entered the war with a great shortage of all kinds of ships. Demands were tremendous if formidable foes were to be fought successfully in a two-ocean war. The vast majority of vessels employed in the various phases of the war effort had to be built particularly for the purpose in American shipyards during the period of hostilities. It was a herculean task.

A corollary to this shortage and the wartime building program was the enlistment and training of naval personnel to man this vast quantity and variety of ships. The building of vessels and the procurement and training of personnel took time. It was a limiting factor in the timing and prosecution of our military campaigns. It was partly responsible for the need to concentrate early offensive operations in the Atlantic areas and to relegate, for a while, the Pacific operations to a secondary position! Building had to catch up with the need, but this was almost miraculously accomplished by late 1944.

Even so, throughout the period there was a shortage of trained personnel. In the earlier stages of the war the Navy's demand for trained officers and enlisted men was so great for the vessels then available, that the Navy urgently needed Coast Guardsmen to take over the manning and operation of many ships. This demand increased as many new vessels were built, and the urgency of manning Navy vessels never abated right up to the end of hostilities. The Army, also, needed Coast Guardsmen for many of its vessels. These demands, in turn, left the Coast Guard in a position where it was almost continually short of personnel for its own varied activities, especially in certain

ratings. The Temporary Reserve relieved this condition to some extent. But prosecution of the war was a cooperative effort between all the Armed Services, and the Coast Guard, as an integral part of the Navy in wartime, furnished personnel for this manning program to the very best of human ability.

That this effort was very considerable, and the Coast Guard's contribution significantly important, is evident from a few figures given in the Prologue and appropriately repeated here. During the war, the Coast Guard manned 351 Navy vessels; 288 of which were still so manned on 30 June 1945 with 49,283 Coast Guardsmen. It also provided personnel for 288 Army vessels; 262 of which were still in service at that time with Coast Guardsmen numbering 6,851. On that date, the Coast Guard had 171,168 officers and men of whom 80,476 were serving afloat. It is obvious that the vessel manning program for the Navy and Army accounted for nearly 70 percent of those Coast Guardsmen with sea assignments.

The function of most of the larger vessels was the transportation of military personnel and cargo of various types—chiefly the former. The majority of the Coast Guard-manned ships, however, were combat units. The 351 Navy vessels and 288 Army craft and the number of each type manned under this program were:

*NAVY*

| | | |
|---|---|---|
| Landing ships, Tank | (LST) | 76 |
| Patrol Frigates | (PF) | 75 |
| Patrol Vessels | (YP) | 40 |
| Destroyer Escorts | (DE) | 30 |
| Landing Craft, Infantry (Large) | (LCI(L)) | 28 |
| Transports | (AP) | 22 |
| Gasoline Tankers | (AOG) | 18 |
| Cargo Ships | (AK) | 15 |

| Auxiliary Transports | (APA) | 9 |
|---|---|---|
| Gunboats or Corvettes | (PG) | 8 |
| Miscellaneous unclassified | (IX) | 7 |
| Submarine Chasers | (SC) | 6 |
| Auxiliary Cargo Attack Ships | (AKA) | 5 |
| Submarine Chasers | (PC) | 4 |
| Coastal Yacht | (PYC) | 1 |
| Ferryboat and Launch | (YFB) | 1 |
| Ambulance Boat | (YHB) | 1 |
| Gate Vessel | (YNG) | 1 |
| Range Tender | (YF) | 1 |
| Motor Torpedo Boat Tender | (AGP) | 1 |
| Submarine Chaser | (WPC) | 1 |
| Auxiliary Miscellaneous | (WAG) | 1 |

*ARMY*

| Freight and Supply Vessels | (FS) | 188 |
|---|---|---|
| Large Tugs | (LT) | 51 |
| Tankers | (TY) | 22 |
| Freight Vessels | (F) | 21 |
| Army Marine Repair Ships | (AMRS) | 6 |

The vessels involved in actual or potential combat were an integral part of the United States Naval Forces and were engaged in patrol, convoy escort, weather observation, supply, and amphibious landing operations. Activities in some of those categories have been covered in previous chapters. The parts others played in actual combat and landing operations will be made clear in the chapters which follow. We are now concerned, for the most part, with the larger vessels, the duty of which was the transportation of military personnel and war supplies.

The Coast Guard manned 22 of the AP-type transports. One of these was *Wakefield,* formerly *Manhattan,* the story of which is given in the chapter on The Battle of the Atlantic—a story of fire at sea, of salvage, of rebuilding, and of accomplishment as a transport. After being put back into service under command of Captain R. L. Raney, she made 23 round trips across the Atlantic and three across the Pacific, transporting 233,319 persons up to 1 February 1946.

Except for *Wakefield* and *Monticello,* the 13 large AP-type transports were about 622 feet in length, 75 feet in beam, and 17,830 gross tonnage, and had an average speed of 19.3 knots. They had accommodations for about 454 officers and 4,725 troops. Of these, all but *Wakefield* and *Monticello* were commissioned between 20 January 1944 and 30 June 1945. The nine smaller AP-type vessels were 522 feet long, 72 feet in beam, of 12,347 gross tons, and had a maximum sustained speed of

17.8 knots. Troop carrying capacity was about 5,700. These were all built by the Kaiser Company, Inc., of Richmond, California, and commissioned between 7 February 1944 and 20 April 1945.

The Coast Guard-manned AP-type transports were:

*Large Type*

| *Wakefield* | AP-21 |
|---|---|
| *Monticello* | AP-61 |
| *Gen. William Mitchell* | AP-114 |
| *Gen. George M. Randall* | AP-115 |
| *Gen. M. C. Meigs* | AP-116 |
| *Gen. W. H. Gordon* | AP-117 |
| *Gen. W. P. Richardson* | AP-118 |
| *Gen. William Weigel* | AP-119 |
| *Adm. W. C. Capps* | AP-121 |
| *Adm. E. W. Eberle* | AP-123 |

*Small Type*

| *Gen. R. L. Howze* | AP-134 |
|---|---|
| *Gen. W. M. Black* | AP-135 |
| *Gen. H. L. Scott* | AP-136 |
| *Gen. A. W. Greely* | AP-141 |
| *Gen. C. H. Muir* | AP-142 |
| *Gen. H. B. Freeman* | AP-143 |
| *Gen. H. F. Hodges* | AP-144 |
| *Gen. A. W. Brewster* | AP-155 |
| *Gen. D. E. Aultman* | AP-156 |
| *Adm. C. F. Hughes* | AP-124 |
| *Adm. H. T. Mayo* | AP-125 |
| *Gen. J. C. Breckenridge* | AP-176 |

Between them all, they reached the far corners of the world wherever hostilities required American troops. Some trips were made with foreign soldiers. They touched such far flung points as Bombay, Calcutta, Karachi, Shanghai, Melbourne, the Philippines, New Guinea, Ulithi, Guam, Naples, Korranshah (Iran), Marseilles, and Le-Havre, to mention but a few. After the end of the war, most engaged in "Magic Carpet" duty, transporting troops home from Pacific combat areas for demobilization on the "point basis." After the termination of Magic Carpet duty, the Coast Guard crews were removed from these vessels which were then decommissioned. The first decommissioning was on 31 January and the last on 18 June 1946.

The service which these vessels rendered was similar in most cases. Most of their service was in the Pacific. However, some of this was in the Atlantic with voyages to France, Italy, and through the Suez Canal. For example, *USS Gen-*

*eral W. M. Black* made 15 round trips in 22 months—13 in the Atlantic and two in the Pacific. While the ship histories of all of this group are interesting, an account of the service of one of these transports and the mention of another will suffice to give in some detail the type of duty performed by the Coast Guardsmen who manned them.

The transport *General William Mitchell* (AP 114) was named after America's colorful pioneer of air power, General "Billy" Mitchell, and started its service under the command of Captain Henry Coyle. Between 3 March 1944 and 20 August 1944, this vessel made five voyages across the Atlantic; two unescorted to North Africa and three in convoy to the United Kingdom. In each crossing she carried capacity loads of predominantly Army personnel.

She sailed for Casablanca on 3 March, carrying 5,224 Army troops, returning to Newport News on 23 March with rotation personnel and patients. This was followed by another round trip to Casablanca, and after 10 days of availability in New York, she sailed in convoy on 3 May with 5,270 troops destined to take part in the invasion of France for Gourock, Scotland. On her next return trip to the United States she brought 75 officers and 1,950 enlisted German prisoners of war, guarded en route by an Army prisoner escort detachment. The vessel made her final Atlantic crossing for 1944, leaving New York on 24 July with 5,178 troops. On this voyage she achieved the distinction of being the largest naval vessel ever to sail up the narrow channel of Lough Foyle to Lisahally, North Ireland. She returned to Norfolk on 20 August with a contingent of Marines.

*General William Mitchell* then headed for the calmer waters of the Pacific. With 5,188 troops, she left Norfolk 29 August; passed through the Panama Canal; stopped briefly to fuel at Melbourne, Australia; and arrived at Bombay, India, on 8 October. From Bombay, several hundred New Zealand, Australian, and Dutch troops were ferried to Melbourne. She then took on board 1,500 homeward bound U. S. Army troops. Transport *General George M. Randall*, a sister ship, accompanied her both ways between Melbourne and Bombay. The final lap of the voyage took her to Pavuvu, in the Russell Islands, where 3,500 members of the Marine Corps First Division, veterans of Guadalcanal and Peleliu, were em-

barked. This voyage was completed 17 November, at San Diego, California.

After overhaul, the vessel was again under way bound for India on 20 December, under command of Captain John Rountree. Refueling en route was accomplished at Hobart, Tasmania. Both Christmas and New Year's were spent at sea. Joined again by *General George M. Randall* on the Indian Ocean lap and by *SS Empress of Scotland* which was bound for Aden, the transport reached Bombay on 23 January 1945. The return voyage brought back a varied assortment of passengers from India—United States, British, and New Zealand Army and Navy personnel; Chinese Air Force trainees; merchant marine men; New Zealand and Australian Air Force personnel; Red Cross entertainers; and 2,000 rabidly pro-Fascist Italian prisoners of war. The prisoners were debarked at Melbourne, and the New Zealand forces were left at Auckland. On the return trip to San Pedro, California, her passenger list included 195 dependents of American servicemen. These were mostly New Zealand women, but included 60 babies and small children. One baby was born at sea.

A third Pacific voyage began at San Francisco on 19 March 1945. Carrying 3,864 Navy Sea Bees and casuals bound for Tacloban, Leyte, and Guiuan, Samar, in the Philippines, this transport stopped en route at Espiritu Santo, New Hebrides, as well as Guadalcanal, and Manus Island. She arrived in San Pedro Bay, Philippines, on 17 April. The return trip ending in San Francisco on 16 May, after refueling at Eniwetok, brought 2,510 rotatees and patients back to the United States.

Exactly two weeks after V-E Day, *General William Mitchell* set out for Atlantic waters, arriving at Norfolk, Virginia, on 3 June. Ten days of alterations and repairs prepared the vessel for navigating around two-thirds of the globe in the ensuing operation of transporting troops from the European to the Asiatic Theatre. Without passengers, she again ploughed eastward through the Atlantic and arrived at Leghorn, Italy, on 24 June. Here, 5,148 troops were embarked for Luzon in the Philippine Islands by way of the Panama Canal. After brief stops at Naples, Eniwetok, and Ulithi, the ship finally arrived at San Fernando, Luzon, on 11 August. Here, after unloading, troops were brought on board. Others were picked up at Manila and Tacloban, including 1,126 casualties. Loaded with battle weary veterans, including many "high pointers" of the famed American and First Cavalry Divisions, the transport reached San Francisco on 6 September.

Two weeks later she was again under way carrying 4,925 Naval personnel to Guiuan, which was reached 5 October in a non-stop run. *Mitchell* now began her Magic Carpet duty. She proceeded to Hollandia, New Guinea, where she embarked 5,200 veterans of Southwest Pacific campaigns and took them back to Seattle, arriving there on 29 October.

As of 1 November, this transport had thus completed 10 voyages—five in the Atlantic, four in the Pacific, and one covering both. During her 20 months of active duty she had traversed more than 165,000 miles of ocean and had transported 80,858 passengers. She made three more Magic Carpet round trips after which her Coast Guard crew were removed and the ship was decommissioned.

*General William Wiegel* (AP-119) was another of the large AP-type transports. She was initially under command of Captain Thomas V. Awolt. In many ways her service was similar to that just recounted. She was active in carrying troops to the European Theatre in early 1945, and in returning with other personnel, many of whom had been wounded in the Battle of the Bulge. Fresh troops were taken eastward to augment the victorious armies already punching across the Rhine. During these voyages the only enemy activity encountered was in the form of several apparent submarine contacts.

On her first voyage to the Pacific, after passing through the Panama Canal, one of her Army passengers, Miguel Rodriques, became critically ill with a brain tumor. Mindful of the Coast Guard's preparedness to succor sick persons at sea, arrangements were made to have him taken off by a Coast Guard plane and flown to the nearest hospital in the United States. This meant reversing course to a rendezvous with the plane at Soccorro Island, a tiny speck of land off the Mexican coast. The mission was successfully accomplished.

She was also involved in transporting troops from the European to the Pacific combat areas, and made several Magic Carpet trips before being

decommissioned at New York in May of 1946.

The Coast Guard also manned nine auxiliary attack transports. The primary mission of this group of ships was to carry troops to points off the beaches where amphibious assaults were being conducted. The troops were then taken in to the beaches by small landing craft. The story of these ships, which went into the thick of the fighting, will be told in Part IV, The Coast Guard in Combat. The attack transports were:

| Name | Class and Number | Date Commissioned | |
|------|------------------|-------------------|---|
| *Leonard Wood* | APA-12 | 10 June | 1941 |
| *Joseph T. Dickman* | APA-13 | 10 June | 1941 |
| *Hunter Liggett* | APA-14 | 6 June | 1941 |
| *Arthur Middleton* | APA-25 | 8 September | 1942 |
| *Samuel Chase* | APA-26 | 12 June | 1942 |
| *Bayfield* | APA-33 | 20 November | 1943 |
| *Callaway* | APA-35 | 11 September | 1943 |
| *Cambria* | APA-36 | 10 November | 1943 |
| *Cavalier* | APA-37 | 15 January | 1944 |

The manning program for these attack transports, all of which were converted vessels, began even before war was declared. *Leonard Wood*, *Joseph T. Dickman*, and *Hunter Liggett*, for instance, were taken over by the Navy from the Army Transport Service early in 1941. In June of that year they were placed in commission with Coast Guard crews in command of Commander Harold G. Bradbury, Lieutenant Commander Charles W. Harwood, and Commander Louis W. Perkins, respectively. Coast Guard crews manned these vessels until March 1946, when the ships were decommissioned.

The histories of the attack transports read like an account of naval amphibious operations in World War II. Vessels of this group took part in the North African landings, as well as those at Sicily, Italy, Southern France, Normandy, the Aleutians, the Philippines, and the many Pacific islands. Most eventually did Magic Carpet duty after the end of hostilities. They were the object of attack by submarines, airplanes, surface vessels and shore batteries. Not one was lost, but *Cavalier* was torpedoed. After repairs she was put back into Magic Carpet service. *Callaway* was hit by a suicide plane in the China Sea, but was able to continue under her own power.

The Coast Guard manned 15 AK-class cargo vessels—14 of them Liberty ships, all of which were 441 feet in length. These were commissioned between 28 March 1943 and 5 September 1945.

They participated in the various landings in the European and Pacific Theatres. Included among them was *USS Menkar,* assigned to Loran service duty and mentioned in the preceding chapter on the Story of Loran. *USS Etamin,* under command of Lieutenant Commander George Stedman, was attacked by Japanese planes and struck by an aerial torpedo while anchored in Aitape Roads, New Guinea, on 27 April 1944. After the resulting fire was brought under control, the vessel was towed to Finschafen, and later reconditioned for further service. *USS Serpens,* which was carrying ammunition, exploded off Guadalcanal on 29 January 1945, killing 196, leaving only two survivors who were on board at the time. Lieutenant Commander Perry L. Stinson who was the commanding officer at the time, one other officer, and six crewmen luckily were ashore when it happened, and thus escaped.

There were five "attack" cargo-class vessels (AKA) which carried specially trained Coast Guard crews, including landing boat crews for each. The ships carried tank lighters and troop craft. All of these vessels took part in landings— European, Pacific, or both. Most had lively times on occasion. As an example, one experience may be recounted involving *USS Theenim,* commanded by Captain Gordon A. Littlefield.

During the attack on Okinawa some of our forces were ordered to make two successive diversionary feints at landings to confuse the enemy as to the main body of the assault. Japanese broadcasts picked up at this time surprised *Theenim's* personnel by announcing that their ship had been sunk, and that the remains of our battered fleet were "sneaking back to Pearl Harbor." The first chance *Theenim's* crew had to fire at the enemy came later in the still early hours of 1 April 1945, when a Japanese "Val" broke suddenly from the clouds directly overhead and, though fired upon, apparently escaped. On the third day, after two night retirements, *Theenim* hit the Hagushi beaches, and from then until the 15th it was "work and fight." Air raids became a nuisance. "Flash Red" would bring all hands to their battle stations, and unloading was delayed. Guns were at least partially manned 24 hours a day, and the 42 raids in 16 days were never at convenient hours! On the evening of the 15th, one evidently suicide-bound "Oscar" from a group of three incoming

targets was claimed by *Theenim's* crew as a splash. By the 17th, with all cargo finally ashore, *Theenim* was back in convoy and bound for Saipan which she reached on 20 April.

At the same time another of these vessels, *USS Cepheus* (Commander R. C. Sarratt), was also landing cargo at Okinawa. Altogether, this vessel fired upon seven enemy planes, and her fire was believed to have contributed to the destruction of three of them. *Cepheus* boat crews assisted in unloading other vessels, all without casualty.

The Navy allocated to the Coast Guard 18 auxiliary gasoline-oil tankers (AOG). Personnel for these vessels received special training at the Navy Submarine Chaser Training Center, Miami, and at the Coast Guard Yard. The tankers were commissioned between 18 May 1944 and 11 January 1946—mostly during 1944. Their chief mission was to fuel naval vessels engaged in combat operations. One of these tankers, *USS Calamus* (Lieutenant William Hord), was present at the invasion of Okinawa, and downed at least one Japanese plane. Another, *USS Sheepscot* (Lieutenant George A. Wagner, USCGR), was lost by grounding and capsizing in a hurricane off Iwo Jima on 6 June 1945. All were immensely valuable in their support of naval operations at great distances from regular bases.

As a result of conferences with the office of the Vice Chief of Naval Operations, the Coast Guard was directed on 14 January 1943, to man and staff a certain number of vessels of the Landing Craft Infantry (Large) type. On that date a "bob-tail" flotilla of these LCI(L)s was assigned to the Coast Guard. This originally involved manning 24 vessels, together with a Flotilla Staff and two Group Staffs, requiring an original assignment of 84 officers and 661 men. Later, on 10 January 1945, four more of these vessels were manned. The LCI(L)s were first established by the Navy as Flotilla 4, Groups 10 and 11 under the 11th PHIB (Amphibian Command) and were assigned to Commander in Chief, Atlantic Fleet, on 8 February 1943. This Flotilla, under command of Captain Miles Imlay, distinguished itself in various Mediterranean Theatre operations and in the Normandy invasion, mentioned in more detail in a later chapter. Four of the ships were lost during the Normandy invasion on 5 and 6 June 1944. The remaining vessels later returned to the United

States for yard availability, fleet reassignment, and remanning, and were assigned to the Pacific as Flotilla 35, Groups 103 and 104.

These LCI(L)s had varied service in widely separated parts of the globe. The service performed by most was about the same. The experience of *LCI(L)-86* was typical. Commissioned on 29 January 1943, she participated in the Sicilian occupation of 9 July and in the Salerno landings of 9 September 1943. She later went to Falmouth, England, and subsequently took part in the invasion of Normandy.

This vessel departed from the United Kingdom on 5 October 1944, for Charleston, South Carolina, where she remained for overhaul and repair until 4 December. Her crew then underwent amphibious training at Solomons Islands, Maryland, from 10 to 13 December. Loading at Norfolk during the week that followed, she departed on 23 December for Pearl Harbor, and proceeded from there to Okinawa on 20 April 1945, stopping at Eniwetok, Guam, and Ulithi en route. She anchored at Hagushi Anchorage and Nakagusuku Wan, Okinawa, and made smoke to provide coverage for *USS New Orleans* and *USS West Virginia*, as well as smoke coverage and antiaircraft fire for merchant ships off White and Brown beaches.

She opened fire on Japanese suicide planes on 3 June and again on the 11th. At Kerama Rhetto anchorage, which she reached on 14 June, she acted as a smoker to cover ships present, and then made two round trips to Hagushi. During June she made smoke 54 different times and went to general quarters 52 times on air alerts. On two occasions she directed 20 mm. fire at Japanese soldiers on the beach with undetermined results. During July she continued to make smoke and perform other duties at Kerama Rhetto, in Buckner Bay, and at Chimu Wan, Okinawa; there were 25 calls to general quarters on red alerts, and she made smoke 27 times to cover ships in the anchorages. In the first 12 days of August she made smoke at Chimu Wan and carried mail from Buckner Bay. The rest of the month she made smoke in Buckner Bay and carried liberty parties for the Fifth Fleet.

Departing Buckner Bay on 8 September as part of Task Group 52.6 (designated the Wakayama Sweep Group), she proceeded to Wakayama, Japan, to destroy mines cut by sweepers in Kii Suido, and to lay Dan buoys. Going on to Sasebo, Japan, on 19 October, she destroyed mines in "Operation Skagway" in Nansei Shote until 8 November, after which she sailed for Guam, arriving on 2 December 1945. She returned to the United States finally reaching Galveston, Texas, on 19 February 1946. She was decommissioned about six weeks later.

The largest group of Navy ships of a particular type manned by Coast Guardsmen were the LSTs —Landing Ships, Tank. These numbered 76, as against 75 patrol frigates. In January 1943, the Coast Guard agreed to man a "bob-tail" formation of 25 LSTs (later increased to 37), as well as a flotilla of 36 of these ships. The "bob-tail" vessels were not assigned to one particular flotilla but were dispersed among various Navy Command Flotillas; consequently, they reported for duty in many different theatres of operation. LST Flotilla 29, consisting of the 36 vessels, was manned by the Coast Guard in March 1944, complete with all staff personnel. In June 1945, three more LSTs were manned by the Coast Guard, bringing the total to 76.

In accordance with Navy policy, all personnel for Flotilla 29 were processed during a 10-week course with the Amphibious Training Squadron at Camp Bradford, Virginia. Captain C. H. Peterson was assigned as Flotilla Commander. As teams completed training they were sent to Pittsburgh, Pennsylvania, where the LSTs for this Flotilla were being built at the plants of the Dravo Corporation and American Bridge Company. The ships were then ferried down the Ohio and Mississippi Rivers to New Orleans where, after a five-day outfitting period, they were placed in commission. The commissioned ships then reported to the Amphibious Training Base, Panama City, Florida, for shakedown.

The LSTs were twin-screw diesel vessels 328 feet long and with a beam of 50 feet; they were capable of carrying a deadweight load of 2,100 tons. These vessels needed sufficient draft for seaworthiness at sea, yet a shoal draft for landing on beaches. This was achieved by using diving tanks as in a submarine. Seagoing draft was 8 feet at the bow and 14 feet 4 inches aft. After blowing ballast the landing draft was 3 feet 1 inch forward, and 9 feet 6 inches at the stern. The LSTs had bow doors and ramps to allow the exit of tanks, other vehicles, or the unloading of cargo directly upon the beaches or into shallow water. They were able to transport on their decks a fully equipped LCT (Landing Craft, Tank) which was the next smaller of the tank-carrying landing vessels.

The Landing Ships, Tank, participated in virtually every amphibious operation of consequence. They were on the beaches of the Mediterranean, Normandy, the many Pacific islands which were invaded and captured, the Philippines, as well as Iwo Jima and Okinawa. Three of the Coast Guard manned LSTs were lost during the war. *LST-167* was damaged by enemy planes at Vella Lavella on 25 September 1943. *LST-203*, stranded on Nanomea Island in the Southwest Pacific on 1 October 1943. The third, *LST-69*, exploded and burned at Pearl Harbor on 21 May 1944. In addition, *LST-767* was so badly damaged by a hurricane at Okinawa on 9 March 1946 that she had to be decommissioned.

The LSTs were, for the most part, engaged in duty of the same type. Some were active in the Atlantic, others in the Pacific, and some sailed both oceans. The experience of *LST-22* was almost entirely in the Pacific. One of the earlier vessels of this class, she was commissioned 16 June 1943 with Lieutenant L. N. Ditlefsen in command. Succeeding commanding officers were Lieutenant Willie A. Moore; Lieutenant Howard N. Rogers, USCGR; Lieutenant S. F. Rogers; and Lieutenant F. G. Markle.

This vessel joined a convoy to Guantanamo Bay, Cuba, and the Panama Canal toward the end of July 1943 on the first leg of a cruise to the Southwest Pacific. Stopping at Bora Bora, Tutula, Viti Levu, and Noumea, *LST-22* reached Brisbane, Australia, late in September. She then made voyages from Townsville, Australia to Milne Bay, Oro Bay, Lae, Buna, and back to Milne Bay. Early December saw her in Port Moresby, New Guinea, and then she went to Lae with Task Unit 76.3.6 with RAAF equipment and personnel. At Goodenough Island she loaded a Marine cargo consisting of combat vehicles and gear of the First Marine Division. Then in company with a task unit of five other Coast Guard LSTs and two Navy LSTs, she departed on 13 December for Cape Cretin. She returned to Buna and Oro Bay two days later to pick up another load to be delivered at Cape Cretin on 19 December.

On Christmas day, *LST-22* completed loading Marine Corps personnel and joined Task Force 76.2.2 which consisted of two Coast Guard and five Navy LSTs, three destroyers, and *HMAS Reserve*. This Task Force was bound for Cape Gloucester, New Britain. After beaching at Cape Gloucester the following day, the ship underwent her first air raid. Returning to Goodenough Island for another combat load, she went to Saidor, New Guinea, beaching there on 2 January 1944.

The next two months were occupied in resupply echelons. A second trip to Saidor on 8 January was followed by another to Cape Gloucester six days later, and again on 1 February. On the 4th, while on another trip to Saidor, she underwent four "red alerts" during loading operations. Later, she took an LCM in tow from Buna Roads to Cape Cretin. Arriving at Hyane Harbor, Los Negros, on 2 March, she made a support landing during the initial phase of the landings there. While on this assignment, *LST-22* came under enemy mortar fire, and on orders of the Task Force commander, opened fire with the 3"-50 caliber gun on the mortar fire area. During the afternoon she underwent an enemy attack. Although there were no casualties from enemy action, three men were injured by an exploding 20 mm. shell which hit the guard rail. At Cape Sudest, on 4 March, she commenced loading cargo, and then made a resupply run to Seeadler Harbor, returning immediately to Cape Sudest. Three trips to Buna Roads, Cape Cretin, Lae, and Seeadler Harbor consumed the rest of March.

After 14 days at Buna Roads for anchor upkeep and training, *LST-22* loaded cargo at Goodenough Island and carried it to Cape Cretin. Next, she formed Task Group 77.4 for Tanahmerah Bay, Dutch New Guinea, and arrived there 23 April, where the group participated in the initial operation and underwent several "red alerts."

This busy vessel spent the first half of May in runs carrying cargo from Seeadler Harbor to Aitape and Hollandia. On 18 May, this LST was under way for Wakde Island, Dutch New Guinea, with an LCT in tow, beaching there under enemy fire on the 19th. Cargo was discharged under sporadic fire from enemy emplacements on the beach, and one man was wounded. A second trip to Wakde came four days later, and then she took cargo to Biak. Leaving there, she took *SC-699* in tow for Hollandia. After three similar trips in June, she was beached again at Wakde on 6 July. On the 9th she proceeded to Noemfoor, four days after the surprise landing there, and, after unloading, returned to Humboldt Bay. Trips to Maffin Bay, Sansapor, and Alexishafen, New Guinea, consumed the rest of July and August 1944.

Following drydocking and overhaul at Alexishafen, preparations were made for the Morotai operation. With an echelon of LSTs, LCIs, and LCTs in tow, she departed Hollandia on 11 September with cargo and personnel which were discharged at Morotai on 16 September. Just before beaching at Morotai, an enemy plane was fired upon by *LST-22* and was thought to have been damaged. Returning to Hollandia, she moved again to Alexishafen for overhaul and installation of more anti-aircraft guns, returning to Hollandia on 7 October.

The Love-6 echelon, with destination Leyte, Philippine Islands, was formed and departed Hollandia on 23 October. Unloading was carried out 30 October, following a typhoon which the ship rode out at anchor. Returning to Hollandia on 5 November, a trip to Milne Bay followed, and on 19 December, she departed for Aitape for practice exercises with elements of the 43rd Infantry.

On 28 December 1944, George-1 echelon was formed with Lingayen Gulf, Luzon its ultimate destination. Various elements joined until the entire task group was formed before reaching the Philippines. Several attacking enemy planes were seen en route, but only one came within range; this was destroyed by the fire from several LSTs, with partial credit going to the crew of *LST-22*. One casualty resulted when a strafing bullet from the plane went through the thigh of an Army photographer on board.

Two hours before "H hour", on 9 January 1945, LVTs were launched to carry the first assault wave to San Fabian Beach. The ship discharged the balance of its cargo with the aid of pontoons carried from Milne Bay. On the next day the LST departed for Leyte, which had replaced Hollandia as a focal point for future movements, remaining there until 22 January. On the 27th she began a resupply run to Lingayen Gulf discharging cargo and personnel, departing 8 February

ary for Mindoro Island to take on a load for Leyte Gulf.

The next four weeks were spent in Leyte Gulf. Two shuttle trips to Manila were made in April, and short trips to Guiuan, Samar, came in May before going to Hollandia. *LST-22* then went to Madang, New Guinea, to pick up an Australian Tank Company to be transported to Cape Torokina, Bougainville. She then carried equipment for the Royal New Zealand Air and Ground Forces to Jacquinot Bay in New Britain, and reloaded there with Australian Ground Forces for Wide Bay, in New Britain.

After availability at Manus Island for cleaning and painting bottom, she unloaded at Subic Bay on 10 July, prior to departing for Manila. Here she loaded cargo for Palawan, delivered it in early August, and then sailed for Zamboanga, Mindanao. The war was then over, but there was much work still to be done. Various similar trips were made between then and early November. Picking up cargo for the United States, she arrived at San Diego on 12 December 1945, and was decommissioned four months later.

Operations of *LST-22* were almost entirely in the Pacific. Many other Coast Guard-manned LSTs, such as *LST-327*, served in the European area and took part in the invasions. This vessel was under command of Lieutenant A. Volton, and later Lieutenant Ludwig Wedemeyer. She sailed from New York 14 April 1943, for the Mediterranean, preparatory for the assault on Sicily.

*LST-327* was part of the Western Naval Task Force for securing the beach between Licata and Gela, Sicily, in the early June invasion of Sicily. She anchored off Licata Beach and lowered small boats with the first wave of assault troops. After firing on enemy aircraft, she commenced unloading men and vehicles into LCTs, completing the operation in about eight hours. Returning to Bizerte, she made resupply trips to Licata and Palermo, on each journey carrying men and vehicles for the front lines. On return trips she took back many prisoners and wounded. This duty lasted through August.

On 9 September, she was part of the Salerno invasion fleet. Lying a mile and a half from the beach, she encountered heavy shell fire from enemy shore batteries, and withdrew out of range. Later,

**TRANSPORT** *WAKEFIELD* **BRINGS** 6,000 GIs **HOME FROM EUROPE** . . . . her decks are crowded with joyous soldiers home from European battlefields.

THE PATROL FRIGATE WAS A NEW TYPE OF VESSEL . . . . the Coast Guard manned 75 of these ships.

LARGE TYPE TRANSPORT MANNED BY COAST GUARD . . . . *USS Wakefield*, originally the luxury liner *Manhattan*.

ATTACK CARGO VESSEL *AQUARIUS* . . . . the Coast Guard manned several such vessels which took supplies and equipment right along with the invasion forces.

*ARTHUR MIDDLETON* CARRYING INVASION TROOPS . . . . she was a veteran of the Aleutians and eight other important Pacific invasions.

*LST-21*, ONE OF *76* MANNED BY THE COAST GUARD . . . . at anchor in a British port.

ARMY FREIGHT SHIP *FS-177* . . . . many ships of this type carried Coast Guard crews.

SMALL TYPE TRANSPORT *GENERAL H. L. SCOTT* . . . . she takes on a large contingent of Marines for an important amphibious assault.

LANDING CRAFT LOADS TROOPS FOR ALEUTIAN
ATTACK . . . . Coast Guardsmen landed the invaders and
transported medical supplies between ship and beach.

MEN AND SUPPLIES GO ASHORE AT KISKA . . . .
Japanese were found to have abandoned the island before the
Americans arrived.

LSTs LAND TROOPS AND SUPPLIES AT KISKA . . . . the rugged coast line afforded few
opportunities for satisfactory beaching of larger craft.

COMMANDER JAMES A. HIRSHFIELD ON BRIDGE OF *CAMPBELL* . . . . his cutter destroyed *U-606* in a mid-Atlantic battle.

GEYSER OF WATER RISES ABOVE EXPLODING DEPTH CHARGE . . . . these Coast Guardsmen hope to see a telltale sign of the success of their vigilance.

GERMAN SUBMARINE SAILOR IS RESCUED BY CUTTER . . . . the Nazi wears an artificial lung.

REPAIRING HOLE IN SIDE OF *CAMPBELL* . . . . cut by the hydroplanes of *U-606*.

*USS NORTHWESTERN* BURNS AFTER DUTCH HARBOR ATTACK . . . . this old station ship was destroyed by fire after having been hit by Japanese bombers. Sheds burn nearby.—*(U. S. Navy Photo)*

A BATTLESHIP SOFTENS UP THE JAPANESE ON ATTU . . . . the big guns fire at enemy installations in the Holtz Bay area before the landings.—*(U. S. Navy Photo)*

CUTTER ESCORTS CONVOY THROUGH SUBMARINE INFESTED SEAS . . . . deep-laden vessels
head for port after another successful Atlantic crossing.

COAST GUARD COMBAT CUTTER . . . . patrolling the North Atlantic shipping lanes, runs into the fury of a gale.

TORPEDOED TANKER A MENACE TO NAVIGATION
. . . . stern of tanker which was split in two by a Nazi torpedo is sunk by Coast Guard gunfire.

CUTTER *SPENCER* SEEN FROM SISTER SHIP *DUANE*
. . . . these two vessels participated in a mid-Atlantic action
which destroyed a German U-boat.

*CAMPBELL* AFTER CONVERSION TO A COMMUNICATIONS SHIP . . . . her anti-submarine operations in
the North Atlantic were outstanding.

after an air attack during which the crew fired on enemy planes without casualties or damage, she ran in to the beach, got all personnel and vehicles ashore, and retracted to join her convoy. Many resupply trips followed. On one she was in collision with an unidentified vessel, suffering some damage, and on another she suffered a broken oil pump and a damaged generator.

At the invasion of Anzio, on 22 January 1944, she moved to the unloading anchorage early in the afternoon, but enemy shell fire from the beach became so heavy that she returned to her previous anchorage. The next morning, with low doors and ramps opened, she unloaded into four LCTs, which then went in to the beach. Taking on LCVP crews after moving closer to the beach, she fired on five enemy planes. *LST-327* then departed for Naples, from which she made several resupply runs.

A few months later *LST-327* arrived in the United Kingdom on 11 May. On 2 June, she loaded vehicles and men for the Normandy invasion, departing for Southend where she remained until the 5th, when she got under way for the French coast. On 7 June, at 0002, she anchored in the Nan Rhino area. At 1316 she stood in to the unloading area close to the beach, where she unloaded officers and men for Neptune Beach into *HMS LCT-2004* and six small craft. She returned unscathed to London on 9 June, and two days later made a second trip to France. Soon afterwards she was rammed by *LST-534* causing an eight-foot gash, but beached and unloaded. She then took on board 76 German prisoners of war for transportation to the United Kingdom. She made four other round trips to France with vehicles and men.

While working out of English Channel ports, building supply dumps in Northern France, she struck an enemy mine on 27 August, and put in to Plymouth with extensive damage. There she re-mained for more than six months before sailing for Norfolk, Virginia, where she arrived 19 July 1945.

The next largest group of vessels which were Coast Guard-manned were the Patrol Frigates. There were 75 in all, and while some were, from time to time, engaged in combat operations, they were employed mostly in patrol work, convoy escort duty and Weather Patrol. They proved excellent for such duty. The Coast Guard also manned 30 destroyer escorts which were used chiefly for patrol and escort work. The rest of the Navy ships crewed by Coast Guardsmen were of miscellaneous types and few in number. Outstanding episodes involving such vessels will be mentioned in appropriate chapters.

In its manning program, the Coast Guard proved of tremendous assistance to the Navy. In many instances, these Coast Guard-manned naval vessels became integrated with Navy Task Groups and Forces, and carried out their assigned duties with the utmost efficiency and valor. The freight and supply ships, and the large tugs which the Coast Guard manned for the Army, as well as some of the smaller groups of vessels, performed work which was largely unsung, but great credit should go to them as well as to the rest for satisfactorily carrying out their important assignments.

The positive element in war is combat, and from the preceding chapters the reader has gained knowledge of the varied wartime duties of the Coast Guard in relation to defense, security, safety at home, and safety at sea. Many of these activities were directly involved in episodes which were of a combat nature. Some of these have already been related. Part IV, which follows, is concerned entirely with the Coast Guard in combat, and how that Service, as a fighting part of the United States Navy, contributed greatly to the successful prosecution of the war.

Part IV

The Coast Guard in Combat

# Chapter 13

# THE ALEUTIAN CAMPAIGN

WE ENTER NOW upon the story of the Coast Guard in combat. Operations in which the Coast Guard took part were farflung, and many things were happening simultaneously in widely separated parts of the world. We shall divide this portion of the wartime history of the Coast Guard into operations by "theatre", treating each one chronologically, yet being cognizant of other campaigns conducted at the same time. To assist in this, a tabulation is presented on the next page giving the chronology of events in naval operations so that the reader may tell at a glance, the progress being made in the Atlantic and Pacific areas, and how they tied together in the conduct of the war.

The Battle of the Atlantic was under way before fighting broke out in the Pacific. Although our official participation in World War II began with Pearl Harbor, we had participated unofficially in the Atlantic since September 1939, through the means of the "Neutrality Patrol." Trouble in the Pacific had been anticipated, however, and steps had been taken to improve our position in Alaska. The attack on Dutch Harbor in the Aleutian Islands precipitated hostilities there, and it is those with which we are concerned in this chapter.

When war began in Europe in 1939, the Coast Guard already had the nucleus of an organization operating in Alaska. The peacetime strength of Alaska's military defenses consisted of a small Army garrison of about 300 men at Chilkoot Barracks, near Skagway. The Navy maintained a seaplane station on Japonski Island with 216 men and 12 patrol planes; a radio station at Dutch Harbor; and radio direction finder stations at Cross Sound, Soapstone Point, and Cape Hinchinbrook. It was not until 1941 that military construction work began. Then, simultaneously, both Army and Navy began rapid expansion of necessary war facilities.

The Coast Guard played a vital though unspectacular role in this new program. It had been the earliest government agency operating in Alaska. For three quarters of a century, vessels of the Coast Guard and it predecessor, the Revenue Cutter Service, had served continuously in Alaskan waters, assisting other federal departments and reaching hundreds of Alaskan natives in inaccessible regions and in the unfrequented islands of the Bering Sea. Each year the Bering Sea Patrol had visited these remote villages to bring law and order, succor, and safety to the people. The Coast Guard knew Alaska. It was natural, therefore, that the Army and Navy should rely upon the advice and guidance of the Coast Guard in planning the Territory's defense. Coast Guard officials were among the first to plea for an extension of transportation facilities, which were notably poor; for improvement of harbors and navigational aids; and for general defense needs. Coast Guard surface craft, planes, and personnel played appropriate parts in the military operations preceding and during the Aleutian campaign.

As the war build-up progressed, new duties devolved upon the Coast Guard. After the penetration of the Army and Navy into southern and central Alaska, the Coast Guard cutters devoted a great deal of their time to transporting vital war supplies and military personnel. It was impossible to continue all functions of the Bering Sea Patrol. When in April 1941, the United States transferred ten of the newer Coast Guard cutters to Great Britain, the patrol was further curtailed. By the close of 1941 only one vessel was on full-time duty in the Bering Sea. The patrol ceased after Pearl Harbor.

Anchorage, on the Alaskan railroad to Fairbanks, became the headquarters for the Alaskan Defense Command, under Major General Simon B. Buckner, USA. Garrisons were established at

## CHRONOLOGY OF NAVAL OPERATIONS

| Dates | Atlantic | Pacific |
|---|---|---|
| **1941** | | |
| 7 December | | Attack on Pearl Harbor |
| **1942** | | |
| 14 January | Submarine Campaign Starts off Atlantic Coast of U. S. | |
| 1 February | | First USN attack on Marshall and Gilbert Islands |
| 25 March | | USN raids on Marcus and Wake Islands |
| 18 April | | Tokyo bombed by Doolittle |
| 7 May | | Battle of Coral Sea |
| 3 June | | Dutch Harbor bombed |
| 4 June | | Battle of Midway Island |
| 8 August | | Attack on Solomon Islands |
| 7 November | Invasion of North Africa | |
| **1943** | | |
| 3 March | | Battle of Bismarck Sea |
| 11 May | | Attack on Japanese at Attu |
| 9 July | Allies Land in Sicily | |
| 15 August | | Vella Lavella falls |
| 21 August | | Kiska occupied by U. S. |
| 3 September | Allies Invade Italy | |
| 8 September | Allies Land at Salerno | |
| 31 October | | Landings at Bougainville |
| 20 November | | Gilbert Islands invaded |
| 23 November | | Tarawa, Makin taken |
| **1944** | | |
| 1 February | | Marshall Islands invaded |
| 6 June | Invasion of Normandy | |
| 15 June | | Marianas invaded (Saipan) |
| 15 August | Invasion of Southern France | |
| 15 September | | Palaus and Morotai invaded |
| 19 October | | Philippines invaded |
| 24 October | | Battle of Leyte Gulf |
| **1945** | | |
| 16 February | | U. S. Fleet Units attack Tokyo |
| 19 February | | Iwo Jima invaded |
| 26 March | | Ryukyu Islands invaded |
| 1 April | | Okinawa invaded |
| 8 May | "V-E Day"—Germany Surrenders | |
| 24 July | | Japanese Fleet struck at Kure |
| 5 August | | A-Bomb at Hiroshima |
| 9 August | | A-Bomb at Nagasaki |
| 14 August | | "V-J Day"—Japan surrenders |

NOTE: The Battle of the Atlantic began officially for the United States on declaration of war with Germany on 11 December 1941, and continued throughout the war. Despite sinkings right up to May 1945, it was to all intents and purposes won by the end of 1944.

Seward, Kodiak, and Dutch Harbor. In 1942, Canada and the United States, under a mutual defense agreement, constructed a network of bases in the southeastern "panhandle", and others along the southern coast and the Alaskan Peninsula. The Navy extended its chief base at Dutch Harbor, set up air and submarine bases at Kodiak and Sitka, and radio stations throughout Alaska.

Important Army bases were established at Anchorage, Fairbanks, Annette Island, and Yakutat. The Army constructed roads and power plants, laid pipe lines from the Whitehorse oil fields, and built the 1,600 mile Alcan Highway—a stupendous undertaking of immense strategic importance.

After Pearl Harbor, the War Department set up a Northwest Service Command for Alaska to handle all construction and supplies. A new Territorial Guard to replace the old Alaska National Guard was organized. This eventually equipped the 20,000 Eskimos around the fringe of the Bering Sea to defend their homeland. Japanese were rounded up and shipped to detention camps in the United States, and some 500 natives were evacuated from Atka and the Pribilofs.

By our establishment of bases in the Aleutian and Pribilof Islands, within the immediate range of Japanese thrusts across the North Pacific, Alaska was recognized as a key to the security of both the United States and Canada. It served as a vital link across the Bering Strait with our then military ally, Russia, as well as a potential seat of operations for offensive action against many of the Japanese bases. Alaska became the main bulwark of defense of the entire northwest Pacific.

The Coast Guard cooperated with all other agencies of defense. One of its chief contributions was transportation. So great were the demands on the Coast Guard cutters at the beginning of the war that they became, in effect, "glorified passenger vessels" serving as mobile units for the Army and Navy. For all Coast Guard vessels in Alaska, modification of scheduled operations to perform emergency duties for these Services became the normal routine of the day.

With the increase in Alaska wartime traffic, both military and commercial, it became evident that the existing aids to navigation were inadequate. Many new aids for Alaska were approved by the Navy as necessary for the war program and national defense. These were mostly for the region from Sitka Harbor to the westward, encompassing the Gulf of Alaska, the Alaskan Peninsula, and the Aleutian Islands. The prevailing heavy fog and rocky approaches around the Aleutians, where there was almost a complete absence of serviceable aids, rendered the need most pressing. The waters about Kodiak were particularly dangerous. There were few bells or markers west of Dutch Harbor, and no fog signals at all; there was nothing at Attu. Although there was a light at Dutch Harbor, it was not permanently manned; the lighthouse at Unimak Pass was the westernmost attended station.

It was the task of the Coast Guard to remedy the deficiency and to provide adequate safeguards for the main waterway routes from the States, as well as for particular areas extensively used, and to be used, by military patrol craft. Many old aids were discontinued, while new ones were established. Scores of lights, beacons, buoys, and miscellaneous minor aids were established at strategic points. There was a net increase of 30 aids during the war, and in addition, 93 improved fog signals were included in the final total of 1,110.

From the time of the Pearl Harbor attack, a Japanese thrust was expected somewhere in the Alaskan sector, and military preparations were in a race against time. The Aleutians seemed the most probable area. New bases, equipment, communications, planes, ships, and men all had to be put in readiness for the anticipated attack. Work was rushed forward at Dutch Harbor, and naval and air forces were strengthened. A secret airfield was built on the Peninsula at Cold Bay near Kodiak Island, and another on Umnak Island, about 60 miles west of Dutch Harbor. Both were highly camouflaged. Air patrols by Navy PBYs covering Aleutian waters were set up on a full combat basis. Whatever the enemy chose to do, our forces were watchfully waiting.

By May 1942, Captain Ralph C. Parker, USNR, commander of the Alaskan Sector, whose responsibility was to defend Alaska and its coastwise commerce from submarine or other attack, had at his disposal two ancient destroyers, one 240-foot and two 165-foot Coast Guard cutters, several converted fishermen, and ten Catalina planes. This was a pitifully inadequate force, but it was soon augmented.

For months during this defense build-up, Alaska and the Aleutians were otherwise quiet. The Coast Guard was less involved militarily in the coming campaign than in any of the others, though it was represented by combat units or groups in each of the amphibious operations, and performed important service in supplying bases and transporting personnel and equipment. Fortunately, no cutters were lost in the Aleutians, though a number of small landing craft were lost on the beaches.

Rear Admiral Robert A. Theobald, USN, Commander North Pacific Force, had his headquarters on shore at Kodiak through most of 1942. At his disposal was a sizable cruiser task force under

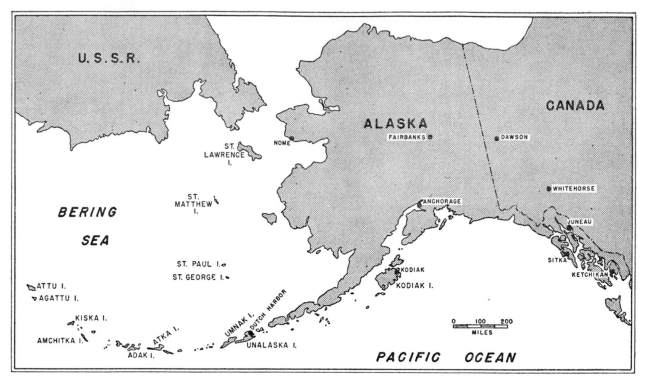

ALASKA AND THE ALEUTIAN ISLANDS

command of Rear Admiral William W. Smith, USN; a destroyer striking group; six S-class submarines; and several Coast Guard cutters, as well as some small craft. Brigadier General William O. Butler, USA, commanded the 11th Army Air Force, which had medium bombers, fighters, a growing group of PBYs, and a few Flying Fortresses. Major General S. B. Buckner, Army commander of the Alaskan Sector, had only a token garrison. This was mostly at Fort Morrow at the base of the Alaskan Peninsula.

Toward the end of May 1942, tension quickened everywhere. The Japanese sent out two task forces, one toward Midway, and the other to the Aleutians. The latter consisted of two light carriers, two heavy cruisers and a destroyer screen. Japanese submarines were reported in the vicinity of Umnak and Unalaska. The headquarters of the U. S. Army Bomber Command and squadrons of medium bombers were moved down the Alaskan Peninsula to Cold Bay and Umnak.

It was learned that the Japanese planned to strike Midway Island, and that a thrust into Alaskan waters would be part of the operation. Accordingly, Admiral Theobald assembled his Task Force 8 to thwart the Japanese Alaskan attempt. He left Kodiak in cruiser *Nashville* on 1 June and rendezvoused with his Main Body of four other cruisers and four destroyers. Efforts to meet the enemy, however, were unavailing, and there was no fleet action in Alaskan waters. Meanwhile, Task Group 8.2—the Surface Search or Scouting Group, under command of Captain Parker at Kodiak—were to be deployed as picket ships in the Pacific and Bering Sea approaches to Dutch Harbor, but were not in position to intercept the Japanese. Only *Onondaga* was at Dutch Harbor. Vessels of this task group were a gunboat, an oiler, 14 YPs, and five Coast Guard cutters—*Haida* (Commander Norman H. Leslie); *Onondaga* (Lieutenant Commander Stewart P. Mehlman), *Cyane* (Lieutenant Commander Leslie B. Tollaksen); *Aurora* (Lieutenant (j.g.) Frank M. McCabe); and *Bonham* (Lieutenant (j.g.) William C. Gill); all USCG.

At this time, the actual military strength of Dutch Harbor was not great. The base, which was still under construction, was garrisoned by a couple of regiments of troops and a few Marines. In the harbor were several vessels, three destroyers, a minesweeper, an Army transport, the old barracks ship *Northwestern,* and cutter *Onondaga.*

Just before dawn on the morning of 3 June, the seaplane tender *USS Gillis* (Lieutenant Commander Norman F. Garton, USN), was near Dutch Harbor and reported possible Japanese planes cruising low over the harbor. Soon afterward, at 0540, Coast Guardsmen on board *Onondaga* sighted the enemy coming out of the grey Aleutian fog, and as the squadron of 17 carrier planes circled the base one of the ground crew identified them as Japanese. Shore and ship batteries immediately opened fire.

On board *Onondaga* general quarters was sounded; battle stations were manned; and all batteries were in action within a few seconds. During the brief period when the Japanese planes were within range, *Onondaga* fired 115 rounds of 3"-23 caliber; 1,400 rounds of .50 caliber; and 500 rounds of .30 caliber ammunition. She suffered no casualties.

Though the attack was of short duration, about 25 American soldiers and sailors were killed; a few barracks and warehouses were set on fire; and a Navy patrol plane was strafed. Only two PBYs were lost. Several enemy aircraft were shot down, and it is believed that several others never regained their carriers. This first enemy assault was probably for reconnaissance purposes, to survey the strength of the base before the main attack was launched.

This enemy attack was followed by an attempt to locate the Japanese surface force by air. A Navy PBY piloted by Lieutenant L. D. Campbell, USN, contacted five enemy vessels about 80 miles off Umnak. On sighting the vessels, this plane was fiercely attacked by a Japanese Zero which so crippled it that a forced landing was required. However, the crew was successfully rescued by Coast Guard cutter *Nemaha.* The Japanese surface force, according to information pieced together from contact reports, apparently consisted of two small carriers, two seaplane tenders, four to six transports, and a full support of cruisers and destroyers. Dutch Harbor may have been their immediate objective.

The invading surface fleet, which had come within 130 miles of Dutch Harbor, withdrew on a southwesterly course, but launched a second attack on Dutch Harbor and nearby Fort Mears that same evening. The attacking force consisted of 18 bombers and 15 fighter planes which approached the harbor from two directions in groups of three planes each. The bombers dropped heavy explosives and incendiaries while the fighters strafed the streets from an elevation of about 500 feet. A warehouse, a few oil tanks, and an empty aircraft hangar were hit. The old *Northwestern* was bombed and destroyed by fire. About 18 more Americans died in this attack. In all, the United States lost six PBYs and five Army planes at Dutch Harbor.

Suddenly, in the midst of the attack, United States Army fighters and medium bombers appeared out of the fog in the rear of the Japanese planes. The latter were taken completely by surprise since they had no knowledge of the two secret Army fields at Cold Bay and Umnak. In stunned confusion the Japanese wheeled to escape, only to find themselves flying directly over one of the secret airfields. The pursuing Warhawks downed at least two Zeros and perhaps two or three dive-bombers before losing the enemy in the fog. At the same time, an unsuccessful air raid was made on the Army post at Fort Glenn on Umnak, about 60 miles west of Dutch Harbor. Many of the attacking Japanese failed to return to their carriers.

That evening, American search planes found the enemy carriers and attacked, doing little damage but losing two planes. However, the Japanese found unexpected resistance and, baffled in their original plans, the task force retired to occupy Kiska, some 700 miles to the westward. Though the first phase of the Aleutian campaign was thus closed, the enemy remained to entrench himself on the islands of Kiska, Agattu, and Attu.

A U. S. Navy report read: "The behavior and size of the expeditionary force gives basis to the belief that the Japanese originally had been assigned to occupy bases on the Alaskan coastal area. But when they found the opposition at Dutch Harbor, and after suffering a tremendous loss of air strength, the expedition is believed to have chosen the landing spot of far-off Kiska as an alternative."

Definite knowledge of the Japanese occupation of undefended Kiska and Attu came only when clearing weather permitted successful reconnaissance, but suspicion arose after 7 June when the usual weather reports failed to come in from the United States weather station on Kiska. On 10 June a PBY scouting plane discovered two ships in Kiska Harbor, as well as numerous boats and small landing craft at Attu where a small Japanese landing party had slipped in under cover of fog; seized the radio station before it could broadcast an alarm; and imprisoned about 90 natives.

When weather permitted, daily bomber raids were directed toward the enemy's newly occupied positions. Eleventh Air Force bombers flew over Kiska on 12 June and bombed two enemy cruisers and one destroyer, setting them afire. Constant preparations were made for the eventual recapture of Attu and Kiska, and naval and military strength in Alaska and the Aleutians was built up in the ensuing months. Reconnaissance planes kept the enemy bases under surveillance, and watched attempts to construct airfields on both islands.

On 14 June, the Japanese returned our calls by bombing a seaplane tender at Atka, and a week later began to reconnoiter Adak, evidently with the intention of establishing an advanced air base there. The Japanese fleet apparently awaited a retaliatory surface attack, which, however, was not then practicable for the U. S. Forces.

On 8 July 1942, a plane of the Royal Canadian Air Force stationed at Annette Island, near Ketchikan, bombed and probably damaged a Japanese submarine. The latter was first seen by a fishing vessel. The Coast Guard cutter *McLane* (Lieutenant Ralph Burns), and Coast Guard-manned Navy *YP-251* (Lieutenant Neils P. Thomsen), searched for it. It was assumed that if the submarine were damaged or a search were suspected, it would seek the nearest spot suitable to lie on the bottom, with engines stilled, and thus evade detection. *McLane's* skipper found a likely 52 fathom spot on his chart ten miles north of where the plane had attacked. *McLane* and *YP-251* worked on a search pattern around this spot with *McLane* on the inside leg operating the only underwater sound equipment.

At 0800 on 9 July, *McLane* made a contact. She dropped a depth charge which failed to explode, but picked up the contact an hour later and followed it. The contact was intermittent and zigzagged, indicating that the submarine was running only at short intervals; then contact was lost. At 1540, *McLane* made another contact; putting about, she followed it for 13 minutes, then dropped four depth charges. Numerous air bubbles rose in the vicinity.

The two vessels cruised around the spot for an hour and a half. Then, as *McLane* was closing astern of *YP-251*, Lieutenant Burns, standing at the bow, saw a torpedo coming which passed under the bow. He ordered full speed ahead in the direction from which the torpedo had come, and *YP-251* dropped one depth charge where the periscope had been seen. At 1805, *McLane* dropped two more depth charges on a contact, and a large oil slick came on the surface. At 1935, *YP-251* reported sighting a periscope and dropped one charge. She turned hard right and apparently bumped over the submarine. *McLane* made a new contact and dropped two more depth charges.

There were no further contacts, only oil and bubbles on the water. *McLane* remained in the area until 0137 on the 10th, and observed these signs as well as flotsam resembling rock wool. Japanese records later revealed that the submarine *RO-32* was sunk in this encounter. Lieutenants Burns and Thomsen were awarded the Legion of Merit.

During the summer there was some activity in the Aleutians. Early in August, we made one unsuccessful attempt by surface ship batteries to bombard Kiska Harbor broadside from ten miles distant, only to miss the fortified area and blast a gaping hole in the uninhabited tundra five miles away. Our submarines were more successful. Early in June one transport had been destroyed in an Aleutian Harbor. On 4 July submarines sank three or four enemy destroyers. On 31 August, five survivors of a torpedoed Japanese submarine were taken prisoner, the first prisoners in the Aleutian campaign.

In August, the Japanese high command decided to abandon Attu and concentrate on Kiska as being the more strategic. Transfer was made by transports and destroyers between 27 August and 16 September. The Americans were unaware of this move. The only contact was made by Japanese submarine *RO-61*, which entered Nazan Bay, Atka, and torpedoed the seaplane tender *Casco*, killing five and wounding 20. The tender beached herself safely and later made drydock in Kodiak. On the following day a Catalina depth bombed the sub and opened seams in her hull, starting a trail of oil which destroyer *Reid* followed until she made sound contact. Two depth charge attacks forced *RO-61* to the surface, and she was destroyed by *Reid's* gunners.

It soon became evident that bases farther westward would be needed for effective operations against the enemy-held positions. In August a task force occupied Adak, about 200 miles east of Kiska, without opposition. On 14 September our first air attack from Adak strafed three midget submarines and a flying boat, sank a couple of minesweepers, and scored several hits on enemy cargo ships at Kiska. Atka, 60 miles east of Adak, was occupied on 20 September, and an airfield was built there.

On 4 January 1943, Admiral Theobald was relieved by Rear Admiral Thomas C. Kinkaid, USN, and Admiral Smith was relieved by Rear Admiral Charles H. McMorris, USN. On 12 January, American forces made an unopposed landing with 2,100 troops on flat, muddy, and uninhabited Amchitka Island where a new fighter strip was to be built only 250 miles east of Attu, and 69 miles southeast of Kiska. The task group which effected the landings on 12 January consisted of four transports escorted by destroyers, while three cruisers and four destroyers provided close support.

A series of heavy air attacks had been made by the Army Air Force in preparation for the Amchitka landing. Two Japanese ships, *Montreal Maru* and *Kotohiro Maru*, both carrying troops and weapons, were sunk on 5 January at Kiska and Attu respectively. The Japanese had decided to reoccupy the latter.

One of the transports engaged in the Amchitka landing was *USS Arthur Middleton* (APA-25), commanded by Captain Paul K. Perry, USCG. The Army personnel carried comprised 102 officers and 2,060 enlisted troops. Reaching Constantine Harbor, Amchitka, on the morning of the 12th, she slipped quietly through the small inlet into the harbor. The order "Lower away all boats" was given, and landing operations were begun. Higgins boats, 36-foot landing craft, and 50-foot tank lighters were loaded with personnel and equipment, and the first "wave" moved in on the shallow rocky beach.

All went well until later that day when a fierce "williwaw" whipped down on the harbor. The buffeting gale threatened all the landing craft. Barges were capsized and sunk or broached on the beach. The number of barges became so depleted that it became necessary to continue the unloading by hand. To save the boats, men donned rubber suits and waded out to their armpits in the freezing water. They unloaded barges and passed supplies back, hand over hand, to keep them dry. The wind increased to gale force before nightfall. Despite every effort, most of the landing barges were wrecked.

During the first day of the landing, destroyer *Worden* (Lieutenant Commander William G. Pogue, USN), became a victim of the gale and treacherous currents, and was swept onto a pinnacle rock near the harbor entrance. She became a total loss. In abandoning ship, 14 sailors were drowned. A Coast Guard landing boat from *Arthur Middleton* in command of Lieutenant Commander R. R. Smith, rushed to the scene, and Coast Guardsmen pulled other boats near the doomed destroyer. Whaleboats from destroyer *Dewey* also arrived to assist. As mountainous seas threatened to swamp the Coast Guard boats, lines were passed to *Worden* to enable the men to slide down into the rescue craft. Returning to *Middleton*, the boats picked up two survivors who were struggling against death in the freezing water. In all, 6 officers and 169 men were rescued from the stricken vessel. While all involved in this rescue performed heroic duty, especially creditable work was done by Ensign J. R. Wollenberg, Coxswains Russell M. Speck, Robert H. Gross, and George W. Prichard, and Signalman John S. Vandeleur. These five Coast Guardsmen later received the Navy and Marine Corps Medal for their outstanding performance of duty.

At 2307 that same day, *Arthur Middleton* herself got into trouble. She was driven aground on her port quarter by the gale. However, her boats continued unloading operations. She remained stranded until 6 April, despite all salvage efforts. Throughout this period of stranding, the attack transport withstood time and again, Japanese air attacks from float-type Zeros based on Kiska. Helplessly aground, unable to maneuver, she presented an immobile target to the enemy, but repelled all assaults without suffering a single hit or scoring any hits on the attacking planes. After 84 days aground, she was finally freed and escorted to Dutch Harbor where she was under repair until 17 June; she then proceeded to Bremerton, Washington, for further drydocking and repair.

With the Americans now at Amchitka, a new base from which Attu and Kiska could be bombed made Japanese positions vulnerable. The Japanese now had two choices—evacuate the Aleutians or strengthen their garrisons, finish airfields, and attack the United States supply line. But sufficient vessels were unavailable to them because of requirements at Guadalcanal and elsewhere, yet they dared not leave and open the Kuriles to attack. So in February the Japanese decided to "hold the western Aleutians at all costs and to carry out preparations for war."

American bomber and fighter raids on Kiska and Attu continued for months. These, and the poor terrain, thwarted enemy attempts to build airfields, and thus reduced enemy raids on our own bases. The enemy airfields never were completed. Kiska suffered most. It was not unusual for Kiska to receive 500 to 600 tons of bombs in a single month.

Our blockade of the Aleutians was now beginning to prove effective. Task Group 16.6, composed of six naval vessels under Rear Admiral Charles H. McMorris allowed very few, if any, enemy ships to get through to the Japanese held Aleutian bases after March. During the spring of 1943, the Japanese took little offensive action, concentrating instead on completing defense installations and airdromes.

With the U.S. occupation of Amchitka, the battle for the Aleutians really began, and our military planners now decided on the next step. The Japanese expected an offensive against Kiska. Though the nearer of the two, Kiska was to be by-passed in favor of Attu in a strategy that was as ingenious as it was simple. With Attu occupied, a pincers operation would be possible from either side of Kiska. Eventual complete success proved the wisdom of the plan.

It had been proved that such military positions could be taken only by invasion. Therefore, an invasion of Attu was staged for the end of April. All through that month naval forces were being outfitted, trained, and assembled for the attack. The 7th Infantry Division was given lengthy and intensive training at Fort Ord, near Monterey, California, and sailed from San Francisco on 24 April. From the 15th to the 30th, ships arrived at Cold Bay, the assembly point, from Pearl Harbor, Dutch Harbor, Adak, and the far away Pacific Coast. The main landing force comprised units of several outfits—the 7th Infantry Division, the

17th and 32nd Infantry Regiments, two battalions of field artillery, the 15th Engineers, and medical units and service troops.

Rear Admiral Kinkaid, Commander North Pacific Area, was in supreme command of all naval operations. For a week before the scheduled date of attack, a battleship group and two cruiser groups were on patrol to the north and northwest of Attu.

Foul weather delayed the start until 4 May. The assault force of 29 ships under the direct command of Rear Admiral Francis W. Rockwell, USN, arrived off Attu by way of the Bering Sea on 7 May, the proposed day of attack, but bad weather delayed their moving in until the 11th.

Meanwhile, the Japanese radio on Kiska had warned Attu of the expected invasion. An alert was maintained on Attu from the 3rd to the 9th after which the Japanese apparently became careless and returned to normal routine. When the attack finally came at 0200 on the 11th, the enemy appeared to be taken completely by surprise.

In anticipation of the Attu action, Admiral McMorris cruised with his task group of two cruisers and four destroyers on a north-south line west of Attu for several days before the attack in order to intercept any Japanese attempt to reinforce the garrison there. On the morning of 26 March the group was steaming 180 miles west of Attu and 100 miles south of the nearest Komandorski Island, when the flagship and a destroyer simultaneously made radar contact on five vessels several miles to the north. Additional vessels were picked up, and preparations for a morning battle were made in all ships. Soon the enemy vessels came into sight. The task group had run into Admiral Hosogaya's fleet of four cruisers, five destroyers, two fast merchant cruisers acting as transports, and a freighter. Hosogaya's intention was to strongly reinforce Attu. He turned his vessels southeastward, except for the transports, the freighter, and a destroyer, to engage the Americans. The Japanese fleet had twice the size and fire power of Admiral McMorris' group.

Action began when the enemy opened fire at 20,000 yards range. For three and a half hours the opposing fleets slugged it out with ranges of eight to twelve miles and without assistance from planes or submarines. It was like an old time fleet action. The battle, which was hot while it lasted, was broken off by Hosogaya who turned from the scene and took a westerly course. There the Battle of the Komandorski Islands ended. Admiral Mc-Morris had fought a brilliant retiring action against heavy odds and all of his ships got "home" under their own power. Vessels of both fleets were battered. *USS Salt Lake City* received the greatest punishment in our fleet, but neither side hurt the other greatly. Tokyo, of course, claimed a great victory, but the fight resulted in preventing the reinforcement of Attu, and this was a large factor in the later recovery of that island by the American forces.

The 2,400 Japanese at Attu were left to shift for themselves after the Battle of the Komandorski Islands; no further attempt by the Japanese was made to send supplies and men to the Aleutians.

Attu is a rugged, mountainous island 35 miles long and 15 to 20 miles across, with sharp crags and snow-summited peaks, some as high as 3,000 feet. Its valleys are covered with moss-grown tundras, with muddy marsh beneath. With little detailed knowledge of the interior, it would be hard to imagine a worse place to invade or one more easily defended.

The enemy had developed two main defense areas on Attu. One was Holtz Bay and the Chichagof sector, including Massacre Bay, Sarana Bay, and Attu village. The airfield at the east arm of Holtz Bay was still unfinished, but the beaches along the bay were well defended. The other defense area was, for the most part, on the high ground at the north end of Massacre Bay, extending 3,000 to 4,000 yards inland. There were no beach defenses in that area. Thoroughly·camouflaged positions, caves, and fox holes dotted the entire northeastern part of the island.

The American plan of attack called for four landings: (1) at Red Beach on the west arm of Holtz Bay; (2) at Massacre Bay in the Chichagof sector, and subsidiary landings; (3) at Austin Cove on the undefended coast north of Holtz Bay; and (4) at Alexei Point, east of Massacre Bay. The strategy was to push the Japanese force into the Chichagof area and divide it into two segments.

As a late April preliminary to the landings, Admiral McMorris' cruisers aided by six destroyers had bombarded enemy installations on the east end of Attu in the Holtz Bay-Chichagof areas for 20 minutes.

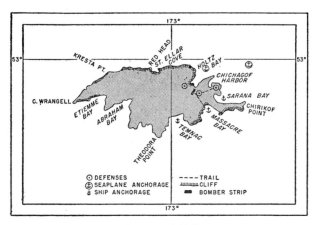

ATTU ISLAND

The main landings began at 1530 on 11 May, and went forward with remarkable precision and expedition, despite the most unfavorable weather conditions. The months of training were well repaid. Strong naval and air assaults on the Holtz Bay and Chichagof areas accompanied the initial movements in that sector. The Coast Guard was represented at Attu only in the landing operations, although a number of Coast Guardsmen were attached to the Navy transports, which included *J. Franklin Bell, Grant, Chirikof,* and *Perida.* After the landings had been effected, boat crews were kept busy carrying the wounded back to the ships.

Within three hours, American forces had advanced inland some 3,000 yards. Later in the day, a beachhead was finally secured at Massacre Bay after a fierce fight in which 10 of our 27 landing barges were sunk. The two main American forces, in the Holtz Bay and the Massacre Bay areas, were then about three miles apart, separated by a ridge in the mountain range. For several days, with little change in the basic positions, the fiercely contested struggle continued in efforts to enlarge the positions and effect a juncture. The Japanese assumed assistance was on the way but, as we have seen, it never arrived thanks to Admiral McMorris and his fleet. The only outside effort came in two abortive and easily repulsed enemy air attacks staged from Kiska 11 days after the fighting began. On the 14th, the weather cleared a little, making possible greater air support for American ground forces. Finally, the two main forces were united on 17-18 May, and the principal fighting was over.

The Japanese withdrew to the ridge around

Chichagof Harbor, and their counter-attack on the 19th was repulsed with heavy losses. Americans, whose casualties had been remarkably light, encircled Holtz Bay, occupied the landing strip, and attacked the pass connecting Holtz Bay with Chichagof Harbor. This was taken, and by the 25th the Massacre Bay force had reached Lake Cories near the village of Attu at Chichagof Harbor. Tokyo admitted that Attu was lost. After a final American drive down the valley, all Japanese organized resistance collapsed. There followed the most spectacular phase of the entire operation.

This was a desperate counter-attack by the Japanese on 29 May. All those remaining alive, even sick and wounded, gathered for a last, hopeless charge on the invading forces. Those physically incapable of fighting had been killed by their own officers. Since their arms and ammunition were running out, the enemy used makeshift weapons, including spears as well as bayonets fastened to long sticks.

Led by Colonel Yamasaka, some 500 Japanese moved down the valley and staged an heroic and fanatical, if foolhardy, attempt to route American forces. Down into the fog they came, with a half insane zeal to kill or be killed to the last man. Taken by surprise, many isolated detachments of American troops were slaughtered before reinforcements could reach them. But the Japanese advanced in the face of overwhelming odds. After charging with the chant "Kill, kill" directly into sweeping gunfire, their charge resembled a macabre dance of death rather than a military advance. After seven hours of fighting, 50 enemy survivors were eventually trapped, where they fought huddled together to the end, some taking their own lives. Only four prisoners were taken.

After mopping up operations, fighting on Attu ceased. Total American losses were 552 killed, 1,140 wounded, and 85 missing, out of a landing force of 11,000. The enemy lost 2,350 killed, with 24 taken prisoner. No Japanese wounded survived.

Attu was speedily made ready as an advance base against Kiska and Japan proper. By early July, the United States had 1,880 Navy personnel and 14,900 Army troops on the island, and on 10 July, nine planes took off from the new Attu base to bomb Paramushiro, the Japanese naval base in the Kuriles.

With Attu in American hands, Kiska was entirely isolated. Shemya Island, 25 miles east of Attu, was soon occupied. During July nearly 4,500 tons of bombs were dropped on Kiska. Vicious air attacks on the last enemy stronghold in the Aleutians continued in August. Between 6 July and 15 August, 15 surface bombardments were directed against the island. One, on 22 July, the enemy accurately interpreted as a preliminary to invasion. After that, each attack was thought to be the beginning of the onslaught.

Rear Admiral Kimura, on orders to evacuate Kiska, arrived in the fogbound harbor on 28 July, and took off the 5,183 Japanese, transporting them to Paramushiro. The Americans never caught on. However, unusual movements on Kiska had been seen by our airmen on and shortly after 22 July. Many submarines had been noticed in the harbor; Kiska radio had gone off the air on 28 July; and great damage to installations was observed, apparently from the bombardments. But the Japanese actually had blown them up! There were several subsequent bombardments of the abandoned island.

As the planned day of invasion approached, a large amphibious fleet rendezvoused at Adak, with Vice Admiral Kinkaid again in command of the fleet. Rear Admiral Rockwell commanded the attacking amphibious force of almost a hundred ships. Major General Charles H. Corlett, USA, was in charge of the ground forces, which totaled 34,426 troops. At daylight on 15 August, the landing was effected under heavy bombardment. The island was found to have been completely abandoned.

The landing was unopposed, of course, but there were casualties. Patrols sometimes mistakenly fired at friends before it was ascertained that there were no Japanese there. Errors of this type caused the death of 25 men, and wounds to 31. Destroyer USS *Abner Read* (Commander Thomas Burrowes, USN) struck a floating Japanese mine and lost her stern, resulting in the loss of 70 men killed or missing, and 47 wounded.

American aerial and sea bombardments and Japanese demolition had wrecked all roads and enemy equipment; tanks, trucks, midget submarines, and sunken surface craft were strewn around the harbor. Practically every object was bullet-ridden.

The bloodless occupation had been a triumph for naval bombardment and an achievement in strategy. The United States had acquired an unbroken string of naval and air bases stretching from Ketchikan to Attu. There were no Japanese left in the Aleutians, and they never returned. The bases were maintained. Though it could not be foretold at the time, the Aleutians ceased to be of military or historical significance for the rest of the war. Nevertheless, the campaign furnished bases which added measurably to the security of Alaska and the west coasts of Canada and the United States, and gave the Americans the initiative in the North Pacific area.

# Chapter 14

# THE BATTLE OF THE ATLANTIC

EARLY EFFORTS of the United States Navy incident to the war in Europe, before Pearl Harbor, were located chiefly in the Atlantic Ocean. The first impact of the war on the Navy was an order from President Roosevelt on 5 September 1939 to organize a Neutrality Patrol to report and track any belligerent air, surface, or underwater naval forces approaching the United States or the West Indies. The fundamental purpose was to emphasize the Navy's readiness to defend the Western Hemisphere. Five days later the patrol was organized. Patrol areas were modified occasionally and forces changed as strength was built up. With the assistance of the Coast Guard, a continuous patrol area about 200 miles off shore, from the Grand Banks to Trinidad, was established in October.

From the beginning of the war in Europe, convoys were used between Canada and England, with the Royal Canadian Navy and the British Admiralty cooperating. At first, merchant skippers preferred to go it alone, and were not interested in convoys. But through war necessity, convoys became the rule. The typical transatlantic convoy of 1939-41 consisted of 45 to 60 merchantmen, in nine to twelve columns, with 1,000 yards between the columns and 600 yards between ships. This early situation was followed by our "short of war" policy, in which a great expansion of shipbuilding occurred. Congress appropriated funds for a two-ocean Navy. In some phases of this "short of war" period of Neutrality Patrol, naval units operated in a way indistinguishable from war.

The local government of Greenland asked for American protection on 3 May 1940, three weeks after the Nazi occupation of Denmark. Rear Admiral Russell R. Waesche, Commandant of the Coast Guard, promptly assigned cutters for special missions to Greenland. That month *USCGC Comanche* landed the honorable James K. Penfield, first United States diplomatic representative to Greenland, at Ivigtut. During 1940 the Coast Guard lent personnel and guns to the Greenland government to guard the cryolite mine, which was so near tidewater that a few air bombs or a U-boat's shells could easily have flooded it. Cutters *Duane* and *Northland*, with Coast Guard planes attached, surveyed the theretofore little-known Greenland coasts, especially the ice-infested east coast where German weathermen were operating, and added a *Greenland Pilot* to the long list of Hydrographic Office publications.

Greenland gave us permission to establish certain facilities. On 31 March 1941, the South Greenland Survey Expedition arrived at Godthaab in the cutter *Cayuga* to locate and survey sites for weather reporting, radar, and radio stations as well as high-frequency direction-finder instruments to detect enemy forces approaching America through Denmark Strait.

These were the days of destroyer-naval base deals with Britain, and the beginning of lend-lease. One part of the American-British Staff Agreement of 27 March 1941, stated: "Owing to the threat to the sea communications of the United Kingdom, the principal task of the United States naval forces in the Atlantic will be the protection of shipping of the Associated Powers . . . in the Northwestern Approaches of the United Kingdom." This meant that, when ready, the United States Navy would take over responsibility for convoy protection. Such protection involved operations tantamount to war measures. The first attack by U. S. naval forces on a German submarine was by the destroyer *Niblack* on 10 April 1941. Thus, the Neutrality Patrol became, to all intents and purposes, escort of convoy.

The numerous casualties to convoys south of Greenland, and the *Bismarck* battle of May 1941, emphasized the strategic importance of Greenland and hastened organization of the Greenland Patrol on 1 June 1941. This activity has been detailed in Chapter 7.

The destroyer *USS Greer*, proceeding independently toward Iceland on 4 September 1941, after tracking a submarine to keep it down, was attacked by that vessel by torpedo, but not hit. This ended the responsibility of the Navy to protect the North Atlantic without authority to shoot. Thereafter, we were in a *de facto* naval war with Nazis on the Atlantic. From this point on, things progressed quite rapidly.

The scarcity of suitable escorts was perhaps the greatest handicap during this period. *CGC Campbell* was employed as escort on Convoy HX-159 in November 1941, and proved so effective that most of her sister ships of the Treasury class were diverted to this duty. These big seagoing cutters had everything that a destroyer had except speed and torpedoes; and seldom does an opportunity to use torpedoes occur in escort-of-convoy. The taking over of the Coast Guard by the Navy on 1 November 1941 made several types of Coast Guard cutters, manned by keen Coast Guardsmen, available for escort duty. The 1,200-ton, 165-foot *Algonquin* class and smaller classes were used on one of the hardest assignments, the Greenland Patrol; larger ones were employed extensively on transatlantic and coastal convoys. Says Admiral Samuel Eliot Morison in his Naval History of World War II; "Their performance was glorious"; their casualties were heavy. The new 2,750-ton, 327-foot "Treasury" class, (named after Secretaries of the Treasury)—capable of 20 knots, and armed with four 5-inch 50-calibre guns, proved able and aggressive escorts. In addition, by 20 June 1942, four 240-foot cutters of the *Haida* class; fourteen large converted steam or diesel yachts; seventeen 165-foot cutters; and thirty-two 125-foot cutters were available for antisubmarine and escort duty. Several Coast Guard cutters, however, had been on Neutrality Patrol since July 1941.

Until the Neutrality Law was amended on 13 November 1941, none of our 1,375 merchant ships had been armed. While armed British merchantmen had fought off the U-boats successfully in 70 attacks since the beginning of the war in Europe in 1939, and had shot down more than 80 planes, our merchant ships were still at the mercy of the foe.

Under this amendment we began to arm our merchant vessels though progress at first was painfully slow.

It was not long after the declaration of war on the United States by Germany and Italy, following immediately on the heels of Pearl Harbor, that a critical situation developed at sea in the Spring of 1942. In the Atlantic, and along the United States Atlantic coast, and later in the Gulf of Mexico, conditions became extremely serious. German submarines operated almost at will, and American tankers were their favorite targets. However, operations were by no means confined to tankers, and vessels of all kinds were sunk in alarming numbers. Survivors by the thousands were brought in to East coast ports. Submarines, singly and in packs, infested the waters. The failure of cargo vessels by the score to reach their destinations with urgently needed oil, supplies, and munitions, further emphasized the crucial need for action. The Navy had a dual responsibility in that it must require every effort to protect allied shipping and cut down the appalling losses and, at the same time, do everything possible to hunt down the underwater marauders. To do this effectively it would be necessary to use hundreds of vessels which the Navy did not have at its disposal. Part of the answer to this was the Coastal Picket Patrol which was instituted off our shores.

A great effort was made to procure for the Coast Guard Reserve a fleet of yachts to be converted to offshore patrol. In the Spring of 1942, such a fleet was procured by purchase, charter, or gift; manned, and set to patrolling offshore areas. The Coast Guard organized these vessels into operational groups which were assigned by Sea Frontier Commanders to restricted patrol stations along the 50-fathom curve off the Atlantic and Gulf coasts. These were the Coastal Pickets. Their duties consisted of "supplementing existing forces employed in antisubmarine, rescue and information duties." While thus engaged, the patrols were instructed to "observe and report the actions and activities of all hostile submarine, surface and air forces" and to "attack and destroy enemy submarines when armament permits." It was chiefly guard duty and the sailing yachts were especially well fitted for this, for they could keep to the sea almost regardless of what Neptune had to offer.

Investigation was important. Coastal Pickets

made scores of contacts by sound device and tracked them down as long as contact could be maintained. Oil slicks were discovered and checked; gunfire was heard and investigated; convoys were notified of the presence of a submarine; and some submarines were located and properly depth-charged. The equipment of these vessels was not known to the submarines. The latter could ill afford to stay in the picket patrol area, and they avoided giving away their positions by shelling, and wasting torpedoes. Finding the pickets quite annoying, they eventually avoided the patrolled areas.

U-boats operated daily in the western half of the Atlantic in January 1942. It was estimated that the daily average was 19. This estimated average increased to 28 in February-April; 35 in May; and 40 in June. The Germans were building 20 or more new 500- or 740-ton submersibles each month. (See Appendix for statistics on vessel sinkings). Airplanes, cooperating with naval forces, helped effectively in meeting the submarine menace, especially in the days of inadequate vessels. When countermeasures along the Atlantic seaboard became reasonably effective, U-boats found better hunting in the Gulf of Mexico and the Caribbean Sea, and raised havoc there. Unescorted merchant shipping received the full fury of this U-boat blitz, and in May 1942, this frontier had the most sinkings (41 ships, 219,867 gross tons) of any area for any month during the war. The Coast Guard then assigned two large, four medium, and several small cutters to the Gulf Sea Frontier as well as several planes. Patrols, planes, and the convoy system with adequate escort, eventually reduced the casualties.

Virtually all vessel movements across the Atlantic were in convoy, and these convoys required protection by adequate escorts. In the earlier days of the war, the escorts were insufficient in numbers to provide the needed protection. Thus, in the first half of 1942, sinkings of vessels in convoy were frequent. It was in convoy escort that the Coast Guard, in the Battle of the Atlantic, lent special assistance to the Navy.

During the first seven months after Pearl Harbor, the duties of the North Russia convoys and escorts were undoubtedly the most disagreeable and dangerous. These convoys were routed by Iceland, around the North Cape, and thence to Murmansk, Molotovsk, or Archangel. Attacks on them usually by airplanes, while under way or in Russian ports loading or unloading, were little short of devastating. Escorting was chiefly by British and United States naval units, and the Coast Guard was not generally involved.

Early operations in the Atlantic were by necessity largely protective, but the United States gradually was able to develop offensive antisubmarine operations with increasing effectiveness. As Admiral Morison says: "The amount of study, energy and expense necessary to combat a few hundred enemy submarines is appalling." Antisubmarine measures included administration, new training devices, schools and analysis-research units, as well as ships, and an air fleet. Refinements of old antisubmarine devices, new devices, and new techniques played a most important part. Depth charges remained highly effective for attack on submerged subs; these were improved, and better techniques in their use developed. Listening devices (sonar) were improved and installed in vessels for picking up sound contacts, and sonar schools were established. Radar enabled the spotting of surfaced submarines at night. High-frequency direction-finders, on shore, and, after October 1942 also in cutters, located surfaced submarines transmitting by radio. The Germans obliged by doing this often.

The Army Air Force responded generously when the Navy called for help. Planes gave very effective air cover to convoys within their limitations, and assisted in spotting and attacking subs. Navy air patrol was important, and blimps were helpful in many coastal areas. The arming of merchant ships was vigorously pursued. Antisubmarine warfare was carried out aggressively by convoy escorts since they were in the U-boat areas and in the best position to make contacts. On contact, the enemy was relentlessly pursued and attacked, and many kills resulted. By the close of 1942 allied air coverage for transatlantic convoys had been extended to an area reaching 400 miles east of Newfoundland, 500 miles south of Iceland and 700 miles west of England. The period of January through March 1943, was probably that of greatest U-boat achievement.

It is probably true that in its influence on the final outcome of the war, the Battle of the Atlantic was second to none. There were many phases. The

Greenland Patrol, treated separately in this History, was almost a subsidiary action of the Battle of the Atlantic. Weather Patrol by Coast Guard vessels was vital to sea and, especially, air operations. Probably the most important phase was the escort of convoys in the tremendous effort to carry men and supplies to the fighting fronts in Europe. Failing that, the land operations would have been futile. Killing submarines was vital if our shipbuilding was to exceed sinkings. After the spring of 1943, the darkest days were over. With more long-range planes, escort carriers, destroyers, destroyer escorts, sloops, and frigates; with better training, doctrine, weapons and devices; the Allies seized the initiative, and in May 1943, 41 U-boats were destroyed. Much trouble still lay ahead, but the Battle of the Atlantic was being won.

However, many dark days preceded this turn of the tide. Out in the Atlantic, submarines and convoy escorts stalked each other unseen during most of the hunt. They tracked each other by sonar, like enemies groping in the dark. Our merchant ships zigzagged to escape when an underwater warning came. Coast Guard and other escort vessels would then swing into action making for the "contact" to give battle. Only when in position to attack would the submarine raise its periscope and fire its deadly missiles. In less than 30 seconds the periscope would be lowered again. Only for these few seconds could the enemies see each other. When periscopes were seen by the escorts, depth charges were dropped on their estimated positions after they had again submerged. The rest of the time our escorts depended entirely upon their echo ranging equipment to estimate the position of the submerged submarine, on which they dropped their depth charges. Day and night the game went on. Not until the enemy finally surrendered could our transports ever count on complete safety.

Vice Admiral Waesche, Commandant of the Coast Guard, summed up the importance of the job of getting supplies to our allies on 15 October 1942: "If America and its allies are to win the devastating war now raging over the surface of the entire globe, the ships that carry food, the guns, the tanks, the planes and other implements of war to our fighting forces on battlefields beyond the seas, must reach their destinations safely. We of the Coast Guard have dedicated everything we have, including our lives, to the proposition that the American Merchant Marine, carrying needed supplies to the far-flung battlefields, shall not be too late with too little. Many of our units have been in contact with enemy submarines and planes and the history of this war will show the extent to which they have engaged the foe. Suffice to say at this time, we are proud of their accomplishments."

By mid-1942 half of our Atlantic merchant ships were being given convoy escort protection on their perilous voyages to and from Europe. Of the United States merchant ship tonnage of 1,000 gross tons or over which was sunk, only 10 percent was being escorted in May 1942. This percentage rose to 50 percent in July 1942, then varied as follows: 20 percent in November 1942; 0 percent in December, 1942; 52 percent in January 1943; 80 percent in February 1943 (the peak); and close to 50 percent through April 1944 except for 5 months which varied from 0 to 28 percent. It was not until December 1942 that total sinkings showed a definite downtrend. The heavy toll of 89 enemy submarines sunk by British and European allied air and surface craft as well as from other causes in the last half of 1942 undoubtedly accounted for much of this decline.

By September 1942, shipbuilding had brought the total tonnage of our merchant vessels to the level of December 1941. From then on, our total merchant tonnage grew at the rate of half a million tons or more a month until May 1943, when the monthly increase climbed to nearly a million tons. Despite continued sinkings, our merchant fleet grew steadily. By April 1944, we had 18,701,370 gross tons, or nearly three times the total tonnage at the time of Pearl Harbor.

In June 1943, the Chief of Naval Operations directed the Coast Guard to assemble and train officers and crews for 30 destroyer escorts to be manned by the Coast Guard. These vessels were 305 feet long, had agile maneuverability, accurate fire power, and especially designed antisubmarine weapons. They carried 10 officers, 13 chief petty officers, and 163 other enlisted crewmen. The German answer to the convoy had been the "wolf pack." During September, October, and November 1943, these 30 destroyer escorts were manned, and together with Navy small carriers and destroyers began to operate as a winning combination against the wolf packs in the Atlantic. These vessels performed most valuable escort service. One, *Leopold* (DE-319), was lost. These Coast Guard forces were supplemented during 1944 with 75 patrol frigates, many of which were used to maintain ocean weather stations while keeping on the lookout for enemy submarines.

Manning the patrol frigates proved the most complex of the various manning projects, because they constituted a large number of units; required the greatest percentage of personnel; necessitated the utilization and promulgation of training facilities; as well as having a wide geographic diversity of shipbuilding yards. Programs had to be continually reorganized to meet Navy requirements, dates of completion, and dates and places of commissioning. Delivery of most of these frigates was delayed over a year, adding to the problems of the manning office.

The ocean weather station program, for which most frigates were eventually to be used, had begun in 1940. The number of stations were gradually increased until after V-E Day, when there were 22 stations in the North Atlantic, 15 being manned by the Coast Guard, with 23 patrol frigates.

In March 1943, officers and nucleus crews for two Canadian corvettes assigned to the United States Coast Guard were sent to Quebec for precommissioning detail. In June the Coast Guard furnished 850 personnel for completely manning these and 6 other corvettes. The following account of a corvette sinking a submarine, written by Nicholas Monsarrat in *Corvette in Action* (Harper's Magazine) typifies the work of these vessels, and others in escort duty.

> Unexpectedly, the U-boat surfaced about two miles ahead of us. I don't know why she came up. Perhaps we had kept her down too long, or she thought she would try her luck at a shooting match, or she may even not have heard us; but we didn't waste time with speculation just then. Our first shot fell short, our second was dead on the line, but over, and our third plowed the water just where she had crash-dived again.
>
> We dropped a pattern of depth-charges for luck, on her estimated diving position, and then began to proper sweep. We picked her up almost immediately and ran in and dropped another pattern; this brought up some oil. Out on a wide turn, and in again; once more the depth charges went over the side; once more, after a pause, there came that series of splitting crashes from below

which told us they had well and truly done their stuff. Another run, and still another; the afterpart was a scene of vast activity—firing, reloading, priming, setting; then the awaited signal from the bridge, and down went the charges and presently the surface of the sea jumped and boiled, and the torpedoman rubbed his hands and called out happily: 'Next for shaving.' One more run, one more series of thunderous cracks, and the sea, spouting, boiling, threw up what we were waiting for—oil in a spreading stain, bits of wreckage, woodwork, clothing, scraps of humanity. . . . Contact failed after that, and though we waited until dusk nothing else worth collecting made its appearance. We had enough in any case.

Meanwhile, good progress was being made against the enemy, and in protecting our shipping. In the last four months of 1942, British Empire and allied air squadrons sank 23 enemy submarines bringing the total for the year to 31. During 1943 the air patrols were extended over the Western Atlantic from Iceland to Brazil. As has been seen, new weapons and new methods of using old ones were being devised and used. In April 1943, our merchant ship losses fell off sharply to 85,174 tons from 233,866 tons in March. They remained below 100,000 tons from then on except in July 1943, when they reached 111,014 tons.

The success of the radar-guided small carrier, destroyer, and destroyer escort combination against the U-boat caused Hitler to reorganize his U-boat campaign. By April 1944, U-boats were estimated to be sinking less than $\frac{1}{2}$ of 1 percent of the ships being escorted in the Atlantic, and it was estimated that the life of an enemy submarine was only 33 percent to 50 percent of the time it took to build it. By April 1943, the number of enemy submarines sunk exceeded that of U. S. merchant ships lost; this was true for the next 12 months with only December the exception.

This tabulation summarizes enemy submarine sinkings in the Atlantic, and emphasizes the efficacy of air attack:

| By | 1942 | 1943 | 1944 | 1945 |
|---|---|---|---|---|
| British Empire and allied air forces | 31 | 86 | 66 | 41 |
| U. S. Navy air forces | 7 | 49 | 18 | 4 |
| Army air forces | 4 | 10 | 14 | 34 |
| Coast Guard airplane | 1 | — | — | — |
| All Surface Vessels | * | 93 | 92 | 49 |
|  | 43* | 238 | 190 | 128 |

Grand Total 599*

* Figures for 1942 surface vessel sinkings are not available.

With this background of the Battle of the Atlantic, and a knowledge of how the Coast Guard operations fitted into this pattern, let us review outstanding episodes involving Coast Guard vessels engaged in convoy escort, weather patrol, and rescue missions.

*Alexander Hamilton,* a virtually new 327-foot cutter, had towed a disabled Navy supply ship, and cast off near the coast of Iceland. At about 1312 on 29 January 1942, the cutter was jolted by an explosion on her starboard side. Although no one saw a submarine, the officers were sure she had been struck by a torpedo, for had it been a mine, the shattering blast would have occurred outside, and not inside the ship. The explosion took place in the engine room, killing all of the engine room crew, and causing live steam from broken pipes to spurt up through the midsection of the vessel.

All hands immediately took battle stations, and perfect discipline was maintained at all times. Depth charges were placed on "safe" so they would not explode should the ship sink. Two shots were fired from a gun and flares were sent up to attract attention. Listing badly to starboard, she settled, but remained afloat for many hours. During this period, 101 men were taken off by the destroyer *USS Gwin.* Another group of men was picked up by an Icelandic fishing trawler. The sea was intensely cold, and the waves were mountainous. However, as *Alexander Hamilton* was being towed into Reykjavik, Iceland, the wrecked cutter suddenly capsized. A few gun shots from other ships sent her to the bottom to prevent her becoming a menace to navigation. Twenty Coast Guardsmen were killed in this action, and six died of wounds.

The tender-class cutter *Acacia* was on temporary duty at Williamstad, Curacao, Netherlands West Indies, when a dispatch was received 12 March 1942, from the Commandant, Tenth Naval District, with orders to proceed, when ready for sea, to Antigua, British West Indies, to complete some unfinished work there. She sailed on 13 March at 0530. At daybreak two days later, a shot suddenly rang out from off *Acacia's* starboard bow, but this did not hit. Nothing had been sighted previously. An SSS message was sent out, giving position. This was acknowledged by several ships. The enemy then kept up a slow fire using machine guns and 3″ and 4″ guns. Many shots were finding

their marks, and several of the crew were hit by shell fragments. Fires started in the wooden upper deckhouse. At 0540 all hands were ordered to abandon ship. At 0600 the enemy submarine, in plain sight, approached the cutter, now ablaze from stem to stern—an inferno of smoke and fire. After further shots, *Acacia* settled rapidly, sinking stern first at 0625. The submarine submerged. The crew of 30 to 35 officers and men in the three lifeboats, moored to a gas buoy awaiting rescue.

Planes soon arrived and flew over the position until the destroyer *USS Overton* picked up the men at about 1430. She put the men ashore at San Juan, Puerto Rico the next day.

The Coast Guard cutter *Icarus* (Lieutenant Commander Maurice Jester, USCG), made a lucky catch at 1625 on 9 May 1942. Using her sound equipment, she caught the new 500-ton *U-352* on her maiden war cruise in comparatively shallow water off Cape Lookout. After firing a torpedo, *U-352* ran aground and was damaged by the cutter's depth charges. The commanding officer decided to abandon ship; surfaced to allow his men to escape; and then scuttled his new U-boat.

During the period of great U-boat activity in the Gulf area, the Old Bahama Channel north of Cuba was the scene of the torpedoing of the *SS Hagan.* At 1330 on 13 June 1942, a search plane sighted a periscope and the submarine *U-157* just below the surface. The Key West Killer Group reached the scene and commenced searching, under highly favorable weather conditions. Coast Guard cutter *Thetis* (Lieutenant (jg) N. C. McCormick, USCG), made sound contact at 1550. She dropped seven depth charges. Each of the other five ships also attacked. Evidence of damage was two pairs of pants, and an empty tube marked "made in Germany." *USS Noa* arrived at 2015, and found the ships making so much wake that no sound contact was possible. They withdrew while *Noa* made a sound sweep. There were no further contacts and searching ceased the next morning with confidence that the submarine had been destroyed. It was later proved that *Thetis* actually sank the *U-157.*

At noon on 28 June 1942, while off the North Carolina coast, the 14,000-ton tanker *William A. Rockefeller* received a crippling blow from the *U-701.* This tanker was then under escort of two Coast Guard cutters and three aircraft. The five counterattacked, but the result was so ineffective that the submarine surfaced that night and sank the tanker. Otherwise she might have been salvaged. An Army plane piloted by 2nd Lt. Harry J. Kane, USA, sank this submarine nine days later. Of the 18 man crew of *William A. Rockefeller* 11 drowned; the rest were rescued by a Coast Guard seaplane.

It took time and experience to develop effective search and attack technique. Sufficient escorts and aggressive patrolling themselves could not protect a slow convoy. One such slow transatlantic convoy was ONS-102—63 ships in eleven columns steaming at eight knots, protected by nine escorts—*USS Leary*; the three big Coast Guard cutters *Campbell, Ingham*, and *Duane*; four Canadian corvettes; and one Canadian destroyer. Commander P. R. Heineman was escort commander in *Campbell*. At 0725 on 16 June 1942, two contacts were made on high-frequency direction finders by Canadian destroyer *Restigouche*. She and a corvette were detached to run them down. At 0836 *Restigouche* sighted a U-boat on the horizon 20 miles from the convoy. When the distance had closed to seven miles, the U-boat dived. *Restigouche* attacked unsuccessfully with depth charges.

*Campbell* now joined in, and formed a scouting line with the two Canadians. At 1300 she sighted the U-boat, surfaced, 13 miles from its previous position and 43 miles from the convoy. Her depth charge attack met with no success. *Ingham*, while still searching on the early morning direction-finder bearing at 1330, sighted another submarine surfaced, and opened fire unsuccessfully at 13,000 yards. The convoy was left alone, however, for 36 hours when, after midnight, a vessel was torpedoed and sunk. *Campbell*, patrolling ahead 5,300 yards, sighted a submarine a few minutes later headed for the convoy, distant 500 yards. This U-boat submerged and was depth-charged without success. Another unsuccessful depth-charge attack followed the next day.

By mid-1942, Army and Navy patrol planes and Coast Guard and Navy escorts sank an occasional submarine, but new construction of U-boats kept adding to the total number employed. "Wolf packs" stretched across convoy routes between the Azores and Iceland, while reconnaissance subs were stationed near convoy termini to keep the packs informed. Every transatlantic merchant convoy was attacked during August 1942.

Convoy SC-100, scattered by an equinoctial storm, lost four of its 24 merchant ships by submarine attack; the escorts, including *Spencer* and *Campbell*, sighted seven surfaced U-boats but could not overtake them.

Sinkings by plane during the second half of 1942 showed some slight improvement over the first half. The planes were very useful, and their spotting of U-boats, signaled to shore or ship, resulted in many attacks by surface craft. At the time, German submarines were under orders to submerge when they sighted a plane, and the air patrol was, therefore, a constant embarrassment to them and indirectly protected shipping. A Coast Guard J4F plane of USCG Squadron 212 based at Houma, Louisiana, and piloted by Ensign Henry C. White, USCG, sank *U-166* off the Passes of the Mississippi on 1 August 1942, (see page 42).

The loss of U. S. Army transport *Chatham* in the Strait of Belle Isle was the first American troopship loss of the war. Convoy SG-6 was a slow convoy under Coast Guard escort. The Coast Guard officers and crews had had slight training in escort duty or antisubmarine work. The convoy departed Sydney, Nova Scotia (Cape Breton), on 25 August 1942, in two groups; the first was *Chatham* capable of 13 knots and escorted by *Mojave*; the slower group consisted of cutters *Algonquin* and *Mohawk*, with three merchant ships, a Navy oiler, and *USS Harjurand*, the last-named capable of seven knots. Air coverage was given for 24 hours, but was not present at 0915 on the clear, calm morning of 27 August when *Chatham* was torpedoed. She sank in 30 minutes. *Mojave* searched for the enemy for two hours but made no contact. She then efficiently conducted rescue operations with assistance from two planes and a small Canadian vessel. About 570 men, nearly all, were saved. *Mojave* then searched until 1700 and returned to Sydney with survivors without notifying anyone of the sinking or of meeting a submarine. A few hours later two ships of the second section were torpedoed at the same place. One was sunk; the other salvaged.

The transport *Wakefield* (ex-*Manhattan*) was one of those manned by the Coast Guard. She had had an exciting and dangerous experience at Singapore when she was damaged by Japanese bombs in a raid in January 1942, while waiting to evacuate some 500 British women and children. One bomb killed everyone in the sick bay. Temporary repairs were made at Bombay and she then returned to the United States. Nine months later, in the Atlantic, she had another harrowing experience which nearly claimed her.

On 3 September 1942, while in a return convoy bringing hundreds of civilian workers from construction camps in the United Kingdom, *Wakefield* (Commander Harold G. Bradbury, USCG), caught fire. When the fire was observed from *USS Brooklyn* (Captain F. C. Denebrink, USN), the latter immediately obtained permission to leave escort position and proceeded full speed to assist, screened against attack by a destroyer. *Brooklyn's* crew had been so well drilled in rescue exercises at sea that when the time came to act every man knew exactly what to do.

Destroyer *Mayo*, patrolling the station nearest *Wakefield*, obtained permission at the same time to close her bow, where hundreds of men were cut off from the stern by flames. *Mayo* went alongside at about 1900. Seven minutes later *Brooklyn* had three lines from her forward deck to the afterpart of the burning vessel. Fortunately, the sea was calm with only a slight ground swell. *Wakefield's* abandon ship ladders, already over the side, were hauled on board the two rescue ships and then men went over them easily. *Mayo* cast off at 1917 with about 247 passengers, and ten minutes later *Brooklyn* left with about 800. Commander Bradbury kept the remaining 450 men, mostly crew members, on board to fight the fire.

*Brooklyn* had not gone far toward the convoy when flames were noticed leaping stack-high from *Wakefield's* superstructure. Captain Denebrink decided to stand by; two destroyers peeled off to protect the two large ships, while *Mayo* rejoined the convoy. At 1947 *Wakefield* signaled *Brooklyn*, "Come alongside same place", and the rescue maneuver was repeated. The burning vessel had set adrift several life rafts and launched 14 lifeboats, some partially manned. Destroyer *Madison* picked up 80 survivors from the lifeboats. At 2015 all hands then remaining transferred from *Wakefield* to *Brooklyn* by rope ladders, Commander Bradbury leaving last at 2032. *Brooklyn*, with 1173 survivors, reached New York 22½ hours later. The transport's entire complement of 1,500 had been saved without serious injury to any man or to the rescuing vessels.

About 24 hours later, *Wakefield* was taken in tow by two ocean-going tugs from New York. A Navy fire-fighting team under Commander Harold J. Burke, USNR, flew out from Quonset; landed alongside; put portable gear on board; and with its new "fog" nozzles sufficiently controlled the fire so that the ship could be towed to Halifax and beached. She burned for eight days before the fires were extinguished. Temporary repairs were then made, and *Wakefield* was towed to drydock at South Boston and practically rebuilt. In May 1944, this great transport was once more in service under Coast Guard command. She subsequently made 23 round trips across the Atlantic and three across the Pacific.

The weather observation ship *Muskeget* had been a Great Lakes freighter named *Cornish* before the Coast Guard took her over. She departed Boston on 24 August 1942 en route to her station about 450 miles south of Cape Farewell, Greenland. She took station on 31 August, and continued with routine duties of making regular reports on weather conditions. The last report received from her came on 8 September when she was awaiting the arrival of *Monomoy*, her relief. On 10 September, *Monomoy* reported she was unable to effect the relief of *Muskeget* due to failure to establish communications. Repeated efforts were made by *Monomoy* to contact the vessel without success. Upon receipt of a report from *Monomoy* sent 13 September, stating she was unable to communicate with *Muskeget*, all aircraft and ships in the vicinity were directed to search for her. This search proved fruitless. *Monomoy*, on return to Boston, reported that from 20 to 35 submarines were daily within striking distance of her particular weather station, near which convoys were numerous and active. After a year had elapsed, with no further information concerning *Muskeget* or any of her nine officers, 107 enlisted men, four civilians, and one public health officer, the entire personnel of the ship were declared officially dead.

The 5252-ton Army transport *Dorchester*, with two merchant ships, departed St. Johns, Newfoundland, in convoy on 29 January 1943. She carried 1,000 tons of cargo; a merchant marine crew of 130; an armed guard of 23; and 751 soldiers, mostly U. S. Army reinforcements for Greenland. An 11½-knot Coast Guard unit consisting of *Tampa*, *Escanaba*, and *Comanche* escorted the convoy. These vessels encountered very cold and dirty weather. Owing to a reduction of speed caused by icing, *Escanaba,* and *Comanche* had difficulty in keeping up. They sometimes had to heave to and remove ice by live steam. Their guns, depth charges, and mousetraps were sealed in by thick ice; sound gear was of little value because of excessive water noises. On 2 February, when the weather had moderated a bit, *Comanche* announced the presence of a submarine in the vicinity. Captain Joseph Greensspun, USCG, escort commander, so informed the convoy. *Tampa* made a 14½-knot sweep 10 miles ahead and 5 miles on the flanks, and at dark reassumed her patrol position.

When about 150 miles from Cape Farewell, *Dorchester* was torpedoed without warning on 3 February at 0355. (See Chapter 7.) Three minutes later, her master ordered abandon ship. *Dorchester* sank rapidly by the bow. There were no rockets or flares; the escort was unaware of the tragedy in the pitch-darkness until after the transport had gone down. Abandon ship was poorly executed; only two of 14 lifeboats were used to good advantage. *Escanaba* and *Comanche* made a fruitless search for the sub, then returned to pick up survivors, while *Tampa* escorted the other two merchant ships to Skovfjord. Recovery of survivors was difficult in the darkness. With the water at 34° and the air 36°, only men of high vitality were still alive. Most survivors were so stiff from cold that they were unable to grasp the cargo nets of the rescuing vessels, much less pull themselves up. Coast Guardsmen of *Comanche* and *Escanaba* heroically entered the freezing water to tow life rafts to the cutters and help survivors on board. Under the circumstances, the rescue of 299 men of the 904 on board *Dorchester* was an outstanding achievement.

Winter weather, 1942-1943, was very bad, with almost continuous heavy gales at sea. Merchant ship losses by marine casualty alone, were 337,852 tons between November and March, inclusive. On 12 February 1943, westward bound Ocean Escort Unit A-3 consisting of eight vessels including *USCGC Spencer* and *Campbell,* took over a convoy of 63 merchant ships. Heavy 50-mile northeasterly gales cut the speed of advance to four knots. Even in this weather, escorts were fueled from three tankers in the convoy on nine out of 14 days.

On 18 February direction finder bearings indicated the presence of submarines. Three days later a large pack was discovered in the vicinity. The cutters ran down two fixes from HF/DF bearings. *Campbell* attacked several times on sound contacts without apparent results. A straggler from another convoy sent an "SOS" 15 miles to the rear, and *Campbell* went to assist, but found no trace of the ship. Meanwhile, *Spencer* and another escort vessel went to help a plane that was attacking three submarines 12 miles away, and assisted in driving them under. Sighting another submarine, *Spencer* attacked it with gunfire and depth charges, but then had to rejoin the convoy which had light escort protection. Subsequently, it appeared that *Spencer's* attack had sunk *U-225.*

There were six attacks on the convoy during the next three days; one submarine was sunk, and several were damaged. Excellent teamwork by the escorts and by RAF Liberators had given good protection to the convoy, but air cover for the next three days was impossible and the enemy submarines made the most of this situation. In the first attack, six submarines were driven off, but another torpedoed *SS Empire Trader.* The 4 escorts then in company did not detect the U-boat. Another freighter was torpedoed six hours later. *Campbell* attacked two submarines with depth charges, and *HM* corvette *Dianthus* attacked with her hedgehog.

*U-606,* which had trailed the convoy, torpedoed three ships that evening. The submarine was depth-charged, but the escort lost contact. Another vessel picked it up, came in fast and attacked. This ruptured the submarine's pressure hull. *U-606* surfaced at a sharp angle, badly damaged, and ran blind on the surface. She was sighted by *Campbell* whose Commanding Officer, Commander James A. Hirshfield, USCG, set a collision course to ram. The cutter was firing with everything she had, and the German skipper was killed. As the submarine turned, its hydroplanes struck the cutter and cut a large hole in the cutter's hull. The sub's senior officer on deck ordered the ship abandoned. Twelve out of 48 Germans were rescued by boats from *Campbell* and from the Polish escort *Burza.* The cutter lay dead in the water several hours, screened by *Burza,* but eventually made port.

Convoy HX-233, consisting of 57 ships in 11 columns, was the most eventful eastbound convoy in April 1943. It was escorted in mid-ocean by an experienced 8-ship unit under command of Captain P. R. Heineman in *Spencer*, which had joined the group from St. Johns, N. F., on 12 April. On the 4th day out *Spencer* attacked on a sound contact without apparent result. The convoy route was changed to elude a closing wolf-pack. On 17 April, four British destroyers joined the escort. Some time later, *Spencer* sighted an object well ahead. She and *HMS Dianthus* began an intensive search at daybreak in a moderate northeast breeze, good visibility, and smooth sea with heavy swell. At sunrise, while these vessels were still searching about 10 miles astern, a freighter in the convoy was torpedoed.

Around noon *Spencer*, back patrolling her regular station, made sound contact on the 700-ton *U-175*. The latter was approaching inside the screen to attack with torpedoes. The cutter attacked, dropping two patterns of 11 depth charges each. The U-boat submerged to 38 fathoms. *Spencer* ran between the ship columns of the convoy keeping sound contact and coaching the cutter *Duane* among the merchant ships. The submarine had been severely damaged by the depth charges and broached 48 minutes after the first contact. She was about a mile from the cutters and astern of the convoy. The Naval Armed Guards on the merchantmen and the crews of both cutters opened a hot fire. The cutters headed full speed for the surfaced submarine. *U-175* was moving slowly in a circle; she returned the fire fatally wounding one of *Spencer's* crew. Fire from the cutters was so accurate and devastating, however, that before *Spencer* could ram, the Germans abandoned ship. With *Dianthus* screening them, the cutters rescued 41 survivors. A boarding party from *Spencer* had time for a good look-around on board the *U-175* before she sank.

Before the convoy reached its destination, *Spencer* attacked another submarine and kept it under, undoubtedly preventing another attack on the ships.

On 13 June 1943, a task unit consisting of *Mojave* (flag), *Tampa, Escanaba, Raritan, Storis,* and *Algonquin*, was escorting Convoy GS-24 from Narsarssuak, Greenland, to St. Johns, Newfoundland. At 0510, observers on board *Storis*, the vessel nearest *Escanaba* at the time, saw a cloud of dense black and yellow smoke and flame billowing upwards from that cutter. No explosion had been heard by the escort vessels and no signals had been either seen or heard. Yet, the 165-foot *Escanaba* had blown up and she sank within three minutes, leaving only small bits of wreckage afloat. She sank so quickly that there was no time to send out signals. *Raritan* and *Storis* searched the area and picked up two enlisted men, but the rest of the crew of 103, including the commanding officer, Lieutenant Commander Carl Uno Petersen, USCG, were lost. The survivors, Malvin Baldwin, BM2c, USCG, and Raymond F. O'Malley, S1c, USCG, had no idea what had caused the explosion. It could have been a mine, torpedo, or internal explosion of magazine or depth charges. On the basis of slim evidence, a torpedo seems the most probable cause of the disaster.

Directly or indirectly, a great number of vessels engaged in the Battle of the Atlantic. These included the coastal patrol boats, which rarely met the enemy, but suffered occasional accident and often fought a grim battle with the elements. For example, on 27 March 1943, *CG-85006* had motor trouble and one crew member was awakened by what appeared to be gas fumes. Soon after, when off Ambrose Lightship on regular picket patrol duty, the vessel was destroyed by an explosion of undetermined cause. She sank rapidly. Of the crew of ten, four were drowned, five others were missing, and only the commanding officer, Garfield L. Beal, CBM, USCG, escaped. He was picked up six hours later by the *SS Charles Brantley Aycock*.

On 2 May 1943, *CG-58012*, while patrolling off Manomet Point, Cape Cod Bay, suffered an explosion in her engine room which blew the pilot house to pieces, and set the craft afire. Ammunition began exploding. A fishing boat, attracted by flares, picked four men from the water a half hour later. A picket boat tried unsuccessfully to extinguish the flames with a hose before the boat sank.

At 2336 on 29 June 1943, *CG-83421* collided with *USS SC-1330*, seven miles north of Great Isaac Light while both vessels were part of an escort for the *SS Jean Brilliant*, Miami to Nassau. The stern of *CG-83421* had two water-tight compartments carried away, but the remaining compartments kept her afloat though water-tight integrity had been impaired. The crew were taken off, and the vessel taken in tow by *SC-1330*. After two hours of towing, the 83-footer sank in deep water. There was no loss of life or serious injury to personnel.

All vessels at times had to battle with the Atlantic and occasionally the Atlantic won. *CGC Wilcox*, a 247-ton former menhaden fishing vessel, had been converted to a patrol craft. Commanded by Lieutenant (jg) Elliot P. Smyzer, USCGR, she departed Baltimore 29 September 1943, sailing down Chesapeake Bay, stopping once or twice for engine repairs. She passed between the Virginia Capes, then with following seas and increasing winds, she rolled heavily. As darkness approached, engine trouble caused several stops. While stopped to repair the main bilge pump, *Wilcox* rolled almost 75 degrees. She began to take water and things looked bad, for the auxiliary bilge pump could only hold its own. Finally, the water got ahead of the pumps. The ship was then east of Nag's Head, North Carolina. With no port handy, Lieutenant Smyzer tried to send an SOS, but the last generator had stopped. The message was sent many times on a portable set, but no one heard it. A bucket brigade of bailers went to work. After another main engine failure, *Wilcox* steamed west for the shelter of the beach.

Shortly after 0800 on 30 September, a tremendous sea swept the superstructure, carrying a man overboard. It was impossible to recover him in the 60-mile wind and 30-foot waves. The engine stopped again. The skipper decided not to abandon ship, for no one could live on a raft in such seas. A ship came close. *Wilcox* flew a distress signal; fired rockets and a 20 mm. gun with tracers; and used a portable blinker; the ship lay to briefly, then proceeded on its course. Water kept rising despite the bucket brigade, and the cutter took a list to port. Finally abandon ship was ordered. The ship sank shortly after being abandoned. In spite of the heavy seas, every man got overboard and away, with Smyzer the last to leave the ship. The rafts were tied together, but Smyzer spent 17 hours riding the seas on a ladder. First a blimp came over and spotted the survivors, then several ships arrived. The entire crew except for the man lost overboard were saved.

On 14 October 1943, another converted menhaden fisherman, *CGC Dow*, ran into trouble. Of only 241 gross tons, the addition of a deckhouse and military equipment had adversely affected the stability of the vessel. Under command of Lieutenant (jg) Edward W. Doten, USCG, she was following orders to rendezvous with *CGC Marion*, and met the latter near Mayaguez, Puerto Rico. She had run into a heavy squall and began taking water. She requested and received permission to seek shelter nearer shore, but the weather and seas grew worse and on the afternoon of 14 October, she asked assistance from *Marion*. She could make little or no headway against the wind and sea. *Marion* came up and asked by blinker if she wished to abandon ship, and the reply was "No." Shortly, however, the engine stopped; *Dow* was broadside to the sea, and it was decided to abandon ship.

*Marion* made a lee, and *Dow* was abandoned by ferrying life rafts carrying six men at a time back and forth to *Marion*. The successful operation was completed at 2020, and the entire crew of 37 were removed without loss of life and with only a few minor injuries. *Dow* grounded a quarter of a mile south of Point Jiguero Coastal Lookout Station near Mayaguez, and the hull and fittings were later sold.

*SS James Withycombe*, a merchant vessel, was aground off Margarita Point, Canal Zone, on 20 December 1943. *CGC Bodega*, a 249-ton, 103-foot ex-whaler, used as a patrol boat and commanded by Lieutenant Thomas M. Duer, USCG, attempted to take off her crew. The sea was heavy. *Bodega* very carefully approached the lee side of the freighter and tried for some time to get alongside, after which her screw jammed and would not turn forward or astern. Attempts to get a line between the vessels were fruitless until one from the freighter's Lyle gun was secured to *Bodega's* bow. The latter was 75 feet to leeward of the freighter. The seas lifted *Bodega* onto a coral reef, and worked her in further until she was hard aground.

One raft was launched from *Bodega* to leeward and the four best swimmers were sent ashore so that a line could be established between the ship and the beach by using the raft as a sort of floating buoy. However, the line fouled on the coral, and they lost contact with the raft. The night passed without further events, except that, save for one, all the life rafts, which had been launched and secured, had disappeared. This one raft was sent to the beach in the morning with seven men. A plane passing over dropped a line between *Bodega* and the beach, and this passed near the bow of the freighter. Everyone was ordered to jump overboard and throw lanyards around the line. When every man was off the skipper followed. Fortunately, the only casualty was the bruised knee of a machinist's mate.

On 14 September 1944, a vicious hurricane swept up the Atlantic coast from Hatteras to New England. Three Coast Guard vessels foundered in this storm. The 125-foot, 220-ton cutters *Bedloe* and *Jackson* (Lieutenant A. S. Hess and Lieutenant (jg) N. D. Call, respectively), had gone to the assistance of a Liberty ship which had been torpedoed off the North Carolina coast and almost driven ashore. She survived, however, and was towed to Norfolk with no casualties.

*Bedloe* was struck four times by towering waves, and tossed like a matchstick in the ocean before going down. All hands safely abandoned ship, and 30 of the 38 on board succeeded in getting a hold on the life rafts. Only 12 survivors were able to hold on until rescued, and 2 officers and 24 men were lost. *Jackson* rolled over completely, and sank. Her men, for the most part, made the rafts, and 20 lived to be rescued. She lost 2 officers and 19 men.

During the 58 hours before rescue, men from each vessel knew the other vessel was in the vicinity, and looked to her for rescue! Added to the torment of parched throats, crowded rafts, and heavy seas, were sharks and Portuguese men-of-war. The stingers of the latter continually lashed the bodies of the storm-tossed men. After more than two days and nights, *Bedloe* survivors were spotted by a patrol plane and picked up an hour later by a Navy minesweeper. Those from *Jackson* were sighted by a Coast Guard plane from Elizabeth City, North Carolina, and many were picked up by a small boat from Oregon Inlet Lifeboat Station, 15 miles away. Coast Guard planes also landed in the swells by the life rafts, and crew members dived into the sea and hauled semi-conscious men onto the wings of the planes, where first aid was administered. After transfer near shore to a Navy vessel, the men were hospitalized at Norfolk.

On the same day this devastating hurricane caused the loss of the 123-foot Coast Guard Lightship #73 on the Vineyard Sound Station, in Massachusetts. This vessel was missing from her position off the tip of Cuttyhunk Island when the storm passed, and all hands, including 12 officers

and men, were lost. Bodies of two of the crew were later washed ashore and were identified. Divers later found that the seas had made a clean sweep of the lightship's superstructures, tearing them off and admitting the torrent of water which sank her.

As the war progressed, convoys crossing the Atlantic under adequate escort met with better and better success in reaching their destinations and delivering their vital cargoes unharmed. Losses of merchant ships and escorts dropped, but occasionally the Nazi submarines let it be known they were still in there fighting.

*USS Leopold*, a Coast Guard-manned destroyer escort (DE-319), with other Coast Guard-manned destroyer-escorts, was with a convoy 400 miles south of Iceland, on 9 March 1944, when she made contact with a Nazi submarine just after dark. *Leopold* attacked at once. The U-boat was almost submerged when spotted, and the gun crews had to work blind. Only a few rounds had been fired when another submarine, lying in wait, fired a torpedo at *Leopold*. The explosion rocked the vessel and the Commanding Officer, Lieutenant Commander Kenneth Phillips, and some others were blown off the ship into the freezing water. The order was given to abandon ship. Most of the officers and men made the boats and rafts successfully, but many slipped into the water and were lost. A storm was blowing and waves were high. About three-quarters of an hour after the explosion, the fore part of the ship broke away.

*Joyce* (Lieutenant Commander Robert Wilcox, USCG), another of the DEs, had dropped behind the convoy for rescue work, but could not stop at the time because a submarine was firing torpedoes at her. *Joyce*'s captain bellowed through a megaphone: "We're dodging torpedoes, God bless you. We'll be back," and the destroyer-escort went away. Soon the stern of *Leopold* rolled over in the heavy seas, and many men, still staying with it, were thrown off; others were washed off as the stern sank lower. *Joyce* returned, but twice while dead in the water picking up survivors, she had to get under way precipitately to evade torpedoes. The final count showed that all of *Leopold*'s 13 officers and 158 of her 186 enlisted men were lost; only 28 survived.

Late in the Battle of the Atlantic, in March 1945, Admiral Doenitz, in a desperate gesture, dispatched eight snorkel submarines to attack the

United States East Coast. So highly organized and efficient were the antisubmarine forces by that time that only three of the submarines got through, the others having been contacted and destroyed in mid-ocean. One of these, *U-866*, succeeded in reaching waters about 100 miles off Halifax where it was reported.

Escort Division 46 was the first hunter-killer group manned by the Coast Guard. Under Commander Reginald H. French, USCG, it comprised four destroyer-escorts, *Pride* (flagship), *Menges*, *Mosley*, and *Lowe*. They went out to track down and destroy *U-866*. In mid-morning of 18 March they picked up a sound contact off Sable Island where the submarine had been lying on the bottom to escape detection. Lieutenant Commander Herbert Feldman, USCGR, Commanding Officer of *Lowe*, ran down the contact, and at 1105 made two depth charge attacks after which oil, splintered wood, and other evidence rose to the surface. Then *Menges* (Lieutenant Commander F. M. McCabe, USCG), attacked and was rewarded by more evidence, including German documents. Not content, other attacks followed. The next day the group returned. *Menges* established another sound contact and attacked with her hedgehog, producing still further evidence. Post-war German records verified this kill.

Later, a task group of two frigates and two destroyer-escorts under Commander Ralph R. Curry, USCG, located *U-857* off the tip of Cape Cod. The destroyer-escort *Gustafson* (Lieutenant Commander A. E. Chambers, USNR), destroyed the *U-857* by hedgehog attacks on 7 April.

On 5 May, only three days before V-E Day, the American collier *Black Point*, proceeding eastward from Block Island Sound in company with other merchant vessels, was torpedoed by *U-853* four miles southeast of Point Judith at the entrance of Narragansett Bay. She sank quickly, and twelve lives were lost. Several Coast Guard 83-footers and *Hornbeam*, *Hibiscus*, and lifeboats and motorboats from nearby stations were sent to the area. Survivors were taken to Point Judith and Watch Hill. Lieutenant Commander L. B. Tollaksen, USCG, in frigate *Moberly*, together with the Navy destroyer-escorts *Atherton* and *Amick*, over which he assumed tactical command, obtained a sound contact on *U-853*, and within a few hours of the sinking, *Atherton*, assisted by *Moberly*, destroyed the U-boat by a hedgehog attack. This completed the destruction of the eight snorkelers which Admiral Doenitz had sent eastward to harass Atlantic coast shipping.

Throughout 1944 and early 1945, while the Battle of the Atlantic was being won by the Allies, German submarines were formidable foes to the last, and there was no room for complacency at any moment. The United States, British, and Canadian Navies, as well as naval units of other Allies, had fought valiantly through all those war years, and the United States Coast Guard, as an integral part of the Navy in wartime, exerted an invaluable influence toward the final decision.

# Chapter 15

# OPERATION "TORCH": NORTH AFRICA

THE INVASION of North Africa was the first great offensive operation by the United States against Germany. After conferences of military planners, simultaneous landings in Morocco and Algiers had been urged by President Roosevelt, but this was turned down by the Combined Chiefs of Staff on 7 March 1942, and sidetracked for some months. Russia was becoming hard pressed by Germany, and urgently called for a "second front." In June came news of the fall of Tobruk and the advance of Rommel into Egypt. The Suez "life line" was threatened. Discussions of the best method and point of attack by the Allies ran into the summer. On 25 July 1942, the Combined Chiefs of Staff reached an important decision; there would be an Anglo-American occupation of French Morocco and Algeria in four months, under the supreme command of a United States Army officer. Lieutenant General Dwight D. Eisenhower was appointed Supreme Commander. The entire project was designated Operation "Torch."

Almost immediately, over-all planning began at the Combined Headquarters at Norfolk House, London. There were many proposals and counter proposals; approvals and disapprovals; and the choice of objectives was in a state of flux for six weeks. Eventually plans began to take shape, and Operation "Torch" had practically assumed its final form by 9 September 1942.

The strategical purposes of the operation were stated by the Combined Chiefs of Staff as:

(1) Establishment of firm and mutually supported lodgments in the Oran-Algiers-Tunis area on the north coast, and in the Casablanca area on the northwest coast, in order that appropriate bases for continued and intensified air, ground, and sea operations might be readily available.

(2) Vigorous and rapid exploitation from lodgments obtained in order to acquire complete control of the entire area, including French Morocco, Algeria, and Tunis, to facilitate effective air and ground operations against the enemy, and to create favorable conditions for extension of offensive operations to the east through Libya against the rear of Axis forces in the Western Desert.

(3) Complete annihilation of the Axis forces opposing the British forces in the Western Desert and intensification of air and sea operations against the Axis on the European continent.

The Joint United States Chiefs of Staff issued the following "concept of United States participation," calling for military and naval forces:

1. A Joint Expeditionary Force to seize and occupy the Atlantic coast of French Morocco.

2. United States forces required in conjunction with the British forces to seize and occupy the Mediterranean coast of French North Africa.

3. Additional Army forces as required to complete the occupation of Northwest Africa.

4. Naval local defense forces and sea frontier forces for the Atlantic coast of French Morocco and naval personnel for naval base maintenance and harbor control at Oran.

5. The United States to be responsible for logistic support and requirements of all United States forces.

During this period of planning, the Amphibious Force Atlantic Fleet was not idle. Under command of Rear Admiral Henry Kent Hewitt, USN, with headquarters at Norfolk, Virginia, the Force organized "Transports Atlantic Fleet" in six divisions, and undertook training of several thousand Navy and Coast Guard personnel in handling landing craft. This training was conducted at the Amphibious Force Training Center at Little Creek, Virginia, and at Solomons Island, Maryland, in Chesapeake Bay, under the direction of Captain W. P. O. Clarke, USN. Army landing force personnel were trained at Fort Bragg, North Carolina. Day and night exercises were conducted in the Solomons Island area; fire support ships held bombardment exercises at nearby Bloodsworth Island.

Over 3,000 Navy and Coast Guard personnel were needed to man the landing craft. Admiral Morison, in his *History of Naval Operations in World War II* wrote: "It would have been desirable to select young men who were used to lobstering, fishing, and other small-craft work, for boat handling is not an art that can be learned in a hurry. But there were not enough such men available. So, as frequently in this war, the Navy had to do the best it could to make boat sailors out of raw recruits who had never seen salt water."

In getting ready for this early effort, which would combine Army and Navy units in one operation, there were many different points of view to be straightened out and reconciled. Army and Navy doctrine on landing procedure differed considerably. Reconciliation was complicated and took time, and training methods had to be changed. An amphibious signal school for Army and Navy communications personnel was established at Little Creek to coordinate the independent Army and Navy systems. There were other complications, too. Some transports did not arrive for training in time to rehearse for day and night landings which were practiced from August to October. Many landing craft had no engines until mid-October. It was nip and tuck, trial and error, all through these preliminaries.

While these preparations were going on, the French situation in North Africa was one which had to be handled in advance with the greatest of care, secrecy, and finesse. In an area teeming with German and Vichy agents, whose provocateurs were always on the alert to intercept, confuse, and threaten, the success of the invasion depended, above all, on secrecy. This meant that the Allied leaders had to use the utmost precaution in seeking the cooperation of French leaders lest a Vichy-controlled "collaborator" be approached by mistake and the entire plan be divulged to the enemy.

Should an approach be made to a single Frenchman who proved unsympathetic to our purpose, we risked the slaughter of soldiers on the beaches of North Africa as well as decisive losses in shipping. Secrecy had to be maintained, yet sympathetic French leaders had to be informed of Allied intentions in order to avoid, if possible, French resistance and consequent fighting with French forces. To some degree, however, this risk had to be accepted.

General George C. Marshall, USA, in his report of the operations, wrote: "The discussions regarding such an expedition had to be conducted on a more or less indefinite basis as to timing. Not until four days before the convoys would deploy off the beaches at Algiers, Oran, and Casablanca were the few Frenchmen we had contacted informed of the actual date for the operation. This, of course, made it extremely difficult, in cases impossible, for these French officials to take all the steps necessary to facilitate our landings."

Prior to the landings, the United States continued to recognize Vichy chiefly for strategic reasons. Admiral William D. Leahy, USN, was our Ambassador to Vichy. Mr. Robert D. Murphy was the Counselor of the United States Embassy at Vichy, but actually he was traveling around in North Africa, and it was almost wholly through him that contacts were made with those French who were to help in the Allied landings. Major General Mark W. Clark, USA, made a secret landing from a British submarine on the Barbary Coast on 23 October to give French leaders military assurance of our intentions.

Thus, while it was certain there would be no bitter and prolonged resistance, if any, once General Henri Giraud and other French leaders had spoken, it was still likely that not all French garrisons would get the word in time, or believe it once it had been passed. The French Navy, through Admiral Darlan, was closely tied to Vichy and loyal to Petain, which meant the risk of naval resistance. Due to the uncertainties, our forces were ordered not to shoot first, but to be ready to shoot fast and plentifully if necessary. Should there be resistance a code signal had been devised to flash throughout the Task Forces that our landings were being opposed. That signal was "Play Ball."

Because resistance remained problematical in spite of the negotiations, steps were taken to insure cooperation just as the landings were about to begin. In a radio broadcast, General Eisenhower issued a proclamation of friendly intentions toward French North Africa, and he instructed French forces to indicate their non-resistance by displaying certain signals. At 0100 in the morning of 8 November, at the moment the landings in Algiers began, and several hours before the landings in French Morocco, President Roosevelt spoke to the French people by short-wave radio, assuring them that the Allies sought no territory and asking for French cooperation against the Nazi regime. He also assured the Spanish government that the invasion was not directed against Spanish Morocco or other Spanish territory in Africa.

These negotiations were going on before and during the transit of the naval forces to the scene of invasion. Along the United States Atlantic Coast plans and preparations surrounded by great secrecy were being rushed. The armada for this operation comprised the largest overseas landing force in world history up to that time. The Western Naval Task Force (Admiral Hewitt), was to land about 35,000 troops and 250 tanks of the Western Task Force (General George S. Patton, USA), at three points on the Atlantic coast of French Morocco. Landings were to be effected at Fedhala, 15 miles northeast of Casablanca; at Mehedia almost midway between Casablanca and the Straits of Gibraltar; and at Safi, 140 miles southwest of Casablanca.

Air cover was important, and four U. S. escort carriers of the *Sangamon* class, converted from tankers, were assigned to the operation with less than half normal shakedown training. *Ranger,* the only large carrier in the Atlantic Fleet, was assigned as the flagship of Rear Admiral Ernest D. McWhorter, USN, who commanded the "Torch" air group. Together, these carriers took 248 planes to North Africa.

The Task Force was divided into a Covering Group (Rear Admiral Robert C. Giffen, USN) of one battleship, two cruisers, four screening destroyers, and a tanker; and three Attack Groups. The Northern Attack Group under command of Rear Admiral Monroe Kelly, USN, comprised one battleship, one cruiser, eight transports, nine destroyers, a beacon submarine, two carriers, two minesweepers, and two miscellaneous craft. The Center Attack Group, commanded by Captain Rob-

ert R. M. Emmet, USN, in *Leonard Wood* as his flagship, consisted of two cruisers, ten destroyers, fifteen transports, six minecraft, two beacon submarines, one tanker, and an air group and screen of two carriers, five destroyers, and a cruiser. The Southern Attack Group, in command of Rear Admiral Lyal A. Davidson, USN, was made up of two cruisers, ten destroyers, six transports, three minecraft, two tankers, a beacon submarine, one carrier, and one ocean tug. In all, this Task Force numbered 105 vessels not including ships' boats and the various types of landing craft which these vessels carried. A mighty armada, indeed!

The French Moroccan operation was to have a counterpart in a simultaneous campaign to seize the Mediterranean ports of Algiers and Oran in Algeria. This, too, was part of Operation "Torch" and was to proceed regardless of developments in French Morocco. The Mediterranean landings were to be the responsibility of the British. Admiral Sir Andrew B. Cunningham, RN, was Allied Naval Commander of the entire "Torch" operation, but gave Admiral Hewitt a free hand in the Atlantic, while he himself directed the Mediterranean campaign.

The Task Force for the Mediterranean operation was divided into the Eastern Naval Task Force, under command of Rear Admiral Sir Harold M. Burrough, RN, with Algiers as the objective, and the Center Naval Task Force, under Commodore Thomas Troubridge, RN, with Oran its destination. Force H of the Royal Navy, consisting of *HMS Nelson*, Admiral Cunningham's flagship, two other battleships, one battle cruiser, three light cruisers, two carriers, and seventeen destroyers, was the covering force for the two Task Forces. It was charged with covering the attack forces during transit, debarkation, and the assault; protection from submarines and aircraft attack; and defense from a possible attack by French fleet units in Mediterranean ports. United States participation was stressed in both sectors. In these landings, about 49,000 United States Army officers and men were put ashore, compared with 23,000 British.

Composition of the Eastern Naval Task Force was a headquarters ship, three light cruisers, two carriers, three antiaircraft cruisers, a monitor, thirteen destroyers, seven minesweepers, seven corvettes, three sloops, and miscellaneous small craft. In the Eastern Assault Force were about 23,000

British and 10,000 United States Army officers and men. The Center Naval Task Force comprised an imposing array of British warships—battleship *Rodney*, a headquarters ship, three carriers, an anti-aircraft ship, thirteen destroyers, eight minesweepers, six corvettes, two former U. S. Coast Guard cutters (*Pontchartrain* and *Sebago*, renamed *Hartland* and *Walney*), as well as many armed trawlers and motor transport ships.

Vessels of the Western Naval Task Force were variously dispersed in several United States Atlantic Coast ports to avoid too heavy concentrations while awaiting fleet movement. Detailed plans were distributed to the ships immediately before departure, but the destination was made known to only a small number in the top command until a short time before arrival. When the time came to sail, most of the Northern, Center, and Southern Attack Groups left Hampton Roads on 23 October, with *Joseph T. Dickman* leading the transports out to sea. The remainder of the Task Force set out from Hampton Roads on 24 October, both groups heading in different directions. Two days later the Covering Group, which had been in Casco Bay, joined the others which had already merged. On 25 October, the Air Group sortied from Bermuda and made rendezvous with the other elements three days later, 450 miles south-southeast of Cape Race, Newfoundland, on about the latitude of Philadelphia.

The Task Force, now complete, with Admiral Hewitt in cruiser *Augusta*, steamed an irregular course east-southeasterly. Various drills were held frequently while en route to acquaint ships' personnel and troops with their stations and duties. The Force reached a point 300 miles west of the Canary Islands on 3 November, then headed northeasterly toward Gibraltar, arriving at a point 150 miles off Casablanca at daybreak on 7 November. There were no submarine attacks during the crossing.

In the Western Naval Task Force there were two Coast Guard-manned attack transports. Both of these were attached to the Center Attack Group, *Leonard Wood* (Commander Merlin O'Neill, USCG) Captain Emmet's flagship, and *Joseph T. Dickman* (Commander C. W. Harwood, USCG).

The Naval Forces for the Mediterranean assault sailed from the United Kingdom in two large convoys, the slower one leaving on 22 October, and the faster one four days later. They passed through the Straits of Gibraltar at night 5-6 November, had air cover during their transit of Mediterranean waters, and reached a point off their objectives on schedule, though not without difficulties. Attached to this force was a third Coast Guard-manned attack transport, *Samuel Chase* (Commander Roger C. Heimer, USCG). This transport was the flagship of Captain Campbell D. Edgar, USN, who commanded "Group Charlie" of eight vessels, one of the three groups into which the Eastern Naval Task Force was divided.

These three Coast Guard-manned attack transports were the vessels in which the Coast Guard participated in the North African landings. It should be said, however, that a few Coast Guardsmen familiar with landing craft also served with Navy crews in *Arcturus, Charles Carroll, Joseph Hewes*, and *William P. Biddle* in the Moroccan assault, and in *Exceller* at Algiers.

For the sake of clarity it will be best to consider first the operations on the coast of French Morocco, and then those in the Mediterranean. Briefly, the objectives of the Moroccan expedition were (a) to capture Casablanca from the land side, (b) to capture the airfield near Port Lyautey, and (c) to capture the port of Safi by direct assault, and then to assist in the reduction of Casablanca.

We have followed the Western Naval Task Force, which included *Leonard Wood* and *Joseph T. Dickman*, to a point 150 miles off Casablanca. Here the great fleet divided; the Southern Attack Group turning south toward Safi, the rest heading again toward the Straits of Gibraltar. At 1600, the Northern and Center Attack Groups separated; the former steaming toward Mehedia, while the latter, with the Coast Guard's transports, steamed toward Fedhala. The precision of these moves is evident by arrivals of the groups at their assigned areas at 2345, 2353, and 2400 respectively!

Military problems facing the advancing armada included the fixed defenses along the Moroccan coast, supplemented by the mobile strength drawn from the French Army, Vichy planes, both Army and Navy; and the French fleet strength at Casablanca. The toughest element of opposition, in case Vichy forces decided to resist, was the French fleet—one battleship, two light cruisers, three flotilla leaders, six destroyers, twelve submarines, and one sloop.

The Center Attack Group with twelve trans-

*(Top) SPENCER* DEPTH CHARGES SUBMARINE . . . . the U-boat was severely damaged and had to surface. *(Bottom) SPENCER,* AT FULL SPEED, BEARS DOWN ON *U-175* . . . . gunfire battered the enemy and the Germans abandoned ship.

TRANSPORT *WAKEFIELD* BURNS AT SEA .... destroyer *Mayo* stands by to help take off some of the passengers. These were Americans who had been stranded in Europe at the outbreak of the war.

COAST GUARD CUTTER *ALEXANDER HAMILTON* SINKING . . . . crew, with perfect discipline, can be seen abandoning ship.

THE ONLY SURVIVORS FROM LOST *ESCANABA* . . . .
Melvin Baldwin and Raymond F. O'Malley.

*JACKSON* SURVIVORS ARE RESCUED . . . . transferring
men to a boat which rushed them to a hospital.

AFTER SEVENTEEN HOURS ON RAFTS . . . . members of the crew of *Wilcox* rest in a
Naval Hospital after their vessel foundered.

*JOSEPH T. DICKMAN*, COAST GUARD-MANNED TRANSPORT . . . . she led the transports to
sea from Hampton Roads, bound for the North African invasion.

EUROPEAN LANDINGS REQUIRED INTENSIVE PRACTICE . . . . Coast Guard landing craft
swarm to the beach in invasion maneuvers in waters of Chesapeake Bay.

UNITED STATES CONVOY EN ROUTE TO NORTH AFRICA . . . . these vessels are carrying men,
materiel and munitions for Operation "Torch."—(*U. S. Navy Photo*)

PERSONNEL AND EQUIPMENT ARE LANDED IN ALGERIA . . . . British-American convoy
unloads on the beach at St. Leu, Department of Oran.—(*U. S. Army Photo*)

AFTER THE ACTION AT ORAN . . . . the salvage job was tremendous. Here a French ship sunk by American vessel is being prepared for raising.—(U. S. Army Photo)

CAPTAIN ROGER C. HEIMER, USCG . . . . commanding officer of transport Samuel Chase.

(Top) TRANSPORT LEONARD WOOD, MANNED BY THE COAST GUARD . . . . this vessel went through the attack at Fedhala unscathed. (Bottom) DIVISION FLAG-SHIP SAMUEL CHASE . . . . leading a charmed life, she earned the nickname "Lucky Chase."

THE LCI FLOTILLA MOVES IN TOWARD SICILY . . . . these Coast Guard-manned vessel are
flying barrage balloons to foil possible enemy strafing.

BOMB POCKED WATERS OFF SICILY DURING THE INVASION . . . . Army contingents from this transport were
hitting the beach as a Coast Guard combat photographer took this picture.

ATTACK TRANSPORT *CAVALIER*, COAST GUARD-MANNED . . . . she and others of her class carried fighting men and vital war materials to enemy-held invasion shores.

CARGO SHIP BURNS AND BLOWS UP . . . . when flames reach the ammunition holds, after being hit by Nazi dive bomber during Sicilian landings.

LAND MINE EXPLODES . . . . as troops disembark and **charge up** the beach toward enemy positions.

CASUALTIES RECEIVE MEDICAL TREATMENT . . . . wounded Coast Guardsmen are treated on landing barge.

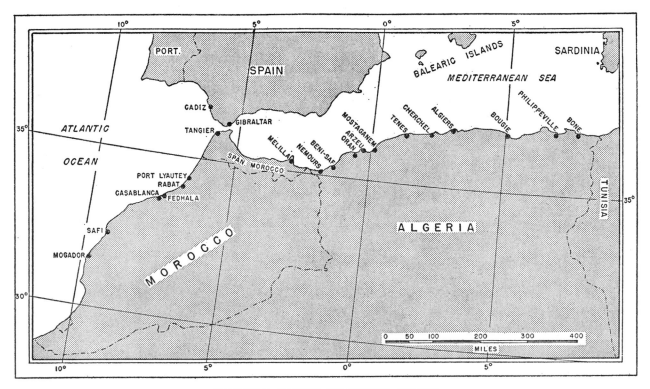

INVASION SHORES OF NORTH AFRICA

ports and three cargo vessels carried 18,783 Army officers and men, 1,701 vehicles, and about 15,000 long tons of supplies. These were to be put ashore at the nearest landing point to Casablanca in the course of four days. Naval personnel of the Group numbered 17,723. Failure of this Group, the most important, meant failure of the entire expedition. The transports took position about six miles offshore north of the town of Fedhala to the east of which were five beaches suitable for troop landings. These were well covered by French artillery, coast defense guns, and machine gun installations.

To alleviate difficulties that small boats would have in finding their way in the dark, the Control Boat and Line of Departure method of finding position, and the Scout and Raider technique of beachmarking were adopted. Problems of fire support were solved by the little LCSSs (Landing Craft Support, Small) with banks of twelve rocket launching racks on each gunwale, which provided devastating fire. The waves of small craft stood in greatest need of protection as they neared the beach and drew within range of hostile light machine gun, mortar, and small arms fire. This was just the time the heavy ships furnishing the preliminary neutralizing bombardment would have to lift their fire for fear of hitting their own men.

The first landing was set for 0400 on 8 November. According to the plan, four beachmarking boats were to be launched from the transports, and were to move into position just outside the line of surf to mark the beaches. When the time came, their identifying flashlights and flares were to show their position to the landing craft. Meanwhile, the transports were to launch their landing craft, man them, and load them with troops, allowing four hours for the process. These craft would then rendezvous with four control destroyers in line before the transports, and the landing boats would be conducted by the destroyers to the line of departure, 4,000 yards off the beaches. At H-hour the boat waves would start for the beaches, accompanied by support boats for protection; they would then land troops, retract, and repeat the operation.

Actually, the first line of four transports, including *Leonard Wood* and *Joseph T. Dickman*, reached their positions on time; hoisted out all their boats and began loading troops into them by 0140.

The troops were loaded in two hours. Other transports straggled in the darkness to find their assigned positions in lines behind the first line of vessels. Due to this delay, sufficient landing craft were unavailable at the scheduled time. Despite borrowing from other ships, the time schedule was upset. Army personnel were slow to move. H-hour was postponed until 0500, when the first assault waves left the line of departure and hit the beaches 15 to 25 minutes later. There was no surf of consequence. Other waves followed. The landings came as a complete surprise to the German High Command.

At this point let us shift our attention to *Leonard Wood*. Embarked on board this vessel were Major General J. W. Anderson, USA, and Staff; Regimental Landing Group 7, Third Infantry Division; and supporting units. In addition there were approximately 3,000 tons of vehicles, supplies, and equipment. In all, this ship carried the following personnel:

|  |  | *Army* | *Navy* | *Coast Guard* | *Total* |
|---|---|---|---|---|---|
| Officers |  | 92 | 28 | 41 | 161 |
| Enlisted Men |  | 1,693 | 122 | 541 | 2,356 |
| Total |  | 1,785 | 150 | 582 | 2,517 |

*Leonard Wood* began lowering boats at 0009. Twelve minutes later, her beach marking boat departed to locate and mark the landing Beach Red 2. All boats were waterborne by 0140. Some delay was encountered in lowering the tank lighters due to the fouling of a block on the boom. Disembarkation of Army personnel and equipment was begun when all boats on the starboard side had been lowered. Some time was lost in loading the first wave because of a failure of six boats (LCP(L)s) to arrive from *USS Procyon*. The first three waves of assault boats left at 0350 for the line of departure. The fourth wave departed at 0400, and the fifth at 0540. Boats of succeeding waves were loaded and dispatched to the beach singly or in groups of two or three in order to expedite disembarkation.

As the boats of the first wave approached the shore, they were illuminated by a searchlight from the direction of Sherki (also spelled Chergui). Support boats immediately opened fire on the light. Shortly afterward there was firing between land batteries at Sherki and Fedhala and the control destroyers near the lines of departure.

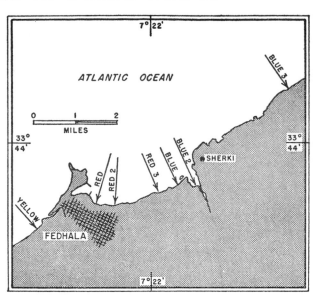

ATTACK AREA AT FEDHALA

In making the landings, many boats from *Leonard Wood* were unlucky because the control destroyer *Wilkes* and the scout boat were out of position. The latter was to take station off the east end of Beach Red 2, where a rocky reef begins, and the landing boats were to leave her to port. The scout boat had been approached by a mysterious and apparently hostile boat before the first waves came in. She had cut her cable and drifted to a position off the rocks. *Wilkes* was out of position to the westward. The first four boat waves, guided by the scout boat's blinker, approached the beach obliquely, and many of the boats ran onto the rocks at full speed. Coxswains were able to retract some, which made their way to the beach; others stayed hard and fast aground. From those, soldiers scrambled ashore over the rocks, and much of their equipment was lost. Out of *Leonard Wood's* 32 boats which made the initial landing, 21 were wrecked. Eight others were lost later that day in landing through the surf.

Fortunately casualities to personnel from these mishaps and from firing by the shore batteries were very light. Troops and equipment continued to move from this transport to the shore in its own and a few borrowed boats. With so few boats available, however, unloading was extremely slow.

Shortly after daylight a small force of French cruisers and destroyers stood out of Casablanca toward Fedhala. They were immediately engaged by cruisers *Augusta* and *Brooklyn* of the Fire Support Group, and were either destroyed or forced back to Casablanca. Enemy planes, believed to have been French, bombed and strafed the landing beaches at intervals throughout the day. These attacks were light and did not seriously interfere with landing operations. No attacks were made on the transports. Heavy gunfiring could be heard occasionally through the day from the direction of Casablanca.

The landing of supplies and equipment continued for several days. Sporadic firing from the shore near Fedhala and from the direction of Casablanca continued until the morning of 11 November, when an agreement was reached with the French, and United States land and naval forces entered the city and harbor of Casablanca.

As *Leonard Wood* lay at anchor off Fedhala in the early evening of 11 November, the U. S. destroyer *Hambleton* and the U. S. tanker *Winooski* were torpedoed. Although severely damaged, they later made port at Casablanca. At the same time, the U. S. transport *Joseph Hewes*, which had several Coast Guardsmen on board, was torpedoed, and sank in 50 minutes. *Leonard Wood* and the other transports sent all available boats to rescue survivors, and most of *Hewes's* crew were picked up from the water. German submarine *U-173* did the torpedoing. Five days later she in turn was attacked and sunk off Casablanca by the U. S. destroyers *Woolsey*, *Swanson*, and *Quick*.

In the late afternoon of 12 November, three more transports, *Edward Rutledge*, *Hugh L. Scott*, and *Tasker H. Bliss*, anchored in the same location off Fedhala, were torpedoed by *U-130*. All three burst into flames. Once again, *Leonard Wood* and the remaining transports sent their boats to the rescue. Well over 1,000 survivors were taken ashore by rescue craft and given medical care.

As a result of this attack, the remaining transports and other vessels at the anchorage off Fedhala immediately got under way, stood out to sea, and steered evasive courses. On the morning of 13 November, they shaped course for Casablanca and stood into the lee of the breakwater where they anchored at 1720. *Thomas Jefferson*, *Charles Carroll*, *Elizabeth C. Stanton*, and *Thurston* preceded *Leonard Wood* into the harbor. The remaining vessels kept at sea until berthing space was available. Later, *Wood* moored to a jetty and completed unloading her supplies and equipment.

*Leonard Wood* stood out of port on 17 November with Army and Navy casualties, survivors, and other passengers—187 in all—to await departure with other transports for the return trip to the United States. She arrived at Norfolk on 30 November.

During this time, *Joseph T. Dickman* was also active in the assault on Fedhala. As she took her position at the head of her line of transports off the port, she had on board about 1,450 officers and men of the 2nd Battalion of the 30th Infantry Regiment, 3rd Division, plus a Navy Sea Frontier Unit, as well as part of the Army Western Task Force Headquarters. The number of troops carried was somewhat less than capacity, but her cargo holds were crammed full. In addition to the regular components of combat equipment and supplies, the cargo was topped off with extra ammunition and provisions.

The troops from *Dickman* were to be landed on a beach identified as the "Wadi Nefifikh", a small indentation of the coast into which a creek emptied. The troops were to seize a small fort (Pont Blondin) on the north side of the Wadi, as well as a bridge crossing it, and other points designated as necessary for defense of the beachhead. A beach to the southward, more suitable for landing cargo, was designated for that purpose. In view of the expected difficulties in retracting the boats, the first five waves carrying *Dickman's* assault troops were to hit the beach nearly simultaneously and trust to skill and good fortune to get back. This beach, lying between two fortified headlands, had the potentialities of a disastrous enemy trap, as well as many natural disadvantages, but the results to be gained by its successful use justified its selection.

*Joseph T. Dickman* began lowering her boats immediately upon arrival. First over was the scout boat, which successfully found and maintained her designated position off the beach. The accomplishments of this boat were important in the outstanding success of the initial landings from *Dickman*.

The plans called for 20 boats to be furnished by other vessels, which, as we have have seen, were slow in taking position. Only one arrived on schedule. About half of *Dickman's* boats were designed to carry vehicles and personnel, and the remainder were to carry personnel only. Immediate revision of the complicated boat landing schedule was necessary. Fortunately, the Commanding Officer of Troops, Major Bernard, was not a man easily flustered; a new schedule was quickly arranged with him which permitted 27 of the ship's boats to make up four and a half of the first five waves and to reach the assembly area ahead of time. Destroyer *Murphy*, acting as control vessel for *Dickman*, escorted these boats to the line of departure and started them in to the beach on signal from the flagship. The destroyer was hit by a shell from the battery on Pont Blondin but was not disabled, and her return fire was instrumental in silencing the battery.

Of these 27 boats, 25 reached Beach Blue 2 and unloaded their troops and equipment just before the fort was alerted. Although their return trip was made under fire, not a boat was lost. They returned to their ship by 0630. Two boats missed their control destroyer; were set to the eastward; and encountered the searchlight and fire from the fort. They landed on the northeast side of Pont Blondin battery and stranded on the rocks, but the troops and crew got ashore safely.

When the beaches were being strafed by planes, one of *Dickman's* boats was shot up. Two members of the crew, Donald LaRue and R. L. Bucheit, were severely wounded. The engineman in the boat, Paul Clark, took charge, placed the wounded men on board a destroyer, and completed the mission of the boat. He was awarded the Navy Cross for his heroic action. C. C. Curry, a Navy Hospital Apprentice attached to *Joseph T. Dickman*, was awarded the Silver Star for his courageous treatment of wounded men along the beach during the plane attacks.

As the day wore on and the unloading proceeded, it was necessary for *Dickman's* boats to assist other vessels in unloading, since many boat losses had been suffered by most of the transports. The beaches continued to get more difficult because of increasing surf and congestion, and finally their use was suspended. When Fedhala capitulated, the harbor became available, but it was too small to accommodate the large amount of supplies being sent in.

During the landings, Ensign Harry A. Storts, USCGR, and a crew of Coast Guardsmen from *Joseph T. Dickman* had an amazing adventure. They were trying to escort three amphtracs

(LVTs) to Beach Blue 2 in the initial pre-dawn landings, using a borrowed support boat. Amphtracs, then experimental, frequently broke down. These did, and by daylight they had drifted so far from their destination that Storts was ordered to take them back along the coast and land them at the nearest available beach. He joined forces with two landing boats carrying antiaircraft half-track batteries. They landed at 0945 on a beach a dozen miles east of Sherki while being strafed by an enemy plane.

French troops were on hand behind this beach and immediately made their presence felt. Ensign Stort's force of 32 Army and nine Navy and Coast Guard personnel dug in, set up their guns, and stood seige. French planes strafed every half hour until dark. They killed five men, but the survivors drove off several French armored cars. Two men put out in a rubber boat after dark to intercept a destroyer; Storts and four others started walking to Fedhala to contact United States forces. The 29 men left behind moved from the beach to a concrete pigpen. They held out there for two days until their ammunition was gone.

Those in the rubber boat missed the destroyer but returned to their ship. Ensign Storts and his party took a night and day before reaching an Army command post near Fedhala. After resting, they were provided with a half-track, a 75-mm. gun, and a rescue squad. On the way back they captured ten French soldiers and took them along, but found that their comrades on the beach had been captured, so they turned back toward Fedhala.

They were neatly ambushed by 150 French-led native troops who wounded or killed everyone in the party. The captors took the American survivors to a French first-aid station at Bouznika, where their wounds were dressed. A French officer then started with them by truck toward Rabat for questioning, but after going a mile the truck was strafed and disabled by a United States plane. Three more Frenchmen were killed. The remaining survivors walked or were carried back to Bouznika, then shipped by truck 14 miles inland to Boulhaut. Next day the fighting was over. A priest conducted Storts and one other survivor of the original party to Fedhala, where they reported on board ship.

The other transports conducted about the same kind of operation as that performed by the Coast

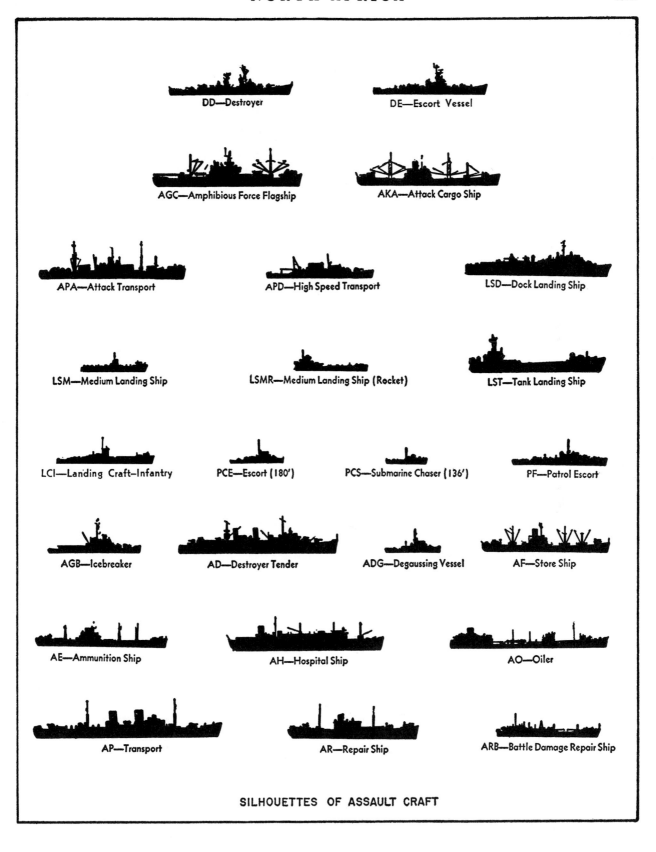

SILHOUETTES OF ASSAULT CRAFT

Guard-manned vessels. In summary, naval bombardment and fighting on shore reduced the resistance points one by one. By nightfall of 8 November, Major General Anderson's 3rd Division had attained all of the objectives in the plan. The Americans controlled the town, the harbor, and the vital bridges. There was sporadic fighting in places, and strafing continued for a while, but Fedhala had been taken.

Considering that the initial landings were made in darkness and on an unfamiliar coast, they went off fairly well. It was the opinion of most senior naval officers who observed the landings, that the Navy men and Coast Guardsmen who handled the landing boats deserved high praise for their courage, persistence, and intelligence, especially in view of their lack of combat experience and brief training. When one wave received heavy fire from Cape Fedhala, one of its boats was hit. The others hesitated, wondering if they should turn back. The coxswain in one landing craft—whether Navy or Coast Guard is not clear—had his bow man break out a large American flag and hold it aloft. The coxswain, standing defiantly at his wheel, led the wave in to the beach.

Admiral Morison pays this tribute in his *History of Naval Operations:* "The best job was done by boats of the Coast Guard-manned *Dickman* on Beach Blue 2, in the estuary of the Wadi Nefifikh, although this was the most difficult beach of all." And he makes this further comment: "The value of previous experience in small boat handling was proved by the superior performance of the Coast Guard, who manned the landing craft of USS *Joseph T. Dickman* at Fedhala."

When *Hambleton, Winooski,* and *Joseph Hewes* were torpedoed on the night of 11 November, *Dickman* sent boats to their assistance. She sent boats again on the following afternoon when transports *Edward Rutledge, Hugh L. Scott,* and *Tasker H. Bliss* were attacked and sunk. After the latter attack, *Dickman* got under way with the other transports, leaving her boats behind to carry on the rescue work. Like *Leonard Wood, Joseph T. Dickman* cruised offshore until the harbor at Casablanca opened up, when she went in and discharged the remainder of her cargo. She left for Norfolk on 17 November. For their heroic conduct and brilliant leadership Captain O'Neill of *Leonard Wood,* and Captain Harwood of *Joseph T.*

*Dickman,* were later decorated with the Legion of Merit.

In the other areas of attack, operations ended successfully. The Northern Attack Group at Mehedia and Port Lyautey began its operations under difficult circumstances. There was plenty of vicious fighting. Fire support from naval vessels was very effective, and in two days our forces finally became masters of the situation. The airfield at Port Lyautey, a principal objective, was captured and secured early on 10 November. By 1030 that day, Army P-40s from the carrier *Chenango* were using the airfield.

With the Southern Attack Group at Safi, landings were promptly effected with a minimum of loss. Resistance by the French, while intense at the time of assault, was quickly quelled and all objectives had been attained in the afternoon of 8 November. There was sharp fighting at Safi itself, with heroic naval action right up into the harbor under the French fire at almost point blank range. All fighting men and tanks from the transports there were ashore by late afternoon on 10 November, and next morning came the armistice.

Meanwhile, when the signal "Play Ball" gave word of resistance, carriers of the Task Force sent up their planes early on 8 November to bomb and strafe Casablanca, French airfields, and other installations along the coast. Admiral Giffen's Covering Group assumed battle formation. Besides destroying and driving off enemy planes, our aircraft made effective bombing and strafing raids on French war vessels and shore batteries at Casablanca. The Navy lost 44 of its planes, but did great damage to French planes aloft and on the airfields.

French naval units at Casablanca were full of fight. Antiaircraft batteries on shore opened up on our planes. The new French battleship *Jean Bart* and a shore battery commenced firings, and the Naval Battle of Casablanca was on. Several French submarines sortied from the harbor, followed by seven French destroyers; they shelled landing craft west of Cape Fedhala, fired on some of our destroyers, and were in turn attacked by some of our planes. Later, the French light cruiser *Primauguet* went out to fight. Our own cruisers and more destroyers joined the fray, and it became an old fashioned naval engagement with planes thrown in. The naval action was watched with interest from *Wood* and *Dickman,* neither of which was involved.

At the end of the fighting, five of our vessels had suffered one hit each. Three men had been killed and about 25 wounded. In addition 40 landing boats had been destroyed by enemy action. The French lost four destroyers and eight submarines. Four other war vessels, including *Jean Bart,* were disabled. The French lost 490 killed and 969 wounded. Coast batteries at Casablanca were still in French hands and operative, although there was only intermittent action after that. The cease-fire came on 11 November, and French Morocco was secured.

While these actions were taking place, the Eastern Naval Task Force was carrying out its assignments in the Mediterranean. As we have seen, this great Task Force passed through the Straits of Gibraltar on the night of 5-6 November, when the Western Naval Task Force was still off Madeira.

In this joint campaign, the British furnished the naval forces with the exception of four United States transports constituting Transport Division Eleven. This Division had left Clyde on 14 October in company with the fast convoy which included 37 vessels. It consisted of Division flagship *Samuel Chase,* Coast Guard-manned and commanded by Commander Roger C. Heimer, USCG; *Thomas Stone* (Captain Olten R. Bennehoff, USN); *Leedstown* (Lieutenant Commander Duncan Cook, USNR); and *Almaack* (Captain Chester L. Nichols, USN). These four ships carried the United States contingent of troops in the Eastern Assault Force of which Major General Charles W. Ryder, USA, was in command. Of the 72,000 officers and men put ashore in Algeria, 23,000 were furnished by the British Army and 49,000 by the United States Army.

Several days before the attack, the Commodore opened his orders and told his officers where they were going and what was expected of them. In turn, men in the ships were informed on the morning of 8 November that the Transport Division was to force a landing at Algiers. Simultaneously, the British forces were to take Oran.

Briefly, the plan was to make a landing and capture the airdrome of Maison Blanche as well as certain villages, and to hold the roadheads and bridges. The airfield had to be taken and held,

since Spitfires would be flown in from Gibraltar to land there. It would also be necessary to reduce a fort on Cape Matifou under whose big guns landings would be made. The final stage called for a cessation and settlement of all hostilities in four days, enabling the British portion of the convoy to move into the Algiers docks and disembark the First British Army whose duty it would be to push Rommel and his German army from the west.

As the Eastern Naval Task Force steamed eastward through the Mediterranean, the Oran Section separated from the group and headed toward its destination. The rest of the Task Force, which continued on, consisted of 19 vessels representing four nations; among them was *Samuel Chase.*

At daybreak on 7 November, when these vessels were about 33 miles off Cape Palos, Spain, the group suffered its first attack. The position was 155 miles from Algiers. Transport *Thomas Stone* received a torpedo hit on her port side. The explosion buckled her stern and disabled her propeller and rudder, and killed or wounded nine sailors. She was forced to drop out of convoy. Another torpedo passed within 50 yards of *Samuel Chase.* Commander Heimer of *Chase,* mindful of the Coast Guard's normal mission of rescue, sought permission from Captain Edgar, who commanded the transport group, to take *Stone* in tow. Citing the order that vessels damaged in convoy must be left behind, Captain Edgar refused. Commander Heimer then proposed to take off the troops, but this suggestion was likewise rejected.

*Stone,* abandoned by the rest, was in no immediate danger of sinking, but had no propulsion. A tug from Gibraltar and two destroyers were sent to assist her. Captain Bennehoff decided to boat his troops then and there, to the extent possible, so as not to miss the assault. It was a courageous decision. Major Oakes and about 800 officers and men, comprising three assault waves, embarked in 24 landing craft for the 155 mile trip. Captain Edgar was notified of this move. Conducted by *HM* corvette *Spey,* which had stood by, the small craft nevertheless encountered difficulties; breakdowns were frequent and the landing boats took water in the mounting seas. Finally, all troops and equipment were taken on board *Spey.* They made

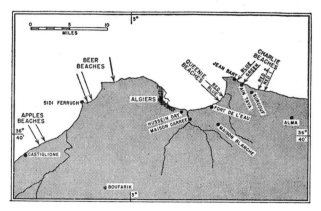

ASSAULT BEACHES AT ALGIERS

Algiers as the fighting ceased. *Stone* was towed to anchor off Algiers, arriving at 1030 on 11 November.

While *Thomas Stone* was thus in trouble, the rest of the convoy steamed on. The Task Force was divided into three main groups designated "Apples", "Beer", and "Charlie", each with a specific area of attack. Group Charlie, to which *Samuel Chase* belonged, will receive our principal attention. It was to effect landings to the east of Algiers Bay and Cape Matifou. "Apples" (all British) would handle landings near Castiglione which was 20 miles west of Algiers, and "Beer" was assigned the area between "Apples" sector and Algiers.

On 8 November, shortly after midnight, Group Charlie moved to a point about 4,000 yards from the beaches. *Chase* and *Almaack* had all their boats launched in about an hour; *Leedstown* encountered delays from equipment breakdown. *Chase's* first wave landed on the beach at 0118. The greatest threat to Group Charlie was a battery of four 7½-inch guns at Cape Matifou. This fort turned its searchlights on the ships and opened fire which was returned by a British destroyer. The fort was finally silenced. The boat waves, however, moved in without opposition, and there was little delay or confusion. After the last wave had departed, the transports preparatory to unloading equipment approached to about a mile offshore.

United States commandos were the first to land for the initial assault. Then followed the infantry, artillery, and tanks. Once the beachhead was consolidated, the troops marched quickly inland, and soon the invaders held all the approaches to

Algiers—rail, highway, and air. The batteries at Cape Matifou and nearby Fort d'Estrees did not interfere with the landings, but the commandos assigned to take the installation at Cape Matifou had been unsuccessful. These two batteries were later bombarded by *HMS Bermuda* and dive-bombed by carrier planes. Americans later marched in to the fort. The airdrome at Maison Blanche capitulated at 0827 and soon thereafter Allied planes from Gibraltar were using it. French troops put up little more than token resistance as gunfire neared the city of Algiers. Sixteen hours after the initial landings, Algiers surrendered.

Inexperience took its toll in this operation, and most of the landing craft were lost as the surf increased during the afternoon. Of all the landing boats from the three transports and the United States merchant ship *Exceller* which carried equipment, only two of ten LCMs, five of sixty LCPs, and one LCV remained. Seven of these boats belonged to *Samuel Chase*.

All French resistance in the Algiers sector ceased on 8 November at about 1900 when General Ryder concluded an oral armistice with Admiral Darlan of the French Navy. Actually, in comparison with landings elsewhere, this operation had been fairly tranquil. As this local armistice went into effect, however, the Germans took over and Group Charlie was subjected to a terrific dive-bombing and torpedo attack by eight German planes. Their chief targets were the transports, which Captain Edgar kept at anchor because of their combined volume of antiaircraft fire.

Escorts went into action. *HMS Cowdray*, a destroyer, suffered a bomb hit and had to be beached. *Exceller* received minor damage from a near miss. One aerial torpedo struck *Leedstown's* stern, destroying her steering gear and partly flooding her after section. While *Samuel Chase* was firing at the planes, two torpedoes were fired at her. As the first torpedo neared her bow it suddenly veered off and passed astern. The second continued straight for the ship but it, too, turned at the last moment and passed between the bow and the anchor chain!

During the night, Captain Edgar was ordered into Algiers Bay, and all vessels, except crippled *Leedstown* and corvette *HMS Samphire*, which stood by her, got under way by daybreak on 9 November. One German JU-88 attacked *Exceller* en route, causing two near misses. Commander Heimer of *Samuel Chase* could not resist trying to assist a stricken vessel in true Coast Guard fashion, but his suggestion to Captain Edgar that he tow *Leedstown* to Algiers Roads was turned down flatly.

*Leedstown*, now a "sitting duck", was attacked at 1255 by two German planes. Three near misses opened seams and increased the previous damage. Fifteen minutes later she was struck on the starboard side amidships by two torpedoes from a submarine or plane, and immediately listed to starboard. Without reasonable prospect of saving the vessel or landing more cargo, the 500 men on board abandoned ship at 1320. Another bombing at 1615 sank her in 20 fathoms, southwest of Matifou.

Upon arrival at Algiers Bay, several of the Group were ordered into the harbor. The rest, except *Samuel Chase* and *Dempo* entered that afternoon. These two ships anchored about two miles southwest of Cape Matifou while awaiting their turn, and were subjected to another bombing from the air. Two near misses damaged *Dempo* slightly. Commander Heimer got *Samuel Chase* under way promptly, and by excellent handling of his ship, avoided damage when she was attacked simultaneously by two torpedo planes. *Chase* and *Dempo* steamed into the harbor the following morning.

During the earlier landings from *Samuel Chase*, a similarity in the names of two beaches caused a small Coast Guard patrol of about 45 men to go to an unspecified beach position. Ensign McLin in command of the patrol was assisted by Chief Boatswain's Mate Hunter Wood, the well known artist. This beach party handled cargo and performed other tasks without rest for long periods. They suffered bombing and strafing attacks on the beach; hid in fox holes; and watched while the Axis bombers were making it hot for the transports. Some of the landing craft bringing in equipment and troops became disabled and, wading deep into cold water, the group hauled the boats in to the beach for repairs. On completion of the work they were ordered to a nearby beach to join another party which, they discovered, was not there.

These Coast Guardsmen reached the other beach just in time to witness the torpedoing of *Leeds-town*. By that time a heavy surf was running. The men of the torpedoed vessel took to life rafts, which floated directly toward the beach where Wood and his men were waiting. Many survivors were thrown from their rafts into the sea, and there was sure to be more trouble when the rafts hit the rocks offshore. Members of the beach party tried to get the survivors to steer the rafts before they hit the surf so as to avoid being battered. They swam out in the icy water with lines to tie to the rafts to enable them to be pulled to shore with the survivors clinging to the sides. In the surf the rafts were tossed into the air, dumping their passengers into the water with danger of being crushed by their own rafts. Thus, the beach party engaged in life saving for five hours without regard for their own safety, fighting against a very strong undertow. Finally, all 480 survivors were pulled to safety, but there were broken bones, contusions and shock, and many survivors had to struggle to keep afloat.

Soldiers from a nearby town, and some French and Arab natives, later joined to assist in the rescue. The French were very cooperative. Even children were at the waterfront with bottles of wine and brandy which they offered the men as they were dragged ashore. Not until the next day did Hunter Wood discover that he had gone to the wrong beach, and so, fortunately, had been on the spot to rescue the torpedoed sailors.

*Samuel Chase* was unloaded by her own remaining boats during the next five days, much of the time under air attack. The ship's complement fought these attacks gallantly, and were credited with having downed three German bombers. The transport received commendation from the British Admiralty for gallantry in action.

While this action was taking place at Algiers, the Center Naval Task Force of British ships, including two former Coast Guard cutters, were carrying out the assaults on Oran and nearby Arzeu, farther to the west. The Army troops landed were mostly Americans. Landings in the Arzeu area proceeded satisfactorily with little or no opposition, though there was sporadic firing. However, as troops worked inland, they encountered stiff resistance at St. Cloud and Fleurus. All resistance near Arzeu was overcome by afternoon of 8 November, and 36 hours later the entire area was well in hand.

The landings west of Oran proceeded as smoothly as those at Arzeu. There was some opposition from two forts, one of which was silenced with bombardment by *HMS Rodney*. The ex-cutters, renamed by the British *Hartland* and *Walney*, carrying anti-sabotage teams of United States soldiers, made a raid into Oran Harbor similar to that at Safi. This foray was executed against terrific odds with the greatest of courage and heroism, but ended disastrously with *Walney* sunk and *Hartland* burned and sunk. Half the men in *Hartland* were killed by point blank gunnery, explosions, and fire.

By 1630 on 8 November, United States Army Spitfires were using the Tafaraoui airdrome 15 miles south of Oran. The next day, two French destroyers sortied out of Oran to fight, but they were put out of action by British warships. Some resistance areas inland were encountered and controlled. On the morning of 10 November, the pincer movement began to exert pressure against Oran and the well-fortified French positions there. Oran surrendered that morning after two columns of troops had entered the city.

*Samuel Chase*, with *Leedstown* survivors on board, and *Almaack* and *Dempo*, comprising what remained of Captain Edgar's Transport Division (except *Exceller* which was not ready to sail), departed Algiers at 1800 on 12 November. They proceeded to Gibraltar and were joined by three or four British transports. Here they formed a convoy under command of Captain Edgar, escorted by British escort carriers *Argus* and *Avenger* and five destroyers.

At 0314 on 15 November, when 120 miles west of Gibraltar, the convoy ran into a concentration of U-boats. *Almaack, Ettrick,* and *Avenger* were torpedoed in rapid succession. *Avenger* blew up with a tremendous flash and roar, a most terrifying spectacle, and went down with almost all hands. She was only a few hundred yards astern of *Samuel Chase*, and heat from the explosion could be felt on board the latter. *Almaack* reached Gibraltar safely under tow and was salvaged, but *Ettrick* sank. *Samuel Chase* remained the only unscathed transport of Division Eleven. She received the nickname of *"Lucky Chase."* With Captain Edgar still embarked, she reached Greenock on 21 November, and returned later to Algiers with reinforcements. The Coast Guard lost no ships in Operation "Torch."

With the successful Allied conquest of French North Africa, the Germans were put on the defensive, and the Allies were able to follow through with their plans for the liberation of the enslaved nations of Europe. Not only was this part of the world prevented from becoming a starting point from which the Axis could initiate an attack on the Atlantic coasts of the Americas, but once in Allied hands, northern and western Africa became a springboard from which the Allied attack was launched against Sicily and on to the mainland of Europe. Operation "Torch" had accomplished its mission.

# Chapter 16

# LANDINGS IN SICILY AND ITALY

WITH OPERATION "TORCH" successfully concluded, and General Montgomery and his British Eighth Army pushing the Axis forces rapidly westward in Tunisia, things were definitely looking up for the Western Allies as 1943 began. The Battle of the Atlantic, while still critical, had eased up a bit. The Russians had taken the offensive against the German hordes. It was vital that the Allies determine the next move expeditiously and carefully to exploit their successes.

The famous Casablanca Conference between the Combined Chiefs of Staff (United States and Britain), President Roosevelt, and Prime Minister Churchill was called in January 1943 to determine the grand strategy and to resolve differences of view, of which there were many. A cross-channel invasion of France from England was discussed, but views were widely divergent, and the Conference ended without a definite commitment on such a move. A strategic compromise of importance was reached involving the postponement of the cross-channel invasion until after 1943; retention of American initiative in the Pacific theatres; and air bombing of Germany. But action of some sort in Europe during 1943 was a "must." Closing immediately with the Germans in Western Europe or Southern France would have been desirable had it been possible with the resources then available. It was not. The United States was still involved in a vast mobilization. The Combined Chiefs of Staff pondered whether this country had the strength at that time to move directly into Italy, and considered whatever might be a better alternative.

On 19 January it was decided that the best and most practical move would be the occupation of Sicily, in order to secure the Mediterranean line of communications; divert German troops from the Russian front; increase pressure on Italy; and to make possible the enlistment of Turkey as an active ally.

The next day a rough plan was formulated for the use of a British force mounted in the Near East, and an American force mounted in North Africa. Two days later, D-day for Operation "Husky", as it was termed, was set for 25 July. On 23 January, just before the Conference ended, Lieutenant General Eisenhower received this directive from the Combined Chiefs of Staff:

> An attack against Sicily will be launched in 1943 with the target date as the period of the favorable July moon. . . .
>
> You are to be the Supreme Commander, with General Alexander as Deputy Commander in Chief. . . . Admiral of the Fleet Cunningham is to be the naval and Air Chief Marshal Tedder the air commander.
>
> You will submit to the C.C.S. your recommendations for the officers to be appointed Western and Eastern Task Force Commanders.
>
> In consultation with General Alexander you will set up at once a special operational and administrative staff . . . for planning and preparing the operation.

At the time of this decision, the Tunisian campaign was still under way and it was assumed that it would not end before 1 May. Until then, there could be no predictions about what troops, ships, and staging areas would be available for Operation "Husky." Planning, therefore, was difficult. General Eisenhower set up his planning staff, elements of which were necessarily widely separated geographically. D-day had been determined on 13 April, but it was not until 3 May that the top planners reached agreement on the method, timing, and locations of the assault on Sicily.

In May, the President, the Prime Minister, and the Combined Chiefs of Staff met again in Washington, D.C. At this conference it was decided to extend Allied influence in the Mediterranean to the point where Italy would be forced to withdraw from the war.

The proposed assault had to be made during a particular phase of a waxing moon; paratroops preferred dropping in moonlight, and ground forces wanted to go ashore in the dark of the moon so as to have their beachheads secured by daybreak. The day finally chosen was 10 July 1943, earlier than the original date. Working out details of the plan occupied several more weeks.

The overall plan finally formulated called for a Western Naval Task Force under Vice Admiral Henry Kent Hewitt, USN, including some British elements, and an Eastern Naval Task Force under command of Vice Admiral Sir Bertram Ramsay, RN, which included certain American units. The Western Force was to assume responsibility for the attack west-northwest of the southern apex of the Sicilian triangle, while the Eastern Force would attack that apex and the coast on its eastern side. American and British divisions would be put ashore to establish beachheads from which a wider base would be established preliminary to capture of the Augusta, Catania, and Gerbini airfields. Forces would then move across Sicily to capture Palermo in the northwest, and Messina in the northeast, the latter a prime objective. Then the two armies would maneuver to trap the enemy north and west of Mount Etna and prevent its escape to Italy.

During the months preceding this campaign, the Task Forces were being organized and their personnel trained. One group underwent intensive training in Chesapeake Bay; the Canadian First Division trained in Scotland. Other forces were trained in North Africa. Rear Admiral Richard L. Conolly, USN, received the new command of Landing Craft and Bases Northwest African Waters, and established his training center at Arzeu, Algeria.

The Western Naval Task Force, charged with landing General Patton's 7th Army on the beaches between Punta Braccetto and Torre di Gaffe, was divided into three Attack Forces.

DIME Force (TF 81), commanded by Rear Admiral John L. Hall, USN, with the 1st Infantry Division (Major General Terry Allen, USA), one combat team of the 2nd Armored Division, and one Ranger battalion, was supported by the U.S. light cruisers *Savannah* and *Boise* and 13 destroyers. This force would handle landings at Gela. A Floating Reserve under Captain K. S. Reed, USN, carried two combat teams from the 2nd Armored Division (Major General Hugh J. Gaffey, USA), and one from the 1st Division. This operated with DIME Force.

CENT Force (TF 85), in command of Rear Admiral Alan Kirk, USN, transported the 45th Infantry Division (Major General Troy Middleton, USA) with the light cruiser *Philadelphia* and 16 destroyers, and was to effect landings at Scoglitti.

JOSS Force (TF 86), under Admiral Conolly, with the 3rd Infantry Division (Major General Lucian K. Truscott, USA) and two Ranger battalions, was supported by light cruisers *Brooklyn* and *Birmingham* and eight destroyers. The objective of this Force was Licata. The 9th Division was held in reserve in North Africa.

The Eastern Naval Task Force transported General Montgomery's Eighth Army of five divisions, and was to put this army ashore between Pozzallo and Cape Murro di Porco.

Operating with these Task Forces were the new 328-foot "landing ships, tank" (LST). They had large bow ramps and were built for grounding on beaches where their ramps could be lowered. Tanks, guns, and vehicles could then roll directly onto the beaches. In Sicily there were "false beaches" or off-beach bars which hindered landings by LSTs, but they had enough water over them to allow 112-foot LCTs (landing craft, tank) to pass over them. Overcoming this obstacle required ingenuity. A causeway of pontoons between the false beaches and the shore was devised and used to good advantage, allowing LSTs to discharge vehicles onto the causeway and thence to shore. Pontoons were brought from the United States, assembled at Arzeu and Bizerte, and slung along the sides of LSTs or towed to their destination. However, there were not enough pontoons to handle all the traffic. Some LCTs which had large hinged sections cut in their topsides, were secured athwartships at the ramp of an LST, and a second LCT was secured athwartships to the first. Tanks were driven across the first LCT into the second, and then transported to shore by the latter.

The LCI(L)s (landing craft, infantry, large) (hereafter designated merely as LCIs), also made their first appearance in Operation "Husky." These were the basic troop carriers, but some were equipped for special duties. These vessels were about 158 feet long, displaced 400 tons, and carried guns on deck. Each had quarters for 25 crewmen and 210 troops. The bridge resembled the conning tower of an old-fashioned submarine. There were two fretted ramps, one on either side of the bow. These were thrust forward and downward allowing troops to disembark into shoal water or onto the beach. However, these ramps proved insufficiently robust for landing in heavy surf and sometimes were wrenched off.

Coast Guard-manned vessels took part in the operations of the Western Naval Task Force. Mobilization and training had progressed considerably in the interval between Operations "Torch" and "Husky," with the result that the Coast Guard was able to participate to a far greater extent in the latter. Attack transports *Joseph T. Dickman, Leonard Wood,* and *Samuel Chase* engaged in the assault phase of the Sicilian campaign, together with the 175-foot submarine chasers *PC-545* and *PC-556,* and the following Coast Guard-manned landing craft except as noted:

| | | | |
|---|---|---|---|
| LST-16 | LCI(L)-85 | LCI(L)-92 | LCI(L)-321 |
| *LST-326 | LCI(L)-86 | LCI(L)-93 | LCI(L)-322 |
| LST-327 | LCI(L)-87 | LCI(L)-94 | LCI(L)-323 |
| LST-331 | LCI(L)-88 | LCI(L)-95 | LCI(L)-324 |
| *LST-381 | LCI(L)-89 | LCI(L)-96 | LCI(L)-325 |
| LCI(L)-83 | LCI(L)-90 | LCI(L)-319 | LCI(L)-326 |
| LCI(L)-84 | LCI(L)-91 | LCI(L)-320 | LCI(L)-349 |
| | | | LCI(L)-350 |

* Anzio Only

In addition, Coast Guardsmen in varying numbers served with Navy crews in transports *Arcturus, Barnett, Bellatrix, Betelgeuse, Charles Carroll, Dorothea L. Dix,* and *William P. Biddle.*

During the build-up stage, submarines of the Italian Navy were not idle. While there was no Italian fleet action, the undersea craft attacked Allied vessels in the harbors of Alexandria, Gibraltar, Suda, and Algiers. For the most part, the Italian surface navy stayed in port, though it performed some escort duty and had occasional encounters. Allied bombing of Italian harbors made it difficult even for the vessels in port. By 1 July 1943, about 10 per cent of the Italian Navy personnel had been killed, taken prisoner, or were missing. A few Axis submarines succeeded

in sinking two American LSTs and about six other vessels at sea in the Mediterranean, but these attackers were almost wiped out by Allied counterattacks. Three U-boats and nine Italian submarines were sunk within a three week period.

Meanwhile, Allied vessels assigned to Operation "Husky" were assembling at various points. The Tunisian campaign had ended on 13 May, and thereafter full concentration could be given the assault on Sicily. The island of Pantelleria, 60 miles south-southwest of the western coast of Sicily, was given several days of intensive air bombing and naval bombardment. It surrendered on 11 June, thus giving the Allies an advance airdrome. The Northwest African Air Force bombed continental and Sardinian airfields to prevent their use by the enemy. They won air supremacy over the Axis in this vital area and destroyed naval and air bases in Sicily. They struck as far north as Leghorn, Italy. Sicilian airports were mercilessly bombed. Few airfields were operative at the time of the main attack.

The Western Naval Task Force was assembled at, or staged through, six harbors along the North African coast between Oran and Sfax. CENT Force gathered at Oran; DIME Force at Algiers. Admiral Hall, in command of the latter, flew his flag in *Samuel Chase.* CENT Force, well equipped, crossed the ocean in 28 combat-loaded attack transports and cargo ships in two convoys, each with a cruiser as escort, and with nine destroyers between them. *Ancon* was Admiral Kirk's flagship. Admiral Conolly's JOSS Force of 276 vessels assembled at Bizerte, with *Biscayne* as flagship. Other elements were at Sousse and Sfax.

Under Admiral Hewitt's command were 580 ships and beaching craft, plus 1,124 landing craft which these vessels carried. Under command of Admiral Ramsay were 795 of the first and 715 of the second to handle the Eastern landings and the follow-up convoys, aside from the covering forces. American ground forces numbered about 228,000, and British about 250,000. If measured by the strength of the initial assault, it was the greatest amphibious operation ever undertaken.

The routes of approach of these various task groups and support forces had to be worked out carefully and thoroughly so that they would not interfere with each other. At the outset, routes were used which, it was hoped, would indicate to

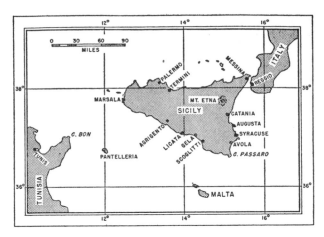

SICILY

the enemy that landings were to be *east* of Sicily. First went the LCIs of the Western Naval Task Force, then an Eastern Naval Task Force convoy carrying the Canadian First Division. DIME Force followed, CENT Force was next, and JOSS Force was last. These movements started on 7 and 8 July, at various specified times from the dispersed locations. Admiral of the Fleet Sir Andrew B. Cunningham, RN, Supreme Naval Commander, sent an inspiring message to every ship in the fleet as it was headed toward Gozo, off the northwest end of Malta, on 9 July.

The weather had been fair for days, but as the ships approached Gozo a nasty, steep sea made up and the wind increased to a moderate gale. Five miles west of Gozo the LSTs and LCIs split up to join their respective forces. Approach dispositions for the three United States attack forces were formed and, even under such adverse weather conditions, the difficult maneuvers were performed in a thoroughly seamanlike manner. Soldier passengers in their quarters below decks became miserable and seasick, and naval and army officers were greatly concerned lest conditions might prevent the scheduled landings. But the Force Aerographer predicted that the wind would die down in time, and plans remained unchanged. Some courses were altered, there were some stragglers, but the vessels proceeded, and the wind fortunately began to moderate at 2230 on the night of 9 July.

As the armada moved toward its objective that day, the convoys were sighted by enemy planes and all German troops in Sicily were alerted.

From then on, contact reports were frequent, and before any landing craft left the transports a state of emergency had been declared in Sicily. Therefore, the enemy was not taken by surprise in the precise sense, but time was short and there was enough surprise for Allied purposes.

The target area of the Western Naval Task Force was the shore of the Gulf of Gela. This shore extends 37 miles from Torre di Gaffe to Punta Braccetto, and includes the small cities of Gela and Licata and the fishing village of Scoglitti. About half of this shore is sandy beach. Rocky points and low cliffs make up the rest. Behind the shores are fertile coastal plains beyond which are mountains.

The attack groups of this Task Force separated in the still rough waters for their rendezvous stations. Three British submarines had reached their positions much earlier. These were waiting quietly in the enemy waters for this moment, and as the ships steamed in toward their three landing areas, the submarines surfaced, and guided the silent transports into their anchorages. It was past midnight on 10 July, all was proceeding according to plan. The ships anchored close enough to shore for the men to see the fires burning from the allied bombs that had been dropping all day long. Battle stations in every ship were manned, and the troops and boat crews were ready.

President Roosevelt assured Pope Pius XII that churches and religious institutions would, to the extent possible, be spared the devastations of war and that the neutral status of Vatican City and other papal domains throughout Italy would be respected. General Eisenhower, in a broadcast, warned the French people in France to remain calm and avoid reprisals through premature action, pointing out that the landings in Sicily were the first steps in the liberation of the European continent.

Following the bombing attacks, which had knocked out several important enemy airfields, destroyed a large number of Axis aircraft, and disrupted local transport and communications, American and British airborne troops descended on the southeast corner of Sicily. Intensive air attacks by Allied forces accompanied the invasion, and widespread fighter cover for the landings was supplied. In all, about 4,000 aircraft were involved.

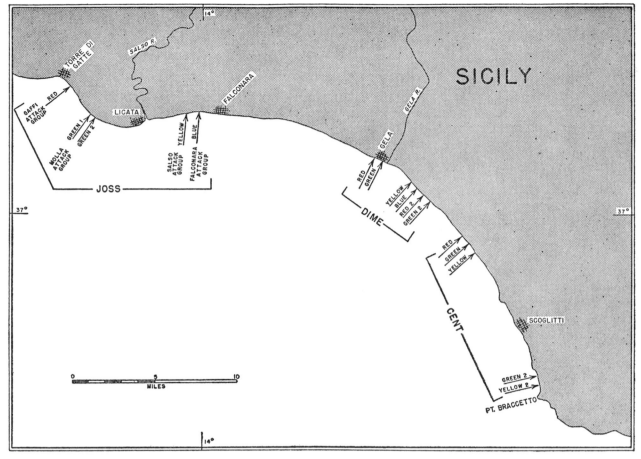

AMERICAN LANDING AREA IN SICILY

Let us now see how the Coast Guard fitted into the scheme of things. JOSS Force, the north-westerly group which had Licata as its objective, included LCI(L) Flotilla Four under the command of Commander Miles H. Imlay, USCG. The landing position of this Flotilla was on the left flank of the beach area. Included in JOSS Force was *LST-327*. DIME Force, the center group, which had Gela as its responsibility, included our old friends *Samuel Chase*, flagship of Admiral Hall, in command of Commander Heimer, and *Joseph T. Dickman* (Commander Harwood). The transport group was commanded by Captain C. D. Edgar, USN, in *Barnett*. CENT Force, under command of Rear Admiral A. G. Kirk, USN, attacked Scoglitti and its adjacent beaches. This was the southerly group in which *Leonard Wood* (Commander O'Neill), played an important part. Also attached to this Force were *LST-16* and *LST-331*.

Our immediate concern will be the operation of DIME Force with its twelve transports including *Chase* and *Dickman*. After moving in off Gela, shortly after midnight on the morning of 10 July, the transports anchored at 0030 in line paralleling the beach about six miles distant, with the LCI and LST lines astern, and with the gunfire support cruisers in their assigned areas on each flank. The plan was for this force to take Gela in the initial phase, first putting Rangers ashore and then the 1st Division. It was hoped that this Division would organize and deploy quickly and capture the Ponte Olivo airfield which was on the plain about six miles inland. It was found out later that the enemy had made special dispositions there to prevent this. According to the plan, the 1st Division would then fan out on the plain and meet other elements of the Army before moving farther inland.

The Rangers were brought into Gela by *Joseph*

*T. Dickman* and two Belgian transports, *Prince Charles* and *Prince Leopold*. Their assignment was a tough one. They were to land on two beaches on either side of a long, 1,000-foot steel pier which jutted out from right under a cliff into the roadstead. It had been hoped that this pier could be seized and used for unloading vessels, especially the LSTs. The scout boat was launched at 0044 and quickly located these beaches two hours before H-hour. The small boats formed their circles about the transports and came alongside; the soldiers clambered down the cargo nets into the heaving, bobbing craft. By 0125 *Dickman* had lowered 30 loaded landing craft, and the Belgian transports soon added 14 British landing boats. A half hour later their subchaser control boat arrived and led the Rangers in. At 0215—right on time—the boats of the DIME and JOSS Forces headed for the beaches. Due to the adverse weather there was an hour's delay in the CENT Force area before the boats of that force, too, raced in for the assault.

*Dickman* had been assigned as a task group leader. Her group was made up of the two Belgian transports, some LCIs and LSTs, one PC boat as the boat group control, and two SCs assigned for secondary control and close fire support. *Dickman's* job was to land not only the special force of Rangers, but also combat engineers and a chemical war service battalion which was to provide artillery support. There was also a unit of the RAF, complete with trucks, bombs, lubricating oil, gasoline, and mats for the airfield.

The paratroops had some light to effect their landings before the moon set; the shipborne units landed afterward in the darkest period. Returning planes passed overhead, flying at about masthead height. Firing on the island could be observed from *Dickman*, particularly tracers firing at the planes. Bonfires were burning on the shore.

*Dickman* could ready a complete unit—lower them and have them ready to start in to the beach—in about twenty minutes. But an hour and a half was available. It was necessary to get the boats clear and dispersed so that if shelling began, casualties would be lighter and most of the men could still carry out their mission. It was also desirable to let the boat control vessels arrive in position so that the landing boats could form and go on with them. Patrol craft were somewhat late in

arriving due to the heavy weather, so the boats went in on their own, but fortunately, the patrol craft were able to catch up with them. *Dickman* kept track of her boats in her radar screens, and was able to assist in their arriving at the right place on the beach.

Getting the first boats in was a very critical phase of the operation because of the difficulty small boats have in running into unmarked beaches. Running six miles with unreliable compasses could cause the boats to get off course as much as two miles. Following the initial waves, landing craft from the transports moved in to the beaches in orthodox fashion and the landings were under way in full force.

The boats went in in waves. The boats with the Rangers formed a line abreast and landed simultaneously on the beach. Twenty-five minutes later the battalion of combat engineers went in. Next were the LCIs carrying the chemical warfare unit with their mortars and immediate ammunition. Then *Dickman* sent some Army DUKWs (amphibious personnel carriers) loaded with ammunition for the immediate support of the troops. The boats ran into some fire on the way in, but the troops were able to get off successfully. One Army lieutenant was killed by machine gun fire. The heaviest fire was received by the boats just after they had retracted. Fortunately, however, the crews escaped with the loss of only one man killed and five wounded. Most of the wounded were able to return to their boats after receiving first aid on board ship.

Equipment loading continued after the first troops were sent in. Boats were assigned from *Oberon*, and some others were available from an LST which did not require them for her own immediate use. These were loaded with ammunition, and stood by awaiting word from the beach that the beachhead had been secured, and instructions on where to land.

There were numerous casualties on the beaches caused by vehicle mines which were planted very thickly. Most of the casualties to the troops, however, were due to personnel mines. Machine guns and small calibre high explosives accounted for some others.

The troops were an unusually able unit, mostly veterans of Tunis and Oran, and most had been especially selected. They immediately went in and around the town of Gela, caught the Italian Staff in their beds, and captured 600 prisoners before daylight. They had so firmly secured the town that Colonel Darby, commanding the Rangers, was able to return to *Dickman* for a noon visit.

*Samuel Chase* was given a key assignment in landing important segments of the Seventh Army near Gela. She accomplished her mission without the loss of a man. Luck, good preparation, and ability to handle small boats as a result of long periods of training were responsible in no small measure.

Combat air patrol over the Gela landings consisted of only two to eight planes at best on 10 and 11 July, and sometimes there were none. These planes were of little help. No Air Force officer with Admiral Hewitt had any authority over them, and the Army fighter-director team in *Samuel Chase* was green at the business. At one time 32 German planes flew over the transport area without interference from Allied fighters that should have been affording protection. But the fire support for the landings from six ships, four organic field artillery battalions, and three infantry cannon companies was excellent. The fire-direction center on board flagship *Samuel Chase* and division artillery headquarters enjoyed close coordination. No troops were hit by the heavy volume of allied fire from various directions—a fact which attests the efficiency of the fire control system and the accuracy of the observers and gun crews.

The LSTs engaged in unloading tanks and heavy vehicles got into difficulty. Sand, too soft for heavy vehicles to operate in successfully, and general beach congestion due to a pile-up of supplies and vehicles, caused considerable trouble. The transports got their men ashore, but urgently needed equipment became available too slowly. Often Army men in unloading details on the beach would be called into action, leaving Navy and Coast Guard men handling the landing craft to do their unloading themselves. Yet, all LSTs finished unloading by 1600 on 11 July.

There were two bombing attacks on the Gela transports in the afternoon of D-day which did little damage, though an LST was destroyed. Air raids of great ferocity on 11 July were well co-ordinated with attacking enemy tanks. Possibly 30 Ju-88s bombed the transport area at 1540.

Liberty ship *Robert Rowan* of the first follow-up convoy was hit by one of these or by artillery on the beach. Resulting fires could not be controlled. Lying only 1,000 yards from *Dickman*, her cargo of ammunition began to explode and she was abandoned forthwith, without loss of life. *Dickman's* boats picked up 92 survivors; other boats and DUKWs rescued the rest. At 1702 *Rowan* exploded with a tremendous detonation, settled to the bottom in shallow water, and burned for hours.

It was in the Gela area that the heaviest resistance to the Sicily landings was met. Opposing the landings was an Axis force estimated at between 200,000 to 300,000 men under nominal command of Italian General Alfredo Guzzoni, but actually controlled by German General Hans Hube. Some German units supported by tanks, and a considerable force of Italian infantry, were beaten back by U. S. troops. The first Axis counterattack came on 11 July, when the 4th Italian Division, supported by a hundred German tanks, struck the American beachhead at Gela. The attack penetrated to within half a mile of the beach at one point but was finally driven off by artillery and naval gunfire. After this attack, Axis resistance in the southern area diminished rapidly. Coastal fighting revealed some poor enemy fighting qualities, and indicated that Italian morale was extremely low. The civilian inhabitants were, for the most part, friendly and cooperative toward the Allied forces.

At about 1800 on 12 July, *Samuel Chase* with Admiral Hall on board, six other transports including *Joseph T. Dickman*, seven destroyers, and other vessels departed for Algiers.

Meanwhile, CENT Force was undertaking the landings on each side of the fishing town of Scoglitti, about 15 miles southeast of Gela. Because these landing were nearest to the Comiso and Biscari airfields, some regarded this as the most important of the attacks. Troops assigned to this force numbered nearly 26,000—over 6,000 more than those landed by DIME Force. The assaults were at two groups of beaches seven miles apart and in each case backed by sand dunes. Behind the coast lay the Camerina plain. The allied planners gave these beaches New England names. The northern beaches were called "Wood's Hole"— *Leonard Wood* was flagship of transports in that section. Those to the south were named "Bailey's

Beach" since Captain W. O. Bailey, USN, commanded the transports in that area.

As CENT Force steamed into position off these beaches, fires and gunfire flashes which were observed indicated that the Air Force was attending to Camerina plain. The Wood's Hole ships anchored about five miles offshore in two lines parallel to the shore. Captain W. B. Phillips, USN, senior transport commander, believed that, in the adverse weather, boats could not be made ready with their troops in time to meet H-hour at 0245. He requested an hour's postponement. Admiral Kirk granted the delay, and this confused the landing craft and scout boats which were, themselves, ready.

Six rocket-mounted scout boats were assigned to support *Leonard Wood's* initial boat waves with a barrage before the landing. Two of the rocket craft sank due to damage in lowering. The remaining four fired 84 rockets into the beach and followed these with smoke bombs to obscure the vision of enemy snipers and to guard against illumination by flares. *Leonard Wood* was the smartest transport in boat handling. She got 28 LCVPs of the first four waves into the water and loaded by 0105, a full hour and a half before the others. She was the first transport at Scoglitti to get her boats ashore, despite heavy seas. After a long wait, the first waves grounded 20 yards off the beach, right on time at 0345. Great difficulty was experienced in swinging the tank lighters, and it was particularly difficult to load vehicles with the boats surging alongside the rolling ship. But the troops which she landed left the boats as fast as the surge of the craft and the surf allowed, and moved rapidly across the beach.

Some of the equipment unloading was done under trying conditions. One tank lighter broached when partially unloaded, and the men were helpless to do anything about it. To make up for that handicap, however, another lighter came in and was unloaded rapidly; she then towed off the one that had broached. Another boat, carrying in a 40-mm. gun, the gun's crew, and heavy ammunition, broached due to lack of proper equipment for removing its cargo expeditiously. Numerous attempts were made to save the boat. All removable gear worth salvaging was taken off. During the day, as other boats broached to, coxswains added their gear to the rest and left two men to keep continuous watch over the boats. Many boats, however, made their run to the beach, unloaded, backed off, and returned to the big ship for more troops and supplies.

Because they were little—or lucky—a good number of the small craft escaped unhurt even when pursued steadily by enemy gunfire. A beach marking boat from *Leonard Wood* set out to mark channels for the LSTs, LCIs, and other small craft. The beach marking crews indicated their first channel with buoys. This was deep enough for the LSTs. Another channel was good only for the LCIs and smaller craft. After this party completed its first assignment, and was leaving for the next, it encountered gunfire. Eventually, it had to withdraw because the attack became too heavy to permit work. Then a shore battery opened up on the boat, and the crew immediately headed out to sea. For fifteen minutes the gunfire continued to follow them but never fell closer than 35 yards.

The transports unloaded men, equipment, and supplies, and most of these got ashore safely. *Leonard Wood* and the others were under frequent attack for four days. *LST-16* (Lieutenant Rufus W. L. Horton, USCGR), was with the Wood's Hole group. While unloading, she discovered an enemy battery four miles distant and fired on it with apparent hits. A destroyer then opened fire on it and put it out of action. *LST-16* then went to Bailey's Beach and discharged DUKWs before beaching. On the 11th while beached and awaiting the construction of a pontoon causeway, she opened fire on several attacking enemy aircraft with uncertain results. After completely unloading, she transported ammunition and supplies, then left for Tunis on 15 July.

The other Coast Guard manned LST in CENT Force was *LST-331* (commanding officer unidentified, Executive Officer Lieutenant W. D. Strauch, Jr., USCG). She carried RAF personnel, trucks and other vehicles, as well as 240 tons of aviation gasoline and aviation equipment for serving aircraft after the capture of Comiso airfield. This vessel reached her assigned area off the beaches while waves were moving in.

On the morning of the 11th, an Axis medium bomber approached *LST-331's* port quarter at 3,000 feet and, while under fire from the LST's guns, dropped a stick of bombs 200 yards off the port bow. At twilight, with the moon to seaward silhouetting the transports for planes approaching the island, enemy planes dropped flares near the transports astern. The LSTs were at right angles to the shore under high sand dunes and they surprised several enemy pilots who were too intent on getting the transports. Holding her fire until two light bombers passed 100 feet above the water on the port side, *LST-331* opened with all available guns. When last seen, one bomber was on fire and losing altitude. Another plane which flew past the starboard side at about 40 feet was taken under fire, and sparks started from the plane as it crashed into the sea. Another approaching the bow at a 45° angle received 90 percent hits and burst into flames, crashing ashore. Despite these diversions, *LST-331* discharged all of her men, vehicles, and equipment by 1830 on 12 July. She then unloaded ammunition from *USS Procyon* and took it to the beaches. She left for Tunis on the 15th.

LCIs surged back and forth, day and night, during the process of getting men and equipment ashore, drawing fire with each new load of reserves taken in, and each load of wounded on the return trip. Beach conditions were poor. Many LCVPs and LCMs broached, and by noon of 11 July, only 66 of an original 175 boats were still serviceable. Supplies and equipment piled up on shore, many boats could not be unloaded for lack of personnel to handle their cargoes, and mechanized equipment bogged down in the soft sand. Occasional air attacks complicated matters.

Despite these handicaps, unloading was finally completed, and the equipment taken off the beach and rolled inland. The little town of Scoglitti was in our hands as D-day drew to a close. On the afternoon of the second day, the Comiso airfield, ten miles north from the coast, was captured. The 1st Battalion, 157th Regimental Combat Team had pushed in to the edge of the Camerina plain. On 12 July, because of a decisive defeat on the Gela plain, German forces began withdrawal from the CENT area as well as the DIME sector. Biscari airfield was taken on 14 July.

We shall now turn our attention to the operations at Licata, 25 miles to the northwestward of Scoglitti, and beyond Gela. Here JOSS Force, under Admiral Conolly, was conducting landings similar to those by the DIME and CENT Forces. Beacon submarine *HMS Safari* had arrived off Licata on 5 July. As the Force approached the area on 9 July, destroyer *Bristol* went ahead, located *Safari*, and took position five miles to seaward of her, and 15 miles from shore. The Force came up, struggling with wind and heavy seas, but with little difficulty took station off Licata.

JOSS Force was divided into four attack groups. The Gaffi Attack Group was to land the 7th Regimental Combat Team of the 3rd Division, which was to occupy the western section of the initial beachhead line. In this group were 7 LSTs, 17 LCIs, and 21 LCTs. The Molla Attack Group was to put the 3rd Ranger Battalion and the 2nd Battalion, 15th Regimental Combat Team, ashore four miles west of Licata, and these were to march on the town. The Salso Attack Group was to land the 1st and 3rd Battalions of the 15th Regimental Combat Team four miles east of Licata. Of these, half were to join the Rangers in a pincer movement against Licata, and the other half were to capture a strong point on a 980-foot hill a mile inshore. Falconara Attack Group were to land the 30th Regimental Combat Team two miles to the east of the Salso group. This team was to take the 1,407-foot Monte Desusino strong points and to contact CENT Force to the east. This group included landing and control craft—10 LSTs. The first wave of 8 LCIs was commanded by Lieutenant Commander A. C. Unger, USCG, and the second wave of 8 LCIs, 9 LCTs, and four SCs, and *PC-582* was commanded by Lieutenant Commander J. A. Bresnan, USCG. Each group had its fire support vessels and transports.

Landings were made in heavy seas and surf, and met varying degrees of resistance. The Gaffi group encountered severe machine gun fire on the beaches, and enemy dive-bombing attacks were vicious. There were fights against machine gun nests and pill boxes ashore, but opposition collapsed after seven hours of naval gunfire support which silenced the more troublesome artillery batteries. Licata was in American hands by 1130 on D-day, having put up no resistance of consequence; the Italian defenders of the town surrendered whenever they had the chance.

In these landings the Coast Guard was represented by *LST-327* (Lieutenant A. Volton, USCG), which landed men and vehicles via LCTs in the Salso and Falconara areas and made several trips from Bizerte with troops and equipment;

and by LCI(L) Flotilla Four which did outstanding work under Commander Imlay, who commanded the Flotilla.

The LCIs were new to this theatre of war. A flotilla of 76 of these craft was outfitted at Norfolk, Virginia, and made a 4,600 mile, 32-day trip across the Atlantic to North Africa in preparation for the landings in Sicily and Italy. The performance of these flat-bottomed landing boats dumbfounded their crews in the Atlantic crossing, for in general, the men who sailed them across had had no faith in them. But the boats went through rough weather with capacity cargoes of ammunition, and reached their destination in time for practice landings before setting out for Sicily.

Of these 76 LCIs, 24 were formed into LCI(L) Flotilla Four. These were Coast Guard-manned. Seventeen of them, known as the LCI Reserve Group, operated with JOSS Force at Licata. They came in with that force and anchored in the rendezvous area at 0200. They were later dispatched to the beaches with their troops and equipment and successfully accomplished their missions under heavy fire.

After disembarking the troops, the LCIs went back to the transport area and took part in antiaircraft defense during a heavy air raid. These vessels were then ordered back to their home ports for more troops to reinforce those they had landed. Maintaining full speed, they made the round trip in two days. During their absence the fighting had gone well, and they took their troops into Licata instead of beaching again. Some of the LCIs were assigned to bring still more troops; others were ordered to act as salvage vessels, messenger ships, and decoys. A few landed troops at Palermo when the American forces reached that port. This work continued until the ships were needed for the next invasion.

After the initial attack, Commander Imlay skillfully assisted in the support and maintenance of the Army at the port of Licata. There he labored tirelessly supervising the clearance of mines, and speedily prepared the port for handling the important equipment and supplies, in spite of continuous enemy fire. His leadership was brilliant. For his services in Sicily and for the outstanding performance of his LCIs, Commander Imlay was awarded the Legion of Merit.

Captain Harwood of *Joseph T. Dickman* also received the Legion of Merit. In addition to commanding that vessel, he also commanded the Naval Task Group which landed assault battalions directly on the beaches fronting Gela. By his sound judgment in planning, thorough indoctrination of his forces, and by his cool and skillful leadership under fire, the assault battalions were expeditiously landed and supported, thereby greatly contributing to the success of the invasion.

Everywhere, the American and British landings had been successful. Naval supporting fire had been extremely effective. After the beachheads had been secured, America's Seventh Army (203,204 officers and men as of 15 July) pushed on and by 18 July the southern half of the island had been taken. The Army overran the western portion of Sicily and entered Palermo on 22 July. Syracuse and Augusta had fallen to the British Army, and several airfields were in Allied possession.

Germany's Marshal Kesselring had conferred with Italy's General Guzzoni and had decided that nothing was to be done except fight a delaying action, despite the German Panzer Grenadiers and the Hermann Goering Division, which had been moved up to fight the invaders.

Kesselring flew back to Rome and informed Mussolini that failure of Italian troops made the defense of Sicily impossible. Hitler assumed that the Italian forces would be eliminated, and said the Germans alone could not push the enemy into the sea. Therefore, he stated the Germans would delay the advance and stop it west of Mount Etna. Axis forces were redisposed with this objective. But it rapidly became apparent to Axis commanders that they could not continue to hold the island, and that after the delaying action, evacuation of forces to the Italian mainland would be required. This whole concept was carried out completely.

Montgomery's Eighth Army found Catania plain a major obstacle, and there was sharp fighting there from 14 to 20 July. While the Allies were closing in on the eastern corner of Sicily, a move completed by 3 August, other important events were transpiring. On 19 July, Mussolini and Hitler met in northern Italy. Hitler berated his Axis partner who wanted more armored divisions and 2,000 more planes to defend Sicily.

Hitler could not spare them, though the 29th Panzer Grenadiers and the 1st Parachute Division were providing reinforcements. During the talks, word was received of the first bombing of Rome. That tipped the scales. Victor Emmanuel III told Mussolini on 20 July that Italy could not go on much longer. On 25 July, the King replaced Mussolini with Marshal Badoglio, and Mussolini was virtually arrested. More German divisions were pushed into Italy from France and Germany.

Italian and reinforced German troops formed a strong, continuous line from Catania around the western side of Mount Etna and to the northern coast and prepared for evacuation to Italy. The enemy put up stiff resistance and employed stubborn delaying tactics. The Allied Armies made slow progress from this point onward. Naval gunfire support was very helpful, but vicious fighting continued to the end. The Germans began their evacuation across the Strait of Messina on the night of 10 August. One week later, General Patton's foremost infantry patrol entered the city of Messina which was tattered, torn, and deserted. Tanks of the British Eighth Army rumbled in two hours later. Sicily had been conquered.

The Axis troops had been successfully evacuated by ferries of various kinds across the three- to ten-mile Strait of Messina, aided by an amazing absence of any really serious attempt by the Allies to stop it. "He who fights and runs away, may live to fight another day." And fight he did!

In reviewing the Sicilian campaign, Rear Admiral Harold Biesemeier, USN, has expressed the opinion that the heroes of the western landings were the crews of the landing craft and beaching craft. Admiral Morison has this to say in his *History of Naval Operations:*

> If landing and beaching craft crews had failed, the entire American part of Operation "Husky" would have failed, and the British would have been left to carry the war into Sicily unsupported. They did not fail: these young sailors performed marvels of valor and miracles of judgment. All honor, then, to these lads . . . since they proved themselves to be strong, brave and resourceful.

On 3 September 1943, Italy signed an armistice with Major General Walter Bedell Smith, USA, in the presence of General Eisenhower. Italy was then officially out of the war, but announcement of its capitulation was not made until 8 September, just nine hours before landings at Salerno had been scheduled.

An attack on the Italian mainland had been considered and discussed by the Combined Chiefs of Staff in May at the meeting in Washington. But definite plans had to await the outcome of the action in Sicily, as well as developments indicating the degree of precariousness of Italy's position. At first an attack at the foot of the "Italian boot" was weighed, but the successes in Sicily caused the Combined Chiefs of Staff to raise their sights. On 26 July, the day after the fall of Mussolini, Operation "Avalanche" was authorized, with Salerno as the target. General Eisenhower was directed to conduct the operation with the forces then under his command—and this directive was confirmed by the Quebec plenary conference held in mid-August *unless* the Combined Chiefs of Staff decided otherwise. Fortunately, they later decided otherwise and gave General Eisenhower additional forces.

As the time for the Salerno attack neared, the Italian Navy, less 49 combat ships which were destroyed, went over to join the Allies. Germany poured her troops into Italy to fight as if it were her own homeland. The Italian Army simply melted away. Italians cooperated with the Allies but were able to be of relatively little assistance.

Ground forces for the Salerno operation were organized into the Allied Fifth Army, and were placed under command of Lieutenant General Mark W. Clark, USA. This Army was divided into two corps—the United States Sixth (Major General E. J. Dawley, USA), and the British Tenth (Lieutenant General Sir Richard M. McCreery), each with two divisions and reserves. The fleet was under the over-all command of Admiral Cunningham, RN. Under him were the Western Naval Task Force (Admiral Hewitt), including all of the amphibious forces in the operation, and the Royal Navy Covering Forces. The two groups of the Task Force were the Northern Attack Force, chiefly British, commanded by Commodore G. N. Oliver, RN, and the Southern Attack Force under command of Admiral Hall. Admiral Conolly commanded the Amphibious Group which was to attack on the left flank of the Northern Force.

The object of the Western Naval Task Force

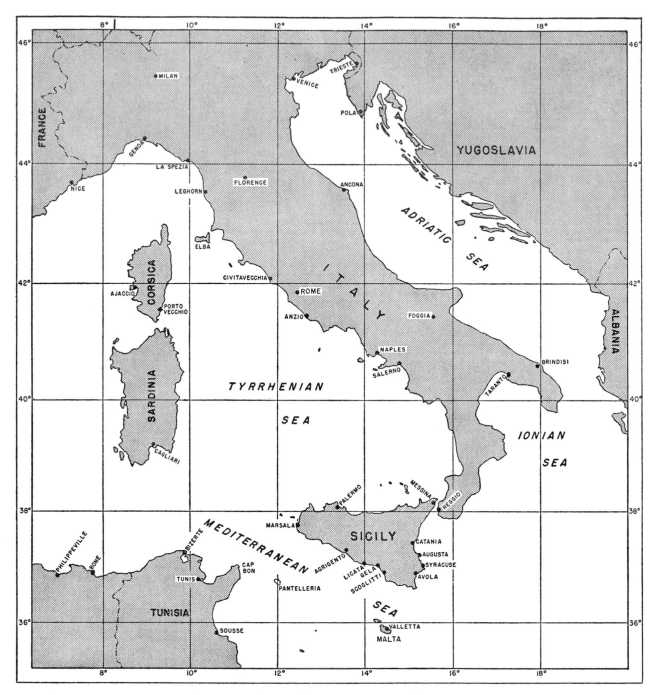

ITALY AND CENTRAL MEDITERRANEAN WATERS

was to land enough forces in the Gulf of Salerno to capture a bridgehead for Naples and to secure the neighboring airdromes. A small task group, partly American and partly British, and including two Dutch naval vessels, was assigned to occupy five islands off the Gulf of Naples.

For several weeks before the Allied Fifth Army invasion, Allied air forces had pounded road and rail communications in the Naples area. On the night before the invasion, the rail yards at Battapaglia and Eboli were hit with about 170 tons of bombs, and 160 more tons were dropped on the roads leading to the beaches at Salerno. On the day of the invasion and every day thereafter, Allied bombers of all types continued their efforts to tie up the rail and road system supplying enemy troops in the region of Naples. In contrast to Axis air activity over the Salerno bridgehead, fighter opposition in the other areas was light. Allied planes also continued to attack enemy communications, troop movements, and gun positions in the southern part of Italy where enemy opposition was encountered.

At about 0400 on 9 September, United States units of the Allied Fifth Army, together with British and Canadian forces, under protection and cover of the Royal Navy and the United States Navy, landed on the Italian mainland. The landings were made along the rim of Salerno Bay, some 40 miles southeast of Naples. United States forces disembarked south of the Sele River, 17 miles south of Salerno. British units disembarked north of the river. Rangers and Commandos also landed between Amalfi and Maiori, west of Salerno. Troops, guns, and vehicles were disembarked according to schedule, despite enemy air attacks on the convoys.

When the Allies landed at Salerno, the Germans were waiting for them. This was not due to any prescience on Marshal Kesselring's part. He knew that the beachhead at Salerno was at the effective limit of Allied fighter range from Sicilian bases and had made plans accordingly. The result was a bitter and bloody battle, which, as it happened, the Allies won only by a narrow margin. The Italian battlefield was of our choosing. But once the fighting in Italy began, the Germans gave every indication that Italy was too great a strategic and political prize to be allowed to go by default. The surrender of Marshal Badoglio's government the day before, did not prevent the Germans from offering strong resistance.

Movement inshore at some points was delayed by a large number of mines which had to be cleared by minesweepers, and on some beaches considerable opposition was encountered. Coast artillery opposed the landings. In resisting the invaders, the Germans had the advantage of strongly prepared positions and artillery emplacements. In addition, the Germans were entrenched in hills overlooking the coastal plain area in which the fighting took place. Secretary of the Navy Knox

described the establishment of the beachhead as the most hotly contested landing in which American troops had ever participated.

Naval forces for the Salerno assault started from Oran, Algiers, Bizerte, Palermo, Términi, and Tripoli. The Southern Attack Force, with 13 United States transports, carried the 36th Infantry Division from Oran. There were also three British LSIs and three British LSTs. The convoy was escorted by U. S. cruisers *Philadelphia, Savannah,* and *Boise,* and twelve destroyers. It departed Oran at 1700 on 5 September. Admiral Hall, in command of this force, sailed in *Samuel Chase.* Admiral Hewitt, in his flagship *Ancon,* sailed from Algiers on the 6th with *HMS Palomares* and three destroyers. All convoys steamed north of the Ægades. Off Salerno they shaped their courses directly to their release points.

In the American sector, the same scouts and raiders who had operated in the Sicilian landings were embarked in the darkness in four LCS scout boats, one for each beach. These were fast, well-muffled gasoline motor boats with some armor protection. *Barnett, Dickman, Carroll,* and *Jefferson* each carried one. The four scout boats found and successfully marked all four beaches. They took their positions a few hundred yards offshore, and blinked seaward to guide the boat waves.

In this invasion, participating Coast Guard vessels were *Joseph T. Dickman* in Section 2, and *Samuel Chase* in Section 1, of the Transport Group under Captain Edgar, of the Southern Attack Group, and vessels of the LCI(L) Flotilla Four under command of Commander Imlay, as well as *LST-327* and *LST-331.* Let us first follow the fortunes of *Dickman,* now under command of Captain Raymond J. Mauerman, USCG.

At 0002 on the morning of 9 September, *Joseph T. Dickman* stopped and drifted in her designated transport area. Her LCS(S) boat, with a scout officer, Lieutenant (jg) Grady R. Galloway, USCG, was lowered at 0020 and departed for shore to locate Beach Green. Lieutenant Galloway located this beach by sighting a medieval stone watchtower called Torre di Paestum against the starlit sky. The lowering of boats commenced at 0015 and was completed in an hour, except for two boats which were damaged. Twenty-one LCVPs and two DUKWs were pre-loaded with boat team equipment and rail-loaded with troops. Eleven LCVPs

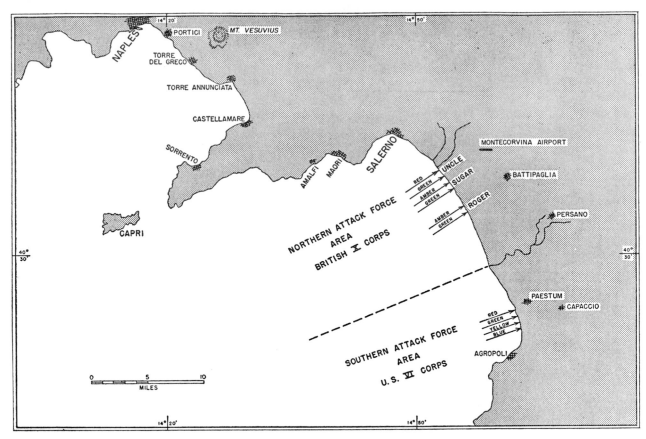

SALERNO AND THE LANDING BEACHES

were pre-loaded with equipment and net-loaded with personnel. The primary control vessel, *PC-625*, led the first three waves to the line of departure. Lieutenant Galloway started blinking green at 0310 from 100 yards offshore, and rocket launchers in his boat were used to silence gunfire directed at the first wave.

All boats landed on the correct beach in excellent line and well spaced, but were ten minutes late in the scheduled time because the primary control vessel was held up by the minesweepers. When the ramps of the first wave were lowered and troops crossed the beach, heavy machine gun fire and high explosive shell fire greeted them from enemy guns.

Quick action by Lieutenant Galloway's scout boat in firing his barrage of 34 rockets caused a lull in the enemy's fire and drew fire to the boat itself. This contributed much to the safe landing and the retraction of the assault boats. While a *Dickman* landing boat of the fourth wave was proceeding away from the beach, a medium calibre high explosive shell struck the starboard side of her ramp and exploded. Several of the boat's crew were wounded. The boat returned to *Dickman* but proved useless thereafter.

Later waves of boats carrying vehicles were not allowed by the beachmaster to land immediately because of machine gun and artillery fire. As a result, there was much congestion outside the line of departure by boats from all the transports. The support boats acted as traffic boats and, when the beaches became tenable, directed the boats to the proper beaches. To assist in landing priority vehicles from *Dickman*, three LCVPs and four LCM(3)s from *Oberon*; two LCM(3)s from *Procyon*; and eight LCM(2)s from *HMS Derwentdale* were used, going in as the 6th, 7th, and 8th waves.

After some delay, unloading of vehicles and cargo proceeded expeditiously on the 9th and 10th, and all unloading was completed by 1600 on the second day. Much of the unloading was done by boat's crews. Boat handling was excellent throughout the operation.

*Dickman's* salvage boat, operating in the vicinity of Beach Green despite artillery fire from shore, assisted and floated many boats, and was able to keep the beach clear of stranded craft. When three enemy bombers attacked the area at 0743 and again at 2140 on the 9th, heavy smoke screens were made by all the vessels. No bombs fell near *Dickman*. At 0445 on the 10th, enemy planes attacked again, and another smoke screen was laid. From 2240 to 2312 on that night, as the transports were preparing to depart, a large formation of enemy bombers lighted up the area with vari-colored flares that apparently marked the limits of the area. The transports were subjected to heavy bombing, but all vessels joined in a barrage of antiaircraft fire and none of the vessels were hit.

*Samuel Chase*, flagship of Admiral Hall, was still commanded by Commander Heimer. As this vessel approached her destination in the transport area, huge fires and severe explosions in the vicinity of Salerno could be seen from her bridge. She stopped her engines at 2350. At 0035, her LCM#1 departed for *Charles Carroll* to become part of their fourth assault wave. At 0130, scout boats *LCS-13* and *LCS-31*, and the *LCVP-21* and *LCVP-26* left *Chase* to escort 58 DUKWs to Red, Yellow, and Blue Beaches of the Casale Greco beach designated for this force. To avoid losing any DUKWs, a board with luminous letters to indicate the beaches was mounted on the stern of each escort lead boat, and a simple set of signals was arranged.

The first wave landed at 0340 amid heavy gunfire of large and small calibre. At 0400, some boats for the fourth wave were lowered and proceeded to transport *Stanton*. Between 0545 and 0600, *Chase* rail-loaded and lowered boats of the second and fourth waves. Major General Fred L. Walker, USA, with 96 officers and 1,168 enlisted men, disembarked. Light artillery of the enemy was shelling the beach and boat lanes, and boats had to proceed with caution due to floating mines. The Sweeper Group, after sweeping the transport area, started to sweep the boat lanes, but was forced to discontinue until daylight because of the many small boats going back and forth. More of *Chase's*

boats landed between 0752 and 0805. Shortly before 0800, the ship fired at a lone JU-88 reconnaissance plane, adding a change of pace to the operation. Troops were all landed, except for port platoon and communications personnel, by 1005 on that morning of 9 September.

Cargo unloading was begun at 0745 with but few available boats. By this time, *Samuel Chase* was 15 miles from the beach, having drifted with the others from the designated transport area. Machine gun fire, floating mines, and light artillery fire on the beaches and boat lanes delayed the landing of LCTs, LSTs, and small boats. As the enemy tanks on shore opposed the assault, they were taken under fire by the fire support group. Late in the afternoon, *Chase* moved in through the swept area, and at 1948 dropped anchor inshore. Most boats returning from the beach brought casualties and prisoners of war. These were brought on board and the casualties were placed in care of the medical department.

As more boats became available, unloading continued more rapidly. But there was no one on the beach to help the boat crews in unloading, and the crews had to manhandle each case or can, carrying it from where it was beached to a point well up on dry shore. This slowed things considerably. Not until the next morning did the crews again receive assistance. It was a repetition of what had happened at Gela. At 0400 on 10 September, unloading operations had to cease due to the congested beaches.

*Chase* resumed unloading three hours later, and her cargo was completely unloaded by 1330. The total cargo unloading time was 25 hours. She began to take boats on board, leaving only those needed for dispatch and possible smoke-laying purposes. When *Chase* reported completion of unloading to the Task Force commander, his reply was "Well done!"

Enemy planes, active throughout the landing operations, were unable to stop the unloading. About six FW-190s bombed and strafed the beaches during the second morning, and these were first taken under fire by *Chase*. Fighter bombers returned about 1435 to give the ships and beach activities another bad time.

At 2215 on 10 September, *Chase* was underway, proceeding through the swept channel to form a convoy of 15 unloaded transports and assault freighters with a ten-destroyer escort. Nine minutes later, enemy planes began dropping flares, and heavy antiaircraft fire was observed astern. Multi-colored flares were dropped all around, illuminating the ships and landing craft. A concerted bombing attack was then made by both medium altitude and dive bombers. Six bombs were dropped close aboard *Chase*, some of which spattered the forecastle with water and jarred the ship, but fortunately there were no hits. Air activity ceased at 2315, and *Chase* continued at ten knots in the northernmost column. Shortly afterward, in a German "E" boat attack on the convoy, destroyer *Rowan* was torpedoed and sunk. Destroyer *Bristol* stood by and picked up 71 survivors, but she herself was torpedoed and sunk soon afterward. Most personnel were rescued by two other destroyers. *Samuel Chase*, still "lucky", moored at Mers-el-Kebir, Algeria, on 14 September.

The work of the Coast Guard-manned LCIs in the Salerno invasion was excellent. All of those involved in the Sicilian landings except *LCI-95* took part at Salerno. The principal work of these vessels was to carry troops and supplies from the staging area directly in to the beaches. Four of these vessels were assigned to proceed with about 30 other Navy landing craft in one of the first convoys, transporting supplies and troops, as well as fuel for the smaller LCTs; delivering these on the beaches; and then standing by in the battle area to act as salvage vessels, to assist grounded craft, and those hit by enemy fire.

The LCIs departed their North African base a few days before the landings, and proceeded under light escort through the swept channels and mined areas en route to a northern Sicilian harbor. Some LCTs and SCs were refueled there. Their stay in harbor was brief and quiet, but during the passage to Salerno, they were subjected to some vicious attacks. About 0530 on 7 September, all the vessels got under way for Salerno, cruising without disturbance from enemy action until 1300 on the 8th. Then the small convoy was spotted by an enemy reconnaissance plane which promptly departed for its airfield with the news. The British destroyer escort fired a few rounds at this enemy without result.

That afternoon the flotilla was suddenly attacked and strafed by a German ME-109F. The

LCIs held their fire as he dived, watching for a chance to give him a few bursts. A flak ship and destroyer fired at him from long range, the former scoring a hit, but the enemy plane descended at terrific speed with all his guns blazing. The LCIs commenced firing and claimed several hits also, but the Messerschmitt's guns never ceased until the plane crashed between two LCIs, showering them with shrapnel and debris. Several men were wounded in the encounter, two seriously. *LCI-319* lost one-fourth of its crew.

Soon afterward, four enemy fighter planes made a dive-bombing attack, coming out of the sun. A destroyer opened fire, giving the first warning. Almost immediately a group of bombs fell near her stern, one narrowly missing the LCI flagship which was in the lead. The explosion put four of the latter's gyro repeaters and magnetic compasses out of commission. One plane dived right over the stern of the convoy and flew up its second column about 100 feet above the water. No ships fired at first for fear of hitting their own men, but soon they let loose. Though hit several times, the enemy appeared undamaged, and after gunning his engine, he headed for home.

The flotilla did not otherwise escape, however, for *LCT-624* was hit squarely by a bomb and burst into flames. The survivors were picked up and the craft sank in a few minutes. The oil slick on the surface burned for hours. That evening the bigger ships arrived, and the bombers shifted their attention to the larger game.

As H-hour approached, and the LCIs and other landing craft waited offshore for their time to go in to the beaches, the night presented an awe-inspiring sight. Countless gun flashes and explosions rent the air as the heavy batteries in the cruisers and destroyers opened up, and fire was returned from the shore batteries. Tracer streams criss-crossed everywhere.

The first waves of invasion craft went in to the beaches in that inferno of exploding shells and smoke. The LCTs with their tanks and the LCIs with their troops were to land at H-hour plus 50-60 minutes, but unexpectedly strong enemy resistance delayed departure. However, as we have seen, small craft were able to sneak in under the barrage and discharge enough infantrymen to keep the enemy busy ashore. Meanwhile, the large cruisers and destroyers continued to fight it out with the shore batteries and with German tanks brought to the beaches to repel the expected invasion.

Fighting had not diminished noticeably by 1030 that morning. American planes spotted and bombed every enemy shore installation. The larger ships then fought a duel with the enemy, forcing him to retreat, which permitted the landing craft to put ashore tanks, trucks, men, and supplies. The LCIs got their troops in to the beach. British destroyers and cruisers moved in nearer shore and shelled German tanks, which, entrenched in the hills, were firing down into Salerno Bay at the Allied vessels. Destroyers laid smoke screens to shield the landing barges and small craft from enemy view, and the landings proceeded according to plan.

As in the Sicilian landings, Commander Imlay played a leading role and was decorated. He was charged with the difficult assignment of bringing the vessels under his command safely through the hazardous course between Bizerte, Tunisia, and the Gulf of Salerno, and his flotilla successfully reached the designated assault beaches at the assigned time despite extremely adverse weather conditions and fierce enemy aerial opposition.

The follow-up work was about the same as in the other invasions. The LCIs left the battle area to load reinforcements, equipment, and supplies, and made several return trips. But the beachheads had been established, and the beaching of troops became a routine matter. It was upon the rapid follow up of reserves and the swift and persistent landing of supplies by the Allied Navies that the Army relied to sustain the attack and give it complete success.

Coast Guard-manned *LST-16*, *LST-327*, and *LST-331* took part in the Sicilian landings under combat conditions, and later several others carried troops and supplies to Italy and Sicily although they were not involved in the actual assaults. These were *LST-21*, *LST-17*, *LST-25*, *LST-175* and *LST-26*. At Salerno, *LST-327* and *LST-331* were involved in the landings under combat conditions, landing troops and supplies under heavy fire.

Without the outstanding support and cooperation of the Allied Navies, experts have agreed, Salerno would never have fallen into Allied hands, and it was more than likely that the Fifth and Eighth Armies would have remained in the heel of Italy. As it was, the Army landed successfully on the mainland of Italy in the face of determined opposition by superior enemy forces.

After the failure of the Fifth Army to break out of the Salerno beachhead, everything depended upon the rate of advance of the British Eighth Army which had landed farther south and assumed the role of a relief force. On 10 September, General Montgomery's army reached Pizzo, 45 miles north of Reggio Calabria. Two days later, part of his army occupied the important port of Brindisi; and on 17 September advance elements of that army made contact with patrols of the American Fifth Army outside Salerno. The first great crisis of the Italian campaign was successfully passed.

After the first failure to entrap German forces in the south, the immediate Allied objectives were the great Italian air base at Foggia, and the port of Naples. With Naples and Foggia in Allied hands, General Eisenhower's troops would have both a first class port of supply and a first class air base at their disposal. Foggia was occupied by the British Eighth Army on 28 September, and, on 1 October, advance patrols of the Fifth Army entered the outskirts of Naples. Before retreating from Naples and Foggia, the Germans had systematically destroyed those bases, and an immense amount of work was required to put them back into shape for use.

Bitter fighting in the next months, although disappointing from the territorial and political views, had an important bearing upon the overall aspect of the war. About 20 German divisions were pinned down in Italy; they could not be used against the Red Army or the main Allied invasion of Europe. Extensive enemy resources were thus being expended in a non-decisive theatre. A steady attrition cut down the effectiveness of German units, though they fought in Italy with all their veteran skill and accustomed tenacity.

The next assault by the naval forces in which troops were landed was at Anzio—known as Operation "Shingle." The landing area selected was a stretch of coastline from Nettuno Beach to the little port city of Anzio, about 125 miles northwest of Salerno, and 30 miles south of Rome. The primary purpose of this attack was to seize and secure a beachhead in the vicinity of Anzio, and then to advance on the Alban Hills; cut the enemy's main

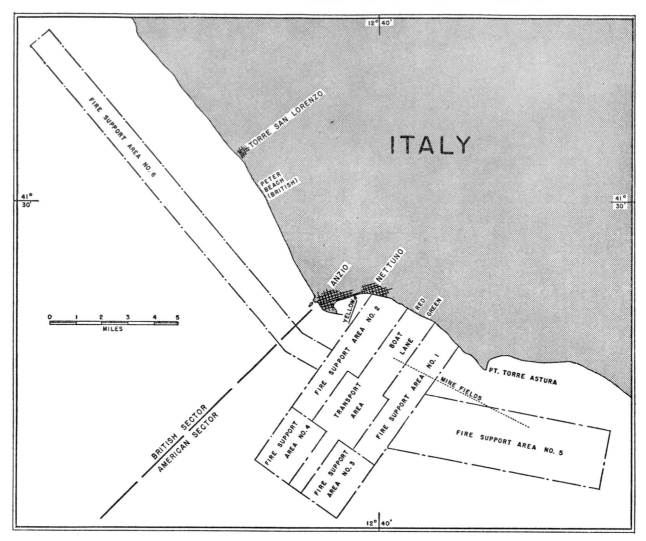

DISPOSITION OF ATTACKING FORCES AT ANZIO

communications southeast of Rome; and outflank the German Gustav and Adolph Hitler Lines by effecting a landing 55 miles to their rear. As an operation independent of the main Fifth Army attack, its chief result was to divert German forces from the main front.

As a preliminary, Allied fighter planes bombed widely diversified targets, including airdromes, rail communications, bridges, and such, and concentrated attacks in locations which might deceive the enemy as to the real point of the coming assault. As the time drew near, attacks were stepped up. D-day was set for 22 January 1944. The amphibious operation was timed to coincide

with a general Fifth Army offensive calculated to tie up the German Tenth Army, which consisted of 13 divisions.

Rear Admiral F. J. Lowry, USN, in *Biscayne*, commanded the American task force. His ships and landing craft loaded their troops at four locations in the Gulf of Naples. They sortied early on 21 January. Admiral Troubridge, RN, in *Bulolo*, was in command of the British task force. They assembled south of Capri in the afternoon of the same day. In these task forces were also some French, Dutch and Greek vessels. Coast Guard participation was in *LST-16*, *LST-326*, *LST-327*, *LST-381*, and *PC-545*. No other Coast Guard vessels were involved. As Admiral Morison put it: "The approach to Anzio beachhead was uneventful—almost ominously so."

H-hour was to be 0200 on 22 January. Deployment of the vessels preparatory to landing was in accordance with custom. The sweepers did their work in the mined waters; rocket fire raked the beaches, and destroyed many land mines; the assault waves moved in to the beaches. There was no opposition, no enemy fire. But as the third wave went in, and *LCI-211* grounded on a false beach, it received heavy machine gun fire from shore, causing many casualties.

About 0800 six German Messerschmitts dive-bombed Beach Red and set loaded vehicles afire. Enemy air attacks increased in number and intensity. Ships gave naval gunfire support to troops ashore and German artillery retaliated lightly. By midnight of D-day, 36,034 men, 3,069 vehicles and large quantities of supplies, 90 per cent of the assault load, had been put ashore.

During D-day, the Coast Guard vessels received their share of fire from enemy batteries, and *LST-326* suffered a few near misses. She moved in to the unloading anchorage, but heavy shell fire from the beach brought orders to discharge her remaining vehicles via pontoon causeway, and she got her vehicles safely ashore. Landing craft then returned to Naples and other ports for reinforcements and additional supplies and vehicles, and this type of operation continued for some time.

On shore, the beachhead had been secured. But the Germans rushed so many divisions to the Anzio beachhead that the Allies were not able to advance inland significantly, and the front remained the scene of bloody fighting for several months. The Anzio beachhead was confined to a small area where the life of the American and British troops was very hard, with practically every square inch of the place hit by German artillery. The Germans continued to pour in even more men and weapons, and so did the Allies. The immediate task of the beachhead force was to hold and strengthen its territory against attacks by strong forces the Germans sent there in an attempt to drive the Allies out. A condition of virtual stalemate existed, with heavy casualties on both sides, until 25 May, when elements of the Anzio forces and those from the forces around Salerno and Naples made contact. On 22 May, the French captured Pontecorvo; the Americans had reached the mountains north of Terracina; and the Hitler Line had been turned. The forces at Anzio broke their bonds and the Allies advanced northward in Italy.

The Italian campaign compelled the enemy to divert hundreds of thousands of troops, tanks, and guns, to the south. He would have preferred to hold these in the west to meet the invasion from Britain. Italy provided a springboard from which the American Seventh Army's landing in southern France was later launched. It supplied a base from which hundreds of American and British bombers were able to operate in a great arc from Bulgaria, Greece, and Rumania, through Hungary, Austria, and Germany to southern France. From Italy, the Allies were able to speed really effective help across the Adriatic to Tito's Yugoslav warriors; send troops to aid the Greeks; and drop scores of tons of rifles, ammunition, and other supplies to northern Italian patriots. Italy was the Allies' foremost testing ground of war. Experience gained in converting Naples' harbor from a tangled mass of wreckage and scuttled ships into one of the world's busiest ports in a few months was in great degree responsible for the speed with which ports in France were made usable after the Normandy invasion.

# Chapter 17

# THE NORMANDY INVASION

THE OPERATIONS in North Africa and the later extension of operations across Sicily and to the mainland of Italy were desirable preliminaries to the main effort of the Allied Forces against the German war machine. The Mediterranean had been freed for Allied shipping. The cross-channel assault had been agreed upon since 1942 as the main operation against Germany, but there had been many postponements and disagreements as to details of the grand assault. It was not until June 1944, that the United States and Great Britain became sufficiently strong to undertake the operation, but the broad tactical plans had been completed and approved by the Combined Chiefs of Staff in August 1943, when the Sicilian campaign was being concluded.

As part of our strategy, the bombing of Germany begun early in the war, was intensified in May 1943; and mounted in volume and effectiveness until the end of the war. Winning supremacy over the German Air Force was a vital preliminary to invasion. Eventually, air bombardment disrupted the German communications system, thus immeasurably aiding Allied ground forces by impeding movements of the enemy.

Tentative plans for the invasion were formulated well in advance by Lieutenant General Sir F. E. Morgan, Chief of Staff to the Supreme Allied Commander, and a staff of United States and British personnel—an organization called COSSAC as a result of that title. By July 1943, an outline of the plan was ready to be presented to the Combined Chiefs of Staff. The operation was to be called "Overlord", and the naval phase alone, "Neptune." The plan was approved at the Quebec Conference, and details were to be worked out further before arrival of a Supreme Commander. The Combined Chiefs of Staff directed that the date of the operation would be 1 May 1944. While the initial plan of this group was ultimately followed in its broader aspects, General Eisenhower, when named Supreme Commander for "Overlord", and his chief commanders decided on considerably expanding the initial assault forces and the front to be subjected to invasion. Thus, on 15 January, when General Eisenhower reached London, the plan was altered in these respects.

General Eisenhower and his top planners decided that the initial assault wave should comprise five divisions, and that the beach area to be attacked should be broad, including an attack against the Cotentin Peninsula with a view toward the speedy conquest of Cherbourg—a port which could be highly useful, especially from the standpoint of logistic support. The area was to be extended to the eastward to include the Ouistreham beaches, to assist in securing the eastern flank and vital airfields in the area. It was believed that support by two airborne divisions was vital in the assault against Varreville beaches—the western end of the assault area, in relatively close proximity to Cherbourg—despite hazards to such an airborne operation.

The larger assault force which General Eisenhower and his planners wanted required an augmented fleet of landing and assault craft. One month's production of such craft in the United States and Britain would make up the deficiency in numbers. The Navy desired additional time for training crews, and the air forces could well use extra time for the strategic bombings of Germany and further wearing her down. Therefore, on 1 February, the Combined Chiefs of Staff authorized postponement of the target date to not later than 31 May but subject, nevertheless, to weather conditions and prospects. On 17 March, General Eisenhower set the date as 5 June, still subject to weather considerations.

By the first week in June, Rome had fallen;

Kesselring was in retreat; the Crimea had been swept clean; and Germany was predicting an all-out offensive by Russia. The enemy was keyed up to a 1 May Allied offensive, and perhaps delay made the enemy complacent. In any event, the delay made possible the availability of additional assault craft and shipping to transport a staggering number of men and vehicles required for the assault. It resulted, however, in the weather being less favorable than on 31 May.

Since an invasion of Europe had been accepted as prerequisite to Allied victory, military preparations had long been under way before this specific planning had taken form. American forces and supplies had been accumulating in England since 1942, with some acceleration the following year. This build-up continued under Lieutenant General John C. H. Lee, USA. But definite plans for the landings in France really began to take shape toward the end of 1943, after the Sicilian campaign.

The logistical problems were tremendous. By July 1943, around 750,000 tons of supplies were pouring into English ports each month, and this tonnage increased until June 1944, when 1,900,000 tons of supplies were received from the United States. The troops already in England needed much of this, but the stock pile earmarked for the American forces, over and above basic loads and equipment, was 2,500,000 tons for the invasion alone. The number of United States Army troops in the United Kingdom had risen from 241,839 at the end of 1942, to 1,562,000 by 1 June 1944.

Commanders for various task forces were designated later in 1943 and early 1944, and they began to arrive in England to assume their duties. The Commander in Chief of the Allied Naval Expeditionary Force was Admiral Sir Bertram Ramsay, RN. Rear Admiral Alan G. Kirk, USN, commanded Task Force 122. Later, the lower echelons of Task Force 122 were broadened into three further task forces. Task Force O was under Rear Admiral Hall; Task Force U under Rear Admiral Don P. Moon, USN; and the Follow-up Force was commanded by Commodore Campbell D. Edgar, USN. Rear Admiral Hall had originally been designated to command the Eleventh Amphibious Force.

With these commands set up, and with the bases functioning, Navy ships and personnel poured into England from the United States in ever increasing volume. The weight of arms, ammunition, supplies, and men spread out in every field, and along almost every lane in the southern part of Britain.

One of the most important functions in the entire pre-invasion program was training. Therefore, each amphibious base conducted exercises for its small-craft personnel. Large scale rehearsals were staged from January through April off Slapton Sands near Dartmouth. They were as realistic as the commanding officers could make them—so realistic, in fact, that one night three German E-boats worked in, sank two LSTs, and damaged another!

As the forces built up to a climax, the RAF and the Eighth and Ninth United States Army Air Forces bombed German communications, supplies, installations, and production and materiel centers, and fought toward air supremacy. By the time of the invasion, the Allied air forces had gained overwhelming mastery of the air. The Navy undertook to neutralize German sea power. They gave special attention to submarines, their bases, and the E-boats in and around the Bay of Biscay, largely by Navy planes through patrol and attack missions. By harassing and holding down the U-boats, the build-up for invasion was made easier.

In an operation of such magnitude it was inconceivable that the enemy would not know that an attack would be made. During the preliminaries, however, every precaution was taken to prevent leaks regarding the true operational intentions against Normandy—where, when, and in what strength.

From the Thames Estuary in the east, to Falmouth, near Land's End, in the west, the ports on Britain's English Channel shore were packed with ships and boats of virtually every kind, including types never known before. There were even floating breakwaters and piers to be sunk in place. Invasion craft were everywhere. As the time for assault drew close, men, machines, vehicles, equipment, supplies, and ammunition moved south to the various ports. All hands turned to in moving materials and loading the ships. There was little sleep for anyone in that last 24 hours before the time of sailing. The commander of the amphibious bases in Britain, Rear Admiral John Wilkes, USN, together with those under his command, did a splendid piece of work. His percentage of readiness

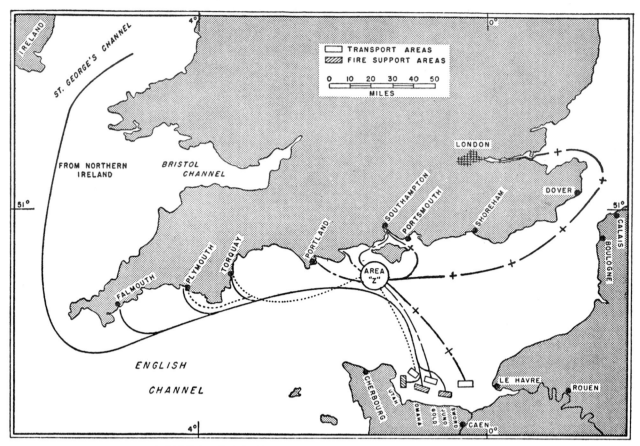

ROUTES OF NAVAL FORCES TO NORMANDY BEACHES

of his ships assigned to the operation was 99.5; the rest being under repair due to a German bomber attack. Out of 2,493 ships under his jurisdiction scheduled to sail, only 13 were unable to do so.

In all, over 4,000 vessels, 2,000 transport planes and gliders, and a million men were assembled. Behind them were other thousands of vessels loaded and waiting to carry reinforcements and all that they would need.

At this point, let us examine the disposition of the naval forces before their departures for the French coast.

The heavy ships of the American Fire Support Groups were assembled in northern Ireland. They steamed south through the St. George Channel, to the west of the Scilly Islands, then northeast into the English Channel, arriving off Falmouth, Plymouth, Dartmouth, and Weymouth at the precise time of rendezvous with transports and other vessels from these ports. Admiral Moon's Task

Force U had assembled at westernmost English ports—Falmouth, Plymouth, Salcombe, and Dartmouth—and moved eastward along the English coast. Admiral Hall's Task Force O was assembled near Weymouth, Poole, and north of the Isle of Wight. His course was generally southeast. The British forces gathered near Portsmouth and Southampton and at various easterly points, and the Thames Estuary.

These assembly areas were widely scattered, and the many different types of vessels, including landing and beaching craft, had different speeds. Yet schedules were arranged so that all vessels from whatever ports, and of whatever types, would arrive off the invasion beaches at the same time. No element of one task force could get mixed up with another without chaotic results. Navigational instruments and abilities ranged from excellent in the larger ships to none at all in the smaller invasion craft.

The Western (American) and Eastern (British)

CAPTAIN MILES H. IMLAY, USCG . . . . commander of
the Coast Guard LCI Flotilla.

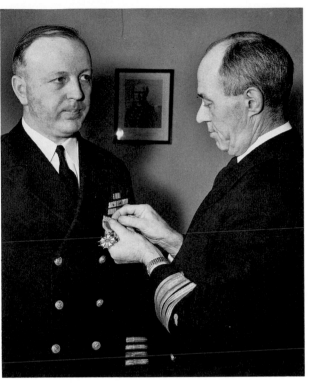

CAPTAIN CHARLES W. HARWOOD, USCG . . . . Admiral Waesche pins Legion of Merit on Captain Harwood.

AFRIKA KORPSMEN ARE ROUNDED UP IN SICILY . . . . German prisoners of war are marched along the Sicilian
waterfront for transportation to a Coast Guard-manned transport lying offshore.

GIs HUG THE BLAZING BEACH OF SALERNO . . . . they hit the ground as
Nazi planes bomb the landing area

MOVING UP THE BEACH AT SALERNO . . . . troops just brought ashore by Coast Guard landing craft
move forward and pass a casualty being returned to a transport.

END OF A SPITFIRE ON SALERNO INVASION BEACH . . . . a Coast Guardsman and a
soldier examine plane which made a forced landing.

LCI FLOTILLA HEADS FOR NORMANDY INVASION . . . . with their barrage balloons, this Coast Guard unit advances
toward the beaches of France to take part in the initial assault.

INVASION BARGE LANDING SOLDIERS EARLY ON
D-DAY . . . . troops storm toward the fire-swept beach after
going down the ramp of a Coast Guard landing barge.

LIEUTENANT COMMANDER QUENTIN R. WALSH,
USCG . . . . he was awarded the Navy Cross for heroism
and bravery during the assault on Cherbourg.

SUPPLIES POUR ASHORE ON UTAH BEACH . . . . LSTs, LCIs, transports and cargo ships disgorge mobile equipment
and supplies to support the conquest for the Cotentin Peninsula.

TWO RESCUE CUTTERS SPEED TO RENDER ASSISTANCE . . . . the 83-footers played a heroic role in saving life and property in the angry waters of the Channel and under fire along the beaches.

LIBERATED FRENCHMEN RETURN TO RUINS OF CHERBOURG . . . . after the battle, French citizens brouse through a salvage depot to gather personal belongings.

TRANSPORT *GENERAL M. C. MEIGS*, COAST GUARD-MANNED . . . . many such transports
kept the supply of reinforcements pouring into the battle areas of Europe.

FREIGHT CARS EMERGE FROM COAST GUARD-MANNED *LST-21* . . . . these cars, ferried from England, were put
ashore in France to expedite the flow of supplies to the Allied Armies on the Western Front.

AMPHIBIOUS FORCES AT NAPLES . . . . preparing for the landings in Southern France.—(*U. S. Navy photo*)

INTO MARSEILLES UNDER SILENT GUNS OF FORT ST. JEAN . . . . a Coast Guard LCVP takes soldiers in to the small boat basin during invasion of Southern France.

ON THE BEACHES OF SOUTHERN FRANCE . . . . two Coast Guard-manned transports among others send men and supplies ashore for the push northward.

Task Forces were under the over-all command of Admiral Ramsay; the Western Force was under the command of Admiral Kirk; and the Eastern Force was commanded by Rear Admiral Sir P. L. Vian, RN. These forces were subdivided to include, altogether, five assault forces, each responsible for the landing of an assault division upon one of the five beach areas to be attacked. In addition, there were two Follow-up Forces. The assault forces for the American Zone were known as Force U and Force O (Utah and Omaha), and were under the respective commands of Admirals Moon and Hall. For the British zone the assault forces were similarly known as Force S, Force J, and Force G (Sword, Juno, and Gold), and were commanded by Rear Admiral A. G. Talbot, RN; Commodore G. N. Oliver, RN; and Rear Admiral C. Douglas-Pennant, RN, respectively.

The section of Normandy chosen for the assault was, broadly, between Cherbourg and Le Havre, and specifically a 50-mile stretch of coast between Varreville on the west (Cotentin Peninsula) and Ouistreham on the east. This section of Normandy was near most of the embarkation ports in England, and near the important communication lines and highways leading to Paris. It was also near the two best French ports on the Channel, Cherbourg and Le Havre, which the Allies had to take to supply an extended drive into the Continent. This coast also afforded the best landing places. Normandy was close enough for fighter plane coverage.

The beaches nearest to Cherbourg were named Utah Beach, and the area farther to the east was termed Omaha Beach. Task Force U was to land the 4th, 90th, and 9th Divisions of the U. S. First Army at Utah Beach; Task Force O was to put the 1st, 29th, and 2nd Divisions of the First Army ashore at Omaha Beach. The British Task Force G was to land the 50th and 49th Divisions, and the 7th Armored Division of the British Second Army at Gold Beach next easterly; Force J was to put ashore the 3rd Commando Division and the 51st Division of the Second Army at Juno Beach, still farther east; and Task Force S was to land the 3rd Division of the Second Army at Sword Beach, the most easterly of all.

We are chiefly concerned here with the attacks on Utah and Omaha Beaches which were the responsibility of United States forces. It was in these operations that most Coast Guardsmen took part. The list of Coast Guard and Coast Guard-manned vessels at Normandy was larger than in any previous operation. Besides *Charles Carroll* and *Barnett*, in which a few Coast Guardsmen served with Navy crews, were the attack transports *Samuel Chase* now under command of Captain Edward E. Fritzche, USCG; *Joseph T. Dickman* (Captain Raymond J. Mauerman, USCG) and a newcomer, *Bayfield*, commanded by Captain Lyndon Spencer, USCG. There were also ten Coast Guard-manned LSTs. Four of these were assigned to the British and operated with their task forces. The LCI(L) Flotilla consisted of 25 LCI(L)s, and was still commanded by Captain Miles H. Imlay, USCG. Also, there was a new Coast Guard unit known as The Coast Guard Rescue Flotilla of sixty 83-foot cutters commanded by Lieutenant Commander Alexander V. Stewart, Jr., USCGR. Specifically, the Coast Guard-manned landing craft were:

| | | | |
|---|---|---|---|
| *LST-16* | *LST-331* | *LCI(L)-91* | *LCI(L)-321* |
| *\*LST-17* | *LCI(L)-83* | *LCI(L)-92* | *LCI(L)-322* |
| *\*LST-21* | *LCI(L)-84* | *LCI(L)-93* | *LCI(L)-323* |
| *LST-27* | *LCI(L)-85* | *LCI(L)-94* | *LCI(L)-324* |
| *\*LST-261* | *LCI(L)-86* | *LCI(L)-95* | *LCI(L)-325* |
| *LST-262* | *LCI(L)-87* | *LCI(L)-96* | *LCI(L)-326* |
| *LST-326* | *LCI(L)-88* | *LCI(L)-319* | *LCI(L)-349* |
| *\*LST-327* | *LCI(L)-89* | *LCI(L)-320* | *LCI(L)-350* |
| *LST-381* | *LCI(L)-90* | | |

\* Assigned to British

The Coast Guard Rescue Flotilla was made up of these 83-footers:

| USCG-1 | (83300) | USCG-22 | (83407) |
|---|---|---|---|
| " 2 | (83304) | " 23 | (83408) |
| " 3 | (83320) | " 24 | (83409) |
| " 4 | (83321) | " 25 | (83411) |
| " 5 | (83327) | " 26 | (83412) |
| " 6 | (83334) | " 27 | (83415) |
| " 7 | (83337) | " 28 | (83416) |
| " 8 | (83360) | " 29 | (83417) |
| " 9 | (83361) | " 30 | (83425) |
| " 10 | (83362) | " 31 | (83428) |
| " 11 | (83366) | " 32 | (83431) |
| " 12 | (83370) | " 33 | (83432) |
| " 13 | (83372) | " 34 | (83435) |
| " 14 | (83373) | " 35 | (83439) |
| " 15 | (83375) | " 36 | (83440) |
| " 16 | (83377) | " 37 | (83442) |
| " 17 | (83378) | " 38 | (83443) |
| " 18 | (83398) | " 39 | (83445) |
| " 19 | (83399) | " 40 | (83447) |
| " 20 | (83401) | " 41 | (83462) |
| " 21 | (83402) | " 42 | (83463) |

| | | | | |
|---|---|---|---|---|
| " | 43 | (83464) | " | 52 | (83500) |
| " | 44 | (83465) | " | 53 | (83501) |
| " | 45 | (83466) | " | 54 | (83502) |
| " | 46 | (83468) | " | 55 | (83503) |
| " | 47 | (83471) | " | 56 | (83511) |
| " | 48 | (83473) | " | 57 | (83512) |
| " | 49 | (83490) | " | 58 | (83513) |
| " | 50 | (83493) | " | 59 | (83514) |
| " | 51 | (83494) | " | 60 | (83516) |

It is interesting to note that all of the Coast Guard-manned LSTs and LCIs which took part in the Sicilian and Italian landings also participated at Normandy. There were 97 vessels manned by the Coast Guard in the Normandy Invasion, not counting the landing craft carried by the transports.

June 1944 saw the highest winds and roughest seas encountered in the English Channel in June in 20 years. D-day had been set for 5 June, and on 3 June many of the slower vessels and those with great distances to go were already at sea. The weather was so unfavorable that D-day was postponed for 24 hours, and the vessels at sea had to turn about and seek shelter, but the great armada moved after that delay.

The courses which these task forces took along swept channels converged into an area of open water about 13 miles south of the western end of the Isle of Wight known as "Area Z." From this point the forces steamed directly toward the assault area. In Admiral Hall's Task Force O were *Samuel Chase*, and also *Charles Carroll* with a few Coast Guardsmen in her crew. Admiral Moon's Task Force U was somewhat smaller than the other and had four transports, *Bayfield* and *Dickman*, the British *Empire Gauntlet*, and *Barnett* (his flagship), with a number of Coast Guardsmen on board. Task Force O was to carry the main assault of the American vessels, spearheaded by the 1st and 29th Divisions. On both sides of the transports, and astern of them, were LSTs and LCIs, many of them Coast Guard-manned. Units of the Coast Guard Rescue Flotilla were variously dispersed among the task forces, as the thousands of ships moved southward toward the beaches of Normandy.

The weather had moderated somewhat, but the sea continued rough, and large numbers of the men were seasick during the crossing. The waves also caused some of the major landing craft to lag astern, while other elements were forced to turn

back. The enemy had concluded that any cross-channel expedition was impossible in such seas, and so General Eisenhower's decision to launch the assault at a time when the weather was so unsettled was largely responsible for the surprise which was achieved. The successful departures from port and the approaches and arrivals off Normandy, despite the severe weather conditions, were a masterpiece of planning and execution.

While the assault forces were being tossed on the dark waters of the channel en route for France, British and American paratroops—four airborne infantry divisions and two paratroop divisions—landed behind the German shore defenses in advance of the onslaught on the beaches. They smashed German coastal gun positions and set up defenses around strategic bridges, villages, and road junctions. Then the night bombers swarmed in. Soon after midnight the bombing commenced, and by dawn 1,136 RAF bombers had dropped 5,853 tons of bombs on selected coastal batteries between Cherbourg and Le Havre. When dawn came on 6 June, minesweepers edged their way carefully toward shore ahead of the invasion fleet. As the vessels approached, there thundered over the horizon the greatest umbrella of air power ever assembled for invasion protection. United States Eighth Air Force bombers took up the attacks, and 1,083 aircraft dropped 1,763 tons on the shore defenses during the half hour before the first waves landed. The seaborne forces witnessed the inspiring morale effect produced by this spectacle of Allied air might and its results as they drew in toward the beaches.

The Allied task forces moved in to their positions. The transports anchored about 13 miles offshore. An impressive array of forces from the Fire Support Group, under command of Rear Admiral Morton L. Deyo, USN, moved in with the transports and other invasion craft. German shore batteries opened fire on the minesweepers which, nevertheless, kept on moving straight toward the shore, clearing a path for the landing craft.

A little after 0500 the Allied battleships, cruisers, and destroyers opened up on the enemy shore batteries and defense installations, and steamed close inshore for the duel. Great fires and smoke arose from the coast.

At the start of the operation, the Transport Area was the point of reference and the focus of all

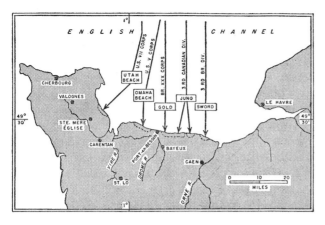

NORMANDY INVASION BEACHES

activities. The troopships lowered their LCVPs, which then assembled off the quarters of the ships to be first unloaded, and then circled about until called alongside their transport to take on troops. Circling kept the small craft in order. The troops scrambled down the cargo nets into these amphibious craft, which then chugged off for the rendezvous circle off the bows of the transports, each roundabout composed of boats that were to hit the beach in the same wave.

Marking the inshore extreme of the Transport Area were the control vessels that guided the first four or five waves of small craft through the mineswept lanes to the beach. Five minutes before the final dash, a light gleamed from each control vessel. When that light went out, the run for the beach began, and the circles straightened out into columns. The control vessels took the troop and gun-laden craft in prearranged waves to the line of departure, about 3,000 yards off the beach. From there, the coxswains could see the beach and recognized from landmarks and detailed charts the spot at which they were to discharge their troops. The control vessels remained at the line of departure, acting as close control of all boat traffic near the beach.

Until the Army signaled that the beach was securely held, the Transport Area remained the heart and brain, the nerve and arterial system of the invasion. Through it passed everything destined for the beach. All messages were cleared through it, for the Naval Task Group Commander and the Commanding General with their respective staffs were there.

Flanking the Transport Area were the Fire Support Areas where the bombardment groups of battleships and cruisers formed to provide the landing forces with artillery support, and to blast any probing artillery fire directed at the heart of the invasion. Destroyers, rocket ships, and gunboats for closer work were ready to charge in with the first wave of the landing craft.

German pillboxes along the coast from Cherbourg to Le Havre had to be destroyed before the assault boats reached the beaches and before the mines, tank traps, obstacles, road blocks, and booby traps could be cleared away. If the pillboxes could have maintained their fire, the invasion would have been a bloody fiasco. Here was a job for naval gun fire.

As a hindrance to any invasion attempt, the Germans had placed underwater obstructions off the beaches. These were pyramids of steel, timber, or concrete, ramps, hedgehogs, and objects of other types, many topped by teller mines. A large number of 50-yard gaps through these obstructions had to be cleared by Naval Combat Demolition Units attached to Forces O and U. These demolition units had been ruggedly trained and were fiercely determined. The men were crowded into LCMs and LCVPs and taken in at the outset, to place demolition charges on these obstructions and destroy them. Constantly in peril from the terrific fire of hostile pillboxes and casements, they ignited their fuses, clearing the way for the landing of troops. Their hazardous and vital mission was successfully accomplished with outstanding heroism and despite heavy losses.

Later, when the beaches were secured and the invasion forces were in control far enough inland to eliminate the enemy shore batteries, the transports moved in closer to speed the movement of troops and supplies to the beach. When safety permitted, the Transport Area was expanded to a general anchorage.

The landing operations went well from the beginning for the Eastern Naval Task Force at the British and Canadian beaches. Preliminary bombardment and aerial attacks had been extremely effective, and opposition on the beaches was relatively light. The sea had abated considerably and landings were made with few craft casualties due to weather. At Utah Beach, also, the landings went off on schedule, demolitions proceeded as planned, and at first there was no heavy enemy resistance.

Task Force U, consisting of about 1,000 vessels of various types, had moved in and the boat waves were hitting the beach. This force, it will be remembered, included the Coast Guard transports *Bayfield* and *Joseph T. Dickman*.

*Bayfield*, Admiral Moon's flagship of Force U, had sortied from Plymouth Harbor, and made the trip without difficulty. All hands went to General Quarters at 2230 on 5 June, and this condition was maintained until time to debark troops. As the convoy approached the coast, gun fire, antiaircraft fire, and bomb bursts were observed in the distance, but the convoy was not molested by the enemy. The vessel anchored in the Transport Area at 0230 on D-day, and all boats were lowered away by 0305.

Twelve of *Bayfield's* LCVPs were dispatched to *Barnett* for use in unloading her troops; the remainder were held in assembly circles to be used by other vessels as required. The sea, whitecaps, and high wind hampered their movement and made loading difficult. *Bayfield* carried nineteen LCVPs, two LCMs, and two LCPLs. Her troops were to be sent ashore in land-based LCMs. These were due to arrive at 0330, but the first did not appear alongside until 0525. They were immediately loaded with troops and despite the delay, the waves of which they were a part reached the beaches only five to fifteen minutes late. The last of the troops and vehicles were loaded into *LCT-526* at 0950. *Bayfield's* boats used by *Barnett* encountered no underwater obstacles, and the first waves met with little opposition on the beach. LCMs landing *Bayfield's* troops met no opposition up to about a mile from the beach. There, considerable fire was encountered, mostly cross-fire between an LCTG and shore batteries, and several boats narrowly escaped being hit.

There were two casualties to *Bayfield* personnel. Jessie G. Patton, Seaman Second Class, USCGR, in the crew of a stranded LCM, was injured by shell fragments while on the beach. Ensign Mason C. Daly, USCGR, was injured by fragmentation of a shell while landing cargo on the beach.

Three heavily loaded LCVPs assigned to *Barnett* grounded off the beach, swamped when discharging troops, and had to be left there. The troops starting chest-deep in the water, waded ashore without mishap. The boats were later recovered. The stranded LCM to which Patton belonged received shell bursts which put about 40 holes in the hull and broke the ramp. The ramp was temporarily repaired by the Beach Party; the boat returned to the ship, and was put in first class operating condition. As the invasion progressed, *Bayfield* worked in closer to the beach.

Although primarily functioning as Admiral Moon's flagship, this transport also served as a Service Force. In her capacity as Headquarters Ship for the Commander Force U, it seemed generally assumed that she was prepared to act as supply, hospital, and accommodation ship, information center, and oiler, and to perform any other needed service. The crew were called upon to extend themselves far beyond ordinary duties for many days. To meet the needs for dispatch, work, and smoke boats, it was necessary to put boat crews on a watch-and-watch basis—twelve hours on and twelve off. Boat maintenance men salvaged and repaired not only *Bayfield's* craft but also many others. Even though repair facilities were later set up ashore and repair vessels became available, there was still a steady stream of boats to *Bayfield* which the other facilities could not handle.

Before the accommodation ship arrived, and afterwards when warranted, survivors were taken on board, given medical attention, fed, and accommodated. Efforts of the medical staff, headed by three doctors and one dentist of the U. S. Public Health Service and one Navy Medical Officer, were heroic. By 17 June, 419 casualties had been taken on board and cared for. Treatment ranged from appendectomies and amputations to dressing gun shot and shrapnel wounds. Of these casualties, 307 arrived in one night and included 75 wounded prisoners of war. Each of the 307 was examined and given necessary care before removal to other vessels for evacuation the following morning.

*Bayfield* was attacked by bombers twice, and suffered one near miss that caused minor damage in the engine room. Enemy air activity required General Quarters at least once almost every night up to 16 June. After that, no air activity was experienced over the anchorage.

On 19 June, when Navy *LST-523* struck a mine and sank, *Bayfield* was again called upon to act as rescue, emergency, and hospital ship. All available boats were dispatched to the scene of the explosion, and 49 casualties and 75 survivors were taken on board, cared for, and outfitted. Two bodies were also recovered.

From the afternoon of 19 June until the morning of 23 June, heavy weather brought activities virtually to a standstill. *Bayfield* sent those of her boats which were in the water to the beach and to the protection of the breakwater, since they could not be hoisted on board due to the heavy seas.

*Bayfield* departed for the United Kingdom on 25 June, escorted by minesweepers at first, and then across the Channel escorted by a destroyer screen. For his exceptionally meritorious service for the part he played as Commanding Officer of Admiral Moon's flagship and the invaluable support rendered by his vessel, Captain Spencer was awarded the Legion of Merit. Also, in gratitude, the French Resistance Government, then headed by General Charles de Gaulle, awarded him the French Croix de Guerre.

*Joseph T. Dickman*, also of Force U, anchored in the Transport Area off Utah Beach at 0240 on 6 June. She had begun to lower boats even before anchoring. Unloading of cargo began at 0305, ammunition at 0401, and troops and vehicles soon afterward. Her boats went in to the beaches as scheduled, and began returning with casualties at 0800. In the initial assault, she landed 1,833 troops and 130 officers, seven jeeps, eighteen M-29s, five one-quarter ton trailers, 38 miscellaneous hand-drawn carts, and a considerable amount of explosives with little difficulty. All of her troops landed in her own boats, and reached the beach without a serious casualty to a single soldier. However, during the landings, seven of her LCVPs were lost. By 1145 all cargo had been unloaded, all troops debarked, and the remaining boats returned. All were hoisted by 1308 and *Dickman* prepared to get under way after exceptionally fast work. She stood out of the Transport Area at 1438 with 153 wounded and three dead. Two of her crew members were missing. One was killed in action when his landing craft received a direct hit and sank, and the other was wounded in action and taken to the U. S. destroyer *Shubrick* for medical attention.

Transports formed a single column for the return trip with *Barnett* as guide. After crossing the Channel, *Dickman* stood in to Portland Harbor at 2337 and anchored at 0119 on 7 June. All but 43

casualties were removed by an English lighter to Examination Service, Weymouth. *Dickman* then moved to Falmouth Harbor. *USS LCT-148* took off the remaining casualties.

The transport moved then to Plymouth Harbor on the 12th, embarked troops, and on the 14th joined a convoy proceeding to the Utah Transport Area. She debarked her troops there in a little over two hours. *Dickman* then departed in convoy for Falmouth Harbor and remained there until the 19th. Two days later she steamed to Loch Long Anchorage, Scotland, and remained there for the rest of the month.

*Samuel Chase* was with Force O, which attacked Omaha Beach about 20 miles to the east of Utah Beach—a much larger force with a tougher assignment. *Chase* sortied from Portland Harbor at 1727 on 5 June, and steamed with her convoy to the Transport Area off Omaha Beach, anchoring there at 0315 on 6 June. She had already lowered her scout boat, which had proceeded to its assigned duty. At 0510 she began lowering her landing boats, and at 0530 commenced debarking troops. The waves moved in to the beaches. Unloading of vehicles began shortly before 0800.

In spite of the effects of heavy naval and air bombardment at Omaha Beach, German opposition there was fierce and deadly—the most disastrous and damaging in the entire invasion. Casualties were heavy, and heroism great.

The landing operations followed the usual pattern, and by 1100 all vehicles and three Piper Cub planes had been unloaded by *Samuel Chase*, and all hatches were secured by 1150.

During this time, the Coast Guard-manned *LCI-85* (Lieutenant (jg) Coit T. Hendley, Jr., USCGR), hit a mine while going in to the beach. She careened through a jumble of beach defenses, got her ramps down, and began debarking troops. During the process, enemy fire blew off one ramp, killed 15 men, wounded 40, and set fires in three compartments. Small boats from the transports assisted in getting the remaining soldiers ashore. Despite all this, *LCI-85*, taking water slowly, returned to the Transport Area. She went alongside *Samuel Chase* just as unloading had been completed, and the wounded and dead were transferred to her by cargo boom. *LCI-85* then backed away and a salvage tug went alongside to determine if she could be saved. But she settled by the bow, capsized, floated for a while, and was then sunk by a demolition charge.

While the unloading of cargo was going on, casualties in a continuous stream were taken on board *Samuel Chase* from small craft. About 15 LCVPs which could be spared were sent back to the beach to help in unloading the LCIs. But at 1530, *Chase* began hoisting in her boats as they returned, preparatory to leaving the Transport Area. Six of her boats failed to return, having become casualties from gun fire, underwater obstacles, or swamping.

*Chase* got under way in convoy at 2006 and arrived at Weymouth Bay at 0536 on 7 June. She transferred her survivors, injured, and dead, which totaled 322 to a British tug. On 19 June, she proceeded to Loch Long Anchorage, Scotland.

Captain Imlay's LCI(L) Flotilla again did outstandingly fine work in the Invasion of Normandy. These small troop carriers performed duties similar to those which they carried out in the landings at Sicily and Salerno. The LCIs, assigned to Assault Groups 0-1, 0-2, and 0-3, assembled in the English Channel ports with their particular task forces; and accompanied them on the cross-channel voyages to the invasion beaches. For instance, the LCIs of Convoy Group 0-1 departed Weymouth about fourteen hours before H-hour, and proceeded with ten Coast Guard Rescue craft abreast of the transport section of the convoy for most of the trip. Captain Imlay, in *LCI-87*, was in this group which led the LCI section of Assault Force O.

The LCIs went in with troops at both Utah and Omaha Beaches. Most of the early waves of LCIs were unloaded into LCMs. The German 88s on shore promised to give plenty of trouble, and this unloading undoubtedly saved many of the LCIs for later work. This type of unloading was slower than landing directly on the beaches, but it avoided some risks such as heavier enemy fire and grounding on runnels and sand bars. Later, these landing craft went in to the shore. One way or another, the troops were successfully landed, although not without some casualties. During the operations, four Coast Guard-manned LCIs were lost—*LCI-85*, already mentioned, *LCI-91*, *LCI-92*, and *LCI-93*.

*LCI-91* (Lieutenant (jg) Arend Vyn, Jr., USCGR), approached a beach in the Omaha assault area, and proceeded through a maze of stakes topped by teller mines. She beached and began to debark troops in the face of heavy enemy fire. A crew member led a guide rope through the obstructions to the beach, and the LCI moved forward as the tide rose. On retracting, because stakes blocked further progress, the ship hit a teller mine which exploded on her port bow, killing several men and tearing a two-foot hole in the bow above the water line. She still had 200 troops to unload. *LCI-91* beached again 100 yards away, and part of the remaining troops got ashore. Then there was a violent explosion forward, followed by a blast of flame which enveloped the well deck. Since damage to the hull prevented retracting and the flames could not be controlled, the ship was abandoned.

When *LCI-92* (Lieutenant Robert M. Salmon, USCGR), went in to the same beach to land her 192 troops, she found *LCI-91* in flames and landed in her lee to use her smoke as a screen. She had cleared the outer obstacles when a terrific explosion on her port side rocked the ship, starting a fire, and spraying the forward deck with burning fuel oil. The crew battled the flames. Almost simultaneously, a shell exploded close aboard. Aground on a runnel, she started to unload troops under heavy rifle and machine gun fire. After all were ashore, an attempt was made to retract but the fire was intense and gaining, and Lieutenant Salmon ordered the ship abandoned. Fortunately, there were no casualties among the crew.

On her first trip in to Omaha Beach on 6 June, *LCI-93* (Lieutenant (jg) Budd B. Bornhoft, USCGR), encountered little enemy action and landed her troops. She made her second trip in the afternoon on a rapidly falling tide, passed over a sand bar and started to debark her soldiers. With about 25 troops still on board, the enemy found the range and several heavy batteries concentrated on the ship. One soldier was killed and four seriously wounded. The crew suffered five shrapnel casualties and two other men were seriously injured. After all of her troops were ashore, *LCI-93* retracted but grounded firmly on the bar astern. She had received ten direct hits; two through the pilot house; two in the bow; and the rest along the port side. Small boats were called alongside, to evacuate the wounded first, and then the crew. The vessel was so badly holed that no further attempt was made to save her.

These four LCIs were the only Coast Guard-manned LCIs lost during the entire war. They were in the midst of the hottest fighting in the Normandy invasion. The other LCIs of Captain Imlay's flotilla encountered light-to-severe enemy fire during the initial and earlier subsequent landings, but survived to carry on under quieter conditions. *LCI-83* and *LCI-88* received damage during the invasion, but after overhaul and repair performed further useful service. After the main assault phase, the LCIs were engaged in a variety of pursuits; they served as fire fighting ready ships and salvage ships; towed pontoons, causeways, and LSTs; directed small boat operations; served as channel guides; transported reinforcements to France; and performed other operational and logistical duties.

During a storm on 10 June, *LCI-319* towed two ammunition barges out of mined waters. For this devotion to duty her Commanding Officer, Lieutenant (jg) Francis X. Riley, USCG, later received the Bronze Star. The vessel also received damage during the severe storm on 20 June.

*LCI-83* (Lieutenant G. F. Hutchinson, USCGR), stood in to Omaha Beach at 0830 on 6 June, but was halted because of obstacles. A small boat went alongside to take off troops and succeeded in removing 36. A shell then smashed through the bulwarks, killing three men and wounding 13. An hour later, another boat took off 36 more troops. This process was slow and the Commanding Officer decided to try beaching again. In going in, a mine blew up through a troop compartment, causing extensive damage and injuring several men, but all troops except those wounded succeeded in getting ashore. The crew carried the casualties to the beach and turned them over to the medics.

The damage control party immediately commenced to patch the big hole, when word was given to abandon ship. Soon the tide left the ship high and dry. Demolition crews cleared away the obstacles astern while the crew waited on the beach. It was then planned to save the ship if possible, and each man was given an assignment, such as starting the pumps, securing plywood for patching, and pumping excess fuel overboard.

After the work was done, with one compartment still flooded because repairs were impossible there, *LCI-83* backed off the beach. Much equipment was jettisoned to lighten the bow, which was down seven feet. With pumps going, the motors operat-

ing, and the ship floating, Lieutenant Hutchinson tried to request permission to return to England, but could not contact the proper authority. The ship drifted all night in the Transport Area, her pumps keeping even with the water. The next morning permission was granted and *LCI-83* returned to Weymouth, England, under escort and was beached. She was later put back into service.

One of the best salvage records was that of *LCI-84*, though she was not designated as a salvage vessel. She served for a month as a fire fighter off Omaha Beach, but was instrumental in salvaging six vessels. *LCT-2037* had landed her troops and had struck a mine in doing so. *LCI-84* found her in a sinking condition with engine room and quarters flooded tied alongside an LST. The LCI began pumping her at 2300 and continued all night. Her men were in the flooded compartments to keep the strainers on the hoses clean. Water was low enough in the morning to allow temporary repairs. The ship was then backed up to a tug and towed to England, where she was made ready for further service.

On another occasion, *LCI-84* beached an engineless coaster which was sinking inside the Mulberry breakwater, one of those fabulous breakwaters built off the Normandy beaches by sinking floating units in position. While being pumped out she was pushed higher on the beach as the tide advanced. *LCT-999* was another vessel found in trouble. She was fully loaded and sinking 400 yards off the beach. The LCI commenced pumping and pushed her onto the beach so that her vehicles could be unloaded at the next low tide.

The coaster *Craigside* was found one night sinking a mile and a half off the beach with 13 feet of water in her engine room. *LCI-84* began pumping, gained on the water, and beached the craft. The LCI stayed alongside and repaired some of the holes. As the tide came in, *Craigside* was pumped and pushed farther up the beach and on the next low tide the salvage crew assumed responsibility for further repairs. DUKWs were unloading her during the whole process.

Six of the ten Coast Guard-manned LSTs took part as units in Forces O and U on the Omaha and Utah Beaches. The other four were attached to the British units farther east. Not one was lost. These vessels moved in to Normandy with the convoys; carrying troops, vehicles, and equipment of varying types. Some towed Rhino ferries—a development of the famous Seabee pontoon causeway—large rafts of pontoons which were powered with huge outboard motors. These were loaded from LSTs and then moved in to the beach, where they also served as floating piers over which LSTs could run their vehicles to shore.

Once these vessels had discharged their loads in the initial assault, most of them returned to England for reinforcements, both personnel and vehicular, and crossed the Channel many times. *LST-261* (Lieutenant Commander L. I. Reilly, USCG), serving with the British units, made no less than 53 channel crossings. On their return trips they were usually loaded with casualties from the beaches and the fighting inland.

The experience of *LST-21*, also assigned to British units, was typical of that of most vessels of this class. After loading 20 officers, 205 men, and 73 vehicles of the British Army at Southampton, England, on 1 June, *LST-21* (Lieutenant Charles M. Brookfield, USCGR), proceeded to an anchorage off the Isle of Wight, where a Rhino ferry and Rhino tug were secured and towed toward Normandy in convoy. En route, the Rhino tug broke loose and drifted off, but the Rhino ferry was cast off as planned in the assault area at 1210 on 6 June. At 1350, *LST-21* discharged six DUKWs from her ramp. At 1446, shells from a German 88-mm. gun began falling near the ships in the area. The first load was taken in to the beach at 1540 by Rhino ferry. At 1915 the LST went in to shore to meet the Rhino ferry which was laboring through a tidal current, and took on 13 casualties from a DUKW. The remaining vehicles were debarked at 2240 via the ferry, and the vessel went to her anchorage. A few minutes later, an air attack occurred and several sticks of bombs struck the water near her, causing no damage. A dive bombing attack followed the next day before the vessel left for Southampton.

*LST-21* returned from Southampton to Normandy on the 10th with 40 vehicles and 146 Army personnel. She beached during an air attack at 1649. Five hours later having unloaded, she retracted, and the next day joined a convoy for the Thames River. Here she took on 31 ammunition trucks and 131 Army personnel and returned to Normandy on the 13th. Taking a British LCT in tow on the 15th, she arrived at Calshot, England.

*LST-261*, which initially carried some of "Montgomery's Desert Rats" and tanks for the British Eighth Army, was bombed without damage; took a mine close aboard which necessitated some hand steering; had some casualties on her main deck; and was rammed by a British merchantman in a dense fog.

No particular difficulty was experienced by *LST-326* during the invasion, and she made many shuttle trips between England and France. On one of these, on 29 June, while transporting 900 German prisoners of war, she was detached from her convoy to aid the Liberty ship *H. G. Blasdel*, which had been hit and was settling by the stern. A corvette and a smaller craft were taking off casualties, but in the rough seas the small boats could not get the men off the stricken vessel fast enough. *LST-326* sent a boat with a doctor to *Blasdel*, and then moved alongside the vessel which was in imminent danger of exploding or sinking. The roll and pitch of the LST was so much greater than that of the larger ship that the distance between them ranged from sharp impact to nine or ten feet. Two breast lines were formed at the only point possible, holding the vessels about five feet apart, and in this way nine dead, 60 wounded, and 200 other survivors were taken on board the LST. All were Army personnel bound for the French beachhead. The entire transfer was completed in an hour and a half.

On 15 June, an enemy 105-mm. mobile battery opened fire on *LST-331* (Lieutenant W. D. Strauch, Jr.). This was her second trip to the Sword Area, the easternmost British beach. The first shot killed six men in the nearby Navy *LST-307*, and several more shells landed close to *LST-331*. Shrapnel rained on decks and personnel. Those on board who were not engaged in unloading were ordered to take shelter. One officer was wounded by shrapnel when a shell hit the deckhouse. As the LST was unloaded; had no guns large enough to be effective; and might be under fire six or seven hours until the tide changed, all personnel except a skeleton crew were evacuated to the beach. This was good judgment, for 80 to 100 shells were fired at all the LSTs in the next six hours, with *307* and *331* taking most hits. Then shelling subsided. The crew returned and repaired all underwater damage to the hull. In half an hour the ship was waterborne and left the beach.

The experiences of *LST-327* have been recounted in the chapter on Coast Guard Men and Navy Ships.

In planning for the Normandy invasion it was obvious that casualties to ships and personnel would be particularly heavy at the time of assault, and also for some time afterward. The Coast Guard's primary function of saving lives and property at sea and its pre-eminence in small boat handling caused the planners to turn to this Service for rescue operations in this great amphibious undertaking. Although the idea of a rescue flotilla came late—only a few weeks before D-day—it had been created and was on the job. Sixty vessels and nearly 1,000 men strong were ready when the invasion forces got underway for the assault. The work of The Coast Guard Rescue Flotilla One (and only), under the command of Lieutenant Commander Alexander Stewart, USCGR, was outstandingly efficient, vital, and heroic.

After the decision was made to form this Flotilla, things happened fast—they had to! Necessities of war had brought about creation of a large fleet of Coast Guard 83-foot cutters for anti-submarine, patrol, and rescue duties. Coast Guard units from Maine to Key West were secretly ordered to sail scores of 83-footers to New York. Within days, these fast, wooden-hulled craft, manned by one officer and thirteen men, began to accumulate at Staten Island where they were loaded upon decks of Liberty ships, LSTs, and freighters bound for the United Kingdom. These cutters were "processed" for their coming duties under the supervision of Lieutenant Commander Perry H. Simpson, USCG.

Only the skippers and skeleton crews stayed with each 83-footer while crossing the Atlantic, the rest being sent separately and joining their shipmates in English ports. *CG-45 (83466)*, commanded by Lieutenant (jg) Peter Chase, USCGR, like many others, was transported on the deck of a merchant ship. The convoy encountered dense fog between Milford Haven and Plymouth. With gasoline from the ship's lifeboats, the cutter's motors operated the generators which, in turn, provided power for the 83-footer's radar. The merchantman's skipper would have liked the cutter as permanent equipment after this, as it was his first experience with the wonderful seeing power of radar.

Preparation of these vessels and their crews for the invasion took on frantic proportions in the weeks remaining before D-day. Each cutter had to be stripped of its weighty anti-submarine armament. Crews were given intense first aid instruction. Skippers received indoctrination in the complicated operation of the invasion itself. A small repair party of 42 motor machinist's mates and carpenter's mates under the direction of Lieutenant Glenn S. Jennings, USCG, tuned the engines to top efficiency and checked the hulls. On D-day, every 83-footer was operational and ready.

The six-foot freeboard of these cutters posed a difficulty in getting on board men weakened from wounds, shock, and exposure. Therefore, to facilitate rescues directly from the water, scramble nets were made and rigged fore and aft on both sides. To make room for survivors, all excess gear was stripped from the decks. To lift the wounded, regardless of weight, heavy iron davits were constructed and rigged with block and tackle. Huge first aid kits were furnished. Two Assistant Surgeons, Martin R. Boltizar and John S. Micelli, were assigned to the Flotilla by the U. S. Public Health Service. Classes were held morning, noon, and night so that every man in the Flotilla would thoroughly know all phases of first aid. Extra stretchers together with thousands of blankets were supplied. Special rubber life rafts, which inflated themselves on contact with the water, were obtained from the RAF and supplied to each cutter. These proved of immense value in keeping groups of survivors afloat until rescues could be made by the cutters.

These 83-footers were organized into two distinct groups. Thirty were assigned to the British area (Sword, Juno, and Gold) and thirty to the American area (Omaha and Utah). On the eve of D-day, these fleets departed the Flotilla base and rendezvoused with the convoys forming along the channel coast. The trip to Normandy was a nightmare for these vessels due to heavy seas and a bad habit of the transports in going full speed for a while and then suddenly slowing down. However, not one rescue craft was lost during the trip to the French coast.

Only five 83-footers had been assigned to positions between the transports and the beaches. The rest were to stay near the transports, for the greatest disasters were expected here. However, it was barely light before it became evident that the Germans on shore were knocking out scores of small craft, LCTs and LCIs, as they went in to the beach. It was there that the initial rescue roles were played.

From this point onward, Coast Guard Rescue Flotilla One far more than justified itself. Its biggest job was, of course, on D-day. During the invasion, it made 1,438 rescues from the English Channel, but three months later these small craft were still picking survivors out of cold, stormy waters. Sometimes they rescued as many as 100 survivors a day.

As the assault waves hit the beaches, there were frantic calls from the first five cutters, and all but a few of the rescue craft which stayed with the transports went in as close as possible to the beach. Ensign Bernard B. Wood, USCG, made one of the first rescues with *CG-1* less than 2,000 yards off the beach. Forty-seven soldiers and sailors were taken from the water by this cutter only a few minutes after H-hour. The water was bitterly cold, and a fairly high sea was running. The majority were weakened from shock and immersion, and the Coast Guardsmen of *CG-1* went over the side and helped lift them bodily from the water. Shell fire from the beach was falling all around but the cutter kept underway until every man visible was picked up. Assault craft had the right of way, and scores were passing by. This meant that the rescue cutter had to speed in to a group of survivors and then maneuver out of the way as quickly as possible.

The rescue exploits of these 83-footers were so numerous that an attempt to cover even the more outstanding of them in this work would be impossible. The details of many rescues have never even been recorded. We shall recount some of the rescue missions which are typical examples of the heroic work of this Flotilla.

*CG-3* (Lieutenant (jg) William J. Starrett), went in close enough to the beach to rescue the crew of an American tank. After picking up the survivors, several small disabled landing craft with essential personnel and materiel were seen to be foundering. *CG-3* took these in tow and got them close enough to the beach to allow them to make their landing.

Thirty minutes after H-hour, Lieutenant (jg) James F. Smith in *CG-4* noticed that several landing craft with 3″ field pieces had been disabled by gun fire. Despite the heavy surf and continual shelling from shore batteries, *CG-4* towed the craft to shallow water where the gun crews were able to get their field pieces ashore. In the next few hours, this vessel picked 24 men out of the surf and transferred them to hospital ships.

Cutter *CG-2*, skippered by Ensign O. T. Meekings, USCGR, discovered that a number of DUKWs loaded with Army personnel had swamped en route to the beach. Although a heavy surf was running and there was great danger of the rescue craft hitting underwater obstacles, this cutter made many rescues, taking on board several unconscious survivors. En route to the hospital ship, artificial respiration was administered to the more seriously wounded, and not a single death occurred on board the cutter.

These vessels proved of great value aside from their actual rescues. *CG-8* (Ensign Richard S. Peer), was sent to stand by a large troop-laden British steamer which had received a direct bomb hit and panic on board had broken out. There were many casualties, and the ship began to burn fiercely. Ensign Peer discussed the situation over his loud hailer with the skipper of the steamer, and indicated that he was standing by to take off casualties and survivors if and when necessary. This conversation could be heard by all in the stricken vessel, and the presence of this one small craft had a quieting effect on the panicky personnel. Commodore Hugh T. England, RN, on board the cutter at the time, officially reported to the British Task Force Commander: "The cool and determined manner in which Ensign Peer informed the master that he was standing by had a most heartening effect on the men and I consider his handling of the whole situation is deserving of the highest praise."

*CG-16* (Lieutenant (jg) R. V. McPhail), tallied up a large rescue job on D-day. This cutter arrived with a group of miscellaneous invasion barges and accompanied some of these right in to the shore. Floating mines were taking their toll of the initial assault craft, and shellfire from the shore was very intense. At 0730 a landing craft converted to an ack-ack ship was hit by a shell a half mile off the beach and sank immediately. *CG-16* engaged in rescue operations. As the last survivor was picked up, a nearby PC was struck by a shell or mine and disintegrated completely. Men and debris were scattered over a wide area. The living survivors were picked up, and all 90 were taken to nearby *Joseph T. Dickman,* where they received medical attention and food.

Soon afterward, *CG-16* sighted an LCT under heavy fire, and sinking by the stern about 1,500 yards from the beach. The cutter maneuvered alongside and discovered that the vessel was loaded with ammunition and on fire. After taking off the wounded, *CG-16* pulled away, but Lieutenant Mc-Phail was told by a survivor that there was still another man with both legs broken on board the ship in a gun tub. Despite the great likelihood of an explosion from the fire raging around the ammunition, Lieutenant McPhail pulled alongside again. Volunteers went on board to get the wounded man, and he was hauled clear just as the LCT turned turtle and sank. The volunteers and the injured man were thrown into the water, but all were saved. *CG-16* had taken on board 126 casualties and one corpse in less than six hours! Lieutenant McPhail and each of his fifteen men received the Navy and Marine Corps Medal for their heroism.

On 16 June, an LCT was seen to hit a mine and begin to sink. *CG-17* (Ensign Alvis Dexter Arnhart, USCGR), found most of the crew still on board or clinging to the wreckage. Twenty-two men were saved; of this number, 19 were stretcher cases and severely wounded. Every man of the 83-footer went on board the LCT to assist in transferring the wounded. While the cutter was tied up alongside, the LCT suddenly sank. The Coast Guardsmen quickly chopped the lines with axes and *CG-17* swung free just in time to avoid being dragged down with the sinking ship. After rendering all possible first aid while en route to the nearest hospital ship, the survivors, all of whom were still alive, were transferred.

In August, a British hospital ship, heavily loaded with wounded, was mined and sank very quickly. In 90 minutes *CG-31* (Lieutenant (jg) Burke I. Powers), rescued 99 survivors, including a British nurse. Most were too weak to climb the cutter's side, so life rafts were thrown overboard to help in keeping the casualties afloat, while every member of the crew of the cutter went into the water to assist the wounded on board. When it was seen that many were unable to swim to nearby rafts and were drifting away with the tide, George C. Betz, Motor Machinist's Mate Second Class, USCGR, and R. T. Seamon, Seaman First Class, USCGR,

remained in the water throughout the entire period, assisting the seriously wounded to life rafts and seeing that they were safe until the cutter could go alongside. Many lives were attributed to their meritorious work.

Cutters *CG-32* and *CG-40* made a rescue which necessitated their crews boarding a sinking destroyer escort to remove casualties even after her decks were awash. Some members of these crews explored half-filled compartments below decks, and in addition to removing 24 survivors, the crew of *CG-32* inspected the depth charges and set them on "safe" before the DE sank. The whole operation took eight minutes. David O. Clark, Sonarman Second Class, USCGR, especially distinguished himself by remaining on the bridge of the DE and freeing one of the DE's crew who had become entangled in a line. With the help of J. S. Jordan, Seaman Second Class, USCGR, the wounded man was rigged onto a stretcher, but all avenues of escape were by then cut off by water. They had to swim for it, and the three were only a few yards from the stricken vessel when it capsized and sank.

Although many rescues were dangerous operations performed "under fire", the skipper of *CG-35* (Lieutenant (jg) George Clark), jeopardized himself and his crew to rescue the crew of a British LCT in another kind of fire. The LCT was carrying a large amount of gasoline when she struck a mine. The surrounding water became an inferno of blazing oil and gasoline. Despite this, Lieutenant Clark sped his craft without hesitation into the area and completed a very exciting, though hot, rescue.

A letter written on Admiralty stationery arrived for Lieutenant Clark. It stated: "I am commanded by My Lords Commissioners of the Admiralty to inform you that they have learned with great pleasure that, on the advice of the First Lord, the King has been graciously pleased to award you the Distinguished Service Cross for gallantry and devotion to duty shown when in command of the U. S. Coast Guard cutter No. 35 in the initial landings of the Allied Forces on the coast of Normandy on 6th June, 1944."

The incident which prompted the British Admiralty to make this award was unknown to the Flotilla or to Clark's brother officers until a memorandum arrived from the British authorities requesting permission to make the award. Lieutenant

Clark's trip report for that period had merely stated: "Survivors rescued, five. Corpses, none. Comments, none."

The U. S. Dispatch (Boat) Service was organized by the Supreme Headquarters Allied Expeditionary Force (SHAEF) on 20 June 1944 for the purpose of delivering registered mail, documents, and certain, often distinguished, personnel from England to France when at first air travel was not possible, and later when absolute security and safety were essential. To do this, six 83-footers from the Rescue Flotilla were detached and temporarily assigned to the U. S. Naval Advanced Base, Southampton. The duty involved nearly continuous crossings of the English Channel from Southampton to the American beaches, and later to Cherbourg.

The period of 19-23 June was extremely stormy off the beaches of Normandy, and most operations had to cease. The peak was reached on 21 June. When the storm broke, many skippers of the 83-footers were able to get underway and get out, but some of these vessels were trapped near shore. The area was so filled with underwater obstructions, unmarked wrecks, and such, that some small craft found it impossible to keep way on, and the wind and sea were too much for their light ground tackle. Many larger vessels dragged anchor and swept onto the beaches. Two of the 83-footers, *CG-27 (83415)* and *CG-47 (83471)* foundered in this storm. One had her whole bottom taken off by some submerged obstacle and sank in 30 feet of water. The other was crushed onto the beach by a stranding LST and became a total loss. No other 83-footers were lost in the entire operation.

One of the chief objectives of the landings at Utah Beach was to put the Army ashore in a position to allow capture of the important channel port of Cherbourg. Despite the Nazis and the weather, the beachheads had held and had grown. The artificial breakwaters served as active "ports" through which flowed all men, vehicles, equipment, and supplies for the great Allied war machine. But to adequately support the growing and advancing armies, a major deep-water port was vital. Cherbourg, lying in the middle of the northern coast of the Cotentin Peninsula, was the immediate need.

In the two weeks after the landings, American troops had driven across the base of the peninsula and isolated Cherbourg which, nevertheless, was heavily fortified. The Americans closed in from the land side. By 25 June, they were fighting in the streets of the city, while the thunder of German demolitions in the port area reverberated from the surrounding hills. On that day, United States and British battleships and cruisers, under the command of Rear Admiral Deyo, bombarded the port from the sea, and were met with intense retaliatory fire from the enemy's shore batteries. Navy planes spotted for the ships in laying down their fire on Cherbourg, and the Army called for fire support wherever and whenever needed. After three hours of intense shelling of Cherbourg, Admiral Deyo signaled for his ships to retire. The heavy guns in the forts had been put out of commission, though some garrisons held out for several days.

At 1500 on 26 June, the German Army and Navy joint commanders at Cherbourg surrendered. On 1 July, the last enemy unit was captured. All resistance in the northern Cotentin Peninsula came to an end, and Cherbourg was in Allied hands. The capture of this port three weeks after the first landings in Normandy, was one of the great strategic triumphs of the war.

Lieutenant Commander Quentin R. Walsh, USCG, while assigned to the Logistics and Planning Section, U. S. Naval Forces in London, had devoted intensive study to determine the capacities of ports to be captured from Germany for handling cargo. He wrote the plans for the occupation and operation of the ports of Le Havre, Rouen, and Cherbourg; arranging for the allocation of personnel and materials at, and the logistics support of, the captured ports. As Chief Staff and Operations Officer with Commander Ports, under Task Force 127, he supervised all the planning of logistics.

He and Lieutenant Frank Lauer, USNR, a Seabee officer, had an amazing adventure at Cherbourg before resistance there had ceased. Between them, they forced the surrender of a Nazi harbor area stronghold, Fort du Homet, taking 300 marine soldiers and liberating about 50 American paratroopers who had been prisoners since D-day. The two entered the fort knowing it had not surrendered. When within shouting distance they told the Nazis that all resistance had ended, but they were not believed. Meanwhile, the Germans covered the two officers with machine guns but held their fire, thinking a large patrol was following them. Only after accepting an invitation to view the situation in the city did the Germans realize that Cherbourg had fallen.

Following the success of the assaults, which had established a good foothold on French soil, there were six weeks of grueling struggle to secure a lodgment area of depth sufficient to build up a striking force great enough to exploit the successes. The flow of materiel and personnel from across the channel continued despite interruptions due to weather conditions. With the capture of Cherbourg, the lodgment area expanded notably, and after portions of that harbor were cleared of sunken vessels and debris, the port became tremendously valuable to the Allied forces.

Allied striking power grew. Fighting was bloody and vicious, but gradually the armies in France gained ground, and by late July the Allies had made a breakthrough in the west. By 12 August, Normandy, west of the invasion area, and substantially all of Brittany except two or three ports were under Allied control.

In the east, the Russian Army was moving forward on a wide front. General Patton's Third Army had broken out of Normandy and was sweeping through France in a great arc toward Paris. A landing of troops on the French Mediterranean shores and a push northward to join with General Eisenhower's forces held great potentialities. The proposal for such an attack was made in 1943 at the Casablanca Conference, and designated Operation "ANVIL." Even before the fall of Cherbourg, plans were being formulated for the invasion of southern France as a subsidiary action of the main effort in the north. The Germans, once fearful of a second front, would then be confronted with a fourth!

Such an operation appeared logical to the enemy and even the point of attack could be closely estimated. Mediterranean ports such as Oran, Algiers, Bizerte, Alexandria, Palermo, and Naples were bulging with shipping; many with a concentration of landing craft. Therefore, the coming operation was not much of a secret and lacked the full force of surprise, but the enemy gave little evidence of acting on such knowledge or suspicions as he may have had.

It was planned to make three separate but simul-

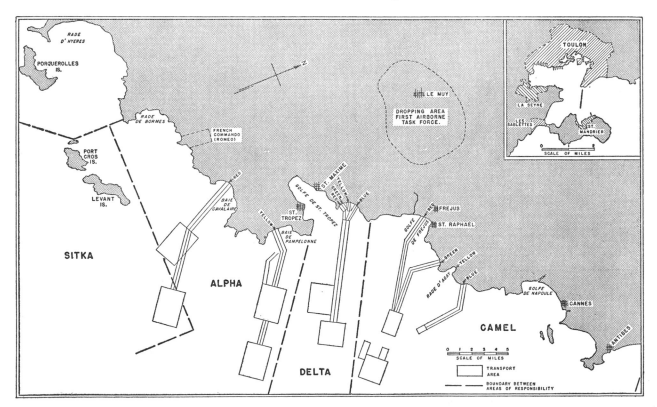

AREA OF ASSAULT IN SOUTHERN FRANCE

taneous strikes from the sea and one from the land; the latter by American and British paratroopers and glider-borne infantry put down ten to fifteen miles inland. Vice Admiral Hewitt was in over-all command of the Naval forces. A task force under Rear Admiral Bertram J. Rodgers, USN, would put amphibious forces of the 3rd Division (Major General J. W. O'Daniel), ashore east of Rade de Hyères. Another under Rear Admiral Frank J. Lowry, USN, would attack the center near Cape Nègre in Bougnon Bay, landing units of Major General W. W. Eagle's 45th Division. To the east, a task force commanded by Rear Admiral Spencer S. Lewis, USN, would set ashore the 36th Division under Major General J. E. Dahlquist. About 800 vessels took part in this assault along the Riviera between Toulon and Cannes.

As in Operation "Neptune", the great variety of vessels in far-flung ports had to reach their objectives at the same time. Landings were scheduled for 0800 on the morning of 15 August. There were preliminary diversions and some sporadic surface actions. Rangers went ashore four hours before the main attack and spiked enemy guns. The big transports anchored in the Transport Areas at daybreak, with landing craft following astern. A hundred vessels of the fire support groups awaited the order to fire. Just to be different, the weather was perfect.

A terrific naval bombardment shook the area. Then naval air power went in to bomb the beaches ahead of the first waves of landing craft. Rocket ships laid down their barrage, and at 0802 the first landing boats touched the beaches. There was virtually no opposition to the landings.

Coast Guard-manned transports engaged in this operation were the familiar *Bayfield, Samuel Chase,* and *Joseph T. Dickman,* and a newcomer, *Cepheus* (Commander R. C. Sarratt, USCG). In addition, Navy transports *Barnett, Charles Carroll, Arcturus,* and *Betelgeuse* had some Coast Guardsmen in their crews. There was also the 327-foot cutter *Duane* (Commander Harold C. Moore, USCG). Smaller vessels were *PC-545* and *PC-556,* veterans of the Sicily-Italy landings, and four LCIs experiencing their first invasion—*LCI-520, LCI-562, LCI-581,* and *LCI-583.*

*Bayfield,* still under the command of Captain Spencer, and serving as Admiral Lewis's flagship,

departed Naples on 13 August with the Commanding General and troops of the 36th Division. In the assault she debarked them near St. Raphael in the easternmost right flank area. *Samuel Chase* steamed into her transport area, and an hour later began debarking her troops for a landing on the beach in the Bay of Pampelonne. There was light enemy fire in that sector, and two members of her boat crews received gun shot wounds. *Dickman* landed her troops in Bougnon Bay in the central area. A coxswain of her crew was wounded by machine gun fire. The LCIs and LSTs also went in and discharged their troops and equipment. After most of the soldiers had been debarked, unloading of vehicles, supplies, and equipment began. Most unloading was completed by evening.

*Duane* departed Naples on 9 August, with Admiral Lowry and General O'Daniel and their staffs on board. After a stop at Ajaccio, Corsica, she left on the 14th, in convoy, and served as guide to the assault area in the vicinity of Baie de Cavalaire, arriving there at 0451 on 15 August. Two hours later, *Duane* with all assault craft, proceeded from the outer to the inner transport area, where she remained until 1612 when she went into Baie de Cavalaire to moor. *Duane* carried a maximum of medical supplies and had augmented her medical personnel. However, the department's facilities were not called into use except for routine medical cases, as she treated no casualties due to enemy action.

The operations went on with little interruption, though there was sporadic fire from shore and some air opposition. Vessels countered the latter with antiaircraft fire, and smoke was made on several occasions. During one raid a Navy LST was hit, caught fire, suffered several explosions, and was finally beached. It was the only vessel casualty on D-day during the landings in southern France.

Within three days, the invasion forces had pushed ahead 35 miles in some places, and, under the leadership of Major General Alexander M. Patch, USA, the Seventh Army was driving northward toward a junction with General Eisenhower's forces from Normandy. By 20 August, they were on the outskirts of Aix-en-Provence, in a drive that virtually isolated the great port of Marseille and the naval base at Toulon, on which they were closing in, following a heavy air and naval bombardment.

Naval forces were active in following up the landings on "the soft underbelly of Europe." Transports and other elements of these forces continued for many weeks to bring reinforcements of personnel and materiel.

The defeat in Normandy and the German withdrawal to the Seine made it apparent that the Nazis had lost hope of holding central and southern France. In mid-France their position was being jeopardized by the growing success of the free French Forces of the Interior. The landings in southern France forced them to speed up their withdrawal. The Allies occupied Marseille on 23 August and Toulon on 27 August—both strong holdouts—and the main force drove up the valley of the Rhone across the German line of flight. Lyon fell on 3 September without opposition. Some of the German force were pushed toward Dijon where they surrendered together with other forces fleeing from the west. The rest retired toward Belfort Gap, and in that area the Allied force from the south made contact with that from the north on 11 September.

France was soon largely cleared of Germans and the liberation was virtually complete. From that point on, until final victory on 8 May 1945, it was an Army campaign supported logistically by naval forces and, for the most part, the work of the Coast Guard in the European Theatre came to an end.

# Chapter 18

# FROM PEARL HARBOR THROUGH THE SOLOMONS

WITH THE COMPLETION of the invasions in the European Theatre, there was a movement of sea power from that area to the Pacific, where it was essential to bring all possible pressure to bear upon the Japanese. This stepped up the tempo of the Pacific War, which, of course, had been in progress during the entire period of the North African and European invasions. The campaign in the Aleutians, already recounted, was almost apart from the campaigns in the South and Southwest Pacific. It cleared the Japanese out of Alaskan territory and occupied some Japanese naval forces which could have been useful elsewhere, but it accomplished little more. The Japanese had proved tough adversaries in the other Pacific areas against which, in the earlier days, the United States was unable to bring sufficient sea power to halt and repel aggression. In those first months there were not enough ships, planes, and trained men; to a large extent European operations had priority.

Yet, the Japanese had to be contained and then beaten. European priority was no reflection upon the importance of the Pacific Theatre, but a two-ocean war with our forces spread too thin would have been disastrous. The defeat of Hitler's hordes in Europe was imperative. Early concentration on one enemy, while endeavoring to contain the other and build up fighting power, was tactically correct.

Progress of the United States and allied forces from the "day that will live in infamy" to the day when Japan was finally brought to her knees was, for the most part, geographically coordinated. Except for the Aleutian campaign, the Pacific War can be treated chronologically, and we shall go back to the time of Pearl Harbor to pick up the thread of operations against Japan.

The Japanese strike on Pearl Harbor on the early morning of 7 December 1941, caught 94 ships of the United States Navy, including eight battleships. Three hours later, the battle was over. The attack virtually put the U. S. Pacific Fleet out of effective action for many months; several large ships were destroyed, others were returned to service only after extensive repairs. In that one air attack the Navy lost about three times as many men as it had lost by enemy action in the Spanish-American War and World War I combined. The resulting deficiency in American sea power in the Pacific facilitated Japanese expansion in the Western Pacific during early 1942.

Pearl Harbor was only the beginning of rapid, well-planned strikes by the Japanese. On 8 December, the day the United States declared war on Japan, the Japanese landed in the Philippine Islands. On that same day there was a three-pronged amphibious landing on the Malay Peninsula. Almost simultaneously, Hong Kong was bombed, and a Japanese army invaded Thailand from Indochina. Guam, the only American possession in the Marianas, was attacked from the air on 8 December, and on the 10th the Japanese landed there. Guam fell after brave but futile resistance. Wake Island lying almost midway between Hawaii and the Philippines, was bombed by sea and air on 8 December, but held out after the only fight in the Pacific War in which coast defense guns beat off an amphibious landing. However, Wake fell on 22 December after a heroic stand.

On 11 January 1942, the enemy landed paratroops and amphibious forces on Celebes and took Tarakan Island off the east coast of Borneo. United States naval forces fought a battle off Balikpapan, Borneo, in the Makassar Strait, which was their first surface action in the Pacific War. It was a tactical victory for the U. S. Navy, but it failed to halt the Japanese advance.

COAST GUARDSMAN DIRECTS TRAFFIC ON BEACH AT GUADALCANAL . . . . landing craft bring in streams of supplies and equipment to the newly-won beachhead.

BRITISH EMPIRE TROOPS RETURN TO *HUNTER LIGGETT* AFTER REHEARSALS . . . . soldiers go up the landing nets and over the side to their quarters.

MARINES HELP COAST GUARDSMEN TO UNLOAD SUPPLIES . . . . landing craft beach at Guadalcanal in the shadow of a Japanese ship which was stranded after the Naval Battle of Guadalcanal.

LANDING CRAFT OF THE FIRST WAVE AT BOUGAINVILLE . . . . Coast Guard boats assemble to take the Marines
to the beaches of Empress Augusta Bay. Mount Bagana, a smoking volcano, rises in the background.

THE COAST GUARD SALVAGES A TWO-MAN JAPANESE SUBMARINE . . . . tender *Ironwood* raised this submarine
from 24 feet of water at Guadalcanal and delivered it to Tulagi Harbor for examination by naval officers.

**A COAST GUARD-MANNED LST BEACHES AT CAPE GLOUCESTER** . . . . she prepares to deliver a big
load of supplies to the American forces of occupation.

WOUNDED MARINE RETURNS TO HIS SHIP OFF TARAWA . . . . Coast Guardsmen bring this casualty on board their transport from the beachhead as the battle raged.

UNITED STATES TROOPS ADVANCE ON MAKIN ATOLL . . . . soldiers pass a large Japanese seaplane, downed by American planes.

COAST GUARDSMEN AND MARINES BUILD A TEMPORARY CAUSEWAY . . . . this assisted unloading as the invasion of Cape Gloucester got underway.

The Japanese landed at Rabaul, New Britain, on 23 January, where the Australians had an advanced air base. The forces of Emperor Hirohito soon expanded their power along the New Britain and New Ireland coasts; then to the north coast of Papua and the northern Solomon Islands. As they went, they established powerful air and naval bases. The enemy occupied Makin in the Gilberts, and other islands in the Marshalls, Carolines, and Marianas. In February, southern Sumatra fell to the Japanese; Singapore surrendered; and Timor, Bali, Borneo, and Ambon were in enemy hands. The Battle of the Java Sea took place on 27 February; this was an attempt by Allied naval forces to halt an invasion of Java, but the Allies had to break off in defeat. Java was taken over by the Japanese.

In the period from December 1941 through March 1942, Japanese Admiral Nagumo had operated one-third of the way around the world; from Hawaii to Ceylon, and from Japan to the northern approaches of Australia. Most of the islands in that great area and a good deal of the Asiatic mainland were then under Japanese control. Allied forces fought valiantly to halt the enemy throughout this period, but the Japanese had the initiative and superior naval forces despite transfers of United States naval vessels from the Atlantic to the Pacific. They forged ahead relentlessly. Nevertheless, the enemy had spread himself very thin. This was the situation when the Japanese tide reached flood stage, and when Colonel "Jimmy" Doolittle's bombers raided Tokyo from Admiral Halsey's carriers on 18 April 1942.

During this period of Japanese aggression, United States naval forces in the Pacific were being gradually augmented. The Coast Guard, however, played no significant part until preparations were being made for the first amphibious assault.

At the time of the attack on Pearl Harbor, the 327-foot Coast Guard cutter *Taney* (Captain G. B. Gelly, USCG), was on routine duty at Honolulu. Within four minutes after the initial attack, her guns were fully manned. She fired on scattering formations of enemy aircraft at about 0900 and at 1135. Just before noon, five enemy planes approached *Taney* from over the harbor entrance on what appeared to be a glide bombing attack on the cutter or on the power plant north of the vessel's berth. *Taney* fired with 3-inch guns and .50 caliber machine guns. While there were no direct hits, the enemy planes were rocked by the fire and swerved up and away.

The days immediately following saw *Taney* patrolling off Honolulu. She made several sound contacts and depth charge attacks. She remained on patrol duty, alternating with USS *Southard* until 22 January. She then escorted steamship *Barbara Olson* to Canton Island in the Phoenix group north of Samoa, and then to Palmyra. *Taney* removed four Department of the Interior colonists from Enderbury Island and from Jarvis Island, in each case destroying the buildings and equipment. She resumed patrol duty at Honolulu on 5 March.

This was about the only Coast Guard duty performed in the Pacific outside of the continental United States and Alaska during that period of the war. There was little wartime augmentation of the number of Coast Guard vessels operating in the Honolulu District.

American naval aggressiveness gradually built up as additional vessels, including carriers, and more planes became available to Admiral Nimitz. The Battle of the Coral Sea on 7-8 May resulted from an American effort to check further enemy advances in the New Guinea-Solomons area and to repulse a Japanese thrust to capture Port Moresby. It was the first strictly carrier versus carrier naval battle in which air action inflicted all the losses and no vessel on either side caught sight of a surface enemy. The battle resulted in a tactical victory for Japan, but a strategic victory for the United States. The capture of Port Moresby was thwarted.

Throughout the early months the enemy's advances, and his increasing strength menaced Allied lines of communication. As the American fleet, damaged at Pearl Harbor, was gradually repaired, reinforcements were consolidated in the Southwest Pacific. In April, it was decided to attempt to halt the Japanese advance by an attack on the Solomon Islands. The two original objectives were the small islands just off Florida Island known as Tulagi and Gavutu. But later in July, when planes observed a Japanese landing field under construction on nearby Guadalcanal Island, from which land-based planes could threaten New Hebrides and New Caledonia, the occupation of that island also became imperative.

Vice Admiral Robert L. Ghormley, USN, became commander of all the United Nations' land, sea, and air forces in the South Pacific area except for the New Zealand land defense forces. Major General Alexander A. Vandergrift, USMC, was to lead the occupation forces as commander of the 1st Marine Division, the first echelon of which reached New Zealand on 14 June.

Meanwhile, the Battle of Midway was imminent. Midway Atoll, about 1,000 miles west-northwest of Hawaii, was at this time the western-most American base in the Pacific. It was coveted by the Japanese, and Admiral Yamamoto planned its capture and occupation. The occupation by Japanese of Kiska and Attu and the attack on Dutch Harbor were subsidiary actions of the main Midway operation. Admiral Nimitz received intelligence as to the Japanese plans, and sent two substantial task forces to meet the attack. These were commanded by Rear Admirals Frank Jack Fletcher, USN and Raymond A. Spruance, USN. In addition a cooperating submarine force under the operational control of Rear Admiral Robert H. English, USN, was made available.

The opposing fleets met on 4 June, and the ensuing three day engagement was one of the most decisive naval battles of the war, and the first serious defeat suffered by the Japanese Navy. Admirals Fletcher and Spruance, with one carrier thrust, destroyed the air power of Yamamoto's fleet despite the latter's superior gun power. It was a battle in which aircraft and submarines did all of the hitting. American aviators destroyed four Japanese carriers and one cruiser, while the Americans lost one carrier and a destroyer. The enemy finally retired without having accomplished his mission.

With our success off Midway, preparations for the Solomon Islands attack were accelerated, and D-day was set for 7 August.

The enemy landed at Ambasi and at Buna on 21 July in a movement down the east coast of New Guinea. The series of enemy land-plane bases which had been established at Rabaul, at Kieta on Bougainville, and on Guadalcanal, together with seaplane bases at Gavutu, Gizo, Rekata Bay, Kieta, and Buka Passage, exposed our Australia-bound convoys to torpedo or bombing attack, and aggressive opposition on our part became still more urgent. Since large enemy ships, especially carriers, had not been observed in southern Solomon waters

since the Coral Sea and Midway battles, it seemed especially desirable to strike at once.

Guadalcanal is a mountainous island 90 miles long and 25 miles wide. It was to be bitterly contested by the United States and Japanese naval, air, and ground forces for nearly six months. Its waters were to be the scene of six major naval engagements, and 50-odd ship-to-ship and air-sea fights.

Assault troops, mostly of the 1st Marine Division were assembled at New Zealand and San Diego. Group Three of the U. S. Carrier Task Force left San Diego on 1 July; it included the carrier *Wasp*, five transports with the 2nd Marine Division on board, and various escorts. Group One of the Carrier Task Force, with *Saratoga*, left Pearl Harbor on 7 July. Group Two, with carrier *Enterprise* and battleship *North Carolina* left Pearl Harbor a few days later. The combined force of transports and cargo ships departed Wellington with their escorts on 22 July.

Vice Admiral Frank Jack Fletcher, USN, in carrier *Saratoga*, had over-all command of the assault forces. Rear Admiral Richmond K. Turner, USN, was given command of the Amphibious Force South Pacific, and flew his flag at Wellington, New Zealand, in *McCawley*, one of 23 transports in the attacking fleet. The Amphibious Force was escorted by eight cruisers, three of which were Australian, and a destroyer screen under Rear Admiral V. A. C. Crutchley, RN. Rear Admiral Leigh Noyes, USN, commanded the Air Support Force of three carriers, a battleship, five heavy cruisers, one light cruiser, 16 destroyers, and three oilers.

Almost the whole force rendezvoused on 26 July at a mid-ocean point about 400 miles south of the Fiji Islands, and rehearsal exercises were then held at Koro Island in the Fijis. Thereafter, about 75 ships headed for the assault. Shore-based Navy and Army planes at Efate, Noumea, Tongatabu, the Fijis, and Samoa were divided into seven task groups which searched a vast area of ocean and conducted antisubmarine patrols as the fleet proceeded toward its objective. An air attack on Tulagi and Guadalcanal began a week before the arrival of these vessels.

The Coast Guard-manned transport *Hunter Liggett* (Commander Louis W. Perkins, USCG), was in the force steaming toward Guadalcanal. Of the 22 Navy-manned transports, 18 carried vary-

## COAST GUARD-MANNED VESSELS
### ENGAGED IN AMPHIBIOUS OPERATIONS IN PACIFIC, 1942–1943

| Name of Vessel | Guadalcanal-Tulagi | Capture, Defense Guadalcanal | Consolidation, Southern Solomons | Tulagi-Loki Point | Vila-Stanmore Kolombangara | Vila-Stanmore-Munda | New Georgia-Rendova | Vella Lavella | Finschafen | Bougainville | Tarawa-Makin | Cape Gloucester |
|---|---|---|---|---|---|---|---|---|---|---|---|---|
| Arthur Middleton | | | | | | | | | | | X | |
| Hunter Liggett | X | X | | X | | | | | | X | | |
| Leonard Wood | | | | | | | | | | | X | |
| LST-18 | | | | | | | | | X | | | X |
| LST-19 | | | | | | | | | | | X | |
| LST-20 | | | | | | | | | | | X | |
| LST-22 | | | | | | | | | | | | X |
| LST-23 | | | | | | | | | X | | | |
| LST-66 | | | | | | | | | | | | X |
| LST-67 | | | | | | | | | X | | | X |
| LST-68 | | | | | | | | | | | | X |
| LST-69 | | | | | | | | | | | X | |
| LST-70 | | | | | | | | | | X | | |
| LST-71 | | | | | | | | | | X | | |
| LST-166 | | | | | | | | | | X | | |
| LST-167 | | | | | | | | X | | | | |
| LST-168 | | | | | | | | | X | | | X |
| LST-169 | | | | | | | | | | | X | |
| LST-202 | | | | | | | | | | | | X |
| LST-203* | | | | | | | | | | | | |
| LST-204 | | | | | | | | | X | | | X |
| LST-205 | | | | | | | | | | | X | |
| LST-206 | | | | | | | | | | | | X |
| LST-207 | | | | | | | | | | X | | |

### NAVY VESSELS WITH A FEW COAST GUARDSMEN IN THEIR CREWS

| Name of Vessel | Guadalcanal-Tulagi | Capture, Defense Guadalcanal | Consolidation, Southern Solomons | Tulagi-Loki Point | Vila-Stanmore Kolombangara | Vila-Stanmore-Munda | New Georgia-Rendova | Vella Lavella | Finschafen | Bougainville | Tarawa-Makin | Cape Gloucester |
|---|---|---|---|---|---|---|---|---|---|---|---|---|
| Alchiba | X | X | | | | | | | | X | | |
| Alhena | X | X | | | | | | | | X | | |
| American Legion | X | | | | | | | | | X | | |
| Barnett | X | X | | | | | | | | | | |
| Bellatrix | X | X | | | | | | | | | X | |
| Betelgeuse | X | X | | | | | | | | | | |
| Crescent City | X | X | X | | | X | | | | X | | |
| Fuller | X | X | | X | | | | | | X | | |
| George F. Elliott | X | | | | | | | | | | | |
| Gregory | X | X | | | | | | | | | | |
| Heywood | X | | | | | | | | | | X | |
| Libra | X | X | | X | X | | X | | | X | | |
| Little | X | X | | | | | | | | | | |
| McCawley | X | X | | | | | X | | | | | |
| Neville | X | | | | | | | | | | X | |
| President Adams | X | X | X | | | | X | | | X | | |
| President Hayes | X | X | X | | | | X | | | X | | |
| President Jackson | X | X | X | | | | X | | | X | | |
| Stringham | | X | | | | | | X | | X | | X |
| LST-334 | | | | | | | | X | | X | | |
| William P. Biddle | | | | | | | | | | | X | |

*Lost at Nanomea.

ing numbers of Coast Guardsmen whose primary duty was to man and operate landing craft. (On the preceding page is a tabulation listing all vessels manned wholly or partly by the Coast Guard in the 1942-1943 Pacific landings, showing in what operation or operations each was involved. The extent of Coast Guard participation at Guadalcanal is made clear.)

The plan of attack called for use of about 19,546 Marines, comprising eight groups. Combat Group A would land at H-hour on Beach Red between Lunga and Koli Points on the north coast of Guadalcanal, and seize the beachhead. The Support Group, with the command post afloat in *Hunter Liggett*, would go ashore at Beach Red; provide artillery support for the attack; and coordinate antiaircraft and close-in ground defense of the beachhead. Combat Group B, to land there 50 minutes later, would seize a grassy knoll four miles south of Lunga Point.

The Tulagi Group, landing at H-hour on Beach Blue on the southwest coast of Tulagi, would seize the northwest section of that island. The Gavutu Group would land four hours later on the east coast of Gavutu Island; seize that island; and press on to adjacent Tanambogo. The Division Reserve Group was to be prepared to land Combat Team B on Gavutu Island and attach Combat Team C to the Tulagi Group. The Florida Group was to land on Florida Island near Haleta at H-hour plus 20 minutes, and secure that village. The Third Defense Battalion was to be ready to land detachments anywhere on receipt of orders. Shore Party commanders would control traffic in beach areas, calling on troop commanders for assistance in handling supplies from landing beaches to dumps.

With these well defined plans, the fleet passed through the southern New Hebrides and northwestward on 3 August and then turned almost due north toward Guadalcanal. On 6 August, an overcast sky and mist fortunately made enemy reconnaissance impossible. At 0300 on 7 August, two squadrons designated "Yoke" and "Xray" separated; the first passing north of Savo Island toward Tulagi and the second passing south of Savo Island along the north coast of Guadalcanal. There was no challenge and the arrival apparently was undetected.

At 0530 the first planes took off from the U. S. carriers. The 15 transports of Squadron "Xray"

steamed along the silent Guadalcanal shore in two columns of seven and eight ships each. At 0613, *USS Quincy* began bombarding the coast, and dive bombers attacked enemy shore positions. At 0647 the transports halted 9,000 yards off Beach Red, led in to the anchorage by *Hunter Liggett*. Boats were lowered and debarkation began. The cruisers and destroyers which were not to give fire support, formed a double arc about the transports as protection against planes and submarines.

Fire support for the landings began soon after 0900 and lasted for about ten minutes. At 0913 the first troops landed on Beach Red between Lunga and Koli Points without ground opposition. Expecting the greater resistance on Guadalcanal, most of our landing forces were concentrated there. This accounted for the comparative ease of the initial landing, as well as the fact that the enemy could, and did, retire to the hills. Despite interruptions caused by enemy air attacks the occupation of the Guadalcanal shore front proceeded expeditiously.

*Hunter Liggett*, the only wholly Coast Guard-manned vessel at Guadalcanal, was one of the largest attack transports in the Amphibious Force; she carried 35 landing boats and two tank lighters; she had 51 officers and a crew of 634. *Liggett's* troops were not to be landed in the assault waves, as they were support, special weapons, and headquarters troops. Therefore, most of her boats were dispatched to other vessels which were sending troops in the first assault waves. Coast Guardsmen in other transports took their landing craft in and discharged troops and equipment.

Opposition to the landings took the form of air attacks which proved very troublesome. At 1323, about 20 Japanese bombers, flying very high, dropped bombs but made no hits, and disappeared over the mountains; this was followed by other attacks. Unloading continued between raids. A Coast Guard Beachmaster and about 40 Coast Guardsmen went to the beach and supervised the landing of the boats, their unloading, repair, and salvage. By 2200 the beach had become so clogged with supplies which were coming ashore faster than they could be moved away that unloading was halted. In all, about 11,000 Marines went ashore during the first day.

At 1054 the next day, 8 August, *Liggett* and the rest of the unit got underway in anticipation

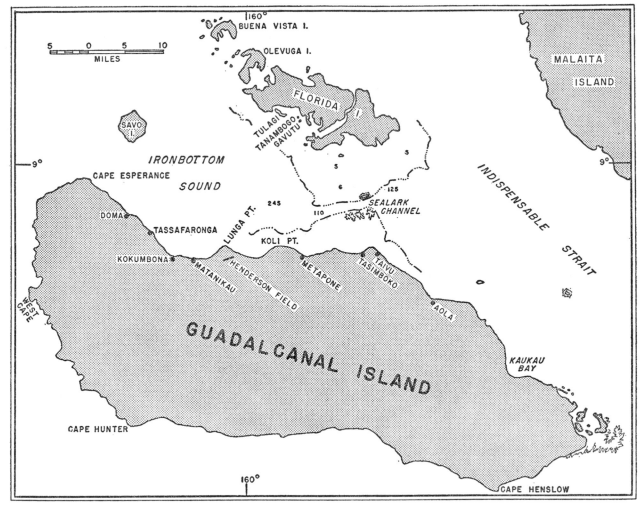

GUADALCANAL AND FLORIDA ISLANDS

of an air attack which came at 1204. Seventeen heavy bombers swept over the rear screen and dropped to deck height before reaching the transports. Four Japanese bombers were shot down by *Liggett's* batteries. Antiaircraft fire from the various vessels accounted for all of the planes! *Liggett* suffered only superficial damage; but a crippled Japanese bomber crashed onto the deck of *George F. Elliott*, which carried some Coast Guardsmen in her crew. This set a fire which burned fiercely, got out of control, and eventually caused the loss of that transport.

During the afternoon of the 8th, Lieutenant Commander Dwight H. Dexter, USCG, and 25 Coast Guardsmen went ashore from *Hunter Liggett* with their landing craft to set up a naval operating base on Lunga Point. Dexter assumed the

duties of Beachmaster. He and his men proved courageous and resourceful, and were indispensable in moving small groups of Marines along the coast. In the evening, Captain W. O. Bailey, USN, with 22 officers and 308 enlisted men from sunken *Elliott* were taken on board *Liggett*.

During the Battle of Savo Island, early on the morning of the 9th, *Liggett* and other transports in the Guadalcanal area again got under way for defensive maneuvering, but returned later to complete unloading. Survivors and casualties from the cruisers *Vincennes*, *Astoria*, and *Quincy*, sunk in the Battle of Savo Island, were taken on board the *Liggett*, bringing the total to 686 American survivors and three wounded Japanese prisoners. At 1510, with *Liggett* as guide, the transport group put to sea, having completed its mission. *Liggett* went to Noumea, New Caledonia, and remained there until September.

Meanwhile, operations were proceeding at Tulagi where landing craft were also handled by Coast Guardsmen, usually with crews of three. The bombardment there began at about the same time as at Guadalcanal. Going into action at 0614, fighters and dive bombers started fires, destroyed 18 enemy planes on the water, strafed the beaches, and pounded the buildings. The ships of Squadron "Yoke" arrived in the transport area at 0637. There were preliminary landings from *President Jackson* east of Haleta, and at Halavo on Florida Island, near Tulagi, and at Gavutu respectively. The Haleta landing was to prevent enemy use of a promontory jutting south from Florida Island to enfilade landing boats on Tulagi Island's Beach Blue. After naval bombardment, the Marines went ashore without opposition.

In the landing at Halavo an enemy battery opened fire at 4,000 yards and was met by fire from three naval vessels. Despite the enemy fire which continued, the Marines landed and were ready to give fire support to troops who were to land on Gavutu. Coast Guardsman Daniel J. Tarr was coxswain of a landing barge at Halavo. Although he encountered withering fire he landed his boatload of Marines without loss of a man, and made several more trips under fire with ammunition and supplies. He was later awarded the Silver Star Medal for "conspicuous gallantry."

Beach Blue at Tulagi was completely surrounded by coral reefs. Because of this, the enemy expected no landing there, and the place was fortified very lightly. With three naval vessels furnishing close fire support until 0755, the boats reached the reef at 0800, where they were halted, and the Marines waded ashore without opposition. By 1012 all of the waves had reached the beach. Shelling by *San Juan*, however, did not dislodge the Japanese on a hill in the center of Tulagi's southwest coast, and two companies advancing along the south shore were held up by heavy machine gun fire from that hill.

At 1026 the first Gavutu wave left *Heywood* in choppy water, and others followed. *San Juan* bombarded, and planes strafed, enemy dugouts near the beach and on the hill with little apparent effect. Hills honeycombed with well armed dugout

fortresses, both on Gavutu and Tanambogo, commanded the shore. The Japanese let the troops land and then cut down many with heavy fire as they crossed the beach. One out of every ten men on this beachhead became a casualty.

The raiders had occupied the western area of Tulagi with no opposition, but the going was exceedingly rough on the eastern end. There, the enemy was sheltered from bombardment in tunneled limestone caves in the cliffs from which they emerged to attack the Marines from machine gun nests and sniping posts in trees. On Gavutu the U. S. troops were greatly hampered by machine gun fire from adjacent Tanambogo, but by 1800 the Marines had control of Gavutu. At Guadalcanal, Combat Group A had reached the mouth of the Tenaru two miles west of Beach Red by nightfall of D-day. At that time no contact had been made with the enemy anywhere on Guadalcanal.

More Marines were put ashore at Tulagi, and at 1500 on 8 August, occupation of the island was complete. By 2200 that day Gavutu and Tanambogo were secured except for a few troublesome snipers. Of 1,500 Japanese on these three islands, only 23 were captured, 70 escaped to Florida Island, and the rest fought fanatically until they were killed. American casualties numbered 248, with eight officers and 100 men killed. But the story was different on Guadalcanal.

The landings on the Islands had been successful everywhere. But the hard fight by the Navy, Marines, Army, and Air Forces for the possession of Guadalcanal went on for 26 weeks! This fight was severe for the ground and air forces on the island, and in addition took the form of naval surface actions, air attacks, and naval bombardments. Reinforcements were poured into Guadalcanal by both the Americans and the Japanese. The Japanese depended heavily on air raids to disrupt and halt both initial and follow-up landings. A large percentage of the attacking planes fell victims and crashed blazing into the sea. Though the enemy destroyed or put out of action several vessels, he did not halt—only interrupted—the landings.

In addition to the Battle of Savo Island, actions related to Guadalcanal included the Battle of the Eastern Solomons which, while not decisive, prevented the landing of 1,500 enemy troops on the island; the Battle of Cape Esperance, also indecisive, was a blow to Japanese confidence in superiority at night fighting; the Battle of the Santa Cruz Islands which at least gained precious time for the United States; and the Naval Battle of Guadalcanal in mid-November, also around Savo Island, which marked a definite shift of the United States forces in the Pacific from the defensive to the offensive. The effect on American morale was little short of electric. In the early part of November fortune at last smiled on the Allies—in North Africa, Stalingrad, Papua, and Guadalcanal.

On 27 September a detachment of Marines, recently put ashore, were fighting along the Matanikau River on Guadalcanal, where unexpected heavy enemy opposition had developed. It became necessary for them to be evacuated. They sighted seaplane tender *Ballard*, and Sergeant Raysbrook, standing in full view of the enemy, arm-signaled their situation to the ship. Signalman First Class Douglas A. Munro, USCG, of South Cle Elum, Washington, volunteered and led in five Higgins boats from *Ballard*. Though under heavy enemy fire, the men were successfully evacuated from the beach. Realizing that the last man would be in greatest danger, Munro placed himself and his boats in position to serve as cover. He was fatally wounded and remained conscious only long enough to say: "Did they get off?" He was posthumously awarded the Congressional Medal of Honor.

During the fighting at Guadalcanal, *Hunter Liggett* and other United States transports with their escorts, made many trips with additional troops and supplies. During these trips they were often greatly endangered by Japanese planes and submarines. On the return trips they took back the wounded. In all, *Liggett* made 14 trips to the island from August through 17 October 1943. The convoys were almost always viciously attacked by Japanese airmen.

The Battle of Tassafaronga on 30 November was the last major sea battle in the waters of the Southern Solomons. The Americans took a severe beating. But there was progress on Guadalcanal. American control became tight and permanent. On 9 February 1943, General Patch sent Admiral Halsey this radio message. "Total and complete defeat of Japanese forces on Guadalcanal effected 1625 today. . . ." Of 60,000 U. S. Army and

Marine Corps troops on that island, 1,592 had been killed in action. Navy losses were even heavier, and several scores of fliers had lost their lives. The Japanese had lost 14,800 killed or missing; 9,000 dead from disease; and 1,000 taken prisoner out of a total of 36,000. Most of the rest had been evacuated. Each adversary had lost 24 warships; though Japanese tonnage lost was the greater. The net result: the island was ours, and the enemy had been turned back!

During this campaign the Japanese had used the Russell Islands, 30 miles off the northwest tip of Guadalcanal, as a staging point for their barge traffic. It was determined to capture these islands, and landings were effected on 21 February. The enemy had already evacuated them.

In the meantime, intensive training for amphibious warfare had been undertaken. Rear Admiral Daniel E. Barbey, USN, a student of amphibious warfare, arrived in Australia on 8 January 1943, and set up two training centers for United States and Australian troops and sailors. Coast Guardsmen, veterans of the North African invasions, were sent there to join the staff of instructors. Programs were started immediately, and the training later paid good dividends.

After their failure to gain command of the air over Guadalcanal, the Japanese constructed an airdrome near Munda Point on the southwest coast of New Georgia Island in the Central Solomons. Cleverly camouflaged, it was not discovered until 3 December, just before its completion. In the next three months, aircraft from Guadalcanal made over 80 raids on the airdrome; cruisers and destroyers bombarded it; however these raids caused little interruption in its use. Meanwhile, the enemy was building a second air base near the mouth of the Vila River on the southern tip of Kolombangara Island, northwest of New Georgia. This had to be taken care of.

The following months were spent in consolidating positions in the Southern Solomons, and in planning and preparing for the next move. The offensive which opened on 30 June 1943 to clear the New Georgia area of Japanese was the first continued land, sea, and air effort undertaken after the capture of Guadalcanal.

A preliminary landing was made at Segi Point on New Guinea on 21 June, but the main land-

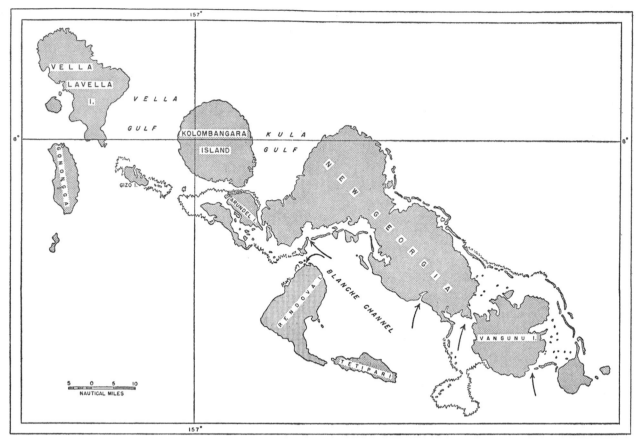

CENTRAL SOLOMONS

ings were made simultaneously on 30 June at several points on Rendova Island, at Viru Harbor on New Georgia, and at Wickham Anchorage off Vangunu Island just south of New Georgia. After diversionary bombardment of the Vila-Stanmore section and of the Buin-Shortland area in southeast Bougainville, 200 miles away, there was a second landing at Rendova Harbor. Several other landings followed at diversified points, many without opposition, from then until 5 July. Transports with Coast Guardsmen in their crews involved in these areas were *Libra, McCawley, President Adams, President Hayes,* and *President Jackson.*

On 5 July there was a landing at Rice Anchorage on the north coast of New Georgia to make possible an advance on the Bairoko-Enogai area, thus preventing enemy reinforcements from reaching Munda from Kolombangara. After a bombardment of artillery emplacements at Enogai Inlet during the night of 4-5 July, when U. S. destroyer *Strong* was sunk by shore batteries, the transports

were unloaded into Higgins boats. The Coast Guardsmen involved in this landing were all in transport *Libra.* Later however, *Hunter Liggett* sent detachments ashore in landing craft on three different occasions. The first comprised one officer and 103 men, the second 88 men, and the third 83 men. These detachments were all sent to the vicinity of Munda, and several of the men suffered wounds.

Following a campaign of four weeks marked by the coordinated use of infantry, artillery, tanks, flame throwers, and air and naval bombardment, Munda airfield was captured. By 1500 on 5 August, all major organized resistance at Munda had ceased, and the New Georgia operation shortly came to a close.

Meanwhile, Lieutenant General Robert L. Eichelberger, USA, had led his troops in some of the nastiest ground fighting of the Pacific War. Since early January he had forced his way up the Papuan Peninsula of New Guinea from Buna to

Nassau Bay where his troops landed 30 June, thereby virtually securing the peninsula. Apart from this, there were also almost unopposed landings in the small Woodlark and Trobriand Island groups between the Solomons and New Guinea.

There had been plans to attack well-fortified Kolombangara, but these were set aside in favor of an assault on Vella Lavella, by-passing the former base with its garrison of 5,000 Japanese troops and an airstrip, and advancing to an island with negligible defenses and no airfield many miles beyond. Vella Lavella lay in the path of the enemy supply routes to Kolombangara and could be used by Allied forces for bases to enable effective patrol of Vella Gulf and Blackett Strait. From Vella Lavella, Japanese shipping and air bases in southern Bougainville could also be attacked.

At dawn on 15 August, Rear Admiral Theodore S. Wilkinson's advance group of seven destroyer-transports (APDs) including *Stringham* with some Coast Guardsmen in her crew, arrived off Barakoma with six destroyers as a screen. They unloaded troops and equipment with no opposition in sight. Within an hour they had completed the operation and departed for Guadalcanal with a screen of four destroyers. Following this, the second transport group consisting of twelve LCIs moved in with their destroyer screen and unloaded, but the process proved slow and landing was done under severe air attacks which were countered by the covering American planes. Then three LSTs came in and finally unloaded, also under attack. In all, about 4,600 officers and men were put ashore in these landings. By the end of two weeks 6,305 men and 8,626 tons of cargo had been landed; enemy planes had been fought off in scores of battles; and only one beaching craft had been lost.

For some weeks after the landings, reinforcement and re-supply runs were made to Vella Lavella, often under air attack. Among the vessels so engaged were *LST-334* with some Coast Guardsmen on board, and *LST-167* which was fully Coast Guard-manned.

*LST-167* departed Guadalcanal in convoy on 24 September and beached at Ruravai, Vella Lavella, at 0745 on the 25th. All of the 77th Marine Combat Battalion's equipment was unloaded by 1115. Two minutes later, three dive bombers came out of the sun and dived at the ship. All 20 guns of the LST opened fire, but before any of the planes were hit their bombs had been released. One plane burst into flames; another began to smoke heavily. Two bombs struck *LST-167*. One struck the main deck port side, exploded, penetrated the deck, and went out through the skin of the ship. The second struck the main deck forward and exploded in the provision room. This started a fire, and flames immediately leapt through the cargo hatch and after ventilators. Damaged electrical circuits cut off power. Dead and wounded littered the main deck. All engines were secured and the ship abandoned.

The living casualties were removed and given first aid at a native dwelling on the beach. Ammunition on the main deck began exploding at 1140, so fire-fighting was discontinued. *LST-167* was still burning the next morning, but the fire subsided at 1530. Two officers and five enlisted men had been killed in action; one officer and nineteen enlisted men had been wounded in action; three enlisted men later died of wounds; and five were missing. The LST was later unbeached and towed to Rendova.

It took until 1 October for the American and New Zealand troops to secure Vella Lavella. An attempt by the Japanese to evacuate their remaining 600 troops led to the important naval Battle of Vella Lavella which was a hard fought action ending almost in a draw, with the Japanese having a possible edge.

After the Allies reached Nassau Bay in New Guinea, General MacArthur decided to take Salamaua, Lae, and Finschafen 15, 30, and 70 miles respectively on up the coast. Australians and Americans captured Salamaua on 15 September. A well coordinated effort by land, sea, and air forces resulted in the fall of Lae on 16 September. In this operation amphibious landings were made about 15 miles to the eastward by a force under Rear Admiral Barbey. *LST-18* and *LST-67*, both Coast Guard-manned, engaged in support landings there on 21 September.

Finschafen was the next goal, and General MacArthur, anxious to press his advantage, set D-day only five days ahead. Admiral Barbey collected a force of eight LSTs, sixteen LCIs, ten destroyers, and four destroyer-transports, and assembled these off Lae on 21 September. This task group moved to a point off "Scarlet Beach" about five miles north of Finschafen where landings were effected before dawn on 22 September.

The enemy, expecting an attack by land, had left only a few defenders in the beach areas, and was completely surprised by the landings. Four Coast Guard LSTs took part in these landings—*LST-18*, *LST-67*, *LST-168*, and *LST-204*. The LSTs beached at about 0700, debarked their Australian troops, and unloaded their cargo under protective air cover without incident. This was finished at about 0930. However, as the LSTs were retracting, a lone Japanese "Zero" fighter sneaked in over the hills and at masthead height dropped two bombs which fell wide of their mark. The LSTs then joined formation and headed south for Buna.

At 1240, six Japanese "Bettys" and 35 "Zekes" from Rabaul approached the retiring convoy. All ships broke formation and weaved at emergency speed. Two enemy planes at high altitude were immediately engaged by the covering aircraft. The escorting destroyers opened fire and two enemy bombers crashed into the sea, one exploding in mid-air. The other bombers broke formation but continued in. Hits were scored promptly on them with the 20 mm. guns of the LSTs. One Japanese bomber hit the water, bounced up again, and burst into flames. Another took direct hits and began to smoke before it splashed into the sea. The remaining bombers were engaged by the U.S. P-38s and three more splashed, one in flames. A P-38 fell nearby, but the pilot bailed out and was picked up by the escorts. It was all over by 1305, and not a single ship had been damaged.

Finschafen was in Australian hands on 2 October.

*LST-203* was a Coast Guard-manned vessel lost while not involved in combat. Having unloaded on the beach at Nanomea Island on 1 October, she tried to retract, but was held fast by a coral reef which caused her to pivot on the bow. With her ramp raised, her starboard door, slightly sprung, did not close fully. A six to eight foot surf pounded her against the reef. Water entered the shaft alley and engine room, and her pumps were unable to handle it. Attempts to save her by U.S. destroyer *Manley* and *YMS-53* were unsuccessful, and after two weeks she was abandoned as a stranded vessel.

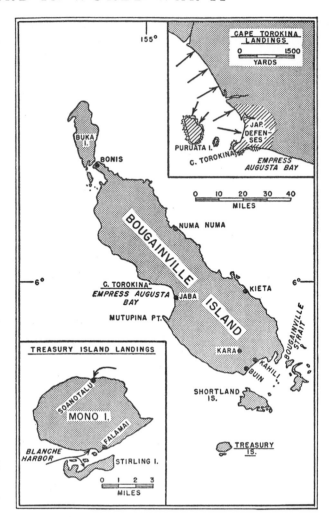

BOUGAINVILLE

Bougainville, 125 miles long from northwest to southeast and 35 miles wide, was the next objective after Finschafen. With only Buka lying beyond, Bougainville terminated the Solomon Island group. An airdrome on Bougainville would make far heavier air attacks on important Japanese-held Rabaul on New Britain possible.

Empress Augusta Bay, in the middle of the west side of Bougainville, was chosen as the place of attack. Landings were to be at Cape Torokina, on the northerly side of the entrance. On 12 October, Admiral Halsey designated 1 November as D-day. It was known that the Japanese had some 40,000 troops and 20,000 naval personnel in the Bougainville area, but that Empress Augusta Bay itself was lightly defended, with only two or three thousand enemy personnel there. As a preliminary to the assault, however, it was necessary also to capture the Treasury Islands, lying 20 miles southwest of the Shortlands, which were just off the southern end of Bougainville.

Rabaul and the airfields on Bougainville were pounded by American planes for several weeks before the assault, a factor which contributed greatly to the success of the coming campaign. Naval bombardments at vital points also were very effective.

As a diversion for the Treasury and Bougainville landings, the 2nd Marine Parachute Battalion made an unopposed landing at Voza, on the southwest coast of Choiseul, 40 miles northeast of Vella Lavella, at 0045 on 28 October. At 1800 on the 29th the Marines met a strong enemy force. The next day they captured Sangigai, destroying installations and killing 72 Japanese. They were later evacuated by LCIs. However, the enemy's attention was completely diverted from Bougainville.

On 27 October, five transport units, including *Crescent City* and *Stringham* with some Coast Guardsmen on board, arrived off Blanche Harbor, Treasury Islands. Preceded by a bombardment from destroyers, the initial wave of troops reached the beach at Falamai on Mono Island, the principal island of the group, at 0626. Almost complete surprise was achieved. The landing was opposed by some machine gun, mortar, and sniper fire but casualties were light. Another landing on nearby Stirling Island was unopposed. At the same time a party was put ashore without opposition at Soanotalu on the north side of Mono Island, where a radar station was to be established. The second echelon, including Coast Guard-manned *LST-71*, arrived 1 November, and the third arrived on the 6th. By that time, mopping up operations at the Treasuries had been completed.

The initial attack force which took the reinforced 3rd Marine Division to Cape Torokina, was under the over-all command of Rear Admiral T. S. Wilkinson. It included 12 transports commanded by Commodore L. F. Reifsnider, USN, in *Hunter Liggett* as flagship, a screen of 11 destroyers, several minecraft, and two fleet tugs. Transports having Coast Guardsmen serving with Navy crews were *President Jackson*, *President Adams*, *President Hayes*, *American Legion*, *Crescent City*, *Alchiba*, *Alhena*, *Fuller* and *Libra*. Only two transports had no Coast Guardsmen on board. This task force, well provided with air cover both day and night, approached Bougainville well to seaward along the southwest side of the Solomons, and arrived off the Cape Torokina beaches at 0645 on the morning of 1 November.

A bombardment by surface vessels and bombing of the landing beaches by 31 TBFs lasted an hour and a half. During the landings, under the blue-grey mountainous island with an active volcano shrouding the peaks with smoke, the destroyers fanned out ahead shelling the beach. Planes which had formed a protective umbrella peeled off and screamed down, bombing and strafing the enemy's machine gun emplacements, many of which disintegrated into muddy holes on the beach. But enough were left to harass the landings. Only 300 Japanese were concentrated at Cape Torokina and on Puruata Island, just offshore, but they resisted stubbornly with heavy machine gun fire.

The first assault wave reached the beaches at 0726. A flare went up from shore as this wave with over 7,000 troops landed. Three more waves went in later. Surf conditions were poor and around 90 LCVPs and LCMs broached and were abandoned. The beaches were found to be narrow and steep, affording considerable trouble in unloading cargo, and some beaches were unusable. Northwest of Cape Torokina the landing was almost unopposed.

Within ten minutes of the initial landings, the first enemy counterattack came from Rabaul in the form of 9 "Vals" and 44 "Zekes." All the transports immediately got underway, headed for the open sea, and maneuvered for two hours. Above, a dog fight was in progress. A bomber streaked for *Hunter Liggett* but suddenly banked away, losing altitude rapidly. Destroyer *Wadsworth* had the closest call—a near miss. Unloading was resumed at 0930, but was interrupted again in the afternoon when 100 enemy carrier planes swooped down from New Britain. They were repulsed by fighter planes and again none of the ships were hit. In the meantime, *American Legion* grounded on an uncharted shoal. Seven enemy bombers poised over her for the kill, but a destroyer's antiaircraft fire drove them off. In eight hours of working time, 14,321 Marines and most of the supplies (6,200 tons) had been landed at a cost of 70 killed and missing, and 124 wounded. Half of the enemy force had been killed, and the remainder had fled inland.

With night coming on, and most transports unloaded, all twelve transports got underway and headed back toward Guadalcanal. But four still had vital supplies for the Marines, and Admiral Wilkinson detached them at midnight to return to Empress Augusta Bay. Commodore Reifsnider in *Hunter Liggett* was to accompany them. As the other transports withdrew, a cruiser force under Japanese Admiral Omori sortied from Rabaul. Admiral Wilkinson then ordered the Commodore and his transports to resume retirement to the south. Rear Admiral A. Stanton Merrill, USN, with his Task Force 39, consisting of cruisers and destroyers, met the enemy off Empress Augusta Bay on 2 November. In this vicious surface and air encounter, Omori was prevented from getting at the transports, and the battle ended in a victory for Admiral Merrill's task force.

A second echelon of the landing and occupation force of eight LSTs and eight destroyer-transports, including *Stringham*, protected by Task Force 39, arrived off Cape Torokina at 0700 on 6 November. After much difficulty in beaching the LSTs, unloading was completed and the vessels retired about midnight. Coast Guard-manned *LST-70* and *LST-207* were in this echelon. As *LST-70* was leaving Puruata Island she was taken under fire by the Japanese shore batteries. In an enemy air attack soon afterward she was bombed and strafed, and one man of a gun crew was struck in the leg.

Air battles over Bougainville continued for many days. By 14 November, 33,861 men and 23,137 tons of supplies had been put ashore at Empress Augusta Bay. Not until then had the beachhead been secured. Bougainville was virtually in Allied hands by the year-end. During this period, naval activity at Bougainville was chiefly reinforcement, re-supply, and removal of wounded. Engaged in these activities were *LST-334* with some Coast Guardsmen in a Navy crew, and *LST-70*, *LST-166*, and *LST-207* wholly manned by the Coast Guard. On one of these re-supply trips *LST-70* and *LST-207* each shot down one enemy plane. The LSTs finished the year making runs between Guadalcanal and Bougainville.

While these operations were going on, another important assault was being prepared and exe-

cuted in the Gilbert Islands, which included the Tarawa, Makin, and Abemama atolls. This group lies about 1,000 miles north of the Fiji Islands and roughly 1,200 miles east-northeast of Bougainville. The attack on these islands had been planned as early as mid-1943. Elaborate training and preparations occupied much of the period until November. About 200 vessels were assembled at various places to carry or escort 27,600 assault troops, 7,600 garrison troops, 6,000 vehicles, and 117,000 tons of cargo.

The vessels were organized into three main forces. The Northern Attack Force (TF52) was under the command of Rear Admiral Richmond K. Turner, USN, in *Pennsylvania*. This Force mounted at Pearl Harbor, and was destined for Makin. Its six transports included *Neville*, with some Coast Guardsmen on board, and Coast Guard-manned *Leonard Wood* (Captain Merlin O'Neill, USCG). In addition there were four battleships, four cruisers, three escort carriers, an LSD (landing ship, dock), and three LSTs.

The Southern Attack Force (TF53), commanded by Rear Admiral Harry W. Hill, USN, mounted in New Zealand and Efate, and was destined for Tarawa. In this force were 16 transports, including Coast Guard-manned *Arthur Middleton* (Captain Severt A. Olsen, USCG), three battleships, five cruisers, five escort carriers, 21 destroyers, one LSD, and some LSTs.

Fast Carrier Forces Pacific Fleet (TF50) was under command of Rear Admiral Charles A. Pownall, USN. With eleven carriers, it was the greatest carrier force assembled up to that time, and was divided into four groups, each with supporting war vessels and a special mission. In addition to these three forces, land-based planes searched the Gilberts every day from 16 November, with incidental bombing, particularly on Makin and Tarawa.

These great striking forces got underway from their widespread points of assembly, so as to arrive at their destinations at the prescribed times. The slow LSTs started first. The Makin group was discovered by the enemy on 18 November and subjected to several undamaging air attacks. Soon after daybreak on 19 November the Northern and Southern Attack Forces sighted each other. At about 0530 on 20 November, the transports and other vessels moved into their assigned

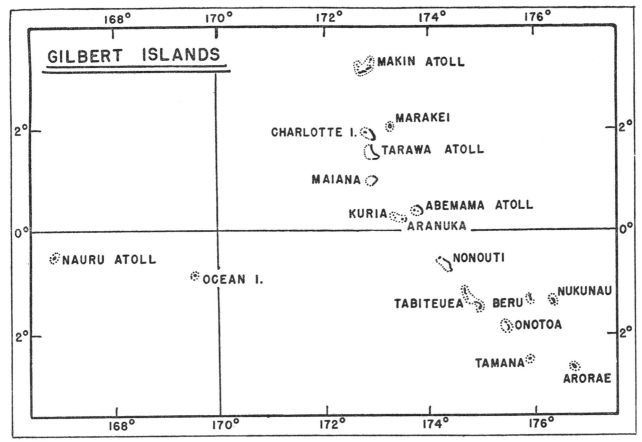

GILBERT ISLANDS

areas, and landing boats were swung out ready to lower.

Let us first see what happened at Makin, where only one island, Butaritari, was defended. The transports anchored 5,000 to 7,000 yards off the beaches. The weather was perfect for the landings. *Leonard Wood*, veteran of the Mediterranean actions, commenced lowering her LCVPs at 0603, with soldiers already in them. Carrier planes finished a two-minute bombardment of the shore. A naval bombardment followed, with salvos from the battleships *Pennsylvania*, *New Mexico*, and *Mississippi*. Light and heavy cruisers joined in, and the whole fire support group blazed away until 0824. There was no reply from shore for the enemy had nothing to reply with.

There were 1,788 officers and men of the 165th Combat Team of the 27th Division, U. S. Army on board the *Wood*. Her first boats landed at 0840, and other waves followed. On the return trips, the boats evacuated casualties.

The landings at Makin were made on two beaches, on the southern and western ends of the island. The coral reef off the south beaches had twelve to eighteen inches of water at low tide—not enough to allow boats to get to the beaches over the reef. This meant using LVTs entirely to unload boats at the beach. There were eight waves of landing craft, most of which were directed to one of the beaches, as coral conditions at the other necessitated its abandonment, causing confusion, delay, and damage to landing boats. Fortunately, there was only slight enemy resistance. By the 22nd, 409 officers and 6,098 men had been landed to engage an estimated 600 to 800 of the enemy. The island was weakly defended, but it took until 1300 on 23 November to completely secure it.

On 24 November, some troops were re-embarked, and the U. S. destroyer *Hughes* transferred 150 survivors from the sunken carrier *USS Liscome Bay* to *Wood*. Altogether, 245

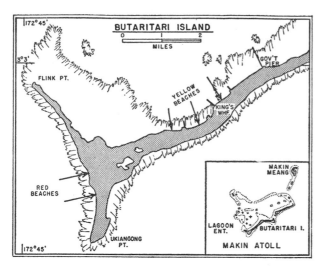

LANDING BEACHES AT MAKIN

casualties from six vessels were taken on board. Some Coast Guard coxswains and their crews had worked for four straight days without leaving their boats. At 1435 on the 24th, *Leonard Wood* stood out to join a convoy and departed for Pearl Harbor, where she arrived on 2 December.

The Japanese reacted to the Makin operation with surface vessels which were relatively innocuous; with submarine attacks which did some damage; and with various air raids which were deadly. Carrier *Liscome Bay* was sunk; numerous vessels were damaged; and there were many casualties.

While these landings were in progress at Makin, the attack at Tarawa, 100 miles to the south, was taking place. This was one of the most intensely fought amphibious operations in the entire war. Betio, with an area of only 291 acres, was the fortified island of the atoll. The entire island was surrounded by a shallow coral reef which extended from 500 to 1,000 yards offshore. As Admiral Morison put it: "Every square foot of it could be defended, and almost every foot was defended." The Japanese system of defense was extensive and complete; the installations were amply manned and bravely defended. U. S. carrier plane attacks on 18 and 19 November had done considerable damage to the enemy airfield which had a strip 4,000 feet long.

At 0355 on 20 November, Admiral Hill's Southern Attack Force reached its position off Betio, and

the transports anchored in their designated areas. Boats were immediately lowered and unloading began. The LST group, with its cargoes of LVTs, arrived shortly afterward. The Coast Guard-manned *LST-20*, *LST-23*, *LST-69*, *LST-169*, and *LST-205* were in Task Group 54.7, which carried garrison troops.

Boats for the initial assault were lowered by 0430. Enemy shore batteries opened fire at 0507 and the U. S. ships commenced firing two minutes later, ceasing at 0542 in anticipation of a dawn air strike scheduled for 0545. This was delayed until 0610 due to a misunderstanding, thus giving the Japanese batteries 20 minutes for firing on the transports without opposition. H-hour was then changed from 0830 to 0900. Counter battery fire was resumed at 0605; the air bombardment was over in seven minutes; and at 0622 an intensive naval bombardment began which lasted until 0855. The first wave of assault troops did not reach the beaches until about 0917, and in this interval the enemy was able to concentrate his men at the point of impact. This, and an unpredictable tide which stranded many landing craft, resulted in very heavy initial casualties.

Beginning with H-hour, six waves of landing craft (LCTs, LCVPs, and LCMs) were scheduled to land in 25 minutes. The first three waves of LVTs had little difficulty in crossing the reef and no underwater mines or obstructions were encountered. However, all waves were under heavy fire. About 95 percent of the LVTs reached the reef and 85 percent reached the beaches. The fourth, fifth, and sixth waves of LCVPs and LCMs could not pass over the reef and troops and equipment were put ashore by loading into LVTs or onto rafts, or by landing at the pier which extended out across the reef to deeper water. Troops attempting to wade ashore over the reef, other than along the pier, met intense fire and suffered heavy losses.

*Arthur Middleton*, which was in the Aleutian campaign, had arrived with the other transports, and her Marines were debarked into LVTs sent from other ships. Transports with Coast Guardsmen on board serving with Navy crews were *Heywood*, *Bellatrix*, and *William P. Biddle*. The first waves were ashore at 0917. They were stopped almost immediately against a barricade running

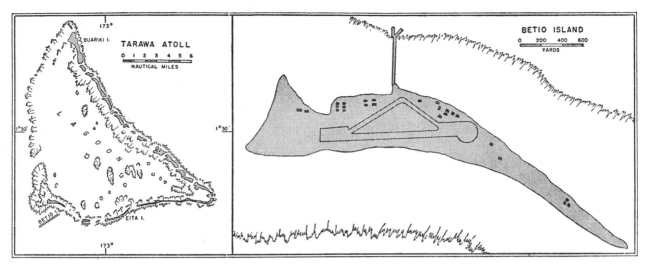

TARAWA AND THE SCENE OF ATTACK

parallel to the beach and 20 yards inland. By mid-afternoon the issue was still in doubt. No suitable beachheads had been established, and so there were no beach parties. After leaving the beaches many LVTs drifted about, some in the lagoon, apparently leaderless. Later in the day nearly 200 other landing craft, most of them loaded with either troops or supplies, were still floating around in the lagoon, unable to discharge. It was not until the next morning that order was restored.

By noon on the 21st, several beach parties had established themselves ashore. The fighting on the island was still bitter, but the situation showed marked improvement. *Middleton's* beach party consisted of three officers and 43 men with Lieutenant (jg) Robert Hoyle, USCG, in charge. They remained ashore for five days handling the boats and equipment. Two of *Middleton's* officers were wounded.

Late in the afternoon of the 21st, troops were landed unopposed on Buariki Island, adjacent to Betio, and also on the western side of Betio. Mopping up operations on the western end of the island proceeded on the 22nd and 23rd, assisted by air and naval gunfire and artillery on the shore. The enemy was pushed to the east. By early afternoon of the 23rd, the enemy had been annihilated and Betio was secured. The Transport Division remained at Tarawa until the 29th, and *Middleton* acted as a receiving ship for Marine casualties from the fighting ashore.

The total number of troops in the Marine Landing Teams used in the attack was about 15,545. Of these, 913 were killed or were missing, and 2,037 were wounded. In both Services the total number engaged was 18,313 out of which there were 3,110 casualties, or 17 percent. Of the probable 4,800 Japanese and Koreans on the atoll, all were killed except 17 Japanese and 129 Korean laborers, who were taken prisoner.

The occupation of Abemama, 75 miles southwest of Tarawa, was an almost bloodless side-show to the main operation. A small Marine landing force went ashore there at midnight of 20-21 November and secured it on 25 November, all Japanese there having been killed or wounded by naval gunfire or by committing suicide. Coast Guard-manned *LST-19* was in Task Group 54.11, which carried garrison troops to Abemama.

While this campaign in the Gilbert Islands was being carried out, preparations were made for the next strike to the northwest of the Solomons, and we shall return our attention to that area. New Britain, in the Bismarck Archipelago, lies between the northern Solomons and New Guinea. Cape Gloucester, its western end, was not far from where Allied troops were pushing up the coast of New Guinea. On the island's eastern end, 250 miles away, was the great Japanese air and naval base of Rabaul. General MacArthur believed that Cape Gloucester must be taken in order to protect the passage of naval vessels through the Vitiaz and

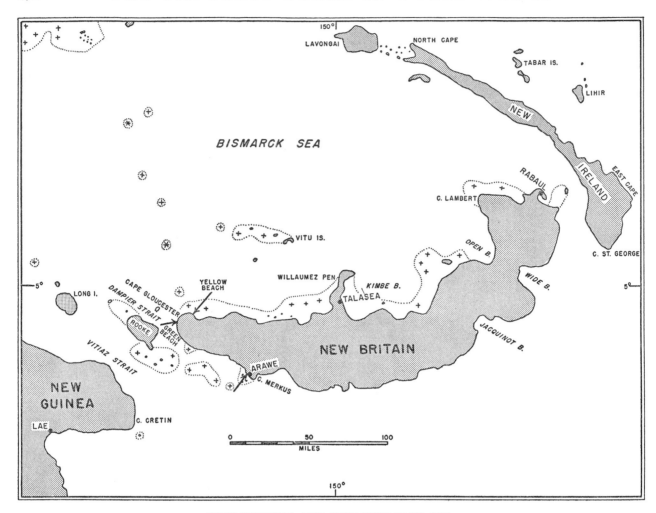

NEW BRITAIN AND THE BISMARCK SEA

Dampier Straits between New Guinea and New Britain. The plan called for an attack at Arawe on the southern coast of New Britain, and then one at Cape Gloucester.

A small amphibious force under Admiral Barbey's command arrived off Arawe on 15 December. The usual landing procedure was followed, though it was not a smooth operation. Finally, beachheads were secured, but they and the landing craft were subjected to heavy bombing by enemy aircraft. Once ashore the troops had little difficulty although 42 men were killed or seriously wounded. One vessel was sunk and six were damaged. This landing had little value except as a diversion for the main action at Cape Gloucester. The Coast Guard was not involved at Arawe.

The Japanese had occupied Cape Gloucester in December 1942. One year later it was estimated that about 10,000 Japanese troops were in the area, principally in two rear sections which were natural positions for defense against forces advancing northwesterly up the coast.

Admiral Barbey's VII Amphibious Force handled this operation, and put ashore the 1st Marine Division under Major General W. H. Rupertus, USMC. Admiral Crutchley's mixed Australian and United States cruiser division covered the operation and gave fire support. The attacking force consisted of a first echelon of ten destroyer-transports including *Stringham;* a second echelon of ten LCIs; six destroyers acting as escorts including the Admiral's flagship *Conyngham;* and five miscellaneous craft. The cruiser bombardment unit consisted of four cruisers with eight destroyers. Five more echelons consisted of 24 LSTs with their various escorts of destroyers

A DIRECT HIT ON THE ENIWETOK AIR STRIP . . . . naval gunfire preceded the attacking
Marines as they advanced to capture the Japanese installation.

COFFEE FOR THE CONQUERORS OF ENIWETOK
. . . . these Marines, after two days and nights of fighting,
are back on their Coast Guard-manned transport.

SAVING AN AMERICAN LIFE ON THE BEACH AT
ENIWETOK . . . . medical corpsmen and Coast Guardsmen
give plasma to a wounded comrade who fell in the onslaught.

FRIENDLY RECEPTION AT EMIRAU ISLAND . . . .
Polynesian natives meet the Coast Guard and volunteer their
services as stevedores.

ROLLING THE DRUMS AT BIAK . . . . barrels of oil for
American planes and vehicles are delivered on the beach at
Biak by a Coast Guard-manned LST.

COAST GUARD-MANNED LSTs AT TANAHMERAH BAY, HOLLANDIA . . . . nosing in to the beaches, these landing
ships bring men and equipment for the advance in Dutch New Guinea.

NAVY LST BEACHES FOR THE SARMI LANDING . . . . a Coast Guardsman
of the beach party flags the vessel in to its beaching position.

LCIs OF THE SECOND WAVE BEACH AT SARMI . . . . while landings were not difficult at Sarmi, these troops had three months of jungle fighting before them.

LCIs CLOSE IN FOR THE INVASION OF CAPE SANSAPOR . . . . an LST, manned by the Coast Guard, decks brimming with equipment and supplies, follows with anti-aircraft guns manned to meet enemy attacks from the sky.

THE DAWN LANDING AT NOEMFOOR . . . . invaders cram the topside of a Coast Guard-manned LST
as landing craft go in for the attack.

AMMUNITION AND SUPPLIES COME IN AT SAIPAN . . . . landing craft pour in with
materiel to support the vicious fighting ashore.

INVADERS COME ASHORE AT TINIAN . . . . landing craft from the larger vessels offshore are halted by shallow water about 100 yards from land. The attackers wade in.

TROOPS SWARM ASHORE UNOPPOSED AT MOROTAI . . . . the enemy garrison had fled to the mountains.

THE PRE-INVASION BOMBARDMENT OF ANGAUR . . . . a Coast Guard landing barge carries troops in to the beach while naval guns blast the shore to neutralize the enemy.

AMPHIBIOUS TANKS DASH TOWARD BLAZING ANGAUR . . . . they move in with the first wave as the fleet eases up in its shelling of enemy emplacements.

BLACK SMOKE SHROUDS WRECKAGE OF CHARAN-KANOA, SAIPAN . . . . the sugar refinery still burns as Coast Guardsmen look over the pier where vital supplies were finally landed.

*CALLAWAY* TAKES CONVOY POSITION OFF LEYTE . . . . this veteran of Pacific invasions
appears peaceful enough in the waters of Leyte Gulf.

HELL BREAKS LOOSE OVERHEAD AS BARGES HEAD FOR LEYTE BEACHES . . . . Coast Guardsmen take in
troops as American and Japanese planes duel to the death.

and other craft. Coast Guard participation was entirely in LSTs, except for a few men in *Stringham*. These LSTs were numbers *18, 22, 66, 67, 68, 168, 202, 204,* and *206*.

Preceding the landings, the U. S. Army Air Force attacked the area on 21 out of 31 days, dropping 4,500 tons of bombs. Air strategy was unusual in that nearly all offensive strength was sent against enemy defensive ground positions rather than first against enemy air strength. This lessened ground opposition, but it did permit the Japanese to mount an intense air offensive against the landing operations.

Landings at Cape Gloucester began at 0745 at points six miles east and west of the Japanese airstrip after a 53-minute naval and air bombardment on the morning of 26 December. Although the landings themselves were unopposed, and Allied fighters turned back an enemy air attack during the morning, a Japanese attack in the afternoon succeeded in sinking destroyer *Brownson*, and near misses caused damage to destroyers *Lamson, Mugford,* and *Shaw,* and to *LST-66*. On the first day of the action 12,500 troops and 7,600 tons of equipment were landed; 2,400 additional troops, and 3,500 more tons of cargo went ashore the next day. At noon on 30 December, the Marines occupied the airstrip. Enemy air opposition, which was vicious, came wholly from Rabaul, and was concentrated in the first few days; it then quickly faded, due to pressure on Rabaul by South Pacific air forces.

During the air raids on the landing operations, *LST-22* was attacked by a dive bomber which she probably destroyed. *LST-66* was credited with shooting down three Japanese planes. Two of her men were killed and seven were wounded from near miss bombs. *LST-67* brought down one "Val" with her 40 mm. fire. *LST-68* claimed one enemy plane. Two Japanese aircraft and possibly another were shot down by *LST-202*. Two "Vals" were accounted for by *LST-204*, which suffered minor damage from several near misses. The Coast Guard gunners gave a good account of themselves!

It was not until 14 January 1944, that Allied control of Cape Gloucester and the Straits was secured. The Marines lost 248 killed, and 772 wounded.

The year 1943 had been one of hard fighting on the sea, on the ground, and in the air. But the Japanese were being worn down and pushed toward their homeland; their tide was beginning to ebb, and the Allies were moving forward with mounting power and at an accelerated pace as the New Year dawned.

# Chapter 19

# THE SWEEP TO THE PHILIPPINES—1944

As the third calendar year of the war opened, Allied forces kept up their pressure in the advance toward the Philippines. There was still a long way to go. Mindanao, the southernmost major island of that group, was over 1,500 miles from Cape Gloucester. In the 2,700 miles of ocean between the Gilbert Islands and the Philippines lay the Marshall Islands, the Carolines, the Marianas, and various minor groups. It had taken from August 1942 until December 1943 for the Allies to advance up the Papuan Peninsula, and from Guadalcanal to Cape Gloucester—only about 800 miles. In the year 1944, however, the advance against Japan was to sweep over much greater distances and vast areas of ocean, in a relentless pursuit of the enemy.

On 24 December 1943, Admiral Barbey had been directed to land the 126th Regimental Combat Team of the 32nd Infantry at Saidor, about 110 miles northwest of Finschafen on the New Guinea coast on 2 January 1944. This would be the third major operation by the VII Amphibious Force in 18 days. The landing at Saidor preceded by air and surface bombardment, was made on schedule on the morning of 2 January from destroyer-transports, LCIs and LSTs. Four Coast Guard-manned LSTs were in the initial landing, and five others went in later. So sudden was the attack, that the Japanese garrison fled from its breakfast tables, leaving food half consumed. The 7,200 American troops meeting only light resistance swept ashore on both sides of Saui Point, which was quickly overcome, and moved a mile inland to capture the airstrip. American forces were thus placed some 75 miles beyond Australian units driving up the Huon Peninsula coast. Many Japanese were trapped between the two.

The Japanese island base of Truk, in the Caro-lines, posed an enemy naval threat to any Allied operation northward of New Britain and New Guinea. The battles in the Gilbert Islands had been a step toward the neutralization of this threat, but that was not enough. It became essential to move northwest of the Gilberts and capture the Marshall Islands, chief among which were Kwajalein, Eniwetok, Jaluit, Majuro, and Wotje.

Original planning by the Joint Chiefs of Staff for the attack on the Marshalls dated back to July 1943, and called for action in January 1944. After various modifications, the final plan was accepted by Admiral Nimitz. It provided that undefended Majuro would be taken first to provide a good anchorage; that Kwajalein would be assaulted simultaneously at both ends the next day; and that Eniwetok would be taken as soon after that as possible. Four strongly defended atolls with airfields would be skipped—Wotje, Maloelap, Mili, and Jaluit.

Vice Admiral R. A. Spruance, USN, commanded the expeditionary force from *Indianapolis*. Rear Admiral Richmond K. Turner, USN, in *Rocky Mount*, was Officer in Tactical Command. Major General Holland M. Smith, USMC, commanded the ground forces. The Northern Attack Force, under Rear Admiral Conolly, was to take Roi and Namur Islands in Kwajalein Atoll. The Southern Attack Force, directly under Admiral Turner, had Kwajalein Island where an enemy bomber strip was under construction as its objective. Admiral Hill in Coast Guard-manned *Cambria*, commanded a third amphibious unit consisting of a Reserve Force and a small Majuro Force. The Reserve Force was to stand by at Kwajalein, but move on to attack Eniwetok if not needed there. The combined forces comprised 297 vessels, aside from a fast carrier task group and submarines. Troops to be landed numbered 54,000.

Air operations against enemy bases in the Marshalls began before the Gilbert assault, and then were stepped up when new American airfields in the Gilberts became operative. These attacks virtually destroyed enemy aircraft and shipping in the Marshalls before the landings took place. The Japanese made almost no attempt to meet the threat against their Marshall bases except with the forces already there.

The Majuro Attack Group, which included flagship *Cambria,* and the Reserve Group, departed from Pearl Harbor on 23 January and separated 30 January. The former proceeded to Majuro and the latter, under Captain D. W. Loomis, USN, went on to stand by at Kwajalein. The Majuro force steamed into its assigned area on 31 January, expecting to find three or four hundred Japanese on Darrit Island. The V Amphibious Corps Reconnaissance Company of the 1st Marine Defense Battalion, landed on the entrance islands at 2100 without incident or opposition. More men were put ashore on Dalap and Uliga Islands; they found no enemy. There were no Japanese on Darrit Island and only four in the entire atoll! The next day the task group entered the lagoon, and Admiral Spruance was notified that Majuro had been secured. For several months in 1944, Majuro Atoll was a staging point and springboard for most of the Central Pacific Fleet operations.

The Northern Attack Force Initial Transport Group included six vessels among which were attack transport *Callaway* (Captain D. C. McNeil, USCG), and *William P. Biddle* which had some Coast Guardmen on board. In addition, there were screening destroyers, minesweepers, powerful fire support units, and a carrier group. The Main Attack Detachment consisted of eight attack transports and the Coast Guard-manned attack cargo transport *Aquarius* (Captain R. V. Marron, USCG), as well as several auxiliaries, destroyers, minesweepers, and LSTs. The Southern Attack Force was similarly constituted, and included attack cargo ship *Centaurus* (Captain George E. McCabe, USCG), which was also manned by the Coast Guard.

These forces staged through the Hawaiian Islands. After a relatively uneventful trip they reached the Kwajalein area on 30 January, and the Northern Force took its position for the assault.

Kwajalein is the world's largest coral atoll. It is 66 miles long from northwest to southeast, and at most 20 miles wide. There are 97 islands and islets on the chain-like reef surrounding the lagoon. The area of the lagoon itself is about 840 square miles, but the total area of the islands is only 6⅓ square miles. At the southernmost tip is Kwajalein Island; at the northernmost Roi and Namur; and at the westernmost, Ebadon—the only islands large enough for military installations.

D-day was 31 January. Roi and Namur, the objectives of the Northern Force, were subjected to an intense bombardment, which, it was later discovered killed a large proportion of the 3,700 Japanese defenders. The initial landings were made at 0952, in a heavy surf by a Landing Team of the 4th Marine Division on Ennuebing Island and then on Maliu Island, both a very few miles from Roi. By 1200, both islands had been secured against very light opposition. Boats and amphibious vehicles then reassembled for an attack against Ennumennet and Ennubirr Islands, near Namur. The first waves struck those beaches about 1515, with support of destroyer and LCI fire including rockets and smoke screening. Those islands were secured by 1645 with 34 enemy killed. By 2000, all islands immediately adjacent to Roi-Namur had been captured. Transport Division 26, which included *Callaway,* lay outside the lagoon and sent supplies and artillery to the islands already taken, while other units proceeded to sea for the night.

On the same day, U. S. carrier planes bombarded Roi and Namur. At 0645 on 1 February, fire support units assisted by artillery from the smaller captured islands nearby, bombarded those islands at close range. Landing craft were not ready and organized at H-hour which was, therefore, postponed until 1100. Beaching at Roi, where Combat Team 23 was put ashore, was fairly orderly despite a heavy rain squall. The airfield was found to be largely deserted. Half of some 600 Japanese defenders there had been killed in the bombardment. A coordinated attack at 1500 quickly overcame organized resistance except in a small sector on the north coast. Mopping up operations were completed the next morning.

Combat Team 24 had little trouble at the beach

on Namur, but strong opposition developed from an intricate network of defenses as soon as the enemy recovered somewhat from the effects of the preliminary bombardment. The attack was resumed at 0915 on 2 February, with the support of tanks brought over from Roi. All organized resistance ceased at 1215.

It still remained to mop up all islands within 13 miles of Roi and Namur. Since little opposition developed, landings were made by reconnaissance units, with reserves available in case of resistance. On 7 February the last of those islands was occupied.

Namur and Roi, once pretty wooded islands, had hardly a tree left standing after these operations. Two weeks later the islands had been cleaned up and Quonset huts erected; American planes were using the airdrome; and the Marines were there to stay.

The Southern Attack Force, with Kwajalein Island as its objective, carried Army troops of the 7th Infantry Division (Major General Charles H. Corlett, USA) which had captured Attu and occupied Kiska. The force steamed in from Pearl Harbor, reaching its destination on schedule. The plan of attack was similar to that of the Northern Attack Force, with initial landings on small nearby islets.

Before dawn on D-day, troops were landed on Gea and Gehh Islands. The former was at the southeast entrance to Gea Pass, one of the few entrances into the lagoon. Opposition there was light. Of the 130 Japanese who had gone ashore on Gehh Island, armed with machine guns and rifles, none survived. Ninni Island was taken without resistance, thus securing islands on both sides of Gea Pass, through which the minesweepers entered the lagoon. At 0915, landings were effected on Ennylabegan and Enubuj Islands against light opposition. Artillery was immediately landed on Enubuj, nearest Kwajalein Island. In the late afternoon, Transport Divisions 6 (including *Centaurus*) and 18 transferred their troops to LSTs. These troops were the Regimental Combat Teams 184 and 32 that were to make the assault on Kwajalein Island the next day.

The naval bombardment of Kwajalein Island began on 30 January. On 1 February, after three hours of final naval gunfire preparation against the island, the first wave reached the beach at 0930, followed quickly by others. These landings were well executed and right on time. Resistance was light and scattered; the devastating bombardment had destroyed all organized positions for 300 yards inland, and had terrorized the defenders, reducing their effectiveness. It was largely responsible for the speedy capture of the islands with relatively few casualties. As the invaders advanced, the enemy's resistance stiffened. By 1700 the troops had reached a line about one-third of the way up the island, but the Japanese fought viciously, and it was not until 1530 on 4 February that organized resistance ceased. Meanwhile, the occupation of the smaller islands nearby was effected, and completed on the 6th. Out of the total enemy strength of 8,600 on Kwajalein Atoll, 8,122 were killed and 437 taken prisoner. Total American strength was 41,446. Of these, 372 were killed, 1,582 were wounded, and 82 were missing.

In the Attack Force Reserve Group for the operation against Kwajalein Atoll was Transport Division 20. This consisted of *Leonard Wood*, flagship, commanded by Captain Merlin O'Neill, USCG, and *Arthur Middleton* (Captain S. A. Olsen, USCG), *Heywood* with some Coast Guardsmen on board, and *President Monroe* and *Electra*. Since the capture and occupation of Kwajalein went exceedingly well, the Reserve Group was not needed in the initial operation; therefore, it entered the lagoon the day after the attack and stayed until 15 February.

The success against Kwajalein made it possible to advance the date for the attack on Eniwetok Atoll from 10 May to 17 February. The ships were ready, and the troops of the Reserve Group were available. Eniwetok Atoll, the westernmost of the Marshalls, lies 330 miles northwest of Kwajalein. There are 30 small islands on the coral rim. The three principal islands used by the Japanese were Engebi in the north (with an airstrip), and Eniwetok and Parry in the south. Eniwetok Island is about three miles long and up to 2,000 feet wide, covered with cocoanut trees and encircled by a sandy beach. Parry Island is slightly smaller. Three passages afford entrance into the lagoon. There were about 1,200 Japanese troops on Engebi, 900 on Eniwetok, and 1,300 on Parry. Most were recent arrivals. Engebi was the most heavily defended, with earthworks and coastal defense guns.

The Task Group for this assault consisted of 89 vessels including flagship *Cambria;* ten transports among which were *Leonard Wood,* flagship of Captain Loomis commanding the transports; *Centaurus, Arthur Middleton,* and *Heywood;* nine Navy LSTs; six LCIs; a fire support group of battleships, cruisers, and destroyers; together with six carriers of various types and their screens of cruisers and destroyers, minesweepers, and auxiliaries. The force carried about 8,000 assault troops, mostly of the 22nd Marines and 106th Infantry, under command of Brigadier General Thomas E. Watson, USMC. These moved up from Kwajalein.

D-day, 17 February, was one of preliminaries. Counter-battery fire on the islands flanking the Eniwetok Lagoon entrances began at 0700, with no return fire. Minesweepers proceeded into the lagoon, followed by LSTs and LCIs through Wide Passage, while the battleships, cruisers, and destroyers entered through Deep Entrance. The same pattern of attack was made on all three islands, assaults being made one at a time. Each island was continuously bombarded from the time of arrival until the troops were put ashore. Landings were made on the lagoon beaches mostly from LVTs.

At 1318 on D-day, unopposed landings were effected on two small islands along the reef about four miles eastward of Engebi. Assault troops, loaded directly into LCVPs from *Heywood* and *Arthur Middleton* (at this time under command of Captain G. W. McKean, USCG), landed on Engebi at 0843 on 18 February. The first wave was led by *Middleton's* boats. The ship's beachmaster, Lieutenant (jg) Robert Hoyle, USCG, announced that the beach assigned to *Middleton* had been secured by 0930. One beach party member was wounded in action. Hoyle later received the Silver Star, and Malcolm Anderson, RM3c, USCGR, and Russell Alson, RM3c, each received the Bronze Star. Enemy resistance was quickly overcome. Except for isolated positions the island was secured at 1600. American losses were 78 killed, 166 wounded, and seven missing. The Japanese dead numbered 934.

During the afternoon of 18 February, all ships involved except *Leonard Wood* and *Ashland* (LSD) moved from Engebi to Eniwetok. Preliminary naval gunfire was very effective. Landings were made there on 19 February. Sniper and mortar fire was encountered by the landing craft and it increased steadily until the last wave landed. Only light losses were sustained by the troops as they went ashore, and resistance was light for the first several hundred yards; thereafter, the enemy conducted a stubborn defense. At 1800 half the island had been taken but it was not entirely secured until 1740 on the 21st. At Eniwetok, the Japanese lost 704 dead as against 34 Americans killed, 94 wounded, and three missing.

Parry Island was even more strongly held. Accordingly, that island was subjected to continuous harassing bombardment from 18 February until the morning of the 22nd, when landings began at 0900. The first wave met rifle and mortar fire, but casualties were few. During these landings, Lieutenant (jg) John M. Johnson, USCGR, the first wave guide officer from *Middleton,* in an LCVP, went alongside Navy *LCI-442,* a rocket fire ship of the first wave, which had been hit by an enemy shell and had burst into flames. He learned that the magazine was on fire and that the ship was in imminent danger of blowing up. A number of dead and injured were lying on the deck. Lieutenant Johnson and members of his boat crew removed the injured to their LCVP and transferred them to hospital ship *Solace.* All the Coast Guardsmen involved received the Navy and Marine Corps Medal for their heroism.

The naval bombardment had raised havoc with the enemy. At 1924 the island was declared secure, but mopping up operations continued into the 23rd. Losses to American troops at Parry were 57 killed, 261 wounded, and 16 missing. One thousand twenty-seven Japanese were buried.

Vessels wholly or partly manned by the Coast Guard, which were engaged in the Marshall Islands and other Pacific combat operations during 1944 and the campaigns in which they participated are listed on the following page.

After these operations in the Marshalls, there were 28 islands and atolls in that group which had not been reconnoitered or occupied by United States forces. A systematic and methodical occupation of the Lesser Marshalls was then undertaken, by-passing only four atolls—Wotje, Maloelap, Mille and Jaluit—which remained in enemy possession.

While the Marshall Islands were being taken over by United States forces, further progress was

COAST GUARD-MANNED VESSELS ENGAGED IN AMPHIBIOUS OPERATIONS IN PACIFIC—1944

| Name of Vessel | Saidor | Marshalls—Kwajalein | Majuro | Eniwetok | Green Island | Admiralty Islands | St. Mathias Islands | Hollandia | Wakde Island | Biak Island | Marianas—Saipan | Guam | Tinian | Noemfoor Island | Cape Sansapor | Peleliu | Angaur | Morotai | Leyte | Mindoro |
|---|---|---|---|---|---|---|---|---|---|---|---|---|---|---|---|---|---|---|---|---|
| Allentown | | X | X | | | | | | | | X | X | | | | | | | X | |
| Aquarius | | | | | | | | | | | | | | | | X | | | X | |
| Arthur Middleton | | X | X | X | | | | | | | X | | | | | | | | X | |
| Bisbee | | | | | | | | | | | | | | | X | | | | X | |
| Burlington | | | | | | | | | | | | | | | | | | X | X | |
| Buttonwood | | | | | | | | | | | | | | | | | | | X | |
| Callaway | | X | X | | | X | | | | | X | | | | | | X | | X | |
| Cambria | | X | X | X | | | | | | | X | | X | | | | | | X | |
| Cor Caroli | | | | | | | | | | | | X | | | | | | | | |
| Carson City | | | | | | | | | | | | | | | | | | X | X | |
| Cavalier | | | | | | | | | | | X | | X | | | | | | X | |
| Centaurus | | X | X | X | | | | X | | | X | X | | | | X | | | X | |
| Coronado | | | | | | X | | X | | X | | | | | X | | | X | X | |
| El Paso | | | | | | | | X | X | | | | | X | X | | | X | | |
| Etamin | | | | | | X | | X | | | | | | | | | | | | |
| Eugene | | | | | | | | | | | | | | | X | | | | X | |
| Gallup | | | | | | | | | | | | | | | X | | | X | X | |
| Glendale | | | | | | X | | X | | | | | | | X | X | | X | | |
| Hutchinson | | | | | | | | | | | | | | | | | | | X | |
| Leonard Wood | | X | X | X | | | | | | | X | | | | | | X | | X | |
| Long Beach | | | | | | X | | X | | | | | | | | X | | X | | |
| Muskogee | | | | | | | | | | | | | | | | | | | X | |
| Ogden | | | | | | | | | X | X | | | | | | | | | | |
| Orange | | | | | | | | | | | | | | X | X | | | | | |
| San Pedro | | | | | | X | | X | | X | | | | | | | | X | X | |
| Spencer | | | | | | | | | | | | | | | | | | | X | |
| Sterope | | | | | | | | | | | | X | | | | | | | | |
| Tupelo | | | | | | | | | | | | X | | | | | | | | |
| Van Buren | | | | | | | | X | X | X | | | | | X | | | | | |
| Woodbine | | | | | | | | | | | X | | | | | | | | | |
| FS-367 | | | | | | | | | | | | | | | | | | | | X |
| LST-18 | | | | | | X | | X | X | X | | | | X | X | | | X | | |
| LST-19 | | | | | | | | | | | X | | X | | | X | | | | |
| LST-20 | | | | | | | | | | | | | | | | | | | X | |
| LST-22 | X | | | | | X | | X | X | X | | | | X | X | | | X | X | |
| LST-23 | | X | X | | X | | | | | | X | | X | | | X | | | | |
| LST-24 | | | | | | | | | | | | X | | | | | | | | |
| LST-26 | | | | | | | | X | X | X | | | | X | X | | | X | X | |
| LST-66 | X | | | | | X | | X | X | X | | | | X | X | | | X | X | |
| LST-67 | X | | | | | X | | X | X | X | | | | X | X | | | X | X | |
| LST-68 | X | | | | | X | | X | | X | | | | X | X | | | X | X | |
| LST-70 | | | | | X | | | | | | X | X | | | | | | | | |
| LST-71 | | | | | | | | | | | | X | | | | | | | | |
| LST-166 | | | | | X | | | | | | X | | | | | | | | | |
| LST-168 | X | | | | | X | | X | | | | | | | | | | X | X | |
| LST-169 | | | | | | X | | | | | X | | | | | | | | X | |
| LST-170 | X | | | | | X | | X | X | X | | | | | X | | | X | X | |
| LST-201 | | | | | | | | X | | | | | | | | | | | | |
| LST-202 | X | | | | | X | | X | X | | | | | X | X | | | | | |
| LST-204 | X | | | | | | | X | | | | | | X | X | | | X | X | |
| LST-205 | | | | | | | | | | X | X | | | | | | | | X | |
| LST-206 | X | | | | | X | | X | X | X | | | | | X | | | X | X | |
| LST-207 | | | | | X | | | | | | | X | | | | | | | X | |

NAVY VESSELS WITH A FEW COAST GUARDSMEN IN THEIR CREWS

| Name of Vessel | Saidor | Marshalls—Kwajalein | Majuro | Eniwetok | Green Island | Admiralty Islands | St. Mathias Islands | Hollandia | Wakde Island | Biak Island | Marianas—Saipan | Guam | Tinian | Noemfoor Island | Cape Sansapor | Peleliu | Angaur | Morotai | Leyte | Mindoro |
|---|---|---|---|---|---|---|---|---|---|---|---|---|---|---|---|---|---|---|---|---|
| *Alhena* | | | | | | | | | | | X | | | | | | | | X | |
| *Bellatrix* | | | | | | | | | | | X | | | | | | | | X | |
| *Crescent City* | | | | | | | | | | | | X | | | | X | | | X | |
| *Fuller* | | | | | | | | | | | X | | X | | | X | | | X | |
| *George F. Elliott* | | | | | | | | | | | X | | | | | | | | X | |
| *Heywood* | | X | X | X | | | | | | | X | | X | | | | | | X | |
| *Libra* | | | | | | | | | | | | X | | | | | | | | |
| *Neville* | | X | X | X | | | | | | | X | | | | | | | | | |
| *President Adams* | | | | | | | | | | | | X | | | | | | | | |
| *President Hayes* | | | | | | | | | | | X | | | | | | | | X | |
| *President Jackson* | | | | | | | | | | | X | X | | | | | | | | |
| *Stringham* | X | | | | X | | | | | | X | | X | | | X | | | X | |
| *William P. Biddle* | | X | X | | | | | | | | | X | | | | | | | | |
| *LST-334* | | | | | | | | | | | | X | | | | | | | | |

made in the waters off New Guinea. Green (Nissan) Island, lying north of Buka Island at the northern end of the Solomons, became a desirable objective. Since it was only 117 miles from Rabaul, it could be used to harass that base as well as Kavieng on New Ireland, and halt Japanese barge traffic to isolated enemy forces still in the Solomons.

After naval and army reconnaissance of Green Island on 31 January, the Allies returned on 15 February with the 3rd Amphibious Force under Admiral Wilkinson. This force consisted of eight destroyer-transports including *Stringham* with some Coast Guardsmen; twelve LCIs, seven LSTs, six LCTs; and numerous smaller craft, all screened by 17 destroyers. Among the LSTs were Coast Guard-manned *LST-23*, *LST-70*, *LST-166*, and *LST-207*. Covering the landings were two cruiser task forces under Rear Admirals W. L. Ainsworth, USN, and A. S. Merrill, USN. These task forces met opposition only from the air and suffered but one hit (on *St. Louis*) which killed 23 men and wounded 30.

Fear of killing friendly and cooperative natives caused cancellation of the usual naval bombardment prior to the landings. The LCIs and LSTs were subjected to a pre-landing attack by 15 "Vals" which did negligible damage and were driven off by antiaircraft fire and covering fighters. In all, 5,800 troops of the 3rd New Zealand Division (Major General Barrowclough) landed unscathed. Additional troops, landed later, brought the total to 16,448. In four days Green Island was secured. By the end of February a fighter strip was nearly completed, and the airfield was in use in early March.

On 16-17 February, timed to coincide with the assault on Eniwetok, Rear Admiral Marc A. Mitscher's carrier task force struck hard at the formidable Japanese base at Truk. This attack virtually wiped out the aircraft concentrated there and destroyed 32 enemy naval vessels, mostly cargo ships. Two days later, most of the remaining enemy planes at Rabaul were flown to Truk, ending the effectiveness of Rabaul as an air base. The final isolation of Rabaul was achieved on 20 March when Marines landed at tiny Emirau Island, in the St. Mathias group, north of the Bismarck Archipelago. *Callaway* and cargo transport *Cor Caroli*, both Coast Guard-manned, participated in this operation, together with 22 Navy-manned vessels. The Marines landed without a scratch.

The Admiralties are a group of rugged, mountainous islands just below the equator at the head of the Bismarck Sea, about 300 miles north northwest of Cape Gloucester and 200 miles off the New Guinea coast. The largest of the group are Manus and Los Negros, which are barely separated by

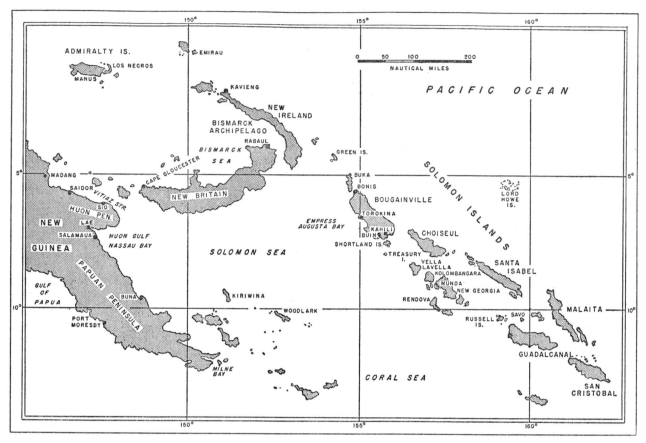

BATTLE AREAS OF THE SOUTHWEST PACIFIC

a narrow channel. Almost enclosed by islands to the north is Seeadler Harbor, large enough and deep enough for any fleet. The Japanese had substantial airfields on the two largest islands. By capturing the Admiralties, about 100,000 by-passed Japanese troops would be sealed off to starve in the Bismarck-Melanesia area, and a strategic location would be acquired for the Allied forces.

Enemy air strength had ebbed fast in this area, but reconnaissance had established that Los Negros had plenty of enemy defenders. An attack force under Rear Admiral W. M. Fechteler, USN, assembled at Oro Bay, New Guinea and, weighing anchor on the afternoon of 27 February, headed north. It consisted of eight destroyers and three destroyer-transports carrying units of the First Cavalry Division, preceded by two cruisers and four destroyers.

*Etamin* (Lieutenant Commander G. W. Stedman, USCG), a Coast Guard-manned cargo ship, as well as a number of LSTs with Coast Guard

crews, were involved in the landings at the Admiralties. These were *LST-67*, flagship for the Manus assault, and LSTs *18, 22, 66, 68, 168, 170, 202,* and *206.* Also taking part at various times were patrol frigates, a new class of vessel. Four of these—*Coronado, Glendale, Long Beach,* and *San Pedro*—were Coast Guard-manned.

The attack force arrived off Hyane Harbor, Los Negros, on 29 February. After a short bombardment landings were effected at 0815 with no opposition from the beaches. Considerable crossfire, however, was experienced by most boats as they passed between the harbor entrance headlands. Light resistance was offered at Momote airfield, which was quickly seized. Patrols moved north and southwest from the airstrip, establishing contact with the enemy, who counter-attacked during the night but were repulsed with heavy losses.

The next echelon consisted of two destroyers and two minesweepers and six LSTs. Each LST towed an LCM. When this echelon arrived at 0900 on 2 March they found a serious situation at the beachhead. The enemy was bringing up additional forces and United States B-25s were strafing and bombing the beachhead. The LSTs went right in through the narrow entrance. As they beached they came under mortar fire. Coast Guard-manned *LST-202*, which was nearest the enemy, opened up with her 3-inch and 40-mm. guns, as well as the .50-caliber machine guns that she was carrying on deck as freight. The other five LSTs did the same. In the midst of all this, they opened their bow ramps and unloading began. They were completely unloaded by 1700, and then returned to New Guinea. By 9 March, about half of Los Negros was in Allied hands; Americans had lost 116 dead and 434 wounded, while the Japanese killed numbered 1,288. Fighting continued throughout March.

On 15 March, after an air and naval bombardment, units of the First Cavalry Division were landed with little opposition on the northeast coast of Manus Island. Despite some enemy fire, they quickly seized the Lorengau airfield. Stubborn resistance was met on the 16th, but shelling from destroyers and artillery gave effective support. Two weeks later, all major resistance had been overcome, and probably not over 900 effective enemy troops remained. At least 2,594 Japanese had been killed up to that time.

The Admiralty Islands were to all intents and purposes in Allied control by 3 April. Seeadler Harbor, now available for use by Allied navies, became an air and naval base which proved a powerful element in the defeat of Japan.

The reconquest of New Guinea had gone far, and Allied armies had moved up half the length of the giant 1,200-mile-long island. To complete this, it was decided to push far to the northwest, and seize the coastal area in the vicinity of Aitape and Hollandia, thus by-passing and neutralizing the enemy's holdings in the Hansa Bay and Wewak areas. American and Australian surface units were organized to carry out the amphibious landings.

Admiral Barbey was in over-all command of the operation. The attack group was divided into three forces. The Western Attack Group (Rear Admiral Barbey) would land at Tanahmerah Bay; the Central Attack Group (Rear Admiral W. E. Fechteler) at Humboldt Bay wherein lay Hollan-

dia; and the Eastern Attack Group (Captain Alfred G. Noble, USN) at Aitape. These groups comprised a total of 161 vessels. In addition there were the reinforcement group with 50 ships, as well as escort carrier groups and covering forces. Twenty-one Coast Guard-manned vessels took part in these operations. *Etamin* was in the Eastern Attack Group. In the reinforcement group were *Centaurus* (Captain McCabe, USCG), and seven patrol frigates: *San Pedro* (Lieutenant Commander C. O. Ashley, USCG); *Glendale* (Commander H. J. Doebler, USCG); *Long Beach* (Lieutenant Commander T. R. Midtlyng, USCG); and *El Paso, Ogden, Coronado* and *Van Buren*. These frigates acted as an antisubmarine screen and joined in the bombardment. Commander Frank D. Higbee, USCG, commanded a group of six LSTs in the reinforcement group. Out of 37 LSTs in all groups, 12 were manned by the Coast Guard. These were LSTs *18, 22, 26, 66, 67, 68, 168, 170, 201, 202, 204,* and *206*. Altogether, the United States vessels embarked 25,430 Army personnel for the assault landing. Reinforcements brought the total to 45,000.

Following air and naval bombardment this powerful force landed at Hollandia and Aitape on 22 April. Landings were made at two points near Hollandia, on the shores of Humboldt Bay east of the airfields, and in Tanahmerah Bay, northwest of the fields. The landing at Aitape, over 125 miles east of Hollandia, took place at the same time. Beachheads were quickly established at all points against virtually no opposition from the surprised Japanese, many of whom fled into the mountainous interior. Towns and airfields were captured in relatively short order. On the 23rd, an amphibious force landed on Tumelo and Seleo Islands just off the Aitape beachhead. Seleo was quickly overrun but stubborn resistance was encountered on Tumelo.

Enemy airfields in western New Guinea had been under heavy air attack for several days before the landings. Naval aircraft destroyed 13 enemy planes in air combat and 88 on the ground. Aside from two minor attacks, the landings were unchallenged by the Japanese air forces. This amphibious operation virtually isolated 60,000 enemy troops caught between the Allied forces at Madang and those at Hollandia and Aitape.

On the night of 27 April, while anchored in

Aitape Roads, *Etamin* was attacked by Japanese planes. At about 2300 an aerial torpedo struck her starboard side rupturing the shell plating and shaft alley about 10 feet above the keel. The explosion sprayed gasoline over the after part of the ship. Gasoline and fumes came in contact with the hot furnaces and boilers, and an explosion set fire to the engine room, severely burning three crew members. As the ship settled fast at the stern, Commander Stedman deemed it advisable to beach her, but there was no power. An LCT tried to tow her to shallow water but could not move her. In view of the danger of further explosions, all of the 200 crewmen and 150 Army personnel were removed without apparent loss, although later two bodies were discovered in a hold. *Etamin*, with about half of her cargo still on board, was finally towed to Finschafen for salvage. The three seriously burned Coast Guardsmen were flown to Port Moresby. This was the only serious damage suffered by any naval vessel in the entire Hollandia operation.

The landings had gone well. Resistance was met at various points as the troops moved inland, and ground fighting was not completed until 6 June, when the operation was officially declared closed. United States losses in the entire campaign were about 550 killed and 3,600 wounded. About 14,000 Japanese were sacrificed.

The advance along New Guinea was carried out as rapidly as possible, with a series of assaults all pointing toward Mindanao in the Philippines for which a target date of 15 November had been set. In a period of about three months, in four operations at Wakde, Biak, Noemfoor and Sansapor, the Southwest Pacific Forces moved west from Hollandia to Vogelkop, the northwestern end of New Guinea, 550 miles away. All seaborne operations in this advance were conducted by Admiral Kinkaid's Allied Naval Forces. The sea was the only road. Cover and close gunfire support were always provided by cruisers and destroyers under Rear Admirals R. S. Berkey, USN, and V. A. C. Crutchley, RN. Motor torpedo boats and Army Air Forces also took a leading part in the assaults.

On 17 May, Allied forces from Hollandia moved nearly 125 miles west to capture Wakde airfield and gain a new bridgehead at Arara, on New Guinea opposite the Wakde Islands. The

Transport Task Unit assaulting Wakde Island was composed of Navy and Coast Guard-manned LSTs all under the command of Captain Frank D. Higbee, in *LST-18*. Other vessels manned by the Coast Guard were patrol frigates *Van Buren, El Paso,* and *Ogden,* and LSTs *22, 26, 66, 67, 170, 202,* and *206.*

Landings followed the usual pattern, with preliminary bombardment of enemy positions at Wakde, Sawar, and Sarmi. The Arara landing was unopposed and a beachhead eight miles wide was gained without casualties. A minor landing was made on Insoemanai Island nearby, and a major uncontested landing was made on the 18th at Insoemoear Island on which the airfield was located. Enemy troops at Wakde fought furiously until they were wiped out. After mopping up operations, all resistance ceased by the evening of the 19th. American losses in the entire assault were 41 killed, 135 wounded, and one missing in action. The Japanese lost 759 killed. However, in the Sarmi-Maffin Bay region west of Arara, dirty jungle fighting kept up for over three months.

The next move took Allied forces 180 miles beyond Wakde to Biak Island, the largest of the Schouten Islands, lying off Geelvink Bay near Vogelkop. Biak was important as a site for a base from which to operate heavy bombers. Allied air forces worked over Biak in anticipation of the assault. After the 41st Division and most of its equipment had been embarked, the assault force of six LSTs, eight LCTs, and 15 LCIs with their smaller landing craft sailed from Humboldt Bay on 25 May. In the attack force or follow-up forces were the Coast Guard's patrol frigates *Van Buren, Coronado,* and *San Pedro,* and all their LSTs which had taken part at Wakde except *LST-202,* plus *LST-68, LST-204,* and *LST-205.* The covering forces of Admirals Berkey and Crutchley joined the next morning.

After the usual bombardment, landings were made on 27 May near Bosnek village, about eight miles east of Mokmer airfield, easternmost of three. Because of the fringing coral reefs offshore, troops and supplies were loaded into small landing craft some distance from shore. These were stopped by coral about 100 yards from the beach and the troops had to wade in through water nearly waist deep. Fortunately, no opposition was met on the beach, although Biak held about 10,000 Japanese—nearly as many troops as the invaders. The bombardment had driven enemy troops to prepared positions on high ground overlooking the narrow coastal flat. There they offered determined resistance and had to be blasted from hillside dugouts and natural caves.

Some of the stiffest resistance of any in the New Guinea operations was encountered around the airfields, with especially bitter fighting on the 29th and 30th. It was not until 6 June that Mokmer airfield was captured. The assault engendered a naval battle off Biak on 8-9 June which was indecisive, though Japanese reinforcement attempts were thwarted. Stubborn defense continued until 22 June, when the first Allied fighters began operating from Mokmer. These airfields provided forward bases only 900 miles from Davao in the Philippines, and less than 600 miles from Palau, putting the latter within easy range of land based bombers. The cost to Allied ground forces was 438 killed and 2,361 wounded, but cases of disease numbered 3,500.

With Biak under control, the next allied objective in the New Guinea area was the island of Noemfoor, about 60 miles to the west. It is a circular island about nine miles in diameter, surrounded by a coral reef, and rising in jungle covered hills up to 700 feet high. The Japanese had built three airfields there, so Noemfoor was an attractive target. The landing force was built around the 158th United States Infantry Regimental Combat Team reinforced by artillery, anti-aircraft, tank, engineer, and service units totalling 7,078 men.

Air bombardment began 20 June and lasted until 1 July. There was no air opposition because enemy aircraft had been sent to Saipan to contest the landings there. The naval bombardment which preceded the landings rendered the enemy defenders almost worthless. The Naval Attack Force which moved to Noemfoor included Coast Guard-manned LSTs *18, 22, 26, 66, 67, 68, 202,* and *204*. Patrol frigates *El Paso, Orange,* and *San Pedro* also served at Noemfoor.

Shortly after dawn on 2 July, landings were effected as scheduled and went off well. It was necessary to transfer cargoes to the smaller shallow draft LCIs which could successfully drop their ramps on the jagged end of the reef. Transfer of heavy Army equipment between the ships was a delicate operation, and Coast Guard LST skippers demonstrated their "know-how" gained from months of amphibious experience.

By noon of 2 July, Kamiri airfield had been secured, and before evening a good beachhead had been established. Paratroopers were landed on 3 and 4 July in a spectacular manner. Dozens of DC4s went in low over the island and dropped hundreds of paratroopers while above them A20s and P38s swooped and darted to keep at bay any prowling "Zeros." Reinforced by the paratroopers, the infantry captured Kornasoren airfield on the 4th. Namber airstrip was taken the next day. This gave the Allies seven air bases at the south of Geelvink Bay—all within 800-900 miles of the Philippines and within bombing range of important Netherlands East India enemy bases. The only landing casualties were leg and ankle injuries from the rocky terrain.

Mopping up in the hills of Noemfoor took time, and the operation was not officially terminated until 31 August. Allied losses were 66 killed or missing, and 343 wounded. Japanese losses were 1,900, including 186 captured.

The final stop in New Guinea for General MacArthur's return journey to the Philippines was Cape Sansapor, near the northern extremity of the Vogelkop Peninsula, 200 miles beyond Noemfoor. It is barely 600 miles from the southern tip of Mindanao.

The expeditionary force for Cape Sansapor, commanded by Admiral Fechteler, got underway from Toem and Wakde at 2300 on 27 July, and consisted of 11 destroyers, five destroyer-transports, 19 LCIs, eight LSTs, four PCs, and a fleet tug. Included in this force and in follow-up activity were the Coast Guard-manned LSTs *18, 22, 26, 66, 67, 68, 170, 202, 204,* and *206*. Patrol frigates *Bisbee, Coronado, Eugene, Gallup, Glendale, Long Beach, San Pedro,* and *Van Buren* were engaged in patrol activity in the area.

Landings in six waves were achieved without opposition at 0700 on 30 July, and within a few hours the objectives had been attained. No preliminary bombardment of the beaches was necessary or desirable since complete surprise was wanted. Amsterdam and Middleburg Islands, off nearby Cape Opmarai, were also occupied during the day. The only enemy contact was with a small force about six miles east of the beachhead.

This operation placed Allied forces between the only two major bases remaining to the Japanese in New Guinea—Sorong, 60 miles to the southwest on the western tip of New Guinea, and Manokwari, with 15,000 Japanese, 150 miles to the east. Airfields in the Sansapor area were begun immediately, bringing into effective bombing range northeastern Celebes and eastern Borneo; regions bordering two of Japan's principal routes to the East Indies through the Straits of Makassar and the Molucca Sea. As the New Guinea campaign drew to a close, large numbers of the enemy had been cut off and trapped behind the advancing front.

During the New Guinea operations just recounted, one of the great amphibious undertakings of the Pacific War was being planned for and executed in the Marianas. This group of 15 islands extends in an arc for 425 miles. The southernmost, and the only ones of military and economic importance, are Guam, Rota, Tinian, and Saipan. The first and last are about 120 miles apart; they lie roughly 1,200 miles north of the Admiralty Islands and the same distance east of the Philippines.

American bases and airfields established in the Marshalls, Admiralties, and north central New Guinea threatened enemy bases in the Carolines, Netherlands East Indies, and the southern Philippines. Allied attacks by land and carrier based aircraft had rendered Japanese communications to the Carolines insecure, and enemy air strength in that area had deteriorated. Severe losses had been inflicted on Japanese shipping by submarine, air, and surface forces. Nevertheless, the enemy was rapidly strengthening his position in the Marianas. To continue pressure and extend American control to the westward, the southern Marianas were selected as the next amphibious objective.

The assault force for the Marianas was formidable indeed. Under the over-all command of Admiral Nimitz, were the Fifth Fleet (Admiral Raymond A. Spruance, USN), the Reconnaissance and Patrol Submarines (Vice Admiral Charles A. Lockwood, USN), the Service Force Pacific Fleet (Vice Admiral William L. Calhoun, USN), and three other forces also under Admiral Spruance. These were the Joint Expeditionary Force (Vice Admiral Richmond K. Turner, USN), the Fast Carrier Forces (Vice Admiral Marc A. Mitscher, USN), and the Forward Area Central Pacific, (Land-Based Aircraft) under Vice Admiral John H. Hoover, USN.

The Joint Expeditionary Force was divided into two attack forces and one Floating Reserve. The Northern Attack Force for Saipan and Tinian remained under the direct command of Admiral Turner, and carried the 2nd and 4th Marine Divisions, reinforced, under Lieutenant General Holland M. Smith, USMC. This force mounted in Hawaii and on the West Coast. In it were 37 transports, including Coast Guard-manned *Cambria* (flagship of Admiral Hill), (Captain C. W. Dean, USCG); *Arthur Middleton* (Captain S. A. Olsen, USCG); *Leonard Wood*, flagship of Transport Division 20, (Captain H. C. Perkins, USCG); *Callaway* (Captain D. C. McNeil, USCG); and seven with Coast Guardsmen in their Navy crews: *Alhena, Bellatrix, Fuller, George F. Elliott, Heywood, Neville,* and *Stringham.* In addition were LSTs *166, 19, 23,* and *169.* Each Attack Force had its own bombardment group.

The Southern Attack Force for Guam was under command of Rear Admiral Conolly, and carried the 3rd Marine Division and 1st Provisional Marine Brigade under Major General Roy S. Geiger, USMC. It mounted in the Guadalcanal-Tulagi area. This Force included Coast Guard-manned *Aquarius* and *Centaurus*, and LSTs *24, 70, 71,* and *207*, among the 30 vessels of that type. Cargo ships *Cor Caroli* and *Sterope*, both manned by the Coast Guard, were included as well as these Navy vessels with some Coast Guardsmen in their crews—*William P. Biddle, President Jackson, President Hayes, President Adams, Crescent City, Libra,* and *LST-334.* In addition, cutters *Woodbine* and *Tupelo* served as mobile service bases.

The Floating Reserve, commanded by Rear Admiral William H. P. Blandy, USN, carried the 27th Division, U. S. Army, reinforced, under Major General Ralph Smith, USA. *Cavalier* (Captain R. T. McElligott, USCG), Coast Guard-manned, was in the Reserve Transport Group. All of these forces moved up to the Marianas at the same time.

It was a vast operation on a scale slightly exceeding that of Operation "Torch" at North Africa. The combatant ships and auxiliaries numbered 535, and carried four-and-a-half reinforced divisions comprising 127,571 troops. Admiral Turner had set 15 June (nine days after Normandy) as D-day for Saipan but left the dates for Guam and Tinian dependent upon events at Saipan.

While the plan called for the initial amphibious

assault to be made at Saipan, both that island and Tinian were subjected to heavy air and naval bombardment beginning on 13 June. The bombardment group encountered no opposition.

At dawn on 15 June, fire support vessels took their stations and poured their fire into the two islands. In the meantime, the transport and tractor groups carrying the troops, artillery, tanks, ammunition, supplies, and other equipment arrived off the western coast of Saipan. A heavy air strike along the landing beaches was made between 0700 and 0730, and intense pre-assault close range naval bombardment of the landing beaches commenced at 0800. A diversionary demonstration by two divisions, including *Arthur Middleton,* was made in the north while the actual landings occurred. Several waves of boats without troops were sent beachward, then recalled. At 0840 regular landings in the usual fashion were made on eight beaches along a four-mile front on the southern part of Saipan's west coast.

The assault was successful despite heavy mortar, artillery, and machine gun fire from the enemy which caused heavy casualties. Several LVTs were lost, some overturning in the surf. In the first half hour about 8,000 troops, with nearly 150 LVT(A)s operating as light tanks in support, were landed on Saipan. A beachhead was established in spite of the high casualty rate. Throughout the remainder of the day, reserve troops, emergency supplies, ammunition, tanks, and artillery were landed. By 1800 nearly 20,000 troops had been put ashore. In the evening most of the attacking ships retired, leaving designated fire support vessels, *Cambria,* most of the LSTs, and various small craft.

During the Saipan landings the Japanese made a living hell out of a pass leading into the lagoon off Garapan, about five miles north of the main landings. Many Americans died as they tried to negotiate it. While bullets whizzed overhead and shells fell nearby, Coast Guard Lieutenants (jg) Clifford L. Benson of Maspeth, Long Island, and Truman C. Hardin of Springfield, Missouri, while probing about a shallow lagoon found a channel through the coral reef which led to the sugar refinery pier at Charan-Kanoa. Through it they brought sorely needed supplies and reinforcements at a crucial point in the battle for the beachhead.

Use of this channel saved the day for the beleaguered Marines in the vicinity. One of the first boats to use it delivered 30,000 rounds of desperately needed ammunition. Another brought in blood plasma and medical supplies. Three tanks as well as troop reinforcements were delivered through the channel. As scores of small craft filled the lagoon, the intensity of the enemy fire increased. Coxswains bent down and steered on bended knee, popping up occasionally for a quick glance at their course. The supplies landed gave the Americans the necessary superiority to defeat a strong counter-attack, and when the action ended the Marines were in possession of the refinery and the ground surrounding it.

The military conquest of Saipan was divided into three distinct stages; first, the establishment of a beachhead which gave control of the southern portion of the island; second, the fight for control of the central mountainous area; and third, the defeat of remnants of the enemy in the northern part. In the 25 days following the landings, the Japanese defenders of Saipan were defeated after some of the stubbornest and most vicious fighting in the Pacific Islands. However, it was not until 10 August that Admiral Spruance announced that capture and occupation had been completed. Out of 67,545 troops landed, Americans counted their casualties at 3,100 killed, 13,099 wounded, and 326 missing in action, which was a very high percentage. The final count of Japanese dead was 25,559—just about all there were.

Though Tinian, near Saipan, had received a thoroughgoing bombardment, Guam was chosen as the next point of attack, with 18 June originally selected as the target date. The severe resistance at Saipan, however, caused postponement. The Japanese, as a result of the action at Saipan, diverted strong naval forces from the Philippine area toward the Marianas to engage the American naval forces, and this resulted in the Battle of the Philippine Sea. The famous Marianas "Turkey Shoot", in which attacking enemy planes were spectacularly decimated, was a preliminary. Though badly hurt in the main battle, the enemy fleet escaped and the net results were disappointing to the United States Navy. From 18 to 24 June, until the conclusion of this battle, and the end of Japanese threat to American amphibious forces in the Marianas, the task force designated for the Guam attack retired and advanced in an area east of Saipan and finally returned to Eniwetok for additional preparation and planning.

The new "D-day" for Guam was set for 21 July.

For some time before the main attack, surface ships and aircraft first neutralized, and then knocked out practically all the enemy antiaircraft and artillery batteries on Guam, and destroyed virtually all enemy aircraft there. Not a single piece of enemy artillery was brought to bear on the transports when the landings finally took place.

In the assault on Guam, 19,423 Army troops and 37,292 Marines were employed. During the night of 20-21 July, the transports steamed around the southern tip of the island and moved into their assigned positions. As the ships approached the beaches on 21 July, a heavy pre-landing air attack on enemy positions took place from 0715 to 0815. There was simultaneous naval gunfire for the first time in Pacific amphibious operations. The landings were carried out in the customary manner, with planes still attacking enemy mortar and artillery positions a mile inland.

At 0830 the first wave from the Northern Group landed on the Asan beaches, and from the Southern Group at Agat, nine miles to the south. Due to the heavy bombardment, enemy opposition to the landings was relatively light. By 1130 the entire 3rd Marine Division, with essential equipment, was ashore on the northern beaches. The 1st Provisional Marine Brigade was landed on the southern beaches by 1100, and the 305th Regimental Combat Team of the 77th went ashore in the afternoon.

Beachheads were established and the two forces joined on 27 July. The Japanese contested vigorously, but all organized resistance ended by 9 August. Complete elimination of the remaining pockets of stubborn defenders in exceedingly rough terrain, however, was not effected until 14 November by which time 17,238 of the enemy had been killed and 463 captured. American casualties were 1,289 killed, 5,648 wounded, and 148 missing.

In the meantime, Tinian, 10½ miles long and 5 miles wide, was receiving attention. Its capture was perfectly planned and executed. Admiral Hill assumed command of the Tinian Attack Force, and the day for the assault was designated as 24 July. Threat from the damaged Japanese fleet was considered negligible and American naval forces adequate, to prevent serious interference. No significant attacks by enemy planes had been made in the Marianas since 8 July. Enemy air bases at Guam, Rota, and Pagan had been effectively neu-

tralized. The Japanese forces on Tinian had been subjected to aerial and naval bombardment since 11 June and their effectiveness had been impaired.

Task Force 52, which attacked Tinian, consisted of 214 vessels of which 174 were in the amphibious groups, 16 in the Carrier Support Group, and 24 in the Fire Support Group. Included were Coast Guard-manned *Cambria, Cavalier, LST-19,* and *LST-23,* and also *Fuller, Heywood,* and *Stringham* with Coast Guardsmen in their crews.

Movements of all vessels from Saipan to Tinian were executed on 24 July in good weather and without incident. The attack forces assembled off two landing beaches on the northwest shore of Tinian, with a deceptive feint at Tinian Town to the south. The Japanese had expected the assault to be made at the town, and with concentrated forces opposed the feigned landing with intense mortar and artillery fire. Battleship *Colorado* and destroyer *Norman Scott* suffered severe personnel casualties when taken under fire by a previously undetected shore battery. The feinting force withdrew after two "tries" and landed to the north in the afternoon. Surprise as to the real location of the assault was satisfactorily achieved.

In the real landings farther north, the first waves landed at 0742 on one beach and at 0750 on the other. They were opposed by rifle and machine gun fire. Numerous land mines and booby traps were encountered. By 1000 the Marines had advanced 500 yards inland and had closed the gap between the beaches. All troops of the 4th Marine Division were ashore in the afternoon and landings by the 2nd Marine Division were underway. A secure beachhead had been won by nightfall with very light casualties to the assault troops. It took nine days to secure the entire island, during which time 5,546 Japanese had been killed and buried and 404 prisoners had been taken. American casualties were 290 killed, 1,515 wounded, and 24 missing.

With excellent planning and precise execution and despite heavy casualties, the Marianas campaign drew to a satisfactory close. Success in New Guinea, already recounted, placed American and cooperating forces in a position to develop the long scheduled attack on the Philippines. There remained, however, a few Japanese strong points in the Philippine approach area which had to be secured. These were Peleliu, Angaur, Ngesebus, Ulithi, and Ngulu in the Carolines, and Morotai in the Halmaheras. Possession of these islands would reduce the distance between the American perimeter and Mindanao by half.

Morotai and Peleliu were invaded on the same day—15 September. Let us first see what happened at Morotai, about 250 miles west northwest of the Vogelkop Peninsula. It is the northernmost island of the Halmaheras. Admiral Barbey's VII Amphibious Force undertook this operation, with Admiral Berkey's bombardment force, and Rear Admiral T. L. Sprague's carrier force working over the island preparatory to the landings. The Amphibious Force was to put ashore 16,852 Army troops. Included in the landing, re-supply, and patrol forces were 19 Coast Guard-manned vessels—*Burlington, Carson City, Coronado, El Paso, Gallup, Glendale, Long Beach,* and *San Pedro,* and *LSTs 18, 22, 24, 26, 66, 67, 68, 168, 170, 204,* and *206.* A large unit of LSTs and miscellaneous cargo vessels was under the command of Captain Frank D. Higbee, USCG.

Landings began at 0830 and were accomplished without any incident or opposition, and the airfield was promptly taken. The small enemy garrison of probably 200 on the island had fled to the mountains. Two light enemy air attacks that night and the next day did no damage. Reinforcement and re-supply landings followed, and in another two weeks there were 45,000 troops on Morotai, and Army planes were flying from a newly Seabee-built airfield.

The simultaneous landing at Peleliu was a different story. The operations in the Carolines directly or indirectly involved about 800 ships, 1,600 aircraft, 19,600 soldiers, 28,400 Marines, and 202,000 Navy personnel. As early as 6 September, carrier-based fighters swept Japanese installations in the Palaus, including Peleliu, and nearby Angaur. In the following days air and naval bombardment there was intense.

The attacking naval forces for the Palaus were under command of Rear Admiral J. B. Oldendorf, USN, who took tactical command of the force attacking Peleliu. Rear Admiral R. W. Hayler, USN, commanded the Angaur group. Coast Guard-manned vessels at Peleliu were *Aquarius, Centaurus, LST-19,* and *LST-23.* Those at Angaur were *Callaway* and *Leonard Wood.* In addition, at

Peleliu, were *Cresent City, Fuller,* and *Stringham.*

At 0830 on the 15th, Marines of the 1st Division went ashore on the southwest shore of Peleliu, landing opposite the airfield against heavy enemy opposition which resulted in almost 200 landing casualties. Since Peleliu was surrounded by reefs, the Marines were landed in tracked landing craft which had little difficulty with the offshore obstacles. A wide beachhead was quickly established. But landing supplies was another thing. The reefs off Peleliu were strewn with coral heads and boulders and were too shallow for even smaller landing craft to pass over. Consequently the cargo had to be transferred from the transports to small boats, and then to amtracks before it could reach dry land. When the wind rose after the first landing, swells made it impossible to beach these smaller craft. Only LSTs could work through the rolling seas and the pounding surf between reef and beach.

During the blow that followed, three LSTs used as lighters to carry food and ammunition the last critical hundred yards to shore, went aground and broached, and pounding against the ragged reef tore their bottoms out. Other LSTs finished the job. Day and night the work went on, while to seaward *Aquarius, Centaurus,* and other ships worked ablaze with cargo lights despite danger from planes and submarines.

The defenses on Peleliu were among the strongest which had been attacked in the Pacific. Japanese resistance was stubborn, vicious, fanatical, and fought from well prepared positions. Progress ashore was slow and counterattacks numerous. However the airfield was captured by the following noon. After six long days of bitter fighting the famous pillbox-studded height known as "Bloody Nose Ridge" was taken. By the 26th enemy forces on Peleliu had been surrounded, but it was not until mid-October that the assault phase of this operation was completed.

On 17 September, troops of the 81st Infantry Division commanded by Major General Paul J. Mueller, USA, were landed on Angaur Island, an incredible tangle of brush and caves, six miles south of Peleliu. The troops debarked from *Callaway, Leonard Wood* and other transports, following a magnificent barrage by planes and surface vessels. The landing was made at two beaches on the northeast and east coasts against light opposition. By nightfall the two beachheads had been joined. After three unsuccessful Japanese counterattacks the next day, the island was secured on 20 July. However, the mopping up of enemy remnants, some holding out in caves, continued until 22 October.

The capture of Peleliu and Angaur cost the United States 7,794 casualties, mostly on Peleliu, of which 1,209 were killed or missing. Japanese dead totaled nearly 12,000.

Rather uneventful landings were made at several other points, with little or no participation by the Coast Guard. Elements of the 81st Infantry Division not needed at Angaur were dispatched to Ulithi Atoll, about midway between Guam and the Palau Islands. Troops landed at Ulithi on 23 September with no opposition; it was discovered that the island had been abandoned by the Japanese. Its value was chiefly as a shelter for large surface forces. On 28 September, Marines landed on Ngesebus and Kongauru Islands inside the lagoon north of Peleliu, and both were secured within a few hours. Ngulu Atoll, about 100 miles south of Yap Island, was occupied by United States forces on 16 October, and the decks were now clear for the advance to the Philippines.

Some attention had been paid to the Philippines earlier in September. Task Force 38, consisting of three Task Groups, cruised undetected off Mindanao on the 9th. One group under Rear Admiral L. T. DuBose, USN, eradicated an entire Japanese convoy which was carrying cargo desperately needed by the enemy. Soon afterward U. S. carrier plane attacks were made on the islands of Leyte, Samar, Cebu, Negros, Panay, and Bohol. These strikes destroyed 373 enemy planes, ten cargo ships, a transport, two precious oilers, three escort craft, and many smaller vessels. On 21 September, Luzon was attacked by air, after which very little was left floating in Manila Bay. Sixty-six Japanese planes were destroyed in the air, as well as many more on the ground. The September attacks accounted for more than 1,000 Japanese planes and over 150 ships. A good beginning!

General MacArthur and Admirals Nimitz and Halsey determined to move up the planned operations against Leyte from 20 December to 20 October if possible. The Joint Chiefs of Staff, in conference at Quebec on 15 September, received and granted their requests for this change, and ordered the invasion of Leyte for 20 October. The various naval forces spread over the Pacific assembled at diverse bases and anchorages to prepare for the coming campaign. The logistics problems were staggering but were adequately solved. With time short, preparations were pushed to the utmost.

The over-all command in this operation was General MacArthur's; Vice Admiral Kinkaid was in charge of naval operations. The new organization of the Seventh Fleet under Admiral Kinkaid called for three Task Forces—77, 78, and 79— with Admiral Kinkaid also commanding TF 77, Admiral Barbey TF 78, and Admiral Wilkinson TF 79. Task Force 77 included Fire Support, Close Covering, Escort Carrier, Beach Demolition, and other groups. The 6th United States Army, commanded by Lieutenant General Walter Kreuger, USA, comprised the landing forces, and these assembled at Hollandia and Manus.

In the Seventh Fleet, participating in the Leyte campaign, were 738 vessels of which 157 were combat ships, 420 amphibious types, 84 patrol, minesweeping, and hydrographic vessels, and 73 service ships. Of the vessels taking part in the assault at Leyte and in the follow-up, 35 were Coast Guard-manned and seven carried Coast Guardsmen in their Navy crews. This was by far the Coast Guard's greatest representation in any Pacific operation up to this time. The 35 Coast Guard-manned vessels were:

| | | | |
|---|---|---|---|
| Allentown | Cavalier | Ogden | LST-68 |
| Aquarius | Centaurus | San Pedro | LST-168 |
| Arthur Middleton | Coronado | Spencer | LST-169 |
| Bisbee | El Paso | LST-20 | LST-170 |
| Burlington | Eugene | LST-22 | LST-204 |
| Buttonwood | Gallup | LST-24 | LST-205 |
| Callaway | Hutchinson | LST-26 | LST-206 |
| Cambria | Leonard Wood | LST-66 | LST-207 |
| Carson City | Muskogee | LST-67 | |

Vessels with some Coast Guardsmen were *Bellatrix, Crescent City, Fuller, George F. Elliott, Heywood, President Hayes,* and *William P. Biddle.*

In his operating instructions, General MacArthur had given Admiral Kinkaid heavy responsibility:

"The Navy will transport and land the Army inside Leyte Gulf; will sweep the mines and clear underwater beach obstacles; will sink opposing surface forces and clear the skies of enemy planes;

THE STARS AND STRIPES RETURN TO THE PHILIP-
PINES . . . . supplies are brought in to the war-ravaged
beachhead.

COAST GUARD BEACH SALVAGE UNITS . . . . were
usually assigned the hazardous job of rescuing disabled
landing craft.

TWO LSTs, MANNED BY THE COAST GUARD, ON LEYTE BEACH . . . . sandbags are used to build a pier to the jaws
of the ships to facilitate the landing of equipment.

GENERAL MAC ARTHUR BACK ON PHILIPPINE SOIL
. . . . he chats with two of his commanders after going ashore
at Leyte and fulfilling his famous promise.

INVASION TRAFFIC MOVES ASHORE . . . . the Japanese plane fell victim of heavy ack ack fire from the Task
Force which established the beachhead.

JOYOUS FILIPINOS MINGLE WITH AMERICANS AT LEYTE BEACHHEAD . . . . American liberation forces are
welcomed by a throng of Philippine citizens, half-starved, war-torn, but happy.

LSTs MANNED BY THE COAST GUARD BOUND FOR LINGAYEN GULF . . . . this Flotilla slogs its way through the China Sea to land men and equipment for the attack on Luzon beaches.

JUBILANT FILIPINOS SWARM OVER LINGAYEN BEACHES . . . . they welcome a Coast Guardsman, one of the first American liberators to land, with unbridled joy.

THESE LSTs WERE AMONG THE FIRST TO DROP RAMPS AT MANILA . . . . with the capital city of the Philippines free from Japanese, the harbor bustled with activity. Soldiers and supplies were brought into the liberated city.

THE FIRST WAVES SURGE IN AT IWO JIMA . . . . smoke from naval bombardment still rises from the beaches and Mount Suribachi as the invaders strike.—(U. S. Navy Photo)

will hover air power over our long attack and support convoys; will prevent the Japanese from reinforcing Leyte from the west; will clear all adjacent waters for future operations; will press a submarine offensive and at the same time provide lifeguard services and will establish in Leyte Gulf a naval force sufficient to support current and future operations."

The main part of the attacking fleet, which would land 193,841 Army troops, assembled at Seeadler Harbor in the Admiralties, and the rest at Hollandia. Admiral Halsey's Third Fleet cruised in offlying waters before and during the invasion to prevent enemy surface interference, and to give strategic support and launch strikes should this be necessary. The great invasion force got underway on and after 11 October, the slower vessels first. General MacArthur sailed in cruiser *Nashville* which accompanied Admiral Kinkaid's group. En route, a typhoon complicated things, particularly for Admiral Oldendorf's Bombardment and Fire Support Group. Many of the smaller vessels were damaged.

Leyte is the eighth largest of the Philippine Islands and had a native population of over a million. It is 90 miles long north and south, and roughly 30 miles wide. To its east is Leyte Gulf, a broad, 40-mile square body of water guarded on the north by the Island of Samar, and on the east by Suluan, Homonhon, and Dinagat Islands with 10-mile wide passages between them. These were mined. To successfully operate in Leyte Gulf it was desirable first to capture these three islands.

Preliminary landings were made, and U. S. Rangers put ashore on 17 October at Dinagat and Suluan Islands, which commanded these approaches to Leyte Gulf, and at Homonhon Island on the 18th. Patrol frigate *Gallup* participated in the former and *Bisbee* in the latter. Minesweepers then removed mines in Leyte Gulf, and demolition teams investigated landing beaches. Bombardment ships entered the Gulf on the 18th, firing on shore installations, while carrier planes from the Third and Seventh Fleets neutralized Japanese airfields.

By nightfall on 19 October, the main attack force approached Leyte Gulf, the vessels streaming their mine-severing paravanes. As the ships passed in by Homonhon Island, the Rangers blinked that all was well. Inside the Gulf, the vessels fanned out for their assigned areas.

From dawn until 1000 on 20 October, all bombardment ships laid down a methodical, destructive fire against enemy positions. Air strikes were made by planes from Escort Carrier Group 77.4, commanded by Rear Admiral T. L. Sprague, USN. LCIs delivered a rocket and mortar barrage. Landings were scheduled at four Leyte beaches in the northwestern part of the Gulf and on both sides of Panaon Strait to the south. At exactly 1000 the first wave hit the beaches followed closely by others. The troops encountered light enemy resistance in the landings except at Red Beach, where they were harassed by mortar fire.

An advance beach party of four Coast Guardsmen who landed on Red Beach from an LCVP attached to *Aquarius* were the first Naval or Coast Guard personnel to land on Leyte after the bombardment. Captain Higbee, in command of a fleet of landing craft, went ashore with the first wave. One man in a Coast Guard invasion barge wrote:

"We weren't more than two hundred yards offshore when the first enemy shell fire splashed in front of us. The soldiers dropped to a crouch as one man. There was another splash to our right and then another to our left. All you could see now across the straight line of twelve boats were the tips of brown helmets and erect figures of twelve coxswains standing behind their wheels. Then over the deafening roar of the bombardment behind us, we heard the singing whine of a mortar shell. We could see the geyser shoot up just behind us. Seconds later, the barge jarred its flat nose up on the sandy beach. In seconds more the ramps were down and the soldiers were running out, crouched low, their rifles ready. The invasion had begun."

Native Filipinos were everywhere; around two thousand had gone through the battle lines to safety. Their high spirits were reflected by their smiles of approval. Sailors fed them K-rations, and doctors set up first aid stations to treat those needing attention. Most had not been harmed by the terrific bombardment, but their homes were in shambles.

Anticipated strong Japanese air opposition to the landings did not materialize, and only a few enemy planes appeared over the beaches. Considerable air opposition developed later, however.

The assault waves and the reserve battalions were all ashore in the forenoon of D-day. Four hours after the first soldier had stepped ashore on Leyte, General MacArthur tread triumphantly along the beach and made his historic speech to the assembled Philippine patriots. He began: "This is the Voice of Freedom, General Mac-Arthur speaking. People of the Philippines! I have returned. By the grace of Almighty God our force stands again on Philippine soil, consecrated in the blood of two peoples."

That first day the 1st Cavalry Division captured Tacloban airstrip and the next day the capital city of Tacloban. Lieutenant General Walter Kreuger took command of all Army forces in the Leyte area on 24 October. On that day additional landings were made on the north side of Leyte Island and on Bacol and Samar Islands.

The Japanese Navy was not going to take this invasion lying in harbor. Fleets put to sea from Brunei in Borneo and from Kyushu in Japan, under Admirals Kurita, Shima, and Ozawa. These fleets attacked American naval forces in Philippine waters in three viciously fought battles between 24 and 26 October at Surigao Strait, off Samar, and off Cape Engano. The three related actions known as the Battle for Leyte Gulf, placed Admiral Kinkaid's shipping perilously close to disaster, but Admiral Halsey's forces successfully met the enemy and the battle finally ended in a decisive defeat of the Japanese. The enemy lost by sinking three battleships, one large and three light carriers, six heavy and four light cruisers, and eleven destroyers. The United States Navy lost by sinking one light cruiser, two escort carriers, two destroyers, and one destroyer-escort. Thus, the Japanese naval threat to the Leyte landings ended. The Japanese Navy, as a fighting fleet, ceased to exist.

On the morning of the 25th, an enemy plane was sighted dead ahead of *LST-207*. The plane went into a dive, releasing a bomb which landed 100 yards off the LST's starboard beam. Shortly after noon another plane dived from the clouds and all starboard guns fired until the plane disappeared, smoking, back into the clouds. In a third attack, while *LST-207* was underway, she opened fire at 800 yards and numerous hits were made on the plane. The plane disappeared in a trail of smoke, after it had dropped a bomb 300 yards to

port. Later an enemy medium bomber was seen diving. The LST opened fire at 1,800 yards and scored immediate numerous hits. The enemy banked sharply, and when 1,000 yards from the ship, burst into flames as the LST's shots repeatedly struck its engines and fuselage. Such attacks continued for weeks, and saw the first of the "suicide planes", or "kamikazes."

By the end of October, troops pushing inland against growing enemy resistance, had captured the Japanese airfields and controlled practically all of Leyte Valley. But enemy troops were being ferried from Cebu to the Ormoc Peninsula of Leyte to reinforce the Japanese defenders. Though the American advance was being slowed it continued relentlessly. The land fighting on that island proved to be the toughest in the South and Southwest Pacific since Guadalcanal.

The United States Navy continued to bring troops, supplies, and equipment into Leyte through the Gulf. Reinforcement and re-supply kept many Coast Guard-manned vessels busy in the months immediately following. Though the Japanese Navy left Leyte Gulf alone, enemy aircraft peppered the area with troublesome, if not disastrous, raids. The Coast Guard vessels had their share of excitement. Kamikazes, instead of being a novelty, became something of a habit with many unpleasant results. On 12 November, during a re-supply landing, a suicide plane crashed *LST-66's* boat deck, killing eight men and wounding fourteen. During this attack *LST-68* destroyed one plane and probably destroyed another. *LST-168* got two planes in another attack.

On 5 December, while patrol frigate *Coronado* was escorting a 39-ship convoy to Leyte, the starboard side of the convoy was attacked by an enemy bomber which did no damage. Later, another enemy plane flew in low on the port side. *Coronado* went to general quarters and began firing. As the plane passed ahead, it launched a torpedo which hit *SS Antoine Saugrain's* stern. "Cease firing" was ordered as the plane crossed *Coronado's* bow, but a few more rounds were fired, killing a Coast Guard officer who had placed himself in the line of fire and was not observed by the crew. *Saugrain*, by this time dead in the water, was again hit by a torpedo from another "Oscar", and, settling slowly, she was abandoned by all hands. *San Pedro*, *LST-454*, and *Coronado* put boats over to pick up survivors. *Coronado* received on board 223 Army troops, eight Navy gun crew members, and 31 merchant seamen including *Saugrain's* master. The dead ship was attacked again a few hours later, and *Coronado* fired on the plane scoring hits at 1,000 yards. *Saugrain* stayed afloat and was taken in tow by *LST-454*, but the next morning she took a third torpedo and sank.

United States forces had cleared the Japanese from most of eastern Leyte by early December. The enemy, with about 35,000 troops, still held the western part of the island. These were being supplied through the port of Ormoc. On 6 December, a Task Group left Leyte Gulf, and, proceeding without incident to Ormoc Bay, landed elements of the 77th Division in the usual fashion near Ormoc. The American craft in this action and in the first re-supply echelon were subjected to heavy attacks by enemy aircraft, including kamikazes, losing two destroyers and a destroyer-transport to the latter. Marine and Army aircraft intercepted a Japanese reinforcement convoy and sank several ships. The Coast Guard was not involved in action at Ormoc Bay.

The last amphibious operation by the United States in 1944 was at Mindora Island, just south of Luzon. The objective was to provide dry-weather airfields to support future large scale landings on Luzon. An Attack Force was assembled under the command of Rear Admiral Arthur D. Struble, USN, together with Close Covering and Heavy Covering and Carrier Groups and PT boats. The Army Freight and Supply vessel *FS-367* (Lieutenant (jg) R. H. Greenless, USCGR), was the only Coast Guard-manned ship to participate in this landing. Heavy assault troops were not necessary, as only about 200 enemy troops were thought to be in the landing area and only about 500 on the entire island.

The landings were successfully made on 15 December, but the operation was hotly contested by Japanese planes. Air attacks on American positions and shipping were made repeatedly during the rest of December. Two LSTs were hit and set afire; destroyer *Howorth* was damaged by a kamikaze; several merchant ships were damaged; and an ammunition ship was blown up. On 30 December, PT tender *Arcturus* and an LST were sunk. On 26 December, Japanese naval units bombarded U. S. shore positions. By the end of the month, 373 enemy planes had atacked, of which 145 were reported destroyed.

On 30 December, *FS-367* was anchored 300 yards from a Liberty type converted oil tanker, USS *Mariposa*. Despite heavy fire from ships and shore batteries, a Japanese plane succeeded in crash diving *Mariposa* and penetrating the cargo of high octane gasoline. The ship immediately burst into flames. *FS-367* weighed anchor to go to her assistance as a third enemy plane came in for a low-level attack on destroyers patrolling outside the harbor. This plane received a hit which set it afire and it crashed into USS *Ganesvoort* which immediately began to burn and settle.

*FS-367* went alongside *Mariposa* and stayed until all survivors had been taken off. She moved away from *Mariposa's* burning gasoline, but *Ganesvoort*, which was then nearer the fire, requested *FS-367* to come alongside and take off her crew. Because burning gasoline threatened to engulf *Ganesvoort*, *FS-367* began towing her to a safer anchorage. The next day *Ganesvoort*, in a sinking condition, was abandoned by her crew. No casualties were suffered on board *FS-367*.

As the year 1944 ended, United States forces had swept to the Philippines and had established a strong foothold on Leyte and Mindoro. Behind them lay a vast area swept clear of Japanese except for certain pockets which had been by-passed where the enemy was cut off from his supplies, and which were left to become impotent. The Japanese Navy had ceased to be an efficient fighting unit; but enemy air power, especially with its murderous kamikazes, was still a force to be reckoned with. Ahead lay the road to Japan and victory.

# Chapter 20

# FINAL VICTORY—1945

Leyte provided a springboard for the complete reconquest of the Philippines. The New Year found United States forces with their eyes on Luzon as the next major point of attack, and "S-day" had been set for 9 January 1945. In preparation for the Luzon operations, a landing was made on little Marinduque Island, east of northern Mindoro, on the morning of 3 January, partly as a feint to keep the Japanese guessing, and to point to a possible landing in the Manila-Batangas sector. Marinduque's value was that it commanded the eastern entrance to the Verde Island Passage between Mindoro and the Batangas area of Luzon, as well as the Sibuyan Sea.

Luzon is the largest and principal island in the Philippine archipelago. The geographic and productive heart of Luzon is the Central Plain, extending through the center of the island from Manila Bay north to Lingayen Gulf. Around it is mountainous country. The capital and chief city is Manila, which had a pre-war population of over 600,000. Manila Bay, 120 miles in circumference, is the finest harbor in the far East. This had been a main Japanese supply base for the great area to the south. Enemy defenses on Luzon had been weakened by the fighting on Leyte, for General Yamashita had sent five of his best divisions to Leyte and they had been lost.

Pressing their advantage, the United States forces prepared for an attack at Lingayen Gulf on the west side of Luzon, 125 miles north northwest of Manila. To the Americans, Manila, ravaged by the Japanese in those early December days of 1941, was one of the grand prizes of the Pacific War. Lingayen Gulf would open the way for the recapture of this capital city.

The prompt seizure of the central Luzon area and the destruction of its defenses and defending forces, thus depriving the enemy of the northern entrance to the South China Sea as well as securing bases for further operations against the Japanese, were the main objectives of the Lingayen Gulf plan. Establishment of a beachhead was to be followed by an advance through the Central Plain to Manila. Luzon had been attacked by carrier and land-based planes for several months, but there were still more than 70 enemy airfields operating there. It was essential that American planes at Mindoro provide close support in handling an estimated 450 enemy planes in the Luzon-Visayan area. A total of 235,000 enemy troops were assumed to be on Luzon.

As a preliminary, every approach to Lingayen Gulf was covered by submarines. Land-based planes fanned out in great arcs from three bases to detect and prevent enemy surface interference with the coming landings. The Third Fleet patrolled to the east of the Philippines. Admiral Kinkaid's Seventh Fleet was superior in combat strength to anything the Japanese could assemble.

Plans for this operation were similar to those for Leyte. There were the same task force commanders, the same skippers, and the same ships, augmented by some new ones recently arrived from the United States. As at Leyte, there were two groups of amphibious forces, the Lingayen Attack Force under Vice Admiral Wilkinson, and the San Fabian Attack Force under Vice Admiral Barbey. The Bombardment and Fire Support Group was commanded by Vice Admiral Oldendorf, who had won the victory of Surigao Strait. Admiral Berkey was in command of the Close Covering Group of cruisers and destroyers. The Escort Carrier Group which was to provide air cover for the convoys and support troops ashore was under Rear Admiral Calvin T. Durgin, USN. The Reinforcement Group was commanded by Admiral Conolly and the Service Group by Rear Admiral Robert O. Glover, USN. The Seventh Fleet consisted of over 685 ships, not including small craft.

The Coast Guard manned 16 vessels which took part in this assault, and Coast Guardsmen were in seven others which had Navy crews. In the transport groups were our friends *Arthur Middleton*, *Aquarius*, *Cambria*, *Callaway*, *Leonard Wood*, and *Cavalier*. Among the LSTs were these veterans: *LSTs 18, 22, 23, 24, 66, 68, 168, 170, 202*, and *204*. Some Coast Guardsmen were in *Alhena*, *William P. Biddle*, *Bellatrix*, *George F. Elliott*, *Libra*, *President Adams*, and *President Jackson*. These are identified in the tabulation shown on the next page, which also indicates participation by the Coast Guard in the other amphibious operations in the Pacific area during 1945.

Beaches selected for the landings ranged over most of the southeastern and southern shores of the Gulf. The XIV Corps, under Major General Oscar W. Griswold, USA, would land from Admiral Wilkinson's group opposite the town of Lingayen. The I Corps, commanded by Major General Innis P. Swift, USA, would be put ashore by Admiral Barbey on both sides of San Fabian town, farther to the east. The plans called for Admiral Oldendorf to take his heavy ships into Lingayen Gulf three days before the landing, to sweep the Gulf and approaches for mines, and to pulverize shore defenses.

Loading of troops was accomplished by Admiral Barbey's force at Hollandia, Aitape, and Sansapor. Admiral Wilkinson's group loaded at Bougainville and at Cape Gloucester. The distance from Hollandia to Lingayen is 2,150 miles. Both amphibious forces practiced landings before sailing, and then Admiral Wilkinson took his forces to Seeadler Harbor. Admiral Oldendorf's heavy bombardment ships left the Palau Islands, and all forces were on the move on New Year's Day.

All groups took the same general route of approach through Surigao Strait, the Mindanao Sea, and the Sulu Sea, passing west of Negros, Panay, and Mindoro, thence well offshore to the west of Luzon, and entering Lingayen Gulf on southeasterly courses. Japanese planes with their kamikazes were extremely active during the passage.

Advance forces were divided into two main groups, each with six carriers, heavy ships, and screen. The approach of these forces was marked by unprecedented fury from kamikazes. The ships made a daylight passage of Surigao Strait on 3 January. That day the first attack on the spearheading 65 minesweepers and service ships commanded by Commander Wayne R. Loud, USN, occurred in Mindanao Sea when oiler *Cowanesque* was hit. In the evening an unsuccessful suicide attack was made on carrier *Makin Island*. The next day at Mindoro, *Louis Dyche*, an ammunition ship, was hit and completely disintegrated.

Admiral Oldendorf's force, trailing the Minesweeping Group by 30 miles, was first attacked late on 4 January in the Sulu Sea. Escort carrier *Ommaney Bay* (Captain Howard L. Young, USN), received a kamikaze, burned, exploded, was abandoned, and finally was sunk by a torpedo from destroyer *Burns* (Commander Jacob T. Bullen, Jr., USN). The following day Japanese destroyers were chased off near Manila by destroyers and corvettes. That afternoon two dozen Japanese planes attacked; one headed for cruiser *Louisville*, flagship of Rear Admiral Theodore E. Chandler, USN, and crashed into No. 2 turret, miraculously killing only one man, but wounding 58, including the ship's commanding officer, Captain Rex L. Hicks, USN. Suicide planes then hit two Australian ships. Destroyer escort *Stafford* and escort carrier *Savo Island* were hit next, and then destroyer *Helm*.

For two and a half hours the kamikazes carried out their attacks on Admiral Oldendorf's vessels. The Minesweeping Group was similarly victimized. This was just the beginning. Early in the morning of 5 January, General MacArthur requested Admiral Halsey with his Third Fleet to bring in the fast carriers to help neutralize Japanese air in Luzon since land-based air could not handle it alone.

Even so, the two U. S. advance groups reached the Lingayen area on schedule on the morning of 6 January. While 11 escort carriers stood by offshore, the minesweepers entered the Gulf at 0700. The heavy ships stood by in the entrance ready for the bombardment of shore positions, which began soon afterward. The strange sequel to this was that practically no mines were found, nor were there any effective shore batteries. It later developed that guerillas had spent 60 days before the action at Lingayen in clearing the mines, disposing of over 350. But by noontime there was a sprinkle of kamikazes which developed into a rain, and then a murderous torrent!

Admiral Oldendorf moved with his ships into

COAST GUARD-MANNED VESSELS ENGAGED IN PACIFIC AMPHIBIOUS OPERATIONS—1945

| Name of Vessel | Lingayen Gulf | Subic Bay | Nasugbu | Mariveles | Iwo Jima | Palawan | Zamboanga | Iloilo | Negros Island | Cebu | Kerama Group | Okinawa | Malabang | Tarakan | Davao | Brunei Bay | Balikpapan |
|---|---|---|---|---|---|---|---|---|---|---|---|---|---|---|---|---|---|
| *Aquarius* | X | | | | | | | | | | | X | | | | | |
| *Arthur Middleton* | X | | | | | | | | | | | X | | | | | |
| *Bayfield* | | | | | X | | | | | | | X | | | | | |
| *Bibb* | | | | | | | | | | | X | X | | | | | |
| *Callaway* | X | | | | X | | | | | | | | | | | | |
| *Cambria* | X | | | | | | | | | | | X | | | | | |
| *Cavalier* | X | X | | | | | | | | | | X | | | | | |
| *Centaurus* | | | | | | | | | | | | X | | | | | |
| *Ingham* | | | | X | | | | X | X | | | | | | | | |
| *Joseph T. Dickman* | | | | | | | | | | | | X | | | | | |
| *Leonard Wood* | X | | | | | | | | | | | | | | | | |
| *Spencer* | | | X | | | X | | | | X | | | X | X | X | X | X |
| *Sterope* | | | | | | | | | | | | X | | | | | |
| *Taney* | | | | | | | | | | | | X | | | | | |
| *Theenim* | | | | | | | | | | | | X | | | | | |
| *Woodbine* | | | | | | | | | | | | X | | | | | |
| *LST-18* | X | | | | | | | | | | | | | | | | |
| *LST-20* | | | | | | | | | | | | X | | | | | |
| *LST-22* | X | | | | | | | | | | | | | | | | |
| *LST-23* | X | | | | | | | | | | | | | | | | |
| *LST-24* | X | | | | | | | | | | X | X | | | | | |
| *LST-66* | X | | | | | | X | | | | | | | | | | X |
| *LST-67* | | | | | | | | X | X | | | | | X | | | X |
| *LST-68* | X | | | | | | | X | X | | | | | | | | |
| *LST-70* | | | | | X | | | | | | | X | | | | | |
| *LST-71* | | | | | | | | | | | | X | | | | | |
| *LST-166* | | | | | | | | | | | | X | | | | | |
| *LST-168* | X | | | | | | | | | | | | | X | | | X |
| *LST-170* | X | | | | | | | | | | | | | X | | | |
| *LST-202* | X | | | | | | | | | | | | | | | | |
| *LST-204* | X | | | | | | | | | | | | | | | | |
| *LST-207* | | | | | | | | | | | | X | | | | | |
| *LST-758* | | | | | X | | | | | | | X | | | | | |
| *LST-759* | | | | | | | | | | | | X | | | | | |
| *LST-760* | | | | | X | | | | | | | X | | | | | |
| *LST-761* | | | | | X | | | | | | | | | | | | |
| *LST-762* | | | | | | | | | | | | X | | | | | |
| *LST-763* | | | | | X | | | | | | | X | | | | | |
| *LST-764* | | | | | X | | | | | | | | | | | | |
| *LST-766* | | | | | X | | | | | | | | | | | | |
| *LST-767* | | | | | | | | | | | | X | | | | | |
| *LST-768* | | | | | X | | | | | | | X | | | | | |
| *LST-770* | | | | | | | | | | | X | X | | | | | |
| *LST-782* | | | | | X | | | | | | | X | | | | | |
| *LST-784* | | | | | X | | | | | | | X | | | | | |
| *LST-785* | | | | | X | | | | | | X | X | | | | | |
| *LST-787* | | | | | X | | | | | | | X | | | | | |
| *LST-788* | | | | | X | | | | | | | X | | | | | |
| *LST-789* | | | | | X | | | | | | | X | | | | | |
| *LST-790* | | | | | X | | | | | | | X | | | | | |
| *LST-792* | | | | | X | | | | | | | X | | | | | |
| *LST-793* | | | | | | | | | | | X | X | | | | | |
| *LST-794* | | | | | | | | | | | | X | | | | | |
| *LST-795* | | | | | X | | | | | | | X | | | | | |
| *LST-829* | | | | | | | | | | | X | X | | | | | |
| *LST-830* | | | | | | | | | | | X | X | | | | | |
| *LST-884* | | | | | X | | | | | | | X | | | | | |
| *LST-887* | | | | | | | | | | | | X | | | | | |
| *FS-309* | | | X | | | | | | | | | | | | | | |

COAST GUARD-MANNED VESSELS ENGAGED IN PACIFIC AMPHIBIOUS OPERATIONS—1945 *(Continued)*

| Name of Vessel | Lingayen Gulf | Subic Bay | Nasugbu | Mariveles | Iwo Jima | Palawan | Zamboanga | Iloilo | Negros Island | Cebu | Kerama Group | Okinawa | Malabang | Tarakan | Davao | Brunei Bay | Balikpapan |
|---|---|---|---|---|---|---|---|---|---|---|---|---|---|---|---|---|---|
| PC-469 | | | | | | | | | | | | X | | | | | |
| LCI-40 | | | | | | | | | | | | X | | | | | |
| LCI-83 | | | | | | | | | | | | X | | | | | |
| LCI-84 | | | | | | | | | | | | X | | | | | |
| LCI-86 | | | | | | | | | | | | X | | | | | |
| LCI-88 | | | | | | | | | | | | X | | | | | |
| LCI-90 | | | | | | | | | | | | X | | | | | |
| LCI-96 | | | | | | | | | | | | X | | | | | |
| LCI-320 | | | | | | | | | | | | X | | | | | |
| LCI-323 | | | | | | | | | | | | X | | | | | |
| LCI-325 | | | | | | | | | | | | X | | | | | |
| LCI-326 | | | | | | | | | | | | X | | | | | |
| LCI-350 | | | | | | | | | | | | X | | | | | |

VESSELS PARTLY MANNED BY THE COAST GUARD
SERVING WITH NAVY CREWS

| Name of Vessel | Lingayen Gulf | Subic Bay | Nasugbu | Mariveles | Iwo Jima | Palawan | Zamboanga | Iloilo | Negros Island | Cebu | Kerama Group | Okinawa | Malabang | Tarakan | Davao | Brunei Bay | Balikpapan |
|---|---|---|---|---|---|---|---|---|---|---|---|---|---|---|---|---|---|
| Alhena | X | | | X | | | | | | | | | | | | | |
| Barnett | | | | | | | | | | | X | | | | | | |
| Bellatrix | X | | | | | | | | | | | | | | | | |
| Betelgeuse | | | | | | | | | | | X | | | | | | |
| Crescent City | | | | | | | | | | | X | | | | | | |
| Fuller | | | | | | | | | | | X | | | | | | |
| George F. Elliott | X | | | | X | | | | | | | | | | | | |
| Gregory | | | | | X | | | | | | | | | | | | |
| Libra | X | | | | X | | | | | | | | | | | | |
| Little | | | | | X | | | | | | | | | | | | |
| LST-334 | | | | | | | | | | | X | | | | | | |
| President Adams | X | | | | X | | | | | | | | | | | | |
| President Jackson | X | | | | X | | | | | | | | | | | | |
| Stringham | | | | | | | | | | | X | | | | | | |
| William P. Biddle | X | | | | | | | | | | | | | | | | |

the Gulf to bombard the landing beaches, and suffered unmercifully from raids of suicide planes coming out of the sky, details of which need not be recounted here. Captain Karig in his *Battle Report* gives this vivid description:

"Deafening explosions in Lingayen Gulf shook the sea with machine-gun rapidity. Muzzle blasts from sizzling gun barrels, bombs detonating as they crashed against the steel hull of ships or set off as they plunged harmlessly into the water, gasoline tanks bursting into reddish-orange balls in mid-air, ships shuddering from violent magazine eruptions converted peaceful Lingayen Gulf into a zone of total war, a new version of total war at sea—ships versus suicide planes."

In 25 hours, 21 ships had been hit by the Japanese new "secret weapon", the kamikaze. This was the only occasion in World War II when a heavy bombardment force found enemy opposition too hot for it. At 1800 Admiral Oldendorf withdrew his vessels from Lingayen Gulf.

Oldendorf called upon Admiral Kinkaid for additional air power and continuous bombing of all airfields in the area. Kinkaid, in turn, requested aid from Admiral Halsey, who immediately sent his fliers against Luzon the next day. At the high cost of 28 planes (of which 18 were lost operationally) Halsey's airmen destroyed 79 enemy planes, most of which were on the ground, and the Japanese air effort in Luzon was smothered. The heavy bombardment ships re-entered the Gulf, which was then free of kamikazes. The landing areas were shelled, the Underwater Demolition Teams swam to the beaches and reported no beach defenses or underwater obstacles. The bombardment continued on 8 January.

Meanwhile, the amphibious forces which included the Coast Guard-manned vessels were steaming through Philippine waters headed for Lingayen. Ten miles ahead of the main formation was Admiral Berkey's Close Covering Group, with General MacArthur in cruiser *Boise* (Captain Willard M. Downes, USN). Directly astern of the main body were two escort carriers, *Kadashan Bay* and *Marcus Island*. Following them were Vice Admiral Wilkinson's amphibious force of 148 slower landing craft. The armada experienced some opposition from submarines, planes, and destroyers, but this was not especially damaging until dawn of 8 January.

At that time another enemy attack developed about 35 miles off the west coast of Luzon and 60 miles from Manila. *Kadashan Bay* and transport *Callaway* were hit, though both continued on. Two Japanese planes had previously fallen before *Callaway's* guns. The third was downed in this attack, but in falling, it scored a searing blow on the transport's bridge. The attack instantly killed several members of the crew and started a blaze on the starboard side of the superstructure; men were turned into human torches. Flames leaped to the top of the stack and shot down toward the engine room through a ragged hole in the upper fiddley. The blaze was quickly brought under control, however, and *Callaway* continued in her formation. She had suffered nearly 50 casualties—30 killed and 20 wounded.

*Leonard Wood* assisted in the destruction of one enemy plane.

The ships of the Attack Force arrived on schedule at the transport areas in lower Lingayen Gulf. They began debarkation of troops in LVTs and other landing craft at 0715 on 9 January, with the first waves landing at 0930 under cover of a heavy bombardment. The enemy manned no beach positions at Lingayen, and the opposition there was negligible. At the San Fabian beaches, sporadic mortar and artillery fire began at about 1000, causing some damage and casualties to landing craft until the batteries were silenced. After the lethal attacks of the preceding days, the actual landings seemed almost anticlimactic.

The larger transports were unloaded into LVTs, DUKWs, and self-propelled pontoon barges. Unloading continued for several days, although many transports were emptied in time to depart in the evening of the first day. From then until 12 January, a fast and a slow convoy left each day as the rest of the ships were unloaded.

By the end of the invasion day, 68,000 American troops had been put ashore on Luzon, and headquarters for the four divisions had been set up on land. A beachhead 15 miles long and four miles deep had been established. Equipment and supplies landed equaled seven tons per man on the beach! On 11 January, Admiral Conolly landed the 25th Division at the San Fabian beaches, where stiff resistance finally developed.

These operations were not wholly free from assault. *Cambria*, flagship of a transport group, was attacked while engaged in landing troops on 9 and 10 January. She was credited with two assists against enemy planes. Despite smoke screens laid at sunrise and sunset to protect the transports, Japanese suicide planes damaged several screening vessels on the 10th and 12th, sank an LCI(M), and an LCI(G). Toward dawn after the first night the American vessels were attacked by small explosive-laden speedboats of suicide type, and by swimmers, and, later, by more suicide planes. These caused plenty of damage. On 13 January the Philippine kamikazes made their last try, and crashed escort carrier *Salamaua*. Thereafter, resupply and reinforcement convoys arrived frequently in the Gulf. No ships were lost during the return trips to Leyte, though three were damaged by kamikazes.

While operations were going on at Lingayen, Admiral Halsey's Third Fleet penetrated the China Sea. Its fliers took a heavy toll of Japanese planes, installations, and surface vessels, seriously cutting the Japanese supply lines from that area and isolating many enemy outposts.

By 28 January the XIV Corps had progressed to the Clark Field area. The next day, in an effort to cut off Bataan from the Central Plain region, an Attack Group including 22 transports and 35 LSTs, under Admiral Struble, landed the 38th Division (Major General Charles P. Hall, USA) and the 134th Regimental Combat Team—35,000 men—at San Antonio, 15 miles west of Subic Bay. These troops were to support the drive toward Manila. The area was in friendly guerilla hands and the landings were unopposed. The entire Subic Bay area was under American control by 1700 on 30 January. The only casualty was the one vessel in which the Coast Guard was represented in this operation—attack transport *Cavalier*. In returning from this landing, she was torpedoed off Subic Bay by a submarine, but remained afloat and was towed to Leyte.

The drive on Manila began in full force on 1 February, and by midnight of the next day, forces were within 15 miles of that prize. By 4 February, American troops were in the city. Then, for ten days the encircled Japanese were compressed tighter and tighter into a small area, and for three more days there was intense fighting from building to building and from street to street. On 24 February organized resistance ceased, but the last Japanese was not killed until 4 March.

On 31 January, a separate Attack Group landed troops of the 11th Airborne Division at Nasugbu, south of the entrance of Manila Bay. In this force was cutter *Spencer* and Coast Guard-manned *FS-309*, as well as four destroyer transports, thirty-five LCIs, eight LCMs, six destroyers, three destroyer escorts, and twenty-six miscellaneous small craft. The operation was staged from San Pedro Bay, Leyte. The force departed on 28 January, with Lieutenant General Robert L. Eichelberger, USA, Commanding General of the 8th Army, and Major General Joseph M. Swing, USA, Commanding General of the 11th Airborne Division. *Spencer* acted as flagship and guide for the 8th Amphibious Group, under command of Rear Admiral W. M. Fechteler, USN.

The landings were made to outflank the enemy troops defending Manila. There was no return fire after a short bombardment, and the troops landed against light opposition which was quickly wiped out. General Eichelberger, in his interesting book *Our Jungle Road to Tokyo*, had this to say of his experience:

> It was up to me to decide whether to hit or run; and also whether to advance on Manila. At dawn on January 31, I was aboard the command ship *Spencer* with General Swing and Admiral Fechteler. Visibility was excellent, and from deck we could see both the white beaches of Nasugbu and the green mountains of Luzon. Destroyers and rocket-firing LCIs pounded the shore for an hour, and on the landing craft, to quote the graphic phrase of a service reporter, "stomach butterflies nervously flapped their wings."

One PC Control Vessel was lost as a result of suicidal attacks by Japanese "Q" boats on the night of 31 January. Several of these suicide boats were sunk by destroyer gunfire. General Eichelberger further wrote:

> That night (31 January) I went back to the *Spencer*. It was not a restful night because there were a number of attacks by explosive-laden Japanese suicide crash boats. Just after daylight, a little worn, I went on deck and watched a curious cat-and-dog encounter between an American destroyer and a suicide boat. The destroyer was trying to sink the Jap craft with five-inch guns, and pursued it assiduously. Whenever the enemy wheeled and made a direct run at the destroyer, the destroyer zigzagged and took to its heels. In the gay morning sun it seemed like a crazy version of you-chase-me and I'll-chase-you. But it wasn't a children's game. . . . After about fifty rounds of firing, a shell from the destroyer found its target. The boat did not sink; it disintegrated.

Of his experience in *Spencer*, General Eichelberger said: "I found the *Spencer* to be extremely comfortable. Unlike my week en route to Hollandia on a destroyer, the *Spencer* I thought a grand ship . . . outstanding. Discipline on this Coast Guard ship was very fine."

*FS-309* (Army freight ship), moored to a wharf in Nasugbu Bay, was attacked at 0335 on 14 February by a suicide boat containing three Japanese soldiers. A low-lying protective raft of heavy timbers had been placed alongside *FS-309*. As the craft approached closely, a terrific explosion occurred and the smaller boat disappeared, undoubtedly having hit the raft. A large quantity of water and sand was blown on board the larger vessel, and the water had to be pumped from the after crew's quarters and lazarette. *FS-309* suffered no casualties.

After a 35-mile dash, U. S. troops from Nasugbu reached the southern limits of Manila on 5 February. Meanwhile, units of the 37th Infantry Division had continued their advance from the northwest, and units of the First Cavalry Division of the 6th Army had entered the city from the northeast on the 3rd. The fall of Manila was formally announced on the 6th.

It was at about this time (29 January) that *Serpens*, a 14,250-ton Coast Guard-manned ammunition ship at far-off Guadalcanal, exploded while loading depth charges off Lunga Beach, damaging several nearby vessels. The entire ship's complement and 57 Army personnel were killed, with the exception of two officers and eight crewmen, who, luckily, were ashore at the time. This mishap was not attributed to enemy action.

Despite the fall of Manila there was still some cleaning up to do in the Philippines. The Japanese still held Corregidor, and also Mariveles, at the southern tip of Bataan Peninsula. On 15 February, after extensive minesweeping and bombardment, a Task Group under Admiral Struble, in cutter *Ingham* as flagship, consisting of 62 landing craft of various types, with a fire support group under Admiral Berkey, made an amphibious landing at Mariveles Harbor. Enemy fire was received from the north coast of Corregidor, four rounds landing in the transport area and causing several casualties. The enemy batteries were silenced by the fire support ships. *Ingham* was the only Coast Guard vessel in this action. Hitting the beach at the head of the harbor at 1000, troops of the 151st Infantry Regimental Combat Team and the 3rd Battalion of the 34th Regimental Combat Team (4,300 men) quickly seized the Mariveles airstrip and fanned out north, east, and west. Mariveles Harbor was secured the next day.

Corregidor was heavily bombarded preparatory to its attack by U. S. forces. On the 16th, *Ingham* stood in for San Jose Beach in the van of the Corregidor Attack Group. Paratroopers began dropping on Corregidor at 0840, after an hour of heavy air strikes. *Ingham* took station at 1005 about 3,500 yards off the beach and directed landing operations. The first wave landed at 1039, with light opposition, and by 1150 the beachhead had been established and secured. Within 24 hours American troops had split the island in two from north to south against stiffening resistance. The 6,000 Japanese defenders, who had been broken up into isolated pockets, with no means of escape, fought desperately. Corregidor saw some of the bloodiest fighting in the entire Luzon campaign. The east entrance of the tunnel under Malinta Hill was blocked by landslides, caused by the pre-invasion bombardment, and many Japanese were sealed inside. Suicidal explosions spelled *finis* to those defenders. Resistance continued until the end of February, when "The Rock" had been fully regained.

Several other operations in the Philippines followed these actions in Manila Bay. There were an estimated 3,500 enemy troops on Palawan, 270 miles long and 25 miles wide, which stretches southwesterly like a long finger, reaching almost to North Borneo. An Attack Force of 80 ships, mostly landing craft, under Admiral Fechteler, departed Mindoro and made an amphibious landing on Palawan to seize the Puerto Princesa area in mid-Palawan on 28 February. *Spencer*, carrying Brigadier General Harold H. Haney, USA, Commanding General of the 41st Infantry Division (8,000 men), acted as flagship and fleet guide for Task Group 78.2. No other Coast Guard or Coast Guard-manned vessels were involved. Unopposed landings were made at 0845, and two nearby airfields were secured by 1300. Occupation of the Puerto Princesa area assured practical control of Palawan Island and domination of additional important sea lanes. During subsequent mopping-up operations, 12 Americans and nearly 900 Japanese were killed.

Guerilla forces already occupied most of the Zamboanga Peninsula, the western extremity of Mindanao, except for a Japanese defensive area north of Zamboanga City, which included the airfield. Rear Admiral Forrest B. Royal, USN, headed a Zamboanga Attack Group, with Admiral Berkey commanding the fire support ships. Landings were preceded by air and naval bombardment and by the landing of paratroopers. Coast Guard-manned *LST-66*, commanded by Lieutenant Wendell J. Holbert, USCGR, provided Coast Guard participation. This was her 14th amphibious assault. She guided the first assault waves from the line of departure to the beach. Landings began at 0915 on 10 March, at San Mateo, just west of Zamboanga. There was moderate enemy opposition half an hour after the first wave landed. Within the first hour about 6,200 Army and Marine personnel, and one company of medium tanks were landed.

While fighting continued around Zamboanga, landings were also made at Malamaui and Basilan Islands, just to the south. These were virtually unopposed. A further landing was made at Jolo Island in the center of the Sulu chain, and the Sulu Archipelago was in American hands.

The island of Panay had been practically cleared

of the enemy by guerilla forces except for a small concentration in and near Iloilo, the third largest city in the Philippines. A landing was scheduled for 18 March, and the beaches selected were about 14 miles west of Iloilo. The Assault Group was commanded by Admiral Struble, in cutter *Ingham* as flagship and guide. The Group included the Coast Guard-manned *LST-67* and *LST-68*. After some firing by destroyers, the first wave of 16 LVTs landed at 0906. No opposition was encountered on the beach. Fourteen thousand troops of the 40th Division (Major General Rapp Brush, USA) were put ashore, and they advanced rapidly against only scattered resistance. Iloilo city was secured on 20 March, and organized resistance ended two days later.

On the 29th *Ingham* steamed from Iloilo across Panay Gulf, as flagship and guide of an Attack Group which was to land the 185th Regimental Combat Team at Pulupandan Point on northern Negros Island. *LST-67* and *LST-68* were also in this group. Landings began at 0859 and met no opposition. Bacolod Town and airstrip were captured on the 30th. Later, tough hill fighting developed which did not terminate for three months. In this campaign 7,500 enemy troops were killed.

On visits during the capture of Iloilo and the landings near Bacolod, General Eichelberger lived in *Ingham* and found her a "friendly, happy, well disciplined ship."

On 26 March, an Amphibious Group under Captain Albert T. Sprague, Jr., USN, supported by Admiral Berkey's bombardment unit, effected a landing on Cebu Island at Talisay Beach, south of Cebu City. Nearly two weeks of heavy aerial attacks previous to this landing had severely damaged enemy defenses and other installations. Cutter *Spencer* participated in this operation. About 14,000 troops of the American Division of the 8th Army were put ashore there after a bombardment of the beaches. The Japanese had pulled back, and little opposition was met at the shore. Cebu City, largely in ruins from enemy demolitions, was occupied the following day. Enemy forces entrenched themselves in elaborate defenses in the hills, and hill fighting was vicious until mid-June, when cleaning up was completed.

These various actions, followed by mopping up in the jungles and mountains, swamps, and caves,

took care of all Japanese in the Philippine Islands except for Mindanao, of which more will be said later.

While all this was going on in the Philippines, American forces were not idle elsewhere. Another highly important and hazardous undertaking was being planned and executed, in which an impressive number of Coast Guard-manned vessels were to play an important part.

Iwo Jima is about 640 miles south of Tokyo and a like distance north of Saipan. It is one of the few islands of the Volcano, or Bonin, group with enough flat land on its eight square miles for the construction of airstrips. Mount Suribachi rises 550 feet at the southern end, and is joined to the rest of the island by a progressively widening isthmus of volcanic sand. The island has nothing that even faintly resembles a harbor.

United States long-range heavy bombers could make the flight from the Marianas to attack Tokyo and other industrial cities of Japan proper and return, but they could not be given fighter cover for the entire distance. Therefore, Iwo Jima, situated as it is, was of vital importance in the coming assault on Japan. The Japanese had heavily fortified Iwo and garrisoned the island with some 21,000 men, in full recognition of its importance to both Japan and the United States. Iwo's radar station was an effective outpost in the Japanese air-raid warning network. The capture of Iwo Jima by the United States, even at high cost, became a "must."

For six months before the attack, Iwo Jima and Chichi Jima had been subjected to increasingly heavy land-based bomber raids from the Marianas, and later to carrier strikes and surface bombardment.

Admiral Spruance, Commander of the Central Pacific Task Forces (the Fifth Fleet), was assigned to capture, occupy, and defend Iwo Jima, and to develop air bases there. The ships necessary for the assault numbered 900; they were scattered between Hawaii and Ulithi, and had to plan a simultaneous arrival at Iwo. They comprised the Fast Carrier Task Forces; Captain George C. Montgomery's Anti-Submarine Warfare Group; Rear Admiral Donald B. Beary's Logistics Support Group; the Search and Reconnaissance Group of 150 seaplanes and long range land-based planes;

Commodore Worrell R. Carter's Service Squadron; the Attack Force of transports and landing craft of the Fifth Fleet; and other groups, all with their respective screens of destroyers, cruisers, and battleships.

Coast Guard-manned vessels served with Task Force 53 (Attack Force) and Task Force 51 (Miscellaneous Task Groups of the Joint Expeditionary Force). *Bayfield* was in Task Group 53.2. In Task Group 53.3 (Tractor Flotilla which carried troops, equipment, and supplies to be put ashore during the assault phase) were *LSTs 70, 758, 760, 761, 763, 764, 782, 784, 785, 787, 789, 792,* and *795.* In other task groups were *LSTs 788, 790,* and *884. LST-768* was at Iwo Jima after the initial attack. *Callaway* was in Task Group 51.1 (Joint Expeditionary Force Reserves), and *LST-766* was in Task Group 51.3 (Services and Salvage Group). In all, Coast Guard-manned vessels numbered 20. Also in the assault forces were seven Navy-manned vessels with some Coast Guardsmen in their crews—*Alhena, George F. Elliott, Libra, President Adams, President Jackson, Gregory,* and *Little.*

In charge of all Expeditionary Troops was Lieutenant General H. M. Smith, USMC. Major General Harry Schmidt, USMC, commanded the Fifth Amphibious Corps and was in charge of the landing forces, comprising the Third Marine Division, under Major General C. B. Erskine, USMC, the Fourth Marine Division, commanded by Major General C. B. Cates, USMC, and the Fifth Marine Division, under command of Major General K. E. Rockey, USMC. These were to experience the fiercest fighting ever to be undertaken by the Marine Corps, bar none. The fight at Iwo Jima turned out to be the fiercest landing battle in the world's history.

The Landing Force Reserve, Third Marine Division, was kept in areas removed from the objective until after D-day. Employed in the Iwo operation Landing Force were 75,144 officers and enlisted men, of whom 570 were Army Assault Troops, 70,647 Marine Assault Troops of the Fourth and Fifth Marine Divisions, and 3,927 Navy Assault personnel. In addition, 36,164 Garrison Troops were kept intact to take over the defense and development of the island after its capture. These Garrison Troops included 23,830 Army, 492 Marine, and 11,842 Navy personnel.

The Expeditionary Troops employed in the operations thus totalled 111,308.

Beginning on 16 February, the day that Corregidor was attacked, Rear Admiral H. P. Blandy's Task Force 52 and Rear Admiral Bertram J. Rodger's Task Force 54 threw a ring of guns around Iwo Jima and bombarded the island to soften the defenses. Minesweepers swept methodically; planes buzzed overhead. The attack on Iwo came as no surprise to the beleaguered enemy. For three days these forces poured what was intended to be a pulverizing fire on the Japanese of Iwo Jima.

On the second day the Japanese fought back, and ships carrying the Underwater Demolition Teams, and their supporting vessels, suffered considerable damage and many casualties. Sweeping continued, however, and the Demolition Teams, supported by gunboats, scouted the shallow water near the beaches. The larger vessels threw tons of explosives into Mount Suribachi and into high, rocky cliffs. Bombardment kept up on the third day, with the enemy retaliating viciously.

Just before daylight on 19 February, the Attack Force (TF-53), commanded by Rear Admiral Harry W. Hill, USN, arrived off the southeastern beaches. The two Transport Groups reached their areas off the southwestern beaches simultaneously. Landing craft were lowered and loaded. The initial waves of LCMs, LCVPs, LVTs, and DUKWs formed at the line of departure. The bombardment ships let go at Iwo at 0640 and continued their fire until the landings. The first waves struck the beaches at 0900 on a front of 3,000 yards, receiving only a small amount of gunfire initially, but heavy mortar and artillery fire on the beaches soon developed.

Beach conditions were bad. Breaking surf broached some of the landing craft. Picked up and thrown broadside on the beach, they were swamped and wrecked by succeeding waves, sinking deeply into the sand. Wreckage piled higher and higher, extending seaward to damage propellers of landing ships. Troops from the landing craft struggled up the slopes of coarse, dry, volcanic sand which bogged down wheeled vehicles. Tracked vehicles moved only with difficulty. As soon as the beachhead was secured, LSTs and LSMs were sent in, but they, too, had difficulty to keep from broaching. The beaches finally had to be closed to craft smaller than LCTs. Amphibious vehicles were successful in evacuating the many casualties. The beaches were finally cleared of accumulated wreckage, boats and pontoons were salvaged, and damaged ships were repaired by the Service and Salvage Group.

By the end of D-day, 30,000 Marines had been landed. Heavy opposition had developed from the high ground on both flanks, but the Fifth Marines on the left had advanced rapidly across the narrow part of the island, capturing the southwest end of Airfield No. 1, then pivoting southwest against Mount Suribachi. Marines on the right advanced across the steep and open slopes leading up to Airfield No. 1. They suffered heavy casualties from machine gun and mortar fire and from mines placed inland from the beaches.

The landing boats from *Bayfield* and the other transports took terrific punishment exceeding anything previously experienced. Japanese mortar emplacements concealed in the sides of Mount Suribachi and in the high wooded area at the northeast end of the island laid a constant barrage right at the water's edge, where the boats presented motionless targets. Many of the boats were hit. Others broached. Nevertheless, the young Coast Guard boat crewmen, most of them of 'teen age, went in to the beach through shell splashes time and again. Some Coast Guardsmen did not get back to their ships. Those who did were soon off again with another load.

On other assault beaches in previous operations, there had been beachmasters, salvage parties, and beach parties to keep the landing area clear. There was none on D-day at Iwo Jima because no one could remain on the beach. The Marines could keep alive only by moving inland. So the landing boats operated chiefly on the initiative of their youthful coxswains. When a boat was wrecked, it remained on the beach, a swashing, shifting menace to whatever came in next. Boats going back to the transports carried as many casualties as could be brought through the heavy fire to the water's edge and taken on board before the fire made it necessary to shove off.

*Bayfield* took on board 250 to 300 Marine casualties that night. One by one they were gently helped and carried from the landing boats to the deck of the transport, then taken below to the sick bay and crew's quarters. The doctors and pharmacists' mates performed a herculean, merciful task.

The wounded lay helplessly in shell holes, a few yards in, along the entire beach. Many hospital corpsmen were wounded. Although the ships and planes shelled and bombed the Japanese mortar emplacements on Mount Suribachi and elsewhere, the enemy mortar shells continued to rain relentlessly on the beach. There was no safety anywhere, and nothing to do but go forward. The Marines inched their way to the point where they could come to hand-to-hand grips with the enemy. It was the only way they could fight, for they had nothing at first but rifles and hand grenades.

The many Coast Guard-manned LSTs had varying experiences, which blended into the whole operation, with little of the outstanding. Some went in during the initial phase, others later—unloading their troops, equipment, and supplies first into smaller landing craft, and completing the operation by unloading directly onto the beaches. Most withdrew from the assault area at night, and returned to continue the next morning.

For instance, at 0800 on D-day, *LST-784* swung into position off the beach and maneuvered all day to avoid the projectiles which were detonating in the water in her area. On the 20th she moved in to 500 yards off the beach and released five Army DUKWs. They did not come back to the line of departure as planned, and the ship waited for them most of the night. All five had been hit or had capsized in the heavy surf. The LST then launched her pontoon barges, all of which had to be serviced. During this time she had worked 22 miles offshore and was out with the destroyer pickets. Two barges started in under their own power. The LST managed to tow one of the remaining barges to the line of departure, and the fourth barge had to be abandoned.

Plane attacks were numerous. *LST-790* was attacked on the 22nd while in company with two other LSTs and a destroyer escort. At 1510 four enemy planes were sighted coming in abreast, with two more astern. The ships opened fire. All guns of *LST-790* bearing to starboard fired, and the four planes appeared to be hit almost immediately. One exploded in the air, and the other three splashed. Observers claimed that fire from *LST-790* accounted for three. Two days later she beached and finished unloading, landing 30 trucks in 32 minutes.

The troops gained from 100 to 500 yards during 20 February, and captured Airfield No. 1. Some progress was made against Mount Suribachi, and the beachhead was enlarged, making it less vulnerable to counterattack. The beaches, however, continued to be under heavy fire from both flanks, and this hampered unloading, causing many casualties and the loss of considerable equipment, ammunition, and supplies. On the 21st and 22nd, Regimental Combat Team 28, employing flame-throwers and demolitions, advanced against stubborn opposition and succeeded in surrounding the base of Mount Suribachi. On the morning of 23 February, two battalions of U. S. Marines climbed to the rim and surrounded the crater. At 1035 the American flag was raised to its summit. Its capture eliminated enemy observation and fire from the rear, and permitted freer use of the southern beaches.

On 24 February, *LST-792* beached at dusk to unload cargo. She soon underwent one of the first air raids on the island. The crew opened fire, and then received thirteen mortar hits. The LST had to retract from the beach to prevent further damage to ship and personnel. Five men were wounded. While *LST-792* was beached at Iwo Jima, Joe Rosenthal, the Associated Press photographer who snapped the now immortal picture of the flag-raising on Mount Suribachi, went on board for a meal and a little rest, having been on the beach since early in the landing.

The flag-raising on Suribachi, however significant, did not mean the end of fighting. Airfield No. 2 was under control by the night of the 26th, and the Third Marines' position in the center enabled it to support the advance of the Fourth and Fifth Marines through the more difficult terrain sloping to the sea on either flank. The attack continued toward the village of Motoyama and Airfield No. 3. Heavy opposition and difficult terrain held the Fifth Marines' gain to 1,500 yards for many days.

The beachhead was slowly expanded in all directions on the Motoyama plateau in the center of the island. By 2 March, a 4,000-foot runway had been completed on No. 1 Airfield, which was then ready for fighter and transport planes. By the next day the Motoyama tableland and the last of the three airfields were under American control. On 4 March, a B-29 made a successful forced landing

at the airfield. Two days later the first land-based fighters came in to relieve carrier aircraft in effective close support of troops. Little further progress was made until 8-9 March, when resistance toward the beaches greatly diminished, and in the next three days all the eastern coast to within 4,000 yards of Kitano Point, at the extreme north, was secured. Reduction of the defenses of Kitano Point followed, and by 1800 on 16 March, 26 days after the initial landing, all organized resistance ended.

Iwo Jima cost both sides heavily. Japanese dead totaled 21,304, including 13,234 officially counted and buried, and 8,070 estimated sealed in caves or buried by the enemy. Prisoners numbered 212. United States casualties between 19 February and 23 March were 4,590 killed, 15,954 wounded, and 301 missing—a total of 20,845. This was a terrific price, but the objective was vital.

A 790-mile chain of islands extends across the Pacific approaches to the East China Sea from Kyushu, the southernmost major island of Japan, almost to Formosa. These islands are in five groups, the two southernmost known collectively as the Ryukyu Islands. The largest and most important of these islands, lying about in the middle of the chain, is Okinawa, 60 miles long and eight to ten miles wide. Formosa to the southwest, China to the west, and Kyushu to the northeast are all about 400 miles from Okinawa. The immediate group of islands to which Okinawa belongs is known as Okinawa Gunto, of which Kerama Retto is one.

Okinawa was the next U. S. objective after the attack on Iwo Jima. Planning followed the familiar pattern used in the Pacific assaults. Admiral Nimitz, in his directive said:

"The forces under my command are ordered to seize, occupy and defend Okinawa Gunto in order to (a) attack the main islands of Japan and their sea approaches with ships and planes: (b) support further attacks on the regions bordering the East China Sea; (c) sever Japanese sea and air communications between the Empire and the mainland of Asia, Formosa, Malaya, and the Netherlands East Indies." Nimitz named Admiral Spruance as Officer Commanding the Operation.

A preliminary to the Okinawa attack were landings on 26 March at eight small islands of the mountainous Kerama Retto, 15 to 20 miles off Okinawa's southwestern tip. Rear Admiral Ingolf

N. Kiland, USN, commanded the attacking naval forces. Involved were cutter *Bibb* and six Coast Guard-manned LSTs—*24, 770, 785, 793, 829,* and *830*. Troops of the 77th Infantry Division, under Major General Andrew D. Bruce, USA, were put ashore, following bombardment by a battleship and two cruisers of Admiral Deyo's group. The landings, which were successful, encountered only light opposition. *LST-829* had the distinction of landing the first troops to invade and secure Japanese colonial soil in World War II. The landings were well supported by ships' gunfire and carrier aircraft. By the night of 29 March, all of the area was in American hands.

*LST-24*, which was loaded with about 1,300 tons of ammunition, as well as other vessels of the group, underwent several air attacks at Kerama Retto. After the 29th, she remained in the area servicing units of the Fifth Fleet, during which time there were numerous air attacks, some by suicide planes. Navy-manned *LST-447* was hit by one, *Logan Victory* by another, and both ships burst into flame. Many vessels were damaged. An important and unexpected result of these operations was the capture and destruction of nearly 400 suicide boats which had been based on the Keramas. These were 18 feet long, with four-cylinder engines, and were equipped with a depth charge at the stern and a "torpedo bomb" at the bow.

The main attack on Okinawa was getting under way. For nine days before the landing, Okinawa and the adjacent islands were subjected to intensive bombing and shelling by carrier aircraft and surface vessels of the U. S. Fifth Fleet. Admiral Blandy's Task Force 52, with elements of Admiral Mitscher's carrier forces assisting, went in with 120 minesweepers and Underwater Demolition Teams to clear the way and bombard the beaches. On 24 March, Vice Admiral Willis A. Lee, Jr., USN, took battleships and destroyers to bombard the southeastern coast as a deception and to protect the minesweepers, which had preceded Admiral Deyo's fire support ships by a day. On the next day, Deyo's force was attacked by kamikazes, three of which hit and damaged vessels but did not put them out of action. Enemy submarines, both large and midget, roamed the waters and were a constant threat.

Vessels for the amphibious assault had gathered at Guadalcanal, Ulithi, Saipan, Noumea, Leyte, and Espiritu Santo, and from these far-flung bases got under way to arrive simultaneously at Okinawa. This great fleet, under Admiral Spruance, steamed to the south and west of Okinawa to attack its western shore. With the attacking forces was an impressive array of Coast Guard-manned vessels—seven transports, two cutters, twenty-nine LSTs, one PC, and twelve LCIs—fifty-one in all. Cutter *Taney* joined later. In addition, six Navy-manned transports had Coast Guardsmen in their crews.

Enemy troops on Okinawa numbered nearly 120,000, though the total was not known at the time of the invasion. Opposing them in the attacking forces were more than 548,000 U. S. soldiers, sailors, and Marines. Admiral Turner's amphibious force of cruisers, battleships, transports, ammunition ships, cargo carriers, minesweepers, landing craft, and barges numbered about 1,200. There were, in addition, Admiral Mitscher's Task Force 58, comprising 82 ships, Task Group 52.1 of 17 "jeep" carriers to perform combat air patrol, antisubmarine patrol, and support of the ground troops, and a protective ring of destroyers. It was the largest campaign of the Pacific War.

On Easter morning, 1 April, the bombardment ships stood off the beaches waiting for the enemy to make the first move. Admiral Turner's fleet steamed in to the assigned areas with two corps of the Tenth Army, which was commanded by Lieutenant General Simon B. Buckner, USA. Supporting the Third Amphibious Corps under Major General Roy S. Geiger, USMC, were four old battleships, four cruisers, and eight destroyers, steaming in column to the north. The XXIV Army Corps, under Lieutenant General John R. Hodge, USA, was supported by three battleships and four cruisers, which were to the south. Other war vessels were in general support of the assault forces.

During the early hours, three ships became casualties, two of them by suicide planes. One of these, the Coast Guard-manned *LST-884* (Lieutenant Charles C. Pearson, USCG), took a kamikaze and burned brightly; her ammunition exploded. At 0555 the order was given to abandon ship, and men in the water were picked up by the ship's boats and boats from other LSTs and LCMs. At 0731, the heavier ammunition having exploded, Lieutenant Pearson, four other officers, and two enlisted men returned, manned the pump, and brought two streams to bear on the fire. At 0800 three other officers and fifteen enlisted men voluntarily returned to assist. Despite further explosions, the fire was under control at 1100. The vessel was towed to Kerama Retto for repair. Nineteen Marines were killed; one of the ship's company was wounded and one killed.

After a brief wait, hundreds of Navy planes from the carriers swarmed in over the ships to give the ground troops close tactical support. Between 0700 and 1000, over 500 carrier-based planes were over Okinawa, strafing and bombing enemy strong points. Bombardment began on schedule, and at 0830 the first waves, carrying 20,000 men, landed abreast at Hagushi beaches. Incredibly, there was no opposition! Other waves followed. Later in the morning some enemy artillery and mortar fire was received on the beaches, but resistance there was extremely light. Nevertheless, there were seven air raid alerts the first day.

In the days immediately following the Okinawa invasion, things went fairly well. Unloading of troops and equipment went forward with vigor. But on 6 April, 355 suicide planes from Kyushu headed in a mass flight toward Okinawa. What was left of the Japanese fleet sortied from the Inland Sea on a fanatical "do-or-die" mission. First, a group of kamikazes attacked the ring of U. S. destroyers protecting the Okinawa area, and then worked through to the beachhead. The Japanese kept coming in, and explosions were everywhere. Many vessels were hit, a good number were badly damaged and put out of action, some were sunk.

Dogfights swarmed all over the sky. Ships were firing, planes were exploding in the air, splashing in the sea, or hitting their objectives in a burst of flame. This series of enemy strikes was as intense as those of the first days of the Philippine invasion. The attacks were met spiritedly by American planes of the Combat Air Patrol, which knocked down a large number of enemy planes. The raids kept up for several days, but abated somewhat by 10 April. The next day the Japanese turned their fury on Task Force 58, and fighters and ships of that force accounted for 29 Japanese planes. Then the weight of attack shifted back to Okinawa, but American planes shot down 151 of the enemy.

A "suicide fleet" of nine warships, including

Japan's super battleship *Yamato*, under Vice Admiral Seiichi Ito, sortied from the Inland Sea on 6 April to attempt to break up the American attack at Okinawa. Ito could have had more ships, but there was no fuel for them. At 1000 on 7 April, his fleet made radar contact with United States planes. Kerama Retto-based planes kept the Japanese vessels under observation all morning, and Admiral Deyo's surface force of battleships, cruisers, and destroyers charged north to meet the enemy. Planes of two task groups of Task Force 58 closed fast in cloudy, rainy weather. They found their targets. Five of the nine Japanese ships, including *Yamato*, were sunk, one was badly damaged, and three returned to Japan. Thus ended any serious threat from the enemy's surface forces.

*Cambria* suffered only two minor casualties during her ten days at the scene of action. *Joseph T. Dickman*, commanded by Captain Frank A. Leamy, USCG, suffered no damage or casualties, and left on 9 April for Saipan. *Cepheus* and *Theenim* remained in the transport area off the beachhead from 1 to 9 April, except for one night's withdrawal, during which time they were subjected to many air attacks. The prolonged stay in the area offered the enemy numerous targets of which he took good advantage.

In the task groups making up the Joint Expeditionary Force for Phase One of the Okinawa operation was LST Group 85, which included Coast Guard-manned *LSTs 758, 759, 760, 782,* and *785*. *LST-782* served as Unit 12 flagship for Commander W. B. Millington, USCG, and later for Commander S. R. Sands, USCG, of LST Unit 11, part of the Tractor Flotilla. After the initial invasion, Coast Guard-manned vessels were kept active for weeks in landing reinforcements and in making re-supply runs.

Cutter *Bibb* was at Kerama Retto most of the time during the Okinawa operation, and was an almost constant target for Japanese suicide planes. In all, she was subjected to 55 air raids. Later, on 21 June, her guns downed a kamikaze just before it crashed into a nearby vessel which was its intended target.

Coast Guard-manned ships took their toll of enemy aircraft. For instance, *LST-887* shot down one plane off Okinawa the day after the initial landings. During the 15 days in which *LST-788*

EARLY WAVES OF AMTRACKS DRIVE IN TO IWO
JIMA BEACHES . . . . out of LSTs come these amphibians
to land Marines on the fire-raked shore after heavy naval
bombardment.

OLD GLORY FLIES FROM THE SUMMIT OF MOUNT
SURIBACHI . . . . overlooking the hard-won invasion beach
of Iwo Jima.

MOUNT SURIBACHI DOMINATES THE LANDING
BEACHES . . . . the beachhead at Iwo Jima as supplies and
troops went in.

A COAST GUARD BEACH PARTY RESTS AT IWO
JIMA . . . . after three days and nights on the battle-swept
island, these men await return to their transport which lies
offshore.

MARINES LAND AT OKINAWA FROM *JOSEPH T. DICKMAN'S* BARGES . . . . there was no opposition on the beach, but heavy land fighting lay ahead.

A GREAT ARMADA LIES OFF THE OKINAWA BEACHHEAD . . . . troops and supplies pour in for the last major operation of World War II.

COAST GUARD-MANNED TRANSPORT *BAYFIELD*
. . . one of the vessels which participated in several of the Pacific operations.

NATIVE HUTS BURN ON IE SHIMA AS AMERICANS ADVANCE . . . . soldiers move up through a burning village as they drive back Japanese opposition.

COAST GUARDSMEN LAND AUSSIES IN THE BALIKPAPAN INVASION . . . . the first wave hits the beach as heavy **smoke** from a burning oil well rolls over the beachhead.

ON BOARD *USS MISSOURI* . . . . General Douglas MacArthur signing the Japanese surrender document, September 2, 1945.—(*U. S. Navy photo*)

was in the Okinawa region, that vessel scored hits on seven enemy planes and was directly responsible for downing two; one of which splashed 250 yards away and the other only 50 feet off the starboard quarter, missing the ship's conn by a bare 20 feet, inflicting slight underwater damage to the vessel. On the 15th, *LST-789* shot down an "Oscar" to add to a fairly impressive total of enemy planes brought down by the Coast Guard.

An assault on Ie Shima, a small island near the northern tip of Okinawa, and of major importance because of its fine airfield, was a subsidiary action of the Okinawa campaign. On the morning of 16 April, *LST-829* took part in this assault. The 773rd Amtracks and Battalion 1, 306th Infantry, were landed, swiftly overcoming enemy resistance on the westerly slopes, and captured the airfield. But they were soon up against tough opposition around the base of prominent "Sugar Loaf Hill", where the Japanese had constructed a strong line and were holding out in tombs and caves. It was here that Ernie Pyle, noted war correspondent, lost his life on 18 April. For a week *LST-829* followed a schedule which sent her to Ie Shima early each morning and back to anchorages in Naga Wan or off Hagushi every evening. The Japanese defenses on Ie Shima were finally cracked after ten days of fighting.

Rear Admiral C. H. Cobb, USN, the prospective Commander, Naval Forces Ryukyus, and his staff reported to Vice Admiral Turner, Commander Task Force 51, at Okinawa on 11 April, having been transported from Pearl Harbor by cutter *Taney*. This vessel had been converted at Boston to a combined operations-communications-headquarters ship similar to *Bibb, Spencer,* and *Ingham*. *Taney* took station at Ie Shima, and from there Commander Task Group 51.21 directed all local naval activities north of Zama Point. *Taney* was assigned full conduct of Combat Information Center duties. The center was wholly manned by Coast Guard personnel. A complete radar and air-net coverage was maintained, and complete information of all activities, enemy and friendly, was received and evaluated. Orders were issued to all activities for which *Taney* was responsible.

Because of her exposed position to the north, *Taney* experienced a disproportionate share of the actual fighting. She went to general quarters 119 times in the 45 days up to 26 May. She was credited with downing four suicide planes, as well as numerous assists. On 24 June a Japanese float-type seaplane circled *Taney* at low altitude and was splashed by ship and shore batteries.

Coast Guard-manned *PC-469*, while on patrol near Okinawa on 4 May, sighted three small craft at 0035 about 1,000 yards away. When they were identified as Japanese suicide boats, *PC-469* fired and sank one only about 40 yards astern. The two remaining boats cleared to about 600 yards. Illumination was furnished by destroyers, and the PC succeeded in sinking the second. The remaining boat fled, and, though fired on, probably escaped.

LCI(L) Group 103 was under Lieutenant Commander B. A. Walliser, USCGR, and included six Coast Guard-manned LCIs in each of two divisions. With one division at Okinawa and the other at Kerama Retto, these vessels made smoke at night to cover ships of the fire support group and at the same time kept a lookout for suicide boats and swimmers. During the day they were grouped near merchant ships for antiaircraft support and to carry guard mail and staff officers to other harbors. On the afternoon of 3 June, while acting as harbor control vessel in Chinmu Bay, group flagship *LCI-90* was attacked by two Japanese suicide planes, one of which crashed into the starboard side of the conning station, rolling to the deck below and then over the side. Six men and two officers were severely burned, one fatally. Although all radio and navigating equipment in the conn and pilot house was destroyed, *LCI-90* proceeded under her own power, using a makeshift steering wheel.

The story of the ground fighting on Okinawa is long and detailed, and properly belongs in other histories. For the sake of continuity, however, a brief summary is appropriate. The United States troops landed on an eight-mile stretch of beach opposite Yontan and Katena airfields, about 20 miles north of Naha, the capital. Before noon the two airfields had been seized. Resistance on the beaches had been light. Within 48 hours the forces had driven across the island to the east coast. Many enemy troops remained to the south of the beachhead, where most of the major Japanese military and naval installations were located; others retired to the rugged northern part of the island.

As the American troops advanced, enemy resistance stiffened, and by the end of the week, violent artillery barrages were being laid down by both sides. To the north, however, the United States Marines made wide gains against little opposition, and by the 9th had cleared the enemy from practically all the narrow peninsula joining the northern and southern sections of the island. Five days later, the Marines reached the northern tip of Okinawa and virtually occupied Motoby Peninsula.

In southern Okinawa, meanwhile, more determined resistance was being met as the troops moved into the enemy's prepared defenses. By the 10th, Kakazu Ridge, near the west coast, had been taken and lost three times. More than 500 enemy caves were cleared in southern Okinawa before the Army launched an offensive on the 19th. By the 29th, troops of the 27th Division captured Machinato airfield. Beginning on 3 May, the Japanese counterattacked furiously all along the line, but were limited to small gains. At the end of the week United States troops began to advance again, and by 7 May positions had been consolidated along an irregular line from the mouth of the Awa River to the northern end of the Yonabaru airstrip.

By the 17th there were increasing indications that the enemy's supply lines south of Shuri were being sealed off, and that when they lost their communications, their forces would probably disintegrate and break into small pockets. In spite of a ten-day period of heavy rainfall ending 30 May, big gains were made in every sector. A general drive southward was begun by the Tenth Army, as Japanese aerial activity dwindled to the smallest since the Okinawa campaign began.

On 10 June, after a week of swift thrusts into the enemy's shattered defenses and after substantial gains in all parts of southern Okinawa, messages were dropped behind the enemy's line requesting the Japanese commander to open negotiations by 1800 on the 11th, but apparently the Japanese intended to continue the bitter Okinawa battle to the last man. So fighting continued, with all three United States Divisions receiving heavy supporting fire from ships' guns, artillery, and aircraft. Lieutenant General Buckner, Commanding General of the Tenth Army and Ryukyu Forces, was killed in action on the afternoon of 18 June, and command was assumed by Major General Geiger, commander of the Third Amphibious Corps.

On 21 June, after eleven weeks of this vicious fighting, Admiral Nimitz announced that organized resistance on Okinawa had ended. The flag of the United States was formally raised there on 22 June.

Remnants of the once powerful Japanese garrison, however, continued to fight with unabated fury from small pockets in the extreme southern part of the island, until they were overcome. Many of the enemy jumped off cliffs into the sea. Japanese casualties in the Okinawa fighting up to 26 June totaled 111,351, and prisoners numbered 9,398. United States casualties reached 46,319, including 11,897 dead or missing, and 34,422 wounded. These figures include 4,907 Navy dead and 4,824 Navy wounded, among whom were many Coast Guard casualties.

In the final count at Okinawa, the United States fleet lost 36 ships by sinking, although none was larger than a destroyer. Seven hundred and ninety planes were lost—269 in combat, 229 on board damaged carriers, and 292 from all other causes. Two hundred and five men were killed in air combat. The Japanese lost 7,830 aircraft, and, in all probability, 12,000 airmen.

During the Okinawa campaign there were several minor landings. Troops of the 41st Division landed unopposed on 2 April at Sanga Sanga Island, in the Tawi Tawi Group at the extreme southwestern end of the Sulu Archipelago. The Japanese airfield, which was the primary objective, was quickly seized. Bongao Island, nearby, was taken on the 3rd. Occupation of these two strategic islands placed American forces within less than 50 miles of the northeastern tip of Borneo. The Coast Guard was not involved.

Early on the morning of 17 April, elements of the Tenth Corps landed without opposition along the eastern shore of Moro Gulf, in the Philippines, about 100 miles west of Davao, on Mindoro. Some units landed at Parang, others at Malabang. Cutter *Spencer* served as flagship of the amphibious force, which also included *LST-168* and *LST-170*. As this force approached Malabang, a small motor boat put out from shore flying the United States ensign. It was manned by native guerillas and carried three United States Army fliers as passengers.

They explained that the Japanese had fled and that the beachhead was unguarded. Troops were landed and took up pursuit of the fleeing Japanese.

Tarakan is a 160-mile-square, oil-rich island in Dutch East Borneo, about 185 miles southwest from Tawi Tawi. On 27 April, Australian and American warships began a five-day shelling of the area. Three days later, landings were made by Australian units at Tarakan and Sadau Islands. *LST-67*, under Lieutenant John Lence, USCG, the only Coast Guard-manned vessel in this action, anchored off Tarakan on 1 May, furnished ammunition replenishments to the fire support ships, and supplied dry stores, fuel, and fresh water to the various participating vessels. Tarakan was secured by the end of May.

Units of the United States 24th Division, working overland from Parang, moved swiftly through the hills and had reached the west coast of Davao Gulf at Digos by 27 April. They spread out along the coast, while units advancing to the north toward Davao reached the western outskirts of the city on 1 May. The same task force that had operated in Moro Gulf, led by cutter *Spencer* as flagship, swept around the southern tip of Mindanao and landed additional troops and materiel near Digos, where the troops had already cleared the beachhead. Increasing resistance was met in the outskirts of Davao, and house-to-house fighting developed as United States forces drove the enemy from the city and into the hills. Davao's seaport, Santa Ana, was taken on the 3rd, and Davao itself was captured on the 4th.

After a three-day bombardment by units of the Seventh Fleet and an Australian squadron, troops of the Ninth Australian Division landed on 10 June at four points in the Brunei Bay area of British Borneo against extremely light opposition. *Spencer*, representing the Coast Guard in this operation, was command ship for the staff of the 20th Australian Brigade. Besides providing communications facilities for that Brigade, *Spencer* acted as radar guard. Everything went according to schedule, and the ground troops reached all their objectives with little difficulty.

The last combat mission in which the Coast Guard participated in the Pacific was that at Balikpapan, on the southeast coast of Dutch Borneo. This operation was conducted by 300 ships of the Seventh Fleet and the Royal Netherlands

Navy. It was staged from Morotai, the attack force departing there on 26 June, with armored and infantry units of the Seventh Australian Army. *Spencer* acted as alternate flagship and radar guard for the 8th Amphibious Group, commanded by Rear Admiral A. G. Noble, USN, in *Mt. McKinley*. Coast Guard-manned *LST-66*, *LST-67* and *LST-168* also took part in this action. The support force consisted of Seventh Fleet cruisers and escort carriers and elements of the Royal Australian and Netherlands Navies. For three weeks before the landings, which were scheduled for 1 July, the Balikpapan area was subjected to concentrated air assaults, and for two weeks had been worked over thoroughly by naval bombardment.

*LST-67* played an advance part in this operation. She departed Morotai on 17 June, and from Tawi Tawi had a destroyer as escort. She passed through the Makassar Straits on 23 June, a full week before the invasion forces, and anchored next day in Balikpapan Bay. The LST brought in ammunition, which was speedily transferred to cruisers and destroyers which were reducing enemy defenses to rubble.

This vessel was underway on the night of the 25th when Japanese torpedo planes evaded the air patrol. Accurate fire routed the attackers, and one plane, hit repeatedly by *LST-67's* guns, finally crashed in flames a few hundred yards away. The LST took on more ammunition at Tawi Tawi and rendezvoused on 29 June with the main convoy bound for the Balikpapan landing.

Infantry and armored units of the Australian Seventh Division were put ashore on 1 July and met little early opposition other than scattered small arms fire. General MacArthur went ashore with the fourth wave of assault troops and personally directed the operation. Resistance increased as the units advanced inland toward the still burning oil fields and refineries. The city of Balikpapan was encircled by the 9th, and in the following weeks the troops advanced inland. They were consolidating their positions for further advance into the rich oil area when Japan capitulated. At that time, enemy casualties in Borneo were 5,693 counted dead and 536 prisoners. Allied losses were 436 killed, 1,460 wounded, and three missing.

As far as Japan was concerned, the Japanese

military were under no illusions. Defeat at Okinawa was about the last straw, and the last straw was to follow rapidly. Elsewhere, on 1 July, the day of the landing at Balikpapan, 104 vessels of Admiral Halsey's Third Fleet headed out into the Philippine Sea, and then northward to strike heavy blows at Fortress Japan. There were battleships, cruisers, flat-tops, and destroyers. This was to prove the last and decisive blow of World War II. It was a long run, and the days en route were spent in sharpening the fleet for battle. Day and night, a close cover of fighters flew over the ships. Planes from Okinawa flew north daily to hit the Japanese island of Kyushu. Others from the Iwo-Marianas axis pounded the Tokyo area and other cities of Japan.

The Fleet's program was to conduct air attacks on northern Honshu and Hokkaido, and naval bombardment of key coastal cities. The ships rode a weather front but came out of it on 10 July, when carrier planes were launched toward Tokyo. Strike followed strike. There was little opposition. On 14 July, Rear Admiral John F. Shafroth, Jr., USN, led his group of battleships and cruisers to the coast of Honshu and for two hours bombarded the steel-making city of Kanaishi. The next day Vice Admiral Oscar C. Badger, USN, took his heavy bombardment group to within sight of the city of Muroran, on the coal and ore island of Hokkaido, and bombarded for an hour. Not an enemy plane rose to protest, nor did a gun fire from shore.

Most of the remaining units of the Japanese Navy had withdrawn to shelter in the Inland Sea, not far from Hiroshima. On 17 July, Admiral Badger, with his fleet augmented by a British task force, bombarded Mito and Hitachi, industrial centers 50 miles northeast of Tokyo. They ceased to be industrial centers. The next day an air strike played havoc with Yokosuka Naval Base in Tokyo Bay. As Captain Karig in his *Battle Report* said: "The fleet went where it pleased, when it pleased, and stayed as long as it pleased. The mobility of sea power had reached its zenith."

Next, the remnants of the Japanese fleet took a severe beating, as did many airfields. On 25 July, United States carrier planes finished off practically all that remained of the enemy fleet. Then Admiral Shafroth took his ships to bombard Hamamatsu, 120 miles southwest of Tokyo, and other scattered bombardments followed.

The climax of the attack on the Japanese homeland came on 6 August, when the first atomic bomb was dropped from a United States plane and detonated at Hiroshima, making a shambles of the entire city. Three days later, Nagasaki suffered a similar fate, with destruction even greater than that at Hiroshima.

Late in the afternoon on 10 August, Radio Tokyo broadcast in English the first proposal to surrender. The official offer reached Washington through Switzerland 12 hours later, but the Third Fleet continued its attacks. On 14 August, President Truman announced Japan's surrender. World War II came to an end.

Thereafter, occupation forces moved in. These had to be transported and supplied, and mines had to be swept from the waters. Coast Guard-manned vessels joined naval ships in this task, which went on for some months. Troops, eager to return home, were transported back to the United States in the months that followed, and Coast Guard-manned transports were employed in this "Magic Carpet" duty as long as there were troops to bring home.

Though "Magic Carpet" and other war-end activities occupied the Coast Guard well into the next year, the Service was returned to the United States Treasury Department by the Navy on 1 January 1946.

Thus, the United States Coast Guard closed another chapter in its history as a fighting part of the United States Navy in time of war, as it has been in every war following the American Revolution. Its contribution in World War II was on an immense scale in comparison with previous endeavors, but the war, too, overshadowed in scope any fought before.

If there is glory in war, then this Service earned its full share. Its men were as valiant in combat as their brothers in the Naval Service with whom they shared the dangers and the victories. Heroism under fire became commonplace, and the list of Coast Guardsmen who gave their lives that their Country might live is long and impressive. But heroism was not confined to the field of combat. In fulfilling the function of saving lives and property at sea and in guarding our ports, men of the Coast Guard also performed their duties with a devotion and self denial which fully upheld the finest traditions of the Service.

Throughout the war, the Coast Guard motto, *"Semper Paratus"*, was an inspiration and a guide to heroic achievement at sea, in the air, on the coasts, or on the waterfront. The United States may be sure that, as in the past, in peace or war, the officers and enlisted men of the future who wear the shield of the Coast Guard will be "Always Ready."

# Appendix A
## MEDALS AND AWARDS*

### Medal of Honor
*★ Combat citation*

★MUNRO, Douglas A., SM1c

### Navy Cross
*★ Combat citation*

★CLARK, Paul L., F1c
★EVANS, Raymond J., LTJG
★GILL, Warren C. (R), LT

★HIRSHFIELD, James A., CDR
★JESTER, Maurice D., LT
★WALSH, Quentin R., CDR

### Distinguished Service Medal

SMITH, Edward H., RADM

WAESCHE, Russell R., ADM

### Silver Star Medal
*★ Combat citation*

★ALLISON, Samuel W. (R), LT
★ANDERSON, Alvin K., BM2c
★ARNOLD, Arthur A. (R), BM2c
★BRALLIER, Bret H., CDR
★BRESNAN, Joseph A., CDR
★BURKE, Rayner C., LT
★CANTILLON, Mathew P. (R), LT
★CENTOFANTI, Enio J. (R), S1c
★COWART, Kenneth K., CDR
★DANNISON, Byron G., CBM
★DENMAN, Douglas C., COX
★DEXTER, Dwight H., CAPT
★ECKARDT, Garnet H. (R), MOMM1c
★ELMER, Robert E. P., Jr. (R), LTJG
★EMERSON, Robert E., LCDR
★FRITCH, Rollin A. (R), S1c
★GALLOWAY, Grady R. (R), LT
★GARRETT, Arthur O. (R), ENS
★GERCZAK, Joseph (R), SM3c
★GIFFORD, Harry C., LCDR
★GISLASON, Gene R. (R), LT
★GUNTHER, Alvin F., CMM
★HAGGLOVE, Jonas T., LCDR
★HAINRIHAR, Anton J., CWT
★HARRIS, Glen L., SURF
★HARRISON, Benjamin F., MACH
★HENDLEY, Coit T. (R), LTJG
★HOYLE, Robert, LTJG
★HUGHES, Charles J., S1c
★HUNT, James S., CDR

★HUTCHINSON, George F. (R), LTJG
★IMLAY, Miles H., CAPT
★JENNINGS, Damon, CMM
★JOHNSON, Charles F., BM2c
★KING, Sam W., COX
★LAWRENCE, William G. (R), CBM
★LEGATES, Walter L., CWT
★LILLY, C. B. (R), BM2c
★LONG, Wilson K. (R), LTJG
★MANN, Frederick D., BM1c
★MARTIN, Ralph E. (R), S2c
★MILLER, Harold C., BM2c
★MILLER, Jack N., BM2c
★MURPHY, William E., ENS
★NIRSCHEL, Fred W. (R), LCDR
★ONETO, Anthony L. (R), LTJG
★OWENS, Thomas F. (R), S1c
★OXLEY, Gene F. (R), S1c
★PALMER, Walter L. (R), S1c
★PETERSON, Clarence H., CAPT
★SALMON, Robert M. (R), LT
★SCALAN, Bernard E., CDR
★SCHEUERMAN, John C. (R), S1c
★SEUTTER, Donald J. F. (R), SC2c
★SNYDER, Richard T., BM1c
★SPARLING, William A., BM2c
★STRING, John F., Jr. (R), LT
★TARR, Daniel J., SURF
★THOMPSON, Edward C., CDR
★TRUMP, William F. (R), MOMM1c

* Subject to the possibilities of error, the grades and rates listed are those which were held at the time the award was made.

★UNGER, Aden C., CDR
★VYN, Arend I., Jr., LT

★WARD, Robert G. (R), S1c
★WILK, Stanley, LT

## Legion of Merit

★ *Combat citation*
† *Gold Star with Combat V in lieu of second award*
\* *Gold Star in lieu of second award*

★BANNER, Roger H., LT
★BARNARD, Philip E., CBM
★BARTLETT, David H., CDR
†★BERDINE, Harold S., CAPT
  BRIDGES, Howard C., CAPT
★BURNS, Ralph, LT
★BUTCHER, Reginald W., LCDR
★BYRD, John H., CAPT
  CHALKER, Lloyd T., RADM
  COFFIN, Eugene A., COMMO
  COVELL, Leon C., RADM
\*CRONK, Paul B., CAPT
  CULLEN, John C., BM2c
†CURRY, Ralph R., CDR
  DELANO, John S. (TR), CAPT
  DEMPWOLF, Ralph W., RADM
  DERBY, Wilfrid N., RADM
  DONNELL, Kenneth W. (R), LCDR
  DONOHUE, Robert, RADM
★DUCKWORTH, Clifton M., CCM
★DURGIN, Willard L. (R), MOMM1c
★EVANS, Stephen H., CAPT
  FARLEY, Joseph F., RADM
★FELDMAN, Herbert (R), LCDR
  FINLAY, Gordon T., RADM
★FORD, Alexander L., CDR
★FRENCH, Reginald H., CAPT
\*\*FRITZSCHE, Edward H., CAPT
★GILL, Warren C. (R), LT
★GOLENIECKI, John V., BM1c
  GORMAN, Frank J., RADM
  GRAVES, Garrett Van A., CDR
  GULICK, Merle A., CAPT
  HALL, Clarence S., Jr., LTJG
  HALL, Norman B., COMMO
  HALL, Rae B., CAPT
★HARWOOD, Charles W., CAPT
\*\*HEIMER, Roger C., CAPT
★HIGBEE, Frank D., RADM
★HOUSTON, Lewis C., LT
\*\*IMLAY, Miles H., CAPT
  JOHNSON, Harvey F., RADM
  JONES, Leonard T., CDR
  KELLY, Herbert J. (R), LCDR
  KENNER, Frank T., CAPT
  LAWLER, Joseph J. (R), CDR
★LEVY, Harold (R), CHPHAR
  LOWE, William H. (TR), CAPT

★McCABE, Frank M., LCDR
★McCORMICK, Nelson C., LCDR
  McGUIRE, William M., CAPT
\*\*MAUERMAN, Raymond J., CAPT
  MERRILL, Robert T. (R), CAPT
  MICHEL, Carl, RADM USPHS
  MULIERI, Bruno C. F. (R), LCDR
  MUNTER, William H., RADM
  MUZZY, James S., LT
★NELSON, Norman M., CDR
★O'NEILL, Merlin, RADM
  PARK, Charles A., RADM
  PARKER, Stanley V., RADM
★PETERSON, Carl U., LCDR
★PILLARD, Arthur E., CBM
  PINE, James, RADM
★POLLARD, Francis C., LCDR
  REED-HILL, Ellis, COMMO
  REINBURG, LeRoy, COMMO
  ROACH, Philip F., RADM
★ROBERTS, Russell J., CDR
  ROSE, Earl G., RADM
  ROSENBERG, Jacob, CDR
★ROUNTREE, John, CAPT
  RYAN, Michael J., COMMO
★RYSSY, John W., CAPT
  SCAMMELL, William K., RADM
  SCHLESINGER, Rudolph (R), CHPHAR
  SHEPHEARD, Halert C., COMMO
★SLADE, Hans F., CDR
★SPENCER, Lyndon, CAPT
  STANLEY, John T., CDR
★STELMASCZYK, Benjamin, CHRELE
  STRATTON, Dorothy C. (W), CAPT
★SYNON, George D., CDR
★THOMAS, Charles W., CAPT
★THOMPSON, Edward C., CDR
★THOMSEN, Neils P., CDR
  TOWLE, William F., RADM
  Von PAULSEN, Carl C., CAPT
  WEBSTER, Edward M., COMMO
  WENDLAND, James C., CDR
  WEST, Ralph M., CDR
  WHITBECK, John E., COMMO
★WILCOX, Robert, CDR
★WOOD, Russell E., CAPT
  YACCARINO, Joseph, Jr. (R), PHM1c
  ZEUSLER, Frederick A., RADM

## Distinguished Flying Cross

*★ Combat citation*
*★ Gold Star in lieu of second award*

BOTTOMS, Benjamin A., ARM1c
★BURKE, Richard L., CDR
DAVIS, Larry L., LCDR
GRAHAM, Stewart R., LCDR
KLEISCH, August, LT
MacDIARMID, Donald B., CDR

O'NEILL, Louis T., LCDR
PRITCHARD, John A., Jr., LT
SCHRADER, James N., LCDR
VAUGHN, Clement, LCDR
VUKIC, John, LT
★WHITE, Henry C., LT

## Navy and Marine Corps Medal

*★ Combat citation*

ADAMS, Robert H. (R), S1c
ANDERSON, Carleton F., CMOMM
ANDERSON, Langford (R), LCDR
ANDERSON, Robert W. (R), LT
ANDERSON, Ronald R. (R), S2c
ARBUCKLE, Robert W. (R), S2c
ARREGHI, Richard A. (R), ENS
ARWE, Kenneth J. (R), LTJG
BACKER, Arthur E., Jr., BM1c
BALDWIN, John D., Jr. (R), S1c
BARRETT, John A. (R), S2c
BENNETT, Warren, CMM
BETZ, George C. (R), MOMM2c
BETZ, George E. (R), S1c
BILLOS, Harry P., EM2c
BLOOMFIELD, John E. J. (R), S1c
BRADSHAW, Odell I. (R), MOMM3c
BRASWELL, Wheeler M., LTJG
BRIEN, Clyde T. (R), S1c
BRITTON, Mack G., ACRM
BURKE, William E. (R), S1c
BUXTON, Henry L. (R), SPPS2c
CAMPBELL, Leonard W., CBM
CANTWELL, John F. (R), F1c
CARIENS, Richard J. (R), MOMM1c
CARROZZA, Alfonso D., Y2c
CARTER, Sydney G., LTJG
CHASTAIN, Waldron B. (R), SC3c
★CHOINA, Leroy A. (R), S2c
CHURCH, Harry M., S1c
CLARK, David D. (R), SOM2c
COLLINS, John F., MOMM1c
CONE, Burtis P., LT
COULTAS, William F., COX
CRAMER, Louis J., CBM
CUNNINGHAM, Frank M., SOM2c
DALE, Carlos K. (R), LT
DAME, James R., LTJG
DAMEWOOD, Vernon W. (R), BM1c
DAVID, Charles W., Jr. (R), STM1c
DEJARNETTE, Harold M. (R), BM2c
★DEYAMPERT, Warren T., ST2c
DICHIARA, Robert M. (R), S1c
DILORENZO, Edmond (R), S2c
DOAK, Gaylen E., F1c

DUDLEY, Ralph L., COX
DUNNE, Robert J., EM2c
EASTMAN, Jesse E., LCDR
EATON, Philip B., RADM
ELLIS, James D. (R), S1c
FARRAR, Mirl J., Jr. (R), COX
FORD, James (R), LTJG
FREEMAN, James S., LT
FRIEL, John J., Jr. (R), ENS
FRIEND, Charles (R), MOMM1c
★FULLER, Bert P. (R), RM3c
FULLER, Richard L., LTJG
GARDNER, John N. (R), AS
GEHLERT, Gustave A., Jr. (R), F2c
GOUKER, Roy E. (R), LTJG
GOULD, James R. (R), AS
GRAY, William T., LTJG
GREENE, Eugene C. (R), S1c
GROSS, Robert H., COX
HADDEN, Robert G. (R), SM2c
HAMMETTE, Harrell E. (R), RM3c
HAMMOND, Joseph F., S2c
HARLAND, George J. (R), SOM3c
HARRIS, Elmer, GM1c
HARRISON, John P., BM2c
HENDRIX, John T., CEM
HERRMANN, Harry E. (R), S1c
HILL, Walter F. (R), S1c
HUTCHINS, Roy M., Jr., LT
IRWIN, Patrick B., ENS
JASON, Earl L. (R), S2c
JERNIGAN, John L. (R), STM1c
★JOHNSON, John M. (R), LTJG
JORDAN, Jack S. (R), S1c
KALLAS, Peter, MOMM1c
KELLER, William R., CHPHAR
KENDELL, Kenneth G. (R), COX
KIRK, Hobert J., CWT
KLEIN, Jacob Jr. (R), S1c
KOROWICKI, Stanley J. (R), S1c
KRAMM, Herman H. (R), GM3c
KUPAC, Wendel J. (R), SOM3c
KURTA, Stanley B. (R), LTJG
LARSEN, Howard R. (R), S1c
LAWLESS, John D., WT2c

LEE, James D. (R), S1c
LEWANDOWSKI, Edward P. (R), RDM3c
LEWIS, Edwin L., COX
LIVINGSTON, John C. (R), S1c
LOFTON, John H. (R), S1c
LOGAR, Henry J., QM2c
LONGMIRE, James C., GM3c
LYSAGHT, Marshall (R), CBM
MACLANE, Gordon H., LT
McCABE, Michael A., LTJG
McGRATH, Charles J. J., SOM2c
McMANUS, Edward J. (R), RM3c
McMULLEN, Roderick P. (R), F1c
MARTIN, Henry, Jr. (R), S1c
MASSMAN, John D. (R), COX
MEEBERG, Urho I., CM2c
MEEKER, Rex G., F1c
MERRITT, Charles T. (R), S1c
MILLER, Billy L. (R), F1c
MILLER, Harvey J., LTJG
MITCHELL, William G., SK1c
MOSCHETTI, George S. (R), MOMM1c
MUELLER, William H. (R), BM1c
MURRAY, Glen C. (R), S1c
NELSON, Roy C., MOMM1c
NICKERSON, Arthur V. (R), CM1c
NOACK, Roland H., Jr. (R), S1c
OHAYRE, Robert J. (R), LTJG
OLSEN, Bjarne O. (R), RDM3c
PAIN, Rodney H. H. (R), LTJG
PATTERSON, John E. (R), S1c
PAYNE, Ernest W., LT
PETRENKO, John, Jr. (R), CMOMM
PETRONICK, Theodore G. (R), S1c
PFISTER, Arthur F. (R), LCDR
POLLARD, Francis C., LCDR
PRAUSE, Robert H., LT
PRICHARD, George W., COX
PRITCHARD, John A., Jr., LT
RACANELLI, Vito N. (R), SOM2c

RAGAN, Oran D., BM2c
REDIGER, Jack N. (R), S1c
REDNOUR, Forrest O., SC2c
RIGGIO, Jimmie J. (R), MM3c
RISKDAHL, Wayne A. (R), MOMM1c
RITTENHOUSE, Robert F., CBM
ROARKE, Richard C. (R), SPPS1c
RODGERS, Charles D. (R), SPG1c
RUDLING, Walter G. (R), F1c
RUFF, James O. (R), GM3c
SAGAS, Robert (R), S1c
SANDERS, Carvar G. (R), BM2c
SEAMON, Max T. (R), S1c
SEAMON, William E. (R), MOMM3c
SHANK, Harold D. (R), GM2c
SMITH, Richard R., CDR
SMITH, Wilbur R. (R), ENS
SMITH, William E. (R), S1c
SPECK, Russell M., COX
STETKAR, Emil, BM1c
TERRIEN, Ross H., AMM1c
TEZANOS, Joseph (R), GM2c
THOMAS, Horace L. (R), CEM
TILLER, Jennings R. (R), S2c
TILLETT, Forest D., COX
VANDELEUR, John S., Jr., SM3c
VANDERMEER, Douglass D. (R), LTJG
VANDERSCOFF, Charles (R), EM2c
VANN, George D. (R), S1c
VILE, Robert G. (R), F1c
WARD, Thomas W., CBM
WARDELL, Edward (R), S1c
WEST, Milton O., Jr. (R), S1c
WIEGAND, Charles E., BM1c
WILDER, David W., BM1c
WILLIAMS, Fred W., Jr. (R), S2c
WILLIAMS, Robert H. (R), SPPS2c
WOLF, George M. (R), MOMM2c
YOUNG, J. E., QM2c
YOUNGGREN, Richard E. (R), LTJG

## Bronze Star Medal

★ *Combat citation*
† *With Combat V in lieu of second Navy Commendation Ribbon*
\* *In lieu of second Navy Commendation Ribbon*
‡ *In lieu of second Coast Guard Commendation Ribbon*

★AASHEIM, Torlief S. (R), LTJG
★ALEXANDER, Robert T., CDR
★ALLEN, Edward C., LCDR
★ALLEN, Nelson W. (R), SOM2c
★ANDERSON, Eric A., CDR
★★ANDERSON, Malcolm M. (R), RM3c
 ANDERSON, Robert P. (R), CDR
 ANDREWS, Bernard R., Jr., LT
 ANTHONY, Henry M., CDR
★ARNHART, Alvis D. (R), ENS
★BAKER, Lee H., CAPT
★BANKS, George, SC2c
★BARBER, Carter (R), SPPR1c

BARNES, Clifford A. (R), LCDR
★BECK, Rollo (R), BM1c
★★BECTON, Thomas L. (R), LT
★BEEZER, Earl F., BM1c
 BENDER, Chester R., LCDR
★BENDER, John L. (R), LT
★BENNETT, David E. (R), S1c
★BENSON, Clifford L. (R), LTJG
★BERG, Martin D. (R), LCDR
★BOHM, Charles H., BM1c
★BOOTH, John P., LTJG
★BOYETTE, James S. (R), S1c
 BRADBURY, Harold G., CAPT

★BURKHARD, Arthur H., Jr., COX
*BUXTON, Winslow H., CDR
★CASS, William F., LCDR
★CHAFIN, Thurman F., S1c
★CHEEVER, William A. (R), BOSN
★CLAIBORNE, Charles B., LT
★COBURN, Winston T. (R), SOM3c
COLE, Norman R. (R), LCDR
★COLE, Vernon (R), S1c
★COLLINS, Garland W., CDR
★CONNOR, Thomas H. (R), MOMM1c
★CONTI, Edward P. (R), COX
★COOK, Kenneth C. (R), LT
COWAN, Russel, LT
†COWART, Kenneth K., CDR
CROMWELL, Robert P., LCDR
DANIEL, Clarence N., CDR
★DAVIS, Alan W., COX
★DAY, Robert B. (R), LTJG
★DEAN, Charles W., CAPT
DEJOY, Anthony J., CDR
★DIEHL, Herman T., CDR
★*DOBBINS, Clifford F., BM1c
★DODD, Neal D., SOM3c
★DOFBLER, Harold J., CDR
★DOYLE, Ora, LCDR
★EDGE, Robert R., LCDR
★ELLIS, William B., CDR
★ELMER, Robert E. P., Jr. (R), LTJG
★ENBODY, David B. (R), LCDR
★ETHERIDGE, Louis C., Jr., SD1c
★EVERSFIELD, William, S1c
★FARRAR, Arthur (R), LTJG
★FLANAGAN, Eugene L., Jr. (R), LTJG
*FORNEY, John H., CDR
★FORTIER, Gerald A., CBM
★FORTNER, Lawrence T., BM1c
★FRACKELTON, John J., ENS
★FREEMAN, Frank W., MOMM2c
★FRENCH, Reginald H., CAPT
★FRIED, Robert A. (R), BM2c
★FROLICK, Seymour J. (R), LTJG
★FROST, Edwin R., LTJG
★FULCHER, William U., LT
★FULFORD, Nathaniel S., CDR
★GARNER, David (R), RM1c
★GENTGES, Leigh A. (R), LTJG
★GIBBS, Isaac K., CBM
★GILLERAN, Clarence J., LT
★GILTNER, William F. (R), COX
★GLEASON, Friend W., Jr. (R), LTJG
★GOLDMAN, Robert (R), PHM2c
★GORDON, William H., SURG(USPHS)
†GRAY, Samuel F., CDR
★GREEN, Harold W., BM2c
★GRIFFITH, Robert L., LCDR
★GUZIK, Raymond R., MOMM2c
★HAGEN, Paul F. (R), BM2c
★HANNIGAN, John F., BM2c
HARDER, Raymond W., Jr. (R), ENS

★HARDIN, Truman C. (R), LTJG
★HARMON, Freeman H., LT
HARNED, Albert E., CDR
★*HAY, Sidney M., LCDR
*HEARN, Gerard A., LTJG
★HELIGER, Francis J., LT
★HELLMAN, Paul B., LT
†HELMER, Frank V., LCDR
HERBERT, Clarence, CDR
★HEWINS, John S. (R), LTJG
★HIGBEE, Frank D., RADM
HILDITCH, Frank D., LTJG
★HILTON, Robert M. (R), LT
★HOBBS, Robert K. (R), BM2c
★HOPPER, William D., Jr. (R), WT1c
★HOWARD, Sam F. (R), BM2c
HUTSON, John J., Jr., CDR
★IVY, Charles B., MOMM1c
JACOT, Julius F., CAPT
★JADRO, Edward P., LT
★JESTER, Erman E., COX
★JOHNS, Bergum K., COX
★JOHNSON, Henry G., Jr., COX
★JOHNSON, John M. (R), LTJG
★JOHNSON, Owen J. (R), LTJG
JOSEPH, John M., CDR
★KAHN, Lewis, PHM1c
‡KARCH, Joseph J., BM2c
★KARR, Teddy M., COX
★KASHINSKAS, Jerome F., MOMM1c
★KEISER, Edward J., Jr., COX
★KELLAM, John H., ENS
★KELLEY, Thomas N. (R), LCDR
KENNER, William W., CAPT
KIMBALL, Richard S. (R), BM1c
★KROHN, Abraham, S2c
★KRON, Eldred J. (R), LT
★KURTA, Stanley B. (R), LTJG
★LAPLACE, Louis E., Lt
†LEAMY, Frank A., CAPT
★LEE, Melvin S. (R), HA2c
★LENCI, John, LT
LEWIS, Edward E., CHMACH
★LINDQUIST, Karl A. E., LCDR
★LITTLEFIELD, Gordon A., CAPT
★LODGE, Robert K., COX
★LOWELL, James W. (R), LTJG
★LOWERY, George A., CBM
★LUSE, James D., LT
★McCABE, Frank M., LCDR
★McCABE, George E., CAPT
★McELLIGOTT, Raymond T., RADM
★McGILLICUDDY, Leo X., COX
★McGOWAN, W. H., LT
★McKENDREE, William D., S1c
★McMILLAN, William M., BM1c
★*McNEIL, Donald C., CAPT
★McNICHOLS, Stephen L. (R), LTJG
★McPHAIL, Richard V. (R), LTJG
★*MacBRYDE, Ernest P., LCDR

★MacDONALD, Everett W. (R), MOMM1c
★MacKAY, James A., LTJG
★MACKLIN, Edward E. (R), F1c
★MAINA, Everett (R), LTJG
★MALEY, Kenneth P., CAPT
★MARRON, Raymond V., CAPT
MARTIN, John F. (R), LCDR
★MATHIS, Virgil B. (R), MOMM1c
★MAUERMAN Raymond J., CAPT
★MAVOR, Preston B., CDR
★MEEKINS, George Tinsley (R), ENS
★MICHELS, John H., LT
★MIDTLYNG, Thomas R., CDR
★MILLINGTON, Walter B., CDR
MONTRELLO, John, CDR
★MOORE, Harold C., CAPT
★MORINE, Leon H., CAPT
★★MORRISON, William L., LCDR
★MULHERN, Raymond K. (R), BM1c
★MURPHY, Daniel F., Jr. (R), BM2c
MUTRIE, Joseph A. (R), LCDR
NEEDHAM, Clifford G., LTJG
NELSON, Foster O. W., Jr. (R), LT
★NEWELL, Raymond B., LT
★NICHOLS, Rae F. (R), LT
★NIKOLENKO, Nicholas (R), BM2c
★NORTH, James B., BM2c
★★NORTON, James A., LCDR
★O'BRIEN, Austin F. (R), PHM2c
★O'BRIEN, Esmonde F., Jr. (R), LTJG
★OLSEN, Severt A., CAPT
★OLSON, Russell I. (R), RM3c
★OWEN, Robert W. (R), S1c
★OWENS, Francis L. (R), HA2c
★PAINE, James W., LCDR
★PARKER, John L., Jr., COX
★PARKER, Robert K. (R), MOMM1c
★PARRISH, William S. (R), LT
★PATTYSON, Brewster G. (R), ENS
PEDERSEN, Arne C., LT
PEER, Richard S. (R), ENS
★PERKINS, Henry C., CAPT
★PETERSON, Clarence H., CAPT
★PFEIFFER, Arthur, LCDR
★PHILLIP, Gordon P. (R), LT
★POLLACK, Augustus (R), LCDR
★POWERS, Burke I., LT
★POWERS, James A. (R), S2c
★PRESTIDGE, James C., CMOMM
★PUTZKE, Stanley G., LTJG
★RADKE, Charles W., LCDR
★RAHLE, Oliver, LT
★RANEY, Roy L., CAPT
★RAU, Robert C. (R), LTJG
★RAWSTHORNE, John W., Jr. (R), LT
★REEVES, Jack J., BM2c
RICHMOND, Alfred C., CAPT
★RIEDEL, William R., LCDR
★RIGG, Henry K. (R), LT
★RILEY, Francis X., LT

★RISSER, Gordon K. (R), BM2c
★ROBERTSHAW, Jacob D. (R), LT
ROLLINS, Glenn L., CDR
★RUA, Louis (R), F1c
★RUBERTS, Dick W., PHM3c
★RYAN, Billy R., LTJG
★SAIT, John A. (R), LT
★SANDS, Simon R., Jr., CDR
★SARGENT, Thomas R. III, LCDR
★SCALAN, Bernard E., CDR
★SCAMMELL, William K., RADM
★SCHARFENSTEIN, Charles F., Jr., LT
★SCHARFF, Charles W., LT
★SCHEU, Robert S. (R), LTJG
★SCHOPPERT, Kenton P. (R), ENS
★SCOLES, Robert D. (R), GM1c
★SCOTT, Lee R., CDR
★SHIPP, Wallace E., PHM2c
★SIAS, Howard M., LT
★SMART, Ned E. (R), S1c
★SMITH, Edwin F. (R), ENS
★SMITH, James P., LTJG
★SMITH, Richard R., CDR
SMITH, Wallace W., ENS
★SOMMA, Anthony S., CM1c
SOULE, Floyd M., CDR
★STACKHOUSE, Harry A., Jr. (R), LTJG
STARR, John, LTJG
★STEINMETZ, John L., CAPT
★★STEPHENS, Irvin J., CDR
★STEWART, Alexander H., LCDR
★STEWART, Melvin L. (R), LT
STOBER, Carl H., CDR
★STRAUCH, William D., Jr. (R), LT
★SUMMER, John F. (R), LTJG
SUMMERFIELD, Albert J., LT
★SUTINEN, Wesley M., BM1c
★SUTPHIN, Clarence H., BM1c
★SWEENEY, William F. (R), GM3c
SWEENY, Charles A. (R), LT
★SWIERC, Michael J., MOMM1c
★SYNON, George D., CDR
★THARP, Edward R., LTJG
★THOMAS, Charles W., CAPT
THORIGAL, Gordon P. (R), BM2c
★THRESHER, Russell W., LCDR
★TILLMAN, William N., ENS
★TOLLAKSEN, Leslie B., LCDR
★TOWNSEND, Marshall O., SOM1c
★TRESTER, Glenn E., CDR
★TUCKER, Frank A. (R), COX
★TWIFORD, Marvin H., LTJG
★VACLAVEK, John M., Jr., COX
★VanNOSTRAND, LeRoy, LT
★VERNON, Albert B. (R), LTJG
★VETTERICK, Fred P., CAPT
★VITOLANO, Alfred M., COX
★VOLTON, Alfred, LT
★WALDRON, John A. (R), LTJG
WALKER, Paul F., SURG USPHS

WELCH, Richard G. (R), MOMM2c
★WHITE, Howard A., LCDR
★WHITEHOUSE, Henry, LT
★WIGGIN, Philip M., COX
★★WILCOX, Robert, CDR
★WILLIAMS, Wilbert D. B. (R), S2c

★WILSON, William E., BM2c
★WOOD, Bernard B. (R), ENS
★WRIGHT, Sidney G., COX
★★YOUNG, Maynard F., LCDR
ZEUSLER, Frederick A., RADM

## Air Medal

*† Gold Star in lieu of second award*

ADAMS, John H., AOM1c
AIKEN, Roy E., ADC
ALLARDICE, Corbin C. (R), LTJG
ALLEN, Bernard W. (R), ARM1c
†ALLEN, Carl H., LT
BAILEY, Bernard A. (R), LT
BARKER, Lloyd E. (R), AMM1c
BAUM, William S., SURG USPHS
BAXTER, Richard, CDR
BEHRENDS, Curth W., AMM2c
BELL, Claud K., ARM1c
BENNETT, Harold, ENS
BERRETH, William M. (R), AMM2c
BIEBER, Bruce A., GM1c
BIGLOW, Palmer W. Jr. (R), AP1c
†BILDERBACK, Kenneth M., LT
BLISH, Howard J., LTJG
BLYDENBURGH, Raymond, AMM2c
BOGGS, George H. Jr., ARM1c
BOLTON, Walter C., LT
†BOTELER, James C., LT
BOWERS, Maurice L., LT
BOYAJIAN, Edward A. (R), AMM1c
BRANDSTROM, Nels A. (R), AMM2c
BRASWELL, Wheeler M., LTJG
BRESNAHAN, Richard T., ARM1c
BROCKLEHURST, Charles E., CRM
BROCKWAY, Edward D. (R), AMM2c
BROOKS, Jeremiah P., AMM1c
BROWN, Fletcher W. Jr., LT
BROWN, Graham J., AMM1c
BRUNK, Robert W. (R), LT
BURCH, Francis X., AMM1c
BURTON, Joe T., AMM1c
BUSWELL, Charles C., AMM1c
BUTLER, Ralph W., ENS
CADAM, James H. (R), ARM1c
CADE, Ross D., ACRM
CAVIC, George (R), AMM2c
CHAPLINE, William E. Jr., LCDR
†CHILDERS, Earl S., ENS
COBAUGH, Donald, AD1(AP)
COBB, Charles A., ARM1c
COFFEE, Harry D. (R), ARM2c
COFFEE, William H. Jr., ENS
COLE, Norman R. (R), LCDR
COLER, Charles L., LTJG
COLVIN, Robert A. (R), ARM2c
COOK, Lloyd A., AMM1c
CORNISH, James A., LCDR

CORRIGAN, Joseph B., AOM2c
CREEF, Benjamin A., AMM1c
CROMWELL, Robert P., LCDR
CROMWELL, William J. (R), ARM2c
CUPPLES, Andrew J., ENS
CURTIS, George A. (R), AMM2c
†DAMERON, Ben B., LTJG
DAVID, Malcolm J. (R), AMM3c
DeFREEST, David W., AP1c
DeMICHAELS, LaSalle P. (R), AMM1c
†DONAHUE, William E., ARM1c
DONNEL, James A. (R), AMM2c
DONNELLY, Jack W. (R), AMM2c
DURHAM, William N., LT
ECKELS, Harry H., LT
EDDY, Sedgwick R., ENS
EDGMON, Alfred A., AP1c
EISENSTAT, Irving (R), ARM1c
ELLERY, Richard O., AOM2c
EMERSON, Robert E., LCDR
EPLER, Donald F., ACRM
EPPERLY, Vinton A. (R), AMM1c
ERICKSON, Frank A., CDR
ETHERIDGE, Charles S., AMM1c
†EVANS, Gilbert R., LCDR
FAK, Robert (R), ARM1c
FENDLAY, Robert W., ENS
FENNELL, George E., AD3(P)
FERGUSON, Joseph H., AMM1c
FERRANTO, John J. Jr., AOM1c
FERRIN, Glen D., CAP
FINKLEA, James R., ARM1c
FLETCHER, Edward, AMM2c
FROST, Grant N., AMM1c
FRYZEL, Edward S. (R), ARM1c
GALYEAN, Willard E., AMM2c
GERBER, George J., AMM1c
GERBINO, Anthony, ACMM
GERWE, Vincent J., AMM1c
GIGLIO, Samuel Jr., AMM2c
GOODWIN, William B. Jr., AL1
GOULD, Robert C., LCDR
GRAFF, Howard J., AMM2c
†GRAHAM, Stewart R., LCDR
GREEN, James E., AMM1c
GREGORY, Robert L., CAP
GUILLEMETTE, Albert (R), LTJG
GUST, Louis Jr., CAP
HALLOCK, Thomas P. (R), LCDR
HALSEY, Jack, AD1

HARVEY, Herman H., AOM2c
HAYES, James C. (R), RM2c
HAYMON, Otis W., AOM2c
HAZEL, Gordon S., AMM1c
HEATH, James L. Jr., ARM2c
HECKERT, William C., AMM2c
HEDDRICK, John S. (R), AMM1c
HEDRICK, Ernest D., LTJG
HERSEY, Paul F., LTJG
HICKMAN, William L., ARM1c
HINCKLEY, Ralph R., AMM1c
HOGAN, Joseph A., AMM2c
HOLTER, Leonard O., AMM2c
HUCKS, Frank B., AOM2c
HYNES, Thomas J., LT
ING, Edwin B., LCDR
JAMES, Henry C., ARM1c
JOHNSON, John B. (R), ENS
JOHNSON, Reinhold R., LCDR
JONES, Donald L., ARM1c
JONES, Phillip R., AMM1c
KEATING, Robert R. (R), ARM2c
KELLOGG, Glen I., ENS
KENDERSON, Alex G. (R), ARM1c
KIENHOLZ, Robert B., AOM2c
KILBOURN, Rex W., AMM1c
KILLEBREW, William N. (R), LTJG
KIMBALL, Richard S. (R), BM1c
KING, Herbert H. (R), ARM1c
†KLEISCH, August, LT
KNOLL, Arthur N., ENS
KNOX, Roland S., ARM1c
KOTOWSKI, Melvin, AOM1c
KREGER, Sidney E. (R), LT
KROPF, Elba P., AP1c
LANTZ, Walter T., ARM1c
LAWLIS, Robert L., LCDR
LEE, Charles R., CMM
LEISY, Charles R., LTJG
LeNARZ, LeRoy A. Jr., AOM1c
LOCKE, Joyce D. (R), AMM1c
LOCKHART, James B. (R), AMM1c
LOCKWOOD, Charles W., LTJG
MacDIARMID, Donald B., CDR
MacDOWELL, Charles E. (R), LTJG
McCALL, John W. (R), AMM1c
McCORMICK, Joseph T., ENS
McCUBBIN, John D., LT
McCULLOUGH, Joseph W., ARM1c
McGOVERN, Gerald E., LTJG
McGOWAN, Ford, AMM1c
McKERNAM, Samuel S., AMM1c
McLANE, Leon J. (R), AMM2c
McMULLAN, Ira H., LT
McWILLIAMS, Theodore, LTJG
MAGUIRE, Charles C. (R), AOM1c
MAKS, Walter (R), AMM2c
MARSHALL, Raymond E. (R), AOM2c
MASON, Woodrow H., ARM1c
†MATHISON, Elmer P., LTJG

MERRILL, Eddie F., AMM1c
MIGLIORI, Gaetano, RM1c
MILES, Emerson W. (R), LTJG
MOORE, Bernard, ARM1c
MORELL, Donald M., LT
MORRILL, William C., LT
MORTENSEN, Henry E., ARM1c
MRKOBRADA, Walter (R), GM2c
MUELLER, Truman M., ARM1c
NIPPER, Fred A. (R), AOM3c
NOVAK, John (R), RM2c
NYEGARD, Lawrence K., AMM2c
NYSTROM, Donald A., AD1(AP)
OSTERBURG, Ralph E., CAP
OTTEM, Warren L., AMM1c
OWEN, Kenneth B., ARM2c
PAUK, Harold M., AMM1c
PAYTON, J. D., AOM2c
PEPMEIER, Donald L., RM2c
PERKINS, Allen F., LTJG
PETERSEN, Robert J. (R), AMM1c
PINNEY, Herbert W., AMM1c
PROFITT, George L., AMM2c
PROSE, Leroy A., ARM1c
PUGLIESE, Robert A. (R), AMM2c
RADKE, Leonard M. (R), AOM2c
RANDALL, Kirby K., ARM1c
READING, Edward J. (R), AMM2c
RESS, Ruben (R), ARM1c
RICHARD, Leo J., AMM1c
RICHTER, George L. Jr., AD2
RIELLY, Robert B. (R), AOM2c
RIES, Elmer V., AMM2c
RIGGS, James L., LTJG
ROBE, William E. (R), AP1c
ROBERTS, John D., ARM1c
ROZIER, Walter L., AP1c
RUPP, Ralph, AMM2c
SALSBURY, Vaughn E. (R), LT
SCHONING, Rudolph H., ARM1c
†SCHRADER, James N., LCDR
SEIDL, James C. Jr., ENS
SHAW, Harold Z., AMM1c
SHEA, John M. (R), AOM1c
SHEHTANIAN, John H. (R), GM2c
SHELTON, Francis A. (R), LT
SHIELDS, James W. (R), LT
SIERAWSKI, Felix J., ARM2c
SKARDA, Everett A., AP1c
SNYDER, Henry, AMM1c
STEWART, Francis P., ARM1c
STONGE, Joseph E. W., ARM2c
SWAIN, Grover C., RM1c
SWANSON, Ernest M., AMM1c
SWANSTON, William I., CDR
TANGHERLINI, Louis A., ARM1c
TAYLOR, Clifford (R), AOM2c
TAYLOR, Donald E., CRM
TIMBER, William A., AMM1c
TOWEY, Stuart C. (R), AMM2c

TRACY, George R. A., AMM1c
TROMBLEY, James E. (R), GM1c
VOLDISH, Adolph S., ARM1c
WALLACE, Joseph B., AMM1c
WALLACE, William C., LTJG
WALTERS, Herbert, AOM2c
†WARD, Ellis P., ENS
WARNER, George S. (R), LT
WEBB, Harold W., AOM2c
WEEKS, Sherman M. (R), PHOM2c
WELLS, Lyman C., BM2c
WERTIS, John G., AMM2c
WESSELS, Lester F. (R), AOM1c
WHITE, Darrell E., AOM1c

WHITE, George W., AMM1c
WHITE, Henry C., LT
WIDENER, Eugene A., AMM2c
WILLIAMS, Winford C., ARM1c
WILLIS, Hardy M., AP1c
WILSON, Owen T. (R), AMM1c
WOJCICKI, Alfred W., ACRM
WOLFE, Seymour, CAP
WOOD, James A. (R), ARM1c
YEAGER, Joseph A., AMM1c
YOUNG, Oliver S., AMM1c
ZEGOROWSKI, Leos, AMM2c
ZEIGLER, Herbert D., ARM1c
ZINKEL, Warren, AOM1c

## Navy Commendation Ribbon

### ★ Combat citation

ABBOTT, Samuel Jr. (R), SOM3c
ACKERMAN, Andrew G., Jr. (R), CCM
ADAMS, Edward J. (R), LT
★ALEXANDER, Edward A., CWT
ALGER, James A., Jr., CDR
ALLEN, Nelson W. (R), SOM2c
ANDERSON, Chester M., CDR
ANDERSON, Langford (R), LCDR
ANDERSON, Rudolph A., LT
APPEL, Edward L., AMM1c
★ARNOLD, Earlie D. (R), MOMM3c
★ARRINGTON, Charles B., CDR
★ASHLEY, Charles O., LCDR
AUGE, Roger J., LT
AYDLETT, Willard T. (R), CMOMM
★AYERS, Kingdrel N., LT
BACCHUS, R. E. (R), LCDR
BAKANAS, Victor E., LCDR
★BAKER, Henry C. G., BOSN
★BAKER, Ludlow S., LT
BAKETEL, Sherman T. (R), LCDR
★BARNARD, Philip E., CBM
★BARNES, Eddie W., CM3c
★BARRINGTON, Carl A. (R), MOMM3c
BARTON, William H., CAPT
★BATES, Albert J., CBM
BAYLIS, John S., COMMO
BEAL, Ira A., Jr., CGM
★BECTON, Thomas L. (R), LT
★BELL, Ora L. (R), S1c
BENDOSKI, Lawrence (R), STM2c
BENNETT, Louis L., CAPT
BERARD, Gilbert, CCM
BERNARD, Lawrence J. (R), CAPT
BLAUCIAK, Daniel J., S1c
★BLAUHUT, Bernard B. (R), LTJG
BLUNT, Virginia H. (W), LCDR
BONER, Robert M., S1c
★BORROMEY, Romeo J., CDR
BOSLEY, Frederick (R), SK1
★BOVARD, Benjamin L. (R), S1c
★BOYCE, George R., Jr., CDR

★BRASS, Alfred W., ENS
★BRIDGES, Lamar G., CGM
BRIDGES, Lonnie, LTJG
★BRIGHT, Thomas F. (R), LT
BRIERLEY, D. S. (TR), CAPT
BRITTON, Martin M., WT1c
BROOKS, Earle G., CDR
BROSSMAN, Thomas J. (R), WT3c
★BRUNK, Julius J., LTJG
BURDINE, George M. (R), LT
BURHORST, Paul E., LCDR
BURKE, Richard L., CDR
★BURMESTER, Louis E., BM2c
★BURRUS, Luther D., BM2c
★BURT, Robert F., LTJG
BURTON, Watson A., CDR
BUSALACCHI, Charles I., S2c
★BUTLER, Richard (R), S1c
★BUXTON, Winslow H., CDR
★CAIN, William C. (R), LT
CANKAR, Frank (R), LT
★CANTERBURY, Russell E., COX
CAPPS, Robert E., S1c
★CAPRON, Walter C., CDR
★CARLOUGH, Leroy J. (R), S1c
★CARR, Frederick W., Jr. (R), LTJG
★CARROLL, Donald J., S2c
CARROLL, William H., CDR
★CARSON, Robert F. (R), QM1c
CHASE, Peter (R), ENS
★CLARK, Benjamin P., LCDR
CLARK, Eldredge W., S1c
★CLIZBE, Garth D., LTJG
★COBURN, Winston T. (R), SOM3c
★COFFIN, Eugene A., Jr., CDR
★COLEMAN, Eben M. (R), GM3c
★COMBS, Edward W. 3rd., BM2c
★CONKLIN, Randall J., COX
COOMBS, Robert E. (R), CAPT
★COPPENS, John H., BM2c
CORNELL, John H., COMMO
★COUSINS, Morris W., CMM

COWART, Kenneth K., RADM
★COX, Joe M., Jr., BM2c
COYLE, Henry, CAPT (Ret.)
CRAFT, Albert B., Jr., LTJG
CRIMMINGS, John D. (R), LTJG
★CROTTY, Thomas J. E., LT
CROWLEY, Teresa M. (W), LCDR
CRYE, Warren G. (R), BM1c
CURRY, Ralph R., CDR
★CZACHOWSKI, Henry C. (R), MOMM3c
★DANNISON, Byron G., CBM
DEANE, John C. (R), LTJG
★DECARLO, Joseph J., LCDR
★DELAMARTER, Donald E. (R), COX
DEMPSEY, William H. (R), CDR
DENCH, Clarence H., CAPT
★DENK, Michael T. (R), S2c
★DIGIOVANNI, Edward F., STM2c
DILLON, Frederick P., COMMO
★DIRKS, John A., CDR
DIXON, John J. (R), LCDR
★DOBBINS, Clifford F., BM1c
DOLAN, Thomas D. (R), BM1c
★DONAHUE, Robert (R), BM2c
★DORFMAN, Bernard, COX
★DOUGLAS, Sidney W., LTJG
DOYLE, Harry A., BM1c
DOYLE, Paul T. (R), MOMM2c
★DRISCOLL, Thomas F. (R), RM2c
DRISKO, Donald A., AMM1c
DROS, Dirk A., LT
DUFFEY, David L. (R), PHM2c
DUGAN, Clarence L. (R), S1c
★DUNCAN, Albert D. (R), S1c
EATON, Philip B., RADM
EDWARDS, Roderick Y., LCDR
EHLERS, Gosch L., LT
★EICHHORN, Thomas D. (R), S1c
★EISENREICH, Thomas, BM1c
★ELLIS, Merle D. (R), S2c
★ELMER, Robert E. P., Jr. (R), LTJG
ERICKSEN, Earl A. (R), S2c
★ESKRIDGE, Ira E., CAPT
★EVANS, Kenneth E. (R), RM3c
FAIRBANK, John E., CAPT
★FARRISH, James A., BM2c
FELTS, Lewayne N., LTJG
★FERNANDEZ, Valentin R., COX
★FERRARI, Frank J., CMM
★FICK, Edward N. (R), BM2c
★FINCH, Jack H. (R), STM2c
★FINGER, Charles E., LTJG
★FINK, Morton M. (R), SOM3c
★FINLEY, Robert W., LCDR
FIRTH, Thomas J., LT
FISHER, Kenneth J. (R), EM3c
FLOWERS, Roy B., BM1c
FLYNN, Joseph J. (R), CDR
FOGEL, John R. (R), F1c
★FORNEY, John H., CDR

★FORREST, Earl M., COX
FORRESTER, Jack E., LTJG
★FRANCESCONI, Enzo, CSM
★FRICK, Sherman K., LT
FRIED, George (TR), CAPT
★FRYE, Lowell R. (R), LTJG
★GALLOWAY, Grady R. (R), LT
GEHLKEN, Ralph L. (R), CCM
★GEIST, Sidney R., Jr. (R), LTJG
★GELLY, George B., CAPT
★GENAME, Fred J., CMM
GEOGHEGAN, William C. (R), LT
★GEORGE, Howard B. Jr., COX
★GEORGE, Justin V. (R), SC3c
★GEORGE, Melvin F. (R), S1c
GERBINO, Anthony, ACMM
★GIELOW, Francis H. P. (R), GM2c
GILL, Irving L., CAPT
★GLYNN, William M., EM1c
GOODWIN, Stuart B., CBM
GOSCH, Martin E., COX
★GRADIN, Ellis F., LCDR
GRAHAM, Stewart R., LCDR
★GRAMMER, Allen H., LTJG
★GRAY, Samuel F., CDR
GREEN, Harold W., BM2c
★GREENE, Charles A., LT
★GREENSPUN, Joseph, CAPT
GROSSWEILER, Irving L. (R), MOMM3c
★GUISNESS, Carl E., CAPT
★HAAS, Joseph J., Jr., QM3c
★HAFFERT, William A., Jr. (R), SPPR1c
★HAGAN, Marshall J., S1c
★HAIRE, Andrew J., Jr. (R), LT
★HALL, Norman B., Jr. (R), LCDR
★HAMILTON, Raymond E., CBM
★HAND, Robert F. (R), CSPPS
HANSON, Thomas W., F1c
★HARKER, Frank B. (R), LCDR
★HARMER, William G., BM2c
HARRISON, Kenneth S., CAPT
★HARSFALD, Leon (R), SOM2c
★HARTLEY, Harold W. (R), SM2c
HAVLICEK, Joseph W., LT
★HAY, Sidney M., LCDR
HAYES, Phillip C. (R), S1c
HEARN, Gerard A., LTJG
HECK, Stephen B., LT
★HEDGES, Kenneth M. (R), S2c
HEINER, John N., CAPT
★HELMER, Frank V., LCDR
★HENDERSON, John, SURF
HENDRICKS, Charles W. (R), S2c
HESS, Leon A. T., BM1c
★HESTER, Joseph A. (R), ST2c
HICKEY, William L. (R), MOMM2c
★HILL, Thomas E., BM2c
★HILTBRUNER, William C. (R), S1c
★HINDERMANN, Richard L. (R), ENS
★HINDMAN, James G. (R), STM1c

HODGES, Stanley V., COX
★HOFSTETTER, Seymure (R), CPHOM
★HOGUE, Alfred J., LT
★HOLSINGTON, Richard E. (R), SM3c
★HOLIFIELD, James F., CAPT
★HOLLERN, Daniel F. (R), SOM3c
HOLLOMAN, Farrol D. (R), COX
HOOK, Arthur, LT
★HORNE, Richard L., CDR
★HOUGHTALING, Edward H., LCDR
★HOWARD, Douglas F. (R), LCDR
★HOWARD, Robert C. (R), S1c
★HUBER, George F., CBM
★HUDGENS, Edward D., Jr., LT
★HUFF, Carl N., LT
★HUNTER, Harold A. (R), GM2c
HUUS, William A. (R), CBM
IMLAY, Miles H., CAPT
★INGALLS, Howard S., LT
★IRWIN, Charles B., Jr. (R), LT
★JACKSON, William W. (R), PHM3c
JACOBS, Donald G., CAPT
★JANCZYLIK, Joseph P., CBM
JEFFERIES, Robert F. (R), COX
JENNINGS, Glen S., LT
JENSEN, Jens H., LCDR
JEWELL, Henry T., CAPT
★JOB, Walter T., CMOMM
JONES, Roscoe N., Jr. (R), COX
JORDAN, Beckwith, COMMO
★JULIUS, William D. (R), RM2c
★JUMONVILLE, Felix J. (R), LTJG
KAPNER, Harold (R), ENS
★KEENE, Henry C., Jr., LT
★KELLY, James L., CQM
★KELZ, Gerhard K., LT
KENLY, William R., LCDR
★KERRIGAN, Edward P., BM2c
★KERRINS, Joseph A., CAPT
KIMBERLY, James H., CDR
KIMBRELL, John D., MOMM1c
★KING, Roy E. (R), MOMM2c
KINGSLEY, Arthur B. (R), LTJG
KLEIN, Herbert W., AOM1c
★KNAPP, Christopher C., CDR
KNISKERN, Henry P., LCDR
★KOBIALKA, Edmund R., MACH
KOSSLER, William J., CAPT
★KOSTIVAL, Joseph J. (R), S1c
★KREIDER, William J. (R), RM2c
★KRON, Eldred J., LT
★KURTA, Stanley B. (R), LTJG
★KUTZLER, James D., Jr., CMOMM
★KWELBERG, Sam (R), S1c
LACCABUE, Richard C. (R), CSK
LANDEFELD, John W., LTJG
★LANGEVIN, Edmond F. (R), GM2c
LANK, Rutherford B., Jr., CAPT
LANKE, Max H., CPH
★LARAIA, Nicholas A. (R), WT1c

★LARSON, Peter F. (R), S2c
★LASHORNE, Paul R. (R), SM2c
LASTINGER, Claude L., S1c
LAWRENCE, Eugenia (W), LCDR
★LEA, Reedie L. (R), S1c
★LEACH, Warren D. (R), LTJG
LEAMY, Frank A., CAPT
LEBLANC, Theodore, CDR
★LEMAY, Jesse U. (R), MOMM2c
LENDVAY, Paul J., BM2c
LESLIE, Norman H., COMMO
★LEWIS, Aiden E., LT
★LEWIS, Ernest J., BM1c
LEWIS, Stanley E., LT
★LORD, Samuel J., LT
★LORENTZEN, Laurence D. (R), SC3c
★LOUGHLIN, Harry A., CDR
LOWRY, Gilbert M. (R), SC1c
LUMPKIN, John H. (R), LCDR
★LYDON, John M., Bosn
LYNCH, Gilbert I., CDR
★MacBRYDE, Ernest P., LCDR
MacLANE, Gordon W., CAPT
★MacLEAN, Clifford R., CDR
★McCABE, Frank M., LCDR
★McCALL, Daniel F., Jr., PHM3c
McCANN, Gerald R. (R), CSP (PR)
★McGUIRE, Malcolm C., LT
★McLAUGHLIN, Hugh D., Jr. (R), SPCW2c
★McNAMARA, James C. (R), S1c
★McNAMARA, Theodore J. (R), S1c
★McNEIL, Donald C., CAPT
★McNEMER, George W. (R), F1c
★McTAMNEY, Paul F., COX
MAGNUSON, James L., BM2c
MAGNUSSON, Magnus C. (R), LT
★MANN, Robert R. (R), RDM3c
★MARENTAY, Phillip N., COX
★MARSHALL, William J. (R), SM3c
★MARSTON, James G. (R), RDM2c
MARTER, E. Budd III (TR), CDR
★MARTIN, George A. (R), LT
MARTIN, Joseph P., LCDR
MARTS, Arnaud C. (R), CAPT
★MATARAZZO, Orlando J. (R), SC1c
MATHEWS, Eugene T. (R), LT
★MATTHEWS, Richard A., MOMM1c
★MAURER, Norman W., COX
MEALS, Frank M., CAPT
MEHLMAN, Stewart P., CDR
MELLOTT, Davis, LT
★MELTON, Earl (R), MM2c
MERCEY, Arch A. (R), CDR
MERRILL, Robert T. (R), CAPT
★MEYER, Henry A., CDR
MEYER, Ineva R. (W), LCDR
MILLER, Ralph R., COX
MILLER, Raymond M., ENS
★MILLER, Samuel R. (R), CM1c
★MINER, Frank E. (R), LCDR

MINOR, Arthur P., LCDR
★MIRAKIAN, Joseph J. (R), MOMM3c
★MOEHRING, Harold J. (R), SC3c
MOLONY, Donald P. (R), PHM3c
★MONAGHAN, Francis W., MOMM2c
MORGAN, Harry L., LCDR
MORRISON, Walter, LTJG
MORRISON, William L., LCDR
★MOULTON, William H., LCDR
★MOUW, William J. (R), SC3c
★MUELLER, Robert A., BM1c
MULFORD, Robert A. (R), S1c
MURRAY, Russell M., S1c
★NAVIGANTE, Louis, S1c
NILES, Palmer A., CDR
★NIMS, George I. (R), SC2c
★NIRSCHEL, Fred W. (R), LCDR
NIX, Ralph R., AS USPHS
NORMAN, Arvid F. (R), LT
NORTON, James A., LCDR
★OLSON, Carl R. G. (R), F2c
ONEAL, Maltire N., CMOMM
★OWENS, Harry, CMOMM
★PADUR, John D. (R), COX
PAIRAN, William F. R. (R), S1c
★PALKO, George (R), MOMM2c
PALMER, William P., Jr., LT
★PARAS, James, BM2c
★PARSONS, Robert W., MOMM3c
★PATERNA, William J. (R), Y3c
PATRICK, Clyde F., Jr. (R), S1c
★PATTON, William A., Jr. (R), RM3c
★PEARSON, Gustave W., LCDR
★PEGGS, Frederick M. (R), PHM3c
★PELLEGRINELLI, Mario C., COX
★PELT, Harry (R), S1c
★PENNAMEN, Robert C. (R), S1c
★PERLICK, Domenic P. (R), MOMM2c
★PERRY, Anthony, Jr. (R), MOMM3c
PETTERSEN, Petter G. (R), CDR
★PFEIFFER, Victor, LCDR
PICHON, Earl J. (R), S1c
★PLUMMER, John H. (R), LTJG
POIS, Joseph (R), CAPT
POLIHRONOPOLOS, Angelo (R), S1c
POLLARD, Francis C., LCDR
POLLIO, Frank E., CAPT
★POLLOCK, Alvin, COX
PREBLE, Stanley P., BM1c
PRESTON, Allen R. (R), MOMM1c
QUINN, George C. (R), AS
RANEY, Roy L., CAPT
★RAWSTHORNE, John W., Jr. (R), LT
★RAYCRAFT, George E., Jr. (R), LTJG
★REA, Richard F., CDR
★REGE, John H., COX
★REYNOLDS, Francis S., BM2c
RICE, Harold D. (TR), LCDR
★RICE, Richard H., QM1c
RICH, Woodward B. (R), LT

★RICHARDSON, Herbert H., CY
RICHEY, Julius E., CDR
RIDENOUR, Robert G., ENS
★RIDGELY, Randolph, III, CDR
★ROBERTS, Henry T. (R), BM1c
★ROBISON, Charles J., Jr., S2c
RODGERS, Daniel C. (R), MOMM3c
★ROGERS, Harold E. (R), COX
★ROLAND, Edwin J., CDR
★ROLLINS, Glenn L., CDR
ROM, Carl W., LT
★ROOD, Robert F. (R), MOMM3c
★ROSEBERRY, Milmo W. (R), GM3c
★ROSENFIELD, William M., ENS
★ROULLET, Valeriano J. (R), BM2c
RUARK, Herman L. (R), CWT
★RUTKOWSKI, Edward J. (R), SM2c
★SABEL, Karl (R), MOMM3c
SANDERS, Homer A. (R), BM2c
★SARRATT, Robert C., CAPT
★SCHEIBER, Fred J., LCDR
SCHLEMAN, Helen B. (W), CDR
SCHMALL, August, S2c
★SCHMITZ, Oliver E., COX
★SCHOENECKER, Bartholomew J. (R), MOMM
SCHOLTZ, William, LT
★SCHOMER, John L., MOMM1c
★SCHWARTZ, Gerald (R), S1c
★SEIDMAN, Robert B. (R), LT
SEXTON, Floyd J., CAPT
★SHANKS, Leon D. (R), GM1c
SHAW, Phillip E., CDR
★SHIVELY, Bruce E. (R), LTJG
★SHIVELY, Donald E. (R), LTJG
SIEG, James E., GM1c
SINTON, William E., CDR
SMALL, David G., AS
★SMEEDING, Edwin C., Jr., BM1c
SMITH, Charles O., Jr. (R), LTJG
SMITH, Paul V. (R), CBM
SMYTH, Robert A. (R), CAPT
SOLARI, William J., LTJG
SPERBER, Nathaniel H. (R), PHOT
SPRINGFIELD, Leon T., ST3c
★SPROW, Ned W., CDR
★STAHLECKER, Edward F. (R), COX
★STANASZEK, Alfred E., BM2c
STEED, Lamarr W., SM1c
★STEPHENS, Irwin J., CDR
STEPHENSON, David J. (R), F1c
★STEPHENSON, Robert A. (R), SOM3c
STEWART, Gustavus U., CAPT
STILES, Norman R., CAPT
★STINCHCOMB, Harry W., CAPT
★STOBER, Carl H., CDR
STOCKMAN, Roy, LT
STUTTER, Harry E., LCDR
★SUDNIK, Louis F., LT
★SUTHERLAND, Harold L. (R), LCDR
★SWINIARSKI, Henry F. (R), S1c

★TAYLOR, Jesse G. (R), CM1c
★TAYLOR, Edward G., LTJG
TAYLOR, Oliver A., Jr., SOM3c
★THARP, Kenneth C., CDR
★THAYER, Louis M., Jr., CDR
THOMAS, Charles W., CAPT
★THOMAS, Loyd J., Jr., COX
★THOMAS, Robert H. (R), MOMM3c
★THOMPSON, John F., Jr., LCDR
★THOMPSON, Linnie, LCDR
★THOMPSON, Warner K., Jr., LCDR
★THRONEBERRY, William (R), CMOMM
THUFT, William H. (R), BM1c
★TIMBONE, John (R), RM1c
TINKHAM, Ralph R., CAPT
★TRESTER, Glenn E., CDR
★TUCKER, Gaston H. (R), MOMM3c
★TYAS, Henry W., Jr. (R), ENS
★TYNER, Philip B. (R), COX
★UHDEN, Peter P. (R), COX
VAUTRAIN, Charles F. J., LT
VEREEN, Gibbs S. (R), BM2c
★VOLSE, Louis A., LT
★VOORIS, George R. (R), S1c
★VOROBEL, Andrew (R), F2c
VUKIC, John, LT
★WAESCHE, Russell R., Jr., CDR
WAGNER, Austin C., LT
★WALCOTT, Roger N. (R), LCDR
WALDRON, John A. (R), LTJG
★WALDRON, Robert, LCDR
WATERS, John M., Jr., LT
★WATKINS, Thomas H. (R), SOM2c
★WATT, Roy E. (R), SM1c

★WATTS, Merle H., CBM
WEEKS, William A. R. (R), MOMM3c
WEIGAND, Karl (R), MOMM3c
WEINSTEIN, Isadore (R), STM2c
★WEISS, Daniel D., CSM
★WENDLAND, James C., CDR
WESOLOWSKI, Alvin J., ARM1c
★WESTFALL, Neale O. (R), LT
WESTLUND, Carl E., CHMACH
★WETTERMARK, Eugene C., S1c
WHITEHEAD, Reginald E. (R), S1c
★WHITMAN, George F., COX
★WHITTLESEY, George C., CDR
WILCOX, Robert, CDR
WILKIE, Leland O. (R), LT
WILKISON, Harry, LCDR
WILLIAMS, Lawrence J., BM1c
WILLIAMS, Raymond, Jr. (R), CEM
★WILSON, Kenneth E., LT
WINSLOW, Charles E. (R), LT
★WINSLOW, Edward B., LCDR
★WINSLOW, James A., CMM
WISHAR, William, CAPT
WISNIOWSKI, Fred F. (R), S1c
WOLLETT, David E., CGM
WOOD, Russell E., CAPT
★WOODLEY, Harold F. (R), S1c
WOODSON, Jeston V., CGM
★WOODWARD, Milton H. (R), CWT
★WRIGHT, Laurence H. (R), S1c
★WYMAN, James E., BM2c
YOST, William H. (R), CDR
YOUNG, Maynard F., LCDR
★ZITTEL, Karl O. A., CDR

## Army Commendation Ribbon

CAPRON, Walter C., CDR
ERNST, Robert J., LCDR
HASSE, Herbert G., LTJG
HENRICKSEN, John A. (R), LCDR
HOLTZMAN, George W., CDR
HOOSICK, Michael J., LT

JORDAN, Chester L., CDR
KAPLAN, Sidney J., CDR
MOORE, Harold C., CAPT
PELTIER, Norman A. (R), LTJG
STANLEY, John T., CDR
WHITEHEAD, Arthur S. (R), CDR

## Air Force Commendation Ribbon

BROUSSARD, Sidney K., LCDR

## Coast Guard Commendation Ribbon

BALLERINI, Antonio F., BM3 (P)
BANGS, Donald H., BMC (L)
BARNES, Clifford A. (R), LCDR
BATKIEWICZ, Eugene J., AD3
BERLINER, Richard H., RDM3c
BOEHM, Herman, BOSN
BUNKLEY, Charles E., SM1c
BURKE, Rayner C., LT
CANFIELD, John B., AD2

CANION, Kenneth, ADC (AP)
CANNOM, Robert C. (R), LT
CARTER, Thomas H. (R), LT
CICCONE, Richard J., SN
COREY, Dwight E., RDM1c
COREY, Ralph A., SN
DALTON, William H., SN
DAVIS, Louis A., BMC
DILLIAN, James A., LT

DOUGHTEN, Franklin H., BM2 (P)
DOYLE, Bernard J., Jr. (R), LT
DUNN, John F., EN1 (AN)
ESSEX, Charles A., ENS
FEGER, William F., Jr., SA
FIFIELD, Robert E., COX
FINKBONNER, Joseph C., EN3
FORSTER, John W., ETC
FOX, Allen M., ADC
FRYE, Joseph E., PR2c
FUHR, Ralph O., RDM3c
GRIEBEL, Phillip M., RM1 (P)
GRUEN, Raymond A., AO1 (P)
HARDING, Francis J., BM2
HAYNES, Emory H., EN1c
HEALY, Daniel C., Jr., SN
HOFFERT, Roland W., GM3 (P)
HOGAN, Wilbur C., CDR
HOTCHKISS, Delmar R., ENC
HOWELL, Robert G., FCC
HUGHES, John K., COX
JACOBS, Frank J., SN
JOHNSON, Leland L., SA
JOHNSON, William H., QM1c
JOSEPH, John M., CDR
KARCH, Joseph J., BM2c
KATES, Hugh E., AD2c
KEHLER, Gordon L., CM3c
KINNEY, Joseph D., Jr., AT1c
KNOWLES, Ernest, Jr., AL3c
KORPUSIK, Eugene W., SA
KRING, Cyril D., MACH
LANA, Anthony J., FN
LATIMER, John P., CDR
LAWLIS, Robert L., LCDR
LEISING, Charles E., Jr., LCDR
LIVERSEDGE, Charles W., AL2c
LOFTON, Marvin L., AD2c

MacDONALD, James H., ENS
McGEORGE, Glenn W., BMC
McGRATH, Robert E., S1c
MARTINELLI, Enrico W., MOMM3c
MITCHELL, Warren C., LCDR
MONTEIRO, Joseph F., MM2c
MORAN, John A., AD2c
ORMSBY, Ralph L., BMC
PAULEY, Robert W., SN
PERRY, Dennis J., SN
PETERSON, Charles N., AERM3c
PEYTON, Gerdo W., AO2c
PITTS, Donald E., SN
RAY, James F., SN
ROACH, James A., FN
ROY, Alfred J., BM1
RUBINSKY, Herman M., SA
SALINAS, James J., SA
SANSBURY, Lemuel C., LCDR
SCHMIDTMAN, Richard D., CDR
SCHMITZ, Frank C., LT
STEGER, Emil J., EN1c
TEUTHORN, Robert K., EN3c (P)
THOMPSON, Cuyler O. G., BM1c (L)
TIERNEY, James M., Jr., PR1c
TURNER, Allen R., AL2 (P)
VAUGHN, William S., CDR
WAGNER, George W., LCDR
WALLACE, William C., LTJG
WEHNER, Ronald R., EM2c
WENDT, Robert R., MOMM2c
WHITE, Julian E., AD1c
WHITE, Robert B. (R), SR
WILSON, Lewis D., Jr., EM1c
WOHLGEMUTH, Richard S. (R), LT
WOOD, John C., Jr., SN
WUERKER, Alexander W., CDR
YOST, James C., EN2 (P)

## Gold Life-Saving Medal

FITZGERALD, Andrew J., EN2c
HALL, Clarence S., Jr., LTJG
KELLER, Ralph J., BM1c
KIELY, William R., Jr. (R), ENS
LIVESEY, Richard P., SN
MASKE, Ervin E., SN

PERMENTER, Fred, BMC (AN) (P)
REYNOLDS, Marion K., BM1c
ROLLINS, Glenn L., CDR
WEBBER, Bernard C., BM1c
WISNIEWSKI, Leonard, SA

## Silver Life-Saving Medal

AMOS, Arthur L., Jr., CS2
BLACK, Paul R., EN2c
BROWN, Bernard S., LTJG
BROWN, Eugene I., LT
BURKE, Richard L., CDR
CANNING, Bertrum, ACM2c
CARMICHAEL, Gilbert E. (R), ENS
CARPENTER, George L., Jr., EN2
CARTER, Ralph M., Jr., AL2
CLAYTON, Leonard C., SURF

CRAIG, E .R., COX
EASTER, Clarence R., LT
FAHEY, Edmund E., LTJG
FERNANDEZ, John T., ET2
FERRIS, Robert S., AD3c
GOODMAN, Kenneth L., CBM
GRAULICH, Robert, SN
GRCINA, Louis A., EN1c
GUARINO, Ralph, ENC
HALL, Lindel, MACH

HELSETH, Carleton T., PHM3c
HOLBERT, Wendell J. (R), LT
JOHNSON, Frank W., Jr., AL3c
JOHNSTON, John, GM1c
KORF, Herman H., BM1c
KRING, Cyril D., MACH
LaFEVER, Harry, CMOMM
LAMBERTH, Allen J., S1c
LARKIN, Charles E., Jr., ENS
LOMBARD, Edward E., BM2c
McKINNON, Hinton C., SN
McMANN, William W. (TR), CBM
MASON, Edward A., Jr., SA
MAY, Mack D., S1c
MELFI, Vincent A., ETM3c
MORRIS, Albert E., BM3c

NATWIG, John, LCDR
NINEMIRE, Kenneth E., MOMM3c
PARKER, Kermit H., AMM2c
PHELPS, Edward D., EN2c
REILLY, William A., S1c
SANDERSON, Clarence R., SR
SKIDD, George J. (R), MOMM1c
TAYLOR, Philips V., MM3c
TERWILLIGER, Webster G., SN
THOMAS, Anthony W. (R), QM2c
TREMPER, Henry S., LT
VERETTE, Adam, SN
WELCH, James T., SN
WESCOTT, John C., BM3c
WILLIAMSON, Doyle V. (R), COX

## Commandant's Citation

ABBOTT, Henry E. (R), LCDR
ARD, Nelson N., CDR
BECKER, Herman J., CPHM
BERG, Toralv A. (R), LCDR
BOLGER, Jerome (R), LTJG
BRIGGS, Edmund B. (TR), CDR
BROWN, John W. (R), LCDR
BROWN, Miles R. (R), SPPS1c
BUDINGTON, Wm. G., SURG USPHS
BUZA, Joseph E. (R), CARP
CAIRNES, George W., RADM
CALAHAN, Emmet T., CDR
CALHOUN, Ben A. (TR), LT
CHASE, Dwight A., CAPT
CHESTER, Edward P., Jr., LCDR
COMFORT, Thomas A. (R), CPCLK
COOMBS, Robert E. (R), CAPT
CRAIK, James D., CDR
CRUTCHER, Anson H. (R), LT
CULPEPPER, Charles S., LT
DeMARTINO, Marius, CDR
DIMICK, Chester E., CAPT
DONAHUE, James M. (R), LT
DOYLE, Martin A., CAPT
DUGAN, John I., CDR
EILAND, Ralph T. (R), CDR
ELLIOT, Donald G. (R), LCDR
ETZWILER, Charles, CDR
EVANS, Stephen H., CAPT
FEIDLER, Ernest R. (R), CDR
FERRIS, Neckley M. (R), LT
FIELD, Maurice G. (R), LCDR
FLYNN, Joseph J. (R), CDR
FRENCH, Arthur E. (R), CDR
FRIEDLAND, Louis N. (R), LT
GILLIS, Raymond N., CDR
GOODWIN, William M. (R), LTJG
GREENFIELD, Charles E., Jr., LCDR
GUNDERSON, Burton A., LCDR
HANKINSON, Ray L., CDR
HARWOOD, Charles W., CAPT

HERRICK, Carl E. (R), CDR
HILL, David I. (R), CMM
HORDER, Garrett P. (R), LT
HYNES, Thomas J., LT
ISHMAEL, Frank P., Jr. (R), LCDR
JACK, Raymond L., CAPT
JENSEN, Martinus P., CDR
JOHNSON, Sigval B., RADM
JONES, Jonah, Jr. (R), CDR
JORDAN, Beckwith, COMMO
JORGENSEN, William (R), LCDR
KELSEY, Carleton, CDR
KENNEY, George P. (R), CDR
KERR, Evor S., Jr., CDR
KIEFERLE, George R. (R), LCDR
KIELY, Thomas P. (R), LT
KURTH, Donald J. (R), CY
LAYMAN, Lloyd (R), LCDR
LEMARGIE, Paul (R), LCDR
LIPSHIE, Joseph (R), LTJG
LIVERMAN, Horace B. (R), HA1c
LUNDGREN, Gustave M., RELE
McCABE, Michael A., LTJG
McELLIGOTT, Raymond, RADM
McGUIRE, Robert N. (R), LT
McGUIRE, William M., CAPT
MACIONIS, John J. (R), LCDR
MANSFIELD, William N. (TR), CDR
MARTIN, John F. (R), LCDR
MARTINSON, Albert M., CAPT
MAUERMAN, Raymond J., CAPT
MOLLOY, Thomas M., RADM
MORGAN, Gary S. (R), LT
MORTIMER, Ross E. (R), LCDR
NICHOLS, Fred A., RADM
O'CONNOR, Gustavus R., CAPT
PAINE, Stephen (TR), CDR
PAUL, Frank, CHBOSN
PECK, Ira L., LCDR
PENDLETON, Harold I., CHRELE
PIFER, Philip C. (R), LCDR

PLUMMER, Charles C. (R), LCDR
POMEROY, Bobby D. (R), LT
PRALL, Whitney M., CAPT
RAUMER, Fredrick H., LTJG
REICKER, Frederick A. (R), LCDR
RENDLEN, Thomas B. (R), LCDR
RICHARDS, Walter R., CAPT
RICHEY, Julius E., CDR
ROLAND, Edwin J., CDR
ROSENTHAL, Joseph S., CAPT
RUSSO, Philip (R), RM3c
SANTEE, James M., CHBOSN
SHERMAN, George S. (R), CSPX
SIVILS, Talmadge H., CAP
SKIDMORE, Franklin L., BOSN
SOLOMON, Henry E., CDR
STEPANOFF, George V., LCDR
STOFFLE, Merton W. (R), LCDR
STONECYPHER, Wayne O. (R), LT

SUGDEN, Charles E., CAPT
THOMPSON, James L., LCDR
TOMKIEL, Frank, CDR
TOWERS, Charles L. (R), LCDR
TYLER, Gaines A., CAPT
VERNON, Caroline (W), Y3c
WAGNER, Edward P. (R), LCDR
WALTERS, Alvin C. (R), LCDR
WATKINS, Jesse L., S2c
WEBSTER, George E., MOMM1c
WILLIAMS, Gwyn A. E. (R), LTJG
WINSLOW, Charles E. (R), LT
WISHAR, William, CAPT
WOOD, Russell E., CAPT
WRIGHT, James S. (R), LCDR
WRIGHT, Merritt O., BOSN
YATES, Russell E., CDR
ZARILLI, Reuben A., SEN SURG USPHS

## Commandant's Letter of Commendation

ALEXANDER, Wallace J., BM2c
ALLARD, Armand A., BMC
ALSUP, James A., LT
ALTHEIMER, Donald W., ARM1c
AMPHLETT, John R., AL3
ANDERSON, Wallace N., BMC
ARWE, Kenneth J. (R), LTJG
AWALT, Thomas Y., CAPT
AYCOCK, William C., BM1c
BAETSEN, Raymond H., Jr., LTJG
BAILEY, Cecil H., MOMM2c
BANTA, Gareld B. (R), LCDR
BARD, Robert, COX
BARNETT, Francis E., LCDR
BARRETT, James M., LCDR
BARTLETT, Harry I. (R), LCDR
BARTOLI, Joseph, AD3c
BATEMAN, Luther W., Jr. (P), GM3c
BAUER, Howard G., AD3c
BEAVER, Charles N. (P), BM2c
BELL, Herman H., TN
BELL, Joseph H. (R), LCDR
BENNETT, George W., BMC
BENZIE, James G., COX
BERRY, Oliver F., ACMM
BEVIS, Laura D. (W), LCDR
BILZ, Conrad W., LCDR
BINGHAM, Thomas R., SN
BISSEY, Robert M., AP1c
BLACKSHAW, Robert F., AD2c
BOATRIGHT, Douglas D., AD3c
BOGERT, Edwin L. (P), DC2c
BOLDING, James W., Jr., LTJG
BOLTON, Walter C., LT
BOONE, James A., AMM1c
BORNMANN, Adelaide (W), ENS
BOTELER, James C., LT
BRACKEN, Leo M., LTJG

BRACKEN, Robert E., LTJG
BRACKEN, Robert O., LTJG
BRADY, Morey (R), LCDR
BRANNAN, Burl H. (R), LTJG
BRANNAN, Wilburn R., S2c
BRESNAHAN, Jeremiah D. (P), AL3c
BREYFOGLE, Newell D., HM2c
BROWN, Harold K. (P), AL3c
BROWN, Joseph B., EN2c
BRYANT, Jerry C. (TR), LT
BRYZCKI, Leo, ACMM
BURDEKIN, Robert E. (R), LT
BUXTON, Winslow H., CDR
CALHOUN, Charles L., BM2c
CAMPBELL, Gordon R., AL1c
CANNOM, Robert C. (R), LT
CARDENAS, Gilbert, S2c
CARMICHAEL, Horace W., LT
CARPENTER, Albert J., CDR
CARR, Lawrence R., SN
CARROLL, William H., Jr. (R), SM3c
CASCINI, Ernest A., CDR
CASEY, Jack O., MM2c
CAVADAS, Thomas J., F1c
CEBULA, Robert, ARM2c
CERRINA, Joseph O. (R), PHM1c
CHAPMAN, Ganes T., BMC
CHUN, William, Y1c
CINI, Fabio J., S1c
CLUFF, Daniel W., BOSN
COBAUGH, Donald, AD1 (AP)
COHEN, Florence B. (TR), LTJG
CONOVER, Dexter H. (R), CY
COOK, Arthur T., ACMM
CORBALLY, John E. (TR), LT
CORBETT, Walter F., AL1c
COSTLEY, Frederick R., TA
COURTNEY, John J., RM3c

COWART, James G., BOSN
COWING, Charles V., BOSN
COX, Laurence A. (R), LT
CREEDON, William E., CDR
CREELY, J. R. (TR), LT
CRUM, Emerson E., Jr., AT1c
CURWEN, Walter, Jr., LT
DAHLBURG, Theodore A., LCDR
DAHLGREN, Wallace C., LCDR
DAVIS, Gerald M., LTJG
DAVIS, Harry E., CDR
DAVIS, Stacy M., SN
DeCAROLIS, Vito O., MM2c
DeCENZO, John J. (P), BM1c
DELPRA, Attilio E., LCDR
DENNIS, Henry E., BMC
DeSELMS, Raymond C., MACH
DeVOSS, Edwin A. (TR), LT
DINSMORE, Robertson P., ENS
DIVES, Margaret S. (W), LT
DOERNER, Alexander A., SEN SURG USPHS
DOUGLAS, Ralph O., ADC
DREYER, Harry M., SN
DRINKWATER, Earle B., BOSN
DUNN, Francis P. (R), LTJG
DURHAM, Thomas L. (R), S1c
EGAN, John W. (R), LTJG
EHLERS, Erwin P., BM1 (AN)
ELDRIDGE, Cozie, ACMM
ELLIS, Sherman T., SBM
EMERSON, Merle E. (R), WT3c
EMERSON, Robert E., LCDR
ENTREKIN, J. C., AD2c
ERICKSON, Frank A., CDR
EUCKER, Clifford L., DC3 (P)
EURITT, Kenneth E., AO3c
EVANS, Billy K., AL2
FENLON, William G., LT
FISCHER, Charles A. (R), LTJG
FISHER, Alvin N., LCDR
FISHER, Ralph D., LT
FLESSAS, James P., LTJG
FORBES, Thomas B., BM1c
FORWARD, Charles H., LCDR
FRANCK, Kenneth H., ADC (AP)
FRANK, Russell W., DC2 (P)
FRANKE, Radford F., BM1c
FRASER, Donald H. R., ADC (AP)
FRASER, James B., SN
FRASER, Phil G. (TR), CDR
GANONG, Carl F., CAPT
GARDINER, Charles H. (TR), LCDR
GARDNER, Robert E., AL2c
GARFIELD, Montegue F., CDR
GARY, Odelle C. (W), LT
GASKILL, Guy L., EN
GAWRYSIAK, Edward, AMM1c
GEIGHER, Robert K., AEROM2c
GERBER, Lewis F. (R), LT
GIBBON, Waldyn L. (TR), LCDR

GILES, Forest E., ACMM
GILLELAND, Delbert F., AD3c
GLASS, James L., ETC (Z)
GLATFELTER, Ralph E., ATC
GLEASON, Edward W., AD2
GLENDENNING, Robert W., SN
GOLDHAMMER, Walter R., ADC (AP)
GOODWIN, Kenneth R., LCDR
GOODWIN, William B., Jr., AL1c
GOUDE, Gordon S. (R), S1c
GRAY, Charlie O., LT
GRAY, Edward M., BM1c
GRAY, Wilbur D., DC3c
GREEN, Joseph L., CDR
GREENBERG, Balthazar (R), LT
GRUEN, Raymond A., AO1 (P)
GUILDNER, William O., S1c
GUINAN, Edward D., RM3c
GUNTER, Lifford L., CHGUN
HAAG, Chester E., ARM2c
HAAS, Howard L., AMM1c
HALL, Arthur G., CAPT
HALL, Joseph A., MMC
HALL, Richard L., AL1c
HALLEN, Gerald H., S1c
HAMMOND, Winfield J., AL1c
HANKS, Melvin L. (R), CDR
HANSBERRY, Ray A., LT
HANSEN, Charles, LT
HANSEN, Hugo L., EM1c
HARVEY, Frederick J., QM1c
HASSELL, Clayton B., BMC
HAUGHEN, Niels, CAPT
HEFFNER, Charles D., MOMM1c
HENDRICK, John C., AD3c
HENGSTEBECK, Harold J., LTJG
HENNINGER, Hilary E., Y1c
HENRICKSEN, John A. (R), LCDR
HENRY, Bernard R., LCDR
HERPEL, William H., Jr., AMM1c
HEWETT, David G., AL2 (P)
HIGH, Leslie D., LT
HILL, Robert H., SN
HOLLAND, George U., MACH
HOLLE, William F., AD2 (P)
HOLMES, William E., CHBOSN
HOLTZ, Edward W., CAPT
HOOK, Alexander H. (R), LT
HORSLEY, William H. (TR), CDR
HORTON, Joseph K. (R), LCDR
HOUGH, Charles H., RD3c
HOUSE, Roscoe, CAPT
HUCKS, Frank B., AOM2c
HUGHES, Cyril W., AD1c
HUGHES, John F., LCDR
HUNT, Percy J. (TR), CDR
HUTCHINSON, Mark K., CPC
HUTTO, Morgan C., Jr., BMC
JABLONSKI, Gus, Jr., AMM1c
JOHNSON, Earl M., EN1c

JOHNSON, Howard A., LTJG
JOHNSON, Lewis A., CHGUN
JOHNSON, Parker R., CBM
JONES, George, SN
JONES, Jack A., AL2
JOSEPH, Ervin C., AOMM1c
JOY, Richard J., AD1c
KAY, Jean A. (W), LTJG
KEITH, John E., S1c
KELLAR, Dale H., S2c
KELLEY, William H., AD1c
KEMPTER, Mary K. (W), LT
KENDRICK, Milton H., CHMACH
KIRBY, Virginia (W), CY
KNUTI, Leslie A. (R), LTJG
KOSKI, Onni G., AD1c
KRAMER, Everett W. O. (R), LTJG
KROGMANN, Carl F., CAP
KUBAS, Matthew L., HMC
LaMONICA, Angelo A., AL1c
LANG, Richard E. (TR), LCDR
LAUGHLIN, John N. (R), LTJG
LEE, Charles R., CMM
LEE, James R., AO2c
LESLIE, George R., CDR
LIEBERSON, William, LCDR
LIPSHUTZ, Richard A., HM3 (P)
LOCKWOOD, Fred E. (R), RT2c
LOMBARD, Benjamin F., BOSN
LONG, Calvin R., PR3c
LOVEWELL, James A., QM1
LUCY, Carl F., SN
LUPTON, Darrel E., SN
MacLEAN, Norman L., BM3
MacLENNAN, Isabella M. (W), Y2c
McCARTAN, Daniel G., GM2 (P)
McCARTNEY, Willard R., AD3 (P)
McDONALD, Charles H., BM3c
McGOWAN, Gordon P., CDR
McINTYRE, John J. (R), LT
McKAY, Donald E., CAPT
McKEAN, George W., CAPT
McKINLOCK, George J., CBM
McNEIL, Felix J., ADC
MACE, James F., LT
MALLON, William J. (R), LTJG
MALONEY, Arthur J. (R), CY
MANN, Francis J. (R), LCDR
MARONEY, Richard E., BM3 (P)
MARSHALL, Daniel A., YNC
MARTER, William P. F., BM2c
MARTIN, David E., BM3
MARTINSON, Albert M., CAPT
MASSINGILL, Harry E. (R), LT
MATTHEWS, William A., BM2 (ESG)
MATTINGLY, Chester S., BM1c
MAZZEI, Alfred C. (R), CY
MEHLMAN, Stewart P., CDR
MERRITT, Richard B., AMM1c
MEW, Alfred L., BM2c

MIDDLETON, Thomas L., S1c
MIDGETT, Myron V., EN1 (L)
MILLER, Joseph M., Jr., AD1c
MILLER, William, LT
MILLS, Sterling G., AMM1c
MOLONEY, Robert E. (TR), LT
MORAN, Bernard H. (R), LT
MORTON, Fred E. (R), LCDR
MURPHY, Charles J. (R), LT
NAAB, Joseph W., Jr., CDR
NELSON, Clifford E., SEN SURG USPHS
NELSON, Glenn A. (R), CY
NETHERY, George R., AO1c
NEWMAN, Guy R., EN1c
NEWMAN, Harry W., LT
NEWMAN, John W., Jr., S1c
NEWTON, Robert D., S1c
NOEHREN, Henry P., MOMM2c
NORDSTROM, Carl H., DCC
NORMAN, Jimmy R., BM3 (P)
NOWAK, June D. (R), LT
NYSTROM, Donald A., AD1 (AP)
O'HAGAN, David C., CBM
O'HANNA, Matthew B., PH2c
O'HARA, Emmett P., LT
O'LEARY, Edward S., SN
O'LEARY, Robert J., AOM1c
OLIVER, David, LT
OLSON, Louis B., CAPT
O'NEILL, Edward A. (R), LCDR
OPP, Donald M., AL1 (P)
OSBORN, Richard C., AMM3c
OSBORNE, Robert E., GM1c
OTEY, George B. (R), S1c
PACIC, Thomas F., S2c
PALLAM, John M., AD1c
PANTZER, Wilfred F., LCDR
PATE, William M., Jr. (R), BM2 (P)
PEARCE, Allen C., LT
PEISTRUP, Garnard T., AMM2c
PERKINS, Lewis M. (R), LCDR
PERRY, Loren V., ENS
PETERS, Dan W., ET3 (P)
PETERSON, Oliver A., CAPT
PHANNEMILLER, George, CAPT
PHILLIPS, Larry L., AO3 (P)
PHILLIPS, Roger L., QM1c
PINCUS, Philip, RM3c
PITKOFF, Harris, SN
PLATT, Archie F., AM1c
POLAJNER, John S. (R), LT
POPE, Robert R., LT
POST, Duane L. (R), S1c
POWELL, Bobby G., BM2 (P)
PRATT, Mervin F. (R), LT
PRENTICE, William H., CS2c
PRESCOTT, Ben R., DC1c
PUCKETT, Richard H. (R), LCDR
RALL, Frederick R. (R), Y3c
REAMS, Floyd O., BOSN

RICE, Maurice, CDR
ROACH, Cecil C., AD1c
ROBBINS, Merton M., AETM1c
ROBBINS, Meyer, LCDR
ROBERTS, Ernest (R), MOMM3c
ROBINSON, Whelington, BM1c
ROCHE, John D. (R), LCDR
ROHDIN, Adolph A., LCDR
ROHRKEMPER, Henry F., LCDR
ROLL, Clayton E., ADC (AP)
ROSENTHAL, Howard L., AD2 (P)
ROSS, Thomas A., LT (RET)
ROZEMA, Norman J., EN2 (P)
RUPERT, Howard (TR), ENS
SALOVITCH, Michael W., AL1c
SALTER, Adrian, CHBOSN
SANDSMARK, James M., SN
SANFORD, Hoban B., CHRELE
SAPP, Edward V., AMM1c
SATTERLEE, Richard T., AO2c
SCHIAVO, Frank J. (R), EM3c
SCHOENFELD, L. Kenneth (TR), CDR
SCHONING, Rudolph H., ARM1c
SCHRUBB, Carl C. (R), PHM2c
SCHWEITZER, Charles (R), MOMM2c
SCRIPTURE, Doris M. (W), LCDR
SEMINGSEN, Earl M. (R), LT
SHAFFER, Harry E., EMC (P)
SHAFFER, John L., ARM1c
SHARP, Henry S., CDR
SHEEHAN, Francis C., AL1c
SHELTON, Clarence E., BM3 (P) (ESG)
SHEPARD, Roland P., Jr., BM2c
SIEGFRIED, Harry B., EN1c
SIEMENS, Abe H., LT
SILVER, Ronald B., ET3 (P)
SIMMONS, James P., ARM1c
SLATON, Billy J., RM3c
SMACK, Zadok H., BM1 (L)
SMILARI, Julius J., AMM3c
SMITH, Anderson, BM1c
SMITH, Channing P. (TR), ENS
SMITH, Ellison H., AD1c
SMITH, Gerhardt, HMC
SMITH, Lytle C., ACMM
SMITH, Robert W., LTJG
SMITH, Wesley D. (R), LCDR
SNYDER, Henry, AMM1c
SOMERVILLE, John M., ARM1c
SPARACIN, Joseph G. (R), ENS
SPEAKER, John B., Jr., LT
SPRINGER, Helmut W., BT3c
STAHL, John C., BMC
STEEG, Edward G., BM2c
STEELE, Lee W., S1c
STELLBERGER, W. F. (R), LTJG
STETKIEWICZ, Francis R., AL3 (P)
STROBLE, George (TR), LCDR
STUDLEY, Carl S., LCDR
STYRON, Earl, SN

SULLIVAN, Charles J. (R), LCDR
SUTHERLAND, John W., LT
TAFRO, Victor J., SN
TAYLOR, Arthur V., AL1c
TENNYSON, L. B. (R), LT
THIELE, Herbert A., SN
THOMETZ, George F., Jr., LT
THOMPSON, Howard J., C SPX MSCR
THOMPSON, John E., CRM
THOMSEN, Neils P., CDR
THURSTON, Norman D. (R), S1c
TIFFT, Paul W., Jr., LT
TRAX, David L., Jr., QM1 (P)
TURNER, J. C., BMC
TURNEY, James F., HM1c
VANELLI, Francis A., ACMM
VanLOPIK, Evan, LCDR
VARLESE, Catherine F. (W), LT
VAUGHN, Mont. (TR), ENS
VAUGHN, Ruby B. (TR), LTJG
VRANCKEN, William L., CBM
VREELAND, Robert H., AD3c
VUKIC, John, LT
WAGNER, George W., LCDR
WALTERS, Allen S., SN
WAMBY, Donald S., SN
WATERS, Harold C., CGM
WEBB, Robert E., LT
WEBER, Roy H., AP1
WEBSTER, Andrew H., BM1c
WEED, Oscar D., CDR
WEEMS, Benjamin F., ADC (AP)
WEITZEL, Christian A., ADC (AP)
WESOLOWSKI, Alvin J., ARM1c
WESTERBERG, Merwin E., AMM1c
WHALEN, Mark A., LCDR
WHEELER, Philip H. (R), LCDR
WHELTON, John P. (R), Y1c
WHIDDEN, Charles D., PR3c
WHITE, Edmond F., BM1c
WHITEHURST, George W., AD2c
WHITFIELD, Edwin C., CAPT
WHITFIELD, James W., AM2c
WIDDOWS, Harold E., PR2c
WILCOX, Ben C., LCDR
WILDONGER, Dorothy M. (W), CCS
WILLIAMS, Milton B., LT
WILSON, Donald J., SN
WISE, Gerald F., SN
WOLFSTONE, Hyman H. (TR), LCDR
WOOD, Charles K., ENC (L)
WOOD, George V. (R), LT
WOOD, Thomas S. (TR), ENS
WOODMAN, William H., ETC
WOODSON, Ferdinand (R), F1c
WYATT, Dorothea E. (W), LT
YATES, Heulette C., ENC
YOUNG, R. M., CMOMM
ZIFFERBLATT, Irving (R), AMM1c

# DECORATIONS AWARDED BY ALLIED NATIONS

## BELGIUM

### Order of Leopold II

#### *Commanders*

BOLTON, Walter C., LT
BROWN, Fletcher W., Jr., LT
ERICKSON, Frank A., CDR
FISHER, Alvin N., LCDR

GRAHAM, Stewart R., LCDR
GUILLEMETTE, Albert (R), LTJG
KILLEBREW, William N. (R), LTJG
KLEISCH, August, LT

#### *Companions*

BAILEY, Aldrich G., CHPHOT
BERRY, Oliver F., ACMM
BRYZCKI, Leo, ACMM
ELDRIDGE, Cozie, ACMM
GAWRYSIAK, Edward, AMM1c
JABLONSKI, Gus, Jr., AMM1c

O'LEARY, Robert J., AOM1c
OSBORN, Richard C., AMM3c
SCHONING, Rudolph H., ARM1c
VANNELLI, Francis A., ACMM
WATSON, James E., CPHOM
WESTERBERG, Merwin E., AMM1c

### Order of the Crown

#### *Commander*

MacDOWELL, Charles E. (R), LTJG

#### *Officers*

DAVIS, Larry L., LCDR
GIFFIN, Alvin H., CDR

SCHRADER, James N., LCDR

### Military Medal

ALTHEIMER, Donald W., ARM1c
COOK, Arthur, ACMM
HAAS, Howard L., AMM1c
HALLEN, Gerald H., S1c
HERPEL, William H., Jr., AMM1c
JOSEPH, Erwin C., AMM1c
MERRITT, Richard B., AMM1c
MILLS, Sterling G., AMM1c
PEISTRUP, Garnard T., AMM2c

ROBBINS, Merton M., AETM1c
SAPP, Edward V., AMM1c
SHAFFER, John L., ARM1c
SIMMONS, James P., ARM1c
SMILARI, Julius J., AMM3c
SMITH, Lytle C., ACMM
SOMERVILLE, John M., ARM1c
WESOLOWSKI, Alvin J., ARM1c
WHIDDEN, Charles D., PR3c

## BRAZIL

### Order of Military Merit

McKEAN, George W., CAPT

### Medalha de Campanha

ADDISONE, Charles J. (R), PHM1c
ARANGO, Hasdrubal (R), MUS3c
BAKST, Jacob (R), CPHM
BALL, Harry N., SK1c
BARR, William W. (R), LT
BERRY, Walter V. (R), STM1c
BEVERLY, Leonard P., MACH
BOCKIUS, Peter L. (R), BM1c
BRAGDON, Edgar F., PHAR

CACCIAMANI, Henry J. (R), SM1c
CARIBO, Cletis L., LTJG
CUNNINGHAM, Almond L., LCDR
DAHL, Henry E. (R), SC1c
DINAN, James A., CHRELE
DOTY, Edward T. (R), ST3c
EISKAMP, Albert G., CM1
FABIK, Theodore J., CDR
FOGARTY, Warren V. (R), SK2c

GRIFFITHS, Douglas C. (R), S1c
GRILLY, Alverardo (R), S1c
HABERCAM, Julian W., SURG USPHSR
HALFERTY, Francis W., LTJG
HAWORTH, Francis R. (R), LTJG
HOFFMAN, Elmer H., CY
HOOVER, William B., SURG USPHS
JORDAN, Donald E., SP1c
KNOX, Edmond L. (R), COX
KOVALSKI, John C., CMM
LAUTER, Herman A. (R), COX
McCAFFREY, Timothy, EM1c
McKEAN, George W., CAPT
MAKREZ, Louis J., CBM

MARLOWE, George A. (R), PHM2c
MATLOCK, Donald C., SC1c
MELE, Vito A. (R), MM3c
PENTECOST, John R., ELE
PETERSON, Erwin H., S1c
PHAIR, James F., (R), LTJG
RHODES, Earl K., CDR
ROWLANDS, Hugh O. (R), PHOM1c
RYER, John S. (R), Y1c
SADLER, Hobert E., CARP
SOUZA, Emanuel J., CBM
TENCH, William R., SURG USPHSR
WILBER, James A., LCDR

## CANADA

### Air Force Cross

KLEISCH, August, LT

## CHINA

### Order of Yum Hui

RINGLER, Eli T., CHBOSN

## DENMARK

### Cross of the Order of Dannebrog

COMMANDER OF THE FIRST DEGREE
PINE, James, RADM

COMMANDER OF THE SECOND DEGREE
vonPAULSEN, Carl C., CAPT

## DOMINICAN REPUBLIC

### Order of Trujillo

HILTON, Carl H., CDR

### Order of Military Merit

HILTON, Carl H., CDR

## FRANCE

### Croix de Guerre

*With Palm*

RICHMOND, Alfred C., CAPT

*With Silver Star*

ALLISON, Samuel W. (R), LT
HENDLEY, Coit T. (R), LTJG
HUTCHINSON, George F. (R), LTJG
IMLAY, Miles H., CAPT

KIRSTINE, Lance J., LCDR
SALMON, Robert M. (R), LT
UNGER, Aden C., CDR
VYN, Arend I., Jr., LT

*With Gold Star*

FRITZSCHE, Edward H., CAPT                     SPENCER, Lyndon, CAPT

## GREAT BRITAIN

### Order of the British Empire

ANDERSON, Robert P. (R), CDR                  JONES, Leonard T., CDR
DICK, George W., CDR                          POLLARD, Francis C., LCDR
ERICKSON, Frank A., CDR                       WAESCHE, Russell R., ADM
JOLLY, William H. (R), LCDR

### Distinguished Service Cross

CLARK, George C., Jr., LTJG                    REILLY, Louis I., LCDR

## HAITI

### L'Ordre National Honneur Mérite

BRASWELL, M. T., CDR

## ITALY

### Order of Saints Maurice and Lasarus

LAWLER, Joseph J. (R), CDR *(Two Awards)*

### Order of the Crown of Italy

*Commanders*

LABROT, William J. (R), CDR                    PELL, Claiborne (R), LT
MULIERI, Bruno C. F. (R), CDR

## POLAND

### Polonia Restituta

*Second Class*

WAESCHE, Russell R., ADM

## UNION OF SOVIET SOCIALIST REPUBLICS

### Order of the Fatherland

*First Class*

POLLARD, Francis C., LCDR                      WILCOX, Robert, CDR

*Second Class*

HAY, Sidney M., LCDR

## Appendix B

## MERCHANT VESSELS LOST

| Year | Month | U.S. Merchant Vessels (1000 Gross Tons or Over) (Gross Tons) | U.S. Merchant Vessels Lost (1000 Gross Tons or Over) (Number) | U.S. Merchant Vessels Lost (1000 Gross Tons or Over) (Gross Tons) | Per Cent of Lost Vessels Being Escorted (Per Cent) | Enemy Submarines Sunk (Number) |
|------|-------|------|------|------|------|------|
| 1941 | December | 6,720,042 | 16 | 83,390 | 0 | 14 |
| 1942 | January | 6,562,387 | 23 | 117,642 | 0 | 9 |
| | February | 6,679,541 | 30 | 166,578 | 0 | 2 |
| | March | 6,627,382 | 30 | 193,987 | 6 | 9 |
| | April | 6,462,204 | 38 | 203,303 | 0 | 4 |
| | May | 6,599,854 | 44 | 233,416 | 10 | 6 |
| | June | 6,626,264 | 55 | 289,790 | 17 | 6 |
| | July | 6,534,965 | 42 | 245,762 | 50 | 15 |
| | August | 6,386,375 | 18 | 116,552 | 44 | 16 |
| | September | 6,833,855 | 29 | 160,366 | 40 | 12 |
| | October | 7,211,128 | 25 | 161,980 | 26 | 17 |
| | November | 7,792,803 | 25 | 183,362 | 20 | 17 |
| | December | 7,998,845 | 10 | 43,211 | * | 13 |
| 1943 | January | 8,157,590 | 19 | 112,724 | 52 | 11 |
| | February | 8,982,158 | 21 | 135,911 | 80 | 23 |
| | March | 9,524,223 | 36 | 233,866 | 78 | 16 |
| | April | 10,103,746 | 12 | 85,174 | 66 | 17 |
| | May | 10,734,772 | 11 | 71,569 | 50 | 47 |
| | June | 11,653,386 | 13 | 88,631 | 14 | 20 |
| | July | 12,599,147 | 16 | 111,014 | 28 | 49 |
| | August | 13,360,524 | 6 | 37,009 | 57 | 28 |
| | September | 14,316,163 | 10 | 69,613 | 40 | 14 |
| | October | 14,651,203 | 9 | 46,554 | 54 | 27 |
| | November | 14,747,658 | 5 | 35,387 | 0 | 22 |
| | December | 15,702,484 | 16 | 96,676 | 2 | 11 |
| 1944 | January | 16,612,799 | 11 | 78,981 | 55 | 18 |
| | February | 17,265,093 | 7 | 51,357 | 47 | 28 |
| | March | 17,782,125 | 10 | 64,510 | 26 | 27 |
| | April | 18,701,370 | 8 | 55,264 | 55 | 27 |
| | May | 19,319,396 | 1 | 7,176 | 0 | 30 |
| | June | 19,853,365 | 4 | 24,989 | * | 35 |
| | July | 20,624,890 | 29 | 182,120† | * | 29 |
| | August | 21,199,262 | 4 | 25,877 | * | 34 |
| | September | 21,464,022 | 1 | 7,143 | * | 25 |
| | October | 21,462,400 | 1 | 7,176 | 0 | 16 |
| | November | 22,321,600 | 3 | 24,550 | 0 | 15 |
| | December | 22,965,375 | 12 | 70,263 | 0 | 12 |
| 1945 | January | 22,845,515 | 3 | 15,745 | 0 | 15 |
| | February | 23,665,715 | 8 | 50,570 | 0 | 30 |
| | March | 24,395,942 | 9 | 95,288 | 0 | 36 |
| | April | 24,779,882 | 7 | 52,655 | 0 | 65 |
| | May | 25,353,072 | 1 | 5,353 | 0 | 29 |
| | June | 25,389,505 | 1 | 7,176 | 0 | 3 |
| | July | 25,878,200 | 1 | 7,194 | 0 | 3 |
| | August | 26,146,500 | 0 | | | 1 |

* Details unavailable.
† Includes 24 old vessels (145,475 tons) sunk for breakwater, San Lopenzo Beachhead, France, July 16, 1944.

## Appendix C

# SUMMARY OF NOTABLE COAST GUARD
# ESCORT OPERATIONS IN THE ATLANTIC

| Name of Escort | Outstanding Operations |
|---|---|
| CGC Algonquin | 21 March 1943—Rescues 22 SS Svend Foyne<br>31 May 1944–March 1 1945—Weather Patrol<br>18 April 1945—Attacks Submarine<br>1 July 1945–12 August 1945—Weather Patrol |
| CGC Bibb | 3 April 1942—Attacks Submarine<br>3 August 1942—Attacks Submarine<br>26 September 1942—Rescues 61 SS Penmar<br>7 February 1943—Rescues 202 SS Mallory<br>9 March 1943—Attacks Submarine—Rescues 3 SS Coulmore, 2 SS Bonneville, and SS Melrose<br>26 May 1943—Attacks Submarine<br>9 July 1943—Attacks Submarine<br>20 April 1944—Attacks Submarine<br>23 April 1944—Attacks Submarine<br>12 June 1944—Plane Attack Bizerte |
| USS Brisk | 1 August 1932—Attacks Submarine<br>27 August 1943—Attacks Submarine |
| USS Calcaterra (DE-390) | 14 May 1944—Submarine Attack<br>7–8 March 1944—Attacks U-Boat Hideouts—Spanish Moroccan Coast |
| USS Camp (DE-251) | 18 November 1944—Loses Bow in Collision |
| CGC Campbell | 24 February 1942—Attacks Submarine<br>27 May 1942—Attacks Submarine<br>16–20 June 1942—Attacks Wolf Pack<br>15–22 September 1942—Attacks Submarine<br>23–29 October 1942—Six Convoy Vessels Sunk<br>21 February 1943—Attacks Submarines<br>23 February 1943—Rams and Sinks U-606. Damaged by Collision<br>7 October 1943—Attacks Submarine<br>10 May 1944—Air Attack |
| CGC Comanche | 4 April 1942–8 May 1942—Greenland Survey<br>18 July 1942—Established Ice Cap Station at Comanche Bay<br>3 February 1943—230 saved—678 Lost SS Dorchester<br>15 December 1943—Rescues 29—USAT Nevada<br>14–24 March 1944—Weather Patrol<br>1 October–1 March 1945—Weather Patrol<br>20 June–30 September 1945—Weather Patrol |
| CGC Duane | 9 February 1942—Attacks Submarine<br>17 September 1942—Attacks Submarine<br>3–6 February 1942—Dorchester Rescue<br>17 April 1943—Helps Sink Submarine; Rescues 22 Crew<br>14 June 1943—Attacks Submarine<br>7 August 1943—Attacks Submarine<br>15 August 1944—Invasion of Southern France |
| USS Durant (DE-389) | 14 May 1944—Attacks Submarine<br>12 July 1944—Air Attack<br>11 May 1945—U-873 Surrenders |
| CGC Eastwind | 4 October 1944—Captures German Weather Station East Greenland; Little Koldewey Island 12 Prisoners<br>15 October 1944—Captures German Trawler Externsteine; 17 Prisoners |
| CGC Escanaba | 15 June 1942—Rescues 22; USS Cherokee<br>3 February 1943—Rescues 133; SS Dorchester<br>13 June 1943—Escanaba Sunk; 101 Lost |

| Name of Escort | Outstanding Operations |
|---|---|
| USS Falgout (DE-324) | July 1944—Picks up 4 German Aviators Shot Down |
| USS Forsyth (PF-102) | 15 May 1945—U-234 Surrenders |
| USS Gulfport (PF-20) | 11 March 1945—Attacks Submarine |
| USS Harveson (DE-316) | 25 November 1943—Collision with "OK Service VII"; Crew Abandoned Ship Taken Aboard Harveson<br>14 December 1943—Collision with SS Wm. T. Barry<br>27 February 1944—Forces Submarine to Surface. Submarine Later Sunk by British Aircraft |
| USS Hurst (DE-250) | 25 February 1944—Rescues Survivors SS El Coston |
| CGC Icarus | 9 May 1942—Sinks U-352; Take 32 Prisoners<br>6 February 1942—Attacks Submarine<br>10–16 June 1942—Attacks Submarine<br>26 September 1942—Rescues 8 SS Tennessee<br>17 December 1942—Sunk U-626<br>27 January 1943—Attacks Submarine<br>7 February 1943—Rescues 22 from 5 Vessels<br>18 March 1943—Rescues all hands SS Matthew Luckenback<br>20 March 1943—Attacks Submarine<br>13 May 1943—Attacks Submarine<br>24 August 1943—Attacks Submarine<br>15 September 1943—Attacks Submarine |
| USS Joyce (DE-317) | 9 March 1944—Rescues 28; USS Leopold<br>15 April 1944—Sunk U-550 (With DE's Peterson and Gandy). Took 12 Prisoners |
| USS Lansing (DE-388) | 14 May 1944—Submarine Attack<br>12 July 1944—Air Attack |
| USS Leopold (DE-319) | 9 March 1944—Sunk South of Iceland. All 13 Officers and 158 of 186 Enlisted Men Lost |
| USS Lowe (DE-325) | 18 March 1945—Sunk U-866 along with DE's Menges, Mosley, and Pride |
| USS Marchand (DE-249) | 25 February 1944—Rescues 50—SS El Coston |
| USS Menges (DE-320) | 20 April 1944—Rescues 113; USS Lansdale (DD-426) sunk by Enemy Air<br>3 May 1944—Stern Blown off by German Torpedo off Algeria. 2 Officers, 29 Men Killed<br>18 March 1945—Sinks U-866. (Along with DE's Lowe, Pride, and Mosley) |
| USS Merrill (DE-392) | 7 March 1944—Operations Against Submarine Hideouts; Spanish Morocco<br>14 May 1944—Submarine Attack<br>12 July 1944—Air Attack |
| USS Mills | 1 April 1944—Rescues Survivors SS Jared Ingersoll and Extinguishes Fire Adjoining Magazine |
| USS Moberly (PF-63) | 6 May 1945—Sunk U-853. Along with USS Atherton (DE-169) |
| CGC Modoc | 21 January 1943—Rescues 128, SS Svend Foyne |
| CGC Mohawk | 27 August 1942—Attacks Submarine<br>22 November 1942—Rescues 25, SS Barberry<br>15 July 1943—Helps Float USAT Fairfax<br>7 October 1943—Attacks Submarine<br>28 October 1943—Attacks Submarine |

| Name of Escort | Outstanding Operations | Name of Escort | Outstanding Operations |
|---|---|---|---|
| | 28 March 1944—Attacks Submarine | USS Ricketts | 25 February 1944—Rescues 33; El Coston and |
| | 3 April 1944—Attacks Submarine | (DE-254) | Murfreesboro |
| | 18 May–August 26, 1944—Weather Patrol | USS Savage | 1 April 1944—Air Attack off Algiers |
| | 8 December 1944—Attacks Submarine | (DE-386) | |
| | 10 May 1942—Attacks Submarine | USS Sellstrom | 29 March 1944—In Air Attack off Gibraltar |
| | 22 July 1942—Attacks Submarine | (DE-255) | 9 April 1945—Rescues 18; San Mihiel |
| | 27 August 1942—Rescues 293; USAT Chatham | CGC Southwind | 15 October 1944—Assists in Capture of German Trawler Externsteine. East Greenland; |
| | 2 September 1942—Attacks Submarine | | 17 Prisoners |
| | 1 October 1942—Attacks Submarine | CGC Spencer | 7–8 March 1942—Attacks Submarines |
| | 21 October 1942—Attacks Submarine | | 12 May 1942—Rescues 52 SS Cristales and |
| | 3 September 1943—Attacks Submarine | | Mont Parnes. Attacks Submarine |
| | 9 October 1943—Attacks Submarine | | 22 July 1942—Attacks Submarine |
| | 9–27 October 1944—Weather Patrol | | 21 February 1943—Sinks U-225 |
| | 8 April 1945—Attacks Submarine | | 24 February 1943—Attacks Submarine |
| | 25 May 1945–14 August 1945—Ice Patrol | | 25 February 1943—Attacks Submarine |
| USS Mosley (DE-321) | 20 April 1944—Knocks Down German Plane in Air Attack off Algiers | | 8 March 1943—Attacks Submarine; Rescues 35 SS Guido |
| | 18 March 1945—Sunk U-866 Along with DE's Menges, Lowe, and Pride | | 9 March 1943—Attacks Submarine |
| USS Muskegon (PF-24) | 24 April 1945—Attacks Submarine | | 2 April 1943—Attacks Submarine |
| CGC Nemesis | 24 February 1942—Attacks Submarine | | 17 April 1943—Sinks U-175; Rescues 19 Crew |
| | 23 March 1942—Attacks Submarine | | 18 April 1943—Attacks Submarine |
| | 21 May 1942—Rescues 28, SS Fajadeoro | | 29 June 1943—Attacks Submarine |
| | 7 June 1942—Rescues 27, SS Suwied | | 1 December 1943—Attacks Submarine |
| | 5–6 July 1942—Attacks Submarine | | 21 March 1944—Attacks Submarine |
| | 3 August 1942—Attacks Submarines | CGC Storis | 24 June 1942—Attacks Submarine |
| | 17 August 1942—Attacks Submarines | | 8 August 1943—Escorts Convoy to Frobisher Bay, Canadian Arctic |
| USS Newell (DE-322) | 20 April 1944—Rescues 120; USS Lansdale (DD-426) | | 18 December 1943—Searches for Survivors; USAT Nevada |
| CGC Nike | 6 February 1942—Rescues 38; Tanker China Arrow | | 7 July–31 October 1944—Northeast Greenland Operations against German Trawlers |
| | 5 May 1942—Attacks Submarine on Surface | | 6 March 1945—Attacks Submarine |
| | 9 May 1942—Attacks Submarine | | 20 July 1943—Assists USAT Fairfax |
| | 14 May 1942—Rescues 9; Tanker Portrero Del Llano | | 1 May–14 August 1945—Ice and Weather Patrol |
| | 16 May 1942—Attacks Submarine | CGC Tampa | 30 May 1942—Attacks Submarine |
| CGC North Star | 12 September 1941—Seizes Buskoe (Nor.) First Naval Capture World War II | | 3 June 1942—Refloats SS Montrose; Aground |
| | 13 August–23 September 1942—Services East Greenland Stations | | 3 February 1943—Escorting SS Dorchester when Latter was Sunk |
| | 23 July 1943—Attacked by German Plane off Jan Mayen Island | | 5 May 1943—Attacks Submarine |
| | 31 August 1943—Investigates German Camp Sabine Island, East Greenland | | 30 September 1943—Attacks Submarine |
| USS Pert | 30 November 1943—Attacks Submarine | | 17 December 1943—Searched for Survivors USAT Nevada |
| USS Peterson (DE-152) | 15 April 1944—Sunk U-550 (with DE's Gandy and Joyce) | | 3 October 1944—Attacks Submarine |
| USS Poole (DE-151) | 28 August 1944—Attacks Submarine | | 21 June–6 September 1945—Ice Patrol |
| | 30 August 1944—Rescues 2; SS Jacksonville | CGC Taney | 20 April 1944—Air Attack |
| USS Pride (DE-323) | 4 May 1944—Sunk U-371 off Algiers along with USS J. E. Campbell (DE-70), Sengelee (FR.DE), Alcyon (FR.DD), Blankley (Br.-DD), and Sustain (U.S. Mine Sweeper) | | SS Paul Hamilton Sunk; 504 Lost. USS Lansdale Sunk |
| | 18 March 1945—Sunk U-866 along with DE's Menges, Mosley, and Lowe | | 24 May 1944—Attacks Submarine |
| USS Ramsden (DE-382) | 1 April 1944—Shot down German Bomber in Mediterranean | CGC Thetis | 13 June 1942—Sinks U-157 |
| USS Rhodes (DE-384) | 1 April 1944—Knocks Down German Plane. Extinguishes Fire on Merchant Ship | CGC Travis | 8 February 1942—Attacks Submarine |
| | | | 20 December 1942—Assists SS Maltram |
| | 9 April 1945—Rescues 6 from Tankers St. Mihiel and Nash Bulk in Collision | CGC Triton | 21 February 1942—Attacks Submarine |
| | | USS Vance | 14 May 1944—Attacks Submarine |
| USS Richey (DE-385) | 9 April 1945—Rescues 32 from Tankers St. Mihiel and Nash Bulk | | 14 July 1944—Air Attack |
| | | | 11 May 1945—U-873 Surrenders |
| | | CGC Vigilant | 22 February 1942—Rescues 2; SS Pan Massachusetts |
| | | | 9 May 1942—Attacks Submarine |
| | | CGC Woodbury | 16 February 1942—Rescues 40; Tanker E. H. Blum |
| | | PC-556 | 19 July 1943—Repulses Attack on Convoy by Enemy E Boats off Syracuse, Sicily |
| | | | 24 January 1944—Anzio Landings; Air Attacks |

# INDEX

Names of Coast Guardsmen who received medals and awards are omitted from this Index unless mentioned otherwise. See Appendix A.